DEDICATION

TO THE BOYS OF OUR GREAT COUNTRY

To the wonderful crop of our future Manhood, whose wholesome enthusiasm over our undertaking was a constant source of inspiration, I lovingly dedicate this story.

Forty Million Hoofbeats

by
Frank Heath

The Long Riders' Guild Press

www.thelongridersguild.com

ISBN No: 1-59048-072-4

To the Reader:

The editors and publishers of The Long Riders' Guild Press faced significant technical and financial difficulties in bringing this and the other titles in the Equestrian Travel Classics collection to the light of day.

Though the authors represented in this international series envisioned their stories being shared for generations to come, all too often that was not the case. Sadly, many of the books now being published by The Long Riders' Guild Press were discovered gracing the bookshelves of rare book dealers, adorned with princely prices that placed them out of financial reach of the common reader. The remainder were found lying neglected on the scrap heap of history, their once-proud stories forgotten, their once-glorious covers stained by the toil of time and a host of indifferent previous owners.

However The Long Riders' Guild Press passionately believes that this book, and its literary sisters, remain of global interest and importance. We stand committed, therefore, to bringing our readers the best copy of these classics at the most affordable price. The copy which you now hold may have small blemishes originating from the master text.

We apologize in advance for any defects of this nature.

ACKNOWLEDGMENT

I wish to acknowledge my sincere appreciation of the assistance cheerfully tendered me by officials of the Bureau of Roads and the Division of Maps of the Interior Department in selecting the most feasible routes through lands where a horse traveling on his own feet "into some part of every State in the United States" could survive, living off the country for the most part.

I also found the forewarning given me by Dr. T. S. Palmer, of the Biological Survey, regarding certain poisonous herbs, very valuable.

I found very useful too Farmers' Bulletin No. 1030 (Feeding Horses), by Mr. G. A. Bell, former Senior Animal Husbandryman, and Mr. J. O. Williams, now Senior Animal Husbandryman in Horse and Mule Investigation, Bureau of Animal Husbandry, when it came to constant changes of feed, which was one of our major problems.

I am indebted to Mr. Williams, and to the officers, Col. Sterret, then Chief of the Remount Division of the Army, Maj. Cedarwald, former Acting Chief, and Maj. C. L. Scott, First Assistant in 1925, for checking my calculations as to what seemed the least possible time in which I could, within reason, with ordinary luck, accomplish such a feat within the possibilities of a good ordinary horse of the right type. Also, these officials obliged me with any information at their command in establishing the fact that, to the best of their knowledge, such a feat had never before been performed. They particularly helped me in checking my tentative schedule. Most of these gentlemen saw us off on our trip.

Upon my decision to undertake this story, the officials of the Department of Indian Affairs were very obliging in verifying facts of which I was not quite certain in the "Indian Country," and in proffering me some cuts, and also the use of the Department Library. The same is true of the Bureau of Ethnology. In fact, I have always found our Government officials very courteous to one who knows what he wants to know and why.

TABLE OF CONTENTS

BOOK I

BOOK II

BOOK I

Chapter I

SELECTING A HORSE

LIKE a true Irishman, I love a horse. I appreciate him as does an Englishman, as a noble comrade in sport. The squeak of saddle-leather was balm to my soul. I had a strong desire to give the undertaker a run for his money, and too, to add something to my desultory education.

Finally, early in 1925, I decided to undertake a trip—I would start from the Zero Milestone near the White House on April 1, 1925, at noon—"To hit some part of every State in the United States and return to Washington, riding the same horse, the horse traveling all the way upon his own feet."

No sooner had I announced my intentions than I was deluged with offers to sell me "just the horse for the purpose." Most of them were priced ridiculously low for a horse of required quality. On investigation I found none of these filled the bill. Evidently my announced intention was taken as a joke.

Now I would not for an instant have the reader believe that there were no good horses in our part of Maryland. But a race horse was not what I wanted. He is too fiery, for one thing, and he has not the "bread basket" to carry feed to do him for long distances. We have some very good show horses—or jumpers. They too were not my type. What I wanted was a road saddle horse. He is scarce here—no proper place to ride him. Park trails, etc., are not comparable to country roads.

Having exhausted the local market, I began to correspond with various dealers at a distance. An exchange of letters with the Morgan Horse Farm in Vermont soon convinced me that their horses were too expensive for me, though I had intended to use a Morgan if possible. A letter from a dealer two hundred miles away, in the foothills of Virginia, assured me that he had "exactly the horse I needed at $125.": that he was sound of hoof and good-looking in every way, though "bob-tailed" as a result of having all the hair pulled out by having another horse tied to it, but that would soon grow out. On

3

the strength of this description, I went to see the horse. He proved to be not only "bob-tailed," but "rat-tailed," never would have any more tail than a rabbit. Besides he had one foot that I knew would not hold out.

I learned that a "kid" who worked for this man had a little black mare which he "might sell." She was not the type of horse I had in mind, but she seemed to come the nearest yet offered me. I knew that she had a constitution like iron, a good bone, and ligaments and tendons like whip-cord. She was a little too young—only six— and was too short-legged. She had been allowed to acquire a "dirty little jig" that some might call a trot. I thought perhaps I could get her out of that. She was a good jumper. I decided to buy her, and if she did not "pan out," trade her on my way back for the best I could get. All Virginians love a horse that can jump. I did not believe the kid when he told me she weighed a thousand pounds, but she did on the scale, so compact was she—too compact, in fact. I thought $100 was too much for her, but the boy was adamant—I could take her or leave her. I took her.

Borrowing a light saddle and bridle from the dealer—later shipping it back—we got started toward home at 9 a.m. I rode the little black thirty miles before 3:30 p.m., and had not fazed her. But I felt as if my backbone and some other things were about jolted out of me. As I rode along, mentally saying things about a fellow who knew no better than to presume that any horse would take the place of cash in the purchase of another and choicer one, two men hove in sight. One was mounted on a rather leggy solid bay mare with brown markings, with a good middle and short back. Her walk was easy and nimble, with a stride that carried her forward forcefully. I noted that she carried the large man with ease both to herself and rider. This man led a little mule, while a younger man, riding a pony, was 'fanning' the mule. As we approached more closely, I noted the bay mare had hazel eyes that could show fire on occasion. The slightly Roman nose denoted grit. A strong jaw indicated good digestive ability, and wonderful teeth. At a glance, I could see no blemishes save some slight 'wind-galls,' and several scars as though she might be a "scrapper." A certain indescribable knowing expression in her eye caused me to wonder whether she had ever killed a man.

"There's my horse," I told the little black, "and she is in the hands of traders. I'm going to give you the darnedest swappin' you ever got." And I did. It took the dealer four minutes to extract from me ten dollars in addition to Blackie. My new mount was coming ten that spring (this was February, 1925). She stood so proud and queenly that, on a sudden impulse, I renamed her "Gypsy Queen."

I believed I had the horse I wanted, but I meant to test her out. She had already had a pretty hard day's jaunt, and I rode her about ten miles to the next town. I found her very springy and easy to ride. A man rode alongside on a pretty fair horse. With Queen in an easy trot—a kind of fox-trot—we put his horse into a keen lope.

Now, there are a few gaits that I cannot find to be standardized in books—and fox-trot is one. The term is differently interpreted in different localities. I believe the nearest correct is that a horse steps well out, quite rapidly, placing the hind feet in the tracks made by the front feet. The Ozark mountaineers so interpret the term, as do some other practical horsemen. The horse does not jolt the rider, nor does the rider post. The horse does not lead perceptibly. It is a gait a horse cannot keep up too long, for it is too fast.

From a fox-trot I could easily change her to what I call a 'jog.' By 'jog' or 'jog-trot' is generally meant a kind of easy, long, swinging trot. In this gait Queen led almost imperceptibly—just enough so that I caught part of my weight on the stirrups, automatically, at every alternate step, but did not leave the saddle. Outside of a walk, which was our principal gait, this was her best road gait. From any other gait I would swing her into a 'posting trot,' which is not a very good trot for the road where we were continually approaching uneven footing. Then too, she had a 'dog-trot' often called erroneously a fox-trot, sometimes referred to as a 'squaw-trot'—four trots in all. It means that a horse (more usually a pony) just patters along. It is a very good prairie gait, and does not strain a horse or greatly jar one who, from long habit, automatically uses his feet as springs and lets his shoulders go lax. In the army it is referred to as 'slow trot.' On the range it is called a 'cowboy trot.'

Queen was not good at the canter. When she broke into that she wanted to run. Of course, running was not to be thought of in our case. Her best gait on our trip was just a good walk. We rode mostly in a walk. She had two distinct walks—a quick snappy one which she assumed "in society," being very proud, and a long strong stride she took automatically on the open road.

I referred to her as Kentucky Morgan: by which I meant there was every indication she came from the Morgan family of the Kentucky saddle horse, an offshoot of the American saddle horse. Then too, Gypsy Queen was said to be a Morgan by those who knew her.

As I brought her through Washington, she was as full of capers at the strange sights as any green ten-year-old would have been, but harder to handle than some.

As we proceeded on our way, a large, modern steam shovel lumbered toward us on its creeping caterpillars with its tremendous shovel dangling in the air many feet in advance. Queen was extremely fearful of it. The Irish engineer obligingly stopped the works. But just as I was having some difficulty navigating past it, off went the pop-valve. Queen took the bit in her teeth, as the saying goes, and lit into a dead run. It was raining, a cold February drizzle. The slick pavement was doubly slippery. I was wearing awkward old gloves. Being unable to control her with one hand, I made, from force of habit, a grab with my right hand for the right rein in order to 'see-saw' her from side to side, to check her speed by throwing her slightly off her balance. At the time her mane was long. Inadvertently this interfered with my right hand grasping the rein, which, as I gave a hard pull on the left, threw her altogether too much off her balance. She seemed to lose all four feet. With unexpected agility, however, she alighted on all fours and kept right on going until I finally got a proper hold on her reins. At last I had her turned about, and by slow degrees worked her back to the snorting iron monster. There was a good deal of rearing and wheeling (and she could wheel as quickly as any horse I ever straddled).

"Git the hill out o' this," quoth the Irish engineer, "before that harrs kills ye!"

"I might as well let her kill me as to let her beat me out at this stage of the game," I replied.

When we departed thence, we left in a walk. I had not punished her. She had received her ABC's in learning that when I patted her on the neck, assuring her that something was 'all right,' she could depend upon it.

SCHEDULE—Subject to Change

Objective: To Hit Some Part of Every State in The Union With One Horse and Return to Washington on or before July 1, 1927.

FRANK M. HEATH, of Silver Spring, Md.
Riding Gypsy Queen.

Place	Miles from Last Place Estimated	1925
Washington, D. C.	—	At Zero Mile Stone Via
Silver Spring, Md.	8	16th St. and Ga. Ave.
Baltimore, Md.	40	Laurel and St. Denis
Bel Air, Md.	25	
Havre de Grace, Md.	15	
Elkton, Md.	15	Perryville
Wilmington, Del.	20	
Philadelphia, Pa.	25	
Trenton, N. J.	30	
New Brunswick, N. J.	30	
New York, N. Y.	40	Jersey City
New Haven, Conn.	75	
Providence, R. I.	100	
Boston, Mass.	40	
Portland, Me.	100	
Rutland, Vt.	175	Fryeburg, Me.
Middlebury, Vt.	30	
White Hall, N. Y.	30	
Utica, N. Y.	125	
Syracuse, N. Y.	40	
Buffalo, N. Y.	125	Niagara
Cleveland, Ohio	200	
Toledo, Ohio	100	
Somerset, Mich.	50	

	Mo.	Date	Day of Week	Time
Lv.	April	1	Wed.	P.M.
Ar.	April	1	Wed.	P.M.
Lv.	April	2	Thu.	A.M.
Ar.	April	3	Fri.	A.M.
Lv.	April	4	Sat.	A.M.
Ar.	April	4	Sat.	P.M.
Lv.	April	5	Sun.	A.M.
Ar.	April	5	Sun.	P.M.
Lv.	April	6	Mon.	A.M.
Ar.	April	6	Mon.	P.M.
Lv.	April	7	Tues.	A.M.
Ar.	April	7	Tues.	P.M.
Lv.	April	8	Wed.	A.M.
Ar.	April	8	Wed.	Night
Lv.	April	9	Thu.	P.M.
Ar.	April	10	Fri.	P.M.
Lv.	April	11	Sat.	P.M.
Ar.	April	12	Sun.	P.M.
Lv.	April	13	Mon.	P.M.
Ar.	April	15	Wed.	P.M.
Lv.	April	18	Sat.	P.M.
Ar.	April	20	Mon.	Night
Lv.	April	21	Tues.	P.M.
Ar.	April	24	Fri.	P.M.
Lv.	April	25	Sat.	P.M.
Ar.	April	26	Sun.	P.M.
Lv.	April	30	Thu.	A.M.
Ar.	May	3	Sun.	P.M.
Lv.	May	5	Tues.	A.M.
Ar.	May	12	Tues.	A.M.
Lv.	May	13	Wed.	Night
Ar.	May	13		
Lv.	May	14	Thu.	P.M.
Ar.	May	15	Fri.	Night
Lv.	May	16	Sat.	P.M.
Ar.	May	21	Thu.	P.M.
Lv.	May	22	Fri.	P.M.
Ar.	May	23	Sat.	P.M.
Lv.	May	25	Mon.	A.M.
Ar.	May	30	Sat.	P.M.
Lv.	June	1	Mon.	A.M.
Ar.	June	10	Wed.	A.M.
Lv.	June	11	Thu.	P.M.
Ar.	June	15	Mon	A.M.
Lv.	June	16	Tues.	A.M.
Ar.	June	17	Wed.	P.M.
Lv.	June	18	Thu.	P.M.

SCHEDULE—(Continued)

Place	Miles from Last Place Estimated	1925 Via	Mo.	Date	Day of Week	Time
Elkhart, Ind.	100		Ar. June	22	Mon.	A.M.
			Lv. June	24	Wed.	A.M.
Valparaiso, Ind.	60		Ar. June	25	Thu.	Night
			Lv. June	26	Fri.	P.M.
Schererville, Ind.	25		Ar. June	27	Sat.	P.M.
			Lv. July	1	Wed.	A.M.
Joliet, Ill.	35	Chicago or Chicago Heights	Ar. July	2	Thu.	A.M.
			Lv. July	6	Mon.	A.M.
Ottawa, Ill.	40		Ar. July	7	Tues.	P.M.
			Lv. July	8	Wed.	A.M.
Sheffield, Ill.	40		Ar. July	9	Thu.	P.M.
			Lv. July	10	Fri.	A.M.
Davenport, Iowa	40		Ar. July	11	Sat.	P.M.
			Lv. July	13	Mon.	A.M.
Des Moines, Iowa	200		Ar. July	23	Thu.	P.M.
			Lv. July	27	Mon.	A.M.
Omaha, Neb.	150		Ar. Aug.	5	Wed.	P.M.
			Lv. Aug.	20	Thursday	
Topeka, Kan.	200	Lincoln—Optional	Ar. Aug.	29	Sat.	A.M.
			Lv. Aug.	31	Mon.	P.M.
Miami, Okla.	200	Garnett or Burlington	Ar. Sept.	12	Sat.	A.M.
			Lv. Sept.	14	Mon.	A.M.
Springfield, Mo.	100	Joplin, Mo.	Ar. Sept.	19	Sat.	A.M.
			Lv. Sept.	21	Mon.	P.M.
Powhatan, Ark.	175	West Plains	Ar. Oct.	3	Sat.	P.M.
			Lv. Oct.	5	Mon.	P.M.
Marion, Ark.	90	Jonesboro	Ar. Oct.	10	Sat.	A.M.
			Lv. Oct.	12	Mon.	A.M.
Memphis, Tenn.	15		Ar. Oct.	12	Mon.	P.M.
			Lv. Optional			
Indianapolis, Ind.	600	Optional whether by way of Florence, Miss., Nashville, Tenn., Louisville, Ky. (700 miles) Or Fulton, Ky., Hopkinsville, Ky., Princeton, Ky. Layovers optional. May reach Indianapolis Dec. 1, 1925, and put Gypsy Queen in winter quarters until Mar. 15, 1926, to save re-acclimating in spring, or moving her too much in winter. In last case during interim will probably raft down Mississippi to its mouth. Get back any way possible to Indianapolis by Mar. 15, 1926.	Ar. Mar.	15	on or before	

1926

Place	Miles	1926	Mo.	Date		
Indianapolis, Ind.			Lv. Mar.	25	on or before	
Chicago, Ill.	175		Ar. April	5	on or before	
			Lv. April	15	on or before	

SCHEDULE—(Continued)

Place	Miles from Last Place Estimated	1926 Via
Hazel Green, Wis.	200	Via Rockford, Ill.
Waterloo, Minn.	100	
Albert Lea, Minn.	125	
Sioux Falls, S. D.	150	
Huron, S. D.	150	
Aberdeen,		
Morbridge, S. D.	100	
Bowman, N. D.	150	
Miles City, Mont.	150	
Billings, Mont.	150	
Livingston, Mont.	100	
Yellowstone, Wyo.	50	
Livingston, Mont.	50	
White Hall, Mont.	75	Lewis and Clark Cavern Nat. Monument
Butte, Mont.	50	
Missoula, Mont.	125	Philipsburg
Coeur d'Alene, Idaho	150	St. Rigies Pass
Spokane, Wash.	40	
Portland, Ore.	350	Pendleton and The Dalles, or Pasco and Goldendale
Eugene, Ore.	125	
Medford, Ore.	150	Grant's Pass
Weed, Calif.	200	Carter Lake, a circuitous route. Siskiyou. Optional.
Redding, Calif.	70	Side trip to Lassen Volcanic Nat. Park. Optional.
Roosevelt, Calif.	150	
Carson City, Nev.	150	Reno, Nevada
Carl Inn, Calif.	250	Sacramento, Stockton. Optional. Privilege cut across. (Visit to Yosemite Nat. Park.) Fresno.

	Mo.	Date	Day of Week	Time
Ar.	May	5	Wed.	
Lv.	May	7	Fri.	
Ar.	May	11	Tues.	
Lv.	May	13	Thu.	
Ar.	May	18	Tues.	
Lv.	May	20	Thu.	
Ar.	May	26	Wed.	
Lv.	May	28	Fri.	
Ar.	June	2	Wed.	
Lv.	June	3	Thu.	P.M.
Ar.	June	5	Sat.	P.M.
Lv.	June	7	Mon.	A.M.
Ar.	June	10	Thu.	P.M.
Lv.	June	11	Fri.	P.M.
Ar.	June	17	Thu.	P.M.
Lv.	June	18	Fri.	A.M.
Ar.	June	24	Thu.	A.M.
Lv.	June	25	Fri.	P.M.
Ar.	June	30	Wed.	P.M.
Lv.	July	2	Fri.	A.M.
Ar.	July	5	Mon.	P.M.
Lv.	July	7	Wed.	A.M.
Ar.	July	8	Thu.	P.M.
Lv.	July	10	Sat.	P.M.
Ar.	July	11	Sun.	P.M.
Lv.	July	12	Mon.	P.M.
Ar.	July	15	Thu.	P.M.
Lv.	July	16	Fri.	P.M.
Ar.	July	18	Sun.	A.M.
Lv.	July	19	Mon.	P.M.
Ar.	July	24	Sat.	P.M.
Lv.	July	26	Mon.	A.M.
Ar.	July	31	Sat.	P.M.
Lv.	Aug.	1	Sun.	P.M.
Ar.	Aug.	2	Mon.	A.M.
Lv.	Aug.	16	Mon.	P.M.
Ar.	Sept.	1	Wed.	P.M.
Lv.	Sept.	15	Wed.	A.M.
Ar.	Sept.	18	Sat.	P.M.
Lv.	Sept.	22	Wed.	A.M.
Ar.	Sept.	25	Sat.	P.M.
Lv.	Sept.	27	Mon.	P.M.
Ar.	Oct.	5	Tues.	A.M.
Lv.	Oct.	6	Wed.	P.M.
Ar.	Oct.	8	Fri.	P.M.
Lv.	Oct.	13	Wed.	A.M.
Ar.	Oct.	20	Wed.	P.M.
Lv.	Oct.	21	Thu.	P.M.
Ar.	Oct.	26	Tues.	A.M.
Lv.	Oct.	27	Wed.	P.M.
Ar.	Nov.	7	Sun.	P.M.
Lv.	Nov.	10	Wed.	A.M.

SCHEDULE—(Continued)

Place	Miles from Last Place Estimated	1926 Via	Mo.	Date	Day of Week	Time
Visalia, Calif.	150	Fresno or short cut.	Ar. Nov.	15	Mon.	P.M.
			Lv. Nov.	16	Tues.	A.M.
Sequoia National Park, Calif.	30		Ar. Nov.	17	Wed.	P.M.
			Lv. Nov.	19	Fri.	A.M.
Bakersfield, Calif.	100	Delano or short cut.	Ar. Nov.	23	Tues.	P.M.
			Lv. Nov.	24	Wed.	A.M.
Pasadena, Calif.	100	Optional. Los Angeles, Hollywood.	Ar. Nov.	27	Sat.	P.M.
			Lv. Dec.	13	Mon.	A.M.
Bagdad, Calif.	175	San Bernardino - Doggett, or cut across.	Ar. Dec.	21	Tues.	P.M.
			Lv. Dec.	22	Wed.	P.M.
Needles, Ariz.	100	(Hot across here.)	Ar. Dec.	24	Fri.	A.M.
			Lv. Dec.	27	Mon.	A.M.
Flagstaff, Ariz.	200	Hackleburg	Ar. Jan.	4		
Holbrook, Ariz.	100	1927	Ar. Jan.	9		
			Lv. Jan.	10		
Gallup, N. M.	50	Petrified Forest—St. Johns. Optional.	Ar. Jan.	11		
			Lv. Jan.	12		
Ship Rock, N. M.	100	Navajo Ind. Res.	Ar. Jan.	16		
			Lv. Jan.	17		
Cortez, Colo.	40	Mesa Nat. Monument	Ar. Jan.	19		
			Lv. Jan.	21		Night
Bluff, Utah	50		Ar. Jan.	22		P.M.
			Lv. Jan.	23		
Cortez, Colo.	50		Ar. Jan.	25		
			Lv. Jan.	26		
Aztec, N. M.	75	Optional route.	Ar. Jan.	28		
			Lv. Jan.	30		
Gallup, N. M.	150		Ar. Feb.	6		
			Lv. Feb.	8		
Grant, N. M.	80	Optional route.	Ar. Feb.	11		
			Lv. Feb.	12		
Los Lunas, N. M.	70		Ar. Feb.	14		
			Lv. Feb.	15		
Hot Springs, N. M.	125		Ar. Feb.	19		
			Lv. Feb.	21		
Mesilla Park, N. M.	75		Ar. Feb.	23		
			Lv. Feb.	25		
El Paso, Texas	35		Ar. Feb.	27		
			Lv. Mar.	3		
Austin, Texas	600	Ft. Stockton	Ar. Mar.	21		
			Lv. Mar.	23		
Houston, Texas	200		Ar. Mar.	30		
			Lv. May	2		
Baton Rouge, La.	275	Beaumont, Texas	Ar. May	7		
			Lv. May	9		
Mississippi City	85		Ar. May	11		
			Lv. May	12		
Mobile, Ala.	40		Ar. May	13		
			Lv. May	14		
Pensacola, Fla.	40		Ar. May	15		
			Lv. May	16		
Tuskegee, Ala.	200	Optional.	Ar. May	21		
			Lv. May	22		
Atlanta, Ga.	125		Ar. May	27		
			Lv. May	28		
Charlotte, N. C.	250	Via Spartanburg, S. C.	Ar. June	6		
			Lv. June	7		

SCHEDULE—(Continued)

Place	Miles from Last Place Estimated	1927 Via	Mo.	Date	Day of Week	Time
Roanoke, Va.	175		Ar. June	13		
Lexington, Va.	—	Natural Bridge	Lv. June	15		
			Ar. June	16		
Lewisburg, W. Va.	50	White Sulphur Springs	Lv. June	17		
			Ar. June	18		
Staunton, Va.	100	Warm Springs	Lv. June	20		
			Ar. June	24		
Warrenton, Va.	75		Lv. June	26		
			Ar. June	29		
Fairfax, Va.	30		Lv. June	30		
			Ar. June	30		
Washington, D. C.	15		Lv. July	1		
			Ar. July	1		Noon

Chapter II

WE ARE OFF

ON March 31, 1925, I rode Queen under her pack to Washington, less than ten miles, and put her up at a feed barn.

We arrived at the Mile Stone four minutes late, that is, at 12:04 p.m. Our objective was to be back in Washington on July 1, 1927, at noon.

Some people who were waiting for us told me the reporters had come promptly at twelve o'clock—and left. It developed they had gone in a bunch to keep some appointment at the White House that could not be postponed. They came back shortly after, as did the Army Officers, Colonel Sterrett, Major Scott and Major Cedarwald, who was Assistant Chief of the Remount Division, early in the World War, later Acting Chief, and since then Secretary of the American Remount Association, and Editor of "Remount."

All the Washington papers bore notices of our departure. Most had pictures. There was a general news broadcast. Our local home papers also gave us a send-off.

A few of the boys, and particularly a lot of my kid friends, rallied at the Legion Hall in Silver Spring around a camp-fire. We left there about 10 p.m.

We stayed that night at our little cabin home. A few hours' sleep and then at last we were off. Away from the previous excitement, out on the quiet country road, Gypsy Queen seemed listless and down-hearted. Did she sense what was before her? At any rate, she was tired. The main reason was obvious. It (the reason) had been forced upon me the day before. Our pack was much too heavy. Like some old maid, I had thought that I simply must have certain things, until the load, with the saddle, weighed one hundred pounds by the scale in passing through Silver Spring. I made up my mind then and there that we could not carry with us all the conveniences of civilization and keep going. A few things went over the bank. A friend had invited us to stop at noon for dinner. It was while devouring his chicken that I decided to separate my pack into two parts—one for things immediately necessary—the other containing articles with which I could temporarily dispense. The bare essentials we carried with us. My friend delivered the rest to me in Baltimore next day, to join the parcel-post package that I was sending ahead from place to place. That afternoon Queen 'tripped it off' as though relieved of the proverbial brick house.

Passing a few small farms, mostly truck and poultry, which had been whittled in the past few years out of the second-growth timber which had replaced the intense cultivation of pre-Civil War days, we arrived about 4:00 p.m. at Laurel, famous for its race-track, where we fed. From here, passing dairies and large truck farms that supply the canneries in Baltimore, we arrived at St. Denis, about eight or ten miles south of Baltimore, at 8:30 p.m. We spent over one hour finding a stall. I had led Gypsy Queen from place to place until we had actually arrived in an adjoining small town. All the barns that people told me about I found full of old automobiles or automobile parts. At last I did succeed in finding a narrow, uncomfortable tie-stall in a disused barn and carried loose hay in my arms from a feed store two blocks away. No bedding. The only grain I could procure was corn. I myself slept (?) cold in an old auto. There was no charge for the stall. It developed that experiences somewhat parallel to this were not at all unusual all up the Atlantic Coast, through New England, and on West until we reached the open farming country west of the Adirondacks. Frequently, in town or city, when I inquired for a feed stable—"Feed stable!" they would ejaculate in open-mouthed puzzlement. "Yes—well—livery stable, perhaps," I'd say. Another look of puzzlement would often appear as if they were trying to recall the name of some ancient institution. "Well, where can I get some feed for my horse?" They usually didn't know.

Shortly before noon the following day I arrived in Baltimore and began searching for a stable where, by appointment, I was to meet a newspaper man. It seems to me I chased that stable all over the city. It had been moved several times and finally seemed to evaporate into thin air. At last I located another stable owned by a Mr. Thomas. When I was preparing to leave, having paid the small charge at the stable, the younger Mr. Thomas quietly handed me a dollar, as a 'lucky piece.' He had become interested.

A hard day's travel over continuous pavement (with slight chance to ride on the so-called dirt shoulders) brought us to Bel Air, the home of Booth, the assassinator of Lincoln. The country there is rugged. The soil is stony. There are some small farms—mostly dairies. A large asset is local scenery and tourist trade. There I expected to stay at a barn where I had put up three years previously with a saddle horse I had sold. Imagine my disappointment at finding the barn dark and deserted. As it was the only place I knew about in the vicinity, I groped around and found a box stall and some oat straw, but no hay or grain. I walked to the business section of the town, and after a thorough search, the nearest approach to horse-feed that I could find was a package of rolled oats for table use. I bought myself a can of milk, and shared raw rolled oats with Gypsy Queen.

At Havre de Grace I planned to stay at the race track, thinking that I would have no difficulty in finding lodging there. In my innocence I imagined that Gypsy Queen, the horse that was to perform such a wonderful feat, would be welcomed with open arms by all horsemen. We were about as welcome at the race track as two ragged tramps would be at a society ball. Luckily for me, I met Dr. L. H. Tubbs, a veterinarian, who kept a boarding-stable near the track.

I had noticed him observing us the previous afternoon, as we approached on a slight down-grade that was fairly smooth. She had automatically broken into her running walk.

"I want to see you make that trip," he said. "Come up to the house and have supper."

On the following day, a few miles out of Elkton, Maryland, I noticed that Queen began to favor her left front leg. Although I did not realize it, this was the beginning of a difficulty which dogged our footsteps for the rest of our journey. We were proceeding rather despondently, because Queen was seemingly beginning to fail before she had fairly started, when someone hailed us with "Well, now, what the devil is this?" On looking up, I saw Professor Bartelson, who had been one of my instructors in a vocational training course at the University of Maryland. After a little conversation, he predicted our success, and directed me to friends of his, the Bakers, with whom I spent the night.

> From Signature Book: "Frank M. Heath obtained feed at my farm 10 miles south of Wilmington at noon today, April 7, 1925.
> (Signed) R. L. Richards."

We were passing some real general farms, straw stacks in open fields and all that. It was a prosperous looking community.

As we were leaving Philadelphia that afternoon, I heard "That's him!" from a broad-shouldered traffic cop to another as he humorously jerked a thumb in our direction. "And he ain't got to New York yet," he added. It occurred to me that he was right. This was our ninth day on the road, Queen was slightly lame, my cash was dwindling, and yet we had hardly got away from our own back door. In Philadelphia I had fortunately been directed at once, by some boys, to a feed stable conducted by one Jimmy Ivey. Queen and I were treated as royalty, better, in fact, for at my own suggestion, I was allowed to 'flop' in the shavings—a boon that would doubtless have been passed up by King George or the Prince of 'Whales.' I had been told that Jimmy Ivey could beat any 'vet' in diagnosing lameness. But he could not positively locate that in Queen. No charge.

From Signature Book: "April 11, 1925; Frank M. Heath put up at my barn, 3502 Filbert St., Philadelphia, last night.
(Signed) James S. Ivey."

We entered Trenton and stopped at the Post Office to inquire for a feed barn. There was none that we could learn about. We rode on in the rain, through the city, into the northern suburbs. We had begun to wonder where we were going to stay that night. Looking up, I saw a truck-farmer observing us interestedly.
"What about—?"
"Ride that horse right in here!"

From Signature Book: "April 11, 1925. Frank M. Heath stayed at our place, 2049 Brunswick Ave., Trenton, N. J., last night with Gypsy Queen.
(Signed) Mr. E. B. Van Arsdale."

From Notes. April 11, '25: Left Princeton one p.m. via Carnegie Lake (and C Bridge) and old Brunswick Pike. First day we had fair going most of the way. Beautiful fertile, level land between Trenton and Princeton. * * * * Queen gradually getting over soreness in suspensory ligaments—especially those of left fore. * * * * Been using camp [camphor] 3, clo [chloroform] 2, aconite 1. Quite a lot of rubbing. * * * * Arrived New Brunswick 7:30 p.m. Sat. April 11, country abutting on Old Brunswick Pike. Picturesque. Half a day ahead of schedule. * * * *

April 12, '25: Put up last night with Mr. Vandercrats, a Hollander, a rosarian. Raises about 50,000 roses a year—son a remarkable young man—is in business with father. Gave me a good place for Queen at considerable trouble to himself. I slept in hay. No charge. * * *

Camp Baraton Arsenal, Bonhampton Village opposite. Acres of captured German cannon. Noon, fed at place of Julius Keiser, Bonhampton. He is Hungarian and great lover of a horse. When I asked for water before feeding he said, 'No watta. Feed first time.' So, as Queen was not dry, I let it go at that. * * * * He is engineer for Chas. Bloomfield's Sand and Clay Co. Came to U. S. 1902. Likes U. S. He said, 'I like old country, I go back. No go back no more.' I told him that was the kind of Americans we wanted. * * * *

Reached Elizabeth N. J. about 7 p.m. April 12.
We put up finally at the barn of Mr. Robert Langhampton. His young son was quite enthusiastic over Queen and saved me many a step in locating the things I needed to procure in the town.

From Notes. April 13, '25: Left Elizabeth 9:30 a.m. over Lincoln Highway. Reached Newark 11. * * * * Arrived wooden bridge 1 p.m. Fed. * * * *

Chapter III

A WARM RECEPTION IN NEW YORK

We pulled into Durland's Riding Academy, 66th near Broadway, at 6 p.m., April 13th, two days ahead of our schedule. So far, we had traveled only twenty-nine miles further than our schedule called for. After landing in the metropolis, I remember having traveled many blocks over streets paved with old-fashioned cut-stone blocks, between gloomy-looking warehouses and some factories. Then came small shops, dirty streets, cheap tenements, clothes drying on the fire-escapes, broken window panes, sharp-featured, worried-looking adults, some cats and dogs, a few horse-drawn huckster wagons, and the like—some motor traffic, of course, and the most unruly rabble of street-urchins with whom it has ever been my good fortune to come in contact. I scratched my head and consulted my memory, wondering whether I was, after all, Alice in Blunderland. Was this really America? Italy? Spain? Czecho? Or—where? I was a stranger in a strange city, and seemed to be creating as much disturbance as Gulliver among the Giants. The kids all took after us, the gang augmenting, gaining in force, volume and 'vocabularity,' as we tried to escape. These did not exhibit the usual interest common to childhood. They seemed living only for the moment. Something strange had hove into sight within their horizon. Why not get all the kick out of it while the getting was good? They wanted to see us move. "Pronto! Pronto! Vamose pronto! Porque caballa no vamos? Suse Maria! Vamos!" They were a liberal bunch. They handed us a few over-ripe bananas and oranges that had outlived their usefulness as food. The proverbial ancient egg that usually is supposed to play a part in such receptions was missing. I caught one little devil sneaking up behind with the intention of swatting Queen on the rump with a piece of goods-box. He almost certainly would have received a severe kick had I not faced him with a decidedly negative gesture. We escaped. Queen was pretty well pepped up. As we approached 66th and Columbus Avenue, an elevated train rushed over. That was altogether too much and too sudden for Queen. She took the bit in her teeth, wheeled and ran for more than a block in the dense traffic. But she automatically avoided all collisions. Somehow, between elevated trains, we got her under the trestle and to Durland's Riding Academy. We were assigned to a roomy tie-stall in the basement—two stalls in fact.

In approaching New York, we had ridden via Newark and over a long wooden plank-floored trestle—the Ramp.

It was here on the level footing that the true cause of Queen's lameness penetrated my skull. Before starting I had her shod with rubber pads. Right from the start I was a little dubious about rubber heels. It didn't seem to me just the thing to exclude the air from a horse's frog and sole, and either exclude the water and mud (nature's remedy) or else carry the same old mess under the pad day after day, instead of changing it in every mud-puddle. And yet I knew that horses do wear rubber heels or pads year after year on city pavements. I had studied scientific books and found them recommended. I also knew that we had hundreds of miles of pavement almost right off the reel, and I knew, even then, that a pavement was not what the doctor ordered. So, reluctantly, we started out with pads, intending to remove them as soon as we hit dirt roads. Anyone who has given the matter any thought knows that nature created the horse untold centuries before pavements were ever dreamed of. He is, largely, a prairie animal. The 'spring' or 'springs' within himself are very limited—not nearly enough to absorb the shock of striking a solid pavement. On his natural footing—the earth, the dirt, the 'turf'—the 'spring' is under the horse. To take him from that to an inflexible surface, is like taking the spring from under your automobile—it would not last long.

We learned eventually, and almost too late, that rubber pads on a city pavement are one thing, and on country roads quite another thing altogether. In the city a horse is generally on about the same slope, a slight one, sloping, usually, the same way. If the pad wears out of its natural shape at all, it conforms to the regular slope of the street, maintaining a rather flat, even surface.

"* * * * The joints [referring particularly to the joints of the foot including the ankle or pastern] are therefore hinge joints, though imperfect, because, while the chief movements are those of extension and flexion in a single plane, some slight rotation and lateral movement are possible."

From: Diseases of the Horse, U. S.
Department of Agriculture.

On country roads the slope, even if smooth, is usually more steep. Remember, the rotation of the joints is very slight—that this side flexibility is not enough to take care of a side slope of more than one percent without causing undue strain to the horse. To travel a horse on a side slope that is flexible to the horse's tread is one thing; to put him onto a slope so hard that its surface does not give under his feet (and this will apply in an exaggerated sense to hard hummocks) will certainly cause a tremendous and oftentimes fatal strain on the whole mechanism of the foot and leg. I wish to make it plain that if this rough surface is not sufficiently soft or flexible so that it will give easily under the horse's feet without his full weight being placed upon it, then this is dangerous footing. This is always dangerous if persisted in. Even considering the slight elasticity of the ligaments that bind the joints—of which there is some question—it must be borne in mind that these have their limit of endurance. If strained beyond the stretching-point, there is usually a sprain, sometimes a rupture. In our case it had not come to a rupture. Had Queen been a colt—less firmly knit—a lesion or rupture would probably have occured. But in the case of such great strain, I claim that, even if the ligament does not rupture, it at least loses more or less of its elasticity—like an old suspender—thus depriving the joint of the support of these same slightly flexible (?) ligaments. A horse that has been subjected to such a strain never entirely recovers.

On country roads we had struck a great deal of gravel and broken edges of pavement. The result was that soon the corners of the rubber pad, especially the outside of the left front, wore off, leaving a rounded surface. In trying to avoid the pavement, where to parallel it by a dirt road was impossible (and we found this to be the case generally in large sections of the United States, especially in the Northeast), our next best chance was to try to select roads having a dirt shoulder. We could do this only from consulting detailed maps, or sometimes, more or less reliably, from inquiry. As a matter of fact, these so-called dirt shoulders, particularly in the older settled sections where the roads are narrow and the ground is stony, are such in name only, so far as furnishing any decent footing for a horse is concerned.

We had had these conditions in an exaggerated form most of the way to New York. Sometimes we were directed to a gravel road. The popular delusion is that these are good footing for a horse. This is not true, especially where the gravel is coarse, for the reason that, if it is loose, the horse has no stable footing. If embedded in clay (and that is its purpose—to solidify the clay track), it produces a rough and uneven surface. While these conditions constituted a handicap during more or less the entire trip, particularly had they been nearly disastrous on the very start.

How simple it all was, now that we had the clue. Gypsy Queen was 'rolling out' on her left front foot. She had begun to limp very slightly. There had been continual and increasing strain on ligaments, tendons and joints—a general false adjustment. And yet it had taken this fool of a rider all this time to fully realize just what was going on. He had used liniments, leg-washes and cold water, which helped a little, while the foot continued to roll. All the cold water between us and a place we read of, where there is no water, could not take the place of proper contact between foot and footing. Thereupon I leveled the pad with a sharp knife. This was almost as bad, for the simple reason that, while the side-roll was relieved somewhat for the time, the whole heel, especially the left side of it, was too low in relation to the three-quarter plate that holds it in place. This formed a kind of rocker. No horse outside a child's nursery should be mounted on rockers. His heel should strike the ground simultaneously with the rest of the foot—perhaps a little in advance. He should never 'rock' back on it. As a machine, he was not built to stand the jerk on joints and tendons caused in rocking back.

Our next move was to insert a tapering wedge, or "shim' between the heel of the foot and the pad, on the outside, so as to throw the weight *slightly* off the left side. This shim we held in place by means of slender tacks driven downward through it and into what remained of that part of the pad projecting back of the foot. This helped greatly. But the mischief had been done. A young horse would have quit—one of poorer mettle could not have continued. Queen had to have a rest, repairs, readjustment. Probably every horse has his weak point, if not by nature, then by an error on the part of someone. This had been my oversight.

Inflammation had set in. And here is another beauty (?) of a pad. I could not pack the foot properly. I did use some cold water, but had to go light on it before putting Queen away for the night, for fear of her catching cold. That leg and foot had become Queen's weak point. But she did not enter or leave New York City limping. She was gritty. She would 'grin and bear' a lot.

It was in New York City that we had a special shoe put on that left front foot by old Frank McGuire, shoer for Durland's Academy —an extension shoe, extending slightly beyond the hoof on the outside, to 'brace' the leg against the weakened branch of the suspensory ligament. The foot we had left about 1/32 of an inch high on the outside. As we knew we had still several hundred miles of pavement, we gave her another set of pads. Old Frank McGuire was a wonderful man with a horse's foot. This, by the way, was the only special shoe we had made on the entire trip.

From Signature Book: "New York City, N. Y., April 15, 1925. Frank M. Heath called at this office.

(Signed) Edward J. Quinn,
Act. Captain, Mayor's Office."

On the corner nearest 55th and Fifth Avenue I noticed a mounting-block with steps leading up one side. Upon the block was a woman, well loaded down with avoirdupois and diamonds. At the side of the block, opposite the steps, was a strong horse—also apparently well-fed. One lackey had the horse by the bits, two more were braced firmly against the horse, holding him over near the block, while a fourth was assisting the lady into the saddle. I thought the horse showed remarkably good sense. Possibly he reasoned that as two perfectly good men were paid for pushing him over why should he not do his patriotic duty by pushing back?

It was often well, to be close to Gypsy Queen to guard her against any possible annoyance or tampering with by curious or meddlesome strangers. Too, a horse is a sociable animal. Some high-strung horses will sometimes wear themselves out by being left alone. He craves companionship—not necessarily of other horses. He needs a 'buddy.' Often a dog will do, or a goat—or a man. A horse deprived of contented rest is not much good next day. I learned that Queen seemed to rest better if she knew I was about.

And so it was that I frequently 'hit the hay' literally, sometimes in an empty stall—usually a clean one—rather than supinely quit the task I had undertaken.

While I was out on a useless quest to get 'backing' one day, 'we' had company. There had called to see us Mr. Reese, Manager of the U. S. Morgan Horse Farm, Mr. Williams, horse husbandryman of the Department of Agriculture's Division of Horse and Mule Investigation, Major C. A. Benton, Route Master of the Northeastern Endurance Rides, and Mr. Stillson (?) who, I believe, was Secretary of the Morgan Horse Registry Association. I regretted very much having missed these gentlemen.

I swung into the saddle. We were off. Gypsy Queen was feeling fine. We left New York City via Central Park from Durland's, 66th near Broadway, to 100th Street, to Manhattan (146th) over to 7th Avenue to Grand Concourse, to McComb's Dam Bridge, to Central Avenue, to Yonkers (commercial district), to Police Headquarters. Precinct Number Two.

How different this section was from the one through which we had entered. If ever on the whole trip we enjoyed a complete letting-alone, it was through this aristocratic district—the Grand Concourse. One little incident stands out in my memory. We heard "Hello!" in a refined voice, apparently addressed to us. I looked up just in time to see the flip of draperies, and someone backing away from a window—the sole greeting we received in the city after leaving the Academy. Had someone recognized us, and yet been a little reluctant to openly acknowledge us? My mind flew back for an instant to a remark that had been passed to me by someone at Durland's, to the effect that if I would 'slick up' like Tom Mix I would take better.

In Yonkers I inquired of a traffic cop for Police Headquarters, Precinct No. 2. He happened to be a World War veteran. There was a short, pleasant conversation. I gave him a card and a schedule just because he was interested. He hauled a dollar bill out of his pocket and made me take it. Finally I arrived at the Station. Major Benton had given me the address of a police sergeant there and had suggested that I call on him. ". . . and tell him that I sent you," he had added. The sergeant didn't happen to be in, but the recommendation went just the same. They fixed me up a fine place for Queen, feed and all.

"How'd you like to spend a night in jail?" asked the captain with a twinkle in his eye. "It won't cost you anything."

"Fine!" I replied, adding, "I'm sorry, but it will be my first experience."

I went across the street to a lunch wagon. The proprietor called, "Hello, that's a fine horse I saw you riding in. What's the idea?" I gave him a card, which he read. He went to the till and planked down a half-dollar. Back again to the Station. A quiet chat with the congenial officers and then to bed. I rested well that night on cushions. I had the whole upstairs to myself.

From Signature Book: "April 18, 1925. Frank M. Heath called at this station.

(Signed) Lieut. Cougle, 2nd Pct.
Police, Yonkers, N. York."

Chapter IV

FACING THE 'MIKE'

At noon we stopped in the rain at Silver Lake. I gave Queen her nose-bag and procured a bite for myself from a nearby grocery.

That was a hard day. My notes are a jumble. But I remember passing through some "village" toward evening, in a shower—I think it was Greenwich. The pavement was slick. The rich chimes of an aristocratic church were ringing. Queen was plunging. Some richly dressed girls were giggling. We passed on. By good fortune we dashed into a feed stable in Stamford, Connecticut. We had traveled over forty miles, largely pavement.

From Signature Book: "April 20, 1925. Frank M. Heath with Gypsy Queen put up at my barn in Stamford, Conn. last night.
(Signed) George L. Palmer."

I fed Queen, ate a grocery-store lunch, slept in an adjoining stall, and got a slim, dear breakfast in a restaurant. Left Stamford morning of April 20th.

Over rocky hills, passing many seed-farms, then through a better farming country, but still rocky, we arrived in New Haven about 9:30 on the morning of April 21st.

We had spent the night before with some poor but good-hearted folks whose home was one of those old rundown heirlooms, so many of which we passed, which seem to afford a shelter but not a livelihood. There were about fifty acres of the stony, thankless soil in grass. The man "worked out." These people were hospitable. They kept a dozen or so sheep, some hens, a truck patch. They had a young horse which they were afraid to "break"—not a bad horse. I should have liked to have broken him in, but could not stop. Gave them some practical hints. No charge.

Arriving April 21st at the hamlet of Milford, Connecticut, situated in a lovely little green valley, I was told that by a two-mile detour we would hit the old stage-road via North Milford and North Madison, avoiding a lot of pavement. Queen tripped it off joyously over the soft earth of the old trail, which ran for the most part through practically uninhabited wooded hills. After night had fallen, we arrived at the old stage station at the village of North Madison. Two old-timers on ox-team, stony farms, had "passed the buck" when I applied for accommodations for the night.

As I went along I noticed the scrupulous neatness, forehandedness and economy apparent in these places, ricks of stove-wood, split fine, piled high under sheds, and all that.

Mr. Henry Smith, who lives in the old Inn or Station House of the Old Boston Post Road of Revolutionary War days (long since abandoned as such) gladly divided with Queen his horse-feed which he buys in small dribs. Up in New England feed is scarce. To part with it is like parting with a tooth. Generous indeed is he who feeds your horse.

This road was through a rugged, mostly wooded, hill country, with many beautiful creeks. The ground all about here was cold and damp from the recently melted snows. Queen had caught a fresh cold. Counting latitude and altitude, we were travelling into a colder climate much faster than the season was changing. It was all un-natural. Queen had shed her winter overcoat in southern Maryland. Her digestive system had become adjusted to some green grass—with which nature opens the season. Her respiratory system had become softened to the balmy influence of northern Dixie. And now—all this. Moving a horse about in early spring is a precarious business at best. Could Queen stand all this? Then too, there was the utter impossibility of procuring just the right kind of feed at all—or most—times. And almost always there was that continual strain or jar that was fast becoming a 'night-mare.' That is hell on a horse.

From Notes. April 22, '25: At Chestnut Hill (Conn.) small fields or patches are divided into smaller ones by walls of boulders loosely thrown together from off the land. Fields also fenced all around with boulders. Still the formation that remains seems to be over half boulders. To me, the wonder is not why the now run-down farms are largely abandoned, but how people ever had the nerve to tackle them.

We came in view of Westbrook lying below in the beautifully fertile valley. We batted our eyes, Queen and I. Could this be true?

Could such barrenness and such bounteousness dwell so close together? Why, of course. For centuries the richer valley had been exacting toll from its poorer neighbor with every fall of rain, every spring thaw.

Passing through Westbrook, we found no feed stable. At the next small town, Old Lyme, we were told that a man named Clark had a large barn. It was late when we applied for a stall and permission to hit the hay.

"Just this morning stored it full of automobiles," began Mr. Clark. "Sorry, Gypsy Queen is pretty tired."

"Gypsy Queen?" came a voice from within. "Why, uncle, that's the horse we were reading about."

"I was just going to say, I have a hay-barn up the street a few blocks. Probably we can fix you up—wait till I get a lantern," finished Mr. Clark. "And come back to the house when the horse is cared for," insisted the "inner voice."

The young lady who owned the voice proved to be a budding newspaper correspondent. She wrote an article and started reading it to us for criticism. It was headed: "Hero Passes Through Old Lyme."

"Whoa," I exclaimed, "Excuse me, I mean, Miss Morgan, we've not done the trick yet, and I don't know as it will be exactly a heroic stunt if we do."

The young lady mailed a newspaper clipping to us via my parents' home in Spokane, Washington.

From Notes. Left Old Lyme 10:30 a.m. over Boston Post Road. Passed through N. London 3 p.m. Road from Lyme to N. London hard and uneven—made no time. Farms still stony—after leaving valley. Not so bad as yesterday.

The country traveled during the day was rather stony but fairly prosperous looking. Small farms of various kinds lay along the highway and every small town seemed alive with factories.

We had been trying since about five o'clock to find some place where we could get feed and stall together.

At 8:30 p.m. in the darkness, we arrived at the home of Mr. D. G. Saunders. He was about to retire. Nevertheless, he was very courteous and considerably interested. He gave us a stall. We had fed corn that day at noon. This night it was some kind of patent cow-feed —or nothing. I parked my better judgment and gave Queen the cow-feed. I knew it wasn't right, but hadn't the heart to refuse. I had decided to pull out early next morning to try and reach a point where proper feed could be obtained. We left early. I had thought it necessary to politely decline Mr. Saunders' invitation to breakfast.

From *Signature Book:* "Stonington, Conn., 5.45 a.m. (1½ N. E. of) April 24, 1925. Frank M. Heath with Gypsy Queen just leaving my place here.

(Signed) D. G. Saunders."

From *Notes.* April 24, '25: Had breakfast and grazed Queen at home of Fred H. Savage, 1½ miles north of Westerly. They are great horse lovers. No charge.

Noon found us at Hope Valley. The principal feature of this town, which hardly had the appearance of a town at all, was a factory on a stream, the power from which was utilized. The product was fishing-lines and, I believe, fishing-nets. At the general store I bought a lunch. I asked for feed. Carl Smith, the principal employee, got it for us from the feed-shed. His eye had taken in Gypsy Queen —and the entire situation. He would accept no pay for the feed. He almost dragged me into the shed and made me take a dollar. He was dressed very commonly. I wondered if accepting this was working a hardship on him. "Oh, I don't know," he said, "I draw a salary here, another modest one as town marshall, and I gotta few acres up on the hill where I raise truck that I sell to the natives."

As I left Hope Valley, Carl Smith, knowing the difficulty in securing feed and a place to stay, had directed me to the dairy farm of Colvin Brothers, Cranston, R. I. I arrived at this place at 8:30 p.m. My introduction from Smith was sufficient.

This dairy farm was a very large and modern one with carefully selected cows. The available hay was second-growth alfalfa. For grain, we had more of some kind of cow-feed. In spite of myself, these days, I was treating Queen's digestive apparatus about as scientifically as does a mother when she turns her kid loose among the melons and cucumbers and green apples in the good old summer time.

We had had that day all kinds of road-pavement, crushed granite, dirt. Another feature which I had begun to learn to classify was so many miles of "good side," by which I meant I had good traveling by the side of the road. My notes indicate that on that day we had 'jogged' ten miles, and had trotted three miles. My schedule was beginning to crowd us. Right now, for the first time, we were a few hours behind schedule. I had been checking up. I made out, that between New York and Boston, we would have traveled about forty-three miles more than the schedule called for.

There was no charge at leaving Colvin's Dairy Farm at 6:30 the morning of the 25th.

From Notes. * * * * Arrived Helleg's barn, Pine Street, Providence, at 8:30 a.m. Called at P. O. Got shave, hair-cut, square meal. * * * *

From my parcel post package, I had dug up a clean khaki suit and a clean shirt. Thus disguised, I called at The Outlet (Providence's principal department store). With my introduction from Mr. Freedman, who called on me at Durland's and presented me with a hat, I was cordially received. Several of the salesmen denoted pleasure in tipping us a quarter on receiving a card and a schedule. They also complimented me on my new hat. Finally, I believe it was the general manager took me up and introduced me to Mr. Samuels in his inner sanctum. Mr. Samuels was really quite a remarkable man. One used to meeting people could read more in the flash of his eye than those who judge people through books could get from a volume of biography or autobiography. He seemed genuinely pleased at my having called. "Why, you look just fine—well-dressed for the occasion." He picked up the phone. "Gimme the *Journal.* Leon Samuels speaking. Got a good news article. Send up a reporter right away— some bright fellow." He pushed a button. "Take a letter," he said to a stenographer who appeared from nowhere. He dictated a letter to our friend, Mr. Freedman, conveying his appreciation of his having sent me. She was gone. A young lady appeared on the scene, evidently a saleswoman. To a question from Mr. Samuels, she replied "Yes." "What's that, young lady?" he reprimanded. "Yes, sir," she corrected. "Well, that's *better.*" She vanished.

"We'd like to have you meet our radio audience," said Mr. Samuels to me. Again he pushed a button. In popped the announcer of The Outlet Broadcasting Station. I was introduced. "I believe our audience would appreciate a few words from Mr. Heath, the Horseback Traveler. . . . And now, Mr. Heath, will you excuse me." (Until such a time, setting an hour.)

The announcer took me in hand. I was alloted three minutes with the suggestion that I outline what I had to say, and see if I could read it within that amount of time. I took a seat facing the audience, comprised largely of customers who had just dropped in.

A song or two were rendered, a local band gave some music, then the 'Mike' was turned upon me—or I was turned loose on the 'Mike' —I don't know which. The announcer was so competent and suave, that I cannot imagine anyone becoming excited in his skillful hands. I was as cool as a cucumber. I indicated that I would appreciate it if he would give a few details leading up to what I was doing, and why, and all that. He did so, and then gently pressed me up to the 'Mike.' We were keeping very close check on time. I had just two minutes left. I had already gotten the idea that I could read the audience that I was to reach through the microphone—their attitude toward us and all that—through the cross-section represented in this local audience. I knew I could not be expected to say much in two minutes—just a kind of a "Hello, Everybody! The announcer has already told you about all there is to say in general. Mr. Samuels thought perhaps you'd like to meet us here." I assured them that Gypsy Queen was doing fairly well, and that I, myself, traveling largely for my health, as the gentleman had announced, was feeling fine, except that I had caught a cold one night from being compelled to sleep in a bed because horse-stalls were scarce. The studio audience seemed to think this was funny. The three minutes were about up. Without moving away from the microphone I asked the announcer, "How's that for the first time?" The local audience roared. In a flash the announcer was at the 'Mike'. "Mr. Heath asks, 'How's that for the first time?' I think he did pretty well—don't you? Thank you, Mr. Heath." It was over. Followed a short interview with a reporter with an appointment for a photograph as I was leaving. Then came the appointed time when I was to take my leave of Mr. Samuels. He again expressed his appreciation of my having called. It occurred to me all at once that this man Mr. Samuels seemed to be a pretty big man for such a small state.

Near four o'clock the *Journal* photographer met us at the rear of The Outlet. It was extremely cloudy. The picture which appeared in the Providence Sunday *Journal* next day, looked like the 'last rose of summer!' The caption above it:

"FRANK M. HEATH LOPES INTO TOWN ON
'GYPSY QUEEN'

HE IS ON A TOUR OF EVERY STATE IN THE UNION AND FINDS NEW ENGLANDERS MOST HOSPITABLE IN THE COUNTRY. MR. HEATH, A WORLD WAR VETERAN, IS GUEST OF MR. SAMUELS WHILE IN PROVIDENCE"

I am preserving this clipping for the benefit of my children's children. Is it not indisputable proof—newspaper proof—that their 'grand-dad' was once the guest of, presumably, a millionnaire?

From Signature Book: "(Signed) Joseph H. Gainor, Mayor,
Providence, April 25, 1925."

We left Providence at 4 p.m. At six o'clock we arrived in the rain at the home of Mr. C. D. Betts, Attleboro, Mass., just a few miles out of Providence. We had stopped on the way out and procured some necessary drugs. No good fairy could have directed us into better hands or a more congenial environment. Mr. Betts greatly loved and appreciated a horse. He himself had a big, fine gray. In his barn was everything that any horse, well or sick, might wish for.

When we had reached Providence that day, Queen was badly off her feed—all 'out of kilter'—on account of the unsuitable concoctions I had fed her. At noon I had given her a large bran-mash with about one dram of Nux Vomica, a little ginger, and a pinch of salt to give it flavor.

That night I had fed another bran-mash with Nux, ginger and iron—no grain. Next morning I could see that I had done the proper thing. I had 'swept her out' with a huge bran-mash—just in time. I had got rid of the indigestible mass that had lain too long in her digestive tract. When I had put her in the barn the night before I didn't know whether she'd come out the next morning alive or not. She had been plainly sick. A longer retention of this 'mess' would without a doubt have caused inflammation of the stomach and intestines. This is usually fatal to horses.

The weather was damp and cold. Mr. Betts came out, shortly after I had 'hit the hay,' and spread two heavy blankets over me. Nothing would do in the morning but I must stop for breakfast. We were treated as guests.

From Signature Book: "Frank H. Heath stayed at our place last night with Gypsy Queen, leaving about 7:30 for Boston.
(Signed) C. D. Betts,
26 Scott Street, Attleboro, Mass."

Chapter V

BOSTON

It is hard for one not familiar with a horse's digestive apparatus to fully realize the tremendous amount of energy that is lost to the horse in continual haphazard changes of feed. For in such cases, we must often either feed the horse altogether too little, or else do him greater damage by putting him out of condition. Without boring the reader with the theory of proteins and carbohydrates, let us say it is well known amongst horsemen, that a sudden change from corn to oats—and, more particularly, from oats to corn—is very likely to make a horse sick. (It is always safer to change onto oats, for the reason that oats are more nearly the horse's natural feed. For one thing, they carry their own roughage, and therefore lie more lightly in a horse's digestive tract.) Corn not only lies heavier, more compact, but it is much more likely to ferment.

It will be seen by this that, while we had pulled Queen through, she was by no means in first-class condition. She had, however, a lot of stamina upon which to draw, and she was such a type that she would go as long as there was a breath left in her.

It was Sunday morning, the 26th of April. Our schedule called for us in Boston that P.M. The schedule had the distance estimated at forty miles from Providence, or about thirty-seven miles from Attleboro, which I found to be about right in actual miles, if we considered "Boston" as just inside the city limits. This was at best a pretty severe test for a half-sick horse. I grazed Queen at noon beside the road near a creek, and gave her part of the oats which Mr. Betts had put in the nose-bag. About one o'clock we pulled out from there.

We had been directed to about twelve or fifteen miles of 'dirt' road (by a short detour) which I found to be the kind I learned to designate in my notes as R. I.—rough and inflexible. I was beginning to learn that 'dirt' road meant nothing, sometimes worse than nothing, unless I knew what kind of dirt road. Oftentimes the expression 'dirt road' is a misnomer altogether. It may be composed largely of boulders, to the extent that the horse is not relieved of the jar, but in addition to this, must suffer the strain of an uneven surface —a dirt road may really be composed of dirt—but what kind of dirt? If it is clay that has been roughened or 'ridged up' and then baked by sun and wind, this is really the very worst footing imaginable, for the very reason that it must necessarily bring the side-strain on muscles, tendons, and particularly the hinged-joints. The horse, having no proper place to set his foot, goes flinching and hobbling along.

It was here on this rough dirt road between Providence and Boston that Queen's lameness began to return. For here, as often, having. once entered upon these conditions, it was utterly impossible to escape such footing—roadside, field or whatever. For a little way we had the other extreme, what I learned to call 'wallow-sand,' loose sand so deep that a horse flounders in it. We passed through rather barren country—almost a 'no-man's land' between two great industrial areas. Passed a large old shell of a house that remains in my memory. Seated about it, on this Sunday afternoon, were people plainly bearing the stamp of toil. In approaching Boston, inquiring for a stable, we were told repeatedly that 'there are lots of stables in Jamaica Plains,' (a suburb). I had determined that we should at least cross the city limits that day, so as to enter Boston on schedule time, April 26, Sunday, P.M., if it took a leg.

We crossed the city limits into Boston about 6:30. We found one solitary feed stable locked up and the man gone. But everyone was friendly. Our picture had come out that morning in the *Boston Globe Pictorial*, and such things act as a kind of sponsor. Friends scampered and phoned here and there and either found no one at home, or every riding academy filled to overflowing. Finally, by mere chance, someone got the Longwood Riding Academy for us. It was late, but the boss had an attack of indigestion, so someone was up to answer the phone. That's how close the rub was. We had had many miles in the darkness or in the glare of the arc-lights to nearly half-way across western Boston. This was the first time we had traveled any considerable distance at night-time in city traffic. Queen was very nervous. Did a good deal of shying and plunging. Just as it seemed she was reaching the limit of her nervous endurance, we met up with the bridle-path—in the southern extremity of Longwood Park. We had a couple of miles or so of this comparative quiet and easy footing. We rode into the Academy at eleven P.M.—

Queen right up on the bit, but the several stands in the cold night air had done her cold no good.

I had fed oats that morning and noon, with a good fill of grass also at noon, and a few oats we had with us at eight P.M., while those good fellows were trying to find a stall for us.

We had made that day a good forty-five miles, all but seventeen of which was pavement, to half-way through Boston. Based on deductions arrived at from experience, it has since occurred to me that Queen had put out that day as much in "endurance and durability" as in traveling ninety miles on a good dirt road in the country. I estimate it this way: One mile of pavement takes more out of a horse than two miles of good dirt; one mile of road that is rough and inflexible, the same—at least as much. By inflexible I mean that it is so hard that it will not give under the weight of a horse. On a 'bumpy road,' the horse, given time, will learn to choose his footing, but it is tortuous at best. On a side-slope or a road that is 'ridged-up' this is no choice. One mile of strange dense city traffic reduces a horse as much as three miles of good dirt road in the country. (There is the nervous strain, and it is a strange fact—or is it strange? —that I always found that Queen required and would assimilate twenty per cent more feed under such circumstances.) To continue, a mile of coarse gravel road takes more out of a horse than one and one-half miles of good dirt: a mile of what I call 'wallow-sand' is almost incalculably hard on a horse. I hope I have sufficiently clarified this matter so that the reader will readily understand just what I mean later on, when I speak of 'theoretical miles.' And while we are on the subject it might as well be understood that when we exceed in actual and 'theoretical' what a horse is able to travel in actual miles on natural footing, we must eventually pay back with tremendous interest what we have overdrawn. If the road is hard and jars the horse or if it is rough and strains the horse, he must be given more time while on the road and also more rest. If you don't believe this, ask your veterinarian.

We must keep the horse within his natural gait, or speed. To 'extend' him means disaster. We must keep him within his gait not only on good footing, but he must have time to take care of himself on whatever kind of road we are traveling today. So if in the future, you think we are taking you over the old trail too slowly, remember that a horse has his limits. In the long run he is a self-repairing machine. His repair-shop can work only so fast. Whether he can 'come back,' depends largely upon whether he has become merely fatigued or is ruined. The fact that some inexperienced or unthinking person has decreed that a horse must cover so many miles does not qualify him to do it.

When we arrived at Longwood's they were waiting up for us. This was a small stable in the western suburbs. The foreman and his family lived in a cottage close by. The lady came out with a cup of hot coffee. I had a comfortable bed, spread on the barn floor. At eleven-thirty I again gave Queen a twelve-quart bran-mash with more iron, ginger, and Nux Vomica. I am not sure but that the ginger was a mistake. It is good for the digestion but opens the pores of the skin. It is fine where the horse is kept comfortable in one place, but I question my wisdom in giving it on this occasion, when there was no telling how soon she would be exposed to sudden changes of weather or temperature.

From Signature Book: "Longwood Riding Academy, (Boston) Mass., April 28, 1925. Frank M. Heath with Gypsy Queen put up at this stable from 26, 11 P.M. to 1:30 today.
(Signed) P. J. Griffin."

Mr. Griffin was the foreman. On leaving, he and the Scotch groom told me that "only as a matter of form—to keep the books straight—they'd have to make an entry of $1.00." They were proud to have had us with them. My preconceived notions that all Bostonians were niggardly and unsociable had been knocked into a cocked hat. Meanwhile during this day and a half in Boston, I had been taking care of Queen's legs, plenty of rubbing with some good liniment. I also leveled the rubber pads again. By so doing I temporarily arrested the lameness.

On April 28th, at 1 p.m., we pulled out of Boston, one and a half days ahead of schedule. Queen was full of pep. That night we put up at Stoneham, in an empty barn, which I managed to make fairly comfortable by stuffing the cracks. There was no bedding. Queen did not lie down. I fed her another bran-mash.

Chapter VI

MIXING A HORSE'S COMPLEXES

ONE of the first indications of Western civilization, it seems to me, might have been the segregating of passing traffic into two streams—right and left. In other words, the beginning of the adoption of some kind of system. (Whether some bright child first suggested this to his elders after having communed with the ants does not seem to be a matter of history.) I have been told that in China they still have no particular rule for passing (this was 1925) though their civilization is thousands of years older than ours. "East is East and West is West." I sometimes wonder if this apparent failure of some of the Eastern civilizations to lay down certain fundamental rules of behavior has not played an important part in retarding their progress.

Certain things we learn to do automatically. The horse, like man, is largely a creature of habit. In the U. S., as everyone knows, traffic passes to the right. A horse, from habit, turns out to the right when he meets other traffic. Naturally, he becomes used to meeting the passing traffic on his left. To put the traffic on his right, is to 'mix his complexes'—to use a modern term.

Many of the narrow roads that link up the small towns through which we passed in going north from Boston, became established long before Ben Franklin discovered electricity. Any thought of electric cars was as remote, comparatively speaking, as Mars. It is probably safe to say that considerably less than a hundred years ago—some two hundred years after those roadways and property-lines were established—came the first car-lines (horse or mule-drawn). To have split these narrow roads or streets by placing rails in the centre, as is usual in the more modernly planned thoroughfares, would have left no room for traffic on either side. So, they had to be placed on one side. Here, then, for a considerable distance north of Boston, these roads presented a very vexatious new problem. Queen had thoroughly acquired the habit of turning right, having traffic on her left. Now we butted into this proposition of having traffic, including electric cars, automobiles and buses, as often on

34

her right as otherwise. I am a strong advocate of the idea that a horse has more intelligence than he is generally presumed to have. I do not give him credit for having more intelligence than the average human being. It does seem to be a fact, however, that the average horse has more sense than a great many human beings exercise. A man becomes, to a certain extent, an automaton. He turns to the right. He has often been known to dodge, from habit, squarely into the path of an automobile or a train of cars. How, then, could anything else be expected of Queen than that she should become confused or frightened of all this traffic on her right? It was hard to prevent her from acquiring the habit of wheeling, which she did once or twice, in spite of me, in order to avoid this. Several times, to get away from this unaccustomed condition at any cost, she jumped over the stone wall dividing a property from the roadway. I knew this would not do. For one thing, the opposite side of the stone wall was not always a safe place to light. It might be boulders. There might be stumps or stubs where trees had been cut off, leaving sharp points. Still worse, as it once happened, she landed right in the middle of a flower garden. The lady, who was working there with a rake, was not expecting us. We did not seem to be altogether welcome. We jumped back. I made up my mind then and there that, in some way, Queen must be taught to obey me. For her own safety as well as mine, she must let me be the judge. I am not sufficiently versed in English to be table to make a horse at all times understand the why's and wherefore's. I believe I made it clear, some time back, that Queen was capable of taking the bit in her teeth, refusing to be guided thereby. Some other means must be resorted to. Once or twice I had to have recourse to the fairly well-known trick of giving her a sharp 'swat' on the side of the head. I greatly dislike to do this. First, because, to me, it looks cruel and cowardly to be everlastingly beating a horse about the head, and secondly, there is danger of causing an ulcer on the maxillary bones. So, in place of this, on the next occasion, I took a firm cross-hold of the reins in my right hand, well down on the neck, with the loose ends of the double-pointed reins in my left hand as a quirt. Being somewhat ambidextrous, I was able to play a rapid, sharp tune on her left jaw with the reins. She was about to leap one of these walls. I started playing this tattoo. She recoiled. She came down on the right side of the wall. As she lit, I had time to count one street-car and two buses. I had no time to count the automobiles. We were gone from there.

Chapter VII

WEST FROM PORTSMOUTH

BUCKING a cold ocean breeze and some rain on the way, we arrived in Portsmouth, N. H. in the rain on the afternoon of April 30th. We had passed through a pretty fair agricultural district, truck largely, and had had as a rule no unsurmountable difficulty about stable or feed. Roads had been good, bad, and indifferent. Queen's cold was still giving me concern.

From Signature Book: "Portsmouth, N. H., April 30, 1925. Frank M. Heath with his mare, Gypsy Queen called here 2 p.m. today.

> (Signed) Geo. H. Ducker,
> Chief of Police."

It developed we had already traveled some sixty-five miles further than our schedule called for to Portland, Maine. So I decided to drop out Portland and strike west. I was glad I had had the foresight to make our schedule flexible—that is, "subject to change," as plainly stated in the heading. The fundamental purpose, however, must stand at all costs—*we must hit some part of every state on our own feet.*

We crossed over into Kittery, Maine, and back to Portsmouth.

From Signature Book: "Kittery, Me., April 30, 1925. Frank M. Heath called at this office at 3:05 p.m. Horse Gypsy Queen in good condition.

> (Signed) Arthur O. Goodwin,
> Town Clerk."

From Notes. Figuring up distances I find that:

Before N. Y. [New York City] extra	49	miles
Between N. Y. and Boston	41	"
Between Boston and Portsmouth	15	"
Total [extra miles] to Portsmouth	105	"

Portsmouth to Rutland, Vt. via Portland would have caused us 215 miles travel. Portsmouth to Rutland direct estimated about 135 miles. Meaning that when we should have reached Rutland, Vt. we would have saved about 80 miles. The mileage from Portsmouth to Rutland from records proved to be 133 miles.

From our hurriedly (and worriedly) taken notes, including a special note, taken down at the time in Notebook No. 1, as of April 30th and May 1st, 1925: "*Traveled* month of April, 1925 to Portsmouth, N. H. 634 miles, or 21 [miles] per day [counting every day]. [Actually] traveled 26 mi. per day [counting days traveled]."

We had learned a lesson. How silly I had been in presuming our "estimated mileage" would be nearly accurate enough to use as a basis for record of miles actually traveled. Instead of all these deductions I decided simply to keep a daily record of the miles actually traveled that day, together with condition of roads, etc.

Also from now on the narrator will quote largely from notes, etc., instead of trying to iron out the abruptness. This is a record. Why try to make it read like literature?

After spending a very comfortable night at the combined shoeing shop and feed barn of a Mr. Jas. J. Morrison, we left Portsmouth the next morning, May 1st, five days ahead of the time scheduled to leave Portland, Maine.

Up hill, down dale, we passed farms where house, out-buildings and barn were almost invariably attached. In this country I was now passing through, farming had given way largely to pasturage. Cows were the chief source of income. We saw more horses, even meeting a few horse-drawn rigs—also more difficulty in finding accommodations.

On the afternoon of May 2nd, we arrived in Concord, N. H. There we found good accommodations at a regular feed barn.

We struck west from Concord on the morning of May 3rd. Soon we arrived on Putney Hill. I let Queen nibble grass as I took in the quiet view.

From Notes. May 2, '25: (Some 50 miles west of Portsmouth, N. H.) 11:30 a.m. Arrived Suncook, in a beautiful fertile little valley—(From west of Portsmouth Pop is 'tonic'—feed is 'baiting'—also doughnuts still are 'fried-cakes.')—Had Queen shod in front. Lugs top of shoes on toes. Also tightened hind shoes. Fred Marcott. (Fair—only $2.25.)

The reader may be wondering about those 'lugs.' From Portsmouth west, we had not had so much pavement. In many respects the footing had been much easier on Queen. She was, nevertheless, more or less 'sore'—a little inclined to go 'stubbing' along. A good many of these roads were surfaced with a kind of finely crushed granite. This naturally cut out the toes of her shoes and also the hoof at the toe (above the shoe—but not into the quick). Hence, in the new shoe, I had lugs—a small-size toe-calk—welded into the top of the shoe instead of the bottom, so as to take up this space. It also protected the toe from further wear, and incidentally gave added weight to the toe, which had a tendency to make her throw her feet out and prevent the stubbing. I also had her pads leveled off and replaced.

Via Warner and Bradford we arrived at South New Bury and were directed to View Inn, on the shore of beautiful Lake Todd, as a likely place to keep Queen. We spent the night very comfortably among good-hearted people.

Passing next day, May 4th, south of Lake Sunapee, we came upon the remains of the previous winter's snowdrifts. At noon we put up at a farm near Mt. Sunapee, where a lady told me the delicious dewberries go to waste by the ton. Here, too, the principal income was from pasturage and cows.

We spent the night of May 5th with the Boyds, seven miles east of the summit of the Green Mountains. We were in Vermont. We have passed today through a dairy country of rich Canadian bluegrass in patches, some rugged scenery, a little farming, a very little lumbering. Here in the foothills the soil is, in places, somewhat stony. I observed some farmers picking small rocks in the fields— nothing, however, like that described in passing one day through Connecticut. These small rocks, as the farmer expresses it, "keep coming up." The fact that this is a dairying country accounts for the soil being kept up.

My host would not hear of my 'hitting the hay.' I slept in a feather-bed. The night was cold. There was a heavy frost. In the morning Queen was shivering when I opened the door of the double-constructed barn. All through here, as well as near the summit of the Adirondacks, later on, I generally found the horse-stalls of a stable to be built inside of a great barn. The partitions were doubly constructed reaching from the ground floor to the floor above, so that the horses were protected from the severity of the northern winters in this mountain altitude, first, by the main hay-barn, and then by the inner structure. It was inside of such a stall that I found Queen shivering next morning. Here, the buildings were not attached. By the way, the cold she caught coming up the coast was not being helped by this change of climate. I was still giving her Nux, iron and ginger, together with a little Vapo-rub in her nostrils and rubbed into her throat at the larynx and the glands. (Since then I have substituted an ointment made by mixing lard, three parts, and turpentine, one part.)

The charge for our meals, bed and lodging was very light. I carried away a cake of maple-sugar made by the Boyds. It is a local product.

Over the summit and down the west slope of the Green Mountains, we arrived at Rutland.

From Notes. May 6, '25: . . . 5:30 p.m.—Conniff's barn via Mt. Holly, E. Wallingford, N. Clarendon.

Traveled 26 mi.—jogged 14 mi. Much up and down hill. Good roads. Dirt mostly—but little too rough for safe trotting. First half distance very rugged (over divide.) Rest of way broken. Some fairly good dairy farms. 8:40 p.m., after visiting *Rutland Herald*, visited Legion Post. Well received.

Leaving Rutland May 7th, I made the discovery that Queen could easily jump more than twice her length. We were riding along a dirt road through mostly meadow country. Here the right-of-way was fortunately of a reasonable width. The roadway, which was much of the way graded well up, was usually springy turf, almost marsh, on one or both sides. Queen bounded along on this, unconsciously or otherwise enjoying the 'spring' of this peat-like soil— which greatly rested her. Every little bit, in traveling on this strip of turf, we would come to a drain-ditch of considerable depth and width. We found it much easier to jump these ditches than to be everlastingly climbing the grade and back again to escape them. While Queen could not be classed as a jumping-horse as compared with the typical Maryland or Virginia 'jumper,' that is, a high jumper, I found that she could easily hop over a ditch as wide as her length. This would mean, when you come to think of it, that she jumped, allowing a little to start and stop on, more than twice her length. In other words, a seven foot ditch involved a leap of more than fifteen feet. This almost accidental discovery of the distance she could "broad jump" with comparative ease, came in very handy several times later on.

*   *   *   *

MIDDLEBURY REGISTER

May 8, 1925

MORGAN HORSE GETS MOST SEVERE TEST FRANK M. HEATH, RIDING GYPSY QUEEN, WILL HIT EVERY STATE

Riding a Morgan grade mare, Gypsy Queen, Frank M. Heath of Silver Spring, Md., entered the grounds of the U. S. Morgan Farm, Weybridge, at a lively trot at 7:30 last evening. Heath is to be a guest at the horse farm until next Wednesday.

Heath is a great admirer of the Morgan horse. He is now engaged in a stunt which will give this remarkable animal a severe test. Starting on the back of Gypsy Queen, from Washington, D. C., on April 1, Heath plans to hit some part of every state in the Union with one horse and return to Washington before July 1, 1927. The objects of this trip are health, recreation and education, of which Mr. Heath is getting a great deal, and to prove that a good horse, properly handled, is capable of making this trip, never before accomplished by any rider or any horse.

So far Mr. Heath's horse is standing the rigors of the trip remarkably well, and Gypsy Queen was pronounced in fine shape by Superintendent Reese, upon the arrival at the Morgan farm. A schedule of the trip was made out for Heath in Washington, but he is not following it technically, or to the letter. He has ridden approximately 733 miles to date, (My review shows 805 mi.—Author.) at an average of 20 miles per day, and 24 miles for every day he was in the saddle. * * * *

Mr. Heath says that his local Legion Post extends a cordial invitation to all legionnaires who may at any time be in Washington, to visit the Post.

Mr. Heath says that he finds the Morgan Horse Farm very interesting and requests all those who wish to see his mare to call at the Government Farm. Gypsy Queen is a dark bay with black markings.

*   *   *   *

From *Signature Book:* "This is to certify that Frank M. Heath arrived at the U. S. Morgan Horse Farm last evening about 7:30.
(Signed) H. H. Reese."

From U. S. Department of Agriculture Circular 199:
"Breeding Morgan Horses at the
U. S. Morgan Horse Farm."
H. H. Reese, Animal Husbandman,
Animal Husbandry Division, Bureau of Animal Industry.

FOUNDATION OF BREED

"The Morgan breed of horses was established by a single stallion whose potency was so great that he left many descendants that looked and acted like him even after his blood had been much diluted. This stallion was Justin Morgan. During his early life he was the property of a school-teacher by that name, who lived near Randolph, Vermont. Justin Morgan was foaled about 1793 and died in 1821.

According to the meager records available, Justin Morgan was a small but powerful and quick horse, standing considerably under 15 hands. It is said that he could outwalk, outrun, or outpull any of the horses in his section of the country. Very little is definitely known of his ancestry. One investigator collected evidence showing that he was sired by the Thoroughbred stallion, True Briton, also called Beautiful Boy, a horse that traced in direct male line to Byerly Turk, and many other traces of Arabian blood. Another investigator contends that he was sired by a Dutch horse, which in turn came from Arabian stock. Which of these theories is correct is not important today. The presence of only five lumbar vertebrae in many Morgans supports both theories of Arabian foundation. * * * * Prominent writers have contended that the Morgan added stamina to certain trotting-horse families, for which the Morgan breed deserves considerable credit.

In the early days many high-class Morgan stallions and mares were purchased at attractive prices and taken to other sections of the country, and, while a few scattering studs were pure bred in their new locations, many of them were absorbed by the Standardbred and the Kentucky Saddle Horse breeds."

Chapter VIII

WINDING THROUGH THE ADIRONDACKS

From *Signature Book*: "May 13, '25. Frank M. Heath left this morning about eight o'clock.
(Signed) H. H. Reese."

From Notes. May 13, '25: * * * * Noon: We are lunching by the roadside 5 miles north of Shoreham, 7 mi. S. of Middlebury. I have today passed through a fine dairy country. Good buildings. Mostly good grass. Queen feeling pretty good. Cold broken. Cough nearly gone. Still some nasal discharge—still feeding G.I.N.—with little C.S. Discontinued tar on tongue—seem to aggravate cough (probably clogged bronchi)—for three days have been giving one—two oz. coal oil (on tongue with syringe). * * * Later—she has just cleaned up 4½ lbs. oats—eating grass. 4:30 p.m. (13th) *Arrived* farm of Mr. C. E. Riley, Shoreham, Vt., one mile E. of Lake Champlain.

The old man was a little reluctant about keeping us. It was almost too late to cross Lake Champlain that night and take a chance of getting accommodations on the other side. The Rileys had a strong sorrel horse, eleven years old, which they said had never been ridden. They wished to have him ridden.

"What's the matter with him?" I asked.

"Oh, he just wants to run away," replied the old man.

"If that's all, I'll ride him—if you will keep us," was my reply.

"All right," was his answer. He showed me the horse. I 'interviewed' the horse. We seemed to understand each other. After playing with him awhile I put the saddle on him and let him stand while we all went in to supper. When the meal was over we—the old man, his son, and myself—started to the horse-stable.

"Let's go out and see the show." It was the lady of the house addressing some one inside. It was plain that she was referring to the sorrel and myself.

"I don't believe there is going to be any show," I took upon myself to remark.

I brought the horse out, gently tightened the girth, saw that everything was 'ship-shape,' and climbed aboard. "What part of the farm was he working on last?" I asked. "Back there in that field we've been plowing with him," said his owner, indicating some sod which had recently been turned over. Not forgetting to keep a firm seat, and giving the horse his head to a reasonable extent, while not allowing him to get away with it altogether, I started off into the field. When he wanted to trot, I let him trot, while I maintained a firm seat. I rode him all over the field—up and down and back, occasionally talking to him as a fond father might to a wayward son. When we came back past the building, I expected, that if anywhere, there would be the circus. He showed some slight signs of rebellion, but by now he seemed to have got it into his head that I was the captain of the ship. He went where I steered him. I rode back to the barn and dismounted. The 'show' was over. Next morning at the breakfast table it came out that years before someone had undertaken to ride this horse, and, as the lady who 'wanted to see the show' expressed it, had been thrown 'higher than Gilderoy's kite.' These people, knowing the undertaking I had before me, though evidently not taking it as seriously as I, had deliberately inveigled me into riding this 'outlaw' horse, simply for the fun they expected to get out of it. They had no intention of ever riding the horse. Right there, I made a resolution that never again on this trip would I take the chance of getting my neck broken by riding outlaw horses for people's amusement. When it came time to settle at the house, the lady charged me nearly hotel rate, reminding me kindly that they had several little mouths to feed. I paid the bill without comment. I walked out and saddled up, remarking to the old man that I thought we were about square as far as the horses were concerned.

The Reeses had, with me, been very much interested in my choice of routes. The United States Touring Map, from which I had compiled my schedule, showed two easterly and westerly roads. Ours ran in almost a half-circle, going nearly direct south from Middlebury (which is located near Morgan Horse Farm) over some kind of a road—by way of White Hall and Saratoga Springs to Schenectady, where we would have struck the main tourist route, No. 42, to Utica and then to Syracuse as per schedule. The only alternative which I could choose from my map was to Ticonderoga, west to Schroon Lake, S. to near Chestertown, then N. W.—W.—S. W. (in a half-circle) through the mountains, finally coming out of the mountains at Utica. Neither was very practicable. The one would take us south, out of our way, onto a much traveled tourist-highway. The other would take us north and then back, through a lake country evidently sparsely settled, where either grazing or feed would very likely be hard to procure at this time of year. Both these routes we discarded in favor of the more direct route—presuming that there was one—which would be by Ticonderoga, southwesterly (south of Schroon Lake) to Chestertown. From there, as the crow flies, it is about seventy-five miles southwest to Utica. As a matter of fact it turned out that we actually traveled over this route one hundred and fifty-three miles to Rome, in place of Utica, Rome being according to the map some fifteen or twenty miles northwest of Utica.

Meanwhile, Mr. Reese phoned by long distance to a country postoffice, at a point where we should, logically, cut across, to know if it were possible for one on horseback to get anywhere near directly from there to Speculator, N. Y. The reply was that it could be done by resorting to frequent inquiries. Speculator was practically one-third of the way across, in a direct line to Rome—though as actually traveled the route was very crooked. From a point about two-thirds of the way across there was, as indicated by the State Map, a considerable choice in roads to Rome.

From Riley's I rode across the flat land to Larobee's Point, a little town, the east landing of the ferry over Lake Champlain. There we waited probably half an hour in the cold breeze which was coming over the Lake. The ferry arrived. It was of the scow type with a rather low railing and a single chain across the two ends, as is common with such ferries. The distance across the lake was considerable. The waves were rolling pretty high. Queen was rearing and plunging. She was almost hysterical. Several times I was in doubt as to whether she would jump overboard, carrying me with her. I had dismounted and was keeping a firm hold on both reins just back of the bit in such a manner that it would, in fact, have been a difficult stunt for her to have leaped overboard with my 125 pounds dangling from the strong bridle. Meanwhile, of course, I did my best to soothe her. Finally we got across. We were much relieved when we arrived on the other side.

Here we detoured slightly to visit old Fort Ticonderoga. I was struck with the apparent flimsiness of what once was a fortification. I believe that modern rifle-balls would easily pierce these walls today.

They would certainly be no protection against modern artillery. Leaving the Fort we passed through Ticonderoga.

From Notes. May 14, '25: * * * * Entered foothills of Adirondacks soon after passing through Ticonderoga. Passed west of Lake George, about 2 p.m. Took winding dirt road to Graphite, an old, half-deserted graphite mining town. Stopped at 5 places, trying to get accommodations for Queen, before succeeding. 6th place, got good warm stall, good hay—bought grain at another place. Supper, breakfast, bed [at Zera Frazier's] only $1.00. Many deserted small farms between here and Ticonderoga.

Traveled: 22 miles. Extra detour to Fort, 2 mi.—by misdirection, 2 mi.—hunting stable, 2 mi.—Road, 3 mi. west from Ti. very hard and rough surface. About 3 mi. paved, good "side," bal. dirt, much steep grade. Queen tired but good appetite, etc. This place is practically at summit of the Adirondacks (1½ mi. E.) on Fenimore Cooper Trail, on State Highway to Horicon and Chestertown.

May 15, '25: Left Frazier place 7:30. [On getting ready to leave I noticed the old man and his son plowing—or rather rooting—amongst the boulders with one horse and a large old single-shovel plow. The old man seemed to have all he could do to handle the plow.] 1:30 p.m. Feeding Queen by roadside 1 mi. N. E. of Horicon, near Lake Brant. * * * Passed Summit at Swede Mt. fire signal sta. A long lake at Summit. Passed north of lake to get dirt road. Summer resort just opening. Passed only 2 farms this morning. First 3 miles west of Graphite all woods. Very fine view from west slope. 4:30 ard. Chestertown—found "tight" box-stall in one end of old shed at Feed Store of Harry Perry. * * * * Let Queen feed ¾ hr. on grass. * * * * Got good supper at boarding house for 50 cts. * * * *

Traveled: 22 miles. Detour N. Brant Lake for dirt Rd. 3 miles —by misdirection 1 mile.

At noon we stopped at the home of Robert Richard, four miles west of Weavertown. This old place had been in the family for five generations. The personal recollections of the grandfather of the sixteen-year old boy who acted as my host, were very clear in the mind of this boy—about Indians, surveyors, etc. The farm had quite evidently seen its best days. The house, once quite a building, was fast crumbling. The young man mentioned the resources of the place. It seemed to have a ridiculously small number of sheep and cattle compared to the acreage. The boy told me that his father was working their team of horses on the public road some sixty-five miles away. I was invited in to dinner, which proved to be an excellent meal. The family was intelligent. Books lined the walls. Some man had driven in to shoe a horse. He happened to have a bag of oats in the back of the buggy. Generously, he gave me a feed of the precious grain for Queen. Queen's cold was sticking with her to quite an extent. I was beginning to worry—not that I believed it was anything contagious—at least as yet. I had had her examined before leaving Silver Spring by a veterinarian, and once or twice on the way. I was becoming sensitive about appearing, perhaps, to be careless as to spreading contagion. I mentioned to this young boy the fact that she had a cold and suggested that I had better feed her outside. . . . "Out of the mouths of babes and sucklings cometh Wisdom"—Solomon. The boy glanced at the mare. "Oh," he said, "she's all right. Bring her in. You see," he continued, "you've been exposing her to some pretty strenuous conditions. This is pretty well north and fairly high altitude. Here it is still early spring—the season of colds. In fact, most of the local horses have colds." (A fact which I had noticed.) "You'll soon be down out of the mountains now," he went on, "into a warmer climate and plenty of green grass, and that'll be the end of your horse's cold." This proved actually to be true. As soon as we got down out of the mountains to where there was plenty of green grass, her cold left her. That was many years ago. With the exception a very slight cold once or twice, she has never shown any of these symptoms since, which then alarmed me.

From Notes. May 16, '25: * * * * 4:30 ard. Fox Lair, summer home of R. A. Hudnut, perfume king, of N. Y. Mr. Harry Armstrong, foreman. 15 miles s.w. of Weavertown, via Johnsburg and farm of Robt. Richards.

Traveled: 26 miles. Extra, by error, 1 mile. About 2 miles west of Chestertown very hard and rough. Balance dirt or good "side." Many steep hills. Queen feeling pretty fair—nasal discharge still bad. Crossed 2nd and west divide at Weavertown.

This place consisted at that time of about 1200 acres. The house of the Superintendent, Mr. Armstrong, where we were guests, was located on the edge of a beautiful natural meadow of considerable extent. On the rolling hills, probably a half-mile south of this, were the main buildings, it might be safe to say, acres of them—large horse-sheds, etc. A golf course lay nearby. About here it seemed impossible to cure hay properly. A little was spread out on an old hay-rack to air. It was mouldy. Queen had been out on the young grass which to me did not seem to contain much nourishment. The Superintendent, a native mountaineer, a very intelligent and hospitable man, was not niggardly with the oats. As a fool would do, I fed Queen some of this mouldy hay in addition to the oats—though I knew better. This gave her a temporary set-back. That night I slept in a good bed. Had a wonderful supper and breakfast. Had a very interesting conversation with the Armstrongs. Something in his attitude made me know better than to offer to pay, either cash or in voluntary services. I had been a guest. This Superintendent had not seen any of the Hudnuts for several years—they were in Europe. The road through which I entered and left Fox Lair is not shown on the map. A short distance southwest of the estate the road on the local map, but not on mine, turns much more duly south than the direct course we would take 'as the bird flies.' But in this place there was no road in our general direction so far as Armstrong, a native of these parts, knew. He referred me to old Henry Girard, at Griffin—on the highway that ran way south of the direct line to Speculator. This place was situated on the east bank of the east Branch of the Sacandaga River. I was given to understand that if there were anyone in this part of the country who could direct me, it would be Henry Girard, a very-old-timer. I arrived there about noon, had some kind of lunch, and fed Queen in an old dilapidated barn, over the plank approach of which we had carefully to feel our way. As nearly as I can remember, Griffin consisted of this barn and the old, old wooden hotel building. There had been a postoffice at Griffin, but it had been discontinued for lack of patrons. Girard could tell me of no way across this wilderness.

I insisted that there should be some shorter way than by Wells, which is still further south, but I was told as persistently that there was no way through. So I went on south to Wells, somewhat of a town, lying on the river far below the east and west forks. Here I crossed the Sacandaga above the town, over what I remember to be a pretty fair, rather high old bridge. After this, I took what is shown on the local map as a dirt road, running through the mountains, back north toward Speculator. From Speculator my next objective was

Lake Piseco—which would take me back S. W. from Speculator—causing us to make an inverted V. Piseco (on Lake Piseco) was almost directly west of the Fuller place. The round-about road via Speculator was terribly rough surface, clay all chopped up when wet, and now dried into hard bumps.

From Notes. May 17, '25: * * * * 4:45 p.m. Arrived place of Wm. Fuller, 4 miles N. W. of Wells (via Wells). Fuller is a good-hearted chap, let me keep Queen in old, but comfortable shed—box-stall inside. I slept in one stall. Plenty poor hay for Queen. * * * * Oats. Only 25 cts. Had supper with Mrs. Grace Olmstead.

Traveled: 20 miles. Jogged 1 mile. * * * * Dirt road very narrow—last 4 miles. (At Elvard postoffice discontinued—this was formerly Fuller's postoffice.) Followed Sacandaga River from Fox Lair to Wells. Then N. W. 4 miles to Fullers. This is an old dilapidated place—with small new house. Good soil. Plenty manure going to waste. No garden. Hustlers—run market in Wells and Speculator. Good fishing, wild life. Tourists attention.

May 18, '25: 8 a.m. Getting ready to leave here (Fuller). * * * *

The local road-map I was carrying showed a road cutting off the inverted V, but I was told by all that it had been abandoned. Mr. Fuller, with whom we stayed that night, near the junction of what had been a road, told me that the last he had heard of its having been traveled, was six years before, when he had managed with some difficulty to lead a cow across there. The country through which it led was a wilderness. But, as the road by way of Speculator was through dirt, hard and uneven, and twisted Queen's joints grievously, I decided to try the cut-off. Some instinct seemed to tell Queen that this was a hazardous proposition. I was walking. She tried to run back. Nevertheless, when we came to a creek, she stepped from stone to stone across it. As we approached the 'hunter's lodge' we had been told about, we came to a foot-bridge consisting of two logs over a boggy-looking swale. To try putting Queen over this bridge would have been disastrous. Had I been foolhardy enough to try it, she would have put a foot through the uneven opening between the logs. So, reluctantly, she started across the bog. I was on the bridge. Half way across—down she went! The floating bog had broken through. Where the bottom was, God knows. With an intelligence

almost human Queen started swimming, as it were, with her hind
feet, while placing first one foreleg and then the other full length
upon the partly yielding bog or sod or peat (call it what you will)
ahead of her. As that hold gave way she got another until she reached
footing on the far side. Still some people will say that a horse doesn't
know anything. A horse, in swimming, does not show his front feet.
In climbing, he climbs principally with his hind feet. It is well
known that in jumping a ditch, for instance, if a horse loses his hold
with the hind feet, he is gone. In performing this feat Queen had
climbed with her front feet, while *swimming* with her hind feet—
something entirely unusual in the horse of today. Who shall say at
what point in our evolution a horse's—or man's—superimposed intelligence merges with instinct? Or to what extent we are still gov-
erned by the instinct of some predecessor—nobody knows how many
millions of years back? In the above case Gypsy Queen had recourse
to the instinct of whatever marine animal preceded the horse in that
stage of evolution covered by the "Marine Age." Have you any
other solution?

When Queen emerged from this slough there was not a dry hair
on her. It took me over an hour to remove this soft mud from her
by means of scrapers which I improvised from pieces of bark and so
on, and rub her dry with wisps of grass. I also had to do a good deal of
cleaning on the pack and saddle before they were fit to replace.

This hunting lodge was on a kind of island surrounded by this
floating bog. There had been a wagon track approaching this old
lodge from the west, the direction in which we were traveling. With
great difficulty I found what appeared to have been a wagon track,
almost obliterated. This wagon track had run across a bridge, the
abutments of which still stood. I believe these abutments were built
of logs, evidently sunken to a solid formation. I poked a stick through
perhaps a foot of floating bog. Below this seemed to be the same
slush. The floating bog would carry me but not the horse. Queen was
standing with her front feet on the first abutment or sill, taking it
all in. The gap would require a jump of about twice her length. Not
so bad for a standing jump—what? She was sizing that up too. "Jump,
Queen!" I commanded, and over she went, getting a clean hold on
the opposite sill with her hind feet.

On we went—over log, under fallen tree—scarcely able to distinguish where the old road had been. Queen went down into what
must have been quick-sand beneath the turf. A scramble with the
front feet—a pull against suction on the back ones—a sucking sound

—the feet were out. One of the rubber pads had been 'sucked' out of place as far as the nails allowed even tearing loose from one or two of them. I toggled this up. Down went one hind foot between the entangled roots of a beech tree where the earth beneath had been washed away. The foot was in a trap. "Stand still, Queen," I cautioned her, "Don't move." She didn't. I pried open the jaws of the trap with a long stick. "Now pick it up, ol' girl!" She lifted her foot out.

That noon, having come upon a trail that penetrated from the far side of the wilderness, Queen was feeding and I was lunching on Mrs. Olmstead's short-cake. Queen came over and put her head down close to mine, saying as plain as a horse can talk, "You meant all right, but something told me that was a hard place." "Queen, you're a wonderful pal," I told her.

We were, by now, well over the line into the State Park (which does not mean that all of this land was owned by the State).

> *From Notes.* May 18, '25 continued: (Taken immediately after emerging from the Wilderness.) Observed considerable scraggly but fair-sized timber—various kinds. Here on a S. E. slope I observed instance of reforestation. Evergreens (I believe spruce) set out in rows five or six feet apart. Very few 'blanks.' Trees two to four feet high. * * * *

This trail we had come upon brought us out onto the highway, at the village of Lake Pleasant, at the south end of Lake Pleasant, instead of at Speculator, at the north end of the lake.

> *From Notes.* May 18, '25 continued: 4:30 p.m. ard. home of Herbert Aird, Piseco, N. Y. (on highway at west end of Lake Piseco). World War vet. Queen in basement barn. Supper, bed. Helped on fence. S. S. (Subscription to Stars and Stripes). Sleeping in house—breakfast—no chg. Queen fine.
> *Traveled:* 18 miles, May 18th. Extra by twisting through 'jungles'—1 mile.

We were now, at Lake Piseco, in the heart of much tourist country —or rather of the summer vacationist region.

We left Herbert Aird next morning. Twisting around between the lakes, through miles and miles of country where more farms are abandoned than otherwise, where the principal meal-ticket is a few cows, a patch of potatoes maybe, a little garden, balsam pillows, antiques, fresh air, a little scenery and tourists or vacationists—we are a little way down the west slope.

Having passed a sawmill or two, we arrive at the place of Mr. Bussy and family, fifteen miles southwest of Morehouseville. It is too high here for successful farming, but Mr. Bussy spends part of the money he makes from sawing timber off the places he buys up, in "trying to farm anyhow." It is the 19th of May.

The trees are just leafing out. Moss here has a tendency to smother out the grass. Mr. Bussy tells me that he has bought up about 1,000 acres, farm by farm—old estates at forced sale. The young folks have all left for the city, and the old folks let us hope for a more congenial clime. He pays around $2.00 per acre, he tells me. That is what the state is paying, he says, for land for the purpose of reforestation.

Over more miles where the main meal ticket apparently is extracted from the tourist in return for milk, eggs, meals, beds and antiques, and we are down in the foothills. We come suddenly upon some good dairy farms. Down, down we continue to drop until we stop tonight at Trenton, N. Y. The climate is as different from last night's environment as summer is from early spring, for there is actually that difference in one day's ride. And a hard day for Queen it was—that down grade.

From Notes. May 20, '25: 6 p.m. Ar'd barn of C. S. Heckland, Trenton, N. Y., via Remsen.

Traveled: 21 miles. Jogged ½ mile. Dirt 15 mi. Pave. 6 mi.

Here the lush grass is eight inches high, the air is full of the sweet perfume of fruit blossoms and the hum of bees. And with warm weather and green grass Queen's cold disappears.

Leaving Trenton next morning, May 21st, we traveled through what seemed like a fairyland farming country. At noon we stopped in a shower of rain and I got permission to feed Queen in the dairy-barn of a good farm. The young man invited me to the house for dinner. It was a little late. The meal was just over. So was the shower. The young man went out in the field with a tractor. The old lady set on the table a good hot meal. The conversation had not proceeded far when she asked, "How do you manage to keep the police from picking you up?" "I don't know what you mean," I replied. "Why should the police want to pick me up?" "For bumming," she replied. "Who is bumming?" I asked, half indignantly. "The young man, whom I took to be a member of the family, invited me to the house to have some dinner." Looking past her I saw the old man sitting against the wall, apparently rather amused. I caught his mood. "Lady," I said, "I've been told that either an argument or unwelcome food is bad for the digestion. If you'll be so kind, since I've been invited to the house, as to allow me to finish the meal in peace, I'll pay you anything you ask." I could see the old man chuckling. "Oh, you have some money, then?" she queried. "Lady," I chirped cheerfully, "I have more money than some folks have hay." (I was certain this was true, since "some folks" have no hay at all.) The old man could scarcely suppress his giggles. She looked interrogatively at my clothes which were pretty dirty and almost in tatters. "Oh," I said, "my clothes. I dress that way because I am naturally democratic. I feel more at home with the common people." This time the old man laughed outright. She cut loose and laughed too. The young lady of the house was still looking a little skeptical, as though wondering if they were entertaining a tramp. "I am in the newspaper business," I informed her. The fact is, I had forgotten I was still an agent for the "Stars and Stripes." The girl looked much relieved. The old lady, meanwhile, was putting on the dessert. "Well," she said, "you just finish your meal and welcome. You're a man we don't meet every day."

I was now back in the country of regular roads. Someone suggested, "Why not take the old Erie Canal tow path and avoid the regular highways?" I decided to try it. On a bridge entering Rome we met a well-dressed man driving a fine automobile. He was very civil. This bridge we were on was over some old canal. Its direction did not suit me. It came in from the north. "This is the Black River Canal," he explained. "The old Erie—what's left of it—you'll strike over in the west part of the city." I saw him studying us.

"Say, where you figuring on staying tonight?"

"Figuring on making about five miles and 'hitting the hay' in some farmer's barn."

"Say, a rest won't hurt you or your horse. I've traveled some myself and I love to talk with a traveler. I wish you would 'hit the hay' at our house. You go . . ." (and he gave directions how to reach the place). Out in front, there's fine blue grass. Let the horse feed there while I go get permission to put her in a barn I know about. I'll phone the folks—they'll be looking for you."

"But I'm as dirty as the devil—haven't had a shave for ten days. I better go over town first. I—"

"Too much time fooled away. I have all kinds of razors and everything."

We sat up late, exchanging experiences. Mr. Wallace, my host, gave me a great deal of the local traditions.

Late that night I sat down on the edge of the bed in the guest-room, and made in my Notebook this entry:

This is, indeed, a strange life. One night I curl up in an empty stall, the next I am being entertained like a prince.

From Signature Book: "Rome, N. Y., May 21, 1925. F. M. Heath is a guest at our home for the night.

(Signed) H. F. Wallace."

From Notes. May 21, '25: Traveled: 16 miles. Side trip to Mr. Wallace's place 1 mile. Pavement 9 miles. Balance, hard rough dirt.

THE ROME SENTINEL

MAY 22, 1925

ON 18,000 MILE HORSEBACK TRIP WORLD WAR VETERAN STOPS HERE—HEATH ON GYPSY QUEEN WILL VISIT EACH OF 48 STATES

* * * * Leaving Rome this morning he headed Gypsy Queen west, planning to reach Buffalo Saturday afternoon by way of the old Erie Canal towpath. He prefers country byways to the improved roads.

"The strain on my horse is not because of the number of miles," he said, "but because of the hard footing for her. Then, too, changes of feed, various climates and strange stables make it hard for the old girl."

Weighing 120 pounds himself, he carries with him on the horse packed saddle bags that weigh 60 pounds. (Error: He meant the horse was packed 60 pounds dead weight.—Author.) Other equipment he mails ahead. Gypsy Queen averages about 24 miles a day. (When traveling.)

* * * * Little incidents here and there add interest to the trip. Heath nearly lost his horse in the woods near Lake Pleasant, when, coming over a back road, the animal stumbled into a blind bog.

(Slight error: Queen did not *stumble* into the blind bog. She broke through the upper peat.—Author.)

So far he's been in the States of Maryland, Delaware, New Jersey, Pennsylvania, Connecticut, Rhode Island, Massachusetts, Maine, Vermont, and New York. The other 38 lie ahead of him and his good horse, Gypsy Queen.

Comment: As stated, we had actually traveled, from Chestertown, fully twice the distance as the crow flies. A reasonably close check of the map indicates that in miles we had traveled approximately the same distance as we would had we traveled by way of Schenectady. We had gained, however, in theoretical miles and therefore in the saving of horse flesh. About one fourth of this distance on the southern route would have been over a much-traveled and presumably paved highway. Besides, look at the experience we had!

From Notes. May 23, '25: 5:45 p.m. Ar'd at barn of J. J. Collins, 208 S. Beach St., Syracuse, N. Y.

Traveled: 22 mi. Jogged ½ mi. Very wet, slippery.

May 24, '25: Leaving barn of Mr. Collins, 8:45. Had feed, blankets, in barn—no chg. Quite a talk with Mr. Collins. * * * * Noon: Feeding by rd. side on luscious grass, excellent feed, crushed oats, ground corn and molasses, contributed by Mr. Collins. (This excellent feed was Collins' own invention.) He is a great horse lover. Pavement several miles through Syracuse. Onto tow path. Detour 1 mile. * * * Back on tow path. Detouring again 2 mi. acc't trespass notice and gate. Will soon be back on path. Cold rain last night. Cold now with both raincoats on. Snowing at 2 p.m. (slight flurry.) * * * * 4:45 p.m., Ar'd farm of Norman H. Hard, Jordon, N. Y.

Traveled: 24 mi. 2 mi. detour onto lateral by error. Jogged 3 mi. Land along canal heavy, black, * * * * Off to south low-lying hills. Good looking farms.

Chapter IX

SOUTH OF THE GREAT LAKES

OVER more rolling country devoted to mixed farming, dairying and truck, over roads more or less stony when not paved, we arrived at a place near East Rochester on May 25, 1925. We were with difficulty keeping up with our schedule. Something had happened to further interfere with Queen's left front foot. Not far back I had stopped at noon in a town. I gave Queen the nose-bag at a black-smith shop. There happened to be there a horse belonging to the proprietor which was newly and well shod. Queen's front shoes being pretty well worn, I decided to have her reshod in front. I thought I made it plain to the proprietor that I wished to have the left front left 1/16 of an inch high on the *outside*, with the shoe projecting also on the outside as much as was permissible in reason —that is, as much as could be done and still get a good hold with the nails. I was very hungry, and went in search of lunch while she was being shod. When I returned and looked at the foot, I was so damned mad that I knew better than to open my head except to pay the bill, and remarked, I'm afraid a little sarcastically, that they "certainly had given me a fine job of shoeing!" The foot had been shod exactly the reverse of my instructions. Why he did it, God knows. I had made it plain that it was the *left* side of the *left* foot that I wished made a little high and prominent, and supposed that any horseshoer would know that I meant the left side when the foot was on the ground. It could be presumed that a thoughtless man, believing he was following instructions, might, in picking a horse's foot up—sole up—with the foot between his knees and his back toward the horse's head—get the right side of the horse's foot con-fused with his *own left* hand, and thus leave the shoe prominent on the *right* side of the foot in place of the *left* side. Anyhow, it will be seen that a lot of mischief had been done. Instead of the shoe being prominent on the outside, some of the hoof was actually filed away and the shoe prominent on the *inside*. Also, the foot, instead of being a little high on the outside, was positively a little

low. Instead of supporting the strained ligaments and properly adjusting the bearing, the desired result was reversed. We were in a pretty
pickle! Too much had been taken off the foot to allow a resetting
of the shoe without destroying too much of the hoof. It will be seen
that to attempt to set the nails outside of the holes that had been
made in the shoeing would not be possible if we expected them to
hold. No 'shimming' up of the shoe could be attempted. If ever a
man worked to save a leg, at the same time keep going, 1 did during
the next month. Fortunately, creeks or wells of cold water were
plentiful. So was good old mud. We made fairly good time anyhow,
but had fallen a little behind our schedule. Upon getting this terrible
job of shoeing just mentioned, I determined to never again absent
myself while Gypsy Queen was being shod.

Some twenty-eight days had expired since that terrible mishap in
shoeing (usually Queen went from four to six weeks between shoeing). I found an old man who was one of the best shoers I have ever
met. We reshod Queen all around, the hoof meanwhile having
grown to the extent that it was possible to shoe her properly.

> *From Notes.* May 28, '25: Leaving Mr. Bush, 7:30. Horse,
> bed. No. chg. * * * * Gave formula for spavin blister—they
> have a spavin horse. Noon, feeding by rd. side ¼ mi. west of
> W. Henrietta on oats contributed by Mr. Bush. * * * * Tra
> versed fine mixed farming country, slightly rolling. At West
> Henrietta took first cash sub. in long time. Met Mike Serne and
> Eddie Rimmers, State Troopers.

Most of these State Troopers were now dismounted, using motorcycles instead of horses, except in winter. Once only, before this, I
had caught a glimpse of two mounted on horses. By the way, I had
had a little amusement, off and on, over this State Trooper business.
It seemed a little strange that I, a few times, had been mistaken for
a trooper, seeing that I was dressed in khaki, while all troopers that I
saw were dressed in blue—though they may have worn khaki later
in summer. Once I was hailed by a little old man who gave me 'an
earful' about a 'petting party' lane near his residence, and wanted
to know what we were 'going to do about it.' "I am sorry, friend," I
had replied, "but so far as I am concerned we'll just have to let 'em
pet." He looked at me in half-indignant astonishment. "Ain't you a
State Trooper?" "Not guilty," I told him as I rode on.

From Notes. May 28, '25 continued: 5:30 p.m. reached farm of John Skinnington, Mumford, N. Y. 2 miles E. of Caledonia. Had been turned down 5 times—began to worry. Passed gypsum mills.

Traveled: 25 miles. Jogged 3 mi. Good side nearly all the way, via (from E. Rochester) Pittsford, West Henrietta, Scottsville, Mumford. Fine mixed farming country. Queen fine except left front leg.

May 29, '25: Leaving farm of Mr. John Skinnington 7:45 a.m. Horse, meals (slept in hay), no chg. Showery. Noon, feeding at farm of Mr. Robt. Mattice, 1 mile west of Le Roy * * * * (hot day)—lunch at store. 6 p.m. Ar'd farm of Mr. J. L. Townsend, Batavia, N. Y., 2½ mi. west center Batavia. (3½ mi. west S. T. [State Troopers'] Barracks.)

Traveled: 25 mi. Jogged 3½—fair side except Batavia.

I was never more hospitably entertained than at Townsend's. Here I learned a little trick in keeping down the 'road founder' in Queen. By 'road founder' is meant the inflammation that would get into a horse's feet simply from continual pounding on the road, especially when hard. Aside from the strained condition of some ligaments, we had this generally to contend with also. It happened that Queen was given a large pen in a straw-shed which had been used principally for cows. Straw was plentiful. I bedded her very deep, but her feet worked through down into the 'barnyard poultice.' She came out in the morning with feet as 'cool as cucumber.' Now in future, should I speak of 'barnyard poultice,' you will know what I mean—and that it had its origin with the genus bovine. I remember particularly that the soil on this farm was very rich, and the country all around seemed fertile and prosperous. Mixed farming.

From Notes. May 30, '25: Leaving farm of Mr. J. L. Townsend, Batavia, N. Y. * * * * 8 p.m. Ar'd place of Louis J. Schwendler, 1989 Clinton St., Buffalo, N. Y.

Traveled: 35 miles. Jogged 5 miles. Fair side 20 mi. Pavement 5 miles. Very rough hard road, 10 miles * * * * Country rather flat, soil sour and cold.

Special Note: Total to Buffalo 1153 mi. as corr.

From Signature Book: "1989 Clinton St., Buffalo, N. Y. May 30, '25. 8 p.m. Frank M. Heath, with Gypsy Queen, has just arrived here.
(Signed) Lewis J. Schwendler."

From Signature Book: "This is to certify that Frank M. Heath has called at my office, June 1, 1925. He is making a tour of the country.

(Signed) Frank Y. Slocumb,
Mayor of Buffalo, N. Y."

From Notes. June 2, '25: 8:30 a.m. Just leaving home of Lewis Schwendler. * * * Noon, between Athel Springs and Bay View, feeding near shore of Lake Erie. On Yellowstone Trail. Very poor dirt 'side' so far. 5:30 p.m. Reached farm of Mr. James McIntosh, Derby, N. Y. Keeps tourists. Garage. Wants stallion 'second-hand.' (Mr. McIntosh had several polo pony brood mares running in pasture. He delegated me to look out for a suitable stallion to breed with these mares. He said he wouldn't mind going as far as two or three hundred miles with his truck to get it, if I found one at a reasonable price.)

Traveled: 26 miles. 1 mi. by misdirection. Poor to fair 'side,' —23 mi. Pavement, 3 mi. Country level. Ground baked hard as a brick. All along Yellowstone Trail to 10 or 15 mi. out of Buffalo—residence lots. This is where [Yellowstone] trail leaves the Lake Shore. Beyond this I observed several good-looking vineyards. (For miles the principal product was grapes. At least one team was generally working continually upon each of these grape farms with a horse-cultivator—of the type often referred to as a horse hoe). Also several men with hand hoes were generally employed.

From Notes. June 3, '25: Leaving place of Mr. McIntosh, 8 a.m. Horse, bed, meals—no charge. Need rain. None for 2 months. I trimmed horse's feet—put back on axis—and gave several useful formulas. Noon, feeding by wayside, 1 mile west of Irving, N. Y., on oats contributed by Mr. McIntosh, and a 'hot dog.' Quite hot, but fine breeze. Farmers setting out acres of tomato plants. N. Y. cannery at Irving. 5 p.m. Ar'd farm of Walter Ingham, Sheridan, N. Y. Observed Jersey cows from Buffalo west.

Traveled: 24 miles. Fair to poor 'side' on Y.S.T. [Yellowstone Trail] via Derby, Silver Creek, Irving. Country slightly rolling. (Back 3 miles from Lake). Soil not quite so hard. Needs rain badly. Vineyards continue. Mixed farming.

June 4, '25: Leaving place of Mr. Ingham 8:15. * * * *

Horse, n.c. [no charge] Meals, $1.00. Sold gun, $1.50. 10:00 a.m. passing Fredonia. Citizens dedicating monument to discovery of 1st gas well in U. S. Detoured off Y.S.T. onto Webster (dirt) Rd. via Chautauqua. 11 a.m. met Neal Madigan who gave me address of Hoyt Averil, North East, N. Y., who has lame horse. * * * * [Author's note: Here notes in places are illegible due to the note-book becoming soaked in a heavy storm.] Notes continued: * * * * This, like surrounding farms, is devoted, mostly to the cultivation of Concord grapes. Average yield 3 tons per acre. [We had passed several farms devoted to the raising of a variety of white grape.] * * * * 4:45, reached farm, or vineyard, of Sam Foti, Westfield. * * * * They are industrious Sicilian people—2 children. Paying for 40 acres for which they gave $200 per acre. * * * * (The children ran from me, and soon their mother appeared. She greeted me civilly. Her husband came up and eyed me suspiciously. He said, "If a man is a bum, he lose his life!" To myself I said, "Just for that I'm going to stay, unless you definitely send me away." Thereupon I picked up a hoe and followed them both back to the grape-vines for an hour or so. The woman out-hoed me.) Ground is very hard and dry. Home is ¼ mile from Lake Shore. Owned place 15 years.

Traveled: 23 mi. 2 by detour. 3 miles pavement. 6 mi. fair 'side.' 14 dirt.

Mrs. Foti talked intelligently and civilly about grape-culture and of the country thereabouts. I became convinced that grape-farming is not as poetical as it sounds. It involves a great deal of hard work and not any too much profit. The evening meal was served by 'lamp-light.' It was an Italian meal. Spaghetti and cheese was the main dish, with a great pitcher of fine fresh milk and another of wine. 'Sam' was in an amiable mood. My diligence with the hoe had convinced him more than any talk could have done that I was not a 'bum.' I questioned whether it would be best for me to drink both wine and milk. "That's right," he said, "You drink wine, you drink wine. You drink milk, you drink milk. You drink all you want. Me, I drink wine." He did—I believe about half a gallon. I drank milk—all I wanted.

From Notes. June 5, '25: Leaving place of Sam Foti, 7:15 a.m. * * * * 3:45, little girl, Sara Phillips, riding a piece with me E. of N.E. (North East is the name of a town) on her mustang.

("Dad said to me," she explained, "why don't you ride a few miles with the gentleman and show him the road." She was a bright child. The country here was devoted to truck and berries mostly. In passing the house I had halted to inquire about roads.) 6 p.m. Ar'd farm of Mr. Fraymer, 3 mi. S. of N. E. Hoyt Averil on place. * * * *

Traveled: 28 mi. 5 mi. detour, 3 mi. by error. Pavement 3 mi. [under] construction 4 mi. Bal. fair to poor 'side' or dirt. Passed into Pennsylvania 3 p.m. Grapes gradually giving way to orchards and mixed farms. Very dry and hot. * * * *

June 6, '25: * * * * 7 p.m. Ar'd farm of Wm. Klemm, 2 mi. S. W. Erie.

Traveled: 26 mi.—4½ detour. * * * *

June 7, '25: Leaving Klemms 9 a.m. (?) Good meals. Hay. Oats from neighbor. No chg. 'Helped out' on horse. This was a case of 'chronic sore shoulder.' Gave directions as to proper way of relieving this condition. 4:30 p.m. Ar'd farm of Fred Harmon, North Girard, 18½ miles W. of Erie.

Traveled: 20 mi.—1½ by detour and misdirection. Fair dirt side mostly. Prosperous looking region. Mixed farming. Only a few grapes. Wheat heading out. Not much evidence of drought.

June 8, '25: Leaving home of Everett Struchen (Farmer for Mr. Harmon). * * * * Noon: Feeding Queen at an old farm 1¼ mi. E. of State Line (the Ohio-Penn. State Line) on Under Ridge Road. * * * *

7 p.m. reached country home of A. Westcot, Route 1, West Springfield, Ohio. Country slightly rolling. Mixed farming. Dry. Hot.

Traveled: 32 miles. 8 mi. detour for dirt roads. Fair dirt mostly on Under Ridge and South Ridge. * * * * Dry. Hot.

June 9, '25: Leaving home of A. Westcot, Route 1, 8 a.m. Cooler. Horse, meals, 25c for oats, 10 a.m. reached Astabula. Got shave, material for lotion (Leg wash). * * * * 6 p.m. reached Unionville.

Later waited at a dairy for boss to return. Got quart of milk. Lunched on same and doughnuts. No room. Left about 8:45 p.m. Turned down next place. 9:30, camping at a strawstack 1½ miles west of Unionville.

Traveled: 23 mi. Pavement 2 mi. (Queen sore) Bal. good dirt. Fairly prosperous country. Slightly rolling. Some vineyards.

June 10, '25: Left strawstack 1 mile E. Madison (1½ mi. W.

of Unionville) (Ohio) 5 a.m. * * * * 8 p.m. Ar'd home of
Fred Keyerlever, Euclid, O., R. 1, about 2 mi. E. of Cleveland
Hts. About 12 mi. N. E. center of Cleveland.

Traveled: 39 mi. 9 detour. 4 paved. Bal. fair 'side' and dirt.
Several hills. Via Madison, Painsville, Mentor (via Jackson St.),
Cutland, (Mormon Temple), South Willoughby. Country roll-
ing. Generally prosperous. Mixed farming. * * * * Cold wind.
Mr. Keyerlever a fine good-humored old gentleman alone.
German descent. * * * *

By now it must be patent to the reader that, being of a sensitive
nature, and practically at the end of my resources so far as ready
cash was concerned, I was much perturbed as to how to get along
without being a 'bum.' Day by day, while trying to keep our schedule,
I could feel my face burn with what seemed like a choice between
two very disagreeable alternatives. Either I must abandon the undertaking—and I could not endure the thought of that—or else, as Sam
Foti had it, become a bum. Did the reader ever resort to communing
with his other self, as it were, upon finding himself between the
devil and the deep blue sea? Unconsciously that is what I was doing.
I was constantly soliloquizing: what shall I do in lieu of both these
alternatives? All at once, as though out of the blue, it came to me:
"Why you damn fool, for the last month you've been *giving away*
your experience, professional experience, while feeling that you were
humiliating yourself. From now on seek for and take advantage of
opportunities to exchange your professional knowledge of horses for
your expenses." I was rid of a tremendous burden. I began right
there to start in early in the afternoon inquiring for some man on
or near our route, who loved his horses but had some horse with an
undiagnosed case of lameness. At first this method was not very
successful. The first few times I abruptly approached a man with a
lame horse with my proposition in mind, he naturally would take
me to be a faker. So I adopted a less abrupt method of approach.
It is not in my nature to worm my way into anyone's confidence.
Nevertheless I would ride up to the place I had located, about the
time the farmer would be coming out of the field, and ask to be
put up for the night. Usually, depending on the man's demeanor, I
would say: "I've got to take care of this horse. I'll sleep in the hay
if you don't mind, or under the wagon-shed. I won't burn you out—I
don't smoke, don't carry any matches. I have some lunch with me.
When I get ready to leave, whatever I owe you I will pay." (Bear in

mind, I did not aim to let my finances get below five or ten dollars—which means that I did not take chances on making promises that I could not fulfill if necessary.) Tomorrow or next week would take care of itself. We would cross that bridge when we came to it.

Queen was now in excellent shape. Even the slight lameness was hardly noticeable now in these parts, where we had better footing and plenty of good water and mud. Her coat shone till one could use her side for a mirror. Her eyes were bright. Her muzzle was clean. So she naturally appealed to this man who was a lover of horses. Meanwhile I had showed the man our schedule. We were on time, and by the way, "on time" means a lot to these prosperous northern farmers. The conversation then would usually run about like this: "Say, Mister, you sure understand horses." "Well, there's a lot I don't know about horses. I admit I have handled 'em some. My father was a scientific shoer by the way." I would break in all at once, "If you happen to have a lame horse and nobody seems to understand what's wrong with him—if there's anything I could suggest to help the horse I'll be pleased to do so."

Mr. Farmer, with a sly wink at the hired man, says "Bill, bring old Charlie out here." Out comes old Charlie on the halter.

"Well, he isn't lame today," I tell Mr. Farmer, "but he goes lame in the left hind foot sometimes, particularly when he's been out on the rough hard road."

"Well, that's right," says the farmer, "but how the devil can you tell?"

"Why, to me it's obvious."

"How?"

(We were standing directly behind the horse. I had seen to it that the horse was standing on practically level ground.) "Had you noticed that the horse is off balance in that foot?"

"Off balance?"

"Yes. It's a case of malconformation—that is, the weight doesn't come in the center of the foot. He steps on ground which does not readily conform to his tread. The foot rolls more or less, throwing a strain on the tendons and particularly on the suspensory ligaments, and indirectly a pressure on some nerve or other." I have sprung a new one on Mr. Farmer. He understands, perhaps a little vaguely.

"Here's an illustration," I say. I look around for a stone which will roughly represent the coffin-bone, inside the hoof. I pick up another one much smaller, an inch or so in thickness. I place this as nearly as possible in the center of the larger stone. Then I get hold of a long slim stone, a little stick, or maybe a corn cob. This represents the long pastern. I place it in the center of the smaller stone. Then I bear down on whatever represents the long pastern. The improvised coffin-bone, the short pastern, and the long pastern, all remain upright one upon the other. In other words they do not buckle. Mr. Farmer and hired man, and whatever other members of the family have gathered round, understand this at once. Then I make a slight change. I slip my improvised short pastern over very slightly to the right or toward the inside of the foot. Next I slip my improvised long pastern over a little to the right of center—remember we are standing behind the horse. Again I bear down on the long pastern or corn cob or whatever it is. The joints buckle slightly, the right side sinks down, the outside, or left side of the hoof of the left foot does not sink down in proportion. "And there you are," I remark.

"Well, now," says Mr. Farmer, "I see that plain as day. I gotta book my Congressman sent me. It says something about a horse being off balance—sometimes off his axis. It gives a lot of lines and explanation—but I'll be darned if I could ever understand them."

"I get you, Mr. Farmer. I was brought up on a farm myself, have owned a few farms—though I never was much of a farmer. I realize full well that a man working, including chores and so forth, from five in the morning until eight at night, doesn't feel much like concentrating. That's the reason I've used this simple illustration. You see, Mr. Farmer, your horse is a mechanical structure the same as your barn. If a corner of the foundation gives way, a strain is thrown upon the whole structure. It is bound to lean. The whole framework of your building—or of your horse—is thrown out of alignment. Once the building is wracked or thrown out of alignment, or out of balance, it will keep on getting worse, especially if let alone. Once the supporting ligaments are strained or stretched they will not support the joint that they are supposed to support.

"There seem to be two schools of thought about the suspensory ligaments that support the ankle. One is that 'all ligaments except those of the neck are inelastic.' The other, and it seems to me the more correct one, is that the suspensory ligaments are slightly but strongly elastic. In other words, when a horse puts his weight or part of it on a foot upon sod or turf, or upon ground in the field that is soft enough to conform to the pressure of his foot, these ligaments do not stretch, but support the slightly imperfect hinge joint. If, on the other hand, the nature of the footing is such that it resists the pressure of the foot under a portion—say half—of the horse's weight, then these ligaments must stretch a little. Otherwise how could both sides of the foot find a bearing on the ground, or road or—much worse—the pavement? Over hundreds of miles I have studied this part of the horse's anatomy. I am convinced that an ordinary road horse can stand with impunity about a one per cent "side angle" on surface that is inflexible under his weight. To me it seems obvious—and experience teaches—that if we continue to stretch these slightly elastic ligaments they will eventually lose their power of elasticity. The ankle will lose its support. Henceforth it is a chronically strained ligament. It will never fully recover—especially in an adult horse. The best we can do is to keep the horse off all rough and inflexible surfaces, try to avoid strain in pulling, traveling and jumping, keep the horse well nourished, give plenty of mild work or other exercise. And *above all* pare or shoe the foot so as to brace against the unbalanced condition—whether the malconformation is natural or not. And that is where the experience comes in."

"I understand that now," ejaculates Mr. Farmer. "Say, where's that horse of yours?"

"Why she's round back of the barn eatin' grass," volunteers the school-boy. "She's been all round, helped herself to the water, n'everything."

"Well, put her right in here," says the farmer to his son. We remove the saddle. "Come on, Mister, supper's ready."

Between supper and late bed-time we have reshaped the foot as far as possible (the reader well knows how), and very likely looked over another horse or two, saying nothing of a more or less delightful conversation. Chances are nine to one that there is no charge. I have been treated like a prince. The chances are about even that Mr. Farmer slips a dollar into my hand inoffensively, possibly two. Certainly he has filled our nose-bag for the noon feed. Probably the lady has pressed a cold lunch upon us for noon.

This is about a sample of how we usually got by in a farming community where horses were largely used, without sacrificing our pride. Remember this was in 1925-26-27. Also observe by our Map we did not cross the great wheat belt in Kansas where tractors are used almost altogether on the large farms. Of course, there were some large stretches where for various reasons this method of getting along did not apply. Once more we will cross those bridges as we come to them.

Of course, the reader will understand that this talk I gave Mr.

Farmer is only one of many ways in which I often was able—through experience—to "help out" on a horse. It might be a chronic sore shoulder. It might be chronic indigestion, or it might be intestinal worms. It might be a horse that "bolted" his feed. It might be one of those misunderstood horses that are called "bad" but are only ticklish. Such a horse squirms and raises hell in general when some fellow touches him very slightly for fear of arousing his temper. All this horse craves is to be handled with a firm touch instead of being treated like a sissy, or we might have a balky horse.

From Notes. June 11, '25: (Leaving Mr. Keyerlever) Warm barn—feed—blankets—breakfast—no chg. * * * * Arrived Miles and Corlette Sts. in Cleveland via Glenville 4 p.m. Left Cleveland 7:45 p.m. Ar'd 10 p.m. at farm or small dairy of "Italians" (in south suburbs of Cleveland).

Traveled: 24 mi.—10 mi. detour. Pavement 4 mi. 4 mi. very bad dirt. Bal. dirt.

Special Note: June 11, '25 (Just before entering Cleveland.) 1st. Will arrive Cleveland 1 day late. 2nd. Distance Buffalo to Clev. 265 mi. (to Its.) [Italians] or 46 mi. [Clerical error—65 mi.] more than schedule. Distance over all to Cleveland (S. E. sub. where spent night) 1418 mi. 3rd. Average travel, Buffalo to Cleveland, 23½ miles (per day) 4th. Average, over all, approx. 20 mi. (per day).

June 12, '25: 7:30 a.m. Feeding, breakfast, at Brooklyn Heights, S. of Cleveland, with Mr. and Mrs. Henry Merkle. No chg. Fine people. Farmers. Country rolling. Prosperous. Dry this year. * * * * 8 a.m. Leaving Merkle's place.

From Signature Book: "June 12, 1925. This is to certify that Mr. F. M. Heath of Silver Springs, Md., riding Gypsy Queen, has eat breakfast with us this A.M. at Brooklyn Heights, Ohio at our address.

(Signed) Mrs. Henry Merkle,
1256 Schaef Rd., Cleve. O."

From Notes. June 12, '25, continued: 9 a.m. Leaving Brooklyn Hts., the most prosperous truck farm and green house section yet witnessed. Noon, feeding. Lunch at store. Farm of E. Rindfleisch, Brock Park, O. * * * * No chg. for oats. 7:45 Ar'd farm of Mr. W. L. Jenkins, West Dover. * * * * Need rain.

Traveled: 32 mi. 14 detour. Good 'side' all the way. Via Arlington Hts., Brock Park Rd. N. 1 mi. to Mastic Rd., Kennedy Ridge Rd., Butternut R to Porter Rd. to Center Ridge Rd. (We were back again on the Ridge Roads west of Cleveland—all this jostling about in extricating ourselves from the "Wheel.") Am now (night of June 12, '25) 16 mi. W. of Pub. Sq. [Public Square] Cleveland—101 miles to Toledo. Traversed good truck farm district.

June 13, '25: Leaving Mr. Jenkins, 7:45. Horse, blankets, no chg. Ar'd Elyria, O. 11:30 a.m. Queen shod behind. Dinner, shave, material for Z. O. (Zinc ointment). Just leaving 2 p.m. 6 p.m. Ar'd farm of W. G. Bullock, Oberlin, O. * * * * after being turned down 6 times. English people. First were doubtful. 1 week previous tramp whom they kept stole car.

I had been turned down six times. Nowhere yet had I been quite so universally 'turned down.' When Mr. Bullock (the seventh one) had looked me over, he shook his head. I expressed myself something like this: "Well now, that's funny. If I were begging, it would be a little different. Someone must have been doing something around here that he oughtn't to." "That's it," spoke up his wife, "about a week ago we let a man sleep in the hay-mow. When we got up in the morning our car was gone. It wasn't much of a car, but it was the best we had. We haven't seen it since—or the man either."

"Well," I said, "I see it all now, and of course I don't blame you. Nor do I blame anyone in the community for being leery of strangers after that. Of course, if it were worth while for one to stop and make a deduction, he might presume that a person would not be traveling as I am and stealing cars at the same time. I know you're not going to keep me after what has happened to you, but if you will give me two or three minutes of your time, I'd like to convince you, just the same, that all people who are traveling are not thieves. Such ones as you mentioned work a great injustice on the honest traveler."

As I said this, I fished out a couple of postcards with our picture, and handed them to Mr. Bullock. I saw him looking intently at the picture and went fishing for some letters. "That's enough," he said. "Put your horse in the barn." "And come in and have a bite to eat," invited his wife. Their evening meal was over, but she set on a bounteous cold meal. "I hope you don't think all English people are snobs," she remarked. The funny part of it was, the whole neighborhood was going to some school 'doings.' It was the end of a semester. The Bullocks went also, leaving Queen and me in sole possession of the place. I had expressed a desire to do some 'washing up.' Mrs. Bullock handed me a tub, soap, washboard and a bucket with which to draw water from the cistern. About twelve or one o'clock that night Mr. Bullock looked in upon us in the hay-mow with a cheerful grin.

From Notes. June 13, '25 continued: *Traveled* 22 mi. Jogged 1 mi. dirt 1 mi. Pavement 3. Bal. fair 'side,' dirt or cinders. * * * *

June 14, '25: Leaving Mr. Bullock 9:45 a.m. * * * * Ar'd at farm and hot-dog stand of Mr. H. A. Charles, 6 p.m., 4 miles west of Wakeman.

Traveled: 17½ miles. 13 miles good dirt and cinders. 4½ miles very bad 'side.' Flat country. Mixed farming. Best wheat seen on trip.

Meet Mr. H. A. Charles and family. Mr. Charles is a renter in a good productive locality. The land is flat and fertile. His barns are so full of last year's hay that he hardly knows what to do with the new crop. The farms about here are pretty good sized. But Charles rents the farm which they *owned*, free of debt, before the World War. He lost his head, he tells me, during the land-boom, ran in debt for more land at two or three times the price at which he could make it pay interest, and lost what he had.

One means, aside from the hot-dog stand and the farming, by which they had determined to retrieve the old place, was poultry. I could see that they didn't understand the game, as in fact most farmers do not unless they have had a course in poultry. I had a college course in it and was busy all morning making poultry-house drawings and answering questions.

From Notes. June 15, '25: Leaving Mr. Charles 8 a.m. Feed, meals, no chg. Nice people. 4:30 p.m. Ar'd farm of Stimson Bros., Mechanicsville, R. 3. * * * *

Traveled: 18½ mi. Detour 3½ mi. * * * * Level. Soil and crops much better. Hard rain. Pulled me in early. Some sulphur wells.

June 16, '25: 7:30 a.m. Leaving Stimson Bros. No chg. Gave formulas etc. * * * * 5 p.m. Ar'd farm of Mr. Samuel Cuns, 4 mi. W. of Fremont.

Traveled: 22 mi. 6 mi. pavement. Bal. good 'side.' R. 2 (Yellowstone Trail). Level. Black corn land. Mixed farming. Sugar beets.

June 17, '25. Leaving Mr. Cuns 7:30 (a.m.) No chg. Poul. lec. Oil well on farm. (This oil well like several I had passed was an old well exhausted to the extent that it was on pump. Also gas was obtained from the well. Mr. Cuns was using the natural gas from this well. I believe the power that operated the sluggish pumps was obtained somehow from the pressure of the natural gas.) 11 a.m. Just dodged into a barn in time to avoid a hard rain. Passed a number of oil pumps—mostly idle. * * * * Ar'd farm of Clarence Goodman, Line City, O. * * * *

Traveled: 29 mi. Pavement 1 mi. Bal. fair 'side.' Yellowstone Trail, wide right-of-way. Dirt track on side mostly. Country level. Good. Some stony places. Mixed farms.

From Signature Book: "Line City, June 17, '25. Frank M. Heath with Gypsy Queen is staying at our place tonight.
(Signed) Mrs. Clarence Goodman."

From Notes. June 18, '25: Leaving Mr. Goodman 7:45 a.m. Horse, meals, bed, no chg. Formulas—feet. 10 a.m. Hit Maumee. * * * * Left Maumee 7 p.m. 8:30 p.m. Ar'd farm of Fred MacDonald, Route 2, Maumee.

Traveled: 10 mi. (6 to Maumee) 5 paved, bal. fair to poor 'side.' Level. Black land—much mixed farming. (P.M. by trolley to Toledo, to draw, go through, and forward parcel post package. While there called at office of the 'Toledo Blade.' Back to Maumee, 4 mi. W. to MacDonald's.)

Special Notes:

1st.—Cleveland to Maumee [few miles south of] (Toledo), 147 miles.

2nd.—Total to Maumee 1565 miles.

3rd.—160 mi. more than schedule.

4th.—Am three days late in time, but—

5th.—Am at least 5 days [travel] ahead in miles [called for in] schedule.

6th.—Average miles per day Clev. to Toledo 21. * * * *

From Signature Book: "June 18, '25. Frank Heath called here.
(Signed) R. A. Werneke, City Ed.,
Toledo Blade, Toledo, O."

From Notes. June 19, '25: Leaving Mr. MacDonald 8:15 a.m. No chg. (Worked on horse's feet.)

11 a.m. Lunching—feeding Queen at home of a nice Polish boy who accosted me by the wayside 11½ mi. West of Maumee. Struck into sand (poor land—level) and Polacks—West of Mt. Cleve. Noon: Feeding Queen 13 mi. West of Maumee. Have just passed myriads of grasshoppers. 3:40, Turned N.W. at point 19 mi. W. 1 mi. S. of Maumee, to take dirt rd. to Whiteville, Mich. 5 p.m. Am in Delta, O. Crops and soil excellent. [Notes here obliterated except for fact we arrived Sam Coleman's place at 6 p.m.]

Traveled: 25 mi. 2 mi. by misdirection. Sand rd. 23 mi. Rough, 2 mi. Meals, bed at home of A. E. Russa, R. 1, Delta, O. No chg. Poul. lec. Horse, no chg. vet. lec.

June 20, '25. Leaving [Name obliterated] 7:45 a.m.—10:30 a.m. crossing Michigan line 18 mi. N.W. of point where we turned yesterday toward Mich. (Estimate: 26 mi. detour to hit Mich.) Noon: feeding Queen, eating chicken pie at home of Carroll Service, R. 2 Jasper, Mich., ½ mi. N. of Ohio-Mich. line. 7:30 p.m. Ar'd farm of Gail Bulkley, 2½ mi. S.E. of Morenci, Mich. R. 4, after being turned down 5 times. Skipped M. [Morenci] to avoid pave.—also to see lame horse off axis [off balance].

Traveled: 27 mi. Dirt 23 mi. Country traversed fair (some sandy—mostly level). ½ places empty.

From Signature Book: "Jasper, Mich., June 20, 1925. Frank M. Heath with his mare Gypsy Queen stopped at our farm here today at noon.

(Signed) Mrs. C. C. Service."

From Notes. June 21, '25, Sunday: Leaving Mr. Bulkley 11 a.m. * * * *

From the original, written on a sheet out of some notebook: "Morenci, Mich., June 21, '25.

"To Whom it may Concern:

Frank M. Heath stayed at my farm last night with Gypsy Queen.

I have a horse that for 8 months has been constantly very lame in right front, baffling all examiners. Mr. Heath put the horse back on his axis' as he expressed it. [Back on his balance would have been more correct, perhaps.—Author] The horse walked off much better at once. I feel satisfied that he properly diagnosed the case.

(Signed) Gail Bulkley."

These are the facts. All along our track up here, we found pretty good footing. But as for unshod horses, the theory that a horse's hoofs will just naturally wear off and should never need trimming, frequently does not work out. Take this Bulkley horse, for instance. His hoofs just kept on growing until "they covered the whole farm," as the boy said. The hoofs had actually grown down and outward until they extended at least an inch and a half beyond the white line—or the union of the wall and the sole of the foot. Of course, eventually something had to happen, and what happened in this case was that half of the rim of this right front foot had broken off somewhere near the point to which it should have been trimmed. As I remember, this half that broke off was on the inside of the right front foot. The outer half of the rim, for some reason or other had not broken off. When the horse stepped upon the hard ground, it will be seen that the outside of his foot was something like an inch higher than the inside. It seems to me that it should not take much imagination to realize what happened. There was more difference in the height of the two sides of the foot than either the slight flexibility of the imperfect hinge joint, or the slight elasticity of the suspensory ligament—or both—could stand. This brought about probably a near rupture of those ligaments, together with a terrible pressure on the surrounding nerves.

From Notes. June 21, '25: * * * * 6 p.m. Ar'd farm of Mr. Wm. McGowan, Fayette, O., R. 15, 1½ mi. west of Zone.

Traveled: 14 mi. Detour 1½ miles. Fair sandy rd. or 'side' all the way via Angola Rd. * * * * Mr. McGowan is 81. He was born near here in Michigan.

Mr. McGowan had a grown son and daughter who conducted the place. He told me that he, with an axe, had cleaned his farm when a much younger man. It is generally conceded that cleared timber land is not as fertile as good natural prairie. Still this grand old man was proud of his accomplishment. "A good axe can do a lot for a man," he remarked.

From Notes. June 22, '25: Leaving Mr. McGowan 7:30 a.m. No charge. Queen quite sore last night. Stood in mud 2 hrs. Still sore, especially left front. Inclined to "roll" acc't poor shoeing, and rock back acc't pads worn. Have kept middle cut out and 'shimmed' up heels twice—once just now. But *must* have reshod at once. * * * * 8:40 p.m. Ar'd farm of P. A. Dick, Edona. * * * * 2 mi. E. of Columbia, O., after being turned down 9 times though I repeatedly offered to pay and offered indisputable proofs. * * * *

Traveled: 24 mi. 10 mi. very bad side, bal. poor to good dirt. Country, soil, crops, fair. Mixed farming. Level, getting rolling near Columbia.

From Notes. June 23, '25: Left Mr. Dick's 8:15 a.m. No chg. Advice on horse. 3:30 p.m. Ar'd shop of Free Patterson, Angola, Ind. Passed State line 9:30. * * *

Traveled: 16½ mi. macadam mostly. Country rolling, soil sandy. Crops poor. Put up at barn of Mr. Monahan, Angola. Had Queen shod front, F. Patterson.

It had been nearly a month since that almost disastrous job on Queen's left front foot. The reader sees that I had been having a great deal of trouble, which was increasing. The hoof had grown sufficiently to permit reshoeing. For several days before reaching Angola, I had been inquiring for a horse-shoer. Had been told of several 'blacksmiths.' It wasn't 'blacksmith' I wanted. We limped by them. By the time I arrived at Angola, I was satisfied that this Free Patterson was a *shoer.* A short conversation with him decided me. Carefully we cut the clinches and removed the shoe without tearing the hoof, pared down so as to level the foot. Then we left the shoe a little prominent on the left, as it should be. Here I introduced a new scheme of my own. I knew that I still had considerable pavement to cross in places. Many of the medium-sized towns through which we passed in escaping the cities, we found paved, the pavement extending a few miles beyond the town, usually, on either side. So I deemed it necessary to shoe Queen once more with pads in front. I also knew that it would be advisable to dispense with these pads before there would be need for reshoeing. It has been explained that these commercial pads are held in place by a three-quarter shoe, leaving no shoe under the heel. But I, with my sharp knife, continued the depression on back and used a full-length shoe, so as to permit cutting away the pad inside the shoe when I was ready.

That last sixteen-and-a-half mile day had been pretty painful for her. We saved the situation just in time. After I had used plenty of cold water until bedtime that might, she went much better for a considerable time.

This little town had peculiarities of its own. At the barn where I stopped, the man who sprinkled the streets was keeping his team. The sprinkling, he told me, was paid for, not by the town, but by certain individuals or firms, in front of whose places he sprinkled. If they didn't pay—he didn't sprinkle.

From Notes. June 23, '25 continued: * * * * Washed up, etc. Feel bum right side. Also right internal—old trouble. Eating rolled oats and milk.

June 24, '25: Leaving Mr. Monahan 8 a.m. Slept in barn. Hay, 50 cts. Noon, feeding and eating at farm of Mr. Mortorff, Ashley. Had passed rolling country. Soil varies from sand-hill to excellent 'beaver-dam.' Here (region of Monahans) level. Black loam. Mixed farming. Truck. Sugar-beets. 7 p.m. Ar'd farm of Wm. Walter, 1 mi. E. of S. Milford, after being delayed by a heavy rain. Turned down 5 times.

Traveled: 20 mi. Detour 1 mi. Gravel rd. via Pleasant Lake, Ashley, Helmar. Rained hard 5 p.m. Country continues rolling. Mixed farming. Some truck. Sheep.

From Signature Book: "Ashley, Ind., June 24, 1925. Frank M. Heath with Gypsy Queen this day took dinner with us today.
(Signed) Ira Mortorff."

From Notes. June 25, '25: Leaving Mr. Walter 7 a.m. Horse, meals, bed, no chg. * * * * 6:30 p.m. Ar'd farm of Earl W. Brown, 6½ mi. S.E. Goshen. * * * *

Traveled: 30 mi. ½ by error. Dirt all way. Via N. of Milford bet. Long Lake and Whitner (?) along air mail route. Rolling. Mixed farming—some peppermint (Considerably raised as a standard crop in the United States, adapted to low, flat land.) Rained 11 to 1.

June 26, '25: Leaving Mr. Brown 9 a.m. Showery. Fine man from Devil's Lake. No chg. Large family. Boy, 14, very clever and anxious to learn of horses.

This boy, it seemed, had been determined from childhood to become a veterinarian—just had to be. I sat up till 9 o'clock giving him instruction even drawing diagrams for him of the inside of a horse's foot, explaining 'axis,' etc. Had a hard time to get away from the kid next morning. The previous evening he had crawled out on a log foot-bridge that spanned a creek, with Queen's halter shank in one hand, and tied her where she stood in the cold water and mud to her knees. A couple of hours later he crawled out again and brought her in.

From Notes. June 25, '25 continued: * * * * Reached farm of Martin Wagner, 6 p.m., 6 mi. W. 1 mi. N. Wakerusa.

Traveled: 21 mi. * * * * Via 2 mi. S. of Goshen, 7 mi. S. of Elkhart, 1 mi. N. of Wakerusa. Country rolling, soil varying good black to sandy. Crops fair.

June 27, '25: Leaving the Wagners 7:30 a.m. * * * * 10:30 rested on a rock by the wayside while Queen took her mid-forenoon rest and nibble. Passed over about 5 mi. flats—some very fertile beaverdams. Drained cooperatively. Some peppermint. Now in rolling country again. Alternating woods and clearing. Corn good. Grain medium. 10 a.m. passed U.S. Air Mail emergency landing field. * * * * 6 p.m. Ar'd farm of John Pommert, 2 mi. W. N. Liberty. * * * *

Traveled: 20 mi. 1 mi. detour (½ mi. R. 5 and return.) Via Air Mail Rt. to 3:15. * * * * Country slightly rolling, some timber. Mixed farming. Crops poor.

June 28, '25: Leaving Mr. Pommert 9:15 a.m. Has sick horse —laryngitis. * * * * Fed Queen 2 ears of corn, some alfalfa last night. 3 ears corn this morning (Oats were not available, so fed a little of this corn.) Meals, no chg. Noon, feeding at Oak Grove, Jersey Farm. 7 mi. S. W. N. Liberty. John Rush tenant. Clark Rush, owner. *Large round barn 60'* (feet diameter) Silo in center 12' x 47'. Place is in center of former Kankakee Marsh, several thousand acres Delta land. Mastodons' skeletons. 3:30 p.m. eating at farm (420 acres) of Mr. H. Shepherd, from which stretches level delta as far as eye can see in all directions. 7 p.m. Ar'd farm of Mr. Paul Bent, 4 mi. S.E. Union Mills. * * * *

Traveled: 28 mi. Detoured 8, error 2. Dirt and gravel. Via "Jersey" farm and Kankakee Marsh. Crow Island to west side marsh. (Offset) south 6 mi. Made 16 (off sets) (some of them diagonal) and one 'loop' (by error). Marsh extends 30 mi. S.

from here. 'Island' very poor soil, also shore. Passed over
hundreds of acres beaver-dam. Crops only normal. Much stock—
hogs, horses, mules. Alternating woods, ditches. (Much of this
marsh had been tile-drained. It was told me that some of these
crops being hardly normal was caused by the imperfect
drainage.)

From Signature Book: "Union Mills, Ind., June 29, 1925.
Frank M. Heath with Gypsy Queen at our farm took supper and
breakfast with us.

(Signed) Mrs. Paul Bent."

From Notes. June 29, '25: Leaving Mr. Bent 8:20 a.m. They
are starting in poultry. Drew plans. Horse, meals, bed, no chg.
3 kids. Good eats. 10:30, passed sorghum mill—lady says sorghum
pays. Traveled [traversed] country slightly rolling. Alternating
between sandy hill and beaver-dam bottom. Ditches. Coming
into flat country (going west.) Good crops. Noon, feeding at a
farm 2 mi. E. Wanatah. * * * * 2:10 passing Wanatah. 4 p.m.
1 mi. S. Valparaiso. 8 p.m. Ar'd Porter Co. (?) Farm after trying
3 places. (No feed other places.) 5:15 stopped ¾ hour—advised
on horse—$1.00.

Traveled: 28 mi. 3½ detour. 6 dirt. Bal. fair 'side.' Via Wanatah 2½ mi. S. 1. N. Bal. W.—level P.M. to S. of Valparaiso,
then rolling. Crops fair to good.

June 30, '25: Leaving Porter Co. Farm 7:15. * * * * Noon,
eating farm Clarence Goodrich, Crown Point, R. 6. No chg.
Ar'd Schererville—John Schutz, 5 p.m.

Traveled: 23 mi. 2 detour, 3 paved. * * * * Bal. dirt. Jogged
(i.e. offset) S. 2, N. 3. Hit Lincoln H.W. (highway) 2½ mi. E.
(east. i.e. of Schererville.)

Special Note:

1st.—Distance Maumee to Schererville 289 mi.

2nd.—Average per day, Mau. to Sch. 22½ mi.

3rd.—Average total to date 20 mi. approx.

4th.—Total (miles) to date (i.e. from Washington) 1854 miles
(approximately)

5th.—More than schedule (i.e. Wash.) 190 miles.

(We were 3 days behind in time, but 9½ days ahead in miles.)

July 1, '25: Side trip to Chi. few miles north of Schererville,
by trolley. Called on Abells. (The Abells were a family that I

had met and ridden with on a train about 4 or 5 years previously.)

July 2, '25: Leaving Mr. Schutz 7:15 a.m. No chg. for barn.
* * * * 8:45 crossing Ill-Ind. line, on Lincoln Hy (highway)
* * * * 6 p.m. Ar'd farm of Edward L. Watson, Captain
(W.W.V.) (World War veteran.) Frankfurt, Ill., R. 1 (14 mi.
E. of Joliet.)

Traveled: 22 mi. Gravel or side. Via Lincoln Hy. and Sack
Trail.

July 3, '25: Leaving Captain Watson 7 a.m. No chg. 11 a.m.
Ar'd Joliet, Hill Crest Rr., near home of Mr. George L. Morris,
W.W.V.

Traveled: 14 mi. 4 mi. gravel 10 side—of Lincoln Highway.
Crops Schererville to Joliet fair. Corn good. Level country.

From Signature Book: "Joliet, Illinois, July 4, 1925. Frank M.
Heath arrived here yesterday A.M. Will leave tomorrow.

(Signed) Geo. L. Morris,
Hillcrest Rd."

From Notes. July 4 and 5, '25: Spending 2 days in camp.
Frank Abell of Chi. is with me. Later: Spent quiet day in camp.
Accepted invitation to dinner with Sr. Morrises. Slept in barn.

July 6, '25: Breakfast in camp. Left 6:15. 8:45 a.m. soaking
Queen's feet in mud hole. 5:15 Ar'd farm of Mr. Tom
Thompson, Newark, R. 2.

Traveled: 27 mi. Pavement 4 mi. Side 4 mi. Bal. dirt. Level.
Black corn land.

July 7, '25: Leaving Mr. Thompson 8 a.m. Horse, meals, slept
in hay—no chg. Advice. 6:30 p.m. Ar'd farm of Mr. S. W.
Bragg, Ottawa. * * * *

Traveled: 25 mi. 2 by error. Dirt. Via Lisbon, Otta Rd. to
E. of Dayton. Then via Dayton and on West and S. (having
crossed Fox River.) Region Fox River rolling. Here level. Black
soil. Corn rank. Oats fair. Hay poor. Horse, meals, no chg.

July 8, '25: Leaving Mr. Bragg 7 a.m.—11 a.m. to 2 p.m.,
feeding, eating, advising on sorrel mare with chronic laryngitis
(presumably heaves). At farm of Wm. Kelly (Tenant). 12½
mi. N.W. Ottawa. 8 p.m. Ar'd farm of Mier Bros., Zearing, Rt. 1
—6 mi. N. 26 mi. W. Ottawa.

Traveled: 30 mi. (needless offset) (Back on long distance line
4 p.m.) Dirt. Jogged (offset) 1 mi. Very hot. Corn good.

July 9, '25: Leaving Mier Bros. 8 a.m. No chg. Advice. Noon, feeding, eating, farm of Mr. Sweederton (?) Largest corn seen. (Shower 11:30 to 1.) 7 p.m. Ar'd Mr. J. P. Larson, Wyanet, Ill. Pop. 800 to 900.

Traveled: 27 mi.—offset 3 mi. S. Dirt side or gravel. Hit "Cannon Ball" R 7, 5 p.m. (Passed 1 mi. N. Princeton 3 p.m.) Country slightly rolling. Corn not quite so large. Oats better. Mixed farming. Some dairying. Hogs on all ILL. farms. Extra good gardens.

July 10, '25: Leaving Mr. Larson 7:45. Horse, breakfast, hit the hay (no chg.) Advice. 10:30 a.m. Mrs. Roy Gottschall and Bro. overtook us 2 (mi.) E. Sheffield—took photos. Noon, feeding, lunching in Tourist Camp at Sheffield, Ill. Just "held up" by reporter. 7 p.m., feeding, eating farm of W. R. Winter, Annowan (?) Ill. Le. 8:30. 10 p.m. camped by Rd. side 20 (?) mi. N.W. of Sheffield.

Traveled: 30 mi.—2 mi. detour (N.W.S.) * * * *

July 11, '25: 5 a.m. leaving camp by Rd. side. Queen gave us scare twice early in night, by breaking loose. 6 a.m. feeding at farm of Fred Newman, Cambridge. * * * *

Chapter X

WEST FROM CHICAGO

The Sheffield Times
July 16, 1925
"MAN ON HORSEBACK" PAYS
SHEFFIELD VISIT

*On Tour Touching Every State in Union to Demonstrate
Possibilities of Horse*

Frank M. Heath, a former regular in the U. S. Army and a
member of Cissel Post No. 41, American Legion, of Silver Springs,
Maryland, passed through Sheffield Friday night on his schedule on
a horseback trip to hit every state in the Union. Heath left Washington, D. C., April 1, 1925, with the above object, and must return
to that city on or before July 1, 1927. Incidentally along the way he is
imbibing health and an education, but the object of the trip is to
prove that a horse properly handled can make this long journey
in a given time.

Mounted on Gypsy Queen, a ten-year-old Kentucky whip Morgan
cross, he crossed all of the northern coast states and doubled back
over New York and Pennsylvania, and had been in Ohio, Michigan
and Indiana when he arrived in Sheffield, having covered 1,970
miles, and was 230 miles ahead of his schedule. He stated here that
his worst going for the horse was in crossing the White, Green and
Adirondack mountains. Stopovers for rest are made as much as
possible in the country, as aside from points on the scheduled route
which he must make, Heath avoids the cities and the hard pavements
to spare his horse. He estimates that one mile of congested city
pavements or two miles of our ordinary state aid hard roads tire his
horse more than three or more miles of dirt roads, and frequent
detours were made in this state to avoid the pavements of the direct
route. He left Illinois behind Saturday and out in Iowa where the

mud and the tall corn abide, Heath and Gypsy Queen will find some of the best going in all their big trip. * * * *

* * * *

From Notes. July 11, '25: continued: 2:15 p.m. left front shoe loose. Met Mr. Carl Westerlund, Orion, Ill., R. 1, who assisted in fastening shim under shoe. Fastened with wire, aid of pliers.

The reader will remember that in Angola, at the shop of Free Patterson, we put under the pad a full length shoe—instead of the three-quarter shoe, having cut the heels of the pad to admit the full length shoe—with the intention of cutting out most of the rubber pad, leaving only the rim that was between the hoof and the shoe. This we had done. The left branch of the rubber strip back of the nails, in this particular case, had become crowded from between the bottom of the foot and the shoe, probably on account of the foot still being inclined to roll, because of the weakened condition of the suspensory ligaments which should have held the joint in place. It will be seen, then, that this left side of this rubber (I guess we may call it packing) had slipped out of place. We simply replaced this strip and wired it securely to that branch of the shoe where it extended back half an inch or so beyond the heel of the foot. She had started in limping again. After we had replaced the strip or packing onto the shoe she walked off without a limp.

From Notes. July 11, '25 continued: 9:15 Ar'd Tindel School House No. 67, 9 mi. S. of Rock Island.
Traveled: 33 mi. detour (or error). Dirt. * * * *
July 12, '25: (Sunday) Rained last night. Camped in old shed by School House. Climbed gate. Queen under tree. (Wild sweet clover here was as high as my head.) Very hot (99 today). * * * * 10:15 a.m. leaving camp. Going west. * * * * Noon Ar'd Taylor Ridge, Ill. 27 (?) miles S. W. of Davenport, Iowa.
Traveled: 6 mi. side. * * * * Country level. All crops good.
Special Note:
1st.—Joliet to Taylor Ridge 178 miles
2nd.—More than schedule bet. Jol. and T.R., 52 miles
3rd.—Daily average Jol.—T.R., 22 mi. approximately
4th.—Total to Taylor Ridge 2,052
5th.—Total average (miles per day) 19.27 miles (roughly)
6th.—More than schedule (to Davenport) 243

From Signature Book: "Taylor Ridge, Ill. (16 miles S. W. of Davenport, Iowa), July 12, 1925. Frank M. Heath and Gypsy Queen arrived here at noon today.

(Signed) John Buck, General Store."

From Notes. July 13, '25: Camped last night on covered scale at stockyards, Taylor Ridge, Ill. Queen in good pasture. Leaving T. R. 7:45 Sold Lit. (Literature, or cards and schedules.) $1.15 (exp. $1.05) * * * * 3:15 coming down hill into Miss. River Valley Proper (i.e. River Bottom). 4:15 crossing high bridge. No craft in sight larger than fishing boat. Taylor Ridge to Muscatine 21 mi. 7:15 arrive farm of J. A. Hass, 3 mi. S.W. of bridge, Muscatine. Address Fruitland, Iowa, R. 1.

Traveled: 24 mi. Pavement ½ mi. Bal. dirt. * * * *

July 14, '25: Leaving Mr. and Mrs. J. A. Hass (and niece) 9 a.m. No chg. (Gave poultry lecture.) Muscatine Island formerly produced large quantities water melons. Now sweet potatoes, etc. Showery this A.M. Very muddy. * * * * 6:30 Ar'd Chautauqua Grounds Tourist Camp, Columbus Junction.

Traveled: 21 mi. (one mile side trip to camp) Pavement 1 mi. Bal. dirt. * * * * Country slightly rolling. Crops fairly good. Some very prosperous [farms]. Some herds Herefords. Melons N. of Fredonia.

July 15, '25: 6:30 leaving tourist camp Col. Junc. Hit Ainsworth. Tightened shoes, wired rubber "strips" to shoe. * * * * 7:15 Ar'd farm of Mr. J. M. Godfrey, 2½ mi. W. of Washington, Ia., Rt. 5.

Traveled: 24 mi. * * * * Pavement 1 mi. Bal. dirt. * * * * 2:30 got Queen down in mud creek in effort to soak feet. Had to remove pack, took over 1 hr. to clean up. * * * *

As I see it now, after much experience and much observation, there are two kinds of so-called quicksand. We hear or read occasionally (and it is true without a doubt) of a man or a horse becoming suddenly and entirely sucked down, never to be recovered, in quicksand. I sometimes wonder if in such a case the quicksand is something like quicksilver. There's another kind of so-called quicksand, usually of a bluish cast, that is a kind of sandy mud, or possibly it might be designated as 'quick-mud.' This has been mentioned a time or two in this narrative. In this latter a horse, or man, would generally settle until he is held as in a vise, providing he stays there, and more particularly if he flounders about in the same spot. If he keeps

moving forward he has a chance to get through and out. It was in
such as this, in the bottom of a small creek, flowing under a bridge,
that Queen went down—almost. When I saw her going down, I at
once put her in motion (I being dismounted) until she floundered
herself clear through under the bridge. Meanwhile I encouraged her
to turn left—and she knew right and left as well as we do. Bringing
her to the left brought her out where the sod was more substantial,
to the point that it sustained her body. A substantial, tough sod.
There I let her rest while I stripped her of the saddle and pack. After
she was thoroughly rested she drew first one foot and then the other
out upon the sod, much as she did the time she went down in the
bog north of Wells in New York. I led her up to a farm house a
little distance. There was a large tank of water warmed by the sun.
There was no one at home, but I helped myself to the water, and
gave her a thorough bath all over. It took me probably half an hour.

From Notes. June 16, '25: Leaving Mr. Godfrey 7:30 a.m.
* * * * Mr. Godfrey is a practical horseman. Could give him
no advice. * * * * *He induced me* to try bandage on Queen's
left front. * * * * Ar'd pasture opposite Mr. Bakehouse.
Camped [in fence corner]. Carried mud up hill for Queen's foot.
(This was a good quality of mud. I carried it quite a way up a
steep bank and wrapped Queen's foot in it in an old gunny sack.)
Traveled: 27 mi. Dirt. (We fed sheaf oats that night. Had
'eats' with us).

July 17, '25: 5:30 a.m. Leaving camp. * * * * Noon: Feeding, lunching at farm of J. W. Sawyer, ½ W. 1 mi. N. of Delta,
Ia. * * * *

From Signature Book: "Delta, Ia., July 17, 1925. Frank M.
Heath is feeding Gypsy Queen at my farm here, noon today.
(Signed) J. W. Sawyer."

From Notes. July 17, '25, continued: 5:30 p.m. Reached farm
of Mr. Wm. Bell, 5½ mi. N.E. of Oskaloosa, Ia., R. 1.
Traveled: 22 mi. (1 mi. side for camp site.) Dirt. * * * *
Hilly except Skunk River bottom. Crops fair. Hay heavy. Oats
heavy.

July 18, '25: Leaving the Bells 8:30 a.m. * * * * 9:30,
stopped at a farm to replace shim. The shim had worked loose.
Ar'd Oskaloosa Tourist Park 11:45 a.m.
Traveled: 9 mi. (3 through city). Paved. 2 blks. Bal. dirt.
Hilly, W.S.W.

Special Note:
1st.—Muscatine to Oskaloosa, 108 mi.
2nd.—Total to Oskaloosa, 2179 mi. (roughly)

July 19, '25, Sunday: Spending day quietly in Tourist Camp (Fair Grounds) Oskaloosa, Ia. Washing up. Tired, need the rest. Queen still a little sore. Have resorted again to the "old simple remedy" (cold water). Feeding R. oats. Had shoes soled, repaired, leggings sewed, yesterday P.M.

July 20, '25: Leaving Tourist Camp, Oskaloosa, 9:45 a.m. A. W. (Billy) Wiesman, Box 114, Mgr. Queen still sore in ligaments. On advice of Mr. Wiesman (old race horse man) decided, at last, to use Absorbine. Mr. W. gave bandages.
* * * *

From Signature Book: "Tourist Camp, Oskaloosa, Iowa. Frank M. Heath stayed in our camp from July 18 until July 20, leaving at 9:45 with Gypsy Queen.

(Signed) A. W. Wiesman."

Oskaloosa is one of the places that lingers fondly in our memory. Everybody seemed to get a joy out of entertaining travelers. The Camp was free. They wanted us to feel entirely at home. No suggestion that we should trade with anybody. Billy Wiesman spent quite a lot of time helping me to find just what we wanted— Absorbine, cotton—*gave* the bandages.

From Notes. July 20, '25 continued: 2 p.m. Just accosted by Mr. W. H. Barrouman, Sup. Washala County, Ia., Home and Asylum. He contributed $2 check (first over 1.00). Address Oskaloosa, Ia., County Home. 4 p.m. Crossing Des Moines River. 6:30 Ar'd farm of Mr. F. R. Harrington, Harvey, Ia.
* * * *

Traveled: 16 mi. Dirt—Westerly—Winding—Hilly. Crop good. More grass. Groves. Some sheep. Queen some sore. Using Absorbine, cotton bandages.

July 21,' 25: Leaving Mr. Harrington 7:30 * * * * 10:30 Passing worked-out mine. [soft coal]. [Old] Colored man and wife in shack [Care takers] Watered Queen. [Water was scarce here.] 3 p.m. Feeding Queen at farm of F. B. Marsh, Knoxville, R. 5, No chg. (Formula for thrush.) 6, Replaced shim left front. 7:30 p.m. Ar'd farm of Burt James, Knoxville, R. 9. * * * *

Traveled: 20 mi. (detour 1 mi. suburbs Knoxville). Paved 1, Bal. dirt. Via R. 24. Winding.

June 22, '25: Leaving the James 8 a.m. * * * * 6:30 p.m. Farm of Mrs. O. Wellons, Indianola, R. 1 1 mi. E. Indianola. * * * *

Traveled: 19 mi. Dirt. Country rolling. Crops good. Hay fair. Plenty pasture.

July 23, '25: Leaving Mrs. Wellons 10 a.m. * * * * 6 p.m. reached farm of Guy Fogler, W.W.V., Patterson. 8 mi. E. Winterset, after 4 'turn downs.' (I believe the 'turn downs' were on account of Queen limping again. You recollect some distance back, the narrator strongly suspected a lame horse was not a very good recommendation for the rider.)

Traveled: 21 mi. Paved 1 mi. Bal. dirt—detour 1. Via Wickman, R. 24. Country fair bottom land. Crops fair. Dry.

July 24, '25: Leaving Foglers 9 a.m. after good night's rest. * * * * 1 p.m. feeding, lunching in Tourist Camp (City Park), Winterset, Ia. Good company. 6:45 Ar'd farm Orie Hart, Winterset, R. 6, 9¼ mi. W. Winterset.

Traveled: 18 mi. (1 side to camp) Via R. 24. Gently rolling. Crops fair. Dry. Sick boy. Queen in mud.

July 25, '25: Leaving Mr. Hart 8 a.m. Cool. Slight showers in night. * * * *

Here, the country and conditions being very similar, I am dropping out the details of five days travel, to save space and the reader's patience.

From Notes. July 31, '25: Leaving Mr. Berchart, 9:30 a.m. Horse, meals, blankets, (no chg.) (I remember having straightened a mule's foot.) Noon, 2 p.m., feeding—lunching, Avenue A, Council Bluffs.

From Signature Book: "Council Bluffs, Ia., July 31, 1925. Frank M. Heath stopped at this office at noon today, with Gypsy Queen—outside.

(Signed) J. F. Oliver, Asst. Chief F. D."

Before leaving Iowa I feel inclined to generalize on some points that came under our observation, especially as I am omitting our daily notes for several days at a stretch—this in order, first, to save space, second, to relieve the reader of the daily grind. What I wish in particular to note is that up to this point in our travels we had seen very few colts—a few in crossing Illinois. I had begun to wonder where our fresh supply of horses would come from after all the old ones were gone. It is true that the public had, even at that date, conceived, somewhat erroneously, an idea that "the day of the horse was over." That tractors were replacing horses and mules on the farm. Now we all know that it is true that on the very large farms in the great wheat belt—of Kansas, for instance—and undoubtedly also on the great wheat farms in the Red River Valley of the North, mostly in North Dakota (neither of which we contacted), tractors are used almost altogether. On some of the medium-sized farms, such as we crossed in Illinois and Iowa, horses are, or at least at that time were, being supplemented, thank the Lord, rather than replaced, by medium-sized tractors. I interviewed many farmers on this point, along our route. The general consensus of opinion was that of one farmer I met driving a fine team of grade Percherons. As he put it:

"A fellow can raise more wheat by using tractors. He can raise a lot more hell—handle a little more money, but he can't gain anything in the long run. Gasoline costs money, tractors *will* wear out and they won't have colts. On the other hand, for instance, I'm going right now to have these mares bred to the best grade Percheron-Norman that I know of. Sorry to say pure bred Normans are very scarce. We have to admit that in that respect our stock is degenerating somewhat. Four or five good colts arrive on our place every year."

"We have profitably pastured more of our land. We certainly have kept our farm in better shape than if we had no horses. Of course, we have not made so much noise, but I feel certain that the money lender is not so likely to get our goat at the end of a decade."

Of course we had observed a lot of fine cattle, corn and hogs. They raise some sheep in hilly sections. They raise a lot of oats. I didn't see so much wheat along our route.

Chapter XI

SOUTH FROM OMAHA

WE crossed the bridge from Council Bluffs into Omaha on July 31, five days ahead of our schedule.

Special Note: Total to Omaha, 2,404 miles [as corrected] Average, 19.4 miles [approximately].

We spent the five days resting Queen in an old orchard in the southern suburbs. The flies were terrible. The tall weeds helped her to brush them off. We were treated hospitably by one George Troxile and family. Had a hard time getting them to accept a dollar or so "for Christmas money for the kids." We were scheduled to remain in Omaha fifteen days—not counting the five days we had gained in crossing Iowa, after having caught up with our schedule (Queen traveling much better in bandages and leg wash). We decided that to try to "exhibit" Queen at that time as the horse who was "doing" all this would be a little premature. So we left Omaha August 5th instead of August 20th. That is, we left Omaha fifteen days ahead of schedule.

*   *   *   *

THE EVENING WORLD, OMAHA, NEBRASKA
Saturday, August 1, 1925
HORSEBACK TOURIST MAKES STOP
IN OMAHA
Leaving Washington in April, He Plans to Visit Every State Within Two Years

HIS HOBBY IS HORSES
———

Up and down the land from north to south, from east to west and back again, streak the motor tourists with shabby and shiny cars

distorted with great tumor-like protuberance of tents and tackle.
"This is the life!" they cry as they pass.

"Horse-radish," says Frank M. Heath, 56, of Silver Springs, Md.
"I never have tire trouble, or run out of gas and oil, I'll travel just
as far on one horsepower as they will on many—and get a lot more
satisfaction out of the trip than they will."

Mr. Heath came to town late yesterday afternoon on his good
horse "Gypsy Queen," a beautiful bay Kentucky Whip-Morgan cross.
It took him four hours to find "hotel" accommodations for his
mount, but that's a common occurrence in town and country in
this gasoline-drenched era, he says.

Who is Mr. Heath?

Well, Mr. Heath is a man, not so very large in size, in khaki
clothes, a veteran of the great war, and a person who knows horses,
their why and wherefore, through a lifetime experience.

Why is Mr. Heath here?

Well, Mr. Heath is riding around and through every state. His
object is to hit every state on one horse and return to Washington
on or before July 1, 1927. He left Washington, D. C. April 1, of
this year and so far has made Maryland, Pennsylvania, Delaware,
New Jersey, New York, Connecticut, Rhode Island, Massachusetts,
New Hampshire, Maine, Vermont, Ohio, Michigan, Indiana, Illinois,
Iowa, and Nebraska.

What makes Mr. Heath do this?

GOOD FOR HIS HEALTH

In the first place he thinks it will be good for his health. In the
second place he is a horseman who loves the horse like a brother
and he hopes to prove the capability, durability and adaptability of
the horse, and wants to help horses, and horsemen.

How does Mr. Heath and his horse draw sustenance from the land?

Well it was this way. Mr. Heath was born at Burr Oak, Ia., and
grew up surrounded by tall corn and horses. During a large part of
his life he seldom strayed far from a horse's house.

During the war he served as "mule sergeant" with various overseas
engineer organizations, and after the war was in the service in a
similar capacity for some time. He served with horses and mules in
the Philippines. (About the time of the Philippine Insurrection.)

"My hobby is horses, but not hobby horses," said Mr. Heath.

In his travels he dispenses horse sense to those who have horses
and need advice about them. If he stops at Farmer Jones' house for

the night, the conversation invariably turns to horses. Farmer Jones' old gray mare has something the matter with her northeast foot. Mr. Heath looks at it, and gives advice from experience. In the morning when it comes to settling accounts, invariably the farmer will not only refuse to accept compensation for bed and board, but tries to force money on Mr. Heath.

Thus he and Gypsy Queen eat!

Mr. Heath says a horse's legs are its underpinning. That if the foundation of a horse, or house either, as the case may be, is wrong, there is bound to be trouble. If the wheels of your car are out of alignment, or you travel far and wide on a flat tire—what's the answer? The same is true of a horse.

Mr. Heath is a horse mechanic—one who has gained much knowledge through experience—and considers it his duty to pass it on.

He is a member of the Cissel Saxon Post No. 41 of the American Legion, Silver Springs. So far he has traveled 2,404 miles, or 207 miles ahead of his schedule.

*   *   *   *

From Signature Book: "August 1, 1925. This is to certify that Frank M. Heath arrived in Omaha on Gypsy Queen July 31, 1925.

(Signed) James L. Dahlman, Mayor."

From Notes. August 5, '25: "Leaving Geo. Troxile and family (S.E. Suburbs of Omaha) 5:45 a.m. * * * * 9:30 (a.m.) crossing Platt River—low bank muddy. 11 Ar'd Plattsmouth via La Platte. Stopped (earlier) at Ft. Crook. 2 p.m. Am having Queen reshod all around. Calks front—plain behind—by John Iverson.

We had traveled quite a distance since shoeing. Had kept left front heel up by replacing the rim of rubberized fiber whenever it worked loose, and once or twice—as the reader will perhaps recall—farther shimming up the outside of the left front heel. So much for the foot. As to the strained ligaments, and the soreness of the leg in general, I was still using this Absorbine preparation by rubbing some into the leg before wrapping, and usually pouring a little into the top of the bandage. I may explain that I first wrapped the bandage twice around the pastern (fairly tight), then, spirally, on up the leg (over the cotton of course), and pinned it tightly with two large, strong safety-pins, instead of cording the leg, which is sometimes done by tying the split end of the bandage tightly. Thus the pressure would be distributed over a three-inch bandage instead of being confined to the width of a string. In wrapping, I worked the slackened cotton into the natural groove between the cannon bone and the flexor tendon. This equalized the pressure, preventing a false swelling between the cannon bone and the flexor tendon. This, the reader will understand, braced the ankle joint against "rolling" outward, thus trussing or reinforcing the ankle and leg in lieu of the natural "truss," the suspensory ligaments—which, being strained or "stretched," did not function fully. I wish to remind the reader that cotton shrinks with moisture. The moisture of the brace (the main purpose of which was to soothe—not anesthetize—the soreness), was to offset by the slight counter-irritant the irritation of the nerves. This brace also stimulated the circulation. I removed these bandages several times a day, partly to air the leg, and partly for rewrapping.

Now about the shoeing at Plattsmouth: first, remember that this long distance we had traveled was mostly over loamy soil, not containing sand or grit enough to cause much wear on the shoes. I believe that somehow, some place, we had had Queen shod one more time in front than behind. Her hind shoes were actually worn down to very thin even metal plates. These we had removed before leaving Troxile's place. There was plenty of hoof to last the 20 miles or so to Plattsmouth. All hoofs had grown abundantly. We could shape them to suit ourselves.

I have been dwelling largely upon feet that were off balance, mentioning only casually anything about a horse being off axis, which means that the heel of the foot is either too low or too high in comparison with the toe. This, as I see it now, may be almost as bad as the foot being off balance, i.e., too short, or too prominent, or too high or too low on one side. Being off his axis, if not allowed to continue too long, may not be as disastrous ultimately. The reason, it seems to me, is that if too low, the strain comes largely upon the Flexor tendon, which would throw the strain on muscles largely, rather than on the ligaments. It throws the strain largely upon muscles which have more of a chance to recover somewhat than a "stretched" ligament. Of course, if this undue strain is continued too long it is pretty likely to cause or aggravate navicular disease, to say nothing of throwing at least some strain upon the posterior branch of the suspensory ligament and causing a slackening of the anterior branch, and a slackening of the extensor tendon in the front of the leg—which throws the whole mechanism out of alignment.

On the other hand, if the heel is too high, it not only slackens the flexor tendon, but also throws the pressure of the coffin-bone against the inside of the wall of the hoof in front, causing a pressure on the sensitive laminae, and in turn a slight slackening of the posterior branches of the suspensory ligament. In fact, it throws all joints in that foot and leg out of alignment. It is well known among veterinarians that this high heel racket is often the cause of stompy foot, cocked ankle, or sprung knee. Take this sprung knee, for instance. A horse's heel has been left habitually too high, throwing the bones of the front leg (saying no more for the present about the ankle), out of alignment, forward. Or, in case the heel is sore, he may flex the knee somewhat to take the pressure off the heel. This may become a habit. This relaxes the muscle to which the flexor tendon is attached. The muscle in time becomes habitually contracted through lack of proper use. A knee has become chronically sprung. Unless a case of arthritis has set in, there is nothing wrong with the joint. Of course, as stated, this does not affect that particular leg alone. It throws the whole frame out of alignment.

We were caught between the devil and the deep blue sea in regard to Queen's left front foot. I had been trying to keep it normal as to axis, as well as balance. Now we had plenty of hoof—a surplus of hoof in fact. The soreness was largely, or at least partly, plainly within the foot. I had begun to suspect a kind of complication between navicular and what we might express as a one-sided laminitis (sometimes called founder) of the left foot. The one-sided laminitis, of course, was traceable to the rolling of the foot. Now it is well-known that navicular is incurable if it has become chronic. It was not certain that she had reached that point. But certain symptoms indicated that she was threatened with this, and that I must guard against it. The treatment (for relief only) recommended for navicular, as all veterinarians know, is to raise the heel, etc. So the horse-shoer and I decided to shorten the toe a little bit beyond normal.

I still believe it possible that had we at that particular time—the whole foot being somewhat inflamed—thrown an excessive strain upon the flexor tendon, navicular disease might have developed. Right then began a case of so-called sprung knee: that is, Queen's left front. I had a hard time keeping this from going over. That is, the heel being a little high, she favoring the heel, the muscles began to become contracted, as stated, through lack of proper or full function. The contracted muscles in turn accentuated the sprung knee until it became almost chronic.

Getting back to the calks mentioned in the notes, that was positively a mistake. I had somehow conceived the idea that mud calks would help to ease a horse down when his foot struck the ground. Sometimes, in a sense, that is true, but in this case, on this good prairie, there was no sense in this. In fact, I have concluded that as a rule more is lost than gained by the use of calks unless they are necessary to keep the horse from slipping.

The fact is that any good road saddle horse, ridden in a walk and properly handled, acquires what is known as a slipping gait. Not only does he gain (though almost imperceptibly) in distance covered, but it prevents, to some extent, what we might call a slackening of the horse's momentum. But—and this is most important—it also relieves the shock of the impact of the horse's foot in contacting the ground. Of course, anyone would know that this would not apply on very much of an up-grade. Also a thoughtful person would know that nature did not intend the horse to be used as a toboggan. We will see the almost fatal results of these calks later when we come into the steep hills of the Ozarks.

From Notes. "August 8, '25: Leaving Mr. Huss 8:30. No chg. Advice. Noon, eating, feeding, farm of W. R. Jones, Brock, Neb., Rt. 2. * * * * Old timer (born here), owns lot of good horses (some prize-winning Percherons)."

From Signature Book: "Heath arrived on my farm today on Gypsy Queen and stopped for dinner and in the meantime rendered me some valuable aid on my horses' feet.
(Signed) W. R. Jones, Brock, Neb."

From Notes. August 8, '25: continued: (I remember particularly his having slipped a crisp dollar bill into my hand upon leaving.) 6 p.m. Ar'd home of John Schlange, Auburn, Neb., R. 1.

Traveled: 18 mi.—1 mi. detour around missing bridge (washed out). 1 mi. side trip to dinner. * * * * By the way of back country Rd. Nearly straight S., winding to cross Little Nemaha River. * * * * Through two farms. Rolling. Crossed ridges of "Limestone soil." Followed lane between hedge rows many miles —abundance elderberries, some wild grapes, plums. Crops poor. Corn, good prospect. Mixed farming, alfalfa.

August 9, '25: Sunday: Washing up. Old clothes about gone.
Boy, 19, Walter, enthusiast about horses, had had a course in
horse training. * * *

August 12, '25: Rained hard in night. Very muddy. Queen
fine. Leaving Mr. Teek 8:30. No chg. Gave "Herbert" advice
on foot. Noon, feeding, dinner, farm of Althouse, Sabetha, Kan.
5 p.m. Reached farm of Mr. Jas. Wilson (colored), Copioma,
Kan. (Address, R. 3, Sabetha, Kan.)

Traveled: 18½ mi. Very muddy. Gently rolling. Mixed grain
and corn good. Mr. Wilson owns part of the 400 [acres] he is
farming—with four boys. Has twelve fine mules. Everything
looks prosperous and well kept up. (We slept in the hay.) Some
orchards in these parts. (During the War Mr. Wilson had
bought mules in large numbers and sold them to dealers who
were selling them to the Government. He bought them largely
on contract.)

August 13, '25: Leaving Mr. Wilson—family, 8:30. No chg.
Advice. * * * * 5 p.m. Ar'd farm of Ed Beam, Netawaka,
Kan. * * * *

Traveled: 22½ mi. Dirt. Gently rolling. Much bottom land—
some wet. All crops good.

August 14, '25: Leaving the Beams 8:30 a.m. No chg. Advice,
formulas. 10:30 at "Recorder" office, Holton. Saw Mr. W. Beck.
* * * * 3:30 p.m., at Patauatomi Indian Agency. * * * *
Talking with clerk G. V. King, Wm. Hale, Indian Police.
Reservation, 11 mi. square. 750 Indians. Farming well. ½ still
under Gov. control. 5:30 p.m. Ar'd farm of Mr. James Vanderblomen, 1 mi. N. of S.E. corner of Reservation. Farming 100
acres—60 acres of good corn. 7 good horses. Corn, hogs, poultry.
Well educated. Children educated. [Mr. Vanderblomen was a
full-blooded Indian. I would hardly have known this if he had
not told me.]

Traveled: 18 mi. Rolling. All crops good, especially alfalfa and
wild hay. * * * *

August 15, '25: Left Vanderblomen 7:30. No chg. * * * *
Ar'd feed yard, Topeka, Kan., 3 p.m.

Traveled: 19 mi. Paved 2 mi. Bal. dirt. Hilly. Crops good.
Immense quantities hay, kaffir corn. Prairie hay. Kaffir corn.
Com. orchards. * * * *

Special Note:
Omaha-Topeka, 181 miles [as corrected]

Total—2,585 [as corrected]. 179 more than schedule. [We were still 15 days ahead of our schedule.] * * * *

August 17, '25: [Laying in.] Rec'd 12 bottles Absorbine from Young Inc. Sold 8, $10.00. Sent 2 P.P. [parcel post package] which I forwarded to Powhatan, Ark. * * * *

Meanwhile having found this to be very effective and very necessary (for this was the basis of the leg wash, or "brace" that I have been mentioning), I had written Young and Company, manufacturers and distributors of this Absorbine, telling them about our trip and sending them some "literature." I wrote them a good letter as to what the Absorbine was doing for the strained leg, and that I did not believe we could proceed without it (and in that, I was telling the exact truth). I also blushingly made it plain that I was getting by largely by means of advising on or treating lame horses, but that cash was almost nil, that I had no objection to their using this letter, and could they kindly send me a couple of bottles of Absorbine. The 12 bottles that I received here at Topeka was the result. I wish to make it plain that I did not sell two thirds of it as a matter of greed, but because it would not be practical to send so much of it ahead by parcel post. They sent a bottle or two once or twice afterwards, which got us through to winter quarters. I have examined their literature which goes out with the Absorbine several times since then, and if they ever used my letter, I don't know it. I believe they did this for us just because they are a bunch of good scouts. The dozen retail would have cost $30.

This, the above, is not an advertisement, it is an expression of my appreciation of one of those kindnesses that some people are big enough to hand out, unbegrudgingly, in behalf of someone in trouble—or a suffering horse—with no ulterior motive. And that reminds me that something done in kindness with no selfish motive is very likely to reflect back. It seems to be a law of nature—including human nature. Had I not helped out many a horse in distress, knowing that I would receive nothing in return except the gratitude of the horses (for it is not true, as some claim, that a horse has no sense of gratitude), the gratitude of the owner probably, and a clean conscience!

From Signature Book: "Topeka, Kan., 212 W. Morris St., August 18, 1925. Frank M. Heath with Gypsy Queen put up at this farm from 5 p.m. August 16th.

(Signed) John Knight, Barn Manager."

From Notes. August 18, '25: Leaving here (Topeka) toward
Miama 8 a.m. * * * * 6:30 p.m. Ar'd farm of Jos. Sargent
(renter), Overbrook, R. 4. * * * *

   Traveled: 27 mi. Pav. 3 mi.—by error ½ mi. Via back roads.
5 mi. E. 22 mi. N. of Topeka. Country rolling, alternating between good and stony land. Crops fair, some corn excellent.
Much Kaffir. A lot of vacant ground. Some flax. Very hot.

   August 19, '25: Leaving "Jim" Sargent 8 a.m. and nephew
Earl Tomlinson. Jolly lot. Batching. Plenty of "grub." * * * *

In inquiring for a place to put up for the night of the day I left
Topeka, I was referred to "a middle-aged man, a young man and
an old man." This proved to be the boss, a middle-aged man, his
nephew, a young man, and his dad, in his seventies, a spry old
fellow. They were good hearted, hail-fellow-well-met.

The water at this place was terrible. During the evening I just
happened to notice a time or two some one of the three would slip
over a little rise in the ground and return. There was some brush
about there. I slept in a bed that night. It was hot. The middle-aged
man slept on the floor in one doorway, and the young man slept
on the floor at the back door. I did not think much of the fact at
the time, it being well known that if there is any breeze on a sultry
night it is on the floor.

The phone rang several times next morning. In this locality they
were "changing help" in threshing. It developed these various phone
calls required the young man to go to help one neighbor, and about
9 o'clock the boss himself was to go to still another neighbor's.
About 7 I was out at the barn. The young man had gone. The old
man was scratch-scratch-scratching away on a horse collar. He said
to me, "S'posin' somebody asked you if you knew anything about
any booze on this place?" I replied that I had neither seen nor
smelled nor was offered any booze.

During the half hour or so that the boss had to wait he told me
a story:

"Last winter there was a young feller came along right in mid-
winter. He was broke—just had to have a job of some kind. Well, I
never like to turn a feller down, so I gave him a job for a few days,
a dollar a day and board. I put him at chopping up some old hedge
trimmings for wood. I was afraid I'd have to get him a wooden axe
for fear he would cut his feet. I took him off o' that. He couldn't
milk a cow—he couldn't harness a horse—he couldn't do nothin'!

This went on for a couple of days or so, and he says one morning, 'Well,' he says, 'I guess I'll go on.' 'Well, suit yourself,' I says, 'You're welcome to stay.' 'Yes,' he says, 'but I am heading for—such a place. I guess I'll travel.' 'Well, all right,' I says, 'I'll take you to town.' I hooked up and drove the young feller to the station, paid him his two or three dollars, and started to buy him a ticket to his destination. The young fellow burst out laughing. 'Say boss,' he says, 'what the hell you doin'?' 'Why, I'm buying you a ticket—you're busted, ain't you?' 'Hell no!' and he pulled out of his pocket bills and credits to the extent of quite an amount. 'What the hell?' I asked the feller. 'Oh,' he says, 'nothin' much. I was sent out here to get the goods on a middle-aged man, a young man, and an old man. Somebody blabbed about there being a little booze, or wine, or somethin'. 'As far as I know,' he says, 'there ain't no booze around here. I couldn't turn a feller in for just about nothin' when he's been as white as you've been.' "

"Well," I said, "you tell the Old Man he needn't worry about me. I ain't seen nothin' either, nor smelled nothin', nor I ain't been offered nothin' to drink." Jim laughed.

We drop out here nearly three days. The conditions had been about as described before, alternating poor and good soil, limestone base. Once we passed a load of coal from some little local mine. We had traveled about seventy miles.

From Notes. August 21, '25: * * * * 6 p.m. Ar'd farm of Chas. Adams, 5½ mi. N. of Iola.

Traveled: 23 mi. 4 mi. gravel and 'side.' Country slightly rolling. Crops fair. * * * * Wild hay, alfalfa.

August 22, '25: Leaving Mr. Adams 9 a.m. * * * * Ar'd Iola (Ice Plant) 11 a.m. Feeding in shade of a large tree.

Traveled: 6 mi. 'Side' (gravel road) all the way. Level. Country very dry. 7 p.m. Put in day trying to arrange to show Queen at Allen County Fair, Aug. 31 to Sept. 4. * * * *

August 23, '25: Got settled for week-end under cattle shed at Fair Grounds about 8 p.m. (last night.) Batching. Oats 16 lbs. 25 cts. Bale prairie hay 25 cts. delivered. 1 p.m. Resting today— washing up—writing letters. I need a rest.

August 24, '25, Sunday: Leaving Fair Ground at Iola for Chanute after trying every lead to exhibit at Allen Co. Fair. 3:30 p.m. Going through Humbolt suburbs. Shacks (colored). Large cement plant. S.E. of Humbolt about ½ mi. Sec. oil

prairie pipe line, Sinclair pipe line. 8 p.m. Ar'd Chanute Fair
Grounds.

Traveled: 20 mi. 6 mi. dirt (back rd.) Pave 2 mi. Bal. gravel
or side. 4 mi. detour to hit Chanute. Country gently rolling.
Valley burning up. Some hay and alfalfa. In Nashoe River
Valley (river bottom) corn fair. Alfalfa. Some oil, some drilling,
Humbolt to Chanute. Large cement plant, Sinclair refinery.

August 25, '25: Had Queen in cattle shed last night. Slept in
straw. Saw Mr.   last night. Am to see him this A.M.
8 o'cl. Leaving Fair Grounds 9:40 a.m. No chance to show.
* * * * 7 p.m. Ar'd farm of M. W. Brocke, Galesburg, R.
1. * * * *

Traveled: 25 mi.—3 mi. by misdirection. 4 mi. gravel, Bal.
dirt. Level country. Grain fair. Corn drying up—½ crop. (few
mi. S. of Chanute burned up.) Much prairie hay. Some water
holes. Alfalfa.

August 26, '25: Leaving Mr. Brocke 8:45 a.m. * * * * 7 p.m.
Ar'd farm of J. W. Roller (owners) Altamont, R. 3. * * * *

Traveled: 22 mi. Dirt. via mostly S. some E. Level. Much
prairie hay. Some corn—some kaffir. Crops fair.

August 27, '25: Leaving the Rollers 9 a.m. No chg. (advice).
* * * * 3:30 p.m. Crossing Kan.-Okla. line about 32 mi. NW.
of Miami. 6 p.m. Ar'd farm of Mr. D. A. Burrows, Address,
Chetopa, Kan., R. 4. *Farm* 12 mi. N.W. at Welch, Ok. * * * *

Traveled: 20 mi. Dirt some stony in Ok. [Oklahoma]
* * * * Here in Ok. first note evidence stretches of prairie
without hedges.

From Signature Book: "This is to certify that Frank M. Heath
arrived at Welch, Okla., Dave B. Burrows, August 27 at 6
o'clock, on Gypsy Queen.

                    (Signed) D. B. Burrows."

From Notes. August 28, '25: Leaving the Burrows. 5:15 Ar'd
at the farm of G. W. Dale (renter), Miami, R. 5.

Traveled: 21 mi. 4 mi. S., bal. E. Dirt. Prairie corn. Mostly
fair. Prairie hay.

August 29, '25: Leaving Mr. Dale. 9:45 Ar'd Fair Grounds,
Miami, Okla. Saw Management. N.G. Waiting to see Carnival
man.

Special Note: Total to date, 2801 miles [as corrected] 195 mi.
more than schedule [we were 14 days ahead of schedule.]

Chapter XII

WE JOIN A CARNIVAL

Q<small>UEEN</small> was fat and bright. But she was just a little sore, and that left knee had now begun to worry me. That high heel theory, or racket, was not working satisfactorily, foot or no foot. I decided she needed a rest badly. That's the reason I had been trying to display her at some fair, in order to at least try to make our expenses while "laying over." At the two places where I had tried in Kansas, I had been given to understand at each place that the fair was neither a circus, a menagerie, nor a side show. It was for the purpose of showing the local stock. Perhaps it was not put up to me thus abruptly; but I got the idea distinctly—and properly—just the same. If we could temporarily join the carnival—the carnival consisting largely of amusement features—a kind of sideshow might go in that case, we thought.

> *From Notes.* Sunday, August 30, '25: Put in day resting. Saw Mr. Isler—Carnival man—Date for tomorrow 10 a.m.
> August 31, '25: Got "spot" at Isler show, Miami Fair. * * * *

Of course, it was understood that any sideshow must have a large "announcement" out front. In Oklahoma, they call that a banner. In discussing the matter with Mr. Isler, I remarked, "Suppose we see if we can get 'em into an argument about it." "Good idea," agreed Mr. Isler. Then he suggested: "Gypsy Queen, Toughest Horse in the World." "All right, I'll give $1,000 to anyone who proves that she is not." "Sounds good," quoth Mr. Isler. (This might sound a little boastful from a man whose ready cash was about five dollars, but—after all, was I not worth more than a thousand dollars!) When "Happy" delivered the banner it read something like this: "*Gypsy Queen, Toughest Horse in the World. $1,000 to Prove that She is Not. See her Alive Today.*" I had paid $2.50 for the sign—too late to start in over again. I straightened the blunder out as best I could with a large pencil. Before I had closed the deal altogether it had

95

been made plain that any attempt to exhibit Queen successfully would be futile unless I had a good "grinder." In Oklahoma a "grinder" is a fellow, usually referred to as a spieler—sometimes a barker. Well, I had to get a "grinder" before I could afford to invest in signs, tents, lights, etc. "There's your man," suggested Happy, pointing out a long, gaunt, knock-kneed, pigeon-toed fellow with an inch-high forehead, a very long, sharp nose, and a kind of a snaky eye. "Hell," I said, "that fellow looks to me like a damn fool." "Well," replied Happy, "it takes a damn fool to stand the grind over and over. You see, an intelligent man couldn't stand it." "Okay," I replied, "He sure ought to be a good 'grinder.'" So I made a bargain with Slim. He was to get one-third of my share of the ticket money. That was fair, he thought. Three way split between The Toughest Horse in the World, her manager, and the "grinder." Now would be as good a place as any to announce that the carnival was splitting fifty-fifty with the fair association. I was splitting fifty-fifty with Mr. Isler (about the usual split). In other words, The Toughest Horse in the World, and her manager, would draw down one-fourth of our gate receipts. Unfortunately for the under-dog, he had to dig up the price of the Banner, fifty cents a day for the tent, rented from Isler, $2.50 that I gave Slim in advance for wiring and lighting the tent.

Slim had just nicely got to work when he informed me that he was "damn hungry." He hadn't eaten a bite all day. Could I let him have a dollar in advance? I handed him a dollar. He disappeared for a while. I finally located him going from one hot dog stand to another, throwing down about anything he could get his hands on. Finally I got him back to work. In this case, as sometimes happens, the "grinder" was also the ticket taker. I had noticed Slim circulating amongst the crowd. When it came to opening, about sundown, all he could say was, "Well, come on buy side tickets, well come on buy side tickets!" Two or three bought tickets. That, of course, put me inside the tent. I had been promoted. I was the lecturer. We certainly did a Land Office business for about half an hour, or for the duration of three lectures—three crowds that filled the tent. Then suddenly business went on the bum. I stepped outside and asked Slim how many tickets had been sold and collected. He had four or five. "How come all that crowd?" "Oh," he replied, "those were all show people. You know," he confided, "a feller with a show is entitled to visit any side show free of charge." "The devil they are," I said. "I wonder who was running all these concessions while that jam was in here. Get the hell out of here!" It looked to me very much as though he had been giving the crowd a cut rate, probably cutting the admission fee to a nickel. "A bird in the hand is worth two in the bush." As the newspaper reporter puts it, he had certainly made a "scoop." The demand for tickets was just about exhausted for that evening. Well, yes, there are fools—and fools.

Along came a fellow called Blondy. "Heck," he said to me, "that fellow's no good, he's a bum, he hasn't even got a bally act." "Meaning?" I asked him. "Why, I've got a bally act, a good one." The situation demanded action rather than delay. "Golden moments were fleeting." At least they should have been golden, or perhaps some small change in silver. "Okay," I replied, "come on with your bally act." It consisted of a cigar box, through each end of which he had punctured a small round hole with an awl. Into these holes he had inserted a twine string. He would hold each end of the string, which of course ran through the box, one hand above the other, with the box near his upper hand. The string being somewhat slack, and therefore slightly fluffed up, gave it a friction-fit in the holes, so that when left slack the box would remain up. Then he began talking to the little box. "Now little box, you stay right where you are until I tell you to travel. All right, now go." He would stretch the string which of course let the box slide downward. "Easy now," he would say, as though he was talking to a team of horses. He would slightly slacken the string, which would cause the little box to slow up a little. "Whoa,"—of course he would slacken the string a little more, which would cause the box to stop again. By this time perhaps a dozen or so people had gathered to see what all this foolishness was about. He sold two or three tickets. Of course, once more I was the lecturer. I got about half through the lecture. Eight or ten more came in. Begging pardon of those that had heard part of the lecture, I began over again. I believe I had two crowds of ten or fifteen people. All at once the potential patrons seemed to have become exhausted, temporarily at least. The lecturer also was exhausted somewhat—temporarily at least. It was hot inside. The lecturer, not wishing to butt in on the affairs of the "grinder," ticket seller, and strange to say, also the ticket taker, slipped out under the back of the tent to get a little fresh air. (The fair association, receiving half the gate money, were supposed to furnish a ticket taker, but somehow they had not yet put one on.) It was only accidentally that the lecturer strolled around toward the front, and what did he see! When the crowd was increasing after sundown, he was selling a few tickets. And a few people were passing into the tent. As he took the tickets, instead of putting them into the box, he would shuffle them a time or two, absentmindedly, being so busy talking, sell the same tickets over again, and put the change in his pocket. "All right," I said, "all holding tickets pass inside and get the concluding lecture of the evening." "Well," remarked Blondy, "I believe I'd better go back to the bleachers and sell some more candy." "I guess that's right," I agreed. "You sold about thirty tickets. Suppose you whack up." He did, whether he had intended to or not. It only amounted, after all, to about $2.00 to me. The junior partner of the firm of Gypsy Queen and Heath closed up for the evening—"a sadder and a wiser man"—but undefeated.

The following day we had a few audiences—three or four tents full, of about twenty, and after that a few stragglers. It was the best day we had. Among the straggling visitors in the evening was one Dr. Cook, veterinary surgeon. He noticed that Queen was standing a little sprung on the left knee. After examining the leg he laid this nearly altogether to the heel being too high. Now the fact is that my ideas of the distinction between a horse being "off axis" and "off balance" had up to this time not been quite clear. There could be a complication of both. I had not placed quite enough importance on the "off axis" business, where "off axis" stood out by itself. Dr. Cook made this all plain to me. My only chance, he said, was to lower that heel, so and so. If possible, he would volunteer his advice on the spot at the local shoeing shop next day. It wasn't possible. Dr. Cook was evidently a very busy man. I got the idea over as best I could to the local shoer. Where I failed in part, was in being afraid to lower the heel too much, all at once, for fear of putting too much sudden strain on the almost chronically contracted muscles, onto which the flexor tendon joined. This was another blunder. I should have lowered the heel to its proper height, depending on the readjustment taking place largely during the three days we still had in camp at Miami, on the soft turf.

Dr. Cook had unhesitatingly verified my suspicion that the lameness originated with the rolling of the foot, and that the false pressure thus caused on the sensitive laminae was the initial cause of the soreness—or, as I have already expressed it, a kind of one-sided (i.e. affecting primarily one side of the foot only) laminitis, or road founder. This, he also agreed, would have a tendency to affect the whole foot, including the navicular. It was made plain that it would be disastrous to follow instructions that are given for relieving navicular disease, by shortening the toe, raising the heel, and so forth. It was hoped that it was still not too late to arrest this approaching trouble by shunting the pressure away from the left side as I had been doing. There was also some discussion of whether all of this foot trouble did not bring some undue pressure on some certain nerve or nerves that farther caused Queen to flex the knee unduly. It seemed that my previous harping upon this "nerve pressure theory" was correct. I could go ahead now with more certainty in my advice on foot and leg trouble. Dr. Cook is one of the men who stands out prominently in my memory of people we met on our adventure.

Having the following week on our hands, and the weather being still very hot, and Queen beginning to respond to the sustained rest, we decided to accept Mr. Isler's invitation to try showing in the carnival the following week at Galena, Kansas. I decided that we would do the best we could by ourselves during the next few days. Almost anything was better than sitting like a bump on a log.

Queen was one of those horses that liked to see what was going on. I was outside the tent mostly. Queen would stick her head out under the flap. She seemed interested in what I was doing. As soon as my back was turned, out popped her head. As soon as I would turn around she would dodge back. This would cause the few people that were sticking around considerable amusement, but it didn't get anybody inside the tent. Something had to be done. Queen had too much time "on her hands." I hit upon a little scheme to occupy Queen's idle time, and at the same time try to arouse some kind of special interest in her. So this is what we did: I went and got a cheap cow-bell. This I rigged from the tent pole in such a way that when Queen pulled the strap the bell would ring. Then I fastened to the strap one of those mammoth ears of Oklahoma corn that I had bought, on the spot, as part of Queen's ration. Knowing that I was coming into a locality where corn would be about the only grain procurable, I had decided to gradually get her used to corn. Of course, she would grab the ear of corn in her teeth. The bell would ring. I would detach the ear of corn and throw a little oats into her feed box. Thus she quickly learned that to ring the bell meant "oats." Meanwhile I had tied her to a stake, so that she could not peek out. I would park myself outside. A few people would come along, perhaps attracted by an occasional jingle of the bell. The bell would ring. I would say to some boy: "Son, step in there and see who the devil is ringing that bell." He would step inside the tent and come out with a grin. "Why the horse is ringing the bell, there's nobody in there but the horse." This would arouse the curiosity of two or three people to the extent that they would blow themselves to a dime to see what it was all about. Our book for that day shows receipts, net $1.00, which means that we must have had thirty patrons. The next day, Saturday, shows no receipts.

From Signature Book: "Miami, Okla. Frank M. Heath arrived in Miami Saturday, August 29, '25 on Gypsy Queen. Displayed her at Carnival until Saturday, Sept. 5.

(Signed) C. J. Fribley,
Pres. Ottawa Co. (County) Amus. Co."

From Notes. September 6, '25: Left Carnival, Miami, Okla. 7 a.m. for Galena, Kan., carnival. Noon, feeding, eating lunch in rear of a miner's plain home about 15 mi. N. E. of Miami. Many zinc mines. (as I remember this was Pitcher, Oklahoma.) 5 p.m. Ar'd Galena, Kan.

Traveled: 31 miles. Via Baxter Springs (and Pitcher, Okla.) Gravel. Very rough and stony 10 mi. First 5 mi. level. Poor soil —dry. Crops very poor—6 mi. N. begin zinc mines. Some patches of corn. Poor, dry—mines to Baxter Springs. B. S. to Galena, rough scrub timber. Around Galena more zinc mines.

About sixteen boys met us about half a mile outside the carnival grounds. The boys were all agog. "You're the man that's ridin' around the world, ain't you?" "Not quite that, boys. Say, boys, I need something to scrape this horse with. I wish I had one of those flat tobacco boxes. They're dandy to scrape the dry sweat off a horse. Don't scratch the skin like a curry comb. You know, boys, that little red box. I guess tiny cigars come in it." Sure they would find one. "All right, any boy that brings me anything I want, gets in free. A bucket of water, for instance, when we come in." When we arrived on the grounds the sixteen boys, more or less, had about six or seven tobacco cans and two buckets of water. About every boy within ten miles of Galena, sometime during the week we stayed there, remembered having brought us something. I had to laugh up my sleeve about this. Finally, as it was announced in the paper, I put on one free night, especially for boys—and was glad to do so.

The different parts of the show were being hauled on to the ground from the Isler train by Mr. Isler's fine, strong team of

Percherons, and assigned positions as they arrived. I believe this process continued well into the next day. I could not get any definite expression out of the lot boss as to where we should set up. Finally, I received a kind of lecture from him which did me a lot of good, which I have never forgotten, and of which it would do some people good to take note. "There are" said he, "other concessions which Mr. Isler would rather see occupy a choice location than this one. You wouldn't expect—would you—that being with us only a couple of weeks, we would disrupt our own arrangements?" "Well," I replied, "I understood Mr. Isler to say that he would try to have us assigned to a place a little less noisy." He smiled wryly, as much as to say, "I'm the guy that's responsible for these concessions." "Did you stop to think, dad, that your little temporary show is entirely out of line with a carnival? Yours is a beautiful horse, I admit that, and your lecture is okay, or would be in its proper place, and at the proper time. But people don't come to a carnival for instruction. They come here to have a lot of fun." "I thank you. I just hadn't thought of that. However, our plans were to spend the week here while giving the horse another week's rest." "Okay, dad, you're welcome, but I'm afraid we can't disarrange our positions." "Wouldn't expect it now," I replied. "Fine, now why don't you get in the shade some place, and take it easy for a while?" We did.

From Notes. September 7, '25: Spent day setting up. Hell of a time—cost me 16 passes for boys. (Of course we did not begrudge the passes.) Took in great sum of 55 cents. (Net.)

September 8, '25: Spending day in camp. Getting Queen shod behind. Writing Mr. Whitacre, S. S. [Silver Springs, Md.] Nat. Bank for Statement. Instructions. Show 40 cts.

September 9, '25: An old Kansas wind. Show 15 cts. Tonight many complimentary tickets. Still I lectured to several groups and individuals of out of town people and several boys who said they paid. Must have sold more than six tickets. Asked Mr. Isler for ticket taker. I had again put on a grinder-ticker seller who also took the tickets.

September 10, '25: Preparing to put on a little Shetland as an additional attraction. (Net receipts) Show 30 cts.

September 11, '25: Money dwindling too fast. Lost Ingersol and fountain pen—cost me $2.50 to replace. Pair paints $2.25. Washing 25 cts.—it all costs—and making nothing. But Queen is walking much better on left front. * * * * Show paid 35 cts.

September 12, '25: 12 p.m. [midnight] Show paid $1.20. Paid boy .25—net 95 cts. Here and at Miami I am out $20.00 [including articles lost or stolen.] Cashed last traveler's check in Miami. On hand $4.50. Galena is an old mining town. Mines (lead and zinc) worked out. Country rough. Town old. Shacks. [Horse] traders.

In pulling up the carnival they had thrown away tubs full of "cherry-cola." Besides hot-dog stands and the like there had been about four "town pumps." The "town pump" was a cheap pitcher-pump, having its lower extremity in a tub of "cherry-cola" under the counter. This "cherry-cola" was cherry color all right, and had some kind of a cherry flavor. Usually there was ice in the tub, for the weather was miserably hot. The fact that this ice melted, adding somewhat to the proportion of water over the coloring and flavoring powder would make practically no difference. If it did, all they had to do was add a little more powder. Well, it was cold anyhow—while the ice held out. I believe this concession was moving right along with the carnival. As they were moving out, I heard one of the concession men say to another, "Too bad to pour all this stuff on the ground. We otta leave some for the old man." They did—about half a wash tub full. For once in my life I had all the "cherry-cola" I wanted. I could have taken a bath in it. Well, it was cold anyhow and the night was hot. Of course, I had turned in the tent which I had rented from the carnival management. We moved over to the livery stable. We could have camped out, but the boiling sun and the flies would have been terrible on Queen. (It is well known among horsemen that flies are less vicious in the shade, even the mild shade of a barn.)

*   *   *   *

GALENA TIMES
Galena, Cherokee County, Kansas
Tuesday, September 8, 1925

HORSEBACK TOURIST HERE THIS WEEK

———

Frank M. Heath, who left Washington, D. C. April 1, 1925, on horseback with the objective to hit every state in the union with his horse Gypsy Queen and return to Washington on or before

July 1, 1927, is spending the week in Galena with the Isler shows who are showing here this week.

Mr. Heath is not connected with these shows, but as he was two weeks ahead of his schedule he decided to spend part of the time here. He has traveled 2,761 miles of his journey and visited 20 states, crossing three mountain ranges. He will have traveled 18,000 miles when he completes his trip. * * * *

He will give a special lecture on horses to boys tonight and Wednesday night at 7 o'clock at the tent at the carnival grounds. Mr. Heath came here from Miami, Oklahoma and will leave next Monday morning going from here to Springfield, Missouri. He is now 195 miles ahead of his schedule. * * * *

* * * *

From Notes. Sunday, September 13, '25: Spent day in Galena —at livery barn of Mr. Frank Ward, 76, old race horse man.

Old Frank Ward is another one of the people who stand out in my memory. I was discouraged, as the notes would indicate. I said something to Mr. Ward about being so discouraged, I had a notion to throw it up. It was hard for me to decide which humiliation would be the greater, giving up the undertaking or becoming a bum, for several weeks at least, while I straightened out the financial tangle. "Don't you ever give it up," said Mr. Ward. "If you do, that'll be the regret of your life. You can make it somehow. I believe people are people, wherever you meet them. I believe you're borrowing some trouble. It won't cost you much anyway, among those people. You can get through. Don't you give it up." This was one lesson I needed, and I got it from him. It was this: How often we turn back, through fear, from something that really would do us good. And how dearly we are punished for lack of self-reliance. A man who turns back at the first difficulty never goes far.

The thought of waiting two or three weeks longer in the heat and flies of Galena was unbearable. Furthermore, we had just time to reach Springfield, Missouri, on schedule. The reader understands that being behind schedule would have lost us a great deal of prestige. Furthermore, it was time for us to get going if we were to reach our destination before the winter set in. So you see there were the two alternatives: Either to quit while the quitting was good, if I must quit, or else go ahead *right now*. I could not get away from old Mr. Ward's brief sentence, "If you quit now, you'll be sorry as long as you live." "I'll not quit, so help me God!" I replied. To prove his sincerity Mr. Ward would not take a cent. He did not extend me "charity" but hospitality and good will. A sensible, placid, kindly old man. We had scarcely broken even during the 2 weeks' sojourn, but the hot spell was broken, the rains were just setting in, the fever was out of Queen's legs and look at the fun I had.

From Notes. Monday, September 14, '25: Raining hard this morning. Ready to start when it lets up. Wrote J. O. Williams, Dept. of Agriculture, appeal for funds (1.25 to 2.00 per day). Gave facts to date. [The response was not favorable.] Also wrote T. K. Sheffield, [Ill.] as to possibility of "barn storming" when I cross my trail. (See Map.)

[Response very uncertain.] [Queen weighed on leaving Galena 1.015 lbs.] 12:30 left Galena. No chg. for barn, feed. * * * * The business people of the town are "waiting for the mines" (lead and zinc) to be put into operation by some big co. 6 p.m. Ar'd farm of Mr. T. N. Estes, Diamond, Mo., R. 2.—10 mi. E. of Poplin.

Traveled: 18 mi. via Joplin. Gravel. (Fine crushed stone gravel that will mesh in, making a really good, flexible surface is practically equal to good dirt. This explanation should eliminate the apparent inconsistency where I have noted "gravel or side." When I write that note, what I really mean is that this kind of gravel is really equal to good side and would count the same in figuring "theoretical miles.") Rolling * * * * Mines 2 miles north, great mountains of tailings. This is called a part of the Ozarks, but there are no mountains in sight as yet, and no large foot hills. People here depend on mines and other employment for cash.

September 15, '25: Leaving Mr. Estes 8:15. No charge. (advice.) * * * *

From Signature Book: "Frank M. Heath arrived at my place 10 miles east of Joplin, Sept. 14 on Gypsy Queen. Stayed over night.

(Signed) T. N. Estes."

From Notes. September 15, '25 continued: "Queen eating good dinner at 220 acre farm of W. T. Ross, Reed, Mo., R. 3. No chg. (advice, formulas). 5 p.m. Ar'd farm of Mr. Jas. K. P. Jennings, 30 mi. E. of Joplin. Old couple—72—old lady

brought chair. Later, 7 p.m. Ar'd farm of Albert Jennings, Sarcoxie, R. 2.—31 mi. E. of Joplin.

Traveled: 21 mi. * * * * Ozark trail from Sarcoxie E.
* * * * Country slightly rolling, soil fair. A great many strawberries, some cow peas. Corn. Oats. A lot of waste land. Scrub
timber. 1 vineyard. Some pretty fair mixed farms. At Sarcoxie
are the large peony and iris farms. * * * * At this point begins the foot hills of the Ozarks. I passed one good commercial
orchard 3 mi. E. of Sarcoxie. Wheat 15 bu. normal. Corn 30.
Strawberries main revenue.

September 16, '25: "Leaving Mr. Jennings 8:45. No chg.
(advice). Mr., Mrs. Jennings and Georgie, a bright boy, 12.
Want book."

The Jennings are another family that stand out prominently in
my memory. They were typical of Missouri hospitality. First, the old
folks. The old lady brought out a chair. The other Jennings was a
son of the old folks. They treated us very hospitably—not charitably.
The boy referred to as "Georgie" wrote me a letter many years later,
inquiring as to whether a book had ever been published, and if so,
where he could get it. He is a young man now.

From Notes. September 16, '25 continued: 5 p.m. Ar'd farm
of Merton Garrison, Mt. Vernon, Mo., R. 6., 5 mi. N.E. of Mt.
Vernon.

Traveled: 20 mi.—5 mi. gravel.—5 mi. macadam. Via Mt. Vernon. Now well into the foot hills. Some grapes. Little oats. Hay,
corn, kaffir. Dairying. Scrub timber. Stony. Passed some log
houses W. and E. of Mt. Vernon. Many pretty good horses. People like them.

September 17, '25: Leaving the Garrisons 8:15 a.m. Only .25
cts. (advice). Noon, feeding excellent corn, growing in very
stony soil, at farm of Austin Davis, Billings, Mo., R. 3. Also
dinner, 23 mi. W. of Springfield. This is right in the heart of the
Ozarks. But no tall Mts. Principal crops corn, wheat (only fair)
—Truck—Dairying. 5 p.m. Ar'd farm of Mr. Homer Robertson,
Brookland, Mo., R. 1. 15 mi. S.W. of Springfield.

Traveled: 15 mi. Very hard macadam full of loose rock. Via
Chesapeake Springs, Republic. Hilly light soil (Post Oak) to
near Republic. Republic is better soil. Still stony. Prosperous
orchards and vineyards. Strawberries best paying crop. Lots of

tomatoes. Better farm bldgs. (Log houses, poor hilly land both west and east of Chesapeake Springs, also shacks. One in particular E. of C. S. where dwelt 2 old bachelors.) Mr. Robertson farms 80 acres. Mostly truck and vineyard. Some crops, Poultry, etc. Good bldgs. Soil good but still stony. Berries this year paid $300 per acre above crates—picking. Tomatoes $75. Rolling, picturesque. "Open view"—no Mts. (as we understand the term in the West) in sight as yet.

September 18, '25: Leaving the Robertsons 7:45 a.m. Noon, Ar'd McDaniel farm. * * * * 4 mi. S. of Springfield. Via battle field—back roads. Dirt, very stony. Plateaus. General [farming].

Traveled: 10 miles.

Special Note:

TOTAL TO DATE: 2916 miles [as corrected].

More than schedule, 210 miles.

4 p.m. Just returned from Springfield. Leaving McD. farm 5 p.m.

THE SILVER SPRING NATIONAL BANK

Silver Spring, Md.,
September 11, 1925.

Mr. Frank M. Heath,
    General Delivery,
        Springfield, Mo.

My dear Sir:

The balance in your checking account is $5.08.
The balance in your savings account is $10.40.
The balance in your Joseph C. Cissel
    special account is $180.44.

I enclose a blank check which may be used to check against either your savings or your checking account, but if you desire any part of the $180.44 balance sent to you, you should ask Mr. Cissel to remit it to you, as the account, insofar as we are concerned, is subject to his control.

Trusting this is the information you desire, I am

Very truly yours,
(Signed) Ira C. Whitacre,
Cashier.

While in Springfield to get mail—and probably I had forwarded the parcel post package—I got to talking with some tourists, and others, in a restaurant. These conversations developed that by the way of West Plains to Powhatan we would have: 1st. rather hard roads. 2nd. I would miss seeing many, if I saw any, real typical hill-billies. (While this was not a sight-seeing trip, primarily, I had heard and read so much, all my life, about hillbillies, that my curiosity was aroused on the subject.) I decided to kill two birds with one stone, probably without any cost in horse flesh, although it would add some sixty odd miles or more to the surplus miles we had already traveled. That is, by having dirt roads mostly, in place of paved roads largely (getting back to the old basis of theoretical miles) we would probably save something in what is known as durability, or remaining fit. A concern (it developed later) was exploiting—or trying to popularize—the "Shepherd of the Hills country." Tourists conducted sight-seeing parties—the Cave of the Story—etc. This was all based upon the still (at that time) very popular book, "Shepherd of the Hills," by Harold Bell Wright. Beginning—so far as our narrative goes—at Springfield, tourists were occasionally induced, through propaganda of one kind and another, to detour off the regular highway to "The Shepherd of the Hills country." Propaganda is a kind of disease like the itch. It's catching. You get it without exactly knowing who or what is responsible. I must have gotten a whiff of this while in Springfield, which may have been the deciding factor in altering our route.

Chapter XIII

AMONG THE HILL-BILLIES

WHEN we left the McDaniel farm, about four miles south of Springfield, we struck practically due south instead of southeast.

From Notes. September 18, '25 continued: 7 p.m. Ar'd farm of Mr. A. M. McSpadden. Battlefield R. 1—8½ mi. S. Springfield.

Traveled: 5 mi. (after McDaniel's.) Hilly. Very rocky. Broken poor side.

September 19, '25: Leaving McSpadden 9 a.m. * * * * 10 a.m., Queen seems to be seeing or hearing things in the brush. I see nothing. * * * * Springfield to Nixa, plateau. At Nixa, got fine view of Ozark Hills sloping south. A kind of a bird's eye view. A—not exactly beautiful—let us say a "pretty view" as far as the eye can see. Pretty, placid, peaceful, poetical it looks at a distance.

Note: Water scarce around here.

5 p.m. Ar'd farm of Mr. C. A. Gance, Highlandville (1½ miles S. of Highlandville).

Traveled: 20 mi. * * * * 18 mi. very rough. Loose rock 2 mi. Dirt. Hilly. * * * * Nixa S. mostly poor land, Post Oak. Small fields, corn, some truck, one *field* excellent corn. Mostly old bldgs. Some vacant. * * * * Passed sorghum (some here also). Some millet. Some sheep. Hogs. Dairy generally, and goats for sprouts and mohair. Principal cash crop strawberries—some orchards. Dry this year. Corn will yield about 30 bu.

From Notes. September 20, '25: Leaving the Gance family 8:45. No chg. Noon, feeding at farm of Perkins, Spokane, Mo. 10 mi. N.E. of Reed Springs, Mo. Came off R. 3 to water at Flatrock Spring—a good one. * * * * 5:20 Ar'd farm of Mr. Chas. Bush, Reed Springs, Mo.

Traveled: 17 mi.—½ side for spring. Via R. 3. Gravel, stony,

14 mi. Bal. dirt. Country hilly, scrub timber. Little corn. Sheep. Some other stock. Old orchards. * * * * Country full of caverns. Passed good spring at cannery. * * * * [Springfield] to Reed Springs, 42 mi.

Soon after leaving the Gances we came into a very broken country. Speaking of cannery, mentioned in the notes, reminds me this was tomato harvesting season. About all they produce, along our route, from a little way south of the Gance place, is tomatoes, south to Reed Springs, in patches ranging from one up to a few acres. It seemed to me that if there was anything else besides tomatoes, it was more tomatoes—excepting that about Flatrock Springs there was some small dairying. We passed teams loaded with tomatoes—usually it seemed to me they smelled plenty ripe.

Just a little beyond, under a bluff, was a little strip of alfalfa along the creek which was formed by the spring. Reed Springs is virtually the northern entrance to the locality they were trying to exploit as the "Shepherd of the Hills Country."

From Notes. September 21, '25: * * * * Leaving Reed Springs 10 a.m. * * * * Reed Springs, little old shacks (or rather, cheaply constructed small residences, some quite old)— about six or more modern cement buildings. No sidewalk grade except W. side. * * * * Spring center of flatiron-shaped plaza. No water system. No light system except private. Good school on top Mt. Up to 2nd high-school. Cow bells. (Tinkling everywhere in the cool of the evening. With their different tones, they seemed somehow to produce music in keeping with the surroundings). Good saddle horses, mules, goats (angora). Two girls one horse [meaning that two were riding one horse—not an unusual sight here.] Tablet at spring enumerates great resources —200 cars tomatoes this year. Quaint characters.

Along the road, nearly from Springfield to Reed Springs, I had seen advertised, "Marvel Cave." As we neared Reed Springs it elaborated somewhat, such as "Marvel Cave is the Cave of the story." (A little more of this later.) Not so far back, in other words more locally, I saw advertised, also on bill-boards, "Fairy Cave," and "Fairy Cave Inn." In talking with Mrs. Bush, a very intelligent, nice-appearing lady, wife of Farmer Bush of Reed Springs, she recommended that I could not very well afford to pass up "Fairy Cave."

Reluctantly I told her that I guessed I'd pass it up, that I had—er—er—a little misunderstanding with my bank, and so must push on as inexpensively as possible. She smiled. "Well," she said, "you take this road and follow these Fairy Cave signs. I am going to suggest to Mr. Waldo Powell, proprietor, that he cannot afford to pass you up. I will guarantee that you will be hospitably entertained for the rest of the day—you probably could get away from there tomorrow morning."

I was, and I did. I found the Powells to be very delightful people. Waldo Powell is a son of Trueman Powell, from whom Wright got his character, "Shepherd of the Hills." The picture that he showed me of his father is the exact picture that was used in the book. Mr. Powell showed me through the cave. He told me about the surrounding country, and, with the same courtesy he would have paid to the Prince of Wales, urged us to stay overnight.

Now, about this "Fairy Cave." It is not large. Every inch of it, I believe, is lined with a beautiful onyx. Mr. Powell, with great industry and considerable expense, has the cave electric-lighted beautifully. He did it himself. I forgot from exactly what source comes the light, but I believe it must be his private plant. But I do remember that it was so arranged that he could throw on bright lights or what you might term a twilight. It would be useless for me to undertake a more detailed description. There is on file at the University of Maryland, along with the immense amount of other data, hardly one-tenth of which is included in this manuscript, a detailed description of Fairy Cave. Mr. Powell has also, largely with his own hands, built a great deal of road leading to Fairy Cave.

From Notes. September 21, '25 continued: * * * * Traveled: 5 mi. Dirt, gravel. * * * * [In arriving at Fairy Cave from Reed Springs.]

September 22, '25: Leaving the Powells 9:30 a.m. after a refreshing night's rest in a real bed. Queen kicking up heels in lot yesterday. * * * * Noon, (Sept 22) Feeding Queen at stable of Homer Johnson, son-in-law of Levy Morell (Uncle Ike). (Uncle Ike, postmaster of the story.) At notch (The Forks) Uncle Ike's P. O. a little cabin about twelve by twelve. A very scanty stock of goods. Uncle Ike 88, Civil War Vet. No chg. Later dinner with Miss Lynch at Marvel Cave Inn. Afterward visited part of cave in company with others. No chg.

Marvel Cave really is quite wonderful and very large—some onyx in places, remains of old ladders used by the Spaniards, presumably, in mining or exploratory operations. It had gotten to be a custom with Miss Lynch to have someone pose as Tutankhamon, the favorite Egyptian mummy of that date (1925). I volunteered to stretch myself out upon the flat table of rock with my nose and toes pointed toward the beautiful blue the same as Tutankhamon. We did not go through the series of caves, which would have taken several hours. So we turned back, especially as Miss Lynch had an appointment soon with quite a crowd of tourists, which would occupy her the balance of the day.

From Notes. September 22, '25 continued: 4:30 p.m. at Evergreen Cemetery, visited graves of the Rosses (Old Mat and Aunt Molly) where a recently erected monument was not yet unveiled. 6:30 p.m. Ar'd at Old Mat's cabin, after taking wrong fork in road E. of cemetery, and cutting through three picturesque old farms. Vining family now on place. Address, J. W. Vining, Garber, Mo. Mrs. knew the Rosses well "when they cooked on the fireplace." * * * * Used to bring corn to old mill on horseback.
Traveled: 10 mi.—2 by error. Very rough.

In order to get back in the right direction, after having taken the wrong fork, we put Queen down slopes that must have been half pitch. I, of course, had dismounted. I remember one time, in particular, that the saddle and pack, although pretty well cinched on, came near slipping over her head. This, and several similar occasions, was doing Queen's knees no good. Arriving at Old Mat's cabin, I asked to be put up for the night. Lester, the boy of the house, and I went into the corn patch and brought in each an armful of the ripened corn stalks, with the little nubbins. He had, a day or two previously, cut his arm with an old saw. For some reason, which I am not capable of understanding, much less explaining, this arm had drawn or twisted way out of place. The bones and joints seemed all right. So it must, I reasoned, be that some muscles or nerves, or perhaps both, were in some way affected by the slight wound. Now it so happened that I was still using, occasionally, when it seemed necessary, some of this leg wash which I prepared from Absorbine. It is well known that there are certain kinds of medicine that, as the saying goes, "If they do no good, they'll do no harm." This I had come to believe was the case with this Absorbine solution. With this in view, I doctored up Lester's arm with a liberal dose of Absorbine solution, which I had with me, wrapping the arm with medical cotton, which we also carried in our pack. Then sopping this full of the solution, I bandaged it well, but not too tightly. Believe it or not, as Ripley says, in the morning the arm was straight. The muscles or nerves, or whatever it was, had relaxed and the arm had resumed its natural position.

From Notes. September 23, '25: Leaving old Mat's cabin, 10:45 a.m.

From Signature Book: "Garver, Mo., Sept.. 23, '25. Frank M. Heath, with Gypsy Queen, stayed here at the old Ross place (Old Mat's Cabin) last night.
(Signed) Mrs. J. W. Vining."

From Notes. September 23, '25 continued: Noon. It had been drizzling rain. Still threatens. So stayed with Vinings to dinner. Looking southward, over on Compton Ridge we see several cabins in small clearings (saw similar Monday from Powells.) * * * * 12:30 p.m., at last leaving the Vinings. * * * * 5:45 Ar'd farm C. E. McClairy, Branson.

Traveled: 9 mi.—7 mi. *extremely rough, stony.* * * * * Few small patches corn. Toms. School—loose shutter.

September 24, '25: Rainy. Leaving the McClairys 10 a.m. No chg. (Advice.) Old barn off foundation. Crops corn, tomatoes, cotton, some grain, cow peas, soy beans. * * * *

As I passed through Branson I made inquiries as to roads on ahead, easterly. No one could tell me much about any road for any great distance ahead in that direction. I was starting in now to find my way to a certain point south of east, largely, we might say, by orientation. Still I was a little dubious about starting across a broken, partly wooded country, for perhaps a hundred miles or more. There was no road showing on my map and I could find out nothing definite for more than ten miles ahead. I learned that there was a well defined road to Harrison, Arkansas, some twenty-five miles south of Branson. But I could learn nothing of any definite road from Harrison east to Powhatan, nearly a hundred miles as the crow flies, which would probably mean one hundred and fifty, at least, through a country that was largely hills. This in itself would indicate a difficult country, when we come to think of it. If the rivers had to twist all through hell (although we understand there are no rivers in that place) what kind of a route would a stranger have to travel on a horse? I had just started out from Branson and had not yet fully made up my mind what to do—undertake to go straight ahead, where I had learned there was no regular road running through for nearly a hundred miles as the crow would fly (if he didn't get lost) to the highway between West Plains and Powhatan, or whether to go on south to Harrison and take a chance of learning of some way through. I met a couple of sensible, reasonable, middle-aged men, natives of the country, just as I was on the point of choosing the latter alternative. I expressed my doubts. "No," one of them said, in a very friendly manner, "I wouldn't go that way if I were you. It might be more difficult than straight east," and he mentioned something about the crooked rivers I had just been talking about. "You can get through east. People live all through that country. They must get in and they must get out at least part way. They must get from one place to another. Your route, of course, might be far from straight, but with your instinct, as you call it, for orientation, and by frequent inquiry, you can get through from this little burg to that little habitation of some kind, from there to the next neighbor in your general direction, and the next, and the next, and the next little town. Finally you'll get through to this northeast, southwest highway." (We were now studying the map.) I thanked him for his kindness and sagacity and started on.

From Notes. September 24, '25 continued: Noon. 1 p.m. Feeding Queen (it is raining) at farm of W. W. Fisher, Mildred, Mo. 1 mile west of Blackwell ferry. No chg. Send card. * * * * E. of Branson met several who knew little of Ozark Co.—or Gainsville. 3:45 p.m. crossing Blackwell ferry. Owen Eubank, ferry man. He seems to be a character—wants book. (He mentioned it first—also helped me out—about the ferry.) Address, Mildred, Mo. Old battered straw hat, broken nose.

Eubank was very affable—he seemed to be somewhat of a dreamer. It struck me that on the "outside" he might have been—let us say— a man of affairs. Or was he, after all, happier and more useful in his present position? When I had asked him about the possibility of fording or swimming the stream (there being a ford a few feet below) he replied, in quaint language, with a shake of his head, "Well, I don't know, mister, the water is mid side to your hoss and purty durned swift. I'd hate to tackle it." He sensed, I believe, perhaps from our appearance or possibly from some expression, that with us quarters were about the size of cart wheels.

From Notes. September 24, '25 continued: 5:30 arrived Cedar Creek, Mo. * * * * Queen in stable of Walter Gable. * * * * Staying the night with Mr. C. C. Collins and family. * * * * Collins family old folks. Three strapping young men of the "Ozark type" and grand-daughter.

Traveled: 17 mi. (In rain mostly.)—7 mi. R. I. (rough, inflexible.) dirt 10 mi. (from Mildred rough and stony.) * * * * Mostly woods—few patches tomatoes, corn, cotton, some alfalfa on White River bottom. Passed 3 or 4 school houses. Cedar Creek a typical Ozark small village. Since north of Reed springs, hogs feeding on acorns—cattle on range. Cowbells. Dairying. Tomatoes.

Getting back a little, I see on an "over" in my notebook the following:

1. Couple on muleback
2. A "burrying"
3. Leaky barns
4. Good Mt. horses
5. 3 saw mills—not far from Cedar Creek

Lumber shingle mill, etc. Shack P. O. Shack store propped up. Plenty log cabins. (These last, of course, apply to Cedar Creek Village.)

Interpreting the above: I met this couple on muleback not far east of Branson. These were tough, wiry little mules indigenous to the community, if that expresses it. They were ridden in what I have described as a cowboy trot—only with these mules the gait was extremely smooth. The people were very plainly dressed. Both the man and woman rode very gracefully. The saddle trees were evidently cut out from selected crooked trees (the whole country is noted for such trees). The road we were traveling was plainly defined. They told me the way to Cedar Creek. They jogged on. A mile or two beyond where they had passed us the mules were tied to saplings beside the road. Off to the left about a quarter of a mile was some kind of a congregation of people. This was a "burrying." A little way beyond this was a track winding around between hills which passed near some pretty plain buildings in a fair-sized clearing. The clearing was planted mostly to cotton. A canvas-covered wagon that reminded me of the one in which our family migrated into Dakota Territory in 1879, stood out in the cotton field. Cotton picking had begun. The wagon cover protected the picked cotton from the rain. It was raining hard when we arrived. A bright, good-looking young fellow came to the door. In much better language than is generally attributed to the hill-billy, he invited me to put Queen in the stable and come in out of the rain. The barn leaked. With him in the house was his sister, a bright, good-looking, well-behaved girl. The other members of the family were attending the "burrying." While waiting for the rain to cease, I learned that all through this Ozark region, when people get sick they are seldom taken to a hospital—in fact, hospitals are hardly available. Besides in this Ozark region it was seldom that the cash income of a family exceeded four hundred dollars a year. If the person needed attention at night, the neighbors "took turns sittin'-up" with the sick. If the person died, seldom was an undertaker called. Some of the older neighbors laid the person out. Others sat up with the corpse. If sufficient money was available among members of the family and the neighbors they would buy some kind of a coffin—if not, a coffin was made by some of the neighbors, and the deceased was honorably, even if cheaply, buried.

While the rain is still pouring we may as well continue with the customs of so-called hill-billies. Here it is to be presumed, of course, that most homes were necessarily of a very cheap construction, whether log cabins or otherwise. If a neighbor's house burned down, anyone within several miles who did not contribute something in work, if nothing else, toward the construction of a dwelling that was just a little better than the one burned down was considered not quite worthy of the neighborhood. Also if the meager furniture were not replaced by as good or better than that lost in the fire (and it usually was replaced) then someone or more people had not been true to the custom of the community.

From Notes. September 25, '25: Leaving Collins family 7:30 a.m. No chg.

I had rendered no service. There was not a horse on the place. There were, however, several fine Jersey cows. The three husky, manly-looking sons were employed in some nearby saw mill, at least part of the time. It was one of these sons who had invited us out to their place from the village. The father, a sturdy, intelligent old gentleman of about sixty, was hospitality itself. The meals were ample. The roof leaked.

    From Notes. September 25, '25 continued: 12:45 p.m. Ar'd farm of W. C. Yandell and O. L. Stallup, 5 mi. W. of Protem, Mo. In the hard rain—soaked through. Fed Queen, dried out, some, by fireplace. Had a lunch (by asking). Asked to stay the night—very reluctantly refused by Stallup (father-in-law). Says the other fellow "quare turned." Later came out saddle up. Mr. Stallup observes that the creek is dangerously high and swift. It also is again pouring rain. Says, "If it don't go down we'll have to keep you somehow." 3:45, rain let up. Creek still swift. Stallup still procrastinating. My feet and back still as wet as sop.
    Traveled: 8 mi. Via Groom (?)—1 by error. Very rough. Poor road. People poor. Windowless houses, etc. (Log house occupied. Never had windows in. Several tow heads in each opening.) Passed lots of rock ledges (limestone formation) and junipers.

Regarding these junipers—a very scrubby, stunted, knotty, crooked juniper cedar tree. This stunted, knotted description does not usually apply so extremely to juniper cedar. I had been wondering all this forenoon how the few people scattered along the trail that we were traveling subsisted. We were passing over, for the most part, a kind of plateau. If there were any crops and gardens I did not see them. I learned later that the sole income of most of these people was derived from gathering peculiar cuts of the twisted, knotty juniper cedars for use in the manufacture of rustic furniture.
    I spent the night in the Yandell's stable which was large and well kept up. Along about ten o'clock, before I knew it, not having heard a sound, biff!—a flash-light in my face. It was carried by the high school boy, about sixteen, who was attending a high school some place—I don't know where. "I brought you out a quilt," he said, and he handed me a little light quilt about one quarter size. I believe he must have raided the baby's crib.
    Shortly after daylight I was dressing. I was also wondering whether

I could spare the price of a breakfast in addition to the meal the day before, for something told me that this would only make an additional large hole in my very small means. This haymow was largely open on the east in full view of five men camping. I believe they came in some time during the night, probably after I went to bed. I didn't remember having seen them before. The aroma of the coffee, the flap jacks and bacon—oh! boy—did my mouth water! Not a word had been exchanged between us. Finally a man who appeared to be the leader says, "Hi buddy!" I said, "Hi!" "Come to breakfast!" Just like that. I said, "Thank you, I will." "Now you just help yourself. There's plenty of it. I'll bet traveling in the rain makes a man hungry."

From Notes. September 26, '25: Leaving Mr. Yandell 8:45 in rain. Chg. $1. Creek down. Took breakfast with campers. Mr. C. E. Arnold, Forsyth, Mo., chief guide on float, Forsyth Cutter, on White River pleasure trip at Elbow Junction, and four others. Later forded creek. Queen a little dizzy.

On the opposite side were several campers with teams. They had waited all night for the creek, or small river, to go down. It was still a little high and swift for them to tackle it with the wagons. "Now, buddy," shouted a man from across the creek, one of these campers, "you start from where you are and you come this way, a little upstream—to such a point." I believe it was marked by an old snag or something. "Better give your horse her time. She won't have to swim but the bottom is probably full of rolling small boulders." And that proved to be so. "You come to this point and watch me. I will signal where to go from there." He did so. Queen often struck these rolling boulders but carefully felt for her footing. Had the water been much deeper she would have had to swim. Our pack was a little above water. Had she had to swim, the current undoubtedly would have taken her down. We turned, as directed, at this point and were soon safe on the opposite bank. These men with the teams did not look or seem to me like the hill-billy as we conceive of them from reading about them. They all seemed like sane, reasonable men.

From Notes. September 26, '25 continued: Fording Shoel Creek S. of Protem. * * * * Noon, Feeding Queen at farm of Clifford Brown, Protem, Mo., 2 mi. E. A field of good corn, typical (of locality.) 1:45 Ar'd Big Creek—swollen. Neighbors

met on road advised me not tackle it. * * * * 2 p.m. * * * *
Unsaddled Queen. Waiting for creek to drop. Came across foot-
bridge—Harry La Mere, Bert Jordan and Jesse Jordan all of
Protem. Am having a fine talk with these men while waiting.
They don't think I am a fool for detouring to see the Ozarks.
As Mr. La Mere expresses it, there is religion in these hills.
"They take care of sick neighbors and bury the dead." Passed
today many quaint log houses, barns, etc. Patches corn, sorghum,
some cotton, gardens, hay of various kinds, including alfalfa.
Open range. Some rock ledges. Some junipers this A.M.—4 p.m.
Invited by Mr. La Mere to spend week end, attend Sunday
School. Gladly accepted.

Harry La Mere and his companions came across the old suspension foot bridge, the floor of which was pretty old and one should
watch his step. It oscillated considerably when walked upon. They
began looking us over. While Queen was nibbling some luxuriant
grass, I had the whole pack, including my note books, spread out on
some flat rocks, trying to dry it out.

"Well, you seem to be traveling," remarked Mr. La Mere. "I
was," I said, "and I am still trying to. A man whom I met a little
ways back who is familiar with the creek and who was riding a big,
strong horse, told me that even with his horse and his knowledge of
the creek, the current took him down a hundred feet." "You were
wise in not tackling it," he said. I had not forgotten that I had many
times been looked upon with more or less suspicion and that as I
would have to stay somewhere around here it might be a good idea
to try to make myself understood.

As stated, my note books and other credentials were drying upon
a flat rock. I noticed Mr. La Mere glance at them. I said, "I have to
get me another note book. I have got this one so full already that I
am continuing through on loose sheets out of a tablet. I have to be
very careful they don't blow away," and I picked up a few of them
along with the note book and casually invited his attention to some
of my notes. He and the other boys became interested. I said, "I
carry a few credentials along just in case." I didn't remind him, but
he had sense enough to know that a man couldn't, even if he was up
to tricks, forge several whole newspapers, and, as his interest grew, I
showed him more and more until he was thoroughly convinced that
I was genuine. "Say," he said, "you are pretty well soaked. You are
tired and your horse is tired. I would like to have you and your

horse stay over Sunday with us and get dried out, and you go to Sunday school with us tomorrow right in that old school house up there." The school house was back a little ways from the creek, located on a large bench of land. "It is too dangerous to try to cross here, but this young man here can take your horse up opposite my place, about a mile, and get across all right." Gladly I accepted the invitation.

From Notes. September 26, '25 continued: 5 p.m. at farm home of Mr. La Mere, 6 mi. N.E. of Protem. "Drying out."

Traveled: 11 mi. Mt. road, rather rough, via Protem. * * * *

Sunday, September 27, '25: Got up early. Cleaned up—a "dull" shave.—at 10 a.m. attended Sunday School at Pleasant Valley School House near Big Creek Ferry and bridge now building. At the request of Mr. La Mere, I made a little talk.

Note: Many toll mills (that is corn mills) everywhere. Some water mills. Mr. La Mere raises some good tobacco. Less than ⅛ acre would bring retail about $50. Has over 400 'twists' besides some smoking. Peanuts also thrive, as do sweet potatoes and yams.

About ten o'clock Mr. La Mere with his family and myself started for Sunday school. Passing along the edge of a table land east of the creek we climbed a crooked rail fence, of which there are many in these parts, and skirted the edge of a large field. I believe the field was cotton, part of which had been picked. Crossing the old swinging foot bridge, soon we were at the school house. A north wind had struck the frame structure a few months previous and twisted it out of plumb, and it had never been righted. The door had to be left ajar because it would not close, but this seemed appropriate. Seldom now did we see a residence that was perfectly plumb or a door that did not drag on the floor or a gate that did not drag the ground. Dame Nature had with one breath given the old school house an artistic twist so the kids might feel at home therein. (But to do these people credit, not long after that they built a stone school house in its place, writes Harry La Mere.)

Tied to the fence were quite a number of pretty good saddle horses and mules with good saddles on, plus a very few vehicles. Standing about in groups were the people. Many of the men, young and old, were dressed in overalls and shirts. Some wore store clothes, usually of a cheap material. Most of the young men wore broad brimmed hats of good quality and high heeled boots to match. They were a "horsy" bunch—which made me feel at home.

Many young couples came and went riding double on a horse or a mule. They have reversed the old colonial style. The girl takes the saddle and the young man sticks on behind. As a means of support he frequently has his arms tight around—well, not the mule! Comely were the girls with a healthy corn-fed complexion. The older people neither seemed or looked by any means dull or unintelligent. We were as yet in the quaint borderland between the primitive and our super-civilization. Many were the high, intellectual foreheads, the expressive eyes. Uninformed people I had met in plenty but not many ignorant—so far. It seemed the whole community round about had turned out. The rain had ceased and the sun shone brightly.

It seemed that all had heard of "the Man that was Riding Through." I was introduced to two or three, but many of the men just started in talking with me without the benefit of an introduction. Uncle Jim said, "I reckon it takes a lot of experience to do what you are doing." We went into the school house. Most of the pine-board seats and benches had been worked upon by jack knives and other instruments of torture. The blackboard looked as though it had been much used and seldom erased. Most of the letters, figures, or examples could be traced upon it even through the fresher markings. There was to me a lesson in physical economy. Why, after all, use the elbow grease necessary to erase thoroughly the old work when leaving it dimly would stimulate the powers of discernment between the old and the new?

We all took seats—that is, most of us. One blue-eyed, curly-haired little fellow stretched out comfortably under the teacher's desk. All too soon he would have to sit up. The old people smiled at him indulgently. The singing began—and oh! what singing! Some good voices there were, as nearly as I could judge—anyhow they were hearty and natural. There was no instrument, and whoever had been entrusted with the tuning fork had forgotten to bring it. But after first this one and then that one had tried an experimental "key" someone would nod approval and the singing would begin in earnest.

I took part, or tried to. I knew that I would "chord" with someone. I didn't want to seem exclusive. Uncle Jim was asked to lead in prayer. The straightforward earnestness of that prayer will accompany me to my dying day. There was none of that "telling God all about it." It was an appeal which would have touched any human heart, when it came to asking God to bless "the stranger that was riding through, and beseeching that he might continue to do good, and that if he was not right he might get right." It seemed the slight assistance I had been able to render was really appreciated.

Thus it happened that when, without warning (except that he had asked me a few questions) Mr. La Mere introduced me to the congregation and told them that in place of the after-Sunday-school sermon, "the Man that is Riding Through will give us a talk." I felt perfectly at ease. I believe if ever I did make a pretty good public talk it was then. I had not made the great mistake that I did a time or two afterwards of preparing notes. I had plenty to talk about and no doubt or insincerity had entered my thoughts. I was conscious of the knowledge I had gained at different times about people and places, but I felt no superiority. Fortune had been kind to me in a way, that was all. I began with my usual outline as to the objective of my trip, and a brief recital of accomplishments to date. Then I cut loose, something like this:

"Many people cannot understand why, when it comes to travel, I prefer this method. Recently we have been reading much of an aeroplane trip across our continent. In describing his sensations the aviator tells us 'the forest looked like green blotches.' Well, to me a forest is much more than that. He sees our rivers as 'silver ribbons.' To me they are living things. They are water. To him, the lakes are 'mirrors.' To me, they are full of life. He sees people moving on the earth far below. To him 'they look like ants.' Well, now, he probably means all right, but as for me, I never want to see my fellow man even in comparison for one instant as 'ants' or anything other than men like myself. I'm afraid the thought might provoke an unhealthy attitude of mind, a false attitude of mind toward my fellow man.

"Aerial navigation is a great thing, much improved. It will save much time—while we resort to all kinds of fool devices in order to pass the time we don't know what to do with. One flies from coast to coast. He knows he has passed over a continent. I ride through the country and have touched elbows and rubbed intellects with my fellow man. I am reminded constantly that I am 'of the earth, earthy.' Luck to aviation. But let no one forget that the machine in which he flies derived its being from out of the earth and that to earth it must return for replenishment and repairs.

"I love a horse because, next to man—or to what man is capable of being—he is God's most noble creature. It is foolish to presume that a horse is a creature of the past. His days of drudgery are about over, thank Heaven. Man, tardily, has harnessed steam and electricity to do the heavy work and gasoline for the speed fiend. But he has not made and cannot make a car that sees, hears and thinks. Do you believe I could make a chum, a buddy, of steel?

"I mean no flattery when I tell you how greatly I appreciate your hearty reception. I was soaked to the skin and you made me feel at home while I dried out by one of your beautiful fireplaces. We were hungry and you fed us. I am ragged and you do not laugh at me or shun me. Why, I have been in places in this good old U. S. A. where, should I presume to address an audience in these rags, I'd have to pass out a lot of little weights with hooks on them for the ladies to hang on their noses. (Giggles from the girls.)

"I enjoy this opportunity of meeting you because here, so far as I know (and we have traveled considerably at different times) is the last phase of quaint simple hospitality and brotherly love without greed. So far as I know these hills are the only section of the U. S. where the miller keeps the toll and gives you back the grist. So far as I know it is the only place where a leisurely respect is shown for the dead. A neighbor dies in spite of your care and a team of mules can take him to the cemetery quickly enough to suit you. It is not necessary with you that the whole family be swamped by the undertaker's bill. To me it seems meet that when a man dies he should rest as he has lived—in this case in rugged simplicity.

"I see among some of you young people a restlessness to 'get away.' Well, that is right. To see more of the world would not hurt you—maybe. But don't nag dad into selling the place to the first stranger that offers him a thousand, two thousand, or three or four thousand dollars. You could not do *anything* with only that much on the outside. Life everywhere is a struggle. Most of the great farms you read about are covered with mortgages. In the great cities life is strenuous mostly, especially among the rich. A woman may be loaded with diamonds and dare not smile or laugh naturally for fear of being thought common.

"Don't let them come in here to exploit these peaceful hills and valleys while you pay the freight. Your roads, for the most part, are as good as the resources of your community can stand or can be made to produce. If tourists' associations want fancy roads, let them be built from automobile taxes, as they are doing on the outside. This country has a great future, but time alone will develop it."

Then I explained how the soil is constantly replenished from the limestone subsoil base, and how, in Europe, I had seen good crops of wheat on such land after perhaps a thousand years of cultivation, while fifty years or less often depletes beyond repair soil with clay subsoil.

I kept my eye on Uncle Jim. When he began to fidget, I, for once, had sense enough to ring off, amid an applause which I believe was genuine.

Getting back to yesterday, Harry La Mere showed me, from the old foot bridge, where they had put in the abutments for a good substantial bridge for vehicles across Big Creek. It seems that a delegation headed by Mr. La Mere had visited the county authorities at Gainesville, the county seat of Ozark County, the county in which we then were. There they had been granted a very good iron bridge which happened to fit in with the requirements here as to width, height, breadth, etc. Much of the work was being contributed by the residents.

Much of the afternoon, after returning from Sunday School, Harry La Mere spent with me, showing me about and telling me more about the local conditions. He had a small piece of land, nearly level with a steeper slope connecting this with an irregular-shaped piece of nearly level bottom land. The wooded bench was mostly scrub oak. All through this region there was scrub oak which produced a lot of hog feed in the shape of acorns. Near one end of this almost wedge-shaped piece below were the buildings, a good garden and some fruit and a small, young orchard. The balance was planted to tobacco, some corn, some grain. No cotton, as I remember. This small portion of this lower bench was irrigated by a spring. They kept a few cows, a team of horses, chickens, etc., of course. Everything about his frame barn, unpainted, was in perfect order. Without a flinch or a bat of the eye, he gave Queen of his precious horse feed liberally.

In speaking about the tobacco, these twists mentioned were the leaves, well cured, treated somehow with molasses and twisted up like an old-fashioned New England fried cake. Of these they sold about so many and kept about so many for him and his wife to chew. I may as well say here that for quite a long distance, extending way beyond what I will describe as the eastern border of the hill-billy locality, probably a large majority of the women I happened to observe could drown a fly at two yards with a stream of tobacco juice.

They made no attempt or pretense at clearing or cultivating the upper bench and side hill. They had learned long since that that would not pay. If they were to do so, more than the profit obtained from the better land would be expended upon the poorer land.

The meals at La Mere's were ample as to quantity. The main course was Johnny-cake or corn bread cut into large sections, probably six by eight inches and three inches thick. There was coffee, of course, with sugar and cream, some "hog meat," and also some home-canned fruit and butter for the corn bread. For Sunday dinner there was also one large squirrel which Harry La Mere had shot on the previous day. They had company that day.

All during the day I had been turning and returning on the porch all of our thoroughly soaked equipment and did some washing.

In the evening, Mr. La Mere and I sat out under the light of the stars, near the out-of-door fire over which, by the way, most of the cooking was done in good weather, until a late hour. Incidentally, he remarked to me that my little talk did the young people a lot more good than any sermon that had ever been preached by some outside preacher with his theology. "Why, you get down to earth, where we are. You didn't preach any sermon or say anything about God that I remember of, but it is inferred from your talk that you believe in and are guided by the same kind of a God that we believe in. Neither you or I, or any of us here, presume to analyze God. Theologians do. Why should we presume to pull God down to a point where he can be analyzed or explained by man? As we see it, if He were such He would not be God. God is God." I was beginning to watch my step and my speech for fear of exposing my ignorance to this so-called hill-billy.

From Notes. September 28, '25: Leaving La Mere's 8 a.m. Nice people. * * * *

From Signature Book: "Protem, Mo., Frank M. Heath with Gypsy Queen stayed at my place from Saturday evening September 26, 1925, to 8 a.m. September 28, 1925.
(Signed) Harry La Mere."

From Notes. September 28, '25 continued: Crossed Little North Fork 12 noon. Passed rough country. Little corn, cane, cotton. Many "throwed out" fields. 6 p.m. Ar'd farm Chas. Owens, Gainsville, Mo., 4 mi. S. W. of.

Traveled: 28 mi. * * * * Rd. rough, rocky most of the way. Afternoon; Farm where fed (noon) and some afterward, *old* orchard. Passed mostly through wooded land—mostly 'culled out' timber. Many abandoned 'farms.' Approaching Gainsville range improves. Mr. Owens has creek place. Raises about everything including cotton. *Principal revenue: cotton, cream, poultry, hogs* (hogs raise themselves on range—good money.) Cattle, horses live on range 9-10 months. Healthy. Good water. Land sells for $2 for bald land (bald hill) to ridge $10. Bottom $50. Good for 35 bu. corn. Alfalfa 1,000 lbs. Cotton. Wages $1 day (and board) up. Owens family Mr. and Mrs., five children.

September 29, '25: Leaving Owens family 8:20 a.m. No charge. 10, reached Gainsville, county seat Ozark County, 250 inhabitants. No drug store. Could not get saltpeter. Saddle horses. Mt. village. (Gainsville, I understand, is 36 miles from a railroad.)

From Signature Book: "Sept. 29, '25. Frank M. Heath arrived with his faithful steed in our little village Tuesday morning, Sept. 29th/25. He reported enjoying his travel through our region.

(Signed) E. W. Ebrite,
Mayor of Gainesville,
Ozark Co., Mo."

*   *   *   *

THE OZARK COUNTY TIMES

Gainsville, Mo., Friday, October 2, 1925
Tourist, Touring the United States on Horse Back,
Arrives in Gainesville

———

Frank M. Heath, of Silver Springs, Md., riding Gypsy Queen, his Kentucky Morgan saddle horse, arrived at this place about 10 o'clock Monday morning from the direction of Taney County, where he visited some of the noted scenic spots of the Ozarks. * * * *

Mr. Heath on leaving Springfield, instead of following his schedule south to West Plains, decided to travel through the heart of the much talked-of Ozarks, going by way of Reed Springs, thence easterly to Gainsville. He was very glad that he made the trip into the Ozarks, the most scenic and interesting country he has ever been in, where the people lived most simply and enjoyed the real pleasures of life, where he found real hospitality, where he always felt secure and among friends. He advised that the people of the Ozarks be slow in giving up their homes to settlers coming in, because no other region offers anything in comparison to the advantages to be found in these beautiful hills and valleys.

*   *   *   *

From Notes. September 29, '25 continued: * * * * 5:20 p.m. Ar'd farm of B. M. Copeland, Elijah, Mo., 15 mi. E. Gainesville.

Traveled: 20 Mi. * * * * Dirt or gravel most of the way. 3:45 crossed north fork of White River. Modern bridge. Passed much "open" land, some cut timber—mostly oak. One or two fair sets farm bldgs. Some abandoned fields. Several old dilapidated orchards, mostly peach. One fairly good apple orchard E. of Uptonville. Many patches cotton. 1 patch tobacco. Some tomatoes. Lot of old log buildings—ruins.

September 30, '25: Leaving Mr. Copeland 8 a.m. (Send 75 cents.) Met Mr. W. R. Penrod of Missouri and Arkansas, hog raiser. * * * *

From Notes. September 30, '25 continued: Noon: Feeding Queen on bank of Bents River at Bakersfield. Corn 10 cents. Self had ice cream cone. Most people here never seem to have heard of Powhatan. One young man says 70 or 80 mis. Druggist did not seem to realize that there was an east line to Missouri.

I was pretty well traveling by orientation, paralleling a few miles north of the Missouri-Arkansas line, zigzagging about from one place to another on any kind of road or trail, and trying to keep some kind of account of how far I was from the east line which should give me some notion of when I would contact this West Plains-Powhatan highway. He says, with his mouth agape, "East line?" "Yes," I said, "east line of Missouri." "You don't mean east line, you mean the *south line.*"

In this town I bought two cents' worth of salt and three cents' worth of vinegar in a bottle with which to make "our own brand" of leg wash. The only ingredient I lacked to make this complete was the saltpeter which I could not get at Gainesville. However, just the salt and vinegar properly used make a very good liniment.

Chapter XIV

THE ARKANSAS OZARKS

From Notes. September 30, '25 continued: 5:30 Ar'd farm of Mr. Virgin Simmons, Moody, Mo.

Traveled: 22 mi. Rough, stony, via Bakersfield by back roads. Same conditions as yesterday. Then fields larger, buildings better, more local crops. Same except more hay.

October 1, '25: Rained hard all night—showery. Leaving Simmons 8:20. No chg. Formulas. * * * *

I HAVE no record of the following, but I remember distinctly, and subsequent notes bear it out, that upon leaving the Simmons, a young man there—I don't believe his name was Simmons, he seemed to be just stopping there or something—asked me into the house and began quizzing me. He kept asking me the same questions over and over, which finally got on my nerves. I believe I got mad and said something like this: "Say, what the hell is the idea of asking me the same question over and over?" He looked kind of funny and said, "Well, I am taking notes for a newspaper." "Well," I says, "if you are taking notes for a newspaper I suggest you write them down." I didn't like his appearance nor his attitude. Somehow he reminded me of a centipede who was about to jump on you. That stopped the interview. Then he suggested that he had a cousin living on my route who would be glad to have me drop in and would be glad to keep me over night, a good fellow, or something like that. I took his address, which will develop later, and started out. The following continuation of the notes will somewhat clarify the day's ride:

From Notes. October 1, '25 continued: Noon, feeding, dinner with Mr. Fred Pope, Viola, Arkansas. Mr. Pope tells story, historical, of Senators Ashley and Sevier in 1840. One was addressed as 'The gentleman from *Arkansas*,' the other as 'the gentleman from *Arkansaw*.' Name was settled by act of legislature in favor of 'Arkansaw.' Mr. Pope runs a 140 acre farm, 30 A. cotton, principal revenue. Pays about $40 to $50 net outside own work. About 2/5 bale. Corn 30 bu. That is average. Out of range hog district. Still in Ozark hills but little more modern buildings, etc. Good school. People here talk United States. 7 p.m. arriving farm of Mr. Lee Bryant. Barn, Arkansas, 3 mi. S. E. of. Two boys, a horse and a mule watching me.

Traveled: 23 mi. via Barn, Arkansas. Patches cotton, some larger. Much in fields in piles, bales out of door. Corn. Old orchards. Learned orchard short-lived here. So some patches "deadened." Dead timber. Abandoned places. Hay, cotton, corn, some cattle, open range. Man headed me off for a horse trade. [These boys had been overtaking us passing us at a faster gait halting to talk with some one along the road until we over-took them and then later passing again and so on. Were they watching us I wondered or were they just two kids on a lark?]

From Signature Book: "Oct 1, 1925. Frank M. Heath ate dinner here today making his tour on Gypsy Queen.
(Signed) F. B. Pope, Viola, Ark."

When I came to this place named Barn, it seemed well named. There was a little store there which resembled a barn made out of rough lumber. It was nearly sundown. Quite a number of farmers were in and around the store. I asked the way to the place of this man Bryant. The way they directed me would have been pretty nearly a horse-shoe and would have caused many miles extra travel. To travel that way would have been two or three times as far as across lots. I said, "Well, it is getting late. My horse is tired and I wanted to make that place." (I had a little note written to them.) "Can't I get through?" One of the men spoke up and said, "I would hate to tackle it in the dark, even though I have lived here most of my life. There is a little trail, and if you get off that you are *lost*." I said, "I will mark it out the best I can on a paper and I will tackle it and save my horse. She is tired now." "Well," he says, "that is your business." I was fool enough to start out to do this. Almost before I knew it, it was dusk in the wooded hills. I was about to lose the little bridle trail, and, by the way, this ground was rough, stony and hilly, probably the reason the road went around, and was un-inhabited. I remember passing one ruin, evidently of something like an old plantation house with two big chimneys. Just as I found myself in this predicament, these two same boys overtook me, and I asked for the Bryant place and if I was headed toward it. Yes, I was headed right and they were going right by there, within twenty rods, and would show me. I sure was glad to avail myself of their offer. They seemed to be nice enough kids, and civil, and I was riding for the most part where it was open enough so that I was abreast of them. Where it was not feasible to ride abreast, two or three times, I fell behind. No sooner would I drop behind them before one or both of these boys would whirl in his saddle, ostensibly to keep on talking, but I began to wonder if they just wanted to keep their eyes on me. We finally came to a fence corner and they said, "Just follow this corner so far and you will see a light and right there will be a little old house and a little new house. That is Mr. Bryant's." I got there at nine o'clock. I believe they were just getting ready to retire. I told Mr. Bryant my predicament, showed him my letter of introduction. I noticed a twinkle in his eyes. I said, "I don't want to try to fool anybody. I have less than a dollar. I expect some money at Powhatan. I have credentials here if you want to look me over and see whether I seem to be O. K. or not." "Oh," he said, "I guess you are O. K." I said, "If you will be so kind as to keep me over night I will certainly send you whatever you say from Powhatan." I was as welcome as could be. The best place we could find for Queen was under the shed on a very steep slope, imbedded full of rocks and small boulders. She could not possibly lie down. We fed Queen and went into the house, and I partook of the best meal I had seen or heard of for many a week. When the meal was over, Mr. Bryant brought out the fiddle. The son and his wife picked the guitar. A boy of ten also played the guitar. Of all the rich tones and perfect chords I ever heard, as near as I can judge, not being a musician, this was the best from amateur players.

About 10:30 the old lady hauled out from some place a feather bed which she spread on the floor in one corner. A table occupied one corner. Each of the other two corners were occupied by a bed. By the way, all through this Ozarks region it is considered the height of inhospitality to allow a stranger to sleep in any outbuilding or otherwise than in the best or one of the best beds available. That is their mark of hospitality. Nevertheless, I had presumed that this feather bed they were pulling out was for the traveler. They wouldn't listen to this for a minute. I occupied the bed that belonged to the old couple and they slept on the feather bed on the floor and the kid with them. The young married couple slept in the corner opposite me.

Meanwhile, I had told Mr. Bryant about this young cousin of his quizzing me. He laughed heartily. They all laughed. "That guy thinks he's damn smart," he remarked. "This gives me a good laugh on him the next time I see him. I will tell him you came damn near catching him!" When I got ready to go, I said, "Mr. Bryant, I appreciate your hospitality and keeping me and the fine meal and fine bed and all that, and I'll send you payment for it from Powhatan." "Oh," he said, "send me fifty cents, and you better not forget to send it, because I might meet you in St. Louis or some place sometime."

From Notes. October 2, '25: Leaving Mr. Bryant 7:30 (send 50 cts.) This is the 1st time people have slept on the floor and given me their bed. Mr. Bryant plays the fiddle—son and wife pick the guitar. Boy, 10, Max, plays guitar. Building bungalow. Several newcomers in past five years. Schools plenty. On hand Oct. 2nd, 94 cts. * * * * 12:15, Ar'd farm Mr. C. H. Bookout, Wiseman. Feeding Queen—no chg. (bumming). (Advice.) * * * * 4 p.m. Ar'd farm of Mr. William A. Vaughan (80, Confederate vet.), Day, Izard County, Ark.

Traveled: 17 mi. Very hilly, stony, little sand. (2 mi. by error.) * * * * Mostly dim and twisted back roads. Mostly scrub timber. Largely post oak, as usual. At Day is a pretty fair valley, 1½ mi. wide. Main crop cotton. Some range hogs and just recently begun vaccinating for cholera. Passed several cheap new residences, new settlers. Land selling for $10 to $30 per acre. Crossed Straw Creek at Wiseman. Later I picked cotton, 1 hour. Got five lbs. but it picks extra hard on account of rain. Earned at regular price seven and one-half cents. Miss Vaughan picked fifteen pounds while I got five. Moral: It takes practice. Queen very comfortable in corral (lot) with privilege of box stall. Hay, corn and sheaf oats. Today, yesterday, passed small patches alfalfa.

Oct. 3, '25: Leaving Mr. Vaughan 8 a.m. No charge. Formulas. * * * * 10: Passing through Ash Flat, S.W. of Hardy, Ark. Nice little town. 1 p.m. Feeding, eating store lunch by a "branch." First signs of blue grass. About two mi. W. of Center, Ark. 3:15 p.m. fording Big Creek (Ark.) 6 p.m. Ar'd farm of

Mr. Frank Thomas, Poughkeepsie, Ark., ½ mi. north of main
road, 4 mi. east of Center.

Traveled: 20 mi., mostly hilly, very stony, some sand. * * * *
Scrub timber (little fairly good). Kind of valley, Vaughan's
east to Ash Flat. Cotton, little corn, some range hogs, few cows,
cattle, horses, mules. Many new small houses. * * * *

October 4, '25: Leaving the Thomases 7:45. No chg. (Advice
on lame mule—off axis.) Mr. Thomas the long, lanky mountaineer we read of with his soft drawl. But on conversing with
him he proves to be a man of good sense and an inquiring mind,
with good, though a little vague, idea of the country in general.
He says that when people come in from elsewhere and try to
show the Arkansan how to farm they always go broke and go
back.

I had been directed to Mr. Thomas' as a place where I would be
welcome over night. That is what took me half a mile off the main
road. I found him back of a hill picking cotton. This was an irregu-
lar small field down under a large hill, a very fertile bottom land.
The crop was excellent. I was welcomed without any hesitation. Mr.
Thomas, Mrs. Thomas, a little girl about nine, were each picking
cotton very industriously. I tried to help. Even the little girl could
outpick me about two to one. It takes practice to pick cotton. I asked
Mr. Thomas, "How come all these 'throwed out fields,' as you
people call them? I have passed several today and all along back."
"Wa-al," he drawled, "you see, shortly after the war cotton was
'boomin', quite a lot of fellers came down here from the north and
bought a piece o' land, and they would go to work regardless of the
way it laid, and clear up the whole durn business and square it right
up. They come from the country where the fields were squared up
and they were just goin' to raise hell, and that is just about what
most of 'em done. They plowed her up good and deep, planted their
cotton, and before the season was over cotton, soil and all was down
at the bottom of the hill some place. I got a lot of that feller's good
soil," he said, waving up above where we were towards one of those
'throwed out fields.' "Well," I remarked, "they don't understand
this business that you read something about these days, called 'contour' plowing." "We don't know nothin' about 'contour' plowin',
but since I can remember, and since my daddy can remember, we've
been plowin' with the lay of the land."

From Notes. October 4, '25 continued: "He says deep plowing spoils the ridge land but is all right in the bottom. Bought 60 A. this year. His little cotton crop will, if price stays up, pay for "hit"—making him 110 acres. * * * *

9:30, Just had to remove bandage to ford a creek. Little back is an excellent spring. By the way, yesterday I saw John Smith, Smithville, Ark., 3 mi. W. of. *Note:* Mr. Smith has 40 A. of land said to contain zinc ore—wants to sell it for $25 per acre net. 3 p.m. Queen lost left half left front [shoe]. Toggled up with burlap. 4:15 Ar'd place of Mr. J. M. Land—just got in barn before hard shower. His son-in-law is the blacksmith (shoer)."

I believe the last shoeing had been on September 4th, at Miami, Oklahoma. We shod her in front with toe calks, and shod her behind at Galena a few days later. Once more I admit that this was a mistake. I just about this time thoroughly woke up to the mistake of using calks, particularly on a road saddle horse. It turned out to be particularly wrong in this case, for the reason that most of the road we traveled after that date was, as the notes bear out, rough and stony. This was on account of my changing routes at Springfield. These calks made it pretty hard on Queen's knees for the reason that there was not soft ground into which the calks would sink as I had anticipated they would. Presuming we had kept to the main Springfield-Powhatan road, it would be reasonable to believe we would have had a lot of good "side." But on the road we traveled, I found that in going down these steep inclines that I have mentioned, the calks prevented her sliding more or less, which would have been better for her, for in sliding, the horse has a chance to brace the knee. Where the shoes are spiked by calks, the foot has to be raised, and in putting it down the weight of the body is thrown onto the partly flexed knee, whereas if the foot were allowed to slide ahead, the foot would advance ahead of the knee, thus causing the knee to straighten instead of buckling, especially when you consider that the weight and momentum of the horse is against it. This buckling, in turn, throws muscles, tendons, and ligaments out of normal position. I realized this almost too late. If kicking myself would have done good—but of course it wouldn't. I had thoroughly learned my lesson, however, at the expense of Queen's left knee, which was getting worse.

It will be understood by any horseman that in order to make either this slipping or sliding practical or even possible the horse must toe square ahead. In other words, he must be built true. I have never seen the theory in print or heard it expressed otherwise, nor do I believe I would ever have discovered the following point (if indeed it is a discovery), which is this: I spoke some way back of what I would call a case of one-sided laminitis. I claim that Queen had within that general comprehension a case of one-sided laminitis in her left front foot. The laminae had been crowded within the left side of the hoof. This caused irritation and inflammation which caused a partial congestion of the circulation. So far it seems to me this should be plain, but the subsequent result had to be beaten into me at the expense of Queen. Everybody knows that if the circulation of the blood is impaired, particularly to the point that it does not nourish the extremities of any certain limb or portion of the body, human or animal, that portion, so far as replacement is concerned, is at best badly impaired. In other words the inside of Queen's left front foot grew much faster than the outside, which means that we could start out today with the foot a little high on the outside, as it should be to brace against the strain. Two weeks from today the foot would be a little higher on the inside, aggravating the strain and again throwing the pressure of the weight of the horse when she stepped on that foot against the outside of the sensitive laminae. And this was just what had happened—this combination which I have just described.

Queen had been stubbing along until the toe of the shoe was worn clear in two. I had been watching it for some time. Inadvertently she stepped on a rock, and off went that side of the shoe taking the nails with it, and a little portion of the hoof outside of the nails. I mentioned toggling it up with burlap. That is, I took a piece of burlap and doubled and redoubled it until I had a thickness of about three-fourths of an inch. This I lashed on the bottom of the outside of that foot and traveled some two or three miles, being careful to have Queen step with that foot where the ground was high on the outside. That is how we got into the village of Smithville.

It isn't necessary to state that I had to have a shoe put on this one foot off which the half had been lost. Generally I made it a practice, if I had to have one foot reshod, either front or back, to have the other shod to match it. So I took Queen to this shop and asked the young man to shoe her in front. A few natives were gathered outside, with some horses. I stepped outside and conversed with them a few minutes. When I stepped back in the shop the young fellow had the shoes removed all right, and was working on

the left foot with a pretty good sharp pocket knife. As I remember
it he was fairly quick. He had this toe pared down a little too much
to suit me. I began, I thought very civilly, to try to tell him how I
wanted these feet shod, and why. Now it developed during my stay
at Lands that this young man was very smart. Some time early in
his blacksmith experience, he had mended a gun stock so neatly
that the break could hardly be detected. On the strength of
that he had become the village paragon. What he couldn't do wasn't
worth doing, and what he didn't know wasn't worth knowing.
"Couldn't nobody tell him nothin'!" So I wasn't so terribly surprised
when he looked up at me as I tried to express what I wanted, with
rather an insolent expression, it seemed to me, and said something
to the effect that he guessed he knew how to shoe a horse, and did I
want him to complete this job or not? Of course I couldn't continue
with the foot in the shape it was in. I knew enough of human nature
to believe it would be worse than useless to try to reason with him.
I looked at the foot. It was fairly level so far as balance was concerned, though off axis. I said, "Well, go ahead. Put on those two
shoes."

At once she began to travel with discomfort, and the knee began
buckling somewhat on every down hill, as it had been doing a
month or two before.

Henry Campbell at Powhatan was also all worked up about the
way Queen was shod. By the way, it was Henry Campbell who gave
me, I believe, the finishing touch in regard to the proper way to
shoe a road saddle horse. It isn't necessary to rehash here our theory
in regard to calks (that they should not be used except in extreme
cases of travel where slippery, as on ice). But the last fine point I
got from Henry Campbell was this: Instead of making the shoe an
absolutely level plate, which, when placed on a flat surface, would
fit all around, he swelled—as he called it—the heels of the shoe,
making it a little thicker on the back, with the back end rather
squared off, so that (to make it perfectly understandable), if the
shoe were placed on a level surface there would be, say, a quarter
of an inch of daylight between the surface and the shoe, half way
between heel and toe. The reason for this was that when a horse
struck any surface that was the least bit flexible, such as fine crushed
stone or crushed gravel, the corners would sink somewhat into such
a surface, thus relieving the jar a little, without at the same time
spiking the foot. I wish to make another point plain. If the road
were a little sidling, it would allow this slightly thickened heel to

sink into the flexible ground—that is the high side—taking a lot of strain off the ligaments.

From Notes. October 4, '25 continued: Mr. Land is keeping me the night. Will send him the price from Powhatan. Mr. McCloud gave us plenty of hay. It had been raining hard. * * * The Lands are raising four grandchildren.

Traveled: 10 mi. Hilly, stony, mostly. Some sand. Copper Creek. 1 mi. W. of Smithville, getting into foothills. More cattle, grass, hay, cotton, corn, wheat, oats. Good poultry, cattle, sheep, hogs. Open range. Good school. Better dressed.

For several days now I had been augmenting my eats (sometimes crackers or cookies bought at a store) with persimmons, which were very plentiful. Somehow or another I didn't get very tired of them. Whether they are very nourishing or not is another question, but they help to satisfy a man's hunger. For many days now our cash on hand had been less than $1.00. The shoeing at Smithville brought us down to the last nickel.

From Notes. October 5, '25. Clear after the rain. Leaving Lands 10:15 a.m. (after having Queen shod in front). Send 75 cts. * * * * (Queen shod front 70 cts.) * * * * 12:30. Feeding Queen at farm Mr. H. P. Campbell, Denton, Ark., 6 mi. E. of Smithville (bummed it). (I had 4 cents which I kept for luck.) Mr. Campbell owns (or controls) 2200 acres, 1000 in cultivation. (He lets it out to share croppers mostly.) Land sells here for about $20. Wants to sell 700 acres. * * * *

Traveled: 12 miles. Hilly (foot hills). Dirt, some stony. Mud most of way. Fairly good old places. This (Powhatan) is an old, old place. Big brick court house on hill. Old saw mill. Took 2 hours to find place for horse—an old ramshackle barn and carry feed one quarter mile. Must sleep at a place they call a hotel. 30 cents. 30 cents for breakfast. 30 cent lunch. This place on Black River. Seemed all right. Good natured folks. Much mail waiting, etc.

Special Note: Fairy Cave Inn (Reed Sprs. Mo.) to Powhatan, Ark. 211 mi. Total to Powhatan 3174 mi. [as corrected.]

This made the distance from Springfield some 68 miles more than scheduled. It will seem we were two days late. Also observe we had traveled two hard days' journey, extra miles. We had seen a great deal that we would not have seen had we not made this detour which, so far as the accomplishments of the horse are concerned, does not count except that in so doing we heaped hardships upon her.

While I was feeding Queen at Campbell's place, he showed me a pretty good saddle horse that he had sold to the owner of a plantation at Beasley, Arkansas. This horse was to be safely delivered. He said, "I don't want to pull any of my boys off the cotton picking. I believe I would rather trust this horse with you anyway." I said, "Well, my horse needs a rest." He agreed with me. "All right," he said, "suppose you leave your horse with me and deliver this horse. It will probably take about three days, two days down and a day back. I will pay your expenses and give you five dollars. That isn't much, but it will give your horse a rest." So the next morning he rode his saddle horse up to Powhatan and took Queen back.

The manager of the plantation at Beasley to whom I had delivered the saddle horse had learned somehow—maybe I had mentioned the fact—that I spoke a little Spanish. He thought this would help in managing the crew of Mexican cotton pickers. He also said something about "he could keep me through the winter at about that price," i.e., fifty per, shack to live in, shed for Queen—I furnish the eats. It will be noticed that this is not so far from a place where, in my original schedule, I was undecided as to where I would spend that winter or just what I would be doing, so this proposition appealed to me for a minute. But there flashed into my mind a conversation I had had many years before in Portland, Oregon, with a veterinary surgeon who had put in a winter somewhere in this same locality. I remembered his telling me that it seemed impossible for him to keep his favorite northern horse from chilling to death on account of the cold fog that would go right through a horse or a man, particularly if they were not inured to it. On inquiry, I found this to be the fact. Right there I decided to beat it north somewhere in the locality of Indianapolis, from about which point I was to start out in the spring of 1926.

From Notes. October 8, '25 continued: This plantation works mostly "niggers." Are 40 pickers shy. Have lost to date ten per cent of cotton. 8:30, Left Beasley with a neighbor back to Marked Tree. 10:20 took train for Black Rock. 1:30 (?) arrived Black Rock (Black Rock is a little old shack town which is the county seat. It is just a few miles from Powhatan. Powhatan had once been the county seat, which accounts for the old court house.) 2:30, Left B. R. in mail wagon, drawn by two little mules, for Denton, near which lived Mr. Campbell. Hilly. Poor old houses. Mail man tells me mostly renters—don't stay. Many places mtgd. The people don't work.

The mail wagon, drawn by this good little team of mules, was a light wagon of the style commonly known as the Democrat wagon. I might say a half-ton wagon with a cover over it. This was only used, however, in case of mud or snow. It sure was muddy now. At other times, an automobile was used. This old fellow seemed to have what appeared to me a very old-fashioned method of driving mules. He kept pulling and slackening on the lines like an old woman, and clucked like an old hen.

At one mail box there stood a man about twenty-two, tight-lipped, awaiting us. "Looks like he expected some mail," I ventured. "Naw," replied the old man, "he ain't expectin' no mail. He give me five cents to mail two letters fer 'im an' he's waitin' to git the cent change back." It was nearly a quarter of a mile back to the house.

From Notes. October 8, '25 continued: 5 p.m. Ar'd Denton— 8 mi. (At Denton a little country store.) Bought rubbers for $1 less than asked at Black Rock. 6 p.m. Went to home, from store with Mr. Campbell. He is batching. He is a prince of a fellow. Has two boys of whom he is very proud, one at West Point, one away at "High." Found Queen O.K.

October 9, '25: Had breakfast with Mr. Campbell. 8:35 left to return to Powhatan. 10:30 Ar'd Powhatan. Queen fine except still not traveling right on left front though some better for the rest. Must have shoes removed, calks cut off. [Also had heels farther lowered with the left side of the left front foot considerably higher and the shoe extending out as much as possible in reason. Swelled heels.] Had to go down river 1 mi. pack hay and corn back. Putting Queen again in old barn of Mr. Hall. Noon: Had, before leaving for Beasley, arranged 'by request' to give a little talk at the court house tonight on my trip, etc. Find they cancelled it on account of weather. 2 p.m. Arrangements under way for me to speak at court house tomorrow, Saturday night. Mr. Campbell's zinc mine near Black Rock. Good outlook. (It seemed there was some trace of zinc through this country.)

During my short sojourn there I picked up considerable general knowledge of the community. It was at the blacksmith shop, while I was getting Queen shod, that I overheard a little conversation that might indicate some of the minor local resources. By the way, Powhatan is right in the Black River bottom and the soil is very productive. I heard one of these men telling another about having backed an open truck under some wild nut tree out in the woods—I believe it was a pecan tree—and having shaken off sixteen dollars worth of nuts. The neighbor asked him where this tree was located. "Well, I ain't tellin'," he replied with a sly smile.

Just what got me into the notion I can't say, but all at once I took it into my head I must have a bath. I had been soaked to the skin several times within the last week, and had changed my clothing a time or two. I couldn't have been very dirty. Perhaps it was just a matter of habit. Where I slept these two or three nights, in this old hotel, I could have taken a shower bath at several points in the room during hard rains—I believe I moved my bed a time or two—anyhow I must have a bath. In this old hotel no bath tub was available, but they rigged me out anyhow. They heated two or three large kettles of water in the fire place, which was provided with hooks, and put a wash tub and towels out for me. The old man turned his back. The old lady and the little girl that was staying with her disappeared up the stairway without so much as bidding me good night. Well, I had a bath anyhow.

The old lady had obligingly allowed me to put Queen in a small lot the previous night, as it was not raining. This had grown up to a rank vegetation suitable for forage. She had intended to save it, she said, for some calves she was buying, but she decided to make that forage a present to Queen, with whom she had fallen in love. She confided to me that she had cleaned up a thousand dollars in buying calves, raising them, and selling them. She had with her own money bought this hotel some years back. And that reminds me, the old lady just loved to cook and set a good table. She served very excellent meals.

The $14.58 which I received from the bank when I reached Powhatan, plus the $5.00 I received from Mr. Campbell, plus the four cents I had upon arriving at Powhatan, was fairly well exhausted after having liquidated my former obligations, paid for the shoeing, bought a raincoat and rubbers and a few other articles of clothing, besides feed and my meals—it will be inferred that my cash balance was pretty small. I said to Mrs. Hall, "Mrs. Hall, I had a little check here. I have paid it mostly out for one thing and another. I have money in the bank where I live. I expect to receive a Post Office order at Carruthersville. I have got just so much with which to pay my expenses from here to Carruthersville." I showed her also two or three Post Office receipts for these small amounts that I had remitted recently. "Can you," I asked her, "trust me for $1.50 of this bill I owe you? I will send it from Carruthersville." "Why certainly," she said. "That is all right." Just as I was leaving the old lady said significantly to me, as she gave Queen a final pat or two on the neck, "Mr. Heath, you know every one thinks you are a Federal Agent." I said, "That is funny. I am sorry. I hope you don't think I am." "No," she said, "I don't. Good-bye."

Chapter XV

NORTH TO WINTER QUARTERS

From Notes. October 11, '25: Leaving Powhatan 10 a.m.
* * * * (We crossed Black River on the old ferry which was
fairly busy. A good bridge across the river was in the building.)
5 p.m. Ar'd farm of N. M. Stone, Light, Ark., via Walnut Ridge.
   Traveled: 23 mi. Gravel 20. Dirt 2. Mud 1. Flat country.
Cotton. Little corn. Some rice. Scrub timber. Cotton damaged
by rain. *Note:* Mr. Stone has two horses for sale $75. I put him
in touch with Henry Campbell near Powhatan. Henry deals in
horses if he can buy them cheap enough and good enough.
   October 12, '25: Leaving Mr. Stone 8 a.m. No chg.
(Formulas). * * * * *

As I approached the Stone homestead the previous evening, a little
before sundown, I met Mr. Stone, his wife, a boy about twelve, and
a little girl, coming from the opposite direction. They were wading
through the water nearly to the top of their rubber boots—all except
the little girl, whom Mr. Stone was carrying piggy back.
   We spent a very pleasant evening with the Stones. They seemed
to be well educated and spoke good United States. I had been
following for about a mile a right-of-way which had been cleared
through the more or less dense woods which might be termed either
swamp or marsh. In reality, it was both. Some grading had been
done and a few bridges begun but none completed, across the low
places which I suppose carried somewhat of a current in floods. In
leaving Mr. Stone's place, he cautioned me very particularly not to
leave the slight wagon trail, which had been made probably in the
dryer seasons, and which could be discerned, not plainly, through
the muddy water, on account of the double track, which would be
free of bushes. That if I got out of that track, even three feet, and
got into one of "them holes" as he expressed it, where large stumps
had been blasted out, we would be lost. "If you ever get into one
of them holes it will be 'good-bye horse and rider.' You will go

right down and never come up." This evidently was that kind of
quicksand which I described many chapters back as the quality which
seemed in a sense to be more nearly related to quick silver, rather
than what I referred to as a kind of "quick mud."

From Notes. October 12, '25 continued: * * * * 5:15 Ar'd
farm of Mr. F. P. Garner, Paragould, Ark., Route 5.

Traveled: 22 mi. via Walcott. 3 mi. swamp flooded. 9 mi.
mud. 10 mi. gravel. Flat to Walcott. 12 mi. Bal. hilly. 1st 10 mi.
woods—a few 'patches' poor cotton. Shacks. But soil good if
developed and drained. Road building (under construction.)
Balance of distance bigger fields, better buildings. (Larger, more
regularly-shaped fields.)

October 13, '25: Foggy. Leaving Mr. Garner 8 a.m. $1.00
* * * * Passing through Paragould.

Paragould was where I had figured on crossing the St. Francis
River over into Cardwell, Mo. In approaching this place I had been
informed that they were about to rebuild this bridge and trestle,
and take a section out in doing so. I hurried to get across before
this bridge was cut. The trestle leading to the bridge was a mile or
so in length, as I remember it. The St. Francis River bottom is well
known as being low and frequently flooded. I met a gang of men
working at the approach of the bridge who informed me earnestly
that to start across that old trap would mean the loss of my horse
almost without a doubt. It was so old and saggy and out of level
in places that my horse would slide off if she didn't go through. I at
once changed my route.

From Notes. October 13, '25 continued: Bridge over St.
Francis River. Learn same unsafe. Going northeast to crossing
at Kennet, Mo. * * * * 5:30 p.m. Ar'd farm of Mr. W. G.
Wimberly, Rector, Ark., R. 4. * * * *

Traveled: 23 mi. via Paragould, Bard, Milltown. Gravel 4 mi.
Mud 10. Sand 9. Flat. Cotton. One or two young orchards near
Paragould. Many shacks but buildings generally better. Good
horses and mules. People well dressed. Observed large drainage
projects.

From Signature Book: "Rector, Ark., R. No. 4, October 13,
1925. Frank M. Heath and Gypsy Queen stayed over night
with me.
                              (Signed) W. G. Wimberly."

From Notes. October 14, '25: Raining. Leaving Mr. Wimberly
8:30 a.m. No charge. (Formulas). Wants Book.

Mr. Wimberly was a school teacher. He believed in "whupping."
He told me of an instance which might seem funny to some, but
it didn't seem funny to me. A young man, a pupil of his in the
grades, had broken some rule or something. He had told the young
man that the only thing that would do him was a "whupping."
They stood toe to toe, eye to eye, for a minute or two, sizing each
other up. The young man says, "I don't know about you giving me
a 'whupping.' Maybe I am as good a man as you are." "Well, maybe
you are," replied Mr. Wimberly, "but I am the teacher. You have
broken a rule. I am going to give you a 'whupping' and you had
better take it. It is necessary for education"—or something like that.
The young man agreed and took his "whupping" and they shook
hands and the school lessons proceeded.

From Notes. October 14, '25 continued: Noon: Feeding at
farm of Mr. J. C. Aiken, 4 mi. N.E. of Leonard near St. Francis
River Bridge. Very large hewn log house. Largest cotton bolls
yet seen [seems a little strange this cotton was not yet matured,
ready to pick. Let us hope it did mature before a flood got it.]
All A.M. have been traveling through St. Francis valley. From
Leonard on larger swamps, cypress and walnut. Passed over
several drainage canals. Road last mile very muddy. (In this
heavily wooded section some pretty large scale land clearing was
going on. If memory doesn't trick me, a logging road penetrated
this section, a very difficult road in the mud. So it would seem
that much of the best of this timber was utilized for lumber,
but great piles of logs were rolled together and were being
burned.) 4 p.m. Ar'd camp of Otto Stout [grading contractor],
4 mi. E. Connett, Mo., among the canals and mud.
    Traveled: 18 miles by way of Leonard, Connett, Mo., St.
Francis River Bridge. 2 mi. sand. 1 mi. pave. 2 mi. dirt side. Bal.
mud and swamp. Flat. Muddy. Good soil. Large veg.
    October 15, '25: Rained in night. Slept (?) on baled hay.
Queen in mud under leaky shed. Plenty hay, oats, corn [con-
tributed] by Mr. Stout. Light supper by C. W. Tidwell who
keeps small store near R. works. Bought lunch goods for breakfast. On hand 27 cents. Leaving [Connett] 7:15 * * * *
4 p.m. Ar'd barn of Mr. Jack Tait, Carruthersville, Mo.

Traveled: 21 mi. * * * 7 mi. swamp and mud (new road). 14 mi. gravel side. * * * * Several plantations. Cotton.

Special Note. Powhatan to Carruthersville, 107 miles. (More than scheduled Powhatan to Memphis, 2 miles.) (Total to Carruthersville, 3,266 miles.) * * * *

By making this change from the original tentative schedule, we had reclaimed, so to speak, about 175 miles of the hundreds of surplus miles we had traveled. Queen's feet and legs had greatly improved between Powhatan and Carruthersville, partly on account of the corrected shoeing, largely on account of the rain (and traveling in the rain actually was good for her as long as I kept her back dry, both because the mud was good for her feet and because the rain was good for the inflammation in her leg).

From Notes. October 16, '25: Raining. 4 p.m. Laid all day account rain and more waiting $50, for which I wrote Joe Cissel on Oct. 11 (would be picked up 12th.) Doping Queen's leg— also back which has developed a little soreness during rainy spell. Have been riding most of time acct. mud and sore toe. Pack is heavy with dampness.

October 17, '25: Clearing. P.M. still waiting on funds from Silver Spring. Queen's back still a little sore—not raw. Mr. Tait loaned me $1.50 Friday night to eat on. I am now "supremely busted." Sleeping on cotton bolls a little damp. Hope to hear from Joe 5:15 today. Have been drying clothes, etc. Patching old pair of britches to wear inside. (Good meals 35 cents.) Got $50 from Joe 6 p.m. just in time to cash P. O. O. before closing.

Jack Tait was an old-timer and a right good fellow. He must get the roof fixed. There was nothing like a good "kivver" in that climate. He had an old, old man working for him about the barn. Each of the three nights I was there, he laboriously lugged each of the two sliding (?) doors to a closed position and rolled a large stone against each. Each morning he lugged them open and placed a stone against them to keep them from tipping away from the barn. They were off the track, or the track had sagged, or something—I don't know just what. After each operation—"Got to get these durn doors fixed. Been goin' to fix 'em for a long time. Just ain't got to it yet."

Carruthersville was quite a mule center. Mules were coming from the north by wholesale and going out retail. This whole locality was quite a place for "swapping" horses and mules.

From Notes. Sunday, October 18, '25: Clearing up. Leaving Mr. Tait 8:45 a.m. Only $1.50 for barn, feed. Very reasonable. 9:15 crossing Powell's ferry. Charge $1.25. [This was the second time I crossed the Mississippi.] * * * * Noon: Feeding at farm of Mr. R. S. Campbell, Ridgely, Tenn. (7 mi. S.W. of)— Still in Mississippi R. bottom. Houses on stilts. Barns on [artificial] mounts. Bottom floods 4 feet (?) nearly every spring. Nearly every farmer has a boat. Soil seems good. Sandy river sediment. 75 per cent land still in woods. Raise cotton, corn. No charge—(formulas).

From Signature Book: "Ridgely, Tenn., October 18, '25. Frank M. Heath fed Gypsy Queen at my place 7 miles S. W. of Ridgely, Tenn., at noon.
(Signed) R. S. Campbell, P. O. Box 282."

From Notes. October 18, continued: 5 p.m. Ar'd farm Mr. T. G. Raines, Winnburg, Tenn. (1 and ½ mi. E. of.) * * * *
Traveled: 20 mi. Gravel 1. Sand 10. Mud 9. * * * * Ridgely a nice clean modern town on a slight ridge. From little W. of Ridgely to Mr. Raines, above usual overflow. Mostly open ground. Fair buildings. Some shacks. Cotton. Corn. Some alfalfa. Heavy soil E. of Ridgely.
October 19, '25: Leaving Mr. Raines 7:45 a.m. No chg. Wants book. Mrs. Raines is one of the Edwards, New York heirs. [Mr. Raines was operating quite a large cotton farm, and had good heavy mules. He said deep plowing was necessary here. Land open, nearly level, good soil. Had some families picking cotton. It was cold when I left in the morning]. 9:45 came to Reel Foot Lake (full of stumps). 10:45, Came to hills. Turning N. between hills and lake. A village. * * * * 4:30 Ar'd farm of Mr. J. H. Grooms, Troy, Route 3, Tenn. (9 mi. W. of Union City, Tenn.).
Traveled: 21 mi. Level to 2:30 at Clayton. Cotton. Corn. Some hay. Hogs. Sheep. Few goats. Ground washes. Mr. Grooms owns 120 acres, some sheep. After entering hills 2:30 p.m., passed a few old orchards. Hills composed of clay. Produces very large heavy corn. Also good cotton and Japanese clover. Red top. * * * *

October 20, '25: Fair. Frost last night. Leaving Grooms 8:15 a.m. Only 50 cts. Old folks. 3 boys and a girl. Two others were in W. W. [World War]. [On or about this Grooms place I observed the erosion was what I would call terrible. Some hills were pretty steep].

From Signature Book: "Union City, Tenn., October 20, '25. Frank M. Heath stayed at my farm here last night with Gypsy Queen.

(Signed) J. H. Grooms."

From Notes. October 20, '25 continued. 10, coming out of hills onto level valley. Mostly open large fields—mostly corn—good. Winter wheat. 11:30, passing through N. of Union City. 12:30, Feeding Queen at farm of Ben Ridley (colored), 2 mi. north of Union City.

I just happened to have learned, inquiring for a place to feed, that this apparently prosperous colored farmer was pretty well liked by everybody. His barn was extremely neat and comfortable and the whole place seemed well kept up. I didn't ask whether he was an owner or a tenant, but he was evidently much interested in his place. Another intelligent-looking colored man was scouting about the buildings with a set of plans, which I believe indicated that he was figuring on some improvements. They treated us fine. Just as I was leaving, a pert, pretty young colored woman met us where the foot path from the house crossed the road, and accosted us pleasantly. I believe I had given Ben one of our schedules. She said, "How many states has you been in now?" "Twenty-two," I told her, and she said, "How many has you got to hit yet?" I made a rapid calculation and said "Twenty-six." She whirled around to the architect who was standing a little back of her. "Dere," she says, "I tole you you couldn't fool dat man!"

From Notes. October 20, '25 continued: 4:45 p.m. Ar'd farm of Mr. W. A. Browder, Fulton, Ky., Route 1. (4 mi. W. of).
Traveled: 20 mi. Dirt. Slightly rolling. P.M., crops, cotton, corn, wheat, tobacco, hogs. Soil good. Building mostly good. Colored help. Bermuda grass. First signs of blue grass.
October 21, '25: Cloudy. Leaving Mr. Browder. No chg.

From *Signature Book:* "Fulton, Ky., Frank M. Heath spent the night with me. Also his horse, Gypsy Queen. Oct. 30.

                        (Signed) W. A. Browder."

From *Notes.* October 21, '25 continued: 9 a.m. in Fulton— remailed P. P. P. [Parcel Post package]. Wrote folks. Hilly. [Young Browder, high school boy, bright fellow, accompanied me as far as Fulton. He had been much interested in Queen]. 4:45, Ar'd farm of Mr. William Wray, "Uncle Bill," Wingo, Route 2. (2½ mi. north of Pilot Oak). 4th trial.

    Traveled: 21 mi. via Fulton, Dukedom, Pilot Oak. Dirt 17 mi. Gravel 4 to Dukedom. Slightly rolling. Dukedom north, low lying hills. Soil fair but much land lying waste. Buildings poor to good. Tobacco, corn, winter wheat. Some stock. Sheep. Some dairying. Sweet potatoes. Tomatoes. Family orchards. [At one of these places where I was passed on to somebody else, who turned me down, the man was just harvesting sweet potatoes. He was drying or curing them in a dugout by means of a wood fire in a stove. That was a new one to me]. Mr. Wray is 71, widower, born on this place but has been in Mo. several years. Batching. Works around the place every day. Fine garden, etc. All kinds garden, orchard, truck about house. Boys in Detroit. Keeps horse for company. Only hay, baled weeds. * * * * [We managed to get a few very small nubbins as grain].

As I pulled into Uncle Bill's place, he was just coming down the road from the other direction with a cushion under his arm. He had just returned from the city with a neighbor. He didn't hesitate a minute when I asked him about staying. Very bright and alert and courteous. It soon developed that he could neither read nor write, greatly to my surprise, for he spoke good English. The fact of the matter is he had been around considerably and confided in me that he had made many political speeches. He felt sensitive about his lack of education and colored up momentarily when he mentioned it. He explained that his daddy was in the Civil War and he had to work all he could and kept on working after the war, trying to hold onto the old place. He served a substantial bachelor's meal. A little after dark a few neighbors dropped in, middle-aged men. I was kind of chilly and was standing with my back to the big open fireplace absorbing the warmth. Mr. Wray and the two other men sat back some ten feet away from me, you might say partly in the shadow.

We were talking horse to beat the band. One of these men was a horse trader. In the twinkling of an eye the old man almost sprang, or at least stepped very spryly toward me, leveled his finger at me and demanded: "Are you a Federal Agent?"

"In that haversack there are newspapers, including those from my home town, statements from people who know me at home, letters received along the road, from my bank and from business men in Silver Spring, where I live, and all that. Of course anybody knows that if a person were mean enough to do so, he could forge a letter. But it wouldn't seem reasonable to suppose that a man could forge quite a number of newspapers, would it? You are invited to examine these credentials." "I'm sorry, but I can't read." "Well," I replied, "let these gentlemen examine them." Neither of them could read either, it seemed. "Well," I said, "I am sorry. There are proofs. If you are not in a position to examine them, I can't help that, can I?" They didn't deny the logic of that, and the subject dropped at that. The rest of the evening passed amicably. The two neighbors went home. A little while before we retired, the old man told me something about some fellow who had called there and got kind of rough—or something. And he showed him a big knife, and told him what would happen if he got funny. He also showed me the big knife, just incidentally, in the way of showing me the knife he had showed the other fellow. A long, slim, wicked-looking, ground down butcher knife, sharp as a razor. Of course the old man showed me this all in good part. Strange to say, I was interested and was not frightened. When we turned in about 9:30, the old man and I slept in the same bed. A very good bed, too—plenty of cover. The nights here in the hills were chilly. I didn't think much about it at the time, but it struck me afterwards that if I had foolishly undertaken to leave the house for any reason in the night, it might not have been so healthy for me either.

Up at daylight—I went out and managed to get a few more nubbins for Queen. The old man had turned his old horse out in the orchard and given Queen his stall. He dished up a good, substantial bachelor's breakfast. Was very bright and cheery and hospitable.

From Notes. October 22, '25: Fair, chilly wind. Leaving Mr. Wray 7:30. Good rest. * * * * Doped up sore hand. Left liniment, formulas. A nice, religious old man. Can't read, but thinks. * * * *

The old man walked down to the gate with us and opened it politely. "Well, Mr. Heath," he said kindly, "We think you are a Federal Agent—but we're not sure. All right—good-bye."

Now that wasn't so bad, was it? He gave me the benefit of the doubt. If there was or had been for a long time, any case around there of where a man had been shot on mere suspicion, I don't know it. I shouldn't like to be found snooping around any place in there, just the same.

In bidding good-bye to Mr. Wray I found a way to press upon him a half dollar. This would leave him no poorer for our having stayed.

From Notes. October 22, '25 continued: 6:30 p.m. Ar'd farm of Mr. Jeff McNeill. * * * *

Traveled: 26 mi. Gravel mostly. Rough. Hard. Via Mayfield, Hickory. Hilly 8 mi. Bal. rolling. Buildings poor to good. Tobacco. Corn. Hay. Some peas. Family orchards. Some stock. Dairying. Last evening (I was putting this down next morning, as of yesterday—I frequently did this) I started (Queen being tired) at 2:30 to "do some work" for a night's keep. * * * * About 4 p.m. started in earnest to find "accommodations." "Turned down" all told eleven times, besides four places no one home. A few flatly declined—others "passed the buck."

Just before leaving I had a pleasant conversation with Mr. McNeill in the corn crib where he was sorting corn. By sorting corn, I mean that some ears were sound and some were not. That which was not fit to be stored was being fed, I suppose, to the hogs. I believe it was Mr. McNeill who pointed out to me that the corn all through this locality had a very peculiar kind of blue mold on the tips of some ears. I was told that this tip was really poison, and he cautioned me to be very careful not to let my horse have any of that. Of course such ears were eliminated in the sorting.

I also learned in the conversation that not far from here was a mine of pottery clay.

From Notes. October 23, '25: Leaving McNeills 6:45—75 cts. Queen did not act well last night (in addition to being sore). I have been crowding her a little on the corn of late, especially two noons on an empty stomach, without hay. My fault. Weed [hay] that night at Mr. Wray's. Filled her up on cold grass—no hay. This was not right. 8:00 this morning Queen showed signs of colic or indigestion. 8:30: Queen has a little colic—evidently indigestion. Unsaddled by roadside, letting her rest and roll. Injected lump of salt in rectum. [Had obtained this lump of salt at nearby farmhouse]. * * * * Queen up, nibbling grass—breaking wind. Had seemed tight. Started on * * * *

This lump of salt I used in lieu of an enema. Of course the enema would have been much better, but there were no facilities for it. I also gave her an "emergency dose." By "emergency dose," I mean that I carried in a little pocket of the haversack, for safety, a one dram vial of equal parts of fluid extract of aconite and fluid extract of bella donna—not nearly so poisonous. An ordinary dose of this mixture—equal parts of fluid extract of aconite and fluid extract of bella donna—for a horse in the condition I have described Queen was in—i.e., not too sick—is 20 drops or 1/3 of a dram on the roots of the tongue. I administered this with a teaspoon, and kept her moving. I want to make it plain that if the aconite were administered alone, a medium dose for a ten hundred pound horse is 10 drops—10 minims. Ten drops of fluid extract of bella donna would be only 1/3 of a minimum dose. I considered the bella donna simply as a dilutant for the more deadly poison, it also being an anodyne.

I believe only twice after this, in the case of threatened colic or indigestion, I gave Queen a minimum dose, i.e. 20 drops of this mixture, on the roots of the tongue, and kept her going, with desired results. I do not recommend this dose for general use. There are other equally good and much safer and better-known remedies. My reason for carrying this small "emergency dose" was that, as it would very seldom be needed, we could not afford to carry one of the best known remedies, which would have entailed carrying nearly a quart. The particular reason for having used the substitute for an enema in this case, was that I strongly suspected from her actions that the large colon was somewhat obstructed. This proved to be the case. The salt had a tendency to dissolve this obstruction.

While Queen was lying stretched out, a couple of natives had stopped to see if they could be of any assistance. They suggested sending or telephoning for a veterinary. I said, "No, thank you just the same. If I can't bring her out now, she will die anyway before I get through." One thing I didn't tell them was, that I couldn't possibly spare the fee that a veterinarian would have charged.

From Notes. October 23, '25 continued: 3:30 p.m. Ar'd Thomas barn, 325 N. Third St., Paducah, Ky.

Traveled: 24 mi. * * * * Pave. 1 mi. Bal. gravel. (No stop at noon). * * * * Queen improved after 9:00 a.m. Emitted much gas. Still bloated tonight. Fed 10 lbs. bran in wet mash (not sloppy). Ate most of it. Timothy hay. Country rolling. Sweet potatoes. Tobacco. Corn. Strawberries. Family orchards. [One] commercial orchard. Observed some beautiful roses—many flowers. * * * *

Special Note: Total to Paducah, Kentucky, 3413 mi. [as corrected].

I did not give Queen a bite to eat from the time I got her up until I reached this place. I had even prevented her from nibbling any grass to speak of. Of course I let her have two or three medium drinks of creek water, not too cold. When I put her in the barn, I took everything out of the manger and gave them instructions not to feed her a bite while I was gone. I went up town, came back with ten pounds of wheat bran, which made nearly an ordinary candy bucket full of mash, mixed up soft, but not sloppy, with hot water. I added to this about two drams of nux vomica, about 1 ounce of ginger—a heaping tablespoonful, half a maximum dose—and a little salt for flavor and for effect. After this I gave her a moderate feed of good clean Timothy hay. In the morning it was plain that I had done the right thing—that I had swept her out. Her appetite was fair. I gave her the rest of the bran mash, which was not soured by now, and a very light feed of good clean oats.

From Notes. October 24, '25: Little rainy. Resting today. Queen O.K. except little sore—left front. Washing up.

Sunday, October 25, '25: Cloudy. Queen O.K. except front —still little sore. * * * * 9:00 a.m. Leaving Thomas barn for Illinois via Paducah Ferry. Nominal chg.

Note: In Kentucky noticed probably larger [percent] 1-horse rigs than elsewhere. Lots of old plugs. Plenty of talk about "swapping." "Water holes."

From Signature Book: "October 24, 1925. A man introducing himself as Frank M. Heath called on me in my office at Paducah, Ky., on the above date.

(Signed) J. M. Bentley, M.D., Mayor."

From Notes. October 25, '25 continued: 10 a.m. Crossing Brookport Ferry—steam—20 cents. Noon: Feeding 3 large ears corn. Eating store lunch by Rd. side 5 mi. Brookport. Level, wet. 4:15 p.m.: Arrived farm Mr. Gus Windhorst, Metropolis, Ill., R. 2. (8 mi. N.)

Traveled: 20 mi. Gravel, flat, a.m. P.M. hilly to 6 mi. N. of Brookport. Mostly open, flat. Wet. Corn. * * * * Alternating scrub timber, clearings. Soil poor. Buildings fair to good. Corn, stock peas, etc. Some dairying. Poultry. Clearer, warmer. Road twisting. Mr. Windhorst calls himself "Low Dutch" descent. Born right here. Father homesteaded adjoining farm about 1855. [At that time] locality all in heavy timber (good timber, oak, poplar, gum). Was mostly burned to clear land. 48 years ago country still wild. Many deer. At present farmers having hard time making ends meet. Wheat as crop played out. Corn averages 40 bu.—this year poor here. Good in bottom west of here. Drouth got upland crops—corn also. Neighborhood mostly German descent—seems prosperous. Americans (i.e. non-German descent) mostly gone. A superior grade of pottery clay (makes "dishes") abounds here near surface. 80 cts. ton delivered in ton car (auto trucks). A great deal goes to Paducah, where they make it into dishes, etc. Mr. Windhorst says 16 years ago he received 1 bbl. flour and 20 lbs. bran for 5 bu. * * * * of wheat. Now they want 13 bu. for bbl. flour and no bran. Or they sell the flour for price of 13 bu. Father used to haul "grists" for neighbors. Cut [cart] wheels off a tree. [Used oxen].

October 26, '25: Cloudy. Leaving Mr. Windhorst 8 a.m. No chg. (Form, etc.) He has evidence of gas and coal on farm. Would lease. Apple trees 60 years old, bearing, healthy. Peach trees stand 35 years, bear alternately. Noon: Feeding, eating store lunch by roadside, 2 mil. N.W. New Columbia. Queen filling on fine blue grass—first in long time. 3:40 p.m. in Vienna. 4:15 p.m. Ar'd farm of Thos. Daniels, Vienna, R. 3, via Round Knob, 1½ mi. N. W. of Vienna.

Traveled: 21 mi. Gravel 1 mi. Bal. dirt—rough. Hilly except 2 (?) mi. bottom. * * * * Alternating bet. scrub timber and brush. [Much] open land lying idle. [Cultivated] fields costly in corn. Some hay, including stock peas, soy beans. 1 patch tobacco. Some good hogs. Some dairying. Residences good.

Barns fair. Fences mostly in good repair. Many farms bear federal loans—some foreclosed.

October 27, '25: Clear, frosty. Leaving Daniels family, 7:45. No chg. (Formulas—lame horse.) Three nice little girls. Noon: Fed Queen fill of excellent blue grass—barnyard of old deserted farm. "Free" corn. Store lunch [augmented by delicious wild persimmons]. Old orchard on place. 4:30 p.m. Ar'd farm of Mr. A. L. Galey, Marion, Ill., R. 5.

Traveled: 23 mi. via Goreville. Dirt. Rough 13 mi. Bal. good. 10 mi. hilly, bal. rolling. Corn. Orchards, peach, apple. Buildings poor to good. Hogs. Dairying.

October 28, '25: Snowing hard—cold wind. Slept in hay [last night]—made protection of bales. Went to nearest neighbor and got permission to stay through storm. Old miner—bought farm $5,000. * * * * 11 a.m. Passing through Marion, Ill. Noon, feeding corn—small farm of Mr. John Labotte (?), miner (coal)—out of work since Mar. 15. Four sons out of work since March. People poor. Most miners poor, out of work more or less. Radical, religious. 3:30 p.m. Ar'd farm of Mr. Chas. Russell, W. Frankford, R. 3—W. Marion 5 mi. E. of Herrin. * * * *

Traveled: 14 mi. Dirt 1 mi. Pavement 2—bad side—muddy. Rolling to Marion. Bal. flat. Little farming (corn) to Marion. Marion [back to] Johnston City to W. Frankford, some farming —corn—wheat—oats.

Note: Since I hit Ill. 2nd time passed much generally abandoned land—probably played out. * * * * [I was told that the fertilizer did not pay for itself].

October 29, '25: Leaving Mr. Russell 7:30. No chg. (Formulas). Fine bed. Mr. Bennett Tate, catcher, Washington Club, son-in-law.

From Notes. October 29, '25 continued: Noon: Feeding cracked corn in Benton—Store lunch.—3:30 Ar'd farm of Mr. H. B. Marshall, Ewing, Illinois, R. 1. 4th trial. Snowing.

Traveled: 20 mi. via W. Frankford, Benton, Ewing. * * * * Pave. 2 mi.—4 mi. side. Bal. dirt. Very slippery, rough. 1 mine N. of W. Frankford (Industrial No. 18). 1 at Benton working— also 3 at Benton idle. 3 (?) mi. timber. Benton, on mostly prairie. A lot of abandoned fields. Corn. Hay. Pasture. Stock. Dairying. (Send book.)

October 30, '25: Cloudy, 2 inches snow. Leaving the Marshalls 7:00 a.m. No chg. (Formulas, etc.) 5 kids. Queen still not feeling good. Some better (?) Noon: Feeding. Eating at place of N. E. Brockman, renter, Mt. Vernon, R. 5, 3½ mi. S.E. of. Later sent them 50 cts. [from Mt. Vernon]. 3:30 Ar'd Mt. Vernon, Ill. 4:00 p.m. at livery barn of ———— (Somehow I neglected to put in the people's name. I am sorry about this, for they treated me very fine, including the use of some blankets).

Traveled: 17 mi. (½ hunting stable)—Via Benton, Mt. Vernon road. Very muddy, slippery. * * * * First 7 mi. had to dig snow balls out of Queen's feet about every hundred feet. We are both tired. It warmed up a little today. Still plenty snow. Came through mostly open country—some poor small farms. Corn. Hay. Few cows.

Special Note: Paducah to Mt. Vernon, 115 miles. Total to Mt. Vernon, Ill., 3528 miles [as corrected].

October 31, '25: Clear, cool. Spending day at the barn, resting, repairing, etc.

November 1, '25: Cloudy. Leaving Mt. Vernon 8:30. Two nights' sleep in office. Only $1.00 (Formulas.) [The $1.00 would easily be offset by Queen's keep]. * * * * [One outstanding feature of Mt. Vernon that I remember was that it seemed to be quite a wholesale mule center]. 4:30 p.m. Ar'd farm of A. W. Bruegge, Centralia, Ill., R. 2.

Traveled: 17 mi. via Walnut Hill. 1st ten mi. rolling. Some old orchards, one young. Some scrub timber. Much idle land. Empty houses. Poor soil. More fruit. "Import" corn. Tractors. Level land. Better buildings.

November 2, '25: Slightly cloudy, warm. Leaving Bruegge family 8:00 a.m. No chg. (Formulas.) Operate large commercial orchard, successfully. Cath. Very conscientious. Hospitable. (Book.) 9:30, Passing through E. end Centralia. Old coal mine, idle two years. * * * * Pumping oil—old well. * * * * 3:15 p.m. Passing through Patoka, Ill., apple center. Mr. Hill, of Hill Brothers, gave us 8 lb. bran (saw picture in Globe Democrat, St. Louis, Mo.) [We gave Queen a good bran mash that night, you bet!]

This was by no means the first time since the last mentioned we had to attend strictly to business in order to keep Queen's vitality up to the requirements of the steady grind while feeding whatever was at hand, often corn not fully matured, and perhaps musty corn stalks for rougage. At best such feed and such unlooked for changes must involve undernourishment. Reckless feeding would mean our sure defeat. We must keep within what the digestive system can stand. If proper feed is not obtainable that is not our horse's fault.

As we had proceeded north from southern Illinois, and feed became more plentiful and more wholesome and there was more blue grass pasture, we saw a few more and better colts—some good young mules.

> *From Notes.* November 2, '25 continued: 4:30 p.m. Ar'd farm of Mr. J. A. Gray, Patoka, R. 1 (4th try). * * * *
>
> *Traveled:* 22 mi. Dirt 4 mi. Paved 1 mi. Bal. side. Level. Apples. Corn. Hay. Dairying. Good soil. Good buildings, mostly. Very few vacant. Good horses.
>
> November 3, '25: Cloudy. Leaving Grays 7:30. Supper, hay, feed. [Fed Queen our bran mash]. Slept in hay. (Form., etc.) Only 25 cts. 7:30 a.m. Eating breakfast with Mr. and Mrs. George Mays. Young couple just starting farming. Own home. Rented land. 10:30 a.m. Following dirt road as directed (as I understood it). Came to end in corn field against swampy creek. Backtracked 1½ miles, equaling three miles by misdirection. * * * * Dirt. Passing town of ————. 11:30. Picked up a lost kitten. Noon: Home of S. E. Cole. * * * * He also gives home to kitten—"on probation." 3:00 p.m. Reached Vandalia, Ill. 4:00 p.m. Barn of John Wier.
>
> *Traveled:* 20 mi. (3 by misdirection). Dirt 2 mi. Pave. 1 mi. Side 17 mi. Level. Good buildings. Corn. Hay. Grain. Dairying.
>
> *Note:* Remailed bag to Mononk, Ill.
>
> *Special Note:* From Mt. Vernon, Ill., to Vandalia, 59 mi.
>
> *Total to Vandalia,* 3587 [as corrected].
>
> November 4, '25: Cloudy, warm—may storm. Leaving barn of John Wier 8 a.m. * * * * Yesterday received bottle of Absorbine, also Junior Absorbine. Slept in old barn. Ate store grub night, morning—Queen a little "off." Noon: Feeding, eating good dinner at farm of Mrs. May E. Ries and son, Ramsey, Ill., R. 2, 1 mi. S.E. of. No chg. (Advice on horse). * * * * 4:15 p.m. Ar'd farm of Gerd Anderson, Hanson, R. 1, 4 mi. N. of Ramsey.
>
> *Traveled:* 18 mi. 1 by error. * * * * Pave. 1 mi. Cinders 2 mi. 15 side. Mostly level. Soil fair. Grain. Corn. Hay. Some old

orchards. Buildings pretty good, several new. Better stock. Good horses. Some hogs.

November 5, '25: Cloudy, warm—may rain. Leaving Andersons 7:30. Good bed. Good eats. Good feed. Queen is fine. 5:30 p.m. Ar'd farm of Mr. Frank Jones, Pana, Ill. 1 mi. N. of R. 5.

Traveled: 23 mi. Via R. 2 to Pana. * * * * Very muddy 15 mi. Pave. 1 mi. Oil road 7 mi. 4 coal mines operating. * * * * Level to Pana. Much waste land. Fair soil. Corn. Grain. N. of Pana, excellent corn, hogs, fine horses.

November 6, '25: Cloudy, clearing. Left Jones family 7. No chg. (Formulas). Little boy with sprained arm, Absorbine.

Note: Queen needs rest. Going 2 mi. S.W. to Farmer Jess Battrell, to try picking corn. Pana, Ill., R. 2. Later on: No good shucking corn—no strength right hand—arm. (Couldn't even keep out of the way. Took up larger portion of Jess' time watching that he didn't knock my block off with a large ear of corn.) 5:00 p.m. Hauled manure P.M. Very tired. Queen in dandy box stall. (No mileage).

November 7, '25: Raining hard. A.M. Queen's stall a little wet. Laying over today ac't rain. Went to Assumption—(no mileage). Coal mine.

Sunday, November 8, '25: Clear, colder. Leaving Battrell family 9:30. No chg. (Form., etc.) [Also we leveled up quite a number of horses' hoofs]. Mr., Mrs., 2 little school girls, 2 small boys.

We might say that Pana was the dividing line between somewhat precarious corn culture and the honest-to-goodness black corn belt that we read about. From Pana on for some distance the principal crop was corn, in large, regular-shaped fields, great large ears of sound corn yielding as high as 100 bushels per acre, perhaps a little more. An ordinary farm through here would usually have two or three corn-huskers in the field, usually one man to one strong team. Always an extra high sideboard on the opposite side from which the man was working, that is, the near, or left-hand side. He had no time to watch whether the ear was falling in the wagon or not. If it did not hit the wagon-bed, it hit the sideboard and bounced into the wagon-bed. He takes one row at a time. The team is trained to straddle the last picked row. It is seldom they come to a dead stop. The man starts in the morning as early as he can see at that time of year. If he does not pull in at noon with at least 40 bushels

of husked corn, by weight, they can't use him on that place. He
often husks from a hundred bushels up. From here on the corn goes
into mammoth corn elevators, usually on a side-track—that is, the
bulk of the crop. Part of it goes into an elevator on the farm, or it
may be in that case, just a large crib, and is shoveled in. This portion
is fed on the farm, very largely to hogs. For the most part, the
corn is elevated by means of an endless carrier, driven by a gasoline
engine. The back end-gate is removed, the wagon-bed tilted back,
so that the corn slides back into the hopper. From Pana north, coal
mines were a minor resource. Through the corn belt they do raise
some oats for feed. Some hay is produced; and blue grass, from here
on north at least as far as Princeton, is indigenous to the country.
We saw little, if any, wheat.

> From Notes. November 8, '25 continued: 3:00 p.m. Mowe-
> aqua. Coal mines, running. 5:00 p.m. Ar'd farm of Mr. F. E.
> Wilson, Macon, Ill. 1 S.W. of—6th attempt.
>   Traveled: 23 mi. via Moweaqua (W. of Assumption). Oiled
> Rd. paralleling No. 2. Level stretch except N. of Assumption
> which is wooded in part. Sheep. Corn. Grain. Stock. Rest of
> way good soil. Corn average 80. Good buildings.
>   November 9, '25: Clear, warmer. Leaving Mr. Wilson 7 a.m.
> No chg. (Form.) Mr. Wilson is one of the finest men I ever
> met. 67. A horseman—also auctioneer. Deals. Broad-minded,
> deeply conscientious, courteous, hospitable. Two sons on "Est."
> (estate) formerly ball players. (The Johnson family—help).
> Xmas card.

I was beginning to have quite a time finding a place to stay. It is
true that in some of these parts I might have timed my day's riding
to hit a city or some small town, but I had learned from experience
that when I did hit such a place, the chances were two to one that
if I got accommodations for Queen at all, it would be in some
cramped-up tie-stall, whereas farm stables usually had more room.
Then again, as the reader will see by the notes, we were now back
in a locality where I usually had a chance to perform some real
service with horses to offset our expenses. The fact is, however, that
since I broke into this locality where corn was the heavy and main
crop, the farmers were almost frantic, one might say, to get that
corn in before winter. The season would compare somewhat with
our Dakota wheat harvests. Any little incident that hampered the

long, hard day's work or the chance to catch a little rest, was resented. So, while the people though here are not at all penurious or discourteous, I was certainly hitting them at the wrong time. If I remember right, I believe they had been working on this Sunday. I had been turned down a few times. I approached Mr. Wilson. He didn't feel like being bothered either. Once more I was almost in despair—the nights were cold. "All I am asking," I told him, "is a place and feed for my horse. I don't mind hitting the hay. I don't smoke or carry matches, so I won't burn you out. I have, as usual, some kind of store lunch." "That's enough," he said, "and you don't have to sleep in the hay, nor you don't have to eat a store lunch. You are my guests tonight. A man that is willing to sacrifice his own comfort for his horse, is O.K. here." Needless to say, we were treated fine.

From Notes. November 9, '25 continued: 11:00 a.m. Ar'd Barry's barn, 240 Wood St., Decatur. Met Manny Wilson (who had something to do with the barn, worked with his dad in the auction business also. Believe the old man had phoned him). Also a reporter. Fed, no chg. 1:15 left Decatur.

* * * *

THE DECATUR (ILL.) REVIEW

Monday, November 9, 1925

———

TO EVERY STATE ON HORSEBACK

Frank M. Heath Arrives from Maryland

A stranger, who rode down the streets of Decatur Monday morning on a beautiful Kentucky-Morgan bay horse, attracted much attention to both himself and the horse, for both were unusual sights for Decatur. The man was Frank M. Heath of Cissel Saxon Post No. 41, of Silver Spring, Md., and the horse was his famous Gypsy Queen on whom he is traveling through every state in the United States, having traveled through twenty-three states and gone 3,582 miles since April 1. * * * *

AHEAD OF SCHEDULE

Mr. Heath is twenty-two days and 180 miles ahead of his schedule and his horse is in fine shape, although it has traveled over 3,500 miles, 1,500 of which was pavement or hard uneven rock surface. He has also traveled through more than a hundred miles of dense city traffic.

Mr. Heath goes from Decatur to Bloomington and from there to Chicago. He stayed with F. E. Wilson of Macon Sunday night. Although he is working or paying his own way his work is being watched with interest by veterinarians and publishers and if he succeeds in making his proposed trip with one horse his efforts will likely be well rewarded.

*　　*　　*　　*

From Notes. November 9, '25 continued: 5:30 ar'd Maroa—no barn. 6:00 p.m. Ar'd farm Mr. C. W. Rogers, Maroa, R. 2.

Traveled: 25 mi. * * * * Oiled road 7 mi. Cinders 2 mi. Paved. 3 mi. Side 14 mi. * * * * Queen in good shape—1st trial after Maroa.

November 10, '25: Cloudy, warmer. Leaving Rogers family 8:00 a.m. ($1.00) 10:30 passing W. Sub. of Clinton. Noon: Feeding, eating, farm of Matt Reynolds, Clinton, R. 7. No. chg. Nice people. 4:30, Ar'd farm of Mr. J. R. Ryburn, Hayworth, 2 mi. N. of.

Traveled: 26 mi. * * * * Oiled road 6 mi. Side (muddy) 20 mi. Mostly level—(few miles rolling). 2 narrow belts somewhat timbered. Bal. prairie, good soil (Black corn belt). Corn. Hogs. Grain. Good buildings. Not so fine as yesterday.

November 11, '25: Clear. Leaving the Ryburns 9:00 a.m. No chg. Fine. Young man, H. S. girl, college girl. Noon, Feeding at barn of Dr. Kyle Galt, Bloomington, 2:40. Leaving Bloomington. No chg. for feed. Met Mr. R. M. Schroeder of Pantagraph (Bloomington Paper.) 3:45, Turned down flat. 4:25, Family displaying several flags 'passed the buck' 4:40, Another flat turn down. 5:00 p.m. Ar'd fine farm of Mr. S. F. Bertram, 5 miles N. of Bloomington. He readily gave me place for Queen and permission to hit the straw and in a business-like manner chgd. me 50 cts. in advance. No suggestion of eats. All this takes the "Armistice" enthusiasm out of me a little.

Traveled: 15 mi. Level. Pave. 4 mi. Side 11 mi. Corn. Grain.

Hogs. Selfish (or desperately busy), except in Bloomington. Looks like rain. Later: Mr. Chas. Willman * * * * came out and had me in to supper afterward. Had me sleep in house and stay to breakfast. (They are living in the house and are Southern people). We had a good talk. This incident makes a vast difference with my attitude toward people's regard for Armistice Day. (After supper, while the men were out taking care of the horses, Mrs. Willman said, "Why, the idea of letting an ex-soldier sleep in the barn and eat a cold lunch on Armistice Day!") Three little girls, one little boy, Jr., age 1½.

November 12, '25: Raining. Leaving Willmans 9:40. No chg. Made me take thermos bottle and lunch. (Send book.) * * * * This is indeed a world of strange contrasts. (Christmas card). * * * * 5:30 p.m. Ar'd barn W. A. Colburn, El Paso, Ill.

Traveled: 15 mi. via R. 2. Pave 7 mi. account mud. Bal. side. Conditions same as yesterday. * * * * (Wrote to Joe for $25).

From Notes. November 13, '25: "Cloudy—rained last night. Leaving El Paso 8:30. * * * * Noon: Feeding corn contributed by elevator man at Woodford. Store lunch."

From Notes. November 13, '25 continued: 2 p.m. Ar'd Minonk. Forwarded P. P. P. * * * * 5 p.m. Ar'd place of Mr. H. S. Ensign, owner-editor of Rutland Record. Readily took us in (to barn)—(2nd attempt).

Traveled: 20 mi. via Woodford, Minonk (2 mi. detour). Pave, 2 mi. Oiled, 7 mi. Side 11 mi. (5 mi. side very muddy). Conditions as yesterday, except several coal mines. Plus alfalfa. Coal, thin veins.

The people here were neither enthusiastic nor optimistic about this mine, which was not running. The simple fact was that the veins being very thin and deep down, this mine couldn't compete with veins that were thicker and nearer to the surface.

From Notes. November 14, '25: Clear. Slept cold in hay last night. Queen fine. Leaving Mr. Ensign 9:30 a.m. No chg. Good eats at Sleinke's (restaurant). * * * * 4:15 Ar'd farm of Mr. Waldo Held (4th attempt), Lacon, Ill. R. 2. * * * *

Traveled: 19 mi. via. R. 2. * * * * Side, sod mostly. Corn. More grain. Hogs. Cattle. 2 mines. * * * * Most mines idle.

Sunday, November 15, '25: Snowing. left Mr. Held 8:40. Horse, meals, bed—only 50 cts. 10:30 a.m. Ar'd Lacon. Saw Buddy (Mark) Belsly. Put up at Lang's Feed Store. [Taken in hand] by Mark Belsly, Legionnaire.

Traveled: 5 mi. Pavement—very slippery. Level to rolling. Corn. Grain. Hogs. Cattle.

Special Note: Vandalia, Ill. to Lacon, 189 miles.

Total to date: 3,776 miles.

11:15 a.m. Talked to a little crowd at Riel's Drug Store. They gave me $1.75 for cards. Fine bunch.

November 16, '25. Threatening snow. Good bed last night 50 cts. Horse only 25 cts. Leaving Lacon 8:30. * * * * [Note: It was chilly—there was a cold northwest wind. A mile or two out, I was crossing a toll bridge. I halted to extract toll from my pocket. "Hey, take your hand out of your pocket! A man that is doing what you are doing—go ahead—luck to you!"] 3:45 Ar'd farm of Melvin Quimby, Putman, R. 2, 3 mi. N.W. of. Wood hauler (i.e. mining props.) * * * *

November 17, '25: Clear. Leaving Melvin Quimby 7:30. No chg. (Formulas etc.) * * * *

Noon: Feeding, eating at restaurant in Tiskilwa. 6:00 p.m. Ar'd Sheffield. * * * *

Traveled: 20 mi. (Gravel mostly.) Alternating woods, prairie. Same.

Special Note: Lacon to Sheffield, 45 miles.

Total to Sheffield (2nd time), 3,821 miles.

Sheffield to Sh. (Sheffield—i.e. "the loop") 1761 mi. (?)

Total, 231 days out: Average over all, 16.1 mi. plus.

Traveled: 182 days or fractions—20.4 approximately when on the road. Average per week 113 miles plus.

From Signature Book: "Sheffield, Ill. 11-18-25. F. M. Heath with Gypsy Queen returned here last night after having passed here last July.

(Signed) E. M. Klock, P. M."

From Notes. November 18, '25: Clear. 4:00 p.m. Out at farm of Roy Gutschall. * * * *

I found Mr. and Mrs. Gutschall out in the field, husking corn. I rode down the lane about half a mile and tied Queen in a fence corner. She got her fill of blue grass within the range of the halter shank. Mrs. Gutschall rode her back up to the barn. She liked horses, too.

After supper, Roy went out to milk the cows. "I don't know how we would make ends meet," he said, "if it wasn't for our Jersey cows." "What!" I exclaimed. "Here in this country where the corn goes a hundred bushels to the acre, and about everything else in proportion—unless it might be wheat! Natural blue grass and everything, and you working like the devil! All these big strong horses, and even a mechanical husker!" "It's the taxes," he told me. "The flat tax on account of the Union School alone is $1.00 an acre, pasture land and all, a year. And that only pays the interest on the bonds. The towns or small cities voted us farmers in on that. We couldn't help ourselves."

From Notes. November 19, '25: Clear, warm, had great visit with Gutschalls. Fine night's rest. Leaving, back to Sheffield, 9:15 a.m. Princeton to see about horse at Fair Grounds.

November 20, '25: Clear, warm. (Returned to Sheffield for the night.) Slept well in Mr. McKee's barn with blankets, o'coat, blouse, etc. Just rec'd P. P. P. 10.00 a.m. Leaving again for Princeton. 12:20, Feeding at Geo. O'Conel place, 1 mi. S. of Wynette. 3:00 p.m. Met Dr. Long, Vet. (veterinarian) and Legionnaire, N. of Wynette. Had quite a talk—fine fellow. 3:30 p.m. Ar'd Princeton (Ill.) Fair Grounds. 4:45. Ar'd Mr. Jester's Stables, Fair Grounds, Princeton, Ill.

Traveled: 14 mi. via Wynette, R. 7. Side, mostly. Country same.

Note: Sheffield to Princeton (Winter Quarters) 14 mi.

Total to Princeton: 3,835 miles.

Estimate: Indianapolis to Hazel Green, Wis. 275 mi.

Estimate: Sheffield to Hazel Green, Wis. 100 mi. (Figured this to Sheffield as it is where we crossed our track.)

Having gained [to apply] on 1926 travel, 175 mi. or 375 more than we figured on traveling this year, which also means that we made up all but (about) 25 mi. of our "Overplus" miles by cutting out Memphis and Indianapolis. [For these surplus miles, see October 23, '25, Paducah, Kentucky.]

November 20, '25 continued: 7:00 p.m. Dr. Long picked me up at Barn, took me to Mr. Skooglin, City Marshal (Chief of Police). He is a fine, plain spoken man. It seems that some light

and thoughtless remark I made about "not being able to find
the Marshal" and that "it would be a good incident in a book,
etc." was either ignorantly or maliciously misconstrued—and
passed on to the Marshal. (Of course this remark was meant to
infer that I was foolish for biting off so much to do in such a
short time "and go back on a return ticket.") On explanation
Mr. Skooglin proved very fair and O. K.

I heard on good authority that Mr. Skooglin was, you might say,
permanent Marshal or Chief of Police—that is, he had held that
position for a long time. He had the nerve. He had stood right out
in the open and exchanged shots with "bad ones." I believe I remember the statement was that he "got his man." I met the Chief a
time or two after that. I believe he was more sensitive than egotistical.
In fact, I recall that in the conversation sponsored by Dr. Long, he
stated, somewhat angrily at first, that he had waited a long time for
me at his office, having gotten wind some way that I wanted to see
him, and was considerably "riled" at my not calling at his office instead of expecting to meet him on the street. I admitted that that
was stupid on my part. He was certainly very fine after that. As I
remember, he had practically a deciding voice in the management
of the Fair Grounds. It was largely in relation to this that I had
wanted to see him, to be sure it was O. K. before I put in there. We
readily received his consent.

The day previous to this I had called at the Fair Grounds, and
interviewed Jim Anderson, who was looking after a lot of sale horses
belonging to Bob Frazier, a horse dealer. I had been referred to
Frazier from Sheffield, not having found in or about Sheffield the
kind of winter quarters I was looking for. Jim had set up in the
Manager's office a stove and a few chairs. Jim had no objection to
our occupying two or three of the box stalls, and it was arranged
that I could batch in the office. We would go fifty-fifty on the fuel
bill. In fact, he thought it might be very good for us mutually in
case any "ruckus" happened among the horses, or anything like that.
Of course it was understood that I was to get the final consent of the
Fair Management.

From Notes. November 20, '25 continued: Later met a bunch
of the boys at the Automotive Shop. Also Mr. Bailey of Republican. All gave encouragement.

From *Signature Book:* "Princeton, Ill., Dec. 1925. F. M. Heath riding Gypsie Queen arrived on Nov. 20. Horse and rider O. K.

(Signed) Frank Higgins, Commander of
Princeton Post No. 125.
[American Legion]

P. S. Mr. Heath's credentials have been examined by special investigating committee and we find them O. K.

(Signed) Frank Higgins, Chairman."

BUREAU COUNTY REPUBLICAN
Thursday, December 3, 1925

———

MAN ON HORSEBACK ON TOUR OF THE UNITED STATES

Frank M. Heath, a former mule sergeant in Uncle Sam's army, who helped with the job of chasing the Kaiser's troops out of France, has gone into winter quarters in Princeton with his pet horse, Gypsy Queen, on which he left Silver Springs, Maryland, the first of last April with the intention of touching part of every state in the Union before the first of July, 1927. Sergeant Heath arrived in Princeton Monday fully three weeks ahead of his schedule and will remain here until March when he will resume his novel journey. He has Gypsy Queen stabled at the Fair Grounds and will also occupy quarters there himself. When he landed in Princeton Monday the ex-mule-sergeant had traveled 3,747 miles of his journey on horseback since he left Washington, D. C. last April. He has been on the road 231 days, of which he has spent 182 in the saddle, making an average of about 22 miles a day. He has already touched 23 states and since last July when he passed through here on the first leg of his trip, he has made a loop embracing Illinois, Iowa, Nebraska, Oklahoma, Missouri, Arkansas, Tennessee and Kentucky, a distance of 1,761 miles. Sergeant Heath and Gypsy Queen avoid the pavement as much as possible and keep to the dirt country roads. Horse and rider are in excellent condition in spite of the strenuous grind and Sergeant Heath is confident he will finish the journey on schedule time. Gypsy Queen is a ten-year-old Kentucky-Morgan mare. Sergeant Heath says she has actually taken on weight on the trip in spite of the fact that she has been on the road practically every day, some days traveling as high as 45 miles. Having to depend on farmers along the way for accommodations for himself and the horse, Sergeant Heath deemed it inadvisable to travel during the extreme cold weather and picked on Princeton for his winter quarters. He has kept a careful record of his trip, and his observations along with his war experiences, make him a very interesting chap to meet. During the winter he will accept a number of lecture engagements.

*   *   *   *

The "Bureau County Record," and the "Stars and Stripes" carried a similar story.

Chapter XVI

WINTERING IN PRINCETON, ILLINOIS

From Notes. November 21, '25: Cool, some breeze. Wrote Joe for $25. Urgent. Ordered feed. * * * *

November 27, '25: Cool, windy. Worked on map, A.M. P.M., rode Queen to office of Bureau County Record, etc. Removed shoes, trimmed feet, lowered inside of left front to relieve strain on left suspensory ligament.

November 28, '25: Cold last night. Working on map. Wrote Young and Co.

November 29, '25: Snowing hard. * * * *

About this time I went to work part-time for Bob Frazier, the horse dealer. I thought I made it plain that I was not physically able to make a full time hand at labor, but that I was handy around horses and was not particularly afraid of them. The work was not especially difficult, but it was a little more than was good for me. I worked altogether something like twenty days, which would amount to about $50. I kept right on batching in the office. I had three good box stalls, one where I kept Queen nights, another where I would turn her in day times when the weather was good, to let the night stall air out, another for feed.

Of course I had been taking pretty good care of Queen meanwhile. The principal care consisted in feeding her just about right, keeping her comfortable, and employing one means or another to try to remove what little soreness remained in the left front foot and leg. I used applications, first of Absorbine, then for a change a concoction of our own, consisting of coal oil, turpentine, a little iodine, and linseed oil. This seemed to work pretty well. The reader may smile at this mixture, the exact proportions of which it is not necessary to mention here. I have a record of them somewhere. Now about the coal oil: I have used coal oil a good deal as a liniment. It can even be made to produce a mild blister by bandaging some. It is much of an anodyne. I believe if coal oil sold for a dollar an ounce, barrels of it would be used as liniment. I had formed the acquaintance of an old man who was a very experienced pharmacist. He owned a drug store in Princeton. He very kindly helped me to check this concoction, and pronounced that none of these ingredients neutralized each other, and verified my suspicion that the body of a certain liniment at that time—and probably now—very largely used, was coal oil.

I would put this on, after I changed, and it really did take out the soreness pretty well, and restored the circulation. I would air the leg during the day, and at night I would wrap it lightly. This concoction would not make a successful liniment for general use for the reason that it did not blend properly. One must shake it and keep shaking it, in application. Otherwise he might get too much of one ingredient and not enough of another. It got us through the winter.

Meanwhile, of course, I kept the feet pared properly. The one great handicap during the winter was lack of exercise as Queen was bare-footed, and the ground was always either very slippery or else very badly chopped up with the horses running over, and then frozen. There was not much not much chance for exercising Queen except in the stall, without cracking up the hoofs. This was not good for Queen, particularly for the reason that Gypsy Queen, largely from habit as I believe now, leaned too much on the right front foot, allowing the left knee to crumple a little, thus allowing certain muscles to atrophy to a certain extent from lack of use, which in turn would have a tendency to hold the knee in a slightly bent position. At the time I was greatly puzzled. Jim Anderson, quite much of a horseman, was also puzzled. He believed that the knee was chronically sprung—and I didn't like it myself.

While it is not my aim to get ahead of the current story, probably the reader will derive more satisfaction if I state plainly now that later I suspected and eventually proved that standing thus on one fore-foot can become largely a habit, and it had become a habit with Gypsy Queen. She improved some with exercise. We will drop this phase of the story for nearly a year. Suffice it to say, she did not suffer unduly from this knee, but on one or two occasions when she went too long without re-shoeing or something, she did favor the foot some, with probably affectation of the nerves in the leg, and consequently this caused her to buckle her knee somewhat, temporarily.

Being, as I now see, unduly concerned about this knee, I once or twice resorted to a light blister. Toward spring, Jim Anderson did not believe I would get far with Gypsy Queen on account of the knee. I believe he was sincere in this. Incidentally, Jim for years had been dealing considerably in horses and was somewhat of a horse trainer himself. He would tackle almost anything. He tried to get me to cancel our trip and work for him, helping him train horses. I don't believe he liked it very well when I declined, although we had no words.

As for myself, I put in a good share of the winter reading everything I could get my hands on in regard to our Southwest, the one part of the United States with which I was not familiar. I was worrying, particularly, for one thing, about how we should get across the long stretches in the Navajo Reservation. I read everything I could get about Arizona, particularly a book entitled "Arizona" by George Wharton James.

Princeton, Ill.,
March 2, 1926.

Mr. George Wharton James,
Pasadena, Calif.

Dear Sir:

I am enclosing a schedule which will give you a pretty good idea as to what I am doing. Please note choice of routes in the Southwest.

I have been reading much of Ariz. and N. M. by yourself, Mr. Alexander Powell and others. But there is still one point that baffles me at this distance: Can I tackle the journey from Flagstaff, Ariz. to Bluff, Utah, Aztec, Col., Ship Rock, N. M., in dead of winter, as per schedule, without running too great a risk of losing or "playing out" my horse?

We travel unattended and depend on the country for subsistence and shelter out of camping season.

While I prefer to finish on schedule, I should rather fall behind two months waiting in California for winter to pass than to lose out altogether.

I am taking the liberty of inquiring of you, as I know you know the country and also have had to do with horses. (My horse will not be hardened to *cold* and exposure, and she requires plenty of feed.)

I am inquiring this early as it seems difficult to receive mail when on the road, and I should choose well in advance which route to take. If I decide to lay over a month or two I may as well take the Western route and spend the time in Pasadena.

Thanking you in advance, I am

Very respectfully,

(Signed) Frank M. Heath.

P. S. We can pack feed enough to run us 60 or 100 miles where road is such that we can walk right along (as three or four days), if we can get weather, water and shelter.

* * * *

1098 North Raymond Avenue,
Pasadena, California,
March 6, 1926.

Mr. Frank M. Heath,
Princeton, Illinois.

My dear Sir:

Your letter of March 2nd, addressed to George Wharton James, has been received. I regret to say that Mr. James is not living, having passed away in 1923.

I would suggest that you write to the management of Hotel El Tovar, Grand Canyon, Arizona, for information concerning the trip you wish to make, from Flagstaff to Bluff, Utah. They will know whether it is a possible trip for you to make at this season of the year, or advisable for you at any season. Or, you might write to the Postmaster at either Flagstaff or Williams, Arizona, and ask to be put in touch with the Head Forest Ranger of the local "National Forest Reserve." The men of the Forest Reserve are usually very reliable, and would be able to tell you in detail as to weather, water, food for your horse, etc.

Arizona is a wonderful country, but distances are often great between habitations, water is often very scarce and perhaps of poor quality—perhaps alkali—and there might be grass for your horse or nothing but sand and rock. At certain seasons the heat is intense. Arizona horses are tough and can eat anything, drink anything and endure anything. Can yours? * * * *

Yours very truly,
(Signed) Edith C. Farnsworth,
(Step-daughter of Mr. James.)

* * * *

From Notes. March 12, '26: Cold, snow. Putting stickers on schedules. (There had been a slight error in them.)

March 13, '26: Yesterday rec'd word from Joe. Believes he can induce Kimball to stay or rent otherwise. Commissioners promise to mend roads. Answering, postponing decision to 23rd. Queen threatened with laryngitis (but feels good, looks bright, appetite good.) Some swelling in throat—giving Pot. (potassium) nitrate form., glycerine, belladonna on tongue, "Heath's Liniment" outside. Vicks, inhale. Self feel "grippy."

* * * *

Transportation Department,
Grand Canyon, Arizona,
March 15, 1926.

Mr. Frank M. Heath,
General Delivery,
Princeton, Ill.

Dear Sir:

Your letter of March 11th and schedule of your trip has been turned over to the writer for attention.

Same has been noted carefully and I am sorry to advise that it would be quite difficult to go from Flagstaff, Ariz., to Bluff, Utah, on a horse at any time of the year, due to the fact that feed stops are few and far between. Believe though if you packed quite a lot of provisions between Tuba City, and Kayenta and then from Kayenta to Bluff that it could be made. March would be a much better month than January or February.

Yours truly,
(Signed) J. E. Shirley,
Manager, Transportation.

From Notes. March 21, '26: Warm. Cleaning up. Darning up. Yesterday and today. Queen feeling fine. Riding 5 mi. today. Left front a little weak. This morning I discovered that the left * * * * muscle just above the knee is considerably smaller than the right. This I believe is owing to her not standing firm on left and to her "right lead" which I make her take to favor left. (This was a damfool thing to do. I should have made her work the left more.) I believe it will "come back" with exercise.

Monday, March 23, '26: Warm. Riding Queen O. K. No word regarding place. Ordered car. Should be ready 26th. Mending barracks bag.

March 25, '26: Warm. No word regarding place. Wired Joe for information. Stated "Returning Friday if not rented."

March 25, '26: Cloudy. 2 p.m. No mail from Joe. No reply to wire. Packing up. Had Queen examined by Vet. complying with commercial law. O.K. Queen weighs 1,000 pounds. Evening, packing for return.

March 26, '26: Cold, cloudy. * * * *

From Notes. March 26, '26 continued: Following is certificate I got yesterday. Insp. agent this morning objected that it must be signed by State Vet or Assistant. I got two copies later from Fred Fawcett, Asst. State Vet.

Princeton, Ill.,
March 25, 1926.

This is to certify that the following described animal, bay mare 11 years old, property of Frank M. Heath, is free from contagious disease to the best of my judgment.

(Signed) Lewis F. Hartzell, Veterinarian,
Princeton, Ill.,
(Signed) Fred J. Fawcett,
Assistant State Veterinarian.

(It is funny about people when a fellow is in a pinch. This vet didn't charge me a cent and the other fellow only took what the law required him to take.)

From Notes. March 26, '26 continued: Yesterday I gave the Bureau County Republican a statement—subject to cancellation if I continue trip, as follows:

Dear Sir:

Owing to reasons beyond my control I am obliged to postpone my trip and look after my small poultry ranch at Silver Spring, Md., which I had believed permanently rented. I can not afford to let it run down. Besides losing tenant cuts off the small income upon which I depended in an emergency on the trip. I am shipping Gypsy Queen back. When I get matters definitely settled I intend to resume the trip right where it is interrupted and complete it. The mare is now in good shape.

My reasons for continuing the trip afterward are the originals: health, education and the scientific test of a horse. Added to these is the reason that I believe it is good for a man to finish whatever he undertakes. [This * * * * article was withdrawn Mar. 31—Author.]

What a blunder this would have been—this retreating and hoping to make good afterwards! Looking the matter square in the face, if we were through—had to retreat—we were *through*. Much concerned, about this time I had a short talk with Frank Higgins. He said something like this: "Well, Comrade, that sure is too bad! If you have to back up now, the public will misunderstand it. They will believe that you have to give the horse a year to grow new hoofs, or something. Anyhow, if you resume the trip after a considerable time and finish, you will not have been making one continuous trip. We are placing great store on your accomplishing what you undertook. We sincerely hope you will be able to proceed." That was all he said. And he was dead right. This emphasizes the importance of the great trouble that Joe had taken and was still taking upon himself in behalf of our undertaking. Anybody would know that this was out of his line of business. Joe is a lawyer. He does not usually fritter away his time looking after small estates. I am sure had it not been for Joe's earnest attention to our affairs, we would have been defeated for lack of funds. Nor should Mr. Whitacre's earnest endeavors be overlooked.

From Notes. March 27, '26: Cold. No word from Joe. Bought more feed. Staying till Mon.

Sunday, March 28, '26: Snowing.

Monday, March 29, '26; Warm, clear.

From Notes. March 29, '26: Snowing, blowing. Had Queen shod by Dick Anderson, $3.00. Later, repacking for trip. Gave paper notice of going 1st, or first day fit to travel. (Later had left hind reset eliminating trailer.)

What I mean by "trailer" is this: Some blacksmiths seem to have an idea that they must extend one branch or side of a shoe way back of the heel. This probably originated from someone trying to give one side of the foot additional bearing. From my point of view, in the light of experience, this should seldom be done, for the reason that if additional bearing on either side of a foot is required, it should be brought about either by an extension shoe, or if that is not possible, by placing that side of the shoe as far out as possible. It seems to me anyone should see, if he thinks about it much, that if the bearing on the outside of a foot should be altered, say at the quarters, it is a great mistake to let that part go and the bearing back of the foot.

The one exception, as I see it, is if a horse is inclined to have what is called broken-down pasterns—that is, if the fetlock drops too much. In that case a trailer on one or both sides might be excusable. Yes, there is one more exception which might happen about once in a thousand times. For example, the reader may remember early in our trip where, for reasons described, Queen got to rolling out on her left front, and particularly rocking back also on the left heel at the same time. Well now, in this case a trailer on the left side was permissible, and I seem to remember having made a notation somewhere of having used one later on to brace the leg. However, a trailer in the ordinary sense, that is, reaching straight back on one side of the foot, particularly in front, would have been wrong, for the reason that in striking the heel first, if the footing had any resistance whatever, one branch of the shoe striking before the other branch would throw the foot in a twist as it contacted the ground.

From Notes. March 31, '26: Storming some.

Decided to stay until Mon. 5th. Many drifts 3-4 feet. Blowing.

April 1, '26: Clear. Roads horrible. Storm coming. Decide to stay until Mon. 5th.

Note: Total expenditure, Apr. 1, '25-April 1, '26 (above earnings) $286.00 or 78 1/3 cts. per day.

Cash on hand April 1, '26—$111.50.

*   *   *   *

BUREAU COUNTY RECORD
PRINCETON, ILLINOIS
April 1, 1926

———

Sergeant Frank M. Heath, late of Uncle Sam's army, who has been in winter quarters at the Princeton fair grounds since last November, expects to start out this week with his horse, Gypsy Queen, on the last leg of his novel horseback journey across the United States. Mounted on Gypsy Queen, a ten-year-old Kentucky Morgan, Sergeant Heath left Silver Springs, Maryland, the first of last April, 1925, with the intention of touching part of every state in the Union before the first of July, 1927. When he arrived in Princeton last Fall, he was three weeks ahead of his schedule and had traveled 3,747 miles after spending 231 days on the road, of which he was 182 days in the saddle, making an average of 22 miles a day. Gypsy Queen came through the northern winter in fine shape and is "rarin' to go," Sergeant Heath said yesterday. The Sergeant claims a world's endurance record for his horse on the strength of last year's performance. In leaving Princeton Sergeant Heath is profuse in his expressions of appreciation for the treatment accorded him, an entire stranger in the community. He and his horse have enjoyed comfortable quarters at the fair grounds all winter and the Sergeant was given free access to the Legion club rooms and the Matson Public Library which he used as a workshop for making maps and compiling the data about his trip.

*　　*　　*　　*

The "Bureau County Republican" ran a similar story.

From Notes. Friday, April 2, '26: Snowing hard.

Saturday, April 3, '26: Thawing slightly. Snowed again last night. Roads still very bad. Had Queen over town—feels good. Reading "Across China on Foot" by Edwin Dingle. Working at bandages.

Sunday, April 4, '26: Thawing. Roads still very bad. Posting books. Addressing tags for P. P. P. Washing, etc.

April 5, '26: Thawing. Roads still very bad. Mending. Reading "The Arab at Home," Harrison.

April 6, '26: Cloudy. Snowed again last night.

April 7, '26: Cloudy, thawing. Rained again last night. Roads still very bad. Bought feed to last to 12th (no travel before then). Writing long letter home.

Princeton, Illinois,
April 7, 1926.

Dear Folks:

Your letter rec'd yesterday. Glad it is spring there. Here this month, so far, has been a regular, typical S. Dak. *March.* It has been one succession of storms—mostly snow. I was ready to pull out Apr. 1 as per schedule; but weather was not fit. Roads were bad. March 30-31st was a hard snow storm. Apr. 1 snow lay anywhere from 6 in. to 4 feet deep. Roads impassable. I postposed departure to Mon. Apr. 5th as such roads would be sure to stove a horse up—especially a soft horse—without getting anywhere. On April 1st I went out about ¾ mile (in exercising) and she was continually balling up and slipping and sliding, to say nothing of wallowing. It took about an hour with wisps of straw to get her legs in any kind of comfortable condition after coming in. I estimate that a mile of such going takes more out of a horse than ten miles of good footing. That may sound like exaggeration, but I don't believe it is. A horse travelling on high "snow balls" fetches an unnatural (though certain) strain on every joint, ligament and muscle. It is even dangerous, especially to a soft horse. Dad will bear me out in that. I thought it ought to be fit to travel by the 5th. On Apr. 2nd it snowed again hard. Apr. 5th it snowed again at night. Apr. 6th it was cold all day—rained at night. So you can see that I could not travel this week either. If it clears up soon I hope to be able to start Mon. the 12th. It is threatening rain again now.

This is a good agricultural section—one of the richest in the world. And when it is wet the good old black mud is almost unbelievable. This state has a very great deal of good concrete roads though most of the roads running north and south in this section are either dirt or gravel. The latter are still in horrible condition (and I am going north from here), and the concrete roads are still almost blocked where lay the snow drifts. Anyhow, I decided long ago that concrete roads are taboo for us. A few hundred miles more of them last year and Queen would never have recovered from the jar. And added to the jar is the side hill inflexible slope that strains a horse's joints and tendons and ligaments. Paved roads in the country are much worse in this respect than ordinary city streets. * * * *

Whenever I meet many people I have to answer many questions—or be snobbish. The question that gets my goat above all others is: "What do you get out of it?" Now to a person who cannot *realize* (and many do) what I "get out of it," to one who counts life itself in terms of dollars and cents, what is the use of trying to answer? Most such would be satisfied were I to give an affirmative answer to the eternal question: "Are you doing it on a wager?" Sometimes I say, "A kind of wager, yes," and ride off and leave them guessing. I wonder how many guess that I mean that I have either to win or lose that which I have undertaken. * * * *

I never accept charity. (I do accept hospitality when extended as such—and it would surprise you the number of people who, when I'm on the road treat me as a traveler—an honored guest.) Still I have just now balanced up my first year's expense and I find that expenditures are approximately seventy-eight cents (78 cts.) per day above earnings. How do I do it? * * * *

From Notes. April 9, '26: Warm. Roads improving fast. P. P., suitcase with o'coat, some other things, to James Norred, 1633 A St. N. E. Washington. Bought Am. Exp. (American Express checks), Princeton State Bank, No. 3420-4327 (10). Writing home.

April 10, '26: Clear, fine. Mailing B. (bag) home to Spokane today. Inclosing this and other notes.

From Signature Book: "Princeton, Ill., April 12, '26. Frank M. Heath, who arrived here last Nov. 20 (at the Fairgrounds) has been here ever since. He is leaving this morning with the same horse under saddle.

(Signed) J. G. Anderson,
109 N. Knox St."

THE AMERICAN LEGION
National Headquarters
Indianapolis, Ind.

May 18, 1926.

Mr. Frank M. Heath,
c/o Ben Francis,
Wells, Minnesota.
My dear Mr. Heath:

Enclosed you will find an item of news which appeared in a special American Legion News Service release recently issued. We are sending it to you in the belief that you will find it of interest to know about this item which appeared in publications all over the country.

Sincerely yours,
(Signed) F. C. Painton,
Director,
American Legion News Service

STARTS ON RECORD TRIP

Silver Spring, Md., April * * * * Frank M. Heath, member of Cissel Saxon Post of The American Legion here, and "Gypsy Queen" are about to start out on the last leg of a world record breaking horseback trip.

Heath, in an effort to regain health lost in the World War, educate himself by travel and "prove by actual test the capability of a good horse," between the dates of April 1, 1925 and November 20, 1925, covered with "Gypsy Queen" 3,747 miles over 23 states and pulled into winter quarters in good shape.

His object is "to hit some part of every state in the Union with one horse and return to Washington on or before July 1, 1927."

BOOK II

BOOK II

HERE we are beginning Book Two, as we leave Winter Quarters at Princeton, Illinois, April 12, 1926. Realizing that Book One is rather tedious, I am adopting a different method in regard to Book Two. As stated in the *Introduction*, when we started out I had not the slightest thought of ever attempting to make a book out of this Trip. But so many people insisted the experience would make good reading that I finally decided I might try it some time. So, before leaving Winter Quarters, I concluded whenever possible to record our whereabouts and anything in particular that I thought might be interesting in letters, most of which are addressed to "Dear Folks,"— my Father and Mother in Spokane, Washington, with the understanding that this meant my other relatives too. I also gleaned a few of the newspaper articles that were published, which would throw some light on our activities.

Our method in traveling and making a living in the agricultural districts through which we passed in 1926 was very similar to those recorded in Book One. These districts will be easily identified by the reader by the agricultural symbols on the map.

We shall make no pretense at keeping a day to day record of the mileage or the conditions of the roads, unless it may be incidentally by an occasional reference to some note which records a fact not brought out in the letters, newspaper article, etc. This method will be used until we reach the Northwest, at about which time and place the humdrum experiences largely leave off and adventures begin. However, I will give the approximate mileage and dates at the end of each lap or leg of the journey, and final mileage will be given at the end of the story.

Chapter I

CROSSING THE GREAT PLAINS

WARREN, ILLINOIS
April 20, 1926
(*Name of paper omitted by oversight*)

WARREN, ILL.—April 20. Frank M. Heath of Silver Spring, Md., a World War Veteran riding a bay horse named Gypsy Queen landed in town yesterday and stayed with Frank Clock. Mr. Heath left Washington, D. C. April 1st, 1925, and he is supposed to hit every state in the Union and return to Washington on or before July 1st, 1927. He has his entire trip mapped out and the date he was to be there. He was to get to Hazel Green, Wis., April 20. He has been in 25 states and will sleep in Wisconsin tonight. He has been in very poor health since leaving the army and expects to be much improved by his return trip.

*   *   *   *

From Signature Book: "Warren, Ill., April 19, 1926. Frank M. Heath with Gypsy Queen is staying at my livery stable here tonight.   (Signed) Frank Clock."

From Signature Book: "New Diggings, Wis. (Stamped) April 21, 1926. Frank M. Heath called here today with Gypsy Queen.   (Signed) C. C. Teasdale, Postmaster."

From Signature Book: "Bloomington, Wis., April 25, 1926. Frank M. Heath with his mare Gypsy Queen put up at my livery barn here from night of 23rd to noon today.   (Signed) J. G. Ervin."

From Notes. April 26, '26: * * * * 3:45 p.m. At ferry (Mississippi). (Prairie du Chien, historical) * * * * 4:30, Leaving McGregor, Ia., via (Route) 13, up river. 6:45, Ar'd farm of Chas. Albright, 5 mi. N. of McGregor, near junction Miss. and Yellow Rivers. * * * *

This was the third time I had crossed the Mississippi. I waited a little while at the river for the ferry. I came in through a suburb of Prairie du Chien. I don't believe I went up town at all.

The map gives McGregor, Iowa, nearly directly across the Mississippi from Prairie du Chien. It seemed to me that the ferry went considerably down stream. I landed at McGregor sometime before sundown. It was a little town, mostly brick, what I saw of it, perched on the east side of the hill.

The road we traveled was, I would say, about half way up the very steep side hill—almost a bluff perhaps two hundred feet high. The railroad ran along the side hill. A train came thundering in from the north between us and the river. Being almost above the train was something strange for Gypsy Queen. I had my hands full for a while.

We passed several shanty boats down below. The men waved at me and I waved back.

I came to a very cheap residence, kind of temporary, you might call it, a shack on the bald side hill, with quite a mound of clam shells, and one solitary large hog in a pen. Saw no other life around there, not even vegetable life. I proceeded a little way beyond and stayed at a small dairy farm. As we were eating supper, a neighbor lady came in, a neat, intelligent-appearing person. It soon developed that she was the wife of the man who lived in the temporary dwelling by the mound of clam shells. Her husband's business was digging and dredging for clams and searching them for pearls. He fed the most of the clams to this big hog. It appeared to me that it must be quite a clammy hog! It also developed that these men with whom I had exchanged silent salutations dug clams for the pearls. The lady said they made—one month with another—pretty fair wages.

* * * *

GALENA (ILL.) GAZETTE
April 26, 1926
TRAVELER MUST TOUCH EVERY STATE IN UNION
Frank M. Heath Then Must be in Washington, D. C. by July 1st (1927)

Traveling men naturally meet with some strange characters while covering their territory, and those whom they meet are frequently of an interesting and educational nature. Wednesday, it was the good fortune of Will Grimm, traveling for the Barrett Wholesale Grocery of this city, to meet an ex-soldier of the World War, Frank M. Heath, who is traveling over the United States riding or walking as the whim dictates, but touching every state in the Union at least once. It frequently happens, however, that it becomes necessary to touch some of the states several times. Mr. Heath left Washington, D. C., April 1, 1925 with the objective to touch every state in the Union and return to Washington on or before July 1st, 1927. * * * *

Mr. Heath was at New Diggings, Wis., on Wednesday, and it is his custom to call at the postoffice and secure an impression of the postoffice stamp as proof of his having been in the state, and it was here that Mr. Grimm met him. He is a very intelligent person to meet, is a world war veteran and had two sons in the world war also. After he was mustered out, he was in poor health and has finally taken this method of out-door life to endeavor to regain his health and incidentally see his own country which he is slowly and deliberately doing. Although Mr. Heath was over the prescribed age for war service, it required over a year's constant effort to get into the game which he finally did, and saw 10 months service overseas and returned in poor health. He is not begging or asking for any assistance, but he is not refusing any offered him voluntarily. So far in his travels Mr. Heath has touched 23 states and crossed four mountains (ranges) and his next stop is Wells, Minn. and after that his trip will be largely through the west and south. * * * *

From Signature Book: "Waukon, Ia., Apr. 28, 1926. Frank M. Heath with Gypsy Queen stayed at my farm here last night.
                                                    (Signed) H. F. Denning."

———

Burr Oak., Ia.,
April 30, '26.

Dear Folks:

I came through Decorah yesterday A.M. I can imagine that it has not changed a great deal since Dad used to drive there or through there fifty or sixty years ago. It must have been a small city then; that's about all it can say of itself now. Just a kind of dear, sleepy old place, strictly a farmer's town, prosperous in an easy going way, population about four thousand.

S. E. of the city a mile or more is an old brick "grist mill" that probably was there when we lived here in Burr Oak.

Apparently the good old days of "toll" are no more so far as flour for the farmer's family is concerned. In fact raising wheat is a thing of the past here, they tell me. But I read a sign over the rusty old door, "Feed ground here." Nor did I hear the same busy hum that doubtless Dad used to hear as he passed some fifty-five years ago, but rather a slight rumble as of some small part of the mill running.

I came into Burr Oak about 6 last night from the south. At first I felt a little disappointed because it didn't quite tally with my childish recollections. I say *quite*, for it does *nearly*. Only the distances appear in some cases too long or too short.

I spotted the site of the log house where begin my earliest recollections; and the other house across the road (the road in which I used to stick fast in the mud—and it's still the same old road)—where we later lived. The creek into which I rolled one day after strangling on the vinegar (in the making) that I was sucking out of the bunghole of the Keg, is still there, south of the same old house, which has been remodeled. But the creek is very tiny now. And the bank has washed down until it is not nearly so steep. The little old wooden bridge has been replaced by a concrete culvert. Silver Creek still flows beautifully. But the Burr Oak trees have been grubbed out. So the pasture where the "hooky" kicked me over when I tried to get milk by using her tail for a pump handle is now only a beautiful blue grass pasture.

The old store—now in ruins—still stands on the west side of Main St. This has become tangled in my mind with Houck's store. But there is across the street a brick—now a harness shop— that the present older residents remember as Houck's store. Old man Houck is "up on the hill," as is also the old Mr. Hobart, "Hily" Hobart, old John Filer and others. The distance from where we lived to the place they pointed out to me as Old John's seems too great. I guess it must have been someone else that chased me across the bridge—Nathan, Gene and me— when we tipped his swell box cutter over; for it seems plain to me that it was the little old bridge just mentioned.

The ruins of the old livery barn just across the creek still stand. Off to the N. W. of where we lived and just across Silver Creek stands an old brick cheese factory—now idle—which I do not remember. The old stone schoolhouse got so small that they built a large brick—in another part of town—to take its place. So the old schoolhouse where I remember having attended for about one hour and from which I had to be dragged by main force because I talked so much that I ruined the discipline, is now only a stony green spot in a field. Even the brick that replaced it got the "wibble wobbles" and was torn down and replaced by a good frame building.

The old town now has three churches. The old Malcolm home still stands, though the last of the Malcolms are gone long ago. The Hobart farm is said to be still intact. I will pass by it tomorrow. The topography of the land tallies with my childish memories—just beautifully rolling. There are many old buildings including modest residences; a few old, old ones and a few not so old. The town is just the dear dreamy old place that you remember, surrounded by a good farming country. * * * *

Say, you remember a Peter Olson who worked in the old shop in Arlington, S. Dak? Well I ran into him here by the merest accident * * * * he has just pointed out where Dad drilled two wells in particular. One was for A. J. Cratsenburg, the other for old John May.

6 P.M. Have been up in Cemetery—a very fine one well kept up by subscriptions. Visited grave of John Filer and Jacob Houck in company with a Mr. Chas. Reed who was 9 when we left here. On returning he showed me where was the original store just across the creek from where we lived. It burned. But getting the location clears it all up so it seems natural. Only I had confused Houck's with this store. Also I must have confused someone else who chased us across the bridge with John Filer.

May 1. Your two cards rec'd at Burr Oak. Leaving this morning. The R. R. left Burr Oak 3½ mi. to the south.

Will have to beat it. Love.

(Signed) Frank.

From *Signature Book:* "Burr Oak, Ia., April 30, '26. Frank M. Heath with Gypsy Queen arrived late last night and is stopping at our place here today.

(Signed) P. C. Olson."

From *Notes.* May 2, '26: * * * * Ar'd farm of Clarence Kingsley, 4 mi. N. Le Roy, Minn., R. 1, via 7 mi. S. Ostrander, 10 S. Spring Valley. Level to hilly. Gen. farming. Dairying. Sheep. Few milk goats.

Traveled: 16 mi.—3 mi. dirt, 13 gravel fair going. Good deep black soil. Clarence Kingsley used to drill wells all around here. He at once mentioned the ruins of Dad's old drilling machine at Preston. Has been well picked. (That is, not much was left of it.) * * * *

From Signature Book: "Harmony, Minn., May 2, 1926. Frank M. Heath with Gypsy Queen stayed at our farm here 9 mi. W. of Harmony last night.

(Signed) Friend Berning."

From Signature Book: "Wells, Minn., May 9, 1926. Frank M. Heath has been here with Gypsy Queen since noon, May 6th.

(Signed) A. B. F. Francis."

We will presume this town got its name of Wells from the numerous artesian wells, by which I mean that overflow through a pipe. Some of these had considerable pressure in 1875 during our sojourn there. When I came through Wells in 1926 I saw no over-flowing wells and was told there were none. I know that around in the region where my relatives lived they were pumping water out of the well in the ordinary way.

A lot of hardship on Queen was caused by the condition of roads that I have described as rough and inflexible, indicated briefly by R. I. This was sometimes a case of where the road was full of rocks, large and small. This would be permanent, of course. But the principal mileage on rough and inflexible roads, especially across the great plains states, especially Minnesota, South Dakota, North Dakota and some of Montana, was dirt that had been punched up and cut up when wet, and then dried. Over such Queen would just go flinching along. It was very hard on her. As stated long ago, a mile of this took more out of her than two miles of good footing. This was especially grievous as we were packing her pretty heavy, particularly when we got over into arid country where we packed field bed and sometimes feed to do us for several days. This dead weight of a hundred pounds and over is simply terrible on a horse on rough roads. I make no apology for the fact that I myself was doing a good deal of walking. Still, with all this, Queen walked me down several times. Sometimes I would be able to drop in behind what I will call a "road repair outfit," which tore up and releveled the road. This made it easier for Queen because she had the best kind of footing.

From about where we hit Iowa the second time, that is, in 1926, west as far possibly as De Smet, it is safe to say that about half the people we met came from Scandinavia or were descended from Scandinavians, at least on one side. The musical sing-song tones were not at all uncommon.

Airlie, Minn.,
May 17, 1926.

Hello Folks:

Sending piece pipestone I got right from ledge on Ind. Res. Yesterday. Use it for paperweight. * * * * We are O. K. Address, Mobridge, S. Dak. Love.

(Signed) Frank.

About this pipestone: I remember well that when the people were migrating from southeast and southern Minnesota they would usually go out—I believe in 1878 was the greatest movement—file on homesteads, do more or less improvement, and come back after their families. The Government granted a homesteader six months in which to get his family settled on the homestead. Several of our neighbors went from around southeastern Minnesota, that is, the region of Spring Valley, and returned by the way of Pipestone, Minnesota, just east of the Dakota Territory line. One family brought back great chunks of this pipestone of the grade that was workable. Nearly every kid in the neighborhood, including myself, had a little of this pipestone to work with. We made rings or crosses, imitation books, watch charms, and what not. It was easily workable with such tools as a jackknife or file. We could bore holes through it with a drill. I now have a piece of this pipestone—the piece I sent to my folks—which I use as a paper weight. I also have a little toy imitation book probably half by three-fourths of an inch in size, and three-eighths of an inch thick, that I made for my mother.

From Notes. Sunday, May 16, '26: 1:30 p.m. Camping on Pipestone Ind. Res. on creek below Winnawissa Falls. Main ledge pipestone little to S. nearly exhausted. Dug up about ¼ mile. (The small workable vein of pipestone, not the granite.) Res. consists of 670 acres. 3:30 visited school ½ N. E. Met Mr. Ansel Carpenter—full blooded Sioux, chief property clerk and others. Sam Ray, Sioux, showed me quarry. Mr. Carpenter gave me three pieces of pipestone as a souvenir. Leaving camp, 5 p.m. Saw Indian Head and Hiawatha hatchet. According to Carpenter there is no Pipestone Tribe. Quarry belongs to Sioux. Indian Joe makes souvenirs, keeps proceeds. 6:15. Ar'd farm of H. J. Farmer, 5½ mi. W. of Pipestone, R. 5 1st try. * * * * Farmers own ½ section farm. * * * *

From Signature Book: "Pipestone, Minn., 5 mi. W. Frank M. Heath with Gypsy Queen stayed at our farm May 17th, 1926. (Signed) H. J. Farmer."

I never saw greater hustlers than these Farmers, young Farmer, the old man and the hired man. By the way, they farmed considerable land besides this half section I mentioned. They had some very good large horses. A colt had arrived on the farm a few days before, and the colt was sick—a very fine, valuable colt. They asked my opinion about this colt and if I could suggest anything. I didn't volunteer any suggestions. It is a long road from a horse's underpinning to a colt that is sick with an infected navel. I did the best I could, however. I advised them first to give the mare a good dose of raw linseed oil, second, to put her on the good fresh grass, third, to give the colt a good dose of castor oil. I had observed that both mare and colt were constipated. Fourth, I advised them to make a large quantity of saturated solution of boric acid, and to keep the navel well washed with this. That was all I could suggest. I wasn't sure that this would save the colt, but the young man seemed to think it would. He was running from the house to the barn and from the barn to where he was hooking up the team. I was just getting ready to pull out. He beckoned me over to him. "Here," he said, "take this,"—handing me a five dollar bill. "Don't tell the old man about this," he said, "if you happen to pass him in the field. He might think it's a little extravagant, but he won't when the colt gets well,"—or something like that.

There is a tribe of Flandreau Indians about Flandreau, but they are said to be very much civilized. The white people are very proud of them. They are quite proud of mentioning the fact that a full-blood Flandreau Indian is a judge in the local court. Miss Farmer, a daughter of the house, was or had been a teacher in the Pipestone Indian School. In relating this to me briefly, she said the Indian girls asked her, "We know we are not far from savages, but why do people make so much fuss about Indian maidens?" "Why," Miss

Farmer replied, "I suppose it is the savage in us that makes you attractive to us." "Savage in you?" The girl was shocked. "White people aren't savages." "No, but we were once, and there is some of it in us yet."

From *Signature Book:* "Flandreau, S. D., May 18th. (1926) Mr. Frank [rest of name omitted by oversight] arrived at our farm located 17 miles west of Flandreau at 4:30 p.m. today.
(Signed) V. R. Lee."

*　　*　　*　　*

DE SMET NEWS
Kingsbury County Newspaper

Kingsbury County, South Dakota, Friday, May 28, 1926

HORSEBACK TRAVELER, FORMER RESIDENT,
VISITS THE COUNTY

———

De Smet had a visit Saturday morning from a man who is riding horseback to visit every state in the Union, and by chance the visitor is a former resident of the county, a pioneer of Arlington vicinity.

Frank M. Heath is his name and he came into De Smet Saturday morning riding his bay Kentucky Morgan horse after more than a year of his jaunt and while in his twenty-sixth state. He had covered 4,413 miles when he stopped to let his horse graze about the tourist park.

The tourist had a little time and we enjoyed a talk with him. It was near the close of the chat that he divulged the fact that his father, M. F. Heath, took a claim near Arlington in 1878 and the family traveled into Dakota the following year, driving a team of oxen from southern Minnesota. Frank Heath, then a boy of ten, grew up in Dakota, spending the next seventeen years here.

Heath knows Kingsbury county well, as he showed in his conversation, and the reason is that he bored wells over much of it, down around Oldham, in Erwin, where he bored the first two— one of them at Leroy Murdick's store—to Bancroft, where again he got the first water.

Mr. Heath is a World War veteran, but a little grayer about the temples than many of them for he got in only by special effort on account of his age. He is 59 today. [I can't dispute this, not remembering the first few weeks of my life distinctly. According to my folks I was born on October 10th or 11th, 1868—another uncertainty. The old clock was on the bum that day.] Most of his life has been spent with horses and it was to care for them that he got in the army, where he served overseas as a "mule sergeant." * * * *

Gypsy Queen, Heath's mount, is a beautiful horse and hardly shows her eleven years. She is half Kentucky Whip and half Morgan, weighs 1,000 pounds, is a bay. She is gaited and her master can call seven gaits from her but travel is mostly on the walk, with an occasional trot of one kind or another. Heath rides a McClellan saddle, weighs but 120 pounds himself but carries 60 pounds of luggage. He walks much, to relieve the horse. * * * *

Life is good, Heath says, and it is his conviction after a year of travel that people are not all money-grabbing, as some would have us believe. He has found them kind, good, courteous to strangers. And Heath thinks he meets folks in a way to really know them. His experience with them is far different from that of the automobile tourist, who he says gets a lop-sided view of the world, meeting only commercial people, who must make a business of serving him. This tourist who rides horseback and stops at farms gets to know the residents of each community in the home surroundings. It is after a year of such experience in the East, the New England States, the Middle West, the South, and the North, that Heath is saying that people are just folks the same as they have always been.

The traveler came to De Smet from Ramona and went on to Huron. He was asked why he did not come by way of Arlington and replied that he had no relatives there and he remembered the hills south of there and so cut across through Ramona to avoid them. * * * *

Huron is on the James River. Aberdeen, our next principal point, is a few miles west of the James River. The James River country is semi-arid, probably always has been except in a few freak years when the rainfall was heavy. It is in the short grass country that we read about. Around 1879 when almost all first and second choice homestead land had been taken about as far west as De Smet, people began to go over into the James River Valley or bottom.

After a lapse of many years, the country had been somewhat resettled since the 1889-90 egress. Perhaps a few of the old ones had stayed. There had been a few fair to good years which had again attracted land-hungry people. One advantage they had over the earlier settlers was the fact that farming on semi-arid land had greatly improved through the adoption of what was known at that time as the Campbell System. The Campbell system meant this: when the ground was not in any crop, or when it was in a crop that could be cultivated, such as corn, a constant shallow cultivation —you might almost call it irritation or scratching—of the surface was carried on, so as to prevent the capillary moisture from reaching the surface and evaporating. In other words you have a dust mulch about an inch deep or a little more. The capillary moisture, by which of course is meant the sweating of the earth from the subsoil, stops then about an inch below the surface. The roots take up this moisture. Every Western farmer knows about this.

Later in many parts, not only in the semi-arid sections of the plains states, but in parts of Oregon and Washington, they began going this system one better. There would not be moisture enough even if conserved in this way to "make a crop of wheat" as they express it, every year, so a great many of the large farmers took to what they called "summer fallow"—first turning under the green weeds and second, keeping the surface cultivated until time to sow the Fall wheat. In that way, it will be seen, two years subsoil moisture went into one year's crop. I don't know whether this last was really considered part of the Campbell System or not, but anyway it was worked. The Campbell System was worked heavily in this semi-arid region previously mentioned. However, there finally same a time when the land became so dry that there was no moisture to conserve, and of course there were no crops—Campbell System or no Campbell System.

Then again, that was about the time that very large teams came into use, whereas previous to this time a great many people, probably the majority of farmers, had used what we ludicrously called a "foot burner" or walking plow. About the time of this egress I have mentioned they were shifting from walking plows to gang plows and larger teams generally. I don't know about this Jim River Valley country, but I know that in Eastern Oregon they used a great many eight-bottom plows, that is, eight plows in one gang, commonly called a Stockton plow, drawn by fifteen or sixteen horses. Whereas when I was a kid you would generally see two or three horses on one harrow, in these later years you would generally see six or eight, and so on. That may give some idea as to how the farmers of this later period could farm with more or less success, land that produced only a small crop.

Most of the wells drilled by settlers were artesian wells. By artesian well I mean a well that overflows through a pipe. This artesian water was very cold. Most of it was very bad with alkali. A few surface or "dug" wells, as they were called, not penetrating to the artesian basin, were also bad with alkali. Once in a while there was good water. We had to watch out for this.

Gypsy Queen seldom missed a feed of grain. Up to now I don't remember of more than one or two cases when I couldn't buy it if Farmer Jones didn't hand it out to me. Here, outside of the city of Huron, I was in sight of one solitary small farm of some kind. I took a bucket or something and went over there. There was no one at home. The granary was open. There was a small bin of oats. I helped myself to about six pounds of oats and put twenty cents on a chip in the top of the feed measure that was in the bin.

In leaving Huron we soon got on a road designated on my map as a dirt road—and it was a dirt road—a road running mostly due north. This ran through a practically level country. It had been graded up with dirt taken from a ditch on each side. These ditches had blown full of the notorious and pesky Russian thistle with which most Western farmers are pestered. This, much resembles a tumbleweed except that it has probably millions of small stickers and is said to produce millions of seeds. When ripe it rolls over the prairies like a tumbleweed, banks up against the fences—if any—lodges behind grades and fills road ditches. Well, these ditches having been full of this, had just recently been burned, presumably by road workers. There were dozens upon dozens of nests of China pheasant eggs, abandoned of course after the fire, but very recently laid, for they were fresh. For several days my principal diet was bread and coffee and China pheasant eggs.

Not until we entered South Dakota had we found much wheat. On west to Huron, north up the James River Valley to Aberdeen, wheat was a principal crop when there was a crop. Passing up the James River Valley late in May, 1926, last year's straw stacks were still bright, never having seen a drop of rain. It is the way of the climate there—semi-arid, long dry spells.

Queen's feet and legs got a good rest from the rough going, traveling much of the way from Huron to Aberdeen in the bottom of the ditch beside the road where the dirt was firm enough but still flexible.

Aberdeen, S. D.
May 20, 1926.

Dear Folks:

We are resting here today, 3 mi. W. of Aberdeen. The water through these parts is generally bad; mostly artesian. I ran onto a well of good water here, a "surface" well; so I thought we better rest while the drinking is good. Grass is still good here too in spite of the drouth. The soil is very good. The farm buildings are good—indicating prosperity for many years, until last year when crops—mostly wheat—were short. * * * * Queen is O. K. But we crowded her a little too much two or three weeks ago in partly catching up with schedule, so have to go a little slow now. But we'll make it.

Next address will be: Bowman, N. Dak.
* * * *

There is nothing special to write. With love.
(Signed) Frank.

Wahpala, S. D.
June 6, '26.

Dear Folks:

Your letter reached me at Mobridge, O. K. This place is 18 mi. from there across the river on the Sioux Res. It is a little difficult getting feed here but haven't missed one yet.

We are O. K. except rather tired. Resting up today. Camping in the ruins of an old Indian log hut, shingled with dirt. It breaks the wind and will, I hope, turn the rain, if it comes. These parts are a little more than half civilized now. Some farming—a lot of range under fence. No danger.
* * * *

A lot of cleaning up and mending to do, so will close. Love.
(Signed) Frank.

Queen needed re-shoeing. Facilities for shoeing, like opportunities for procuring feed, were far between.

After leaving Wahpala we stayed one night at Mahto, S. D., with Chas. Claymore, part-blood Sioux, and his wife, also part-blood, and family. They treated us fine. Claymore was risking 260 acres of wheat and flax, which ground he was plowing with a tractor. Mrs. Claymore had a large garden. Staying with Claymore was his old grandfather, a regular, typical, full-blood Indian.

It was also in Claymore's vicinity, as I mentioned in my notes, that I saw the first prairie dog. As I see it, a prairie dog is not a dog at all. He more resembles a ground squirrel, or chipmunk in build, but he is about the size of an ordinary gray squirrel, and is brown. He has a bob tail like the chipmunk. His ears more resemble those of a squirrel or chipmunk. He doesn't bark, he chirps. When you approach a prairie dog town there will be quite a number of them above ground chirping at you. I have seen this generally mentioned in stories as barking. Just why he is barking—or rather chirping—ask the prairie dog—I don't know. He is very hard to capture. When he is barking at you he is almost invariably right at the mouth of his hole or den, and if you get too close or throw something at him, he just keels over backward out of sight. I have heard it said that he can dodge a rifle bullet. I doubt this, if it is well aimed, but he has keeled over into the hole just the same, dead, wounded, or alive. I wondered if they could be snared in the same way that we used to snare gophers when I was a boy in Minnesota, but I didn't take time to find out. I believe I had read some account of John C. Fremont, the great trail blazer, having eaten prairie dogs.

A prairie dog town is a dangerous place to ride a horse over or through except in a walk. He is pretty liable to break through into some of these dens which are not too far from the surface, perhaps breaking a leg, usually throwing the rider at best.

I have yet to notice the first time in a prairie country where there is a combination of prairie dogs, short grass and any kind of cactus, even the prickly pear, that grain could be raised with any kind of profit, because, while there may be an occasional wet season, the ground is generally too dry to produce a full crop, and frequently there is no crop at all. In other words, if the climate and altitude are really favorable to grain, they are not favorable to short grass, prairie dogs and cactus. If there is irrigation that is a different thing.

From Notes. June 8, '26: * * * * 11:45, Reached McLaughlin via cut-off.

Traveled: 10½ mi. (1½ by misdirection)—Winding. Prairie and prairie road. Very hilly to level. S. E. of McLaughlin a lot of * * * * flax is being planted in large fields. * * * * Tractors. Dry. "New Erie Tractor Farms," 10,000 A. wheat. Putting up in stable back of Mr. A. W. Heath's shop. He is a horseman. P.M. Laying in—Queen very sore. Trying Hanford's Balsam Myrrh.

June 9, '26. Laying over today, resting. Was *tired out myself* last night, and Queen needed rest badly. She has not been *resting* while we were taking it easy lately because she has been laying out in the cold on the cold ground—with improper feed. Here she is in a fine large (well ventilated) stall with good bed, good prairie hay, good oats (¾ rations) and good water. We can easily reach McIntosh (for horse sale). * * * * Ran into a good bunch here. Mr. Heath chgs. nothing for stall. * * * *

From Signature Book: "June 8, McLaughlin, So. Dak. F. M. Heath put up at my barn this 8 day of June, riding Gypsy Queen, and staid over night.

> (Signed) A. W. Heath,
> McLaughlin, So. Dak."

From Notes. June 11, '26: * * * * 12:35 p.m. Ar'd barn of J. S. Forbes [McIntosh] * * * *

Traveled: 10 mi. Dirt. Some prairie. Rolling. * * * * Some wheat, flax, cattle, bronks. * * * * P.M. Attended sheriff sale of range—stray-horses, about 150 head—scrubs. Sold for $12.50 single to $4.00 in bunches. I bought none. Queen better.

This was my reason for having attended the horse sale: The reader is conversant with the condition of the roads generally, with the fact that feed was obtainable only at long intervals. Mostly in here we were practically paralleling a railroad in country that had been farmed more or less—and more or less successfully—for quite a while. There were towns along the railroad about ten or fifteen miles apart, with, of course, a grain elevator in each town. But it was only at about one elevator in three that we could obtain oats. So we often started from an elevator with thirty or thirty-five pounds of oats to last to the next point where we could obtain them. These were added to the already heavy pack. Then we were pretty well north and pretty well up, and I was camping out and sleeping in the open nearly altogether. Our field bed alone weighed probably about forty pounds. It will be seen that our pack was much too heavy for me to have ridden most of the time, or I might say much of the time, for my weight, added to this dead weight, would have been about equal to murder. I myself was practically worn out. Talk about a man walking a horse down! Queen, with this lame leg, improper shoeing, and a pack nearly as heavy as myself, and sometimes when I was tuckered out, myself added to the weight, had walked me to a frazzle. So, knowing that these long distances were ahead of us for a long way, I decided that I must have a pack horse. I thought perhaps this sale might be a chance to pick one up cheap.

All through this country they were very conversant with the fact that wild range horses, the majority of which were useless, must be gotten off the range or else somebody must pay something for the damage they did to the range. It is pretty well understood in that country that generally speaking one horse damages the range more than ten sheep, while the chances are one sheep is worth about as much as a horse, and is certainly much more readily marketed. The range, it will be understood, either by law or custom is in a sense common or communal property, unless it is under fence. If a man has some under fence, that is his pasture. If a man has horses under fence, that is the owner's business. A kind of special tax—I believe it was only one or two dollars a head—was put on horses on the open range. They were rounded up, I believe, once a year. If branded, the owner had a chance to redeem them. If not branded or redeemed, they were sold at auction. So that was the reason of this horse sale. I laid over a day to see if I could buy a suitable pack horse at a reasonable price. The above note from the memo book at McIntosh gives an idea of about how they sold. There wasn't one in the bunch I wanted. Most of them were too young. (Some of them were pretty good, at that.) Most of these horses were very wild, which of course wouldn't do in this case. Two or three of them appeared to be outlaws. My understanding of the term outlaw as applied to a horse is this: It is well known that a horse is ten times as strong as a man, and that no man can handle a horse by physical strength alone. There are very rare cases where a man and such a horse naturally have an affinity for each other to the extent that the horse loves the man as well as the man loving the horse, and the horse will obey the man just because he loves to do so. It is understood that an outlaw horse is not *usually* just a natural-born man-killer. *Such* a horse is impossible under any circumstances. He has no affection, no sense of gratitude. Not one horse in a million, however, is of this kind. This is a type of insanity. If there is any cure for it except a bullet I don't know of it. This horse is a rare exception even *among outlaws.* This affinity between man and horse—the outlaw that has become an outlaw and is not a natural-born killer—is largely a matter of instinct on both sides. The horse may read instinctively something in the man's expression, but he will invariably verify this impression by smelling the man over before he finally takes up with him. It is presumed that the man has the natural faculty of selecting the horse that is amenable to kind, understanding treatment. The horse selects the man, and the man selects the horse.

With this exception, it is well known that no man can handle a horse except by means of some mechanical device such as tripping or the like, or else through some means of deceiving the horse into believing that the man is physically superior. In other words, not letting the horse know that he can get away with the man. Usually an outlaw horse is one which through accident, or otherwise, possibly through the carelessness or misjudgment of the man, has found out that he is greatly the man's superior physically. He is outside the man's law.

While we are at it we might carry this a little further. If this same man we spoke of, who has a natural affinity for horses—sometimes such a man is referred to as half-horse—gets hold of the outlaw horse, presuming that the horse naturally has some sense of affection, then the chances are that the horse will do anything for him. At the same time he might kick the h—e—double out of any person that goes near him. This is what we sometimes refer to as a one-man horse. Of course there are horses that are not quite so extreme in their choice of a master. They will just naturally make up with some people through instinct, and won't have anything to do with others, unless it is to fight them. They will make up with a few.

Take for instance a horse that has killed a man, even if he killed him accidentally or during fright, I don't believe that horse ever forgets that he has killed a man. I believe that some experienced horseman—shall we say a horse psychologist?—can tell by the look in the horse's eyes or make a pretty good guess from the movements of his ears and all that, that the horse has killed a man. I do not know and have never asked whether Gypsy Queen had ever killed a man, but I shouldn't be a bit surprised if she had.

The only horse at this sale that would have done me any good so far as behavior was concerned had one hip knocked down, so I didn't think this would add to our appearance. Therefore we passed on without a pack horse.

There were quite a number of Indians at this horse sale, stalwart young bucks dressed just like the other cowboys, generally fairly high-heeled boots, blue denim overalls with a wide roll at the bottom coming about half way up the boot leg, ordinary shirt, and usually some kind of a jacket if the weather required, possibly a mackinaw, and a five-gallon hat. I didn't notice one of these Indians who attended the sale who resembled the old proverbial Indian of the magazine cover. (I did see a few of these—crossing Standing Rock Indian Reservation.) You would have to look twice at some of these boys to determine whether they were Indian or white. You might guess wrong at that. These boys and the white boys mixed amicably. It would seem that some of these horses that were sold had over-run from the Indian Reservation. Hence I suppose these Indians had an interest in them. I am presuming that whatever a horse brought above the general tax or penalty or whatever you might call it, went to the owner if the horse was branded. One reason I presume this is that I heard one of these Indian boys remark to some of the other fellows as they were carrying me in their car back to town, "Well, we will have a little spending money out of this anyhow."

From Notes. June 17, '26: * * * * 8 p.m. Ar'd farm H. A. Hilden, ¾ mi. W. Reeder, local foreman, Theo. L. Olson. * * * * Still some "pioneer" buildings. Passed one sod house—ruins of others. * * * *

From Signature Book: "Reeder, N. Dak., June 18, 1926. Frank M. Heath stayed at the farm here (¾ mi. W.) last night with Gypsy Queen.
(Signed) Theo. L. Olson, Foreman."

From Signature Book: "Bowman, N. D., June 19, 1926. Frank M. Heath with the mare Gypsy Queen stayed at my barn here last night.
(Signed) M. J. Donahue,
Bowman, N. D.

Bowman, N. D.,
June 20, 1926.
Dear Folks:

Yours of 7th came to me here. We are making it O.K. only we are behind 11 days of the 12 days we started late this spring. Our schedule is that close (here) that we could not hold the time we made up. We probably will reach there 10 or 12 days late. Better late than kill the horse.

We are having cool weather here, which helps. Have been delayed some by rain—caught out in several, but we don't mind that. Am traveling today as we took ½ day off yesterday.

Will you excuse this short note. I'm busy *all* the time except when I'm asleep. Address me next at: Livingstone, Mont. (hold 30 days). * * * *

(Signed) Frank.

From Notes. June 19, '26: 6 p.m. Ar'd place of Clyde Baker, Rhame, N. D. * * * * Country west of Bowman a little more broken. Many buttes, some red, others yellow, in all directions. About ¾ is natural, treeless prairie. * * * *

June 20, '26: * * * * Noon, feeding—own oats, own lunch, at farm of O. J. Olson, 10 mi. E. of Marmarth. Last house E. of Marmarth. 3:30, Entering [a little spur of] Badlands. 5:45, Ar'd Marmarth over Little Mo. Put up in old deserted barn. No hay. Cold showers all day. Feet wet. Bakery closed. Got lunch in tea room—no chg.—Bucked cold wind all day. Country as yesterday. 12 mi. Badlands (in sight). * * * *

For Notes. June 21, '26: Cold wind, clear. Queen very restless last night. Broke loose—hunting for feed. * * * * Having Queen reset in front—she is pretty sore in left. Laying over today. * * * * Elevator man gave me two feeds oats. Shoe man fixed shoe free. Fixed sack on Queen's leg with "suspenders"— burlap. Party shut off water.

About the shoeing. We sure were lucky. Ran into a regular natural born and scientific horse shoer. He knew the inside of a horse's foot and all about it. One of the best jobs of shoeing I ever had done. I didn't even have to explain much to him. He saw it. He leveled the foot properly, leaving it a little high on the outside, made the shoe a little wide, nailed the inside even with the shoe—hoof and shoe even—and actually spread the left side nearly to cover the shoe while nailing. This greatly relieved Queen. She went a long way without much trouble.

Second, about the man shutting off the water. There was a well out in front of this deserted stable where we were putting up—a well with a pump. If I thought anything about it, I guess I took it to be a public well. As Queen's left leg and foot were badly inflamed, on account of the hell she had been through during the last three or four weeks, I was putting in most of my time for a half day before we had her reshod trying to allay the inflammation with cold water. Somehow the pump went wrong, or it may be I had pumped the well dry. A man, who proved to be the owner of the well, came from a residence near by and somehow gave me to understand that I was taking undue liberties with another man's pump.

Third. This led to my adoption of a plan of wrapping the leg from the knee down in burlap to retain the water while not totally excluding the air, so as not to require one-tenth as much water, only dousing now and then to remove the heat. The reason for the suspender was that I didn't deem it right to tie this burlap tight enough that it would not work down. The suspender simply consisted of putting another burlap sack over Queen's withers and suspending therefrom the burlap that was wrapped on the leg. I followed this plan wherever water was scarce for thousands of miles, successfully. It isn't necessary to mention that this moisture from the burlap would also cool and moisten the foot.

From Notes. June 21, '26: continued: Funny Note:—1st thing when I ar'd in the rain last night one of two boys, about 12, asked, 'Say, Mister, you ain't saw no colts?' I hadn't. They found the colts, brought them in out of the rain.

I have a mental picture of those two kids and their mounts. Somehow their demeanor, in spite of the boy's somewhat awkward language—and God knows I have no room for criticism of anyone's English—their solicitude for their colts, the earnest expression of this boy that asked the question, stand out in my memory. Probably twelve, he had outgrown his pants about eight inches, and they were held up by one suspender. Broken rimmed straw hat, red hair, freckled face, sunburnt nose, very earnest gray-blue eyes. If I were able to draw a picture of this boy—or have I? They rode until they had found those colts and brought them in after dark, put them into a lean-to and nailed up the door. They were not going to leave those colts out in the storm, you bet! And they didn't.

From Notes. June 22, '26: Queen much improved by rest, soaking and shoeing. Had good camp, feed, while here. Nice place. Leaving Marmarth 7:40 a.m.—10:00, Crossing state line into Montana. * * * *

From Signature Book: "Baker, Mont. (3½ mi. E. and 1 mi. S. of) Frank M. Heath with Gypsy Queen are here at noon, the 22 of June, 1926.

(Signed) Fred Hasty."

From Notes. June 23, '26: Fair, warm. Queen much better. Slept well in manger. Left Baker 7:10 a.m. * * * * 6 p.m. Ar'd ranch of John Naujoch * * * * across prairie through gates. Rolling to hilly. Ground most in pasture. Some wheat, little rye. Some wheat heading out, other just up.

Traveled: 25 mi. Gravel 8 mi. R. 1. * * * * Bal. dirt, fair side.

Note: Mr. Naujoch was hailed out in 1922-24-25, dried out 1917-1919. This year very dry. Pasture about gone. 1924-25 hail ruined grass and all. Has a bunch of Hereford shorthorn cattle, milking strain. Believes will have to quit. Sod bldgs—and log. Was in Prussian Guards. Son at home has crippled ankle—a good worker. They have a load of oat hay for which they paid $15. Slept in good warm bed. Meals.

June 24, '26: Leaving John Naujoch 8:30 a.m. No charge. Real hospitality. (Formulas, advice.)

Note: Here I got blue gumbo that seems to be of a superior quality for packing feet. * * * *

This is as good a place as any to make it clear what a lot of trouble I had in different parts of the country in finding the right kind of mud with which to pack Queen's feet as one means of keeping down the road fever. Where mud was obtainable I often packed the shoes full several times a day. Up to about this time, usually speaking, mud was mud, some kinds a little better than others. Of course sandy loam wouldn't do much good, even if wet. But all through these different spurs of the Badlands, of different colors and hues, I found that sometimes there was no proper mud available.

And another point I want to make plain parenthetically, is that judging from my experience and what little I had heard, seen and known about adobe, dobie and gumbo, they are, you might say, cousins. Adobe, of which the adobe building blocks are made, is well known. This is generally nearly black. Then there is what in other parts is more familiarly known as dobie. Sometimes what I first mentioned as adobe may be confused with what is more commonly known as dobie. But there is sometimes a difference. You can hardly draw the line. Dobie can be of different colors, generally black, brown, or red. The red dobie is of two classes at least, not easily distinguished by the naked eye. First, there is one kind of red dobie that won't produce anything much but perhaps a little tar weed. Then there is another red clay, either dobie or confused with it, that if cultivated and planted at exactly the right season, will produce more or less of a crop of wheat. But what more particularly concerned us was the fact that I would pack Queen's feet today with some of this red dobie which would have a tendency to allay the fever and moisten the frog. I would pack it again the same night with what looked like the same thing, and it would bake hard as a brick, after having drawn the moisture out of the foot. It was a great detriment. While I am not a chemist, I am presuming it was some peculiar composition that turns the clay dark red.

Then there is still another earth formation commonly known as gumbo, which seemed to be, as stated, a kind of second cousin. Gumbo is more likely to be either black or grayish blue—not necessarily blue clay. This grayish blue gumbo or sort of gumbo as nearly as I could make out, was what I used in packing Queen's feet at Naujoch's place, which was in the proximity of the Badlands. Of course, as stated, I was just trying these things tentatively before applying them over night. So I tried some of this blueish gumbo and it seemed to me equal to antiphlogistin or Denver mud. In fact, there is something much resembling it in looks and in effect which is sold on the market as hoof packing. There was here at this place far from transportation a small mountain of it. If this had been on a railroad track it might have been worth a small fortune. But located as it was, of course I couldn't take it with me.

From Notes. June 24, '26 continued: 6:30 p.m. Ar'd ranch of Billy Mann, 6 mi. S. of Ismay, N. D. First try. Rolling to hilly with red, pink, yellow and white buttes on all sides. Sometime "sawtooth" ranges of rocky hills. Sand banks and sandstone. Some dobie. A few stunted trees on some hills. Mostly in pasture. Ranches 3-4 miles apart. Little grain in poor condition. * * * * Small patches alfalfa, sweet clover. Wheat heading to just up.

Traveled: 19 mi.—1 by error. Prairie road and across prairie through gates. Dirt. Queen missing feed, 1st. time this year. Mr. Mann formerly trained and sold polo ponies and hunters.

Shipped them to England. Was at Green Spring Valley Hunt with car load of grade hunters off range in Montana in 1905. Rode there at some meets. Mr. Redmond A. Stewart was Master of Hounds when Mr. Mann was shipping horses to Balt. Still producing a few good hunters and polo ponies.

For a long time now we had been terribly annoyed by nose flies. I know of no one kind of fly that causes horses more misery than this nose fly. It looks somewhat like the small size bot-fly. It has much the same maneuvers in zigzagging all over h—e—double. The difference in the ultimate operations of the nose fly is that instead of stinging almost anywhere it enters the horse's nostrils and clings there. That is what the flap is for, to keep the fly from darting into the nostril. This seems adequate protection. Hardly did I see a team of horses working without their noses being protected with some kind of a flap. A few wore wire muzzles. All through the country, on a bright day, you might see horses on the range or in pasture going along sliding their noses on the ground with a look of misery in their eyes.

From Notes. June 25, '26: * * * * 6:15, Ar'd camp of Powder River Land and Cattle Co. at Ash Glenn. * * * * Winding through a canyon little W. of Knowlton. Saw some pretty fair pine timber. Passed many very neat, well constructed cabins belonging to P.R.L.C. mostly (two homesteaders.) * * * * About 10,000 head cattle, saddle horses. Do not irrigate but raise —under fence—a lot of Mont. blue joint for hay. * * * *

I spent the night in a cabin with—you might call him a line rider. His most responsible job was counting, not the whole herd, but the marked cattle, as he called them. That is, amongst a bunch of say several hundred head that were on this part of the range, some were "marked"—as to natural color, that is. When this bunch would come to drink, his job was to look out for the marked ones. If any of them were missing, something was wrong and riding must be done. If the marked cattle were all there and the bunch seemed normal, it passed at that, at least for the time being.

Blue joint is a bright grass, the blades of which grow about a foot high or more, with stem growing up from each plant about three feet high, bearing a kind of seed tassel, a little bit similar to broom grass. This makes a very good hay, though the yield per acre is not very heavy. It is not confined to this country. We used to make such hay in South Dakota when I was a kid. It is particularly fine for horses. This hay was put up with buck rakes, at this particular ranch, and the cattle were turned into it. That is, a piece would be fenced off, the cattle turned in until this was fed up, then they would be given access to another section of it.

This outfit here raised their own saddle horses. They never sold a horse or pony. The first time a saddle horse ever lost his feet in running down hill under a rider he was turned out of the saddle horse bunch. All he had to do after that until he died a natural death was to work with several others on a hay rake or buck during haying season. That was not altogether a matter of policy but of humanity.

From Notes. June 26, '26: Leaving 7:45—11 a.m. fording Powder River (pronounced Puder) at Wiles, that is, Geo. Mayer's sheep ranch. * * * * Lot of quicksand in Powder R. Ford at Wiles hard bottom. River deep today (3 or 4 feet). Sometimes 20 ft. and 1 mile wide. (When in flood.) Noon, feeding, getting dinner at Mispah with Mrs. Murphy, 50 cts. Mr. Murphy brought 1st stock cattle from Tex. in 1881 for N. H. Co. 6:15, Ar'd Hill ranch (deserted), former home of Mrs. Sydna Sanders (Sanders a judge) of Butte. Was informed a good spring here. It is covered with scum. Got water fairly clear by use of a bottle. Has "life" in it. Boiling it. Drank little before discovered polly-wogs. Hilly. 2-3 isolated patches grain. Many log dwellings. Saw 9 log bldgs in one group (deserted). Big 2 story log house by barn, etc.

Traveled: 22 miles via winding bottom rd. through hills to Mispah, then Y.S.T. [Yellowstone Trail] through picturesque beautifully colored buttes and hills to here. [Hill Ranch.]

This was one case where it was lucky to be out of luck. I had heard quite a little about the Powder and its quicksands, and would have made quite a turn to get to our next objective, Miles City, had I gone by the way of the bridge. But the bridge had washed out quite recently, so my next best bet was Wiles Ford. I thought I might as well chance it there as at the site of the bridge, seeing that I cut off sixteen miles. I was advised to make diligent inquiries before I undertook the ford, as it was a fact that during these floods the quicksand pockets changed. A way across the river that had been hard bottom last week might be full of quicksand, or as I have previously expressed it, quick mud, today. The old settlers had a way of feeling out this situation, hence the advantage of inquiry. By making inquiry and following the directions we got across O. K.

From Notes. June 27, '26: Clear, warm. * * * * Taking side trip to Venable ranch to see pack horse. Leaving Queen in (wrong) pasture. 11, man took me back to get her. * * * * Mr. J. M. Venable, Miles City, local, handles about 20,000 per year, has about 2,000 on hand usually. Raises about 1,000 colts per year. Keeps about 150 to 500 cattle. Raises little alfalfa, cuts Mont. blue joints, ½ to 1 ton per acre. Orson's Bald Hornet (?) brown belted, white stockings, black white, disqualified Paddy Ryan, world's champion cowboy 1925 at Miles City. Several other noted buckers, including High Tower, a big, beautiful bay—known to all cowboys. Furnishes this year 25 all-white horses for wild horse race at Miles City, 4th July. * * * * Will ship carload to England—London horse show. * * * *

This horse High Tower stands out in my memory. He was large and beautiful for a range horse. As I remember him he was a solid dark bay with brown markings, and so high up off the ground that it would scare a tenderfoot like me to look at him, much less try to ride him. He had that powerful, wilful look about his head, and that eye that we have been talking about, that said plain as day, "You will never conquer me!"

The 20,000 head handled per year mentioned in the note means that this man, as he told me, bought up whole brands, picked out the few that he wanted, and would then ship a trainload or so to the Butte horse cannery, getting four or five dollars a head for them, less freight. It was considered a blessing too to get them off the range.

I had made this side trip in search of a pack horse. He didn't have anything that I wanted as a pack horse. Most of them were wild. He had just run in a big bunch from which to select these horses for the rodeo at Miles City on the 4th of July, including these champion buckers mentioned. The one horse for sale that I thought would be amenable in our circumstances was too badly bunged up. He wasn't good on his underpinning.

I was asked to stay to dinner, as they called it—the midday meal. The main dish was a large portion of boiled beef. I ate heartily of this.

One fellow had a horse he wanted to put in the races, but it had slightly sprained a leg. I tried to explain to him how to treat it with gunny sacking and cold water as described, but he couldn't seem to get the idea—he left it too loose.

Next day I was plugging along toward Miles City when one of the boys from this ranch overtook us, riding one horse and leading another, a show horse. "Hello," he says, "you are making pretty good time." I replied, "Oh, pretty fair considering my horse is tired from the pack." "How did you like that hoss meat you ate yesterday?" he inquired. "Fine," I told him, "best horse meat I ever ate." "The Boss is trying to popularize horse meat. He won't eat any other kind." "Fine," I said, I hope without any change of countenance.

Chapter II

OVER THE ROCKIES

MILES CITY, MONTANA
June 29, 1926

Received of: Frank M. Heath, horseback tripper, twenty-five dollars ($25.00) for one brown mare 7 years old, two white hind feet and branded on right hip, B. H., on left shoulder (   )

(Signed) Ben BigHeade

This was the "pack horse" that broke my leg in Yellowstone Park, Wyoming. I packed her to Mammoth, Yellowstone Park, 300 miles. I never rode this horse one step except from where we were camped on Tongue River to the shop to get her shod.

May 26, 1926

Dear Comrade Heath:

* * * * The interest to Raynor has been paid and I am willing to let the matter of my fee remain until such times as you return, because I realize the difficulties under which you are traveling and that perhaps you will need all avaliable funds before the journey is completed. I do think that if possible you should leave a balance on hand here in case of emergencies, but will leave that to your own judgment. I enclose herewith money order in the sum of $76.00 representing rent for April and May, and also your Legion Card for 1926.

Wishing you continued success,

Fraternally yours,
[From Mr. Cissel—name omitted
through oversight.]

206

THE SILVER SPRING NATIONAL BANK
SILVER SPRING, MD.

June 15, 1926

Mr. Frank M. Heath,
Miles City, Montana.
Dear Mr. Heath:

Replying to your letter of the 5th instant, I beg to advise that Mr. Joseph C. Cissel has deposited the sum of $48.00 in your own name, and stated that hereafter the tenant on your place will make his deposits here. Of course they will be credited hereafter to you, and NOT to Mr. Cissel's account.

Mr. Cissel explained to us that Mr. Kimball had left and that he had secured a new tenant. Mr. Cissel also stated that the amount mentioned above represented that amount due you at this time. * * * *

As requested, I enclose several bank checks for your use.

Yours very truly,
(Signed) Fred L. Lutes,
Asst. Cashier

From Notes. July 1, '26: * * * * 6:45 (p.m) Ar'd place of Coley Tart, E. suburbs Forsyth, Mont. via Y. S. T. Better farms from Rosebud W. Saw one silo. Wheat very poor to fair. Some bearded rye, some pretty fair corn. Stock.

Traveled: 25 mi. Y.S.T. Gravel 16 mi. Bal. dirt, fair side.

July 2, '26: Clear, cool. Slept fine in stable. Horses had fine time in corral. Grass, alfalfa. Mr. Tart bought eggs, fruit, from Spring Valley, Minn. * * * * Leaving 8:15. No chg.

From Signature Book: "Forsyth, Mont., July 2, '26: Frank M. Heath camped at my place last night.

(Signed) Coley Tart."

Myers, Mon.,
July 4, '26.

Dear Folks:

Though we have traveled quite a way more than we expected we will reach Billings the 7th probably, in just the time laid out.

Am laying over here today, 9 mi. S.W. from Myers by a fine spring and shade.

Feed is a problem, but I usually manage to get it somehow.
It's 5:30, and between working, mending, cooking greens, etc.,
and taking good care of legs of two horses, I've been busy all day.

(Signed) Frank.

What a difference it made to get that pack off Queen! Mr. Elwin
Bastain of McLaughlin had given me an old English saddle on
June 9th, which I had mailed ahead to Miles City from Bowman.
After getting the pack horse I used this old English saddle on Queen.
With only this saddle and my weight she tripped it off, while
Cheyenne Belle, a horse four years younger and probably two hundred pounds heavier, slowed up under the same pack Gypsy Queen
had been carrying. This being rid of the pack and having had better
shoeing not far back, added to the fact that I was still using plenty
of burlap and cold water, enabled us from this time on to gain back
a little of the time that we started late from Princeton, instead of
barely keeping even while Queen was gradually going to pieces.

We were passing through a comparatively small irrigation project.
On many of the farms beets were the principal crop. One night I
camped at a kind of a makeshift stable. The vegetation was rank
all about here, with some alfalfa. When outside of the road, we
had been traveling much of the time through an inch or more of
water—it was slightly flooded. This was mighty fine for the horses'
feet, but hell for mosquitoes. Leaving the horses to graze, having
hobbled Cheyenne Belle, I had walked down some forty rods to a
beet farmer's place to get oats. When I got back both horses were
beating it out of there at a gait that made me run to overtake them.
In spite of the hobbles Belle was in a kind of a lope. The fact that
her front feet were hobbled about a foot apart would prevent her
walking much, or trotting, but she was going some just the same.
Queen was following. I managed to get them back to the old stable.
This was about sundown. The air was black with mosquitoes. The
horses were, not frantic, but crazy. I had all I could do to keep them
from knocking me over in their misery and perhaps trampling me
underfoot, for all I know. Anyway, I tied them to posts that happened to be handy at the end of the makeshift stable, and as quickly
as possible took armfuls of the old banking—a combination of straw
and manure—back about twenty-five feet, and built three smudges.
The very slight current of air was shifting from northeast to east to
southeast and back, hence the three smudges. This kept the mosquitoes down. This smudging is a well known trick amongst pioneers.

We used to do a lot of it in Dakota in the early days when the grass was rank and rain plentiful. I believe these were the largest mosquitoes I have ever seen, and the most numerous. If the smoke was too much for the horses, all they had to do was to put their noses to the damp ground.

From Notes. July 14, '26: * * * * 5 p.m. Ar'd Livingstone. Camping in brush N. of city. Spent 1½ hr. investigating, fixing fence. Good pasture, creek (bad water).

Traveled: 22 mi. via Y. S. T. * * * * Gravel, 18 mi., fair side, ¼ distance, Bal. dirt, R. 2. * * * * Rolling to level. Alfalfa in bottom.

Special Note:
Billings to Livingstone, 128.
Total more than schedule, 107 miles.
Total to Livingstone, Mont., 5365 miles.

July 15, 26: Fair. Rained last night. Slept in hay loft of Mr. (name omitted), Livingstone, Mont. Laying over today. Some fever, Queen's left front. Later: Had Queen shod all round new.

July 16, '26: Fair. Leaving camp on "Coney Island,"—7:45. 8:30, leaving Livingstone. 10:45, find have gone 6½ mi. W. Y.S.T. by error—or lack of sign. Right trail (to Gardiner). Had no plain sign while Bozman line showed yellow post. Am saving 1 of the 6½ miles by cutting through ranch of John Tapp and others. * * * * 5:30 Ar'd farm of Focht Bros., 9 mi. S. Livingstone, via Y.S.T., W. of river.

Traveled: 21 mi. (13 by error)—Gravel 10 mi., very poor side, dirt 3 mi. (across farms in returning to right rd.) and stony 8 mi. Followed a creek west and returned. Rolling. After on right rd. followed Y.S.T. but cut over a hill. Alfalfa, stock, very little grain.

Note: Mts. from Billings on, on S. and E., very rugged, rather beautiful, with snow here and there on shady side—none on tops.

July 17, '26: Fair. Leaving Focht Bros. 8:30. Got bread, milk, pasture, no chg. (Advice on founder, formula.) Noon, Quite a way from nowhere and no oats. 12:45, Stopped at a ranch 1 mi. N. Emigrant—no oats. 1:30, In Emigrant—dilapidated, nearly deserted town—no oats. 2 p.m. Ar'd Murphy Ranch, 1 mi. S. Emigrant (Hardy Painter, renter.) Would have had to go 2 mi. to see Painter but for Geo. Larson, hired man, who came to the rescue. Let me have 36 lbs., 50c. P. O. Emigrant. Geo. is

Norwegian. This ranch contains 7,000 acres. Put up 300 tons hay. Have 800 in cult.—have 2,800 sheep on the ranch, mostly in mts. in summer. G. L. (Geo. Larson) here on ranch 8 years (and don't think he owns it.)

George Larson came up on a pretty good strong horse and asked, "Vere you goin'?" Well, I told him I was headed for Gardiner at this time, handing him a card. "Vat vas you askin' de vimen for?" "By gosh, I was asking them for oats. The lady said I would have to see her husband." "Vell, dat's a long vay to go to ask somebody about oats. Ay tank ay let you have some." "Maybe they wouldn't like it," I suggested. "Vell, I guess dey like it all right." So he steered me into the barn, away from the flies, where there was a manger full of good hay, and brought me about a bushel of oats. Then he had to go away. "You stay right hare. Ay be back pretty soon." In about fifteen or twenty minutes he came back. I had quite a talk with him. I said, "You will have to take something for these oats. I wasn't aiming to bum them. Glad to get them at all." "Oh," he says, "Dat's all right. Dem few oats!" "Well," I said, "in order to be sure I haven't raised any family disturbance, I'd better pay you something." "Vell, all right. You might give me fifty cents. I tell de lady you pay. Dat'll be all right vit de ole man too." It was all of two miles down the road that I passed the haying outfit.

From Notes. July 17, '26 continued: 6 (p.m.) At Big Creek—no grass. At Midway—grass scarce (sheep). 6:40, Passed ditch, plenty yellow clover hay—expected to find everything fine at "big old house" described by Geo. Larson. 7 p.m., Through 2 gates, over R.R. to (another) old place—some feed, water scarce —no chance turn out acct. crop peas. 7:30, Reached "old house." Fine creek but no grass. 9 p.m., Ar'd ranch of Geo. A. Pool, 25½ mi. S. of Livingstone, P. O. Carbella, Mont. local. Back ¼ mi. to stack yards.
   Traveled: 29 mi. (½ to stack and return)—Dirt. * * * * Fair side. Rolling to hilly via Y.S.T., W. side. Environs of River Valley narrow mostly. * * * *
   July, 18, '26: Cloudy. Bivouacked at stack alfalfa. No water. Leaving stack 5:45 to get break. [breakfast] went further on reached creek so as to soak Queen's feet. Had hell of a time getting started. Belle rolled with pack, 6:45. Noon, Feeding, plenty of alfalfa in rd. way—by ditch. 1 mi. W. Corwin Springs.

Came through about 5 mi. narrow defile, rugged. Here it is wider. Some ranches, irrigated—small fields alfalfa—little grain. 5 p.m. Ar'd Gardiner, via Y.S.T. * * * * 6:30, Came to "spring" in Yellowstone Park. * * * *

Special Note: Total to Mammoth, Wyo., 5,440 miles.

> July 19, '26,
> Mammoth Springs, Wyo.

Dear Folks:

Address Butte, Mont. I'm O. K., only in little pain from kick. Not serious. Love,

> (Signed) Frank.

From Signature Book: "Yellowstone Park, Wyo. This is to certify that Frank M. Heath arrived at Yellowstone Park Headquarters Station today (July 19th, 1926) riding bay mare known as Gypsy Queen.

> (Signed) Julius L. Green,
> Acting Chief Park Ranger."

> Corwin Springs, Mont.,
> Sunday, July 25, '26.

Dear Folks:

First of all: Don't be alarmed or worry; because I am on the gain and will be on the road again in a few days. But the fact is, Cheyenne Belle came very near breaking my leg last Monday. I still am not able to walk on it. It is discolored from a little above the knee to my toes. She got me right on the knee cap. She is shod, and should receive a prize for good hard kicking. It was my own carelessness. She is an Indian Bronk, and *inclined* to kick, though she is not what you might call *bad*. Where I was camped in Yellowstone Park, three miles in from Gardiner (the northern entrance) is rather an isolated spot on the Old Trail to Mammoth. It is rough and stony and bushy there and a hard place in which to get around. It seemed to be a terrible place for flies of many kinds, especially the old-fashioned horse fly. They were driving the horses frantic. Belle had reached a point of viciousness. It was while I was trying to kill off the horse flies that she got me.

Short of it is, I put in 2½ miserable days there before I felt able to move out. Hobbled about on sticks and got along somehow.

Thursday morning I got packed up somehow. Stopped in Gardiner 1¼ hours in doing a little trading and reached ¼ mi. West of here 2:30 p.m.; having stopped on the way to "give horses the nose bags." Only way I could mount was to get Queen in a ditch.

Here the man's name is Chris Foss. It happened that I had halted here a week ago today on my way in to make inquiries about a camping place and buy eggs. * * * *

It so happens that the place where I started to camp Thurs. p.m. is about the last for many miles where I could get grain and water. Otherwise I might have been fool enough to have gone further. As it is I had ridden too far. * * * *

Pretty soon Mr. Foss came by in leaving the field; we had a short conversation and in true Western style he suggested that "I could have camped back at the Bldgs. under the trees."

"I saw no grass there," I told him, "and thought I'd feed on this." "A little alfalfa hay wouldn't break me," he replied. It looked like rain. He suggested I return to the buildings. I felt so tough I thought I'd "stick it out" where I was and take a chance. * * * * Back came Mildred with an invitation to supper. She helped me mount.

Well, the next morning my leg could not possibly have been sorer than it was. I had ridden too soon and too far; though of course I had to get out of that isolated camp in the Park. I had fully expected to continue on that day. But when Mr. Foss came to the barn, a little late (for they irrigate far into the night) and cheerily invited me in to breakfast, I explained to him that to move on, for a few days, in my present condition was impossible. It didn't take him long to give me to understand that I was welcome to stay until able to travel.

And so I am still here, hobbling about on improvised crutches and cane. And there are three beautiful points yet to relate. None of the family evince any hurry for me to leave, though they are about the busiest bunch I ever saw; the few little things I cannot do for myself are done with the utmost courtesy and unaffectedness. I am regularly at the family table, saving myself lots of pain, cooking. * * * *

I'll reach Butte a few days late. That's the next mail point. With love,   (Signed) Frank.

Corwin Springs, Mont.,
(Near Gardiner, N. Entrance
to Park)
July 29, '26.

Dear Folks:

I guess my leg is a little better; anyhow the swelling is nearly gone; and I can bear a little weight on it. But as this is the eleventh day since I was kicked I *should* be O. K.

So I am going today to the U. S. Veterans' Bureau Hospital at Helena. I wrote up there last Fri. the 23rd and just received a reply. I should have gone long ago, but was not quite clear as to whether I was eligible for admission. Of course this leg has nothing to do with my military service. I had heard that the Reed Johnson bill passed in 1924 gave any World War Vet a right to hospitalization in any V. B. Hosp. But I was not sure whether that part of the law still stood or whether it had been amended as were some other features. Then too the law gives us admittance "if the facilities permit." And of course I did not know whether they were full up or not.

In replying to my inquiry then they sent me a blank to fill out. And they require a certified copy of my Discharge. If I remember correctly my atty. has my discharge along with other papers. If not, it is somewhere with some papers in the box I sent you in 1925 c/o Gene. Don't bother looking for it, or worry about it. I have with me photostatic copies of my Discharge and I feel certain that and V. B. letters I have will admit me.

* * * *

The particular landmarks here that have become most fixed in my dull and aching comprehension are: Dome Mt. on this (N) side to the N. W. It is symmetrical but not tall—the timber line extending to the top. Across the river too is a smaller Mt. the name of which I have not learned. To the east of this is a tall, "slim" or steep Mt., very symmetrical, upon which I never tire of gazing. It is Electric Peak. Still farther to the east is a long (from E. to W.) Mt. in a pocket on this side of which the snow lies the year around.

Well, as Mr. Foss is going to take me to the R. R. Station at Corwin Springs and as I have a few things to throw together I must close. I'm in no pain to speak of when I don't try to walk. The horses are in a good pasture where there are plenty of shade and water, so the rest will not do Queen any harm—

though she is in no particular need of it. This is going to interfere with my schedule. I'll be late getting through the Mts.
between Klamath Lake and Weed, California. But I'll just have
to make it. I'll get to Spokane two or three weeks late. With
love,

> (Signed) Frank.

> U. S. V. B. Hospital,
> Helena, Mont.,
> July 31, '26.

Dear Folks:

Well I arrived here O. K. late the 29th. Phoned out from
Helena, got admittance informally. Yesterday went in Hosp.
car back to V. Bureau in Helena and was formally admitted
simply on strength of a letter I have from Veterans' Bureau in
Wash.—in which they denied my appeal for compensation,
spring of 1925. All the Regional Office here required was my
"C. number." They are treating me fine. I have never come in
contact with a better bunch of Drs. Everybody is good-natured
and cheerful. They are of course going through the usual red
tape.

After I got back here yesterday they x-rayed my knee and put
me to bed. Had supper and breakfast in bed. Think of the contrast between roughing it, as I've been doing, and lying here in
pajamas.

10 a.m. Well, a Dr. just informed me that I have a broken
knee cap. So it's blamed lucky I came here. And I'm very glad
that the law allows me this hospitalization free, or as a part of
the reward for my W. W. service, without being a pauper. They
tell me I'll be here about 6 weeks. Of course I regret this,
especially as it will make me very late in getting through the
Rocky Mts. And of course it knocks my schedule all to smith-
ereens.

I have no intention of abandoning the trip. I hope to keep
traveling all winter once I get started. I'll simply travel six to
eight weeks behind schedule.

11:15 a.m. Two Drs. just looked me over again. Pronounce
knee cap only "partially fractured" which is not quite so bad.
They believe I can leave here in less than six weeks. I hope so.
I need the time. They tell me here that there have been several
new rules in the V. B. and that they believe I can now get some

compensation by re-appealing my case. I am going to try. Don't look for me before some time in Oct. I'm sorry of course; but we can't help it. Don't worry, but rather, feel glad for me that I am so fortunate.

Write me here, U. S. Veterans' Hospital No. 72, Helena, Mont., Ward 3 C. With love,

(Signed) Frank.

P. S. (1 p.m.) There will be no benefit gained to Queen by this layover. On the other hand she will have become "soft" by the time we get started. She was in good shape when I left her. She is in good hands, with Mr. Chris Foss near Corwin Springs, Mont. She, with Belle, is in a pasture where there are plenty of grass, water and shade.

(Signed) Frank.

Any letter (not papers) arriving there for me up to Aug. 20 please forward to above address.

Frank.

U. S. Vets. Hosp., Helena, Mont.,
Aug. 4, '26.

Dear Folks:

Your letter of 2nd with some previous ones was forwarded to me here.

Of course you already have my letter of day or so ago in which I inform you of a broken knee cap. I am getting along O. K. Soreness which extended all up and down leg is nearly gone; not much pain. Knee cap fortunately, and strangely, so they say, while broken square across, was held together and in place by the joint capsule. This means a great deal. It saved me the pain of adjusting or "setting," or worse yet, cutting into and wiring together. It saves the necessity of a cast, which I imagine is not a very pleasant thing in hot weather and it will, I suppose, facilitate a speedy recovery. The latter is very essential as it will, I hope, allow me to get on the road again in time to get over the Rockies before winter—say in Sept. I always was lucky. * * * *

I didn't tell you the particulars of how it happened I got kicked, did I? Well, to begin with, Cheyenne Belle, my pack horse, isn't so very bad. I bought her of a Cheyenne Indian at Miles City for twenty-five bucks. I had turned down several "prospects" all the way from $4.50 to $50.00—saying nothing of one a man offered to give me at McIntosh, N. Dak. if I'd go out of my way 16 miles and return (or 32 miles) after him. But the gentleman told me frankly that he (the horse) was a jug head.

Belle is a pretty fair specimen of Indian bronco—or as the Indian put it, "half pony and half horse." She is rather blocky and will weigh, if she ever happens to get fat, about 1,200 pounds. Brown with white stripe in face, two white feet and several brands. She had packed a roundup bed, so my pack didn't bother her. She neck reins readily and is said to have been used for roping. She has not a bad head except her eye. Back of the eye there is something hard to read. At times (in fact generally) the expression is kind—and generally she is gentle. But on occasion there comes an expression, not of fire, like in Queen's eyes, but of dumbness, like an alligator half asleep.
* * * *

(In other words, the eye had a kind of "sunken" look as though the muscles or nerve about the eye were atrophied. She was a little stubbon generally, and perfectly devilish when her stubbornness was aroused. I very soon taught her to "jerk line" and "right and left." To learn this did not require a high intelligence.)

When we entered the Yellowstone Park at Gardiner, the North Entrance, we were assigned—or relegated—to a spot on the Old Trail to Mammoth, Park Headquarters, about three miles in from Gardiner. This trail is abandoned except "for pack or loose animals" and it appears, saddle animals. I suppose a horse drawn vehicle would be assigned the same camp. * * * *

I started in around and over barren hills, past a meadow and grove of quaking aspens, but no water. I stopped to explore. On we went, and in due time came to a little trickle of water leading into and out of a rather stagnant pool off to one side of where the Trail crosses a kind of bridge. I wondered if this was the "fine spring." The shade was there. And signs of recent campers. Grass in the immediate vicinity was not very evident. The ground was very rough, stony and grown up to brush.

Off to the left, down a steep hill, we had just passed what at a distance looked like a beautiful small lake, high above the river which flows out of it down, what to that locality might be termed the main canyon. Tying Belle to a tree I walked and stumbled down to this lake in search of living water, grass, and a place level enough to camp on all together. The shore was mud, the water stagnant, the vegetation was mostly rushes. Mosquitoes abounded. I scrambled back. Off to the left a little from where I had left the horses I found a small swamp, where grew an abundance of coarse three cornered grass. This grass is not of a good quality. But it was plentiful and as I had brought in a supply of two and a half cent oats I decided it would do temporarily as "filling." Half way between this and the "pool" I found a spot level enough for camp. I unpacked and unsaddled and hobbled Belle in the swamp or meadow. * * * *

The horses were very restless. They didn't like the "meadow." (It was surrounded by dense brush, and full of mosquitoes.) They were forever—then and afterward—seeking the open—and the backward Trail. Belle can travel with hobbles about twice as fast as I can walk. I chased horses until dark, then tied Belle securely, leaving hobbles on as an extra protection, and hit the hay.

Next morning I was up early. Queen having eaten her fill, I, after giving them the "nose bag" tied (Queen) and turned Belle out hobbled. * * * * But I don't trust Belle any more.

After I'd cooked and eaten a bite I went out to the horses. They were frantic from flies. There were seven kinds of flies. There was just the common every day fly, the little dark brown fly about one-third the size of a common house fly, that gather on a horse in spots and take the skin off in patches. They are great strategists, choosing the parts of a horse's anatomy from which they cannot easily be dislodged. There was the deer fly whose bite "stings." There was the nose fly, a pesky little devil about half the size of a bot or nit fly and otherwise resembling him in looks. The nose fly was something new to me until after we crossed the Missouri River at Mobridge, S. Dak. * * * * Of all my experiences with flies the nose fly can deal a horse more misery than any other fly I've ever seen. There was the bot fly, the common old-fashioned horse fly, and dragon flies [Careless error; I meant moose fly, a large black fly.] as large as bumble bees. Imagine, then, what a fine rest (?) my horses were enjoying in this "sylvan" spot!

I decided then and there to get to hell out of that as soon as possible. I had neglected upon entering to learn definitely whether this spring was in Montana or Wyoming. I understood that the state line was "two or three miles in." I decided to leave the horses in the meadow and hustle back to Gardiner to learn definitely whether I had "hit" Wyoming, and if so, get a signature from a Park Official. I turned Queen loose so she could seek either shade, brush, or open. I tied the end of Belle's lead rope to the middle of a pole about ten feet long, thus giving her a chance to move about also, but a certainty of becoming fastened to some obstacle if she tried to go too far. I mean the pole would on such ground be sure to come in contact on both sides of the lead line in a way that would at least check her. She had not and has not as yet become acquainted with a picket line to the extent that I wanted to picket her "solid" and leave her. I did that once when I first got her and gave a rope burn for my pains. Rope burns on pasterns are not conducive to good nature or easy traveling.

Just as I was leaving Belle in the swamp, or meadow, I spied something hiding in the tall grass. I had nearly stumbled over it. Though I had never seen one before I knew this animal to be a very large porcupine or hedge hog. At once it popped into my fertile cranium that I had heard the hedge hog cussed and discussed as an edible. Part of my game is to miss no legitimate opportunity of "subsisting off the country" in a primitive and legitimate manner. By "primitive" I mean that for various reasons I carry no gun. But anything from a mess of dandelion greens to an elephant that I can lay hands on, by either running or outwitting, is my meat. Once I lived largely on China pheasant's eggs for over a week. That was between De Smet and Aberdeen, S. Dak. These birds are so numerous that they are a nuisance and quite tame. One day I "got" one of them. The breast made a couple of dainty meals. Twice I captured a young jack rabbit. Once I "got," cooked and ate a prairie dog. Now don't gag. General * * * * Fremont is said to have eaten prairie dogs. * * * * By the way, they are fat and tender and taste like squirrel. And once I had a mess of frogs' legs. What more natural than that it should occur to me that I might add to my renown as a nature faker by devouring a hedge hog. Suiting the action to the words (or thoughts) I seized a club and dealt the "hog" a cowardly blow on the bean. It didn't throw any quills at me. Then it occurred to me—too late—that I had probably broken one of the Park laws. The principal question I had been asked on entering was: "Have you any fire arms?" I had not shot, but I had *Killed* an animal in the Park.

And how did I know how soon a ranger might be along? I hid the thing in the thick brush. Then I walked three miles to Gardiner. * * * *

Arriving at the gate and inquiring of the man who had assigned me to the camping place I found that "it was just over the line." Upon requesting a signature to the effect that I was "camped in Wyoming" he said he hadn't seen me there; and advised me to ride over to Headquarters with my saddle horse and get a signature there. I decided to do so. I learned, too, that I was camped on "the Old Trail" or bridle trail to Mammoth— or in other words that I was making the trip to Gardiner for nothing. On "going in" in the previous evening I had passed a sign which designated the trail I was taking as "Old Trail to Mammoth." Had I had time to read this it would have saved me this trip. But Belle was on one of her rampages and all my attention had been given to manipulating the jerk line and addressing her in language that is not in the dictionary.

I got back to camp about 1 p.m.—"all fussed up." The horses —especially Belle—were likewise in a tantrum by reason of the seven kinds of flies previously described. It was then that Belle returned evil for good by busting my knee cap when I swatted a dragon fly [moose fly].

Hurt? Well some! Did I faint? Well, I started to, but then I happened to remember that there was no one there to see me faint—so I didn't faint. I picked myself up, and found that I could put my leg through "all the movements" by ignoring the pain. Being able to manipulate my leg was what fooled me. * * * *

Then came the worst part of it; if ever in my life I was sorry for anyone, I was sorry for myself for having killed that hedge hog. It must be disposed of—partly for reasons already explained and partly for the reason that I felt certain I could not travel the next day, and I felt quite certain that owing to the heat I'd soon be reminded through my olfactory nerves of having broken the game laws. Burying the carcass there in the rocks and roots with nothing to dig with and only one leg was out of the question. I must cremate. So hobbling about getting the dried brush and slinging rocks, then carrying them together, I built a "funeral pyre." Then I got the "hog" in place by throwing it a few feet at a time. Determined not to miss this opportunity of "seeing what a hedge hog tasted like" thus settling for myself a moot question, I set about to skin a part of it. In spite of my care I got a few of the quills in my fingers, and I know what *that's* like! Finally, I had all four legs. Then I managed somehow to get the now repulsive thing on to the pile of dry wood and set it on fire. And if ever I smelled a sweet savory smell, this was *not* it. I wondered if it would bring out the Rangers, but it didn't. I guess the wind was in my favor. I fortunately had brought from the spring that morning a small supply of water. I boiled the four legs in a lard bucket suspended by means of a wire which I had previously arranged. I boiled and boiled and boiled that meat. But I had no appetite for that or anything else. I didn't eat a bite of anything. Next day I tried my luck—and my teeth. Was it tough? It was. I mean the "hog" as well as my luck. The *next* night, however, and the following morning—the morning I pulled out—I had managed to stew a kind of gravy from the meat that was fairly palatable on my bread, which had become rather dry.

Getting back to the fire. It got pretty hot; it took a *hot* fire to obliterate the evidence of my rashness. The surrounding vegetation became quite dry. The fire began to spread. I had left by me my only Canteen, not quite full of water. It was dark. I knew that to reach the spring and return stumbling in the dark over stones and brush with water—even a little—would be impossible. I had looked my will power squarely in the face and knew that the pain of such an attempt would master it. So I hobbled around on my stick poking and raking the flames together in the burned area and putting out the burning vegetation, which fortunately did not burn very readily. Several times I caught myself swaying. I knew that if I fell into the fire with clothes by now dry as tinder, I would never get out. Two or three times I narrowly, and by the exercise of all the will power I could muster, avoided collapsing. I must have been in full possession of my faculties, for it occurred to me that *should* I let myself become burned on that fire, it would look exactly like suicide. Funny how in times of peril we glimpse the future. (Is it reflection of our own egotism?) I could hear the news boys shouting all kinds of headlines, airing all kinds of theories as to how it all happened. A few would lay it to accident. Others would ascribe it to temporary insanity caused by the pain, others to chagrin at believing myself incapacitated for finishing my Trip —which had become an obsession.

"I'll fool 'em all," I said to myself. And thus it sometimes happens that a man's egotism saves him.

No sooner had I gotten the fire corraled than the wind rose a little. All I could do was watch that the sparks did not start new fires. Fortunately they did not. * * * *

But the tree from a limb of which I had suspended the wire that supported my "kettle" took fire near the ground and burned about one-third off. I have seldom realized before what a precious thing is water—when a fellow is too lame to go after it. I used about half I had in my canteen keeping the fire down to the point where the sap of the tree—(a quaking aspen) would counteract the remaining fire, after the heat of the now diminishing "funeral pyre" had slackened. "I'll go you 50-50," I said to the tree. "The other half of this water I'll retain for other emergencies." In the morning the fire in the trunk of the tree had gone out. I noticed where a spark had burned a hole through my cotton breeches. Probably I had smothered this when after I had "done all I could do," I crawled into bed—and trusted God. I reasoned that God wants a fellow to do his best, but He does *not* want a man to bring disaster on himself in the end by needless worry or fear.

Next morning Belle was gone. I had the night before, after letting Queen fill up on the rank grass, tied her securely and turned Belle loose hobbled; for one thing this saved me from leading her to water.

After getting myself a cup of coffee, which was about all the breakfast I wanted, I somehow got the light saddle onto Queen, got in the saddle and found Belle about half way back to Gardiner. I slid off Queen, got the hobbles off Belle, got Queen up to a rock, mounted her, and "jerk-lined" Belle back to camp. I tied her to a tree, and then got Queen to support me back to my "bunk." I mean I walked, rather hopped along on my right leg, clinging to Queen's neck with my left hand (and on the off side.) Queen is a fine nurse. She obeyed me implicitly, taking mincy little steps, halting whenever I said "wait a little" and turning ever so little to the right or left as I asked her to do. She is naturally quick, nervous and high strung. But—well, who says a horse don't know anything?

The next morning I could hardly navigate at all. Stayed in camp. Got along best I could. Leg so swollen I had to rip breeches and underclothes to get at it.

The fourth morning I just made up my mind—in fact I'd made up my mind the night before—that I must get out of that, and I did—somehow.

I rolled up, packed Belle as usual, and rode 14 miles that day, stopping at Gardiner for supplies and oats which were to last me back to the farming country. I got to Chris Foss's place. From then till now I've told about.

Sat. P.M.—I've been all this time writing this letter. I'm doing fine.

Yours of Aug. 5th came yesterday. Glad you take the philosophical view of it. Yes, it might have been a lot worse. The fires [there were many forest fires that Fall. Mother had been worrying for fear I would get caught in a forest fire] will all be out long before I can leave here. Anyhow I will look out for them. I am more worried about snow. Still I shall get through. Over the Siskiyous will be a little tough later, but I believe I can make that pass too. I will not be caught in a trap. * * * *

Well, I must close. Love,

(Signed) Frank.

Helena, Montana,
Aug. 16th, '26.

Dear Folks:

Your card of 12th came Sat. 14th. Glad all well.

I've been wondering since I wrote last whether I should have told you all that. Fact is, I wanted to get it off my chest—make a "record" of it and tell you about it at the same time. Hope you are not worrying about the little "inconveniences" I was up against. You must not. It's all part of the game—the game of life. It's part of this trip. "The best laid plans of mice and men "gang aft agley," as Bobby Burns put it. If everything went off as slick as grease what a colorless world this would get to be, wouldn't it? If we made no mistakes—like letting a horse kick us, for instance—what would the world come to? It's the unexpected that gets a kick out o' life. It's also, seriously, the unexpected that develops us. To have followed my schedule would have been comparatively simple. To leave Corwin Springs on or after Sept. 15 and cross the Rockies with a soft horse before the winter shuts me out—well, that will be some stunt, but I'm going to do it.

One of the head Drs. just told me that I'd probably be here for a month yet at least. * * * *

Well, I guess I'll close for today. Love,

(Signed) Frank.

Helena, Montana,
August 31, '26.

Dear Folks:

Just a line today to let you know that I am getting along—somehow. Am up for X-ray today to see whether knee is sufficiently grown together so I can navigate without a splint on leg.

Have been re-revising my route south of Madras, Ore. Will go via Reno, Nev. Sand Springs and across the Mojave desert to Tonopah, Goldfields, Las Vegas and out across the Colorado River near Searchlight. I find on investigation that the footing for a horse is not bad through there in Feb., Mar., and that is when I expect to hit there now after all this delay. The weather is not very severe there and I find that towns and ranches are numerous enough so we can get by. I don't know after all as I as sorry to abandon the regular tourist route. I'll learn more.

I am getting tired of staying here while the fall slips away. Hope to start by the 15th Sept.

There is no news. Love,

(Signed) Frank.

Please keep all my letters. May want to refer to them.

Corwin Springs, Mont.,
September 24, 1926.

Frank Heath,
Helena, Montana.

Dear Friend:

Your last letter received a few days ago, and see by that you may be over here soon, as you expect to be out of the hospital about Oct. 1st. I was glad to hear that, as I think you have had your share of trouble and delay.

It has been very cold and stormy here the last few days but nice again today. Warmed up some. Will commence threshing some time next week. Will sure be glad when this is done so I can get my stock in on the field. Pulled the shoes on Queen quite a while ago and saved them for you, as they are in good shape. But am afraid you will have to shoe her sharp the next time as I expect you will have some frozen ground soon. Queen is doing fine. I think in a couple of days I will take her up and feed her some hay, as it will be pretty hard on her to start out on the soft feed she's been on. I hitched Belle up a couple of times. She is gentle but don't think she was ever worked before, but will make a good little work horse, I think. Well, Frank, no news around here, very interesting. Sure hope your expectations will come true and that you will be out on date you mentioned well as ever again. Family all send their best regards to you. Again wishing you all the luck in the world.

(Signed) Chris Foss.

Fort Harrison, Mont.,
Sun. Oct. 3, '26.

Dear Folks:

Gaining steadily. Will probably get away from here about 8th. Leave Corwin Springs 9th. Mr. Foss writes me Queen is fine. Believe I'll make it yet. Will write before I start. Love,

(Signed) Frank.

From Signature Book: "Mr. Heath was admitted to Hospital No. 72, Fort Harrison, Mont., July 29th, 1926 with a fractured left knee, and is now ready for discharge.

(Signed) B. H. Frayser, M.D.
Oct. 9, 1926."

Vets. Bureau Hospital,
Helena, Montana,
Oct. 9, '26.

Dear Folks:

At last I am ready to start back to Corwin Springs tomorrow night. I hope to leave Foss's place Tuesday, Oct. 12th. Of course I'll have to take it very slow at first. I'll be a little lame for a while, and Queen will be soft as a pumpkin. Altogether I've lost nearly three months. And I don't expect to make it up. I'll be traveling about three months behind schedule during the rest of the trip, and we'll do well if we finish only three months late. * * * *

The weather is fine here again. Barring deep snow you can look for me about Nov. 15.

Write me at Butte, Mont. Always put on letters, "Hold 30 days." With love,

(Signed) Frank.

Up in this country, too, they are rounding up broncos and selling them to the cannery at Butte for $5.00 a head, less the freight.

I had written Chris Foss meanwhile to sell Cheyenne Belle if he could, and put the money in his pocket. In a late letter he informed me that he had sold her to some trapper for coyote bait—or wolf bait. He couldn't even get six or ten dollars for her. And this is the last of Cheyenne Belle so far as this story is concerned. I don't mean this vindictively, don't even blame her for having cracked me on the knee. Poor Belle! She wasn't responsible for the fact that she was ill-begotten. Evidently a cross between a horse that had been bred for many generations in a wild state, no contact with man, one whose intelligence consists entirely of the defensive instinctive type —which, by the way, is a very necessary part of a horse's intelligence, provided the intelligence does not stop there—such a horse, we presume, had been crossed with one of the purely heavy draft type (I do not mean Percheron-Norman), docile and honest but not highly intelligent. Let us presume then that Cheyenne Belle was the result of such a cross. She looked it. In this case physically the blend happened to be all right, but in regard to intelligence, something didn't click. After all, Belle's fate wasn't so horrible. She probably met a sudden and humane death, a bullet exactly in the right place, and after all, she contributed eventually to the destruction—more or less—of coyotes and wolves, the terrible timber wolf that makes life so miserable for other animals, including horses, particularly young foals. The fact is, I believe that horses of this impossible deficiency in intelligence should not be allowed to reproduce, any more than should horses with some congenital physical deformity.

Getting back to Chris Foss: We found Queen fine in spite of the fact that there, high in the Rockies, she had been out in the pasture through two snow storms. Chris and the hired man had tried to get hold of her with the intention of stabling and feeding her as he had said in a letter that he would, but they could not get near her. They told me when I arrived at the ranch that they didn't know how I was going to catch her—didn't believe there was a horse on the place that could run her down. She was with several other horses in a wheat field that had not been worth harvesting, so she was pretty well fed at that. I took her halter rope, went out to get her. She saw me coming and met me half way. I put the rope on her neck, led her in the barn. She had not been in this barn before, but she had hardly stepped across the sill until she saw the oat box and nickered.

The leg and foot which had been bothering us ever since she sprained them rolling on those rubber pads, the corner of which had been worn off by gravel and rock, had not improved. The heel and the inside of her foot had grown down, the knee had again become more flexed. For some weeks Foss and the hired man had been shoeing horses on the ranch and had become fairly handy at it. I fitted the shoes to suit myself, hobbling around on one leg, directed the hired man as to exactly how I wished the feet pared, and he nailed them on for me. She went through to Spokane with this job of shoeing. The foot and leg improved considerably on the way.

> From Signature Book: "Corwin Springs, Oct. 12, '26. Frank M. Heath arrived here July 22nd, 1926, with Gypsy Queen. The horse has been in my pasture ever since and am leaving with her today.
> (Signed) Chris Foss."

We resumed the journey on October 12th. Instead of returning to the Yellowstone Trail by the way of Livingstone, we cut through a mountain pass from Foss' place a little west of Gardiner, and hit Bozman. I had been told that if we got caught in a blizzard in the pass it would be "just too bad," but we tackled it anyway in spite of the fact that it was threatening snow, so that we saved quite a little distance. We heard soon after that it snowed in that pass the night of the day we passed through.

Snow was in the mountains all about us, and it chased us all the way across. As sure as we were past the sight of snow at night, it was visible in the morning on either side of the valley through which passes the Yellowstone Trail. (In a technical sense I don't mean valley either, seeing we had passed over two ranges. What I mean is that of course the trail passes usually between mountain peaks on either side, which makes it usually appear locally or casually to the traveler like a kind of valley, as for instance we are traveling a trail where there is no snow, but piled up on either side of us is snow.)

Farms or ranches in mountain valleys, (alternating with mining towns) provided us means of subsistence. It had been a little cold sometimes. The ground was frozen hard. Every pond of stagnant water was frozen. Once we had put up in an old sheep shed. This was one of the many outlying camps or stations of the Anaconda

C. M. Co. (Copper Mining Company). This company owned thousands of acres of land. This gave them surface rights. Meanwhile they were making it pay its way by running sheep on it. At this point we had left the Yellowstone Trail and were cutting east of Anaconda.

Once or twice, by the way, we had fed wheat hay with the best of results.

From Signature Book: "Missoula, Mont., Oct. 28, 1926. Frank M. Heath put up at the Be Dell Stable last night with Gypsy Queen.

(Signed) Andy Nelson,
Stable Foreman."

From Notes. November 3, '26: * * * 3:30, Ar'd dairy ranch of Mr. John Giachino in E. suburb Mullen, Idaho, Box 244, via Y.S.T. (very winding). Several loops, very hilly.

Traveled: 18 mi. Dirt, 2 mi. R. 2 and frozen mud 7 mi. Gravel 9 mi. (no side). Burned timber—several old sawmill sites. Prospect holes or small mine. 3 big lead and silver [mines] operating. Several dairy farms in valley E. of Mullen. Paid 5 cts. a pound for oats in Mullen. Also paid for a meal abbreviated at both ends. Queen in small warm stall. Hitting the hay. Past divide 2 p.m., then down hill.

From Signature Book: "Mullen, Idaho, Nov. 4, 1926. Frank M. Heath stayed with us last night with Gypsy Queen.

(Signed) John Giachino
Paul Giachino."

From Notes. November 4, '26: Fair. Leaving dairy ranch. No chg. Hay, lunch, breakfast. (Formulas, advice). Mr. Giachino sick, is in Italy. John 20, a very good fellow, works in mine, outside. Large family. Been here 22 years. 11 a.m. Ar'd Wallace, city crowded in between bluffs. Narrow streets.

Wallace is a well known mining city. In approaching from the north, the bluffs were so high on either side that the sun shone in only an hour or two about noon. It was impossible to get off the pavement. The houses, perched on the side hill, came right down to, as I remember it, a flume or deep ditch that made it impossible to get off the pavement. This was a bottle neck. The travel through here was immense. The pavement which was slick to begin with was covered with white frost. I dismounted, you bet. Queen got across, slipping and skating, without going down. I lost my footing. A gentleman coming from the other direction halted to see if I was badly hurt. (By the way, I was still walking with a cane—when I walked.) I indicated that I was all right. He passed on. The city was considerably higher than this pass between the high bluffs. In the streets were several inches of snow. I stopped at the postoffice and we passed on.

North past Coeur d'Alene Lake, through Coeur d'Alene city, through the Fourth of July Canyon and on through the Bitter Roots. I expected to see one long, small, regular canyon. Well, it wasn't. It was up hill and down, turn and twist, like most mountain roads. We had been told that usually about this time of year the snow became so deep that it was practically impassable. The day we passed through, there was a cold, drizzly rain, almost snow. In the mountain tops on either side it was snowing hard. Once I turned momentarily and looked back, on feeling an extra cold blast. There I seemed to be looking directly into a black cloud. It seemed to be rolling toward us, but it didn't catch us. We were on a down grade, and reached a lower altitude where the rain had not yet turned to snow. We just out-traveled it. I heard next morning that it snowed hard behind us that night.

Down into the Spokane Valley, where apples were lying on the ground by the ton—actually by the ton, worth hardly the price of picking. On November 8th we arrived at Spokane, at the home of the old folks, 6,065 miles all told. (This figure may be more or less incorrect. The reader, however, will get the correct mileage of the whole trip eventually. By correct, we mean we are sure that we traveled that many miles and probably more.) We estimated that we must be half way through. We both were in pretty fair shape. Queen's feet and legs were nearly, but not quite, O. K.

Here the writer dispensed with the cane he had used when walking. Ten days was the least time our host of relatives and friends would hear of our staying in Spokane. We had Queen reshod all around before leaving Spokane.

From Signature Book: "Spokane, Wash., 11/8/1926. Met Frank M. Heath with his horse Gypsy Queen as he was entering Spokane.   (Signed) J. M. Nelson, Pastor,
                                      Union Park Baptist Church."

THE DAILY CHRONICLE

Spokane, Wash., Wednesday, November 10, 1926

RIDER AND MOUNT TO SPEND 10 DAYS IN SPOKANE BEFORE GOING SOUTH

Paul Revere's horse was a piker compared with the mount which carried Frank M. Heath into Spokane Monday evening, after taking the former Spokane man through 32 states.

Heath is remaining here for several days visiting his parents, Mr. and Mrs. F. Heath, pioneer residents of the city, who now live just outside the city limits near East Sprague Avenue. He has three brothers, E. C., B. L., and Robert Heath, living in the city. * * * *

Heath's original schedule called for completion of his journey at Washington, D. C., July 1, 1927, but he is now three months behind schedule due to an accident in Yellowstone Park, where he suffered a broken leg.

Chapter III

DOWN THE HINTERLAND OF THE PACIFIC STATES AND NEVADA

WE made good time from Chris Foss' place to Spokane. I had written my parents to expect me on the 15th of November. We left Foss' the 12th of October, and arrived in Spokane on November 8th, a total of 27 days in which we covered 514 miles, an average of 19 miles a day plus, over all.

While I was in Spokane my mother had been worrying a lot about our crossing the desert. The word "desert" has an exaggerated terror for many people who have never had any contact with it, and I might add, it has a terror for some people who have had unfavorable contact with it. The one fear that my mother had in particular was that we might die of thirst in some of these great spaces—not unreasonably so. While my mother never crossed a desert, she was an exceedingly well-read woman. Her fears were fairly well founded. So nothing would satisfy her but that I must provide means of transporting water across these long dry spaces. I had been thinking some about this myself, so the short of it is, I had made in Spokane what I called a "desert water bag"—not the two gallon water bag that is sometimes carried in a car, or the larger water bags, but one that would hold as high as 18 gallons, a bag divided into two parts, one on each side of the horse, with a connecting part to fit our McClellan saddle, with a nozzle in each part, by means of which the bag could be filled through a funnel and siphoned out. I did not chance anything like a spigot at the bottom. This I left with a brother to be forwarded to me wherever I should call for it. We used this twice. We never carried more than eight gallons on the horse.

I foresaw that we would have all kinds of footing, wet and dry, rough and snow and otherwise, so I bought a pair of ladies' laced camping boots—I am not a sissy, but just the same these shoes answered the purpose better because they were very much lighter. However, I had heavy soles put over the light soles. I also bought a pair of good galoshes, which I wore over these when necessary. These came in very handy. Also, one of the boys gave me a pair of heavy-oiled duck breeches. Those also came in very handy. I still had the heavy raincoat I had bought down in Arkansas in the Fall of 1925. I had not been carrying this with me all the time. I had forwarded it to Spokane.

At Spokane I gave the Boy Scouts a talk on our trip up to this point, using the map I had prepared.

On November 19th we left Spokane in a snow storm. We knew it would stop snowing—for a while. We had no intention of sitting down while winter closed the door ahead of us. The old folks were greatly perturbed at our leaving in a storm, but I got them to see the necessity of our keeping as far as possible ahead of winter. The main point in this was that as we proceeded south we were getting into a lower altitude as well as a more southerly latitude. So I finally satisfied them—in a way.

It soon quit snowing, and we did not have much trouble. I laid in a day and a half at Cheney because it rained cats and dogs.

From Notes. November 20, '26: * * * * Noon: Ar'd Cheney, Wash. Barn of Ed Gordon. * * * * Snowed most A.M. Queen balled up badly. Laying in P.M. acc't snow, icy road. Stopped snowing. Queen still off feed.

Traveled: 9½ mi. via country rd. to Cheney. Gravel 4 mi. (no side). Pave. 5 mi.—very slippery. * * * * General farming, apples (many on ground). Poultry.

Sunday, November 21, '26: Silver thaw. Laying in acc't storm. Very slippery. P.M. Loafing in pool room. Queen O. K.

November 22, '26: Warmer, slushy. Leaving Gordon barn 8:45, Cheney 9:30. No chg. for barn. Feed 50 cts. Had left front widened, heel lowered—rest O. K.

Down through the Big Bend wheat country. In the late 1890's I remember that it was questionable whether farming this land was a safe bet or not. It was what we might call semi-arid. The large scale farming, together with this Campbell system formerly mentioned, had largely solved that problem. A thousand acres is a small farm in this section. Everything is done on a large scale. The farmer either makes or breaks.

One great drawback was the destruction caused by jackrabbits. On a small farm of 160 acres, mentioned more commonly as a quarter, the rabbits would generally harvest the crop—the most of it. A man with whom I stayed over night, owner of a small farm, told me that in spite of all he could do the rabbits would take it clean from any side exposed to the prairie, for a distance of from twenty to forty rods. Figure that out!

This country was more or less cut up with canyons. Of course the canyons meant considerable hilly land on each side. The farming was done on the more level space between the canyons, large spaces generally but not always. The rabbits breed and hide in these hills and sage brush and come like a thief in the night and ruin Farmer Jones' crops. A field of less than a half section is only a nuisance. The jackrabbits take practically all of it. Of a township they leave the interior, which the farmer harvests with the great combines.

We arrived at Pasco and over the Columbia River to Kennewick. Kennewick is somewhat of a city. I believe I remember seeing Kennewick as just a kind of jumping-off place. There lingers in my mind a picture of a few old box cars parked there, presumably for the benefit of the section crews. It was out in the desert-like, sandy country, in the late 1890's. West of it is an irrigation project that did not exist at that time.

From Signature Book: "Kennewick, Wash., 11/29/ ['26]. Mr. Frank M. Heath stayed here with his horse Gypsy Queen last night.

(Signed) Farmers' Exchange,
By C. C. Williams."

Kennewick, Wash.,
Nov. 29, '26.

Dear Folks:

Arrived here O. K. last night. Going half way across Horse Heaven Hills to a ranch today. Address, The Dalles, Ore. Love,
(Signed) Frank.

Thence over the Horse Heaven Hills. Along between 1905 and 1915, during which period I resided in Portland, Oregon, I used to hear a lot about this Horse Heaven country, as it was called. It lies in south of Kennewick and is bounded on three sides by a bend of the Columbia River. It is about 25 miles wide from north to south, roughly, and about 50 miles east and west. It is dry, being drained three ways toward the Columbia River. It is low-lying hills, more than semi-arid. It had the reputation of being practically worthless. Now why was it called Horse Heaven? Because it was pretty well strewn with bones of horses. It wasn't heaven in any sense for horses. When the range which was near water became entirely exhausted the horses would feed back toward the interior of this area, which might be called a peninsula, for it was such in a true sense, in that horses couldn't swim the Columbia River. They would drift in here from the one open side of the range that had become barren. They couldn't get out on the other three sides. There was nothing on the side from which they had entered to go back to. They became so weak, partly through starvation and largely through thirst, that they couldn't get back. In a sense they were in a trap, and died there. Crossing the Horse Heaven Hills we ran across one instance of where grain was raised—the one strawstack or sign of grain culture. A few hogs were rooting about the stack. They were not fenced in. They wouldn't leave. Any other protection was too distant. I left Queen to take care of herself, having fed her, and I roosted high up in the straw for fear the hogs would make a dainty meal of me. There were no buildings about this straw stack. I saw one human habitation in crossing these hills. The man and his wife who lived in it had some ground under fence and took in a few head of stock to pasture in the summer months. They had a barn. There was a well quite a way from the buildings that during the wet season furnished considerable water. That is the only water that I heard of in this whole so-called Horse Heaven country. Of course that would not be available to wild horses.

We crossed a ferry to Yumatilla, Oregon. West of Yumatilla is a comparatively small irrigation project, opened somewhere around 1905, and the West Yumatilla project was added to it about 1910, I believe. I am somewhat familiar with this because I heard a lot about it and also saw it develop and progress. Off and on I rode up and down on the O.R.&N. railroad. We found most of the farmers on the Yumatilla irrigation project scratching to make ends meet. It costs a great deal to level the land for cultivation, and it is sand after it is leveled. Then there are always the laterals to dig and maintain. Many of the farm buildings are very poor. There is this advantage though—the range land back in the hills makes a good market for alfalfa which thrives once the ground is in shape. Some of the farmers on this project have their own band of sheep. There is some dairying.

From Signature Book: "Irrigon, Ore., Dec. 1, 1926. Frank M. Heath and Gypsy Queen took dinner with myself and wife today.

(Signed) Chas. H. Stewart."

On west from this irrigation project, paralleling the Columbia River, through a precarious country, where farming is attempted— not very successfully. Some sheep, perhaps a little other stock, too many worthless wild horses, by the way of Arlington. Nearing Rufus we dropped into the Columbia River bottom, in which strip there is some successful farming. Blaylock Island, of which we used to hear a lot in the late 1890's as an island devoted to farming, appeared to lie barren out in the river.

Soon we were at Rufus, Oregon, roughly 25 miles up the river east of The Dalles.

From Notes. December 4, '26: * * * * 9 a.m. Ar'd Rufus. Went 1 mi. west and return to see Mr. Arnold Brady regarding care of horse. Later: Have her in barn of Mr. Cal Brown. Bought feed at Deyos. Brady will care for her.

Traveled: 7 mi. (2 to find accommodations). * * * * Pave (gravel side) 5 mi. Dirt ½. Scenery.

Special Note:
Kennewick to Rufus, 103 miles.
Spokane to Rufus, in place of Portland, 270 miles—80 miles less than schedule from Spokane to Portland.

2 P.M. (Dec. 4) taking bus for side trip to Portland. * * * * 3:30, Passing over tableland by Mosier. Thousands bu. apples on ground. (Particularly south of Hood River—the famous Hood River apple country.) Trees look healthy. 4 p.m., In Hood River. (Arrived Portland that night.)

Portland, Ore.,
Dec. 5, '26.

Dear Folks:

I reached Rufus—25 mi. E. of The Dalles—yesterday, 9 a.m., and came on down here in the afternoon. Left Queen in good hands at Rufus. She is feeling fine. Made 52 miles Thurs. and Fri. and she was right on her metal yesterday (Sat.) morning. Tell Dad I reset left front twice on the way across, lowering the heel each time, so now I have her going about natural. Knee is O. K. since I got her back on her tendon where she belongs.

Our total to Rufus, where we turn south to Lakeview, is 6,168 miles. I am feeling O. K.

(Signed) Frank.

From Notes. December 10, '26: Still waiting draft at noon. Leaving tonight. Left Geo. and Ruth 9 p.m. Ben accompanied to depot. Leaving 10:45 p.m.

Saturday, December 11, '26: Dropped me off at Rufus 3 a.m. Lost hat—nearly let myself drop over 20 ft. wall. Gave hat up until daylight—found then. * * * * Daylight, found hat. Fed Queen, who is O. K. Walked 1 mile and return to see Brady. Neither he nor Brown would accept a cent. * * * * Leaving Rufus 10 a.m. "over the hills."

From Signature Book: "I have been taking care of Gypsy Queen one week while Frank M. Heath was in Portland.

(Signed) A. N. Brady,
Rufus, Dec. 11, 1926."

I made this side trip to Portland to visit my two sons, and cut it short, knowing what was ahead of us, returning to Rufus on the 11th.

At Rufus we had left Queen in splendid hands. Rufus was simply a wheat town. On the morning that we left there we went up a steep grade, a kind of side hill, not straight up, onto the plateau that is known as the Wasco country, devoted almost entirely to wheat. This is quite a large area.

On the second day of this lap a blinding snowstorm overtook me. We had detoured into a dirt road (a wheat road). We reached a farm in the blizzard and they kept us over night. I slept warm in the straw in the barn. They had me in for breakfast. It ceased snowing during the night. We went on next morning. We were between the great fields, the plowed ground off which the wind had filled the roadway full of snow. That day we wallowed in snow from five to fifteen inches deep. It was zero weather. The ground was not so frozen or the snow so packed but that Queen balled up continually. But just the same we hit the main highway at Kent. I believe that fourteen miles was one of the hardest day's travel we had anywhere. We were fortunate in striking a pretty good country hotel and a mighty good place for Queen in a good old-fashioned straw stable. Had straw for roughage and procured some grain somehow. Hotel prices.

We went on through to Shaniko over this main highway which had been opened by the snow plow. We had no snow to wallow between Kent and Shaniko. We stayed overnight at Shaniko. It was cold. I was fortunate in getting a good bed and pretty good supper and breakfast for not too high a price. Queen had to put up with a tie stall and was lucky at that. One point I remember is that here again in this country they were rounding up broncos, shipping them to some cannery or fertilizer factory, not in such numbers as I have mentioned in Montana. Shaniko, as stated, is the terminal of this branch road—I forget the name of it. Shaniko is quite a shipping point for sheep and wool coming in from the semi-arid plains and hills away to the south. A great deal of freight, along in the early 1900's and before used to go from Shaniko away south by great freight teams. Also it was the northern terminus of a stage road serving the back country from Shaniko to Prineville, something over fifty miles in a straight line, further by road.

Considerably north of Trout Creek was the Bolter Ranch. The Bolters were old-timers—pretty good people at that. They had a lot of very fine cattle fattening on alfalfa which they raised in abundance. The cattle range in the hills on either side in summer. This alfalfa culture here and south along Hay Creek was the most intensive it had ever been my lot to behold. It was irrigated, largely through private projects. Two or three crops a year were cut.

The Bolters treated us fine—wouldn't have a cent. Left there next morning, going south along Hay Creek Valley. We waddled through to Hay Creek to the headquarters of the Baldwin Sheep and Land Company, a very large concern. They owned or controlled thousands of acres of range land, and had hundreds of acres of alfalfa land. The headquarters, Hay Creek, is almost like a small town. They have many outlying branch ranches. The weather now had moderated. By accident we ran onto an abandoned house and some kind of a shed about dark. I turned Queen loose and she managed to get a few bites of some grass which had probably been preserved for winter pasture, getting her in before I retired. I thought for a little while she had "pulled out"—but she came out of the darkness at my call.

From Notes. December 17, '26: * * * * 3 p.m. Ar'd sheep camp of Oregon Western Colonization Company, 8 mi. N.W. of Prineville in Ochico Project. Mr. S. E. Jones, foreman. 1st Try. Pineville, R. 1, Box 39.

Traveled: 17 mi. via old [Shaniko freight] rd. Hilly. Dirt (mud), snow, slush. Queen balled badly. Sheep, some cattle, little wheat. Caused first runaway, at bottom of grade S. of Blue Mts.

This was a land and irrigation project that didn't seem to be clicking, as the saying goes, very well, but they were breaking even by running sheep on the land.

Old man Jones treated us fine. We left Mr. Jones at 8:25.

From Notes. December 18, '26: * * * * Leaving Jones 8:25. 11:40, Putting up at Prineville, barn of Si Hodges, Local.

Traveled: 8 mi. Dirt (snow and mud). Balled. Via old Dalles Prineville rd. Level. Ochico. Hay. Sheep. Stock. * * * * Prineville has a R.R. past 8 years.

Special Note: Prineville 6,361 miles. (Rufus to Prineville 129 miles.)

Stories of 3 ft. snow on High Desert. Mail forward from 493 E. 23rd St., Portland, Dec. 17. Note: Not heard from S. S. Bank, reply to request of Nov. 30 for $50. Writing for 50 P. O. O. to Lakeview, Ore. * * * * Laying in P.M. Having Queen shod sharp all round. Sleeping in cabin on good bed. Fire. Horse and all, no chg. Restaurant reasonable. Wonderful view from about 5 mi. N.W. of Prineville. Gorge, symmetrical gap between Three Sisters on left, Bald Butte and Old Grizzly to right. * * * *

What I mean by referring to the railroad in Prineville, was that it had been away back from any railroad until the railroad formerly spoken of went through to Bend and left Prineville considerably to the east of it. Later a branch had been built into Prineville, whether independent or not I don't know. I learned that they had about three trains a week each way. This of course would serve for freight, perhaps for mail, and would certainly be a great convenience for the sheepmen, and this was very much a sheep country. Prineville still had the appearance of being somewhat tough. It was certainly a typical pioneer town, and the people seemed imbued with the spirit of hospitality.

On south over the "High Desert." We were in luck. The weather had moderated. A very deep snow which often strikes there about this time, had obligingly held off. We passed, and again the door closed behind us.

Perhaps the reader has read one or more of the numerous stories that have been written about a particularly tough band of wild horses up somewhere in central Oregon. Some name the place "High Desert," some do not. Some may be more or less of a mixture between fact and fiction, others are more true to fact. There was such a band that used to inhabit the area known as the "High Desert" over which I passed. A good many of them were pretty hard to handle. They and their ancestors had run wild and free for a very long time, nor had they been crossed with civilized horses for any great length of time. They were very strong and very wild, very fleet, almost impossible to capture, and very difficult to subdue. The bunch grass upon which they fed on the plateau was extremely strong feed. There is an old saying that bunch grass puts the devil into horses. And that is true. Then the altitude, the healthy climate, had something to do with their vitality.

As we passed through now the band had largely been eliminated. A few had been captured in this way: during these deep snows, two or three times covering a period of many years, the snow had not been only three or three and a half feet deep, but three and a half or four feet deep. A band of these horses had been caught in this snow to the extent that they actually could not get out. There had been a little hole caused by their trampling and the warmth of their bodies perhaps in some semi-sheltered place, in which case the snow might be still deeper from drifting, and around them it would be so deep that they could not get out. Believing that I understand a horse's nature to some extent, I can understand, too, how these horses, realizing the situation they were in—and horses do realize more than many people imagine—if treated kindly after being rescued, they were not so hard to deal with. I repeat, it is not true that a horse has no sense of gratitude.

South of the High Desert at Alfalfa is another irrigation project. The farmers complained that water was scarce and cost too much. On south, passing east of Bend, over barren hills, we reached Millican. From Millican I had planned to go straight south by the way of Fort Rock—or nearly straight south, to Silver Lake. Fort Rock is fifty miles from Millican, through a pretty rough country.

From Notes. December 20, '26: Cloudy, colder. Slept well in house. Gave Queen blanket. Supper, breakfast, hay, no chg. (Advice on lame horse.) * * * * 3:30 p.m. Ar'd Millican, Ore. Forwarded P.P.P. to Lakeview after taking out foot gear, cap, mits, etc. Discussed rt. with proprietor of store, Mr. W. A. Kahn (?) Decided to go via Four Corners and Lake to Paisley. 4:40, Left Millican carrying 6 feeds R. barley. 6 p.m. Ar'd ranch of C. H. Griffenberger, 3½ mi. S.E. of Millican, Local. 1st try after Millican.

When I mentioned to Mr. Kahn about going south from Millican to Fort Rock, "Why, man," he exclaimed, "It is fifty miles to Fort Rock. They have been working on a road which might guide you, but there isn't one inhabitant in that fifty miles. The nearest you would come to finding any kind of shelter would be some poles over which a tent had been stretched." Of course I knew that would be impossible, and that is where we changed out route. I was much disappointed at receiving no mail. I had expected a letter would have been forwarded from my son in Portland containing a check. Mr. Kahn at first was not going to let me have any horse feed except at the rate at which they usually sold it to horseback travelers through there—it was sixty cents for four pounds. But he finally let me have it for three cents a pound. There was no such thing as staying at Millican over night. He didn't keep anybody, had no room for a horse, and advised me to backtrack some five or six miles to some ranch which we had passed. I told him it went against our religion to backtrack unless absolutely necessary, so we decided to take another route, not so direct.

The Griffenbergers, where we stayed that night, had acquired a quarter section with a good well on it and had a few head of cattle which even this early in the winter were looking pretty thin. The only feed was rye hay. I did not hear of any other kind of hay or grain being produced anywhere near there. Not one in ten of the old homesteaders remained. A quarter section of land where water could be secured, even if it had some buildings on it, usually sold during the egress of the once hopeful homesteaders for a thousand dollars.

From Notes. December 21, '26: * * * * Leaving the Griffenbergers 8:30 a.m. * * * * 1:30 p.m. Ar'd at ranch of Ole Hamstead, 18 mi. S.E. of Millican, local. Via old Prineville Lakeview rd. Dirt (5 mi. R. I.—frozen hard.)

Traveled: 14½ mi. (See above.) Rolling S.E. of Pine Mt. Ole Hamstead is the 1st settler here since 1911. Cattle and horses—large horses. High desert. No habitation between Griffenbergers

and here. Nothing in cultivation (except rye hay). * * * *
Mostly rolling plateau, buttes on all sides, with little scattering
small timber—juniper. Nat. (National) forest two mi. West in
foothills of Cascades. About 2 inches light snow most of way.
Fell last night. No thaw today. This—The Corners—is an oasis,
plenty shallow water. Quite a lot of rye hay. Rye hay is very
strong here.

December 22, '26: Slept well in house. Queen fine. Leaving
Hamstead 8:15. No chg. Helped on chores. [Left] in snow storm.
Ole is a bachelor—45—and a good scout.

Ole, whose dialect was so thick you could cut it with a meat
cleaver, didn't send us away in a snow storm by any means—and it
really was storming. He urged me to stay. The reason I left was that
I had learned that at the end of a pretty good day's travel there was
a place called "The Sink"—meaning a locality much lower than the
country in general. I forget how much lower, but enough, I reckoned,
that it might be considerably different in temperature, which proved
to be the fact. Also, there was less snow there.

Ole drew a diagram for me to guide us past his old homestead on
down by some other marks—I have forgotten what they indicate—
past Walker's Cabin, on the east, twelve miles, a stone cabin on the
right, 18 miles. Beyond that I entered a trail which led to Brooks'
place, 22 miles, in The Sink. Brooks lived on the southwest side of
this trail. On the left hand side of the trail is another stone cabin.
These stone cabins are a mystery to the present inhabitants. It is
believed by some that they were thrown up by John C. Fremont,
and his outfit. There were two habitations between Hamstead's and
The Sink—22 miles.

From Notes. December 22, '26 continued: Noon (1 p.m.).
Feeding (own grain) and eating warm dinner with Geo. Martin,
Lake, Ore., local. Walker Cabin (cow camp of Z. V. Co. No chg.
Snowing. Horseshoe in clouds.) [The first break in the clouds
happened to assume this form, and facetiously we took it as an
omen of good luck.] 8:30, Ar'd ranch of Albert Brooks 16 mi.
N. of Lake, Ore., Local. Via old Prineville Lakeview Rd. Dirt.
1st try. Rd. through E. Ore., some places, old ruts 2½ ft. deep.

Traveled: 22 mi. (See above) * * * * Queen balled up some
last five miles. Sage brush. Juniper covered hills. Some picturesque rocks. Field rye at Hamsteads, one at Walker Cabin, more

in Sink. (They all call this "The Land of Lost Hope.") Passed
¼ mi. W. of ruins of an old stone cabin. No old settler is sure
when it was built or by whom—presumably by soldiers about
1850. Narrow door and windows. Walls about 4½ ft. Shanty
roof. No inhabitants except Walker Cabin, and (name of another, new settler, illegible.)

December 23, '26: Clear, cold. Slept in warm bed. Meals, hay,
1 feed. Queen O. K. (little cold in barn). No chg. "Camp."
(Means a kind of "camp-like" cabin.) Leaving Mr. Brooks. 4
inches light snow. Mr. Brooks' aunt opened P. O. at Lake
(Christmas Lake) about 1900. Noon: Nose bag, camp fire lunch
by a cabin, 10 mi. S. of Brooks place. 2:30 p.m. Ar'd Lake P. O.,
Buchanan postmaster, via old Prineville Lakeview Rd. Rolling.
Dirt. (4 in. snow—Queen balled a little p.m.)

Traveled: 15 mi.—Sage brush, juniper on hills. Stony. * * * *
December 24, '26: Partly cloudy, warmer. Leaving Lake P. O.
8:45 a.m. Meals, horse, bed, $1.75. 25 lbs. R. oats at $1.00.
Noon, nose bag and sandwich by rd. side. "Topography and the
horizon."

Leaving Lake, going south, we soon struck into an old abandoned
stage road. We came to a low hill over which passed a wagon track,
dim under four to six inches of snow, and another track forking off
to our left around the low hill. What fooled me was that a kid at
Lake had told me to take the track around the hill, and also had said
to take the right hand track. Obviously the boy had become confused. An old man had said, "Keep south!"—and that was all I could
get out of him. He was one of those disagreeable men who seem to
believe it is smart to be abrupt. Just as we came in sight of this fork
in the road, this puzzle, a snow storm overtook us suddenly and with
such force that the position of the sun could not be determined. It
happened to be noon. If I could have gotten the direction of the sun
I could have decided which fork ran more nearly south. As it was,
the only thing I could do, having no compass, was to divide the distance between where the leaden sky seemed to meet the earth on
our right and on our left. Ordinarily this would have given us some
idea of direction, seeing that we knew we were traveling southerly.
But it fooled us here, and in a way I never would have dreamed of—
or you either. And it is hard to explain. It was on account of Table
Rock, a high plateau covering a large area on our left, east of us,
which caused a complication in our calculations. An additional point

was that the storm seemed more intense atop of Table Rock, it being probably, at least two or three or maybe four hundred feet higher than the general elevation of the country. (On our side was rather a precipice.) This further lessened the distance of visibility in that direction. The visibility was not great at best on account of the air being so full of snow. I was just about to take the right hand fork over the low hill, which, had we taken it, would have given us about forty miles of broken plateau country without a human habitation, so far as I knew or yet know. It would have been something like Dante's "frozen Inferno"—and no chance to make a fire. The nights were very cold. The altitude there is around 4,500 feet, I found later. It is barely possible that we might have survived. And even had we trudged our way through, we would certainly have been in bad shape. But—just then the snow squall ceased, as suddenly as it had started, and the sun was plainly visible, and instead of the right hand road leading south, as my calculations had indicated, it led south southwest, and the other fork, which according to my calculation without the sun had seemed to lead south southeast, pointed directly south. That is, it pointed directly toward the sun at approximately noon. This is hard to explain to one who never was caught in a like fix, though it came to me plainly enough then and is still quite apparent to me.

Anyway we did not keep the left hand fork that I have been talking about more than five or six miles, at which point it turned southwest, but we kept on south, following some trail or other. The weather had cleared. I could now keep my general direction pretty well by the position of the sun and the time of day. That is one means of traveling by orientation.

From Notes. December 24, '26 continued: 5:15, At sheep camp of Mr. Hoy, by error. 5:40, At home ranch of Thousand Springs Ranch—Hoys. Mr. L. D. Hoy, Paisley, Ore.

Traveled: 20 mi. (1 mi. by error). (Some say 22 mi.) Via old Prineville Lakeview Rd. 11 mi. R. I. Dirt. (1 mi. very rough frozen). 9 mi. very stony dirt. 9 mi. snow over hill 4 to 6 in. deep. Queen balled up badly last 4 mi. Not much snow. Queen is very tired, but comfortable in good quarters with good prairie hay and bed. (Note: Mr. Hoy has been here 21 years.) Today very rough. Sage brush, no habitation seen for 15 mi. Then two cabin shanties. Old rd. some places sage brush so overlaps, followed tracks with difficulty. At other place ruts (often 2 or 3 sets of ruts) worn deep. Great boulders rolled out, still it was very rocky everywhere and very difficult, even dangerous footing for Queen, but she is well. 1,000 Springs Ranch lies just east of center of Summer Lake, which is 15 mi. E. and S., with mountains on west. Rugged hills E. of Ranch. (Valley) Summer Lake was so named by Fremont because after coming out of Mts. to west it "seemed like summer" in the valley. Mr. Hoy cuts about 250 tons of wild hay yearly. Milks about 25-40 cows. Lot of hens —some sheep. Drives to Bend—128 miles.

From Signature Book: "I live on east side of Summer Lake, Ore. Frank M. Heath and Gypsy Queen stayed all night at my ranch Christmas Eve., Dec. 24, 1926.

(Signed) L. D. Hoy."

Over a great barren plain we go next day—all day. It begins to snow again. W-r-r-r! Suppose we are on the wrong track, of which there are several! But no, we intercept the Bend highway as we should. We reach the "Rim." All day long we have not passed an inhabited dwelling or seen a human being—and—there bursts upon our vision a—a—town! Yes, actually, a town. The electric lights are ablaze. It is Paisley, a prosperous town in an irrigated section devoted to hay and stock farms. It is Christmas Eve.

Traversing the fertile Cheuwaken Valley, we pass thousands (it seemed to me it was thousands) of fat cattle. There were at least hundreds of acres of almost marshy land, where the wild hay grew abundantly. This hay was cut in the proper season, buck-raked up into what you could call large cocks of hay, or small stacks. They wouldn't waste any time in moving this hay far. In winter a little piece of this was fenced off and the cattle were turned in until they cleaned up that section. Then the fence was extended until they cleared up that section, and so on.

Then over more hills, snow all the way, following the old Prineville Lakeview Stage Road. Several times we put up at what had been stations, occupied sometimes by the old keepers. Usually we paid. At least one of these places the occupants were running sheep in the hills and cutting wild hay to feed them in winter. At another place on a little irrigation project of some kind there was a little dairying. There was more or less snow all the way to Lakeview, Oregon.

The notebook shows that we again reset Queen's left, lowering the heel, especially inside, using the same nail holes.

From *Signature Book:* "Dec. 28/26. Frank M. Heath with his horse Gypsy Queen stop in Lakeview, Oregon, last night.

(Signed) J. P. Duke."

From Lakeview, keeping on through a fairly prosperous stock and farming country, we reached Alturas, California, on the night of December 30, 1926. It was after dark. Queen snorted some an account of the engine on the little narrow gauge railroad. The engine was also snorting. We had good quarters for Queen in a feed barn where beardless barley was the hay fed and we also fed while there crushed or rolled barley. This was only three cents a pound. We began to find out right then that we must reduce that feed 25% in weight in proportion to oats. A pound of barley will contain 25% more nourishment than a pound of oats. Even with this reduction in weight, I am not sure barley is as safe a feed as oats.

From *Signature Book:* "Dec. 30/26. Mr. Heath arrived at our ranch last night with his horse Gypsy Queen. Stayed over night.

(Signed) Clyde Cogburn,
Dove's Creek, Calif."

From *Notes.* January 1, '27: Cloudy, warm. Slept well in hay except for 12 o'clock noise which I rather enjoyed. 3 fellows had a gal. of whiskey cached in a manger. They came in several times and had a "snort" of it. The purchaser was a liberal hearted fellow—ready to give away his shirt. He was talking of riding Queen in the stall. I kept mum but crept over where I could see, ready to remonstrate if necessary. He forgot to ride. I "borrowed" about ½ pt. of the "corn" for "medicine."

Alturas, Calif.,
Dec. 31, '26.

Dear Folks:

It is thawing today—as it did yesterday. It would be a good day to travel, but Queen needed rest pretty badly. So we are laying over here today. This is the first day she has had off since we left Rufus (E. of The Dalles) and only 1 half day at Prineville. We should reach Reno between the 12th and 15th if we don't get snowed in. Meanwhile don't worry; the "distances" are not great between here and Reno. Feed and grub are a little high here, but not *awful.* 3 cts. lb. for Rolled Barley.

I will soon be down where there is not much cold if nothing happens, and then we'll "move up" as the spring advances, camping out mostly.

Have been very lucky so far. At Prineville they told me there was likely to be 3 ft. of snow on the level on the High Desert south of there "at any time." Well, there was a little snow but we beat the "*big*" snow, with "distances" as high as 22 miles.

Probably there is such a thing as "Luck." But I believe she favors the fellows who uses good judgment but don't sit down and wait for disaster to overtake him, what?

It is mostly cattle ranches for a long way ahead. I find them, generally, very hospitable, even though they charge plenty when they do charge. There is no "penny business" in these parts.

I thought I should be able to write a real letter today, but I seem to have forgotten how. Glad all well there. Love to all and Happy New Year. Address Reno, Nev. Love,

(Signed) Frank.

From Notes. January 1, '27, continued: Leaving Alturas 8:20 a.m. carrying 4 feeds. Barn 2 nights, $1.25.

We followed the Pitt River Valley south toward Madeline. The going was pretty fair. There was snow in the mountains. We passed a sheep ranch or two where they raised alfalfa in the valley, and ranged the sheep in the mountains in summer. There were some cattle, a little dairying—very little grain.

From Notes. January 2, '27: * * * * 1:30 p.m. Ar'd Madeline. Put up at barn of Mr. J. F. Poulson, local, ½ mi. S.E. of M. Dinner, P. O. * * * * Several letters. (Rec'd reply to mine of Dec. 18 to bank. Returns $50.00 check with information only $15.56 to my credit, $15.50 of which he sends. That means Brady is 2 or 3 months in arrears. (Dec.) Writing for statement of rent. * * * * Also writing Joe.

Traveled: 14½ mi. (½ off rd. to ranch and return.) Hilly. Dirt R. I., very stony or frozen. Also either very sticky dobie or ice. Pitt River valley 2-3 mi. Hay, stock and sheep. Bal. "over Mt." to about 1 mi. N. of Madeline. No habitation, P.M. When came into Madeline plain (a valley) adapted to stock range, blue joint grass in valley. Bunch grass and fileree on hills.

Note: Madeline, Calif., 6,570 mi. [This figure was taken before books were corrected.—Author.] Poulson has a large ranch. Going into poul. (turkeys). Large irrigation project depending on snow. Many thousand acres under ditch sold. Abandoned for lack of water.

January 3, '27: Partly cloudy, warm. Slept fine in house. Alfalfa, 1 feed oats, no chg. (Spent 1½ hr. last light on poul. house plans and lecture.) Leaving Poulsons 8:45 with 4 feeds. Shipping 28 lbs. to Wendle. 1 p.m. Nosebag, camp fire, lunch by road. side. 10 mi. S. of Madeline. Overlooking Madeline plain which is really a valley between mts.—or hills, sparsely covered by juniper, and in which is some snow. Snow in valley about gone. Sun out. Road, which is quite muddy, drying up. Much dobie in low places. Dobie hard when partly dry. (Very hard to travel because it clings to the feet). 5,500 feet of elevation. The N.C.&O. RR (narrow gauge) follows in bottom of valley. RR follows E. side mostly. I see deserted places on every hand. Some pretty good bldgs. Also dry ir. (irrigation) ditches. Upland is one mass of stones and boulders but have bunch grass and fileree. 3:35, in Termo—barn—no hay. Started to Ravendale—7 mi. 4 p.m. Crossed R. R. Branch Susanville and Dendle Rds. Never encountered worse case of dobie. Could hardly navigate. 5:30, At deserted place about 3½ mi. S. E. Could barely navigate across. Bldgs. all badly gone, well house best. Camping in that. Lot of work clearing place for Queen. Pump sucks wind. No water except a small puddle. Dug hole trying to let settle to get some for coffee. No hay. Oats. It is warm. Bonfire inside. Saddle for pillow. Old seat cushion minus stuffing. Bread, milk, coffee only.

Traveled: 19 mi. 5 mi. R. I. (stony). Bal. dirt—mud—dobie. Queen tired though I walked all day. Writing by light of fire, 7:45. Later, upset coffee. No more water. Dried up. [After with difficulty getting a little water for coffee, I had dug a hole to facilitate getting more water in the morning. No sooner had I dug the hole than away went the water—into the thirsty earth!]

January 4, '27: Partly cloudy, warm. Mended fire several times [in night]. Warm. Queen did not lie down. Ravendale cemetery, bronco grass. Leaving camp 6 a.m. Muddy—no breakfast—fed last oats. 8 a.m., Ravendale, 75 cts. for 9 lbs. R. oats. (The kind we eat for breakfast.) Tried to slip me two bum sacks. Lady says "all the inhabitants went to war—didn't come back." [I had asked her how it came the town was almost deserted.] 11:30, At Spanish Springs Ranch, first habitation (in-habited ranch) since yesterday A.M. Saw only 3 in distance that seemed to show life. 1 p.m. The proprietor, August Penning, P. O. Ravendale, local, and neighbor Roussel, all insist on my staying over while rd. dries (which it is doing fast). Says the dobie is hell. I am availing myself of their hospitality. Had intended to make McKissic Ranch 10 mi. further on. Queen tired.

Traveled: 9 mi. Level. Dirt. Mud—rather dobie. Description, see above. This ranch was so named because of the numerous springs and the fact that it was first claimed by a Spaniard (but he did not file. Filed on later by present owner.) Mr. Penning has been on this ranch 40 years. Mostly cattle. Raises wild hay and rye hay. Raises some mules and horses. Now engaging in dairy also.

January 5, '27: Clear, warm. Leaving the Pennings 9:30.—horse (hay), bed, meals, no chg. (Advice on crooked feet—straightened feet on jack, * * * * 1:30 Ar'd at Secret Valley Ranch. J. L. Humphrey owner, C. L. Mudgins, Foreman. Address Karlo, Calif. Local.

Traveled: 10 mi. Hilly Country. Rd. dirt ½ way, dobie, very sticky. Wind, sunshine, drying up fast. No habitation 10 mi. Next stop (uncertain) 3 mi. Next Wendle, 21 mi. from here. Passed old lava bed. Stones, mostly lying flat—sage brush—some bunch grass, bronco grass—scattering stunted juniper. This ranch produces wild hay and alfalfa, cattle and horses. (Old McKissie Ranch, taken 1850.)

On finding that we were to cross considerable real desert, Mrs. Hudgins warned me, in crossing a desert where there was a plain trail, never to leave that trail in trying to cut across. The Hudgins knew all about the whole country, I may say, for hundreds of miles around. She told me that in leaving the trail many people got lost and frequently perished. First they would find themselves lost, got confused and get to weaving back and forth or traveling in a circle, and frequently never would get out alive.

From Notes. January 6, '27: Leaving 7:30. Horse (hay), meals, bed, no chg. Note to Doyle at Amadee. *Note:* Mt. Lassen, a volcano, lies about 30 mi. W. * * * * 10 a.m., Met a Pitt River Indian going W. in search of a team to pull his auto out of mud at E. edge Mud Flat. Met him in middle of "West Mud Flat" which was not so very bad for horse as yesterday's wind had dried a crust in places and where not dry was water. The soil is dobie. 10:35 to 11:45, crossing "E. Mud Flat"— about 2 mi. This flat is devoid of vegetation and the dobie seemed at about the worst stage—partly dry. Had to poke mud off shoes constantly. Both wringing wet when we got across. 11:45, Came to E. edge where was Mr. Indian's auto, his squaw and an old one, over a tiny fire. They had been there since last night. Meanwhile two "boys" had pullled car out of mud with rope horses and turned it around ready to try detour. They are on way home near Alturas from Pyramid Lake. Went on little further and gave Queen nose bag, fixed up bite for myself as follows: (Indian women had no water to spare so could not make coffe over their fire as I should have liked—if they didn't object.) (These squaws had a large platter of roasted jackrabbits' legs. I would have liked to buy a couple of these, but the squaws seemed rather sullen, as squaws often do, often for no reason at all, so I let them keep their rabbit legs.) Here there was left a little snow—everything too wet to burn—still spitting snow—so I invented the following "dish" which I have named "The Devil's Gravy." I cut top out of can ½ full condensed milk, put in snow, added some of the O. B. Joyful I borrowed at Alturas, to melt the snow—but it didn't melt. Broke in two eggs in an attempt to make eggnog. O. B. Joyful cooked the eggs. (I remembered a lecture from my teacher when I was about eight or ten years old, to the effect that alcohol would cook a man's brain—I presume this was a temperance lecture. It suddenly flashed into my mind that if alcohol would cook a man's brain, possibly whiskey would cook an egg. It did!) Added a little R. oats which I stole from Queen to thicken so I could eat it with a spoon. A little of this dish goes a long way. By the way, this was the last of the 9 lbs. of R. oats bought in Ravendale day before yesterday—which is all the grain Queen has had. Grain is out of the question in these parts. Snow, cleared about noon, 3:30 p.m. in Wendle. Got oats sent P. P. by Mr. Poulson from Madeline. 5:30, Ar'd Amadee, Humphrey ranch. Putting up with his man, Mr. Doyle, P. O. Wendle. 1st try, prearranged by Hudgins. Doyle gave me good place for Queen. Set up excellent supper. Here are the Amadee Hot Springs and an old hotel. Place is dead now. This was formerly the terminus of the N.C.O. out of Reno and was a live town where freighters and cattlemen hit the Iron Horse. Since building of the S.P., N.C.O. is abandoned, Reno to Wendle, 4 mi. N.W. of Amadee, leaving Amadee a sort of "lame duck."

Traveled: (Jan. 6) 25 mi. Level to hilly. Dirt, R. I. 15 mi. Bal. dirt. See above about mud. Wild hay along S.W. side Secret Valley—which was so named by a poetical cowboy on account of its many "secret springs." Then few miles, two more Humphrey ranches and one other beside "Tranship Ranch" to High Road. Then some 12 mi. very rough and stony (probably old lava bed.) Then down hill about 2 mi. to Honey Lake valley near its N.E. corner to my right looked like large good ranches on the N. end (or N.W. end) of the lake, while an arm of the Sierra Nevada Mts. threw itself around the S.W. end of the Lake, making rather a rugged picture. N.E. of the Lake it is "settled" but most of the places are vacant at present—some partly improved. They are under ditch from Eagle Lake. The Eagle Lake Project. On S.E. from Wendle is level. Some parts seem to me very strong with alkali. Alkali (salt) grass and greasewood is the principal vegetation, though beyond in the foothills are prosperous small farmers. Cattle, spuds, alfalfa, dairy. Still under Eagle Lake Project.

From Notes. January 7, '27: Clear, cool. Slept well in bed. Queen fine. Leaving 7:30. Meals and all, no chg. 10:30. At ranch of Chas. Summer Smith, 5 mi. E. of Amadee. Nose bag, campfire lunch. (Lost note to H. R.) Smiths irrigate 8 or 10 acres from well 70 feet deep, by gasoline motor—another well, 60 ft., windmill. An old irrigation ditch runs along edge of plot (desert) in which there has been no water for years. 10 mi. S.E. Amadee. 3:30 p.m. Ar'd (by chance) at the Caudle Ranch, Mrs. M. O. Caudle, mother, Marvin, son, and Mamie, daughter. P. O. Stacy, local. Via dirt rd. Level, desert.

Traveled: 11 mi. (1 by error in leaving road—see above.) Viewed about 40 places, 5 or 6 of which are inhabited. Three other places show some cultivation. Besides, another—one of the 6—has a small pumping and flowing well irrigation plant. They have a stack of alfalfa. Caudles also have a flowing well 450 feet deep. [The well had flowed, but in this last year it had nearly ceased to flow. Marvin had a windmill and was pumping what water he could with the windmill. He wrote me a year or two later that he had re-established the flow by syphon. I was glad to hear this.] Irrigate about 10 acres alfalfa, 3 crops, about 6 tons per acre. Garden stuff does fair, including corn and tomatoes. The defunct irrigation ditch still continues. Was built 30 years ago, supposed to carry water from Eagle Lake, but only enough water for 10% of land under ditch. (The good farms S.W. of Honey Lake are watered from Swan River.) Scattering ranchers raise cattle and horses. High Rock Ranch is sheep. Soil, Amadee E., alternates between good, hardpan and alkali. Greasewood, sage brush.

Note: Caudle Ranch—10 mi. E. Amadee, 6,708 miles. [This figure was taken before the books were corrected and may not be quite accurate.—Author.]

Twenty thousand dollars cash, earnel as civil engineers by Marvin and a brother, they have sunk in this land. Today they would be lucky to get ten percent of that, says Marvin. Some of this twenty thousand dollars was sunk in the irrigation project mentioned. But they treated me fine, divided with Queen the little alfalfa hay purchased at $10 per ton and hauled ten miles. Not a cent would they receive.

From Notes. January 8, '27: Leaving Caudles 9:30, after attempt at photo. Meals etc. no chg. * * * * (Advice, work on feet.) 11, Leaving High Rock Ranch after much parley by Mr. Peterson about taking trail via Cottonwood River and Mts. Decided on rd.

From Signature Book: "Stacy, Calif., January 8, 1927. Frank M. Heath stopped at our house last night with his mare, Gypsy Queen.

(Signed) Marvin Caudle."

We were trying to get information as to a certain cut-off which seemed dubious, so we decided to take the road, at least for the present. We finally got started from High Rock Ranch at 11 o'clock.

From Notes. January 8, '27 continued: Noon (2:30) nose bag, sandwich, lee of pile of ties on W.P. R.R. [Believe error— S.P.?] few miles E. of Flanigan, site of big derrick. 3:30 p.m. Passing over S. P. and into a canyon, pass between Mts. toward

Pyramid Lake. [Something illegible here about oil wells. There had been some prospecting for oil about here for some time with a cheap drill—compared with a real oil drill—without success— at time when notes were taken.] 4 p.m., Passing Pyramid Fertilizer and Chemical Plant. * * * * [The road we were traveling passed through a shallow pit astraddle of the track. It seemed there were some kind of chemicals which they were trying to exploit as fertilizer. They were not getting very far with the project.] Dusk, striking S. into valley of P. L. (Pyramid Lake). Very rugged, fantastic lava rocks. One resembles a rough pyramid. Later, dim outline several pyramid rocks jutting out into N. end P. L. Later, passing over rugged rd. bet. L. and Mts. Crossing RR crossing. 7:45, Ar'd Whitney Ranch (Mrs. Whitney came here 1880)—W. of P. L.—Pyramid P. O. (Pyramid Lake 48 mi. long, 16 wide—low at present.) Many kinds mineral. Plenty big fish, salmon, trout, and others. Lake heaves before storm and moans though no wind.

Traveled: 28 mi. (½ to P. O.) * * * * Level desert nearly to Flanigan. Bal. rolling to hilly. Dirt, R. I. stony, 10 mi. Bal. dirt. I passed no habitation after High Rock R. except Flanigan ½ mi. to S. and Sec. (Section House.)

This was a pretty tedious day, seeing we got a late start. I was walking a lot, partly on account of the load, partly because it was cold as the devil. About a couple of miles from where we finally reached the Whitney Ranch, after inquiry, I had to hang on to Queen's stirrup to keep my feet. After I had been holding onto it for a little time, Queen stopped. I said, "What's the matter, Queen? Go ahead!" She went a few steps and stopped again, looking around at me knowingly. I expect she was tired too, and my swinging on the stirrup didn't help matters. I rode the rest of the way that day.

From Notes. January 8, '27 continued: No water. Not a spear of grass except few bunches "bronco grass," where fed at noon. This ranch has hay, cattle, cows, horses. * * * *

January 9, '27: Queen comfortable in rather open stable (it is not cold.) Cut the oats last night—(running short.) Slept on spring and mattress in cabin. Warm. Rested this morning. Very tired last night. Leaving Whitney Ranch 10:45. Horse, breakfast, $1.00. Note: Circle S. Ranch, formerly known as Big Cannon Ranch, 3 mi. N.W. of here, German Police dogs, horses,

polo mts. Noon, no stop. Queen colicky. Lay it to too much
alfalfa last night on empty stomach without grain. Gave ½ oz.
Tinc. aconite, 10 dr. (1¼ oz.) Tinc. belladonna. Urine, dung
soon. Still colicky. 1:30, Repeated dose. Better, still some bloat.
3 p.m. Ar'd Sutcliff. Thought best keep Queen moving. Also
$1.00 for meals with no store—bluffed me out. Indian woman
said ranch 3 mi. Passed on. About 4, hailed 4 boys in old Ford.
Said ranch on Reno Rd. Indian ranch—empty. Several miles.
Went right on. Boys gave me 3 big spuds—all grub they had.
Dusq: Pulled up to a very large picturesque rock or pyramid,
where I saw auto, people on pleasure party. Said ranch 3 mi.
Gave me bottle water. (Water in lake not drinkable for man or
beast, on account of chemicals.) 6:30, ar'd Indian Ranch, 23
mi. N. of Wadsworth, Nev. Put Queen in one room (floor removed)—hung poncho over window of other, built camp fire
(floor removed.) Rested and ate spuds with ½ can milk.
* * * * No water. Spread bed on ground by fire. Fed Queen
ordinary feed—grain, no hay. * * * *

Traveled: 20 mi. via local road following W. environs of P.
Lake. Hilly, dirt R. I. stony, 3 mi. Bal. dirt. Very little grass.
Practically no stock in sight. Some very unique Indian homes
at Sutcliff.

From Signature Book: "Pyramid, Nevada, 1/9/27. Frank M.
Heath slept here last night with mare Gypsy Queen.
(Signed) L. S. Whittey,
Act. P.M."

From Notes. January 10, '27: Clear, warm. Wind N. Mended
fire several times—slept warm. Queen did not lie down. Hungry.
Better this morning. No water since 9 yesterday. No breakfast.
* * * * Leaving Indian place, 6:45. 7:45, Ar'd fishing place of
Frank Skimmerhorn, full-blooded Piote Indian, fisherman,
rancher, near S. end P. Lake. Having bountiful breakfast of
salmon, deliciously cooked, biscuit, coffee. P. O. Piote Agency.
Mr. Skimmerhorn was born here. Is about 35 years old. Parents,
all ancestors born here. Mr. Skimmerhorn agrees with all old-
timers that in the past 10 years since water taken from L. Tahoe
for irrigation, lake has fallen a great deal, as in fact is easily
seen. Fears that in another 10 years at present rate, lake will be
entirely dry. Most Piotes depend on fishing for a living. Mr.

Skimmerhorn is owner of ranch where stayed last night. Leaving 9 a.m. 10 a.m., Watered at spring by Lake, ½ mi. off rd.—sulphury, sandy. Noon, nose bag by rd. side, 10 mi. N.W. of Wadsworth. Last of oats. No lunch. Passed few Indian shacks on lake. One old-fashioned tepee. One ranch (?)—log cabin, very little alfalfa at shack of stable. Clouded up about 11. Looks as though snowing in mts. to West. Desolate—practically no grass. 4 head cattle, 3-4 horses, all seen today so far.

The principal reason we hit Wadsworth, some thirty miles east of Reno, instead of Reno, as per schedule, is this: The altitude at Reno is much higher than at Wadsworth. The weather was uncertain. I had been making inquiries in regard to what was probable and keeping my eyes on the forecasts as nearly as possible. Once more we decided to make a run for lower altitude, to try to escape the probable snow. We found we had made a good move. That day Reno witnessed a terrible snow storm—the most terrible in years, I was told. We saw a few flakes. We laid over in Wadsworth. We made a trip to Reno by rail. It was still very wintry there, though the snow had ceased.

From Notes. January 10, '27 continued: Ar'd Wadsworth, barn of T. H. Blundel, Mr. Foster, foreman. 1st try, 4:30 p.m. via local rd. Level to hilly, dirt road. R. I. 12 mi. Dirt, 12 mi. * * * *

Traveled: 24 mi. * * * * Barren, sage brush, greasewood. This Blundel ranch is a good dairy Ranch, cows good. Nearly 160 acres in alfalfa. Modern, well kept.

January 11, '27: Foggy, not cold. Slept well in hay. Queen little sore. Shows some signs of belly ache. No oats obtainable. Mr. Foster free with alfalfa and ground barley, of which fed sparingly night and morning. In corral today. Laying over here. Side trip to Reno via Fernley and motor bus, for Bal. shoeing tools, forward mail, etc. Met Mr. Blundel this morning—a fine, free-hearted fellow.

Special Note. Total to Wadsworth, Nev., 6,780 miles [as corrected.] * * * * Spent day in Reno forwarding mail, etc. Got back to ranch 8 p.m. * * * * Heard from Bank, another check for $12.80, one for $46 wrote thanking Mr. Whitacre. Sent $1.00 to Pyramid. * * * * Got some grub. Nipper, H. S. [horse shoe] nails, etc. [I bought a lath hatchet, had a hole drilled through the handle, a wire loop put in it, carried that snapped to my pack thereafter. I found it mighty convenient.] Colic med. Fare $2.20. All told spent $8.30. (Some remarks about whiskers.) Met Dr. Ball, Red X [Red Cross] lady. Bank cashed checks. * * * *

Reno, Nev., Jan. 11, '27.

Dear Folks:

Yours of Jan. 8 just rec'd here. Came E. of Reno 30 miles to Wadsworth, thus avoiding Mts., snow, and saving a few miles. Here on a side trip to get some things and forward waterbag, etc. * * * * I find I have not very long "jumps." With usually good weather, water bag and so forth of course I'll make it O. K. No "jumps" at all for about 10 days yet. Write next to Tonopah. Love.

(Signed) Frank.

From Notes. January 12, '27: Clear cool. Leaving Blundel place 8:30. No chg. for horse, 5 feeds, 3 meals. * * * * 4:30 or 5 p.m. according to sign (some words here illegible) points where we should reach Ft. Churchill in distance—mistaking bldg. at Appin for Ft. Church ranch. 7:45 smelled a ranch. 8:15, Queen "discovered ranch." 8:30 Ar'd Ft. Churchill Toll Ranch, W. E. Garavanta, Prop. Via Lincoln Hy. to Fernley, 3 mi. dirt rd. (very many and large crooks and angles, S., SE., W., S.)

Traveled: 30 mi. (3 by error). 5 mi. R. I. dirt. Stony 15 mi. Dirt, 10. Queen very tired. (Out of sight of snow, 1 to 4 p.m.) Good irrigated places to few mi. S. Fernley. From there to this place sage brush, greasewood, stony desert. No water. Scarcely a spear of grass. No habitation. Passed 2-3 shafts, probably prospect holes. This farm consists of 4,000 acres, 500 irrigated. Alfalfa. 300 cattle. Horses. [I remember distinctly they had a lot of sheep. I know it was lambing time. Men were up nights.] Old large hotel now used as res. Another ranch S. uses same ditch. R. R. station, Weeks. Camp. [There was a camp or something just across a little creek from the main buildings, where travelers, some freighters, camped.]

January 13, '27: Clear, warm. Slept fine in alfalfa. Queen rested. Leaving 11:15 a.m. Alfalfa, 1 feed barley, cooked in office, no chg. Note: Old Mr. Garavanta came to this locality

1876. Was a good country then. Stock men had been using water out of Carson River since 1858, on natural meadows. Began making ditches 1861 for gardens, etc. Began alfalfa about '70—in '87 came the "nesters." Now everything is going back—especially since too much irrigation with too little water. [So said Mr. Garavanta.]

Note: 10 a.m. (Jan. 13, '27) Sitting on ruins of one of the 22 (brick about 2" to 2½" x 5" x 10") bldgs. of old Ft. Churchill. Bldgs. run from 2 fair sized rooms to one square rm. bldgs. about 25' x 80'. Some walls about 50% intact or more, others reduced to a mere mound. 2 were 2 stories. Some openings square top, timbers still there. Others arched. All have good stone foundations, most of which are in good repair. (Walls about 20" thick—2 bricks.) All surround a "parade ground" on a slightly S. slope a little N. of Carson R. which is now fringed with cottonwood. Vegetation, sage brush, greasewood. Sandy soil. Picturesque hills S. and E. Sierra Nevadas show snow to W. (Ft. Churchill protected immigrants—abandoned 1863 (?)) Bee hives. Loose cattle. Faced rock in foundation—brick moulded. Noon (1:30) Nosebag 7 mi. S. of Ft. Churchill. 3:00, Passing Thompson Smelter. 3:45, in Wahuska—no stable. Bought groceries. 4:15, Ar'd ranch of R. J. Penrose, ½ mi. S. of Wahuska, Nev., local.

Traveled: 16 mi. via local rd. paralleling S.P. Dirt, R. I. 8 mi. Dirt, 8 mi. Level to hilly. Sagebrush, greasewood. Last 8 mi. few small ranches to right (dry)—few prospect holes. Wahuska on alkali flat. Here are fine irrigated farms. Cooperative irrigation from Walker R. Cattle, sheep, alfalfa, spuds. Dairying.

January 14, '27: Clear, cool. Leaving Penrose 8:30. Horse (hay), bed in bunk house, breakfast, no chg. (Advice on lame horse.) 1:30, Yerington—no stable. Spent 1 hr. hunting for stable. (Honey bees out today.) 2:30, At Snyder Ranch, R. J. Snyder, local (about ¾ mi. W).

Traveled: 11 mi. 1 to ranch etc.) Level, dirt. Irrigated valley 2 mi. Not so good bal. way. Alfalfa, sheep, stock, spuds, dairying. (Prospect holes in hills.) Bought 100 lbs. oats 2.75. Poite (?) Indian Village. Work, fair ranch hands.

From Notes. January 15, '27: Cloudy, warm. Slept well in load of hay. Queen rested some. Leaving Snyder 8:30. Hay, breakfast, no chg. (Advice.) Later, Laying over today. Reset

Queen's left front. Lowered heel, spread both—shop of Mc-
Carty. No chg. P. P. 84 lbs. oats to Hawthorn, 16 lbs. to Mina.
* * * *Staying tonight in barn of Ben Barton, a kid.
   Traveled: 1 mi.—Saw Ed. Times.
   January 15, '27 continued: *Note:* Had intended to go S. from
here via Ambrose, Rosacker, Lucky Boy—a mt. pass—to Hawthorn. But everybody tells me pass probably snowed up, so
decided to go via Schurz, a roundabout way, but following valley
through a lower pass, and probably after all not much further.

                                    Yerington, Nev., Jan. 15, '27.
Dear Folks:
   Getting on fine. Resting here today. Queen is prancing and
snorting after a short day yesterday. Still her legs need a rest.
I'll make short days now whenever I can, and save her for a few
fairly long jumps. But none too long. We will make it O. K.
with water bags.
   Have had no snow now for several days, though we just
missed a lot by hitting 30 miles E. of Reno. I am seldom out
of sight of the snow. It is windy here today. Nothing particular
to write. Love,
                                    (Signed) Frank

   From Notes. January 16, '27: Partly cloudy, warm. Leaving
Ben Barton 8:30. Only 25 cts. for hay. 9:00, Leaving Yerington.
11:30, Ar'd ranch of Pete Hendricks, local, 2nd try. 6 mi. N.E.
of Yerington. State Hy. Level, gravel.
   Traveled: 6 mi. (See above). Irrigated from Walker River.
Alfalfa. Cattle. Sheep. Spuds. Dairy. Honey. Poultry. (Walker
River Irrigation district, Smith and Mason Valley.) Average
holding is about 500 acres under irrigation or can be irrigated—
apparently water. (See above.) Owners want to sell part. Prices
run from $30.00 for "susceptible" to $200.00 for that in cultivation. Laying in this P.M. resting Queen. Snowing *hard* in
Lucky Boy Pass 1 p.m. Later, Boys run in 10 wild horses. Had
a private rodeo. Rode 'em all, yearlings too. Some sore back.
Gave away one to a kid for driving same. Offered me one if I
wanted it. Tied a can to tail of a beautiful brown pacer. I hated
to see some of this. This little horse is said to be a "bad one."
He seemed to sense I was his friend so gave me an appealing
look, but what could I do? I should like to own him but couldn't
take him of course. Wild horses are a joke here.

January 17, '27: Clear, cool. Slept pretty well in manger with addition of 5 borrowed blankets. Hung poncho front of Queen to stop draft. Leaving Hendricks 7:15. Hay, milk, no chg. 1:15 p.m. Nose bag, camp fire lunch by irrigation ditch, near rd. 4 mi. W. Schurz on Walker (Indian) Reservation. Stack of hay nearby, owner there (Indian) did not offer Queen any. 4:25, Ar'd Schurz. Putting up stable of J. F. Derig, gen, merchandise.

Traveled: 20 mi. Level to hilly. Gravel, 4 mi., R. I., dirt, 6 mi. Dirt, 6 mi. * * * * Level plain uncultivated. 4 mi. hills. 8 mi. No habitation except old Geo. Hedge. * * * * 1 piece rye—bees. * * * * Then 8 mi. in Walker R. valley. Walker R. Indian Res. well settled (20 acre allotments under Gov. supervision.) Irrigated from Walker R. Alfalfa, some cattle, horses. 6 are shipping cream. Wheat, barley, spuds, turkeys, hogs, gardens, cantaloupes, watermelons. These Indians are industrious and steady. Fences in good repair. Good teams. Good horsemen. Also many indulge in mining. (Rather prospecting.) Paiutes (?) Met Mr. Jack Largen, a Cherokee lately from Okla. Very tall grass—a few horses on range. Fremont came E. of Walker Lake to Schurz on way from Wyoming to Calif., 1846 (?) Schurz named after Congressman Schurz—(?) Walker Lake mts. on W.—snow high up. Other mts. to N. N.E., very colorful, practically treeless. Optical delusion (or illusion)—smoke? water? Neither.

By this last I meant of course that an optical illusion would indicate that either light colored smoke was settled in an apparent hollow in the land, or else that there was a lake of water. While this seemed plain as day, an inquiry proved that it was neither smoke nor water.

From Notes. January 18, '27: Partly cloudy, warm. Leaving Schurz 8:30. Slept well in [old] ice house. (Made bed on dry sawdust.) Passed some very unique rocks—some a mass of rocks corroded together—some small ones—some honeycombed. Below old high water mark are some very beautiful "movies" formed from chemicals in the waters of the lake, gray to yellow. Walker Lake very low—still 60 ft. 500 feet from shore. Hundreds of bass, chubs, silver trout, carp, catfish, ducks, swans, geese, all times of year. Squirrels out today—saw them. * * * * Dusk,

Passing along W. of Lake Walker under overhanging cliffs, past great fissures etc.—about 2 mi. Hy. blasted out of solid rocks. * * * * 6:30 Ar'd place of A. Peterson, 13 mi. N. of Hawthorn, local. Later, putting up in stone stable at his ranch, ½ mi. up in hills to N.W.—unique place. Spring, trees, "a roof of rock."

Traveled: 24 mi. (1 mi. backtrack—1 mi. to stable and return.) Hilly, gravel, 16 mi.—R. I., stony, 8 mi. (Snow nearly to bottom of mts.)

January 19, '27: Clear, warm. Slept warm in vacant stall. Queen O. K. Leaving stable 8:30. Alfalfa, 50 cts. 9:30, Ar'd ranch of Mrs. M. E. Spencer, 12½ mi. N.W. of Hawthorn— local. Stopped to buy ½ doz. eggs. Mrs. S. seemed quite interested in trip. Proposed I lay over today and help butcher a hog. As day's rest will not hurt Queen, and as Mrs. S. needs the help, and as Mrs. S. seems a very interesting woman, I am staying. * * * *

Traveled: 2 mi. Gravel.

This Mrs. Spencer gave one glance at Queen as she was tied at the gate. "Say," she says, "that horse is tired. You can tell by her eye." First she just proposed that I lay over and rest the horse that day. I told her I couldn't impose on people like that, especially a woman. That is the time she proposed I lay over and help butcher the hog. That was a different matter.

From Notes. January 19, '27 continued: Later, noon, Queen in corral and shed with alfalfa. All ready to butcher hog after dinner. Improvised scaffold. * * * * 6 p.m., Had a hell of a time butchering hog. 1st, Wind blew up so hard it was hard to heat water out of doors. 2nd, I didn't rap the big old hog hard enough the 1st time and after the first rap he was hard to approach, but we finally snared him by one front foot and "got him." Then I couldn't get through his hide with what I had believed was a sharp knife. Ran a couple of hundred feet for another, with which I had better success. Then we got a rope on Mr. Hog, a harness on an old horse, and snaked him to the "barrel." (Mrs. S. and I could not budge him.) Then in hoisting him by horse power, one leg of our tripod broke and let the whole durned thing down. We toggled it up and hoisted hog by horse power up to a platform that we had improvised out of an old box, an old door and some rock. But to save our souls we couldn't pull the hog into the barrel. So Mrs. S. escorted the old horse through several gates while I rearranged the togglings, and we finally, by horse power, skillful handling and some language on my part, got the hog started into the barrel. But we could only get head and shoulders in, he was that large. While we were thus engaged the water partly cooled and we had more delay. Finally we got the head scalded and one side. Then we had to switch the old horse back through all the gates on the place and hitch him onto the rear end of the hog to get his head out of the barrel. After we got him out we busted up some old lumber and re-heated the water enough to scald the other side— in places. We shaved the remainder—or I might say the remains. Being too heavy for our "scaffold" we disemboweled him lying down. Then we cut off his head, split him in half and cut each half into three pieces, each of which was all one man could handle. I believe the hog—2 years old—dressed at least 600 lbs. He is now resting peacefully—that is in pieces—on the kitchen table. Queen is resting well in the stable, and I am going to rest in one of Mrs. S.'s several civilized beds. And thus ends another day. Mrs. S. homesteaded this place in 1916. * * * * The place joins Walker Lake. Mrs. S. has had "some little experience" in holding it down. She has rather a good orchard— irrigates about 4 acres from springs on place, and stores snow water. Raises alfalfa (very heavy yields.) Cattle, (very few) hogs, (more) turkeys, chickens. [A grown "tom turkey" brought $12 or $15 as I remember. After starting, she herded them largely in the hills.] She is a good-hearted soul and quite a character, and not easily bluffed. She has had much experience. The water of Walker Lake, she says, possesses great healing qualities.

Jan. 20, '27: Clear, warm. Staying over at S. ranch, resting Queen, who has much soreness in feet and left front leg. Soaking left front. Took cattle to neighbors.

From Notes. January 21, '27: Snowing a little. Leaving Spencer Ranch. Called it even. Eggs, meat, cookies.

Mrs. Spencer objected to our leaving in the storm—urged me to stay—but knowing that Hawthorn was considerably lower, that anyway I was going southeasterly, and as Queen was pretty well rested, I decided to try to beat the snow. But I couldn't get away without taking some grub with me, including a very large cloth bag of cookies.

From Notes. January 21, '27 continued: 4:40, Ar'd barn of Grandfather of Bud Watters, Hawthorn. Hay 35 cts. Lent quilts. Fine boy sleeping in room in barn.

Traveled: 11 mi. Hilly, gravel, 6 mi. R. I. stony, 5 mi. Cleared up. *Special:* Hawthorn 6,901 miles.

January 22, '27: Cloudy. Leaving Hawthorn 7:30. * * * * 10 a.m. Passing several prospect holes, an old mining camp apparently, and a large mill. Noon, Nosebag, cold lunch, sunny side of a large rock. 5 p.m., Sheep camp 4 mi. S. as described by a sheep man I met (looks to me 4 mi. nearly) and probably deserted. So pass it up although still some 11 mi. from Mina. * * * * 8:40 p.m. Ar'd Mina, putting up at Baker Hotel. Queen in a shed. Via canyon road—hilly. [Had substituted Mina for Luning, by which means I cut off several miles.]

Traveled: 35 miles. Gravel 15 mi. R. I. (stony) 10 mi. Dirt, 10 mi. Some snow especially through canyon. Barren—greasewood, sagebrush, stony mostly. Practically no grass—no stock in sight. Few prospect holes. No inhabited dwelling. * * * *

January 23, '27: Cold, clear. Laying in today as next stop, Gilbert, 32 mi. and don't believe it policy to give Queen two long days in succession, especially as back is considerably swollen and some soreness. She is a little off her feed. Soaking back with salt water. P.P. 24 lbs. oats to Gilbert. There are many Indians here. 2,000 men working out of here. * * * * (Rhodes salt put up at R. Salt works.)

There was a large old warehouse on a side track. Some salt (?) had been extracted from the soda, salt, alkali, or call it what you will, crust, that covered the surface. In my exhibits I have one of these sacks. Uncle Sam took a hand in this salt business on the ground that it contained too much borax. I seem to remember that they were selling the stock on hand to stockmen, or something like that. Imagine the effect of this chemical crust and the like sometimes encountered, on Queen's feet.

Mina, Nev., January 23, '27.

Dear Folks:

I am laying over here today. Am laying over *frequently* lately and making a few short days, getting or rather keeping Queen fit for a few fairly long "jumps" ahead. We had 35 miles yesterday—Hawthorne to here—32 tomorrow to Gilbert, and have already mailed oats ahead. Then 32 miles to Tonopah, another day's rest, and on to Goldfield.

We had expected to have to make it from here to Tonopah without a stopping place, as to shelter, but with two springs on the way. Now we learn of the more comfortable way. That will probably be the way of it. Goldfield to Indian Springs—a day out from Las Vegas. Anyhow the (worst?) we will have to do is pack water the last 60 miles, for which we are prepared. From Las Vegas on is quite simple. This is an old mining town. All feed is shipped in here.

The Hotel office—or bar room, is full of miners, prospectors, and other frontier specimens of humanity, and a few Indians. Yesterday I met an old Spanish sheep man—or I took him to be—and here one is reminded that he is nearing a semi-Mexican American locality. The principal product of the country seems to be rugged scenery and prospect holes. There is also a salt mine—or factory, at which they take it from a well * * * * a few miles from here.

For once I have nothing of very great importance to do this P.M., so am going to try to read the paper a little to learn what is going on.

I expect some mail at Tonopah. Better write me next at Las Vegas, Nev. I should be there in 10 days, or two weeks, depending on how long it takes to procure a donkey at Goldfield and teach him United States. * * * * With love,

(Signed) Frank.

From Notes. January 24, '27: Clear, cold. Little warmer. Up 5—breakfast 5:45. Queen dainty about oats. 8 men evidently loafed about stove in Baker Hotel Barroom all night. Leaving Mina for Gilbert 6:30 a.m. Putting piece of old blanket under saddle. Noon, Nosebag, hot lunch in lee of a bluff, 13 mi. S.E. of Mina. Melting snow for coffee. 8:30 Ar'd Gilbert. No stable. Putting up in garage of Mrs. Ione Hatch, wife of Geo. Hatch. Bought bucket of water at Gilbert Club, 15 cts. 2 flakes of alfalfa, 50 cts. Having hot coffee with my lunch with the Hatches. Sleeping in the house—blankets on Queen.

Traveled: 32 mi. Snow at Gilbert. Rock, greasewood. Very little grass. No habitation after leaving Sodaville (4 mi.) to

Gilbert. Gilbert is a mining town—mines not running. Black Mammoth, gold and silver, in litigation. R. R. 12 mi. Haul water from Willow Springs, 4 mi.

January 25, '27: Clear, cold. Leaving Hatch 9:30. No chg. for garage, bed, bucket water (at 5 cts. gal.) Gave kids 25 cts. for candy. Noon (1 p.m.) Nosebag, cold lunch 9 mi. E. Gilbert. 2 p.m., John Noonan stopped, offered to carry pack, P. O. Simon, Nev., local. 5 p.m. Ar'd Millers, an ore mill (a very small part of which was running). Once quite an establishment. A few people here now. Hotel, electric plants, and many old bldgs., and shacks, in ruins.

Traveled: 18 mi. (1 mi. to old barn W. end of town and return.) Hilly except last 8 or 9 mi., which is a sagebrush flat. Dirt 2 mi.—gravel 10 mi. R. I. 6 mi. Desert—stony, greasewood, sagebrush, 6 or 8 cattle—no habitations.

January 26, '27: Cloudy, cool wind. Slept well in small "outbuilding." Queen O.K. Plenty fire—plenty water. Camped. Leaving Miller 9 a.m. Cool N.E. wind. 1:45 Ar'd Tonopah— Putting up at Andy Roush barn. Elevation 6,938 ft.

Traveled: 14 mi. Slightly up grade 9 mi. Last 5 hilly. Dirt 2 mi. Gravel 8 mi. Dirt, R. I. (stony) 4 mi. Barren plain, greasewood, sagebrush (continuation of flat crossed yesterday—Mines, prospect holes). * * * * Later saw people at Times office. Later, Rec'd 7 letters and card at P. O., one from Joe, one from Bank —with statement. Remailed P.P. to Las Vegas. Rec'd pincers, nails. There is some snow here. Seems most like a mining town since Wallace, Idaho.

January 27, '27: Clear, warmer. Laying in. Times having photo taken. Having Queen reshod at Jack Clark's. A good job, $2.50. 5:30 p.m. Just finished all work and lunch. Shipping by Mr. Garside of the Tonopah Times 40 lbs. oats to Springdale, 70 lbs. oats to Beatty (Remick) and 30 lbs. to Indian Spring. Cost me $5.60. Slept O. K. in Andy Roush Barn. Sleeping there again tonight, ready for early start. Letter from home—20 in. snow there.

January 27, '27: Clear, warm, S.E. winds. Leaving Tonopah 7:30. $1.50 for barn, hay, 2 nights.

From Signature Book: "Tonopah, Nev., Jan. 28. Frank M. Heath and his horse Gypsy Queen stop at my barn 2 days.
(Signed) A. Roush."

TONOPAH (NEV.) TIMES

January 27, 1927

CROSSES COUNTRY IN SADDLE USING ONLY ONE HORSE

———

Sergeant Heath Who Served in World War with Engineers Reaches Tonopah with His Gypsy Queen

———

Riding down Main Street yesterday morning appeared a ruddy-faced veteran of the World War astride a sleek, well-groomed dark bay Kentucky-bred mare intent on securing lodgings during their stay in camp. The rider did not care much for his own comfort but seemed deeply concerned about the accommodations for his mount which he treated with all the attentions of a lover. * * * *

Leaving the National Capital April 1, 1925, Sergeant Heath decided his health that had suffered during the war overseas would be benefited by a long campaign outdoors. The only stipulation was that he would be back in Washington July 1, 1927. This part of the contract he voided by an injury to one limb that cost him three months in the hospital and temporarily interfered with his itinerary. On the present lap of his journey Serg't Heath left Spokane Nov. 26th, 1926, arriving Tonopah January 25, 1927 after traversing 1,051 miles and covering altogether 6,949 since hitting the trail. From Spokane he came through by way of Alturas after crossing Oregon and part of Washington.

"I bucked heavy snow at several points, but perhaps the worst," said Heath, "was in the back country east of Kent, Oregon, where the snow was all of six to fifteen feet." [I said 6 to 15 inches, not feet! —Author. I encountered more or less snow all the way to Alturas] * * * *

"One of my greatest problems," added Heath, "was in finding a blacksmith to shoe the mare. In these days of autos the animal blacksmith has disappeared and in order to have proper work done I learned to do it myself. About myself? I love the outdoors and am always ready to camp when night overtakes us, so you will know quite often a blanket on Mother Earth forms my bed. However, I always like to get Gypsy Queen under cover during the night and I never give her the worst of it."

Sergeant Heath works his way by acting as adviser to farmers and ranchers consulting him about their horses or herds and always receives gratuity in return. He never asks for anything and often finds his pay comes in the form of accommodations and meals for man and beast. Where long distances intervene like on the desert the traveler always looks out for the comfort of his mare by seeing she is supplied with her customary oats. In traveling through Nevada the route will be by way of Las Vegas across the Amargosa desert, where careful count has to be made for the daily ration of oats. Yesterday Heath said he would probably buy a burro in Goldfield to carry oats and water on the long trek of 176 miles to Las Vegas.

* * * *

End of newspaper article.   F. M. H.

Goldfield comes next. Thank God we are ahead of the winter—or is winter over? It is January 28, 1927. We are in the northern end of the Amargosa Desert.

Many were the "lifts" we got across the desert. A newspaper man distributed oats for us at intervals along the highway. Railroad crews dropped us off consignments of both oats and hay (grass there was none) at Ralston, on the Tonopah and Tidewater, and again at Bonnie Clair, Death Valley Scotty's railroad station. We zigzag to these points for water at the railroad tanks. Leaving Bonnie Clair, we took an old desert rat's advice and tried to cut off a curve, and were lost in the desert most of that day and night and part of the next day, with one canteen of water, one feed of oats and one meal. Talk about optical illusions! We began to realize how people lose their lives in the desert, and remembered Mrs. Hudgins' warning. We were traveling by the stars that night, and keeping east of the old grade of the old Tonopah and Las Vegas—after we had crossed it—brought us round next morning to Rhyolite, the Ghost City, and thence to Beatty. We had missed Springdale, one of the points where Garside had dropped off some oats.

Beatty, Nev., Feb. 3, '27.

Dear Folks:

We are laying over here today, resting. Queen is fat as a pig and always ready for her oats—which she seldom does without, notwithstanding I send many consignments on ahead since leaving Alturas, Calif. At Tonopah, Nev., for instance, I sent to Springdale 40 lbs., Beatty, 70 lbs., by Mr. Garside, Editor-owner, Tonopah Times. From Goldfield I sent 24 lbs. of oats and 15 lbs. of hay on to Ralston c/o Mr. Kelley—section boss—by the R.R. boys—free of charge. Ralston was 3 miles off the direct route but it saved a "dry camp." From Ralston I sent 12 lbs. oats, 10 lbs. of hay, half of this last consignment, on to Bonnie Clair again by the train crew—free. I had expected to have to pack them. Also the pump man who lives at Bonnie Clair and pumps at both places, took my bed roll (no light matter these days) and my desert water bag—which should still have been in the mail, as I didn't need it yet—to Bonnie Clair on his light hand car.

Bonnie Clair is also a *little* off but by this slight zigzagging I avoided another "dry camp." That is, I again avoided packing water.

Day before yesterday we made 33 miles over pretty tough going and layed out, but reached civilization 9 o'clock yesterday morning. By coming a few miles out of the way and making one dry camp—and it was dry—we struck Rhyolite (the Ghost City) and it paid us well for the little inconvenience. These old ruins "in the middle of the desert" were in 1905-06 a city of 15,000. Some pretty good mines were in operation at that time. Now the sole resident is a Mr. L. A. Mason who lives in The Bottle House, a house literally built of bottles laid in cement. This was restored in recent years by the Famous Players Laskey Company. The ruins of the old Ghost City are used occasionally by them as the background for movies. There still stands the large good school bldg. and two other quite elaborate bldgs. of masonry, one of which is three stories besides a splendid basement. No windows remain, or doors. Perhaps the most striking of all is the splendid depot, also doorless and window-less. The R.R. that once served this old city as well as Carrara (an old marble quarry), Las Vegas and Tonopah, has long been pulled up. I understand the steel was sold to the Chinese Government. The old grade serves in places as a public highway.

Getting back to the old depot. In one room lie the remainders of a large animal—apparently a donkey or burro. According to some of the old-timers he was a bigger ass than those who built the city only in the fact that he leaves his skin and bones there while they got out with theirs. And yet, two or three of the old mines are being worked right now to some extent on leases by individuals who seem to be drawing some kind of an existence from the heart of Mother Earth.

Most of the wooden buildings are moved away—some to this place, others torn down, but many still stand—gaunt ghosts of a past that has been dead only about 20 years. Near by one old foundation lies an old-fashioned blacksmith bellows—what's left of it—that doubtless played its part in blowing things—and prices—up. But like some other windbags it now lies prone.

Near another ruin I saw a warped and checked old chair. Its legs looked tired and wobbly. But still it reminded me that even in those Halcyon days some poor devil probably took time to sit down, more or less.

The hills about Rhyolite are fairly honeycombed with prospect holes. And the large bldgs. of a large mine or two that has coughed up about all it had to give, stand as gaunt testimony that most things at least have two ends—the first and the last—or the front and rear, whichever the case may be. Two or three of these mines did pay for a while.

I must for once backtrack about a mile down toward the flat. On a bench are the much less elaborate ruins of Bull Frog. (Not the old Bull Frog 4 mi. W.) Bull Frog is said by some to have been a tough place, a few having died with their boots on. There is nothing left but a few ruins of shacks.

Yesterday, 11 a.m., we got in here after stopping to have breakfast with Mr. Mason at the Bottle House. (Mr. Mason is working an old mine on a lease.) He also gave Queen a bucket of water, though he hauls it from Beatty, 5 miles. "Have you had any breakfast?" asked Mr. Mason. "Yesterday," I informed him. He laughed a little. "Well, park that horse somewhere a little while." He soon prepared a hearty meal, and it tasted good, you bet!

Arriving here we—especially Queen—were disappointed in finding that Mr. Garside had not yet delivered our oats. He was supposed to have come through a day or two earlier on his way to Las Vegas, where he owns another paper. But on my return from a side trip, of which I will tell you later, I found the consignment for this place and also the 40 lbs. he was to have left at Springdale, both waiting at the Remick garage. Not having been in Springdale the night before as per plan he must have learned somehow (or did he surmise?) that I had passed up that place. These old desert rats are not only wise, but any news travels fast. Here they always seem to know of our arrival several days in advance. Well, I'll simply ship the surplus oats that accrue from missing three feeds and also from the fact that we made provision for a burro which we won't need, on to Searchlight. We'll feed them there.

The reason we will not need the donkey is that we have only one "dry camp" between here and Searchlight, and probably for 400 miles beyond. And now get this: Mr. Remick of this place is going to take in his car, oats, hay, water, and grub to do us at this "dry camp" (that is, it would have been a dry camp) 30 miles beyond Carrara, which is a short day (10 miles) from here, and beyond to the next camp, 22 miles beyond that, where is a spring. The next water, Indian Springs, is only 10 miles beyond that. There is a ranch and hay at Indian Springs. There is another ranch and of course water 25 miles beyond there, and then Las Vegas is only 20 miles.

Now I must go and do a few things before I tell you of my side trip yesterday into "Death Valley."

Feb. 4, '27.

After I did those few little things last night I was so tired all of a sudden that I didn't know whether I was afoot or horseback. So I hit the hay. This morning I'm fine. So is Queen. I'll pull out for a half day to Carrara about noon after another feed. Well, when I arrived here in Beatty, day before yesterday, Mr. Remick told me that three fellows were going into Death Valley with an auto and asked if I wouldn't like to go. I certainly would. So straightway Mr. Remick "flagged" the party until I grabbed my mackinaw. It was about noon and I was hungry, but what of that? I climbed into the waiting car, a Master Six Buick, owned and driven by Mr. E. J. Kennah of Heber City, Utah. He is a musician out on a little vacation, and a good, clean, wholehearted young fellow. With him were also a young fellow named R. Slaughter, also of Utah, another musician, and movie actor. They were taking the third young man 30 or 35 miles on his way to some job he had in view some 50 miles still further west. He was almost a stranger to Mr. Kennah, had met him while playing for a dance (the third man being a pianist) a day or so before. That's the way they do out here. Mr. "Pianist" seems one of those who between being free-hearted and indulgent in O. B. Joyful are most always broke—no matter how much he makes. Such was the party.

As I came along the bluff this morning I saw a road stretching south across a gravelly flat. I thought it must be a good one. After passing back from "the old grade" through the "ghost city" we hit this flat. The car was not driven fast, but all that stopped me from going well on my way toward the beautiful blue every little while was the top—and that's no lie. I soon resorted to hanging onto the back rail of the front seat with one hand and the foot rail of the one in which I sat with Mr. Pianist, with the other. Soon we entered the beautiful rugged hills so full of color. This route is well marked and well watered by springs every few miles, and continues rough.

Here are my notes as I jotted them down whenever we stopped for a few minutes.

12:45 p.m. At N.E. side of Death Valley boundary Pass. Mt. Whitney presents a grand view across the Valley to W. though her top is hidden in cloud.

Little later. Seated near top of a large rugged heap of brown rock, a kind of small mt., we got a good view of a large part of Death Valley. First a bench, beyond which lie to the S.W. a line of rugged, rocky hills. And beyond them the lower floor of the valley. In it are some white streaks. To one famished and half-crazed with thirst they might look like water, as they evidently did to many to their cost in early days. These streaks are alkali. (By the way, all the mirages or "optical illusions" I have seen so far in the desert, with one exception, are easily accounted for in some way.)

1:15. Just came down a wonderful gully, with wide, fairly flat floor, inclining down westwardly at about a 10% grade. Both bottom and banks (which are about 10 to 16 ft. high) are composed of a mess of gravel and small "horseheads." There must, I believe, be a little natural cement in the formation, the walls being about perpendicular. The gully is said to have been made by a cloudburst. It is called Hell's Gate. Soon we came out onto what you might call a great dry sea. The 10% slope still holds, as does the formation. Soon we are at the bottom, 28½ miles from Beatty. To the N. a few miles is the Stove Pipe Wells, leading into the N. arm of Death Valley from the N. to Grapevine Canyon, where is the ranch of Death Valley Scotty, a character well known for five hundred miles around. At Goldfield I was told, for instance, that alfalfa was being hauled from Bonnie Clair to Death Valley Scotty's cattle. Death Valley Scotty's ranch is, I am told by Mr. Remick, a kind of

Garden of Eden, so to speak, in the desert. There are said to be the largest fig trees in the world.

Scotty is a mystery. Peculiar, generous, a lavish spender, just now he is preparing to charter a train—or has already done so—from a Pacific Coast point to New York. He is to make a mile a minute across the continent. He is fond of notoriety. Where he gets the money he spends so lavishly is also a mystery. He is believed by some to possess a secret placer mine of fabulous wealth. Others of his friends wink an eye and say, "Well, he gets away with it and keeps out of jail." He has an irresistible personality, frequently pays with a blank check signed in immense characters, "Walter Scott," which he insists upon the seller filling out in a sum greater than the regular price. He is always in a hurry. He is married and has one son 12 years old. He is said to be just now getting out his biography. His best friends are those who take him for granted and ask him no questions.

This point, 28½ miles from Beatty (from which I sidestepped to tell of Scotty) is on the bottom or real floor of the Valley. The formation is sand and gravel well "flavored" with alkali. There are some fair-sized bare sand domes and some smaller ones covered with mesquite. There is quite a lot of vegetation on most of the floor that we saw except the alkali streaks. There is greasewood, something that resembles dwarf willow a little and has tremendous roots, some species of sage, and something that lies close to the ground, probably fileree. Probably the most beautiful of all is the Death Valley holly.

To the east of us lies the Funeral Range through a pass through which we had just come. To the west the Panamint Mts. frown down upon us. Some snow in them reminds me of what we would have been up against had we not made the second change in our route. * * * *

The day is cloudy and fairly cool, threatening rain. We do not feel any inconveniences on account of either temperature, humidity, dryness, or altitude. But of course this is Feb. 2. There are well marked roads running in all directions, roads that shake up a fellow's liver and give him delirium tremens. At least they make him think of snakes. They are not the "straight and narrow way" though they are narrow. A car that gave us half the road in passing had to be given a push, on account of the sand. * * * *

Mr. Piano Player is striking out for a 50 mile hike west across the mts., accompanied by one blanket, 25 cts. and plenty of nerve. He'll make it.

2:30. On top of a large stony hill in the Valley 68 feet below sea level.

2:50. On floor of valley again, 231 feet below sea level.
* * * *

In the desert are some wonderful colors in earth and stone. In the mts. on either side, you might say surrounding at least the west or N.W. end, dark brown predominates, a wonderful, deep frame for the picture of the lower Valley. Within, taken at a distance especially, a beautiful gray forms the canvas upon which Mother Nature painted the picture in a softer gray (the alkali somewhat resembling water at a little distance), the green of the mesquite-covered sand dunes, the yellow of the larger, or shifting dunes, the silver of the Death Valley holly, the sombre, almost brown of the hills, and in particular some pure yellow golden banks of earth and other banks of a deep green.

As we ascended the long steep grade up out of the valley back toward Beatty, I said to myself—or rather felt—as I sometimes do when in the great open spaces—"What is man that Thou art mindful of him?" * * * *

On our return trip, having lost half (rather two-thirds) of the ballast of the rear seat in Mr. Piano Player, I again had to hang on to keep from perforating the top of the car with my tack head. And I have much respect for a Master Six Buick. But all that could not jar loose from me the mental picture of one of Father Time's greatest wonders, one of Mother Nature's greatest pictures.

Later. I have just been talking with Mr. Remick, whose guest I am so far as shelter and a good fire are concerned, this drizzly day. (The first rain in many months, which, by the way, has caused us to postpone our departure until it quits.) Mr. Remick is an old-timer here, an "Old Desert Rat" as they are sometimes dubbed. He has been across Death Valley in the hottest season. He says practically the only danger, aside from thirst, in the Valley, is over-exertion, or in moving too fast. Death is sometimes brought about from the body perspiration being faster than the perspiration can evaporate. One must not get excited. Once in the very hottest season he had to change a tire right in the middle of the desert. He deliberately took two hours in performing the task of a few minutes, and so lived to tell the story. Water? You never catch an Old Desert Rat without a supply of it.

I wish my arm would hold out while I told you a lot about this place and the people. Suffice it to say it is a typical Western town, supported by some few mines that are still working, some prospectors who are looking for new mines—and occasionally find one—for these hills are full of ore, more or less. Some cattle are also raised on the range. Here they do not have to feed them. The day before I came in here from the N.W., I saw some pretty fair bunch grass, green near the roots, and some white-faced cattle that stuck their tails over their backs at sight of man and horse and struck a clip that would put us to shame.

These people are big-minded and big-hearted. This would be no place for a pinhead or a pinch penny. While he was skinning a flea the Devil would get him sure. He could not survive—and don't. This is one of the reasons he is not here. Another reason is that he is not wanted here. They want Men. And the Desert produces Men. There is plenty of room for them to develop.

Well, I must close. It has quit raining, but it is a little late in the day to start out now. Besides, it is not altogether settled. I'll stay until it is. Probably tomorrow. Another day's rest will not hurt Queen anyhow. We've quite a trail ahead of us yet.

Address Las Vegas. It will be forwarded if necessary. I may run over from there to Pasadena on a side trip—not sure yet. Love.

(Signed) Frank.

Feb. 5th. Stopped raining. Pulling out for Carrara, 10 miles. Don't worry, we'll make it fine.

*   *   *   *

Nine miles beyond Beatty is Carrara, an old marble quarry. The next water is 65 miles. The next habitation is 72 miles. How to make this 65-mile stretch without feed or water was a problem. Water was the worst problem. We sometimes carried feed and grub for that far. But to load Queen with *both* these in the heat and the heart of the desert would have been disastrous and we knew it.

It had been our intention to pack water on a burro over this or similar places. At quite an expense we had had made a special water bag—or twin bags—to straddle our McClellan saddle, which on a former occasion we had used as a pack saddle, riding Queen with an old flat saddle. But to start on this rather long jump, depending on a burro with his slow gait and not able to carry much more than his own maintenance, was considered unwise by these desert men. Those who really know the desert burro do not consider him the infallible creature of story books.

It is Fred Remick, the old-timer, now a garage man, who comes to the rescue.

"Tell you what you do," says Mr. Remick. "When well rested, start at noon and make for Carrara, 9 miles; there is water. I will overtake you next night with your 12-gallon bag full of water and such oats, hay and grub as you shall have laid out. It won't cost you a cent."

And sure enough he overtakes us half way between water holes. When we started to thank Mr. Remick and Mrs. Remick, who had been with him on the 75-mile trip—

"Oh," said he, "don't mention it. We fellows here in the desert love to do such little things just for the pleasure we get out of it. Luck to you. Drop us a card when you get through."

It is worth the whole trip, Mr. Reader, just to rub elbows with the great souls in the desert places. Puny souls cannot survive there. They dry up and blow away.

We fed and watered well and carried from the night's camp eats and grub for the next night and morning, and a few gallons of water in the water bag for noon. The water bag was a mistake.

We reach the distant water hole—the heart of the desert is behind us. We reached Indian Springs the next day. There was an oasis of a few hundred acres. Such hospitality as we met with there means much.

Indian Inn at Indian Springs, Nevada.
February 10, 1927.

Dear Folks:

I arrived here yesterday a little before noon. Mr. Fred Remick had showed up with the water, feed, grub, etc. as pre-arranged and as I knew he would, so we had water to throw at the birds that night. Built up a big fire with discarded ties, which are strewn all along the "old grade" so we fared pretty well. The principal trouble is in such cases Queen is always a little restless, generally does not lie down, making it a little hard on her after all. Next day we didn't have as long a hike as I expected, for the reason that we found a pretty good pool of water that had collected in one of the old railroad ditches from a recent rain. This cut our day down to 24 miles instead of 37. Built another big fire out of ties. Where wood is no object I build these fires in the shape of a large V and build my camp in the open end with the heat and smoke rolling overhead. This makes it seem like summer even on a frosty night. In this light atmosphere the smoke doesn't bother. When you think of it you know it is hard to force smoke to the ground. We have our camp on the lee side of the fire. * * * *

Yesterday I made a trip to Las Vegas, catching a ride with Mr. Lynch, having left Queen here in a pasture at the ranch, intending to have gone last night to Pasadena by rail for a few days visit with Lizzie, but as luck would have it, for the third or fourth time I found that my finances were again in a tangle and I had only a measly little check for $12.80—that being the stupendous sum that Uncle Sam allows me monthly. Another check had gone astray, but fortunately I happened to get it located. Burned up the Western Union wires to the tune of $1.35 so things will come out eventually, in a few days. I forgot to mention that when I left the Inn here for Las Vegas I was heavily laden with a silver dollar and three copper cents. Had it not been for the fact that "Tim," on the strength of a few minutes' acquaintance, my Irish name, and possibly the little red that still remains in my whiskers, had written me a good endorsement to a business firm in Las Vegas who cashed a check for me on the strength of it, I would certainly have been in one of those predicaments into which I so frequently come near tumbling but always manage somehow to get out of at the last minute. * * * *

Tonight and probably tomorrow night I am living luxuriously in a cabin which the Harnedys (the proprietors of Indian Inn) usually rent to tourists, but which they insisted upon my occupying free of charge. It is well equipped and I am living high. Expect to leave for Las Vegas day after tomorrow, arriving there Sunday night. I am through predicting what is going to happen —farther ahead than that. Love.

(Signed) Frank.

From Notes. February 12, '27: Cloudy. Leaving Indian Inn, 8 a.m. No chg. for hay either. The Harnedys built Indian Inn with their own hands out of ties, plastered with cement. You'd

never mistrust the ties. It's a cozy and unique looking place.
* * * * 4:40 Ar'd Corn Creek Ranch about 2 mi. N. of "Old
Grade," 21 mi. E. of Indian Springs, via O. G. and Hy.

Traveled: 22 miles. Level, gravel, 12 mi. Dirt 8, * * * *

Sunday, February 13, '27: Clear, warm. Leaving Corn Creek
Ranch 8:30 a.m. Hay 50 cts. Noon, Nosebag, hot lunch, little
S.E. of Tooley in lee of a clay bank. Very windy. At Tooley is
an artesian well and pond from same. About 2 mi. S.E. of
Tooley in cutting over the clay bank to hit Hy. I ran into
another spring. Some improvements have been made here, apparently some attempt at irrigation. No bldgs. at present. A few
cattle off to one side. 7:30, Ar'd Las Vegas, barn of Bill Morgan,
old-timer, rider pony express. Sprinkling.

Traveled: 26 miles (1 to Tooley). Level, dirt 6 mi. Gravel
10 mi. (Dirt side 4 mi.) R. I. 10 mi. Desert (except as above)
to two or three mi. W. of Las Vegas, where alfalfa irrigated.

Special Note: Indian Spring to Las Vegas via Corn Creek
Ranch and Tooley—48 miles.

TOTAL TO LAS VEGAS, 7,236 miles [as corrected].

From Signature Book: "Frank M. Heath arrived here in Las
Vegas, Nevada, Feb. 13, and his bay mare Gipsy Queen was
on my ranch and they are leaving Friday 21.

(Signed) Bill Morgan."

From Notes. February 14, '27: Got check of $46 forwarded
by Geo. from Portland. (This was the check for which I had
waited in Portland early in December. The envelope was literally
covered with postmarks and forwarding marks.) * * * * Saw
man on Review. Will put Queen in Morgan's pasture—going to
Pasadena tonight. Later, Took 5:30 p.m. train to Los Angeles.

February 18, '27: Clearing. Leaving Pasadena for Los Vegas
5:25 p.m.

February 19, '27: Wreck ahead caused delay. Ar'd Las Vegas,
12:20 p.m. Rec'd $12.86 check from Bank. Nothing from Joe.
Writing Joe stating past facts (letters), suggesting O. K. to
collect rent personally so as to keep tab. But let me know to
whom to apply. Request remittance to Flagstaff—enclosed self
addressed envelope (hold 30 days). Met Joe Pudloff, L. P.
Harris, C. J. Black, "old-timers."

Sunday, February 20, '27: Clear, warm. Got Queen out of

pasture. Review got picture. Note: Borax Smith interested, it is said, in "West End Borax"—30 or 40 mi. N.E. of Las Vegas. Note: Mr. Morgan showed me many desert grasses and other forage plants including muscrew beans, musquette, shadscale. There are many varieties. This I have been calling a "species of sage brush." Horses eat the tips in a pinch. Rabbits feed on it. Note: Mr. Morgan says Death Valley Scotty used to be with Buffalo Bill—also with him (Morgan) in Wild West Shows. Is good rider, good shot. Note: Bill Morgan rode a horse in a race with a motorcycle ridden by a fireman and beat him ¼ mi. Sept. 1925. Also figured as old Pony Ex. rider in hauling mail to man in plane. (This was when they were instituting air mail. I believe this was the first air mail to go out of Las Vegas— at least it was a special demonstration.) * * * * Am sending feed, grub to Dry Lake Tuesday by Mr. Black. Will have it Tuesday noon. Water in Dry Lake after rain. P. P. bed roll to Needles by the Morgans. Feeling tough.

February 21, '27: Clear. Leaving Bill Morgan 6:30 a.m. No chg. for pasture. * * * * Also Bill's brother contributed 2 nights, grain, hay, barn. "Bill" overtook me 2 mi. out, accompanied 4 mi.—riding for beef. 9:45, Came to fine temporary stream water. 11:30, Nosebag, hot lunch, 13 mi. S.E. Las Vegas. 3:15, Looking for spring designated by Mr. Joe Rudloff, 20 mi. S.E. of Las Vegas as in a draw. (See map.) Could find no spring —2 "had beens"—Tried at old cabin also. 4:30, Overtaken 8 mi. beyond by Rudloff and a Cherokee Indian, Mr. Harris. They gave Queen about 2 gal. water—self canteen full. We were within sight of Dry Lake—some water there since rain but very bad place to spend the night. So we "backed up" about ½ mi. to a small tunnel about 5 ft. in. We are there now. Some bunch grass, some fuel.

Traveled: 23½ mi. (Back ½) via Hy. Level to hilly. Pave 1 mi. R. I. 10 mi. Dirt 6 mi. Desert—bottom land—6 mi. No stock beyond bottom. Saw rabbit.

February 22, '27: Clear, warm. Up, 4 a.m.—2 a.m. Queen seemed to see or hear something—was very uneasy. I could see nothing. At dark she had started "back"—overtook her just in time. Prospect holes on divide. Feeling tough with pain in abdomen all night. 7:45, Came to Dry Lake. Rode in to about middle looking for water clear enough for Queen. It had been represented to me as 2 ft. deep. It was scarcely to top of hoofs at deepest. Dipped up canteen full with bucket on string (from saddle) at several dippings. Queen would hardly taste it—thick and brownish yellow. Came out on S.E. Saw "house" across Lake. Approached, found it a car stuck in mud, deserted. Later found *little* better water (mud) in "pot holes" 8 in. deep S. of Lake. (These pot holes consisted of large boulders from which, through some process of nature evidently, the top had been hollowed out, perhaps by freezing and thawing and wind, until the boulder constituted a stone bowl which held the water.) Carried canvas bucket and small one 2 mi. to sign where Mr. Black left feed and grub. Saw him at sign when I was ½ mi. away—signaled. He left feed. An inquisitive fellow was waiting at sign. I stopped 200 yds. away in shade of greasewood. He drove on before I got chance to bum him for water. *Had to unload first.* What made us look more crazy than ever was a 10 ft. board had picked up to boil water with—had it lengthwise on saddle. 10 a.m. Ar'd at above place. Boiling all water and diluting with canned milk. Putting ginger in canteen also. (Queen refused mud.) Had some job removing dobie from Queen. Queen leaving some alfalfa—will carry along. Leaving 12:20. 5 p.m. Dry camp by rd. side 15 mi. Searchlight. Some grass. Plenty cactus to burn.

Traveled: 22½ mi. (2 in Lake extra, ½ from camp). Gravel, 8 mi. R. I. 10 mi. Bal. dirt or mud. Mostly level, desert. Fire of dead cactus. Party gave me drink of water 2 p.m. Beautiful "saw tooth" mts. to N. Rugged to S. Colored desert. No habitation.

February 23, '27: Up 1 a.m. Leaving camp 2 a.m. Searchlight (believe 9 a.m. Queen approximately 40 hours no water).

Traveled: 15 mi. Level to hilly. R. I., gravel, 5 mi. Dirt 5 mi. Old mines and prospect holes last 4 mi.

Special Note: Las Vegas to Searchlight, as traveled, 61 mi. TOTAL TO SEARCHLIGHT, 7,297 miles.

Searchlight is an old mining town. Hills perforated. 1 mine working. * * * * (My intestines are bothering me—cooking vegetables.) [I was also seasoning the vegetable stew with a small piece of beef. Believe it or not, the amount of this stew I ate would have constituted four ordinary meals. I hadn't had a square meal for a long while. This big feed of vegetable stew did me a lot of good.]

February 24, '27: Rainy. Slept well in old shed, barn of Mrs. Weaver. Leaving Searchlight 8 a.m. (clearing). Mrs. Ella Knolls,

Gen. merchandise, gave me first 50 cts. in cash for a long time. [I still have this coin, which I kept as a souvenir.] Am sending 4 meals, 4 feeds, little hay to service sta., 37 mi., by Fred Haganuma (Searchlight, Box 104), a Japanese gardener, 15 mi. E. Searchlight on Colorado River. Irrigates by pumping. Lease with option to buy. 11:30, Mr. Haganuma overtook us. (Mr. Haganuma is one of those gentlemen who stand out in my memory.) Noon, Oats and *plenty* grass (something like bunch grass in places green spears 10 inches high). (This was so far from water that it was not fed down.) Hot coffee and left over vegetables in center of level plain about 9 mi. S. of Searchlight. Cloudy. 5:30 p.m., Feeding, cold lunch, 22 mi. S. of Searchlight. Mosquitoes bothering Queen. Beautiful sunset. Rugged, colorful mts. in distance, E. and W. 11 p.m. Ar'd Arrowhead Service Sta. Refused water—finally gave a "swill bucket" full slop. Queen drank ½, refused bal. in morning.

Traveled: 39 mi. Level to hilly. Gravel 8 mi. 9 mi. dirt or sand. No habitation, no stock. Grass at noon. Some young grass—good feed for sheep.

February 25, '27: Clear, warm. Slept soundly on gravel by side of garage. Up, 6 a.m. Queen was eating my loaf of W. W. raisin bread. Leaving service sta. 7. No chg. for swill (owner handed me last night pkg. left yesterday). 7:30, Ar'd Iris (?) Calif., pumping station of Santa Fe—fuel oil, in charge of "Agent"—late of Canada. Plenty water here, 99% pure and travelers welcome. This is on Main Line Santa Fe. First real train I've seen for a long time. Long lines of refrigerator cars and oil tanks going E. Queen is having time of her life on lush Bermuda grass. Beautiful restful spot. Trees, clean place. Leaving Iris (?) 11. 2:30, Watering at a Sec. house well. 3:30, Feeding, hot lunch, 4 mi. W. of Needles. Lv. 5 p.m.—6 p.m., Camping on bank of Colorado, 2 mi. W. Needles.

Traveled: 15 mi. Hilly, gravel, 10 mi. R. I. 5 mi. Desert.

This was a beautiful camping place, had a little wood for campfire and plenty of water—only the water was black and muddy, and undrinkable, at least for me. A light-colored Mexican-American who was going north with his family in a touring car, camping there that night, very kindly brought me out from Needles my canteen full of water. I was that played out that I guess had it not been for this I would have gone without water.

From Notes. February 26, '27: Warm. Ar'd Needles 7:30.

Traveled: 2 mi. Level, gravel, desert. Putting up at place of Glen Harper, full-blooded Mojave Indian, wife, 2 kids. Camping.

Special Note: Searchlight to Needles via Iris (?), 56 miles. From Rufus, Ore., as traveled, 1,135 miles, 440 less than via Calif. Valley, 400 mi. less than 1926 schedule to Needles, via Portland and Calif. Valley.

TOTAL TO NEEDLES, CALIF., 7,353.

We found it hot at Searchlight on February 23rd. At Needles, California, the flowers were in bloom. We spent Sunday, February 26th, here. Mr. Harper, a full-blooded Mojave Indian, took us in his "skiff" across the muddy Colorado to the Reservation, where the Indians were planting corn, working the river bottom land with spades, or (spuds, a crude spade). Very crude and picturesque are the Mojaves. These people, in their Indian way, were very hospitable. They gave me a cot to sleep on. I cooked over their out-of-door fire the day I laid over there, and they had me in to dinner. Several families, presumably relatives, were camping in what I suppose we would call a compound, at least an area fenced in. One or two were in tents.

From Signature Book: "Frank M. Heath passed through here today on the mare Gypsy Queen." (Date given as February 26 on Postoffice Stamp, on which is also the signature, H. W. Little.)

Needles, Calif.
Feb. 26, '27.

Dear Folks:

Arrived here O. K. early this a.m. Queen and self fine. Resting here rest of day. Will reach Flagstaff about 12th, morn. Write me there.

I'm rather in love with this place. It is a strange mixture of the American and Spanish, North and South—though I guess you'd call it South. The people are "Yankee," Spanish, Mex, and Indian (Mojave). I have Queen at the place of a full-blood Mojave, and am camping there. Harper is the name. They are very friendly, speak good United States. I am in the center of a Mojave village. The houses are of posts, small poles and mud, and are very comfortable. (The type commonly referred to as wattle houses.) Nearer in is the Mex. settlement. The vegetation here goes all the way from northern to tropical. There are several kinds of flowers in bloom. Saw a prairie dog yesterday. With love,

(Signed) Frank.

Chapter IV

EAST TO FLAGSTAFF

From Notes. February 27, '27: Leaving Needles, 11 a.m. Noon, Queen grazing on fine Bermuda grass just E. of Needles by R. R. track. 7 p.m., Ar'd Topock. Left highway like a damn fool, being told by Harper of old rd following R. R. that would save us 7 miles. But all the climbing (over very rough stony ground mostly zigzagging and back-tracking) we have done today is the limit. Country bet. N. and Col. R. very badly cut up with great deep steep gorges or fissures. Several times it looked like a level and straight shot and we had to turn way back. Lost at least 2 miles (worse going).

Traveled: 18 mi. Very hilly and extremely crooked both on highway and off. Dirt 2 mi. Gravel 6 mi. R. I. 10 mi. Desert, no habitation. Ar'd Topock way after dark, did not find pasture described as to left of pumping station. Mistook tank for it. Spent ¾ hr. finding fairly good camp site bet. rd. and river. Good windbreak, no grass, no level place, no hay in Topock. Plenty wood. Had good fire. Slept well bet. 9:30 and 3 a.m. Queen did not lie down.

February 28, '27: Up 3:45. Leaving camp 5. 5:30, Watering at Service Sta. of Don Weston, 1 mi. N. Topock. 6:20, Ar'd ranch of Fred Wyburn, 3 mi. N. Topock, ¼ mi. off rd. where "store man" at N. Topock told me was Bermuda grass. Queen feeding on same to 8 a.m. Nearly missed the place by walking (too low down). Wyburn has old bee-ranch (bees died with foul brood years ago). Wyburn just came in—going into poultry. Fine overflow land—"Marquette" (?) land. Noon, Nosebag, had coffee in a coulee 11 mi. N. of Topock. 5 p.m., Camping in a canyon 4 mi. S. Oatman, ¼ mi. off rd. No water, plenty of that large coarse "bunch grass." * * * * Midnight, Queen much frightened. Got up, dressed feet. Could see nothing but heard some animal plainly. * * * * Built fires all about—quieted Queen. Went to sleep by spells. 3 a.m. Woke suddenly. Saw

large black animal leaving. Might have been a burro but made
no noise. Saw no burro tracks in morning.

About sunset we had swung down off the highway into a low,
wide-bottomed canyon where was some tough grass in bunches. It
happened that in traversing this canyon for perhaps a quarter of a
mile, to find a little shelter for Queen and myself in the lee of a
large bunch of some kind of desert willow, I picked up a board
perhaps ten inches wide and ten feet long, that had been dropped
there by someone. Fortunately it happened that this was full of
pitch and lighted very readily. We camped in the lee of this bunch
of willows mentioned, built a little fire, fed Queen, after letting
her browse around, tied her securely to some of these willows. Up
on the hill, north of us, was some kind of quite large building,
probably housing some mining machinery.

About midnight I was suddenly woken out of my slumber by a
terrible scream, the most terrible scream I ever heard. This scream,
I am quite sure, was from Gypsy Queen. I have seen attempted
descriptions of a horse's scream, but I never happened to hear one,
unless it was Queen then. Did you ever hear a horse scream?

I was awake instantly, slipped on my laced boots, and had a brand
from the fire, near which I had been sleeping, flaming at once.
Queen was more scared than I had ever seen her. She was in a terrible
tremble all over, and was pulling back very hard. I spoke to her.
She let up at that and calmed down somewhat. About that time
I heard a noise—a series of noises it seemed—either human or
animal, or both. Indians sometimes make guttural noises, but I
never heard them utter such as I heard then. It was not a screech,
bark, or howl, but it was something that would make the chills
run down your back. I wasn't sure whether it was some human,
possibly an Indian—maybe a maniac—God knows what! I intended
to find out if possible, so I uttered some language that, had it been
a human being, he would probably have called me. Then I decided
it must be some kind of an animal. Knowing, or at least believing,
that most animals have a fear of fire-arms (and I happened to know
that some wild things know a gun when they see it) I grabbed the
little old lath hatched in my right hand and the brand in the other.
I held the hatchet so as to represent crudely the position of a large
revolver. I went all around indulging in more language. The devil
would have danced with glee had he seen me then. I heard no more
noises. Off to the south of us, ten or fifteen rods, was a dark-colored

object I took to be a burro. Could this have been a bear? After daylight I could find no burro tracks. If it was a bear, did Bruin like the smell of our coffee or our bacon?

I had set fire to the bunches of grass all around. They were so far removed from each other, and the ground between so barren, and there was a little frost, so I felt no danger of the fire getting away. After an hour or so of this, having gotten Queen pretty well calmed down, I lay down and slept more or less the rest of that night—with one eye open.

Stopping with a fine gentleman the next night, who was putting in a small irrigation plant for vegetables for market—a desert rat—I told him this story. I tried as nearly as I could to imitate the sound which I am unable to describe in writing. He said, "Why, you were a little too close to a bobcat's den. Maybe, if it had not been that you started a fire, we wouldn't be enjoying your company just now." Reader, your guess is as good as mine—was it a bear? Was it a bobcat? Or was it both? It sure was something.

From *Signature Book:* "Kingman, Arizona, March 3, 1927. Frank M. Heath arrived here last night at Central Com'l Co.
(Signed) Eddie Hilty."

Over a few small sections devoted to farming, stock and sheep in the hills, across an Indian Reservation, through two hard snow storms, and some difficulty, we arrived at Peach Springs, Arizona, on March 5th.

From *Signature Book:* "Mr. Frank M. Heath arrived here last night with his mare Gypsy Queen.
(Signed) Prop., W. B. Taylor Co.
(Date, on stamp, March 6, 1927.)"
(Stamped, Peach Spring.)

Peach Springs, Ariz., Mar. 6, '27.
Dear Folks:

We are laying over here today. Queen and I both need rest. And of course am cleaning up a bit too. This is an Indian Trading Post. Here the Indian Bureau has resorted to the experiment or expedient of running cattle on the Res. for the Indians. It seems that in most or all cases where the Indians are stocked up and let go their way they eat the cattle or let them go to the Devil and soon have none. I've passed a few such failures.

The Indians here do their own riding and all that under the white supervision. A bunch of their cattle are in corral here now and they look fine and seem well-bred. I've asked no questions but will venture they are a cross between Hereford and Shorthorn. Most of them are white faced, and the shorthorn straight back sticks out. They range most all together.

We are getting along quite well. Have to parcel post oats a good deal yet, which brings them up to about 4 cts. Mailed bed roll from Searchlight (?) here. But will have to pack it a while now. It's fairly cold nights.

We are comfortable here in a corral and shed. It hurts me some to write today so I'll close. Write me at Tuba City, Ariz. Love,

(Signed) Frank.

During the five days since the last notes we had led a fairly rough life, but not impossible, past much indescribable scenery. Here at Peach Springs we put up with one John Nelson, who let us have some feed.

One feature that was becoming outstanding, was numerous small bunches—you may say families—of wild burros. I used to see them down through the desert country along, particularly starting about Goldfield on, to over into Arizona somewhere, and more or less in the great open spaces in New Mexico, wherever the distance from water was great. Perhaps I would see no sign of wild horses or wild cattle, but there would be, now and then, not a band exactly, but a family I would say, of these wild burros, usually some shade of dun color with brown or black markings. As I remember, there would generally be three or four, six or eight, which was the biggest bunch I saw. There would be old ones, two-year-olds, yearlings and colts. They didn't act so wild, although they are said to be hard to capture and handle, especially very strong in the jaw if they happen to get hold of an arm. They didn't pay much attention to us except that they would look at us and kind of look at each other and back at us, as much as to say, "Well, there goes another!"

We arrive at Flagstaff, Arizona, high up in the pine timber. During these six days of which we are giving no record, between Peach Springs and Flagstaff, we had met with some fairly tough experiences. Besides having to parcel post oats from place to place, we had had considerable snow, beginning with rain. At least one night in particular our notes show we slept in a juniper thicket.

Once we had been refused a chance of sleeping in the barn with Queen, so had to resort to a lodging house. Next day the snow, being six or eight inches deep, nearly obliterated the road. We had been the innocent cause of a small covered truck upsetting with a family. The man, in obligingly trying to avoid crowding us off the narrow grade, had himself run off the edge, the grade being so overhung with snow, so to speak, that it was not discernible. Our notes show that the truck rolled clear over. Fortunately no one was hurt, though the truck was badly damaged. Some people coming along helped right it. We were only delayed an hour and a half. The man would accept no apology from me—said none was due, it was an accident. He says, "I don't believe in picking a fuss over every little thing. I'm from Missouri, where people are sociable." Next day while we were making the noon stop under the trees with a big brush fire, they passed us, happily on their way.

One time I remember in particular we would have been without a fire, everything being so wet, had it not been that we found a rat's nest, probably a pack rat, in a hollow log. This made good kindling.

As we approached Flagstaff, the elevation being higher, there was more snow. I believe it was the night before we arrived in Flagstaff that we came to a deserted ranch. There was a young blizzard. The snow was drifting. The house was barren and bleak, no sign of fuel. We took refuge in an old root cellar—Queen and I. With some old scraps of lumber I built a fire inside, figuring that the smoke would escape out of the door. In just a few minutes the place was full of smoke. Fortunately I was able to pick up a scantling and punch a hole through the dirt roof in the back, which cleared the situation. We had not much more than settled down when someone appeared at the door. I wondered for a moment if it was a hold-up. A young man who had seen us traveling and had found some place to put up for the night—an old house—had come over to see if we could spare him and his partner some grub. I had seen quite a lot of fellows, including these two, apparently aimlessly tramping the roads east of Needles. We must take note of the fact that schools and colleges are turning out educated young men much faster than industry can absorb them with our present system. Of course everybody knows this. This young fellow was very gentlemanly and I judged he was one of this educated surplus class who was trying somehow to find his niche. Although he was willing to accept any kind of work.

"I am having quite a time myself," I told him, "to get by." I told him briefly what we were undertaking and why. "I am almost broke but I have a little grub and if you are hungry I will divide with you." "Well, dad," he says, "We have a little grub. A lady gave us a loaf of bread and some coffee which we can heat over a fire in the empty house. I thought you might spare us a little something but you need it worse than we do. Thanks just the same." I wished him luck, what else could I do, bread and coffee was about all I had.

From Notes. March 12, '27: * * * * 5 p.m. Ar'd Flagstaff, Ariz., elev. 6,900 ft. Putting up in old barn of Lightning Delivery (Res. of Mr. Horace Wyatt).

Traveled: 23 miles. Hilly. Pave. 1 mi. Gravel 4 mi. Dirt 18 mi. Several ranches. Entered Coconino Nat. Forest few mi. west.

Special Note: Needles to Flagstaff, 245 mi., 45 miles more than schedule.

Total to Flagstaff, Ariz., 7,598 miles. * * * * Flagstaff county seat Coconino Co.

From Signature Book: "Frank M. Heath arrived Flagstaff March 12, 1927, with Gypsy Queen, and has her in our barn here.
(Signed) Horace Wyatt."

From Notes. March 13, '27: Froze hard last night. Slept warm in barn. Laying over today. Oat hay, little oats. Yesterday rec'd no word from Joe. Sent him night letter requesting him to wire me all available funds—if in bank draw it. (On hand, $.18.) Several other letters.

Flagstaff, Ariz.,
Sun., Mar. 13, '27.
Dear Folks:

Yours of 6th rec'd here yesterday P.M. Had some snow past few days, but got through O. K. Managed somehow to have shelter every night—and feed. Queen is fine. I am pretty well.

We are laying over here today and tomorrow, as must shoe Queen before hitting the Res. And I fear a day or two longer as they again have my finances in a tangle. Should have been some cash awaiting me here, but not a cent or a line. For the 3rd time since last spring I had to wire about funds that should have reached me without any trouble. This time I'll have the expense of wiring money to me. It seems to be a pre-ordained part of this trip that I should have this unnecessary expense and worry constantly recurring. No, don't send me any money. I'll come out O. K. I always do in the "last analysis." There will be a few fairly long stretches across the Res., but nothing but what we can make with safety. There are Trading Posts about every so often. We will rest up in each of them and stock up to last to the next. We won't use pack animal—one is plenty to feed. Will pack Queen and walk. We will be dropping downhill now —where it is a little warmer (it is 6,900 feet here) and it is spring. Then too there are Navajo Indians all along. Some people tell me I could not eat their grub. But I *have* eaten Indian chow and survived. It is doubtful whether I could obtain any horse feed except at the Posts, and they are, in one or two cases, about 40 miles travel apart. But *should* we run out of oats Queen can go on grass and her stamina for a day or two. Water will not be a difficult proposition at this time of year, following the snow.

I will take my bed roll, at least as far as possible. I am told (but perhaps wrongly) that I better not sleep in Indian beds or in Indian hogans (hogans are mud huts) unless I am prepared to take more than one animal with me. I remember, though, of three different occasions in the past when I slept in Indian beds without any serious increase in my family. I'll know more about Navajos in two weeks from now.

When I reach Bluff, Utah, we'll be O. K. As I near "The Four Corners" I learn that there is a good "patch of country" up there. Good white people, oats "n'everything!" * * * *

This is rather a romantic place, a pretty fair city set in Mt. scenery, sunshine and snow. The people we have met are mixed largely with Mexican. I mean that there are many Mexicans and some Spanish. Especially since Las Vegas we hear a good deal of Spanish spoken. I stopped at a dairy farm at Williams where the old folks spoke very little English. They were quite hospitable at that. The kids speak good English and are very bright. They were much interested in Queen, especially the boy Henry 12 years old. The lady is homesick for Spain.

The next address I'm still sure of will be Bluff, Utah. I will be two weeks at least reaching there, so put on envelope, "Please hold 30 days." With love,

(Signed) Frank.

From Notes. March 14, '27: Clear. Rec'd wire from Joe, stating funds forwarded March 12. Two blacksmith shops—both smiths gone S. Made arrangements to have Queen shod to-morrow at shop of A.L.&T. Co. Put in bal. day arranging itinerary to "4 Corners," aided by C. of C. and Sheriff's office. Interview, Sun.

This is the way we "arranged" the itinerary. Every little way somebody had been raving about the fact that we could hit four states at the same point. Maybe they thought they were telling me news—I don't know. I thought every school boy knew it. That is, they know that the four states join. It didn't seem as though most of these people who talked to me about it realized the difficulty of getting there, or that after all, arriving there would be of no consequence so far as our trip was concerned. Nevertheless, the constant dinging away at this got some kind of a bee in my bonnet about it. That is the way I came to go to the sheriff's office. I had heard, which proved to be the fact, that in the sheriff's office were two or three old-timers. especially one, who knew the whole country for a hundred miles or more around like a book. There was a slight possibility that if the going were good from somewhere about or perhaps a little north of Kayenta, and then from the Four Corners out east, and that if it happened that there was subsistance through there—which I much doubted—I could perhaps see this wonderful fact which everybody knows, and possibly cut off a few miles, and still hit all the states. As stated, it didn't seem good to me, but I thought it would do no harm to inquire. I arrived at the sheriff's office, found them a good, congenial bunch, not so excited over what we were doing. They were in the habit of contacting rough stuff themselves and also rough riding. There was one rather slight middle-aged man, dressed strictly cowboy fashion, with high heeled boots, who seemed to be the best posted. "Why man," he says, "it might be possible for you to get there to the Corners, but in getting there and getting out you would wear your horse out if you didn't starve her to death. It is rough, tough and barren." Or something like that. Of course that settled the Four Corners business. I got a lot of good detailed information, however, about different trading posts along the way designated in our schedule, at which we could almost surely get feed and eats. I had a list of these trading posts from this man that I spoke of in particular in the sheriff's office.

From Notes. March 15, '27: Cloudy. Had Queen shod at A.L.&T. (Saw Mill) Co. shop. While came back to town for two more shoes "smith" put a right front with toe calk 1 in. high, no heel (he misunderstood) throwing terrible strain on tendon. Had it removed and calk driven down, but she is sore therefrom—*was* a little sore.

This is the explanation of the toe calks. Some ways back I explained how a horse, particularly a tired horse, would wear the front off the front shoes through the rolling motion of the toe in contact with the ground. I had tried to counteract this by having toe calks made of tool steel and having them welded in and pounded down on a welding heat until they reinforced the toe of the shoe, but at the same time were about level with the shoe. These didn't act as a calk after all, but simply as a means of hardening the toe of the shoe. Of course we had them tempered. I had tried to explain this to the blacksmith at the A.L.&T. Co., which, by the way, was a big sawmill outfit. While I was gone to the city after more shoes he had gotten this one shoe on the right foot—fortunately instead of the left. Had the left been subjected to the same strain, even temporarily, I don't know what would have happened. There were no words about it. It was simply a misunderstanding. They very carefully cut the clinches and took off the shoe, corrected it according to my instructions as above, and put it back on, using the same holes, as per the note. Even that caused a temporary lameness, from which, however, she soon recovered.

From Notes. March 15, '27 continued: C. of C. took our photo. No funds yet. Bought oats $1.00. 37 lbs. Shoe repair 65 cts.—on hand 30 cts.

March 16, '27: Clear, cool. No funds yet. Have to lay over.

March 17, '27: Clear, cold. 8 a.m. No funds yet. Spent last cent for hot cakes. 4 p.m. No funds yet—borrowing $2.00 from Mr. Wayne Shields of the Coconino Sun. 4:30, Having boots further repaired ripped in back.

March 18, '27: Clear, warmer. Rec'd letter with $114—from Joe. * * * * Leaving Lightning Delivery Stable 12:15 p.m. Six days stable and hay, only $1.50.

Chapter V

MOSTLY INDIANS

Going north from Flagstaff we made ten miles that day, mostly through forest reserve—a large body of pine. Beyond the forest reserve was a little settlement, some small farms. We stayed there with Uncle Ben Doney, a very old-timer who had homesteaded here years and years earlier. He was in Flagstaff when it was nothing but a few tents, about the time they were establishing the sawmill.

It was spitting snow a little that day. Uncle Ben told me something about Dove's Tank, a good half day beyond, somewhere in the region of Dead Man's Flat. That is where I was supposed to water and possibly camp. My book on this date would be somewhat vague to anyone except myself. It was cold and I was trying, as nearly as I can make out now, to write some of this by the light of a camp fire, or perhaps the next day. But here are the main points. After some procrastination and a little bit of whipping back and forth, trying to locate a track mentioned by Uncle Ben, and there being as usual different tracks, I gave it up for that day and turned left, that is, back west, into Dead Man's Flat, where there has been quite a settlement. Across a good deal of this Flat, past quite a number of deserted houses, we ran into the place of two bachelors who were really staying with the game. Evidently they were doing some trapping. They had several fine skins about the place. They had no place for Queen, but they pointed out a deserted place where they said it would be all right to stay. There was a pasture there, they said. They didn't know whether I could find any roughage for the horse or not. That day we traveled sixteen miles according to our notes. We arrived at this place early, putting up early on account of the cold threatening weather, instead of trying to locate Dove's Tank, where after all there was no shelter.

From Notes: March 20, '27: Clear, cool. Up once in night to mend fire. Queen up all night. Up 3 a.m. Leaving camp 5:30. Queen don't like the cistern water.

I have unraveled it in some way from the book, and my memory verifies it, that Queen didn't find anything much in the pasture, and came back to the shed. There was a little pile of bean fodder there, which I fed her. This seemed to satisfy her. Had some oats. I slept under a shed beside the campfire.

From Notes: 20, '27 continued: 6:30, At a fork in rd. Took R. to lead to "tank." Will try Queen that water. Later, following old road N.E. Came to track turning E. Sign laying flat says "Dove Tank 1 mi." but I can't tell on which rd. If 1 mi. to right Queen can stand it to Spider Web, 15. Continued on 25 minutes at brisk walk. No sign of Tank, so it must be on other track. Turning W. across rough stony ground to intercept New Rd. off which I turned. (Uncle Ben Doney mentioned an "old Road" —this I take to be it.) Traveled W. nearly an hr. Saw some ditches many of them that looked as though intended to lead rain and snow water to some place. But no rd. though in plain sight of land between mountains beyond, between which and us the Tuba rd. *must* pass. Decided must have passed where New Rd. and Old Rd. came back together. Turned S. Came near passing to W. of Dead Man's Flat, as had gone too far W. Made S.E. and hit near N.E. end of Flat. Struck shanty farthest N.E. No one home. Gave Queen few swallows water out of cistern. Freezing. 2 hrs. since we passed this place. Traveled 5 mi. at least. Can realize how men sometimes perish in these parts. The Ingersoll, the sun, and S. Pass saved us. Later, came past where "old and New Rds." did come together. Crossed rd. Should have kept just N. of fork. * * * * Noon, Feeding, grazing on old grass. Hot lunch lee of rock 13 mi. N.E. Dead Man's F. 3:45 p.m. Ar'd Spider Web Ranch (and Spider Web Tank, a reservoir, now dry) 1 mi. off rd. to E.

Traveled: 26 mi.—1 mi. to ranch, 6 by blunder. Hilly, R. I. 11 mi. Gravel 6. Dirt 10 mi. Desert, prairie, last 15 mi. Saccaton (bunch grass), some gramma grass, few cattle and horses, 2,000 sheep 5 mi. S.E. of Spider Web. This is cattle ranch. Open range. Range goes beyond. Belongs to C. O. Bar Live Stock Co. Drilling for water—several holes 500 to 1,500 ft. Underlie (underlain) by volcanic cinder formation. Own every alternate section. Clay flat where Spider Web is located. Red clay, stone mostly red. Passed some red mts. Entering Painted Desert.

Though the range is free hereabouts, there are practically no other ranches except that of the C. O. Bar between Dead Man's Flat and Cameron, a distance of about 36 miles. To try to describe the rugged country through which we passed next day, March 21st, the grotesque rock formations, the varying colors, would require a volume, perhaps by a geologist, in which, after all, nothing could be conveyed to the layman. It must be seen. The earth we trod most of that day was a hard red clay almost devoid of vegetation. We passed between cliffs of a wonderful brown sandstone carved by Father Time and the wind into all kinds of quaint images.

Toward night we swung off the main highway a little to the west to view the Dinosaur tracks. These tracks are so plain that it is hard indeed to stretch the imagination over the millions of years to the age in which they were made.

The stratum of greyish lava rock upon which the tracks appear seems very thin. It gives forth a hollow sound as though there were at least a thin layer of some softer material below. It is checked, evidently by weathering, into what we might compare to thin uneven mosaic blocks, that could be removed. Not far from the tracks this pavement shows a rough edge which could slough away. It struck me at the time that to reinforce this would not be a bad idea. Passing on through rugged hills we noticed signs announcing "The Petrified Pumpkin Patch." On later investigation I found these "pumpkins" would never have made good pies—not even for the dinosaur. They are concretions.

Leaving Cameron's Trading Post next morning, after a good night's rest on a cot in the store, with plenty of blankets which the proprietor had insisted on my using—free; a good feed of oats and alfalfa—purchased; two good meals which I had cooked over a camp fire (material bought from the trader—without robbery); and some first hand observations of a few Navajo customers, we started on our way. After crossing the Little Colorado over a modern bridge we were in the Navajo Indian Reservation. Cameron's is a point from which tourists turn off the main trail for the Grand Canyon. It is also a hotel as well as a trading post.

About 5 p.m. we emerged into quite a canyon, through which runs the San Juan River, a tributary of the Little Colorado. From this stream are irrigated a few small patches of land—evidently Indian fields. The previous year they had been planted in corn. We passed two or three hogans, all empty. Near one was a kind of corral. Not a sign of forage. Finally we reached the Government

Farm, well kept up. Here were the first human beings we had seen that day.

Along towards noon that day, I was walking, being heavily packed. We were passing through an area where I understood sheep had been recently moved off winter range. We saw one lone sheep which seemed to be affected with some kind of disease or something, which caused its neck to twist round to one side. This sheep may have been left behind purposely. It may be that the herder, probably an Indian, as these were reservation sheep, accused this sheep of being possessed by Schindi—Schindi is the devil. Anyway the sheep ran in circles. Presuming that the sheep was possessed by the devil, then the devil must have departed from the sheep into Queen, something on the order of the Biblical story of the devil passing out of the "man possessed of the devil" into the swine. Round and round Queen chased this sheep in circles, in a lope, with the loose parts of the pack flopping—wouldn't pay any attention to me at all— until finally the sheep seemed to have kind of played out or slowed down, making narrower and narrower circles. I finally got hold of Queen. It is needless for me to try to explain this.

We passed through a canyon between immense cliffs of dark brown sandstone, with streaks of white, as though the two colors had been rained down alternately. There are great chasms, some of which are converted into caverns from being "roofed" by huge slabs of rock that have slid from a higher position. We climbed an incline onto a plateau. At 7:45 we arrived at the "Shekanah Ranch," the trading post and tourist hotel in Tuba City. Here we found plenty of feed and were royally entertained by the Smiths, who run the trading post and also the hotel. We had traveled 24 miles that day, (dirt 14, R. I. 10).

Special Note: Tuba, 7,692 mi.

Tuba was founded by the Mormons long ago, and has since been acquired by the Government. It consists mostly of the Agency for the Western Division of the Navajo Indian Reservation, and the school. Most of the buildings are of brick. Some are of the brownstone previously mentioned, which, however, is not a perfect material, as it "weathers." I noticed at least one case of crumbling.

We laid over a day at Tuba, not so much that Queen needed rest (having traveled from Flagstaff by easy stages so far), as that I wanted to look about. During the day the trader, Jess Smith, and his wife Lillian Wilhelm Smith, the artist, took me for a sight-seeing excursion among their Navajo friends. At the behest of the trader and his wife, an old Navajo, his squaw, and a little girl, all dirty, and all wearing many trinkets, very reluctantly posed for a photograph. At first they peeped shyly from the angle forming the entrance of the hogan, but finally Jess coaxed them out into the open.

We visited the Hopi village of Moenkopi, a few miles southeast of Tuba. Accompanying the Smith party to Moenkopi, was "Hattie," a young Hopi woman (and a very good looking woman at that, bright and clean and well-behaved) who had been doing a large washing for Mrs. Smith. Hattie spoke English.

Down below the lower bench on which stands the old Moenkopi, is an irrigation project including some gardens, old orchards and some alfalfa—all on little benches.

"How old is that dam?" I asked Hattie.

"I don't know," she replied, "Nobody know. Maybe one thousand year."

The Hopi, like all the other Pueblo peoples, are noted for their work in pottery. And by the way, the so-called "Aztec" pottery unearthed in these prehistoric villages (mostly in the cliffs) is not Aztec at all, but was made locally. According to the most reliable sources, there never were any Aztecs north of the Rio Grande.

The Navajo Reservation consists of about 9,503,763 acres. (I am presuming that what is set off as Hopi Indian Reservation and also the Piute Indian Reservation, in southeastern Utah, are both included in this 9,503,763 acres. See map.) The name Navajo signifies "Peaceful People."

I have had a glimpse over many years in many parts of the United States, and contacted several tribes for years, and I will say that next to the Pueblo the Navajo is most peculiar to himself, particularly the Western Navajo. Those in the eastern part of the Reservation are a little more progressive. Between the Navajo and the Columbia River fish-eating Indian there is little comparison. Neither is the Navajo like the (former) meat-eating Sioux. Probably the fact of his composite ancestry has a bearing. They were certainly aggressive and—in their own way—are progressive still. At least they are "wide flung." Many have allotments far outside their reservations. I visited some. The Navajo Reservation has an average elevation of about 6,000 feet which may make a difference. (The highest point, Pastoria Peak in the Carrizo Mountains, is 9,420 feet.)

In 1906 the Navajo were estimated by the Indian office at about

28,500. They are fairly prolific. The women wear long bell-shaped skirts, on a short waist. They wear shawls and are fond of colors. The hair is sometimes worn in a long projecting knob at the back. In the eastern part some still wear the double plait.

The Navajo man today does not, as a rule, dress so differently from the white man, except that, especially in the west more than in the east, many wear a kind of headband with some special significance.

Of course, like a true son of the great out-of-doors, the Indian loves a Stetson or other wide brimmed hat. In addition to this, the older men especially are not only fond of, but really superstitious about certain "bangles" and other ornaments—or which more later. Some of the old men still wear the hair in plaits. The younger generation cut their hair and shave clean.

As Indians go, most Navajo are good workers. Many are employed about trading posts and by the Indian Department. Their main industry outside their flocks is rug weaving. I could not learn of a single instance of Navajo or other Indians bearing blankets woven by the Indians—hand woven. The Pendleton blanket is factory-made, as are other so-called "Indian" blankets. Saddle blankets and belts the Navajo women weave sometimes.

On March 24th, at 9:30 a.m. we left Tuba, in company with Eli Sato, who I understood was Navajo. He rode a pony that seemed nothing but skin and bones and closely matted last winter's growth of hair. He offered to guide us to Red Lake trading post (Tonalea), some 26 miles, by a bridle path which he said in his broken English would be easier than the road. He said he would get to Red Lake at 4 o'clock. At the time I enjoyed a good deal of silent mirth over the comparative condition of the two horses. But I believe that Indian horse gave us the most miserable "chase" we had on the trip—simply by putting Queen off her gait. Half the distance was loose sand and the day was hot. He rode this horse mostly in a fast walk.

"Eli, you make your horse walk too fast," I remarked. "Too much sand."

"Too much sand," replied Eli nonchalantly, as he gave his rack of bones a few more digs with the rope end, while I let Queen into a jog trot to keep up. Had we not been many miles from nowhere, so far as my knowledge of the country was concerned, I would have let the Navajo ride on. But he knew he had the joke on us, and seemed to enjoy it in his silent way.

"Too hot, too hot, Eli. You go too fast."

"Too hot," he agreed, as he shifted easily about in his saddle and applied the rope end. These Indians "ride all over a horse," changing the weight from one (too long) stirrup to the other. The only thing I could do was to fall behind. He allowed us to keep in sight. But finally his horse tired out and solved the problem. The way was rough. At one point we traversed for about a mile a bridle path that was worn from six to ten inches into solid sandstone. At noon we watered at a good cement trough put in by the Indian Department out on the open range. There was an abundance of good water. Queen and I divided our lunch with the Navajo and the Navajo horse.

We had seen no human habitation since leaving Tuba and only one human being, a Navajo. My notes give as the vegetation, "a very little saccaton grass, shadscale, few stunted juniper and cactus, soapweed, Russian thistle." There was absolutely nothing under cultivation—all desert.

That day I had hired Edwin Kawauhaptewa, a full-blooded Hopi who carried the mail and hauled freight from Tuba to Kayenta, to haul our bed roll as far as Red Lake. (He was commonly called K. or E. K., and casually signed himself E. K. The name given here is his real signature.) So for one day our pack was fairly light. Edwin Kawauhaptewa speaks good English and is a right good fellow.

We hear much about the wonderful endurance of these Indian horses, and they are tough. In winter about all they get to eat is sagebrush and shadscale, and some other brush. There is very little grass. The Navajo horse, sometimes a mere pony, but often larger than a pony, seems to derive a rather remarkable strength, or at least a stimulant, from these shrubs, though not much flesh. Like the goat, these horses seem to have become inured to such feed. Both goats and Navajo horses live (we cannot say thrive) where a sheep, even the Navajo sheep, will not. Yet in spite of all this I do not put much stock in some statements I have read regarding these horses. These long rides sound big—I will mention one myself later. But most Indians, like cowboys, have many "changes" of mount. (Eli told me he had about thirty—and I should judge he would need them!) Some Indians are merciless riders, seeming to care not a whoop for the morrow. Like a Mexican, they will worry another ten miles out of a horse after most white men would quit for pure sympathy. It is a strange fact, not recognized by many, that an average horse is capable of doing in one day—and for one day only—

four times as much as he can do continuously. (But the horse does not recuperate the extra energy expended in many times four days, if ever.) By deduction from all this it can be seen that a very false notion might be formed off hand regarding the real lasting endurance of these wild Navajo horses, which after all are only descendants of the mustang. It is true that the footing and the atmosphere are very favorable to a horse through here. A few better horses are owned by the Navajo (that is, larger), as well as some of the other southwestern tribes, and other tribes. Some of these may be the result of having bred the wild mares to larger stallions. But these degenerate in a few generations. Most of the better horses and mules are bought from the whites by Indians generally.

At 5 p.m. we arrived at Red Lake. I was not much surprised to find oats five cents per pound, and alfalfa hay and "grub" in proportion. Everything is brought by truck over very rough roads—if roads you could call them—about a hundred and twenty miles. We laid over at Red Lake until noon the next day, giving us a short half day's ride to Cow Spring. While at Red Lake I was the guest of the Trader, Mr. J. P. O'Farrell, his amiable wife and her mother, Mrs. N. S. Ishmel, formerly a nurse at the Indian School at Shiprock.

Red Lake is an old lake bed of red sand with red clay mixed. In this lake bed are still three large pools of good water fed by underground springs. In the rainy season a lake is formed (from the run-off from the Black Mountains) about two miles long, half a mile wide, and three feet deep.

During my stay at Red Lake I made friends with Hooten Tso (Hotten Zoo)—meaning "Big man." He had been, I believe, a Chief. He wore a kind of Indian costume, and spoke no English except "How-w-w!" He welcomed us to his reservation very profusely.

One feature I noticed at Red Lake was a dipping plant for sheep and goats, put in by the Indian Department. We saw a small flock or two of sheep and goats.

> Red Lake, Ariz.
> (In Navajo Ind. Res.)
> March 24, '27.

Dear Folks:

Yours of Mar. 13 reached me at Tuba City O. K. Glad you are both better from slight attack of "flu."

We are proceeding nicely, by rather easy stages—so far. Water proposition not nearly so difficult as in Amargosa Desert. Oats obtainable too at the Trading Posts. A little high on account freighting them long distance by auto truck (mostly owned and operated by Indians) over rather difficult roads. Still we are glad to get them. Grub a little high—but obtainable. But we continue to meet the same fine class of people (white) that we have encountered in all the West. Especially in S.W. I am getting a lot of kick out of it all. Queen is fine. Have passed over the "Painted Desert." Colors are quite wonderful, but no more so than some other places we have passed—to my notion. * * * * Better address me next Gallup, N. M. With love,

(Signed) Frank.

We left Red Lake at 1 p.m. the next day, March 25th, packed for practically three days to Kayenta. At Bekishibito (Cow Spring) we could get grub but no oats. Queen was well rested and full of pep. Soon after leaving Red Lake we passed between two high upstanding rocks known as "The Elephant's Feet." Far to the north fantastically eroded cliffs appeal to one's imagination. Fragments of prehistoric pottery are as common in the sand hills along the difficult road as broken dishes in a child's playground. Some ascribe this to prehistoric burials—probably correctly. But anyhow I noted the bulk of the pottery corresponded in color with the color of the earth locally. With me it required only a few centuries' stretch of the imagination to see the locality inhabited by the prehistoric people of whom the Pueblos are descendants. And if that was the case there were probably cornfields on the bench lands surrounding the ancient lake. It is too arid for all that now. But if once there was a lake it is not unreasonable to presume that once there was more moisture.

We met two Pueblos (Hopi) with seven burros (two were colts) packed with flour mostly. They were returning to Hotaville, fifty miles from Cow Spring Trading Post. They had traded corn, belts, socks, and dried peaches for the cargo of flour and received some cash in the bargain. All this from Trader Smythe.

One delight in traveling in the great desert is the constant source of surprise. I had heard of Cow Spring. I had pictured a "spring." Imagine my surprise when we hove in sight of a lake a mile or so in length in this comparatively dry season. (But the lake does go nearly dry at times.) Its bottom, I learned later, is rather dangerous on account of quicksands. We did not, in watering, happen to encounter them.

An Indian had told me that there was grass at Cow Spring. And I find, according to Dr. Fewkes, who journeyed there some twenty years earlier, that "when there was water there was a rich mantle of grass." But on our arrival we found no grass at all. We had left the trail before reaching the Trading Post. We scouted around and found a good shelter from the wind in a deep wash. The only available roughage for Queen was some old dry Russian thistles—which are worse than nothing, because they are indigestible even if a horse is starved to eating them. Often we had gone two days and one night without roughage. But the propect of two nights and nearly three days without was too much. So I made a trip to the Trading Post of Mr. L. D. Smythe, about a mile distant, in the bare hope of getting a "little" alfalfa. Cow Spring is 128 miles from the railroad.

"I've got just two flakes that I sold an old Navajo," replied Mr. Smythe when I told him about us.

"But if you've sold it—?"

"Difference is, he hasn't got 'em yet, and your horse is going to eat 'em. I'll handle the Injun all right, don't worry. Heard of you last night. Navajo call you 'Dugi Whitlow,' meaning 'Old Man with Lots of Whiskers.' And they like you. They are stuck on your horse. They call me 'The Old White Man.' But you don't pack that hay over there. You go and move over here—good place in corral for your horse. You're our guest here. No remonstrance. Haven't had a good pow-wow with a white man for a long time." The trader's wife and kid joined in, so off I went and came back bag and baggage—and Queen of course. Mr. Smythe was a very interesting host. He never tired of the subject of Indians. We sat up until nearly midnight. I took down in my notebook a lot he told me first hand.

That the Navajo is very religious there is no doubt, early published beliefs notwithstanding. The Navajos have many well defined divinities. Their hundreds of musical compositions are of a religious nature. Their so-called dances are religious ceremonies, at least mostly. They are very superstitious. Most of their ills, including sickness, they ascribe to the devil, which in Navajo is "Chindi."

Chindi is not visible to mortal eyes, but he is tangible just the same, and what we might call "foxy." Also like the "devil" that was cast out of the one on the shore of a certain sea, he must be "legion," for he is in many places and some people most of the time, if indeed he is not in most places and many people about all of the time. Also, like the devil of Scripture, he can be "cast out"—by the Medicine Men. As he does not have the proverbial swine to enter into—here—we are left to conjecture where he will show up next!

After all, joking aside, why do we call the Navajo, or other semi-civilized peoples, "heathens" for professing about the same things we profess, only in a little different language? Their religion, their interpretation of the supreme power, fits them and their surroundings. The Navajo has a "soul."

Chindi hides in a corner of the dwelling—if there is a corner. It is he, hiding in a corner, that causes the trouble—usually sickness. When chased out of one corner by the Medicine Man or Singer, with his song and his rattle, he dodges into another corner. If there are four corners in the room it takes four Medicine Men to rout him. But if the room is round, one Medicine Man can chase him clear around the wall and on out of the door. It is a fact today that many traders have their store (trading room) round or oval. The superstitious Navajo feels more like spending his money—or other means of trade—if Chindi has no chance to be hiding in a corner. Most Navajo hogans are round. By the way, most traders have a corral and buy sheep, goats, and once in a while cattle of the Navajo and some overlapping or adjoining tribes.

Sometimes a sick person is in a hogan with another in whom Chindi has such a hold that he can't be dislodged, in which case he is carried out of doors to die, so that the song may have its proper effect on the curable. Then they sing until the sick one is cured. If the sick one dies he had too much devil (Chindi) in him.

There is some superstition in relation to their "ornaments." Generally if a sick Navajo has his ornaments in pawn (usually with a trader, as the Navajos are chronic and injudicious borrowers) their friends redeem them for him, often by pawning their own. This applies to all ages and both sexes. These ornaments, beads and jewelry, much of which is hand wrought, are usually buried with the dead.

When a Navajo dies in a hogan, if the Indians are not influenced by the Indian Department, or it may be by the missionaries, the hogan is pulled down by their friends, who each grab the lower end of a pole. This is his tomb. If the person dies in one of the few substantial dwellings, that building is abandoned as a Chindi house, or devil house. Some ascribe the above as the reason more Navajos do not build more substantial homes. This may be a factor, but, as nearly as I can gather at a glance, they prefer the simple, semi-nomadic life. They frequently return to the place of their youth to die.

Some idea of how the Navajo obtains a living outside the revenue from his sheep, goats, a few cattle, rugs, and saddle blankets, may be obtained from this; Mr. Smythe told me that he, at his small store, bought last year over 2,500 pounds of pinyon nuts (and we were still far from the main pinyon forests) and over a thousand dollars worth of bobcat, badger, fox and coyote skins, though hunting is not a main issue with the Navajo. By the way, the Navajo despises and loathes the coyote as being possessed of the devil, and will bring the unskinned beast to the trader for a song rather than skin the coyote himself. The worst name one Navajo can call another is "myiooyazza"—little coyote.

At midnight my hand cramped so I could write no more—not even a scribble. So I went to bed on a cot in the store.

We entered March Pass from the southwest by the old Tuba-Red Lake (Tonalea P. O.)—Cow Spring—Kayenta road, Kayenta being a few miles northeast of where we entered the pass. All day long, after we left the Smythes, we had hiked over more or less broken plains, passing one square cabin or kind of hut made largely of cedar poles and covered with sticks, brush and earth. The fact that it was rectangular meant that it was inhabited, if at all, by one not deeply grounded in Navajo superstitions. This must have been the place Mr. Smythe mentioned as that of an old man who he told me could direct me to a water hole. We had discovered it, considerably off the road to the west. No one was at home. Off to the north of us was a kind of level plain nestling between the hills to our left and those to the right. A slight depression in the ground I thought might indicate the "water hole." It proved to be dry. Quite a sizable band of mixed sheep (Navajo sheep) and goats were feeding on the sage and other brush. I thought I saw a person with them and started that way. I wanted to inquire about water. The herder vanished— just seemed to fade away among the low shrubbery. Two strange looking, good-sized dogs with eyes more like those of some wild animal than a civilized dog, were "working" the band. They seemed well trained. They eyed us suspiciously, but offered no violence.

Leaving the sheep and goats to solve their own problems we passed on again, traveling approximately northeast. We passed some hogans apparently unoccupied, some of them more or less dilapidated. We were looking for the road, off which we had turned in search of water mentioned by Smythe. We saw two Navajo boys. They ducked, but upon our approach revealed themselves diffidently. One of the greatest characteristics of the Navajo is that he—or she—is very diffident. The boys were repairing an old corral. They very obligingly pointed out the road. They either could or would not talk. We communicated by signs. We got back on the road and then built a little brush fire, made a cup of coffee, using the contents of our canteen, fed Queen a ration of oats, let her nibble at a bunch of shadscale (there was no grass) and moved on.

About 3:30 p.m. Edwin K. overtook us. (Remember E. K. as the Tuba-Kayenta mail carrier, a full blood Hopi World War veteran, educated, and a gentleman.) The keg of water so thoughtfully sent through him by Mr. Smythe came in mighty good. We watered Queen well and I filled our army canteen, holding one quart—the one we carried through the trip. It was well we did so, though at the time I had little doubt that I would easily find the water holes Mrs. Lillian Wilhelm Smith of Tuba had told me of as opposite Segi Canyon, at the same time showing me her painting of Segi Canyon, the location of the water. We found them next morning.

Soon after Edwin K. left us the old road dropped down, down, down off the desert plain between rugged cliffs. For a mile or more Queen's shoes made a clanking noise on the bare rock. The gorge widened. Off across the flat to the west we spied a hogan and an old horse or cattle shed and a Navajo field. It being nearly sundown we made across the flat toward them. Here we encountered our first difficulty with those deeply cut crevices in the earth. They are sometimes as much as thirty feet deep, cut by the torrents from rain and snow water. Often these gaps in the earth are deeper than they are wide, and the walls are nearly perpendicular. The earth through which they are cut is a kind of black gumbo, so you will readily understand why the walls do not crumble to about forty-five degrees as would be the case in better soil.

In making for the hogan Queen jumped one or two of these "washes" near the head. They were probably not more than three or four feet across, but deep enough to get us into a nasty mess had she lost her footing on the opposite bank. I was riding, and we were not so very heavily packed as our oats and grub were now reduced to about three meals. Still, with bed rolls, mackinaw, raincoat, canteen of water and other traps, she must have been carrying over a hundred pounds dead weight. I weighed about a hundred and twenty pounds. But she was in good trim and strong. I managed to keep her so, especially in this country where I never knew to what extent I might have to draw on her stamina.

A good old sport was Queen. She cleared that first washout by quite a margin, and as though eager for the fray. After that she was very much alive. Finding the Navajo buildings deserted and desolate, and no signs of water, we made back at about right angles with the track we made first, crossing the flat. We were going back toward the road we had left. This brought us into contact with the wash lower down where it was perhaps ten feet wide and probably twice as deep. Queen almost begged me to let her tackle it, and for a minute I thought she would in spite of me. But I knew we had too much at stake. Now ten feet is not so much of a jump, but when you add to a ten foot ditch the horse's length plus a little to start from and a safe margin on the opposite side it would not be a very safe bet for a horse carrying a hundred and twenty pound rider and a hundred pounds or more dead weight, especially when the bottom is so far down as to make the "lighting" almost certainly disastrous. Then too I had already discovered that large sections or chunks of this gumbo often seemed about ready to part company with the bank. So I reined Queen back up the wash to where it was only about seven feet (making about a twenty foot jump, counting Queen's length at seven feet and three feet at either end to start and stop on). She had hopped over several laterals so easily, and the banks on either side looked so firm, that I first gave her a good look at the ditch, squared her off a hundred feet back, put her into a run, and—over she went, under her own momentum. She still ran quite a distance after landing across the wash. Once before she had jumped a ten foot space where a bridge was out, as previously related, but I was off her. Here I had to go with her. I did not try, and do not believe I could have made the jump, and the walls were too steep to climb. Soon we were back on the old road. It was getting dusk.

I presume the reason the people at Tuba and Mr. Smythe at Cow Spring had not mentioned Laguna Creek, which lay below us in passing the mouth of Segi Canyon, as a source of water for the night's camp, was because they knew it to be almost inaccessible and that at best the water obtained would be dearly paid for in horse flesh. But Edwin K., though very white in his ways for an Indian, had spoken of it when we had met as "a creek"—a mere incident.

Having passed several local openings in the hills to the west, and having found between us and them no sign of water, I began to believe we had passed the water holes, and began a look-out for the creek, while at the same time wondering why my white friends had overlooked mentioning it. We were now in a narrow part of the pass. The going was rough. We were climbing and descending quite steep grades, the "brakes." We crossed a crude bridge. To our right was a little pocket visible in the pale moonlight. Here I had a notion to camp, but the day had been hot and Queen had traveled quite a distance since she had had water from Edwin K.'s—or rather Mr. Smythe's—keg. Leading Queen now, we swerved to the left. We could make out a great chasm between us and the mountains beyond. We came to a great wash, kept well away from it, and followed it to where it met another great wash at an acute angle. At the bottom we heard plainly in the stillness of the night the running of water—or was it the gentle breeze, stirring the pine boughs across the wash to our right? The murmuring sounds of Nature are so neatly blended some times that it takes a better ear than mine to distinguish between them. But anyhow, before us lay a yawning abyss. We turned back. Going north a little farther we found ourselves up against such rugged chasms in the rocks that I knew to attempt a descent in the darkness and the shadow of the trees would be rank folly. So reluctantly, we turned back into the little pocket first mentioned, near the crude bridge. It was 8 p.m. Tying Queen to a bush I soon had a good fire of dried sticks and cedar roots and small stumps. Oats was all Queen had that night—grass there was none at all. But we were well protected from the slight breeze, and as usual when we had no roughage, I gave Queen, near midnight, an extra feed of oats and she did not complain. In fact, some unexplainable expression of her eye told me that she rather enjoyed the adventure. It was partly cloudy, threatening storm slightly. I didn't unroll the bed, because the indications were we might have to move suddenly. A rain floods these canyons.

At 9:20, after a camp supper, I wrapped up in the sack, my raincoat, my mackinaw and the poncho. We had taken two of the old-fashioned grain sacks of very heavy, good, thick material, and merged them into one long sack. From that time on I usually carried quantities of oats, sometimes cans of milk, and so on, in this. Sometimes, as mentioned here, I would simply pull this on over my feet and legs, up under my arms, for protection. If there were oats in the bottom, so much the better. A quantity of oats is not cold like wheat. By the time I piled whatever loose stuff I had over myself and perhaps drew the poncho over my face, I was fairly well protected. I used the saddle for a pillow. Under me partly was my saddle blanket.

From Notes. Sunday, March 27, '27: Clear. Up 4 a.m.—little cold. Leaving camp 5:45. About a mile, came opposite real (beautiful) Segi Canyon shown in Mrs. S.'s drawing. Found by this and stock trails two large holes in rock nearly full of rain water. It did not taste bad to me—Queen would not drink it. Later came upon water hole in rocks described by E. K. Contaminated by sheep. Also creek mentioned by him deep in the rugged canyon. To W. are some of the most beautiful rugged red and brown rock bluffs I ever saw. Later came out upon large mesa between above mentioned bluffs to N.W. and the gray mts. to S.E. in which is considerable snow. Before us to N. are some wonderful peaks, some like the "Needles," some "monuments" and the great tall black El Capitan. About 9 met Edwin K. returning, loaded with sheep and goat skins. Also met Frank and Lee Bradley, half-breed Navajos and farmers of Kayenta. They gave me some valuable information as to finding water between Kayenta and Mex. Hat. Later met son of "stockman" Mr. S. R. Mangum, and made arrangements about hay.

Another feed of oats and hot coffee from the remaining contents of the canteen and we were off for Kayenta, only a half day's travel. As day appeared we had seen the folly of descending to reach Laguna Creek, which besides being at the bottom of a gorge, very deep, was at the bottom of a deeply-cut channel in the floor of the gorge. It struck me at the time that this channel seemed to have been cut most of its depth in recent years. Later investigation proved this to be true. In 1923 the creek bed was about one-third deeper and twice as wide as in 1908. The creek bed is probably (1927) forty feet deep. At this rate it might seem reasonable to presume that less than seventy-five years ago the creek may have been nearly on a level with the floor of the gorge or narrow valley. A crude, pencil drawing, prepared in 1928 when the writer's memory was still fresh, was verified by some of the best authorities in the Bureau of Ethnology.

From Notes. Sunday, March 27, '27 continued:
Special: Kayenta, 7,770 miles.
Noon: Arrived at Kayenta, a trading post (owned by R. Keith Warren) and school.
Traveled: 13 mi. Very hilly to rolling. Loose sand 3—dirt 5 mi. R. I. (solid rock or baked clay) 5 mi. Soil good in some parts of

mesa. Veg. as yesterday. Left trees after 3 mi. Some more skinny ponies. Passed old peach orchard—few trees also across creek. Brown color predominates, some red, dark gray. 2:30, I am extremely tired. Believe must rest tomorrow before 2 hard days to M. H. (Mexican Hat.)

Note: About 6 mi. W. of Kayenta, I. D. (Indian Department) is opening up a 10 ft. vein of pretty good coal, S. of mesa about half way up mt. side.

Later. Camping in old shed in the sand. Putting Queen in old garage attached. Sand under foot. Later, the Bradley boys came down and we talked until about 9. Arranged tentatively for Lee, the younger and married, to take me to the cliff dwellings 9 mi. up Segi Canyon (i.e. horseback from where we left rd).

From Signature Book: "March 27, 1927. Kayenta, Arizona. I had met Frank M. Heath at Tuba March 24th and on March 26th passed going to Kayenta, and today on 27th with Gypsy Queen. I am a mail carrier, Tuba to Kayenta, full tribe of Hopi. (Signed) Edwin Kawauhaptewa."

From Notes. March 28, '27. Cool, clear. Laying in. About 8 a.m. Lee Bradley came down to camp and announced he had sent a man after the horses at 4 o'clock and expected him back at any time. These horses run on the plain and subsist on sage brush—for further acc't see letter.

Kayenta (Nav. I. Res.) Ariz.
Tuesday, Mar. 29, '27.

Dear Folks:

We arrived here O. K. Sunday 27th, noon. We had intended to lay over a day only, not so much this time on Queen's account as my own. I was about tuckered out. Queen is gay. Of course I had planned to spend the day profitably, which in this case was (and today is) in seeing with my own eyes the weaving of the honest-to-goodness Navajo rugs. But on the way, Sunday the 27th morning, I met one Frank Bradley, his brother Lee Bradley and family, and their mother who is a Navajo, (The father was white.) all taking a Sunday ride in an old Ford. They halted and the boys and I had quite a talk. They are rather "white" in their ways and ideas. Frank is an overseas man, was in field artillery and says he took part in the "Opening Ball." He returned recently from Philippines. He has seen much of the world. He is now engineer at the pumping plant at the Indian School here. Lee is Official Interpreter. They carry on some farming and live in a house rather than a hogan. Last night they came down to where I am camped in an old shed and we had quite a parley. Lee mentioned the Cliff ruins about 19 miles southwest and volunteered to treat me to a trip there with him. I gladly accepted his generous offer, you bet.

This is the way it was done. Next morning Lee started Ned, a Navajo youth, out after the horses. He returned here 10 a.m. driving them on foot. Saddling each of them he started out, riding one, to deliver them to us near the mouth of Segi Canyon. We left here in the old Ford an hour later, passing him. At noon we arrived at a spot near which I camped the night before arriving here. There we built a fire, made coffee and ate as only two "adventurers" could. I had provided grub for two meals, as I supposed—but we made two in one, dividing up with Ned when he came up with the horses. (Near at hand were the washes or gullies into which we came so near the night before last.)

1:45 p.m. we left Ned with the old Ford, mounted the little rats of Navajo ponies, which I christened Blackie and Goldie, and started down the steep bank of Laguna Creek. Speaking of horses, for such they are in strength and endurance, though they weigh scarcely 500 each, I never saw their equal for climbing. I'd no more think of riding Queen down and up such steep banks than I'd think of flying—that is, I would not under the circumstances risk what it would take out of her. These horses, by the way, are gentle. They were the two that Lee kept especially for ladies to ride when he was guiding a party of tourists from Kayenta to the Betatakin ruin. Blackie, by the way, had a mane that reached half way to the ground.

We came to Laguna Creek in the bottom of the deep gorge through which it has cut its way in the red sand that forms the floor of a kind of narrow valley lying between the red bluff to the west and the yellow gray cliffs. Crossing this, we went up the Segi Canyon about seven miles over rock, up and down banks as steep as a house roof (about 30 degrees). Whenever we came to a fairly level spot the horses broke into a trot, often a gallop. The Canyon is beautiful, in brown colors mostly. At seven miles we turned to the left up a side canyon and in another mile were at the mouth of the most symmetrical piece of Nature's work I have ever seen. Take a dome and cut it in two halves up and down, look square into one open half, and you have it. This half dome is about 250 feet across and nearly as tall. The floor slopes backward and upward. The "ruins" are of dwellings built of red sandstone laid in red adobe, not caves dug into the rock. Many of the rooms are still intact, roof and all. Roofs are flat, made of poles, thatch and earth. There are about twenty compartments (or clusters—of one or more rooms). Some are granaries or store rooms, the floors of which are at a steep angle. The sleeping apts. and kitchens are more level. One room seems to be a place of worship containing an altar. Another is a children's play house. The whole seems to be built on lines of defense, all deep within the half dome, against its walls. There are two distinct stories. The upper is approachable only by climbing a long pole.

(It seemed that but yesterday the children must have played "housekeeping" in the room evidently built for the little ones. There are the little benches (of rock), the little fireplace, the toy metates set in toy bins.—) * * * *

In our climbing and turning in approaching Betatakin we at one time had crossed a ridge of the gumbo earth many feet high between two washes, with nearly perpendicular walls on either side and so narrow that a slight crumbling or erosion from either side would have sent us over into the abyss. It made my hair stand. I loosened my feet in the stirrups.

"That will cave one of these days," I ventured to Lee.

"Maybe so."

"And then where is your trail?"

Lee grinned slightly.

I was anxious to get back over that narrow ridge before sundown. I dreaded a misstep of Blackie. Lee seemed indifferent about it. He was more concerned about covering the rough old road between the canyon and Kayenta with the old Ford.

"Aren't we pretty near that ridge?" I asked after quite a spell.

"Past it," replied Lee dryly. "We detoured."

"So had it caved while we were in there we would not have been caught in a trap?"

"Not me." And it occurred to me that "in there" would be a bad place for strangers to get lost.

(Signed) Frank.

From Notes. March 29, '27: Clear, fairly warm. Laying in to see rug weaving, etc. Took dinner (supper) with Mrs. J. H. Taylor at Weatherall Ranch. Several friends dropped in. Later Mr. and Mrs. Frank Hughes, traveling, came in. Address, Bowie, Ariz. Mrs. (H.) presented me with a garnet.

THE COCONINO SUN

Kayenta News

Friday, April 8, 1927

Acting as if reaching Kayenta was the dream of her young life, Gypsy Queen trotted into the village limits Sunday and liked the place so well she stayed over for three days. Her rider, Frank M. Heath, of Silver Springs, Md., a suburb of Washington, D. C., is a man fifty-eight years old and served for ten months overseas during the World War, his title being mule sergeant. * * * * Mr. Heath is traveling three months behind his printed schedule as he was laid up two months and ten days from a fractured knee, received in Yellowstone Park, Mammoth, Wyoming, in the summer of 1926 when a horse he had bought for a pack animal kicked him. There were at least six or seven kinds of flies to contend with in the park and he was of the opinion that all the varieties in the whole United States that are troublesome to horses had gathered for a convention there. It was while trying to rid the strange horse of one of these pests that it displayed its ungrateful disposition by kicking him. At the Veterans' Hospital at Fort Harrison, Helena, Mont., he was cared for by Dr. Frazier, known throughout this section as he was formerly in the Government Indian Service at Shiprock. * * * * Arizona is the thirty-fifth state he has visited and ten of them he has struck twice in winding about. So far they have put behind them 7,707 miles and Gypsy Queen is lively as a colt and as full of pep as if she were only starting. She has worn out 17 pairs of shoes. * * * * The traveler could not resist the temptation to see a little more of this neighborhood so Monday Lee Bradley took him to the Betatakin ruins in Segi Canyon. This is quite an honor and proves the lure of the desert, for Mr. Heath does not make side trips to places of interest, as it would consume too much of his time. The gentleman was very much enthused and in his wanderings among the rocks half a mile from this place on Tuesday found what he believes to be dinosaur tracks. * * * *

The two travelers left Kayenta Wednesday on the way to Bluff,

Utah, from there to Cortez, Colo., and on to Gallup, N. M. He was profuse in his praise of the hospitality shown him in the West and especially in the wide open spaces, in sparsely settled communities. * * * *

From Notes. March 30, '27: Cool, windy. Leaving Kayenta 8 a.m., after much photographing. Noon, Nosebag, hot lunch 1 mi. N. of El Capitan. 6 p.m., Came by road to Golding. 7 p.m. Ar'd Golding Trading Post, Monumental Valley, Utah, H. V. Golding, Prop. P. O. Kayenta—just off Ind. Res. 640 acre homestead.

Traveled: 29 miles. Rolling, R. I., 3 mi. Loose sand, 8 mi.—18 mi. (good footing). Strong S. W. wind. Sagebrush, shadscale, soapweed, few scattering junipers, a little gramma grass, stunted cactus. Last 10 miles, getting green toward last. Few horses, sheep, cattle, goats. Traversed Monumental Valley—red cliffs on W., gray on E. to El Capitan. From there on "hit and miss." Passed Mitchell Butte, very symmetrical. 5 miles buttes. Just S. W. of Golding is what the Indians call "The Rock Door" beyond which is a natural bridge.

Note: Made back little S. of W. in going to Golding. Will backtrack 3 mi. (sand) to main rd. Queen drank but little. No hay. Partial windbreak. No good place to lie down. No habitation (in sight all day). Wonderful singing beyond hills.

I had seen no one for hours, and this was the first human voice I had heard all day. We were surrounded by a grand quietude—if that expresses it—as well as grand scenery. All at once this deep, rich baritone voice came to us as though from out the sky—that is, from just over the very high hills at our right. I couldn't understand the words, of course. Mentioning this to Golding, he said that it was a medicine man singing to a patient. Evidently there was an Indian settlement or at least a residence over the hill. Golding is an intelligent man, apparently fairly well educated, not fanatical, and he tells me that these medicine men do perform a good many cures. They give some herb medicine, and soothe or satisfy the mental phase of the ailment, just the same as our own good old home doctors do with a patient.

From Notes. March 31, '27: Clear, cool W. wind. Leaving Goldings. Very nominal chg. for good supper. No chg. for good qrs. in tent. Overseas man. Stable sgt. Engineers. *Note:* He *wants the story. Note:* Seems to me like different variety shad-scale, leaves just coming out, and like tea leaves. Queen likes it. Queen, calling for hay, refuses water. (Golding, like Smythe, has large knowledge of Navajo—says good workers but poorly nourished.) G. also owns dipping plant—barters for sheep, goats. 8:30: Passing several hogans. Found water in arroyo. Doubting whether she will drink, don't go down to it. Golding says we cross water. 8:40, Indian giving name of "Frank" halts us, inquiring abruptly: "Where go?" and "Where come?" We explain. * * * * He magnanimously and majestically stepped aside, saying, "All right, go Mexican Hat." That is where I told him we stay tonight. Noon, Haven't crossed water yet. Nosebag, hot lunch out of wind in dry arroyo about 11 mi. N.E. Golding. 3 p.m. Came upon water (alkali) and a well. Saw a prairie dog. 4:30, Come upon an oil drill—say down 1,400 ft. Another 1,800 ft.—"not deep enough yet, oil below." 6 p.m. Came to brakes of San Juan River—much steep grade. 6:45, Crossing suspension bridge. A cable and carrier cross a little above water—muddy, swift. 7 p.m., Ar'd Bowen's Trading Post, Mex. Hat. (So named after rock resembling a Mex. hat, a big round rock, flat on the bottom, somewhat pointed top, which was balanced on another tall rock at a rakish angle.)

Traveled: 27 mi. (stony)—Very hilly, R. I., 7 mi. Dirt, 10 mi. Loose sand, 10 mi. Vegetation as yesterday. Goats, sheep, horses, cattle. No habitation after 5 mi. except drill outfit. Snow to right and ahead in distance. Rugged scenery, browns and grays. *Note:* Navajos principal means of existence seems to be goats—do not shear them—milk, skins.

April 1, '27: Clear, warmer. Slept well in hay house. Invited to supper by the Bowens. Leaving Bowens 9:10 o'clock. Took wrong road to left, believing large canyon to be river. Bluffs hid real river. Knew by direction must be wrong. Got back when came in sight of canyon in which is San Juan R. 11, Came onto Lime Creek—large spring or rather creek. Queen drinks greedily and often. Noon (12:40), Nosebag, hot lunch at another spring or creek—same arroyo. Soaking Queen's feet—repairing breeches. 4 p.m., Crossing a mesa about 4 mi. in extent. Upon it is pretty fair gramma grass. From above mentioned mesa we came again in sight of "The Mittens" which we passed yesterday 9 a.m. They look very close after nearly two days travel. Snow shows plainly on right and left in distance. We feel it in the air. About 5 p.m. we strike into one of the most picturesque narrow "gorges" yet encountered. In many places it would be difficult to let an auto pass. The turns are often at almost right angles or in small "loops." The floor much of the way is solid rock and quite rough. Between rock ledges is reddish or brown sand—rather a red sandy clay or adobe. The walls of rock are a promiscuous mixture of red, brown sandstone (some of which seems to be in process of turning into stone), and about the same thing in grays and some yellow. Then in places it is of a smoother texture and fairly hard. Sometimes it looks as though the Creator had started out to build these parts in brown, then all of a sudden slapped a mess of gray on top. The whole is fantastically eroded by sand, wind, cold, heat and floods, as indeed are most rock cliffs hereabouts. Then winding through some red hills (Comb Reef) sometimes on a very large scale. 6:30, Crossing a great arroyo, the Comb Wash, near the N. side of which is quite a stream of muddy water. After crossing this we wind our way up a grade out into or graded onto the side of a mt.—up a gorge. It is a long steep climb. I walk, but Queen is glad to stop often and "blow." To our right and very far below lies the great arroyo. A creek empties into it from our side. Beyond it some hills are white—probably alkali. We reach the top about dark, and pass over a divide, through a kind of pass chiseled out of beautiful grey stone—over a divide and then down, down, down a steep grade between a deep canyon on our left and the gray cliffs on our right. We reach the bottom, cross another creek, up another steep hill on opposite side, other hills and out upon another mesa. By the light of the stars we see the cliffs on either hand. Finally we see a light ahead. We take it to be Bluff. It is time. We have traveled about 10 hours. We drop into an arroyo. When we come out we have lost the light. We plod on until 9:15 p.m. Turning we see a bright light to the N.W. Can it be a bright star near the ground? No, it's too large and bright. We believe we must have taken a side trail in the darkness and passed Bluff. Queen is plucky but I know she is tired. We come suddenly near the San Juan. We decide to bivouac for the night. Turning back up the river we tumble into a rocky draw. Up out of that and towards a bluff to the N.W. (The wind is chilly.) Reason—and experience—tells us that the bluff which seems so near may be several miles distance. Saw one prairie dog. We

came into a draw. We follow it down toward the road which
lies between us and the river. Crossing the road again we come
to a deep wash that makes a lovely cave—a fine windbreak. The
water flowing over a rocky ledge had cut it down some 5 feet,
and way under, making quite a cave. I tie Queen to sagebrush,
feed her the one feed I had left. Build a sagebrush fire and by
the light examine the cave for snakes. Spread my blankets on the
sand floor. Then make coffee, eat the remnant of grub I had left
over, and crawl into the cave—that is I start to, when—up comes
a car. I hail it. "Where the hell is Bluff?" I inquire. "Bluff?
About four miles up the river." So I hadn't passed it after all.
"But what light was that?" No one knew. (Must have been the
Evening Star.) Then I rolled in feeling better.

Traveled: 29 miles * * * * Very hilly. Some very steep and
long. Dirt 10 mi. Loose sand, 9 mi. R. I. (often solid rock) 10
mi. Veg. as yesterday plus R. thistles. No habitation. Many
cattle. Some horses. (Comb Reef divides two cattle outfits.)
Cattle, white face, in good shape—many large fine calves. Colors
(in Nature) browns and grays of mellow, restful hues. Gray
predominates E. of "Wash."

April 2, '27: Fair. Up daylight. Leaving camp 7 a.m.—8 a.m.
Ar'd Bluff. Putting up at town farm of Mr. Nielson. Queen in
corral. Plenty alfalfa. Camping in "lot." Oats only 3.50. Eggs
only 25 cts., fine, after paying "the limit." Level, desert to bluffs.

Traveled: 4 mi. Rolling, R. I., 1 mi. Sand, 3 mi.

Special Note: Flagstaff to Bluff, 261 mi. (11 more than schedule.)

Total to Bluff, Utah, 7,855 miles [as corrected].

Bluff is in an oasis between bluffs of gray and reddish brown.
Here are irrigated fields of alfalfa, good gardens, corn, etc. Fat,
contented cows, gentle horses and prosperous appearing people.
The town of 125 people, 2 stores, 1 church, Bishopric, school to
8th grade, 2 hotels. Bldgs. mostly of gray stone—some brick
[made] of adobe. Elevation, 4,400 ft. R. R., Dolores, Colo., 70
mi. 8 p.m., Talking to crowd at Relief Hall (by invitation).

Note: This oasis consists of 172 acres. Bluff founded 1880.
Several artesian wells, 98% pure. Irrigate gardens. [And fields of
alfalfa, if my memory is correct.]

It seems that about everything here was run on a community basis.
The fine white-faced cattle that I mentioned way back just east of

The Combs belonged, the boys told me, to their Cooperative. Everybody works. White I was there I observed they were extending an irrigation ditch, using teams and slip scrapers. The Deacon was working as hard as anybody—a little harder, in fact. He was holding slips. Later he sent one of the boys over to invite me over to his place. His boots showed signs of the rough work he was doing. A rugged, wide-awake man. He was very civil, as in fact all these people were to me.

I had written the Postmasters at Bluff and also at Cortez, N. M., inquiring if oats were procurable in their towns. From each I received a reply that I could get all the oats and other feed I wanted. I found this to be true, at least at Bluff, and presumed it to be true of Cortez, as in there is quite a farming community.

While at Bluff, after making inquiries, I decided to cut east from Bluff, across the Ute Reservation, coming out at Mancos Creek Trading Post, where I would intercept a road given in my schedule, thus cutting off quite a loop saving not only distance, but considerable pretty tough road. This we did.

From Signature Book: "Bluff, Utah, Apr. 2/27. Frank M. Heath arrived here at my place today at 8 o'clock a.m. riding his mare 'Gypsy Queen' and is staying over today.

(Signed) U. A. Neilson."

Bluff, Utah, April 2, '27.

Dear Folks:

I arrived here this morning O. K. Staying over here today. As usual so darned busy I can't say my soul is my own. Making a talk tonight. Love,

(Signed) Frank.

Later: Yours of Mar. 28 rec'd just now. Next address c/o Mrs. E. R. Thomas, Garfield, N. M.

From Notes. Sunday, April 3, '27: Fair. Slept well by haystack. * * * * Leaving the Neilsons 12:30. No chg. for hay. Boys taking pictures (as we left Bluff). 5:30, Ar'd Recapture Creek. After passing a "gray" canyon out of Bluff came to quite a large mesa upon which is fair gramma grass, sage, shadscale, stunted cactus, very few stunted juniper. Then came hills and gray cliffs and bluffs. About 4:30 we came [to] a bluff facing S. of extremely vivid colors in brown, gray and some yellow, a little green, and particularly purple. Fantastic shapes. 5:30 p.m., We are in a

cave facing S. on Recapture Creek. Colors range from very dark
brown (nearly black) to a greenish gray. And from near granite
to sandstone that is hardly stone. These rocks are cut probably
by sand and wind—and washed by torrents of water pouring
down (evidently), possibly in a cloudburst, into every imaginable shape. Many are honeycombed. A great many large boulders
seem to be soft inside, with a harder shell. These are hollowed
out. I have made my bed inside of one of these, half way up the
side of the bluff. It opens to the E. It looks and feels like rain.
If the wind don't change this will afford protection. I fixed a
place nearby for Queen by leveling the sand and removing the
small rocks. She is tied to a stone (staple).

Traveled: 12 mi. Hilly. dirt, 5 mi. R. I., 7 mi. Description
above. No habitation.

Note: In cavern where I am to sleep are some bones, probably
of some modern animal that went in there and died. However,
I never have seen any just like them that I know of—and they
are old. The "cannon bones," if such, are long and straight, the
ribs small (bones are mostly gone—others scattered.) What
puzzles me most is the lower jaw. It somewhat resembles that of
a human—very large—as of some ape or something. * * * *
Teeth very much decayed. About 4 or 5 inches across jaw. Not
being versed in such matters am at a loss (as to how to explain
more adequately). Just for fun I gathered up the bones, put
them into one of the "pockets" in the yellow sandstone, wrote
this on a piece of cardboard and put it in with the bones:

"These bones of the What-Was-It? were discovered [by] myself and Queen. Decent burial by Frank M. Heath, Horseback
Traveler, while camping in this romantic spot on the night of
the 3rd day of April, 1927. 'Let them rest in pieces.' "

Hardly had I finished these "rites" when an owl began hooting
at the silly streak in me that prompted the action. It is beginning
to sprinkle ever so little. The cave is filled with sounds like of a
"jangling" freight train, though I know there is not a R. R.
within 60 miles. Or is it a truck rattling over the stones? It is
neither. It is the wind coming up the creek from the S. and re-
echoing and whistling through and into the ragged rocks. It is
almost uncanny, yet it fills me with a kind of reverence rather
than fear or even awe. It seems like Father Time talking through
the ages. Queen is restless. I have moved her right up against the
ledge close by, having partly leveled a little "shelf" and tied her

to a natural staple in the rock. The sagebrush fire on a little ledge a foot or so beneath my "bunk" lends "fantasy" to it all. I fall asleep half believing myself a "cave man" and not caring a whoop if I were—only I'm glad I have modern grub for breakfast, and Queen is shod, that I don't have to ride bareback, that I haven't a dozen wives to pester the devil out of me, that I have a pair of boots and some breeches—even if ragged—and that I don't have to sleep with one eye open for fear of the "What-Was-It" whose bones I put in the rock.

> Billy Meadows' Trading Post,
> E. McElamo, Colorado,
> April 6, 1927

Mrs. Esther Rockwell,
Rice Lake (Wells) Minn.
Dear Cousin—and Family:
    * * * * We were (originally) routed, (subject to change) to Shiprock, N. M. via Cortez, Colorado. Look at your map and you'll find that Cortez is some 25 miles father N. and about as many further E. as it was necessary for us to go in order to be well within the state of Colorado, (and you of course understand that we have made a long and tedious journey of 304 miles from Flagstaff, Ariz. just for the sake of a "John Henry" from a reliable resident of Utah and another in this state.) Now we make back south. * * * *
    Yesterday, 8 a.m. we left the Post at Montezuma Creek. Though there is some quicksand in the creek in places we succeeded in dodging them. After winding between some hills— always picturesque in these parts—we struck across a small mesa or plain. Then after twisting around through another canyon, the rugged rock walls of which are rich in color, we came onto a larger mesa covered with gray sagebrush and some gramma grass in places.
    Speaking of colored rocks, cliffs and bluffs, the predominating color or "canvas" yesterday and today is a beautiful restful gray. Some places it is brown, varying in the shades enough to delight rather than tire the eye. Varying from this there are banks, sometimes little hills, of purple brown, running into almost black, green, pink, yellow, white—almost. In fact a blending that is indescribable. Any attempt at a drawing of these hills that I have ever seen is a joke. I have never seen in a picture the

mellow tints. They are always overdone—too loud. They excite, while these delight the mind's eye. Or is it partly because these are modified by the greatness of space and glorified by the pure desert atmosphere, while the picture by human hands is "confined"? From the mesas are visible snowclad mts. to N., S. and E. * * * * E. of us is Ute Mt.

About noon we wind our way down another canyon showing just enough of colors to break the monotony. Then we ford Yellow Jacket Creek and are at Ismay's Trading Post. There I fed Queen on 5 ct. oats, and myself on coffee and plenty of canned milk and sugar bread, soft boiled eggs and jam, a meal fit for a king.

We left the Post at 3:30 p.m., accompanied by a Mexican boy on a good fat mule. This boy lives at McElamo, a P. O., a Mexican settlement 2 miles N. of the Post. There is a little farming, gardening, fruit, stock, sheep. Soon I turn off the * * * * road down a steep hill and across McElamo Creek into a bridle path leading Easterly. We came to a dim wagon track turning to the left and took it as directed by Mr. Ismay. We were told to follow the track, turning again to left at a certain point of rock, to Billy Meadows' Trading Post, about 7 miles. This track winds and twists around. Like a blankety blank fool I thought to shorten our path by a bridle trail and "thereby hangs a tale." "The wagon track" to be explicit, was that made by one wagon, of narrow tire, passing one time. Any previous tracks for the most part have been obliterated by erosion, corrosion or tracks of stock, or jackrabbits. Well, after a while I perceived that I seemed to have lost sight of the crooked wagon tracks. I bore back toward the right, being to the left of it. After a while we struck into another wagon track of about the same width. It looked a little dim but I laid it to the texture of the earth. We followed it a long way, occasionally losing it and finding it—or another—again. We had been told that at Billy Meadows' Post was a spring. This track wriggled and twisted its way up a steep incline to the foot of a great hill. There was a spring. And there the track made a loop and doubled back—or rather "pointed" away (and frazzled out). But where the heck was the Post? We had traveled about the length of time it ought to take to travel 7 miles in a walk. It was nearly 6 o'clock. To the left was a little valley—rather a cove. I traversed it in a vain search for an opening—a road turning E. No road, no track. A trail ran up over the

hills to the south. I had been told of a "trail" as well as the
"track." I climbed the hill in search of some sign of the Post. No
Post. A mile or so to the west and south of where we had passed
I saw mirrored against the hills beyond a pool of water. I wondered if thereabout was the Post. I climbed a high hill. No Post
in sight. Looking down and eastward I saw part of a corral. The
other part was hidden by the bluff upon which I stood.

"The Post," I said to myself, "or at least some habitation."
Most posts support a corral. The Trader buys sheep and cattle of
the Indians. I hurried back and brought Queen up. After quite a
search we found a way down over the bluff. You'd hardly believe
it if I told you how that mare, high-strung as she is, can navigate
a difficult path. We reached the bottom and found an unused
sheep camp. There was no hay, no grass there. I looked in the
shack. There hung from the roof a rotten sack containing about
20 lbs. of oats. The mice had been working on them. A large
portion were only hulls. Just the checker—if Queen would eat
them—the hulls made "roughage." Would she eat them? She
would.

No, I didn't swipe the oats—I borrowed them. The first time
I see the owner I'll repay them. Queen must eat. Hurriedly un-
packing and unsaddling I slipped the nosebag onto Queen with
a liberal feed and struck out to find the Post if possible. I still
thought it must be tucked away behind some hill—the spring
fooled me. I needed grub. Fortunately I had, besides coffee and
sugar, one scanty meal. Besides I did not like the idea of spending the next day in locating us. I had begun to suspect that
we were too far north, for, * * * * Ute Peak should be a
little to N.E. of us. It was straight E. I hurried across the small
flat south. It was 6:40 p.m. I took observation of the position of
the moon as a means of finding my way back to the sheep camp
should it happen to get dark. In front of me rose a long hill or
mt. of gray boulders. I surmounted the difficulty to find greater
ones beyond. To the S.W. looked like a pass, a road between
other hills. I scrambled down the steep rough hillside in the
twilight and made for the pass. It proved a hoax—though hard-
beaten by sheep. But on the way I discovered a "tank" of water
(a reservoir here is called a tank). I next went in the direction
of the other pool I'd seen. I found it. No Post. I hollered. I
whistled. No reply.

With the moon over my left shoulder as a guide I started back to the sheep camp—and missed it. "Too far up the bluff," I remarked to me. I turned left following the bluff. No sheep camp. "I must have struck the north arm of the valley," I said to myself. "If so, I'll cross it and should again run into the spring." I crossed it—but no spring. But—I ran into the "pond" again. Back I came and made the half circle of the south arm of the valley, nearly to the camp as I saw later—crossing meanwhile some foot hills. I thought I'd gone far enough west.

"Lost, like the Blank fool that I am," I chided myself. By the light of the moon Old Bobby said 9:15. My legs ached. The corns between my toes were giving me hell. It was getting pretty cool. I had not donned my mackinaw. I'd even neglected to put matches in my pocket. I decided to crawl into the shelter of one of those hollowed out rocks (a kind of cave) and wait for daylight. I started to do so. I put my hand on the skeleton of a sheep. "Be not like dumb, driven cattle," came rolling down to me from Longfellow. "That's right," I thought. "I'll not crawl in there to catch my death of cold and die like the other sheep." I started on. I heard a little noise. "Good old girl!" I said. It was Queen calling to me. She had seen me before I saw her. For the corral was in the shadow of a great bluff—I had just missed it long before. Queen out of the shadow had seen me in the little remaining light of the moon. She was so tickled to have me back that she actually capered about like a collie dog. It was 9:40 p.m. I'd been gone 3 hours and traveled about 7 or 8 miles.

I built a fire and made coffee, ate half the grub, gave Queen an extra feed of oats in lieu of hay, spread my blankets on the ground in the shack, with saddle for a pillow, and went to sleep trying to formulate expressions sufficiently mean to say to the next man that suggested a "cut-off" to me. I've never left the main highway in the mountains but what every mile we saved cost us two in energy.

This morning we left camp 5:40. I had decided to take a look about us in daylight for the Billy Meadows' Trading Post. If I came upon it easily and soon, all right. If not, we would backtrack to the Cortez road and go that way. We had traveled an hour—still studying "language"—when suddenly the unexpectedly we came to the narrow wagon tracks cut deep and plain into the red clay, running S. E. We were going west. Without a moment's hesitation we swung into them. Paralleling them, sometimes obliterating them, was the Indian trail (bridle path) of which I had been told. Sometimes it "cut across." But I stuck religiously to the tracks wherever in sight, and tried to keep a sharp lookout, * * * *   We came to a fence. No one had mentioned it. The wagon tracks ran on through a gate. We ran after them. It was high time we should have arrived at Billy Meadows' if he was 7 or even 9 miles from Ismay's. We passed a gray mule and a brown horse, but no sign of a trading past. "Sold again," I said, "but if the blank track holds out we'll get to Mancos Trading Post in a day or two." We had not seen the wagon tracks for some little time. Also I knew that Meadows was a little way off the main bridle trail.

I saw a man a quarter of a mile ahead coming slowly with his head down. As he approached I said to him: "You are looking for a gray mule and a brown horse."

"Yes," said he.

"Back there," I pointed. "Are you Mr. Meadows?"

"Yes."

"The heck you are!" I said under my breath as he approached. "No one had told me Meadows was an Indian black as the ace of spades!"

"Billy Meadows that way one fourth mile," he told me. "No see road? Turn off back little way. Now you go here."—pointing S.W. over a ridge. "You see tree. You go straight down. No go this way," pointing to the left. "You see Billy Meadows' store."

I followed his instructions. Part way up the hill I ran into Billy Meadows' road. Coming to the top of the hill I saw the Post off across a canyon to the west. The road ran around to the south. So afraid was I of losing the Post that I would not follow the road. "No go that way!" old Henry, the Ute, had told me. It might not be the Meadows' road.

With much difficulty we finally found our way down a pass in the bluff. Also I found more fragments of "Aztec" pottery.

It was lucky I had brought the remaining oats. Meadows had none. But he had grub, of which he set enough on the table for two men, even though hungry, as I was. He also scratched up a little leavings of alfalfa hay for Queen and some corn.

Billy Meadows lives all alone in a room partitioned off from the store. The long, low building is of red stone and situated among the yellowish gray rocky hills. At the foot of one is a fine spring of water containing a little soda. Billy is 66. He came to these parts—these parts means a large scope out here—in 1888.

At first he was in the employ of the Indian Department. He learned the Navajo tongue and finally engaged in trade with them. He is a licensed trader. * * * *

"It's a little slow today," he told me. Still I noticed he had quite a trade. One customer was Little Tom Guadalupe, a full blood Ute weighing about 250. He lives 6 miles this side of Mancos on the trail. He asked me to "stop all night my house," and I may do so. "Other side Shiprock, maybe long way no water." He meant I'd better save my horse while I had a chance. I asked how he was fixed for horse feed.

"Tomorrow, sun here," pointing to the E. horizon, "I go To-yock (the Agency) get alfalfa, get oats. Sun here (pointing west) I come back. You come my house, you put your horse my barn. Him sit down. You come my house. You sit down. Pretty soon, sun here, I come. My wife, my daughter, he is home," he continued, eyeing me critically. I looked him straight in the eye, nodded, and said not a word. He was satisfied. He knows I'm a traveler, not a renegade.

The Indians are greatly interested in Queen.

This is the morning of the 7th. I must pack up and leave "Billy"—after breakfast. You'll excuse pencil and poor writing and spelling. Difficult writing with pen. Arm lame. Will mail it at Shiprock, two or three days' ride ahead, 1st P. O. Best regards to yourself, hubby, the kids and all. Love,

(Signed) Frank.

From Signature Book: "Hilly Meadows Trading Post, East McElamo, Colorado. (10 mi. S. of McElamo P. O., Colorado) Frank M. Heath arrived here 10 a.m. today—April 6, 1927—with bay mare known as Gypsy Queen. He is stopping here tonight.
(Signed) Wm. Meadows,
Proprietor Trading Post."

Mancos Creek Trading Post, Colo.,
20 miles N. Shiprock, N. M.,
April 8, '27.

(A postscript to Cousin Esther, enclosed with letter of April 6th.)

I left Billy Meadows yesterday, 9 a.m. I was told that this place was only 22 miles distant. Probably that is true, as the bee flies. But—the road—for there was supposed to be a "little road"

as the Ute calls a "dim" road, wound and looped around hills
and canyons. Of course you know the little sketch could not
very well describe all these any more than does a highway map,
even had I known all about them. Many times I could have cut
these loops by taking the trail that nearly always cut across. But
there are trails and trails, trails going no place at all, trails
converging, trails branching off and frazzling out. So I was to
keep the wagon road. I've troubles with wagon roads here.
They are often scarcely more than a single track and there are
single tracks everywhere. I mean one may stumble onto one.
And in directing a stranger to take the 2nd left hand "road"
the old-timer usually forgets to count one or two of these
"tracks." If the stranger passes them up on the theory that they
are only tracks, he may pass up the "road." And there you are.
The old-timer tells the stranger to "keep east." The road runs
in every point of the compass in a mile or two. If the stranger
takes it upon himself to strike across in a line toward some
landmark he runs into a precipice and must backtrack. Or, still
more likely, upon a gully cut deep and steep into the nearly
level adobe or dobie flats. These do not show until one nearly
tumbles into them.

At 11:20 a.m. yesterday I came to the gate in the Res. line
fence, which is rather dilapidated. We were on a large mesa
S.W. of Ute Mt. The gramma grass here is good. Queen had not
had much hay the night before and none the night before that.
I let her graze a little. About noon we should have been at
Maryetta Spring. No spring showed up. We followed a cattle
trail some distance to the N. as these sometimes lead to water.
The trail frazzled out. To west was a band of sheep—which
always, here, means sheep and goats. As usual there was with
them a boy on horseback. They were coming our way. I waited
while Queen ate more grass. Finally the boy rode up whistling.
He was friendly and inquisitive. He pointed the location of the
spring a mile away and ¾ mile off the road. He drew me a
diagram on the ground, showing where a "road" crossed the
road I was traveling.

"This side, Ute house, white house this side spring." The
house was a tent. The road a trail. But I made a guess and
found some little pools of water in the bottom of an arroyo
that was white with either alkali or soda, I believe the latter.
Queen would scarcely taste it. I did not know whether I had

found Maryetta Spring or not. I unsaddled, made coffee—and notes—while Queen nibbled the saccaton grass. I forgot to mention, about the time I left the boy I spied six or seven tents off to the S.W. and some more sheep with a mounted herder. Am mentioning these little matters as I go along to give you as nearly as possible the picture of the Ute life and Ute resources. While we are about it, one is seldom out of sight of one to three little bands of horses. These horses are larger and in better condition than those of the Navajo, though I doubt their being tougher.

About 3 p.m. I came to a pretty fair barn and an adobe house. There was quite a piece of good looking ground enclosed by a fence that looked more like white than Indian. A band of sheep that looked prosperous and better bred than most I've seen here were just coming to drink at a reservoir. Just inside the fence toward the house was a little hollow scooped out about the size of a dish pan. In it was water—a faint spring.

Leaving Queen I walked to the house. Squatted about the inevitable campfire were an old squaw, two younger ones, and a little boy. I inquired about the Maryetta Spring. They did not seem to understand. I got permission to water Queen at their Spring. I inquired for the place of Little Tom Guadalupe, half believing this to be it. The old squaw pointed toward Toyock. I noticed a significant exchange of glances, a muttered word or two in Ute. "Is this Little Tom's place?" I asked one of the younger women. She pointed back in the direction I had come. A little laugh went round and I was pretty sure she had told a silent lie. But what was I do about it? I wanted to give Queen as many easy days as possible before the next long siege of hard knocks. But I did not propose to try to force myself in where some of the family didn't want me, much less where women were alone.

I inquired the road to Mancos. They pointed out the one to Toyock, as I learned later to the tune of 6 miles extra. I thought I understood the nasty little laugh that went around.

Going back to the road I dipped water from the little spring into our collapsible bucket and watered Queen. Scarcely had I put the bucket back on its proper strap on the saddle when up rode an oldish Ute, of the typical old type, on a red roan horse with four white legs. This horse and rider, if I was not mistaken, I had seen standing on a hill apparently taking observations of all the little natural movements I have previously described.

"What matter? What matter?" asked the old Ute (I assume he was a Ute) peremptorily.

"Nothing the matter," I replied, trying not to seem to notice his strange behavior. "I am watering my horse, water down there no good. Is that Maryetta Spring down there?"

"Where go?" gruffly.

"Mancos, Shiprock, Gallup."

"Where come?"

"Washington."

"Washington!"—contemptuously. (These Utes seem to hold Washington in contempt—most of them—and anything or any one Washingtonian. I am told that they aver stoutly that Uncle Sam has lied to them repeatedly.)

"Washington! Washington house?"

"No, I just go myself. Ride all round all states"—trying to make him understand by gestures. "Travel 7,890 miles, same horse."

"This Indian country—this no white man country. You go, you *go!*" pointing emphatically up the road.

I took my time in adjusting Queen's bridle. She had gotten one foot over the rein. The old Indian started to chase her. She let fly at him. He fell back. We went on. He went up to the adobe house.

On we went, winding and wondering where was the road that Billy Meadows told us branched off to Toyock. Topping a little rise we came upon two Indians, mounted, off to one side a little way, in a little draw. One of them gave me a friendly wave. I approached them. One of them was the same old buck on the same horse. I had ridden several miles and seen not a hair of him, though I had kept watch. I didn't like this spying on me. The other, the one that waved, was a Navajo and wore some kind of a badge, a kind of police, I believe. (The badge said "Booze cop.")

I inquired for Little Tom. The Navajo motioned the way I had come. I had wanted to believe I was mistaken. * * * *

The old Navajo was a little inquisitive, but in a more civil manner. I tried to talk with him. I did not like being misunderstood. It seemed too much like being suspected of something or other. I showed them our card. "Washington!"—contemptuously. The old Ute started off over a little hill. "Come on," he said, beckoning me at the same time. "Boy." There was a boy to act as interpreter.

Soon we came to a large tepee, a large tent, a pretty good wagon with some good horses tied about it, half a dozen or so big fat Utes—both sexes—and some cur dogs. In the wagon was a boy of about 16. I tried to talk with him. He wouldn't talk, though he nodded when I asked if he understood English. "Been to school?" I asked him. "Say," I told him, "You tell these people I am just riding across here to Mancos and Shiprock, minding my own business. I happen to be from near Washington, but I am not working for the Government. I'm riding for my health, that's all. Good-bye." As I left I heard a contemptuous "Washington!"

Going back toward the road I passed a large band of sheep and goats—or rather I believe goats and sheep, of all colors—except green.

I met Little Tom behind a pretty good little team of mules with a bale of hay on the wagon. Another Indian was trailing a good looking horse with saddle behind.

"Where go?"

"Have to go to Mancos now. Where is your place?" (Here I suddenly remembered that Billy had advised me strongly to go on to Mancos. "You can't depend on them damned Indians," he said.)

"Back there—that's putty good." I described the place of the adobe house, the only house I'd passed in sight of so far on the Ute Res. in fact. It was his.

"I asked your folks and they didn't seem to know where you lived."

"That's putty good!" he laughed. "I tell 'em one white man come, he have 'em stay. They no like. That's putty good! But this wrong road Mancos Store. This road go Toyock."

"I asked your folks—they say this road Mancos Store."

"They no sabe. Now you go s-t-r-a-i-g-h-t that way, you catch-um. You see bi-i-ig flat place. All right. That way (right) you see too big rock. That's putty good. Little farther you see little rock. Mancos Store this side. You cross Mancos Creek then you come store. No go that way (right)—no go that way (left)—go str-r-raight."

I drew a little diagram. I learned long ago to distrust verbal

instructions versus the eye. Once in the desert I looked at one
point while the other fellow meant another. It cost me a lot of
trouble. Tom approved the sketch. It looked only three or four
miles. "Sun here," I said confidently, pointing to the western
horizon, "I come store, what?" He had called it six miles from
his place.

"Maybe." And I thought I saw a twinkle in his rather pleasant
eye.

"Road run my house Mancos—little road."

"Nobody tell me," I said.

"That's putty good joke," he laughed.

I started after presenting Tom with an autographed card and
an invitation to come and see me. As I advanced the rocks
backed away. On and on till sundown. A little fall in the ground
and the rock disappeared. But we had our bearings by a large
niche between two low ridges. We passed through this as darkness fell, and into a low-lying meadow. We struck what we took
to be Tom's "little road." It swerved suddenly to left. We kept
straight on toward the rock which now showed in the moonlight. We came slap up against one of these deep washouts and
had to follow it about half a mile to cross. Here we struck the
"little road" again. After a while the single wagon track became
obliterated by a confusion of cattle tracks. The ground became
very rough and hard. Finally we descended a long steep bank
and came to a creek. I took it to be Mancos Creek. A bridge
crossed Mancos Creek, I'd been told, but I supposed I'd simply
missed the road and the bridge. "The trail must turn around
that turn," I thought, "and up a draw." We're right there now.

We plodded on and on between high perpendicular banks.
We crossed and recrossed the creek. I was afraid of quicksand,
which is not uncommon here. Twice we struck a little but kept
going. One can navigate a small stretch of fairly bad quicksand
with a plucky horse by just keeping going—sometimes. I noted
the results of torrents of water. "This would be a fine place to
get caught in one of those cloudbursts," I kept thinking. Finally
we made a gradual climb up onto a hard, sandy shelf of sand,
clay and a few bushes. This reduced the bank above us from
twenty to thirty feet to about six. I climbed up and looked
about. On all sides was a level dobie plain. Not a house nor a
light in sight. I slid back.

"This is where we camp, old girl," I said to Queen. "Lucky

we've a feed and a little grub." I tied her to a bush, unsaddled, made a bucket of coffee, and gave Queen her oats. Luckily I had given her her fill of the good gramma grass. She didn't suffer hunger.

By the way, it was 10 p.m. A few clouds were scouting about. But I calculated that even should it rain we would be safe on the bench—for a while. I did not unroll, but put on mackinaw, shoved my feet into the grain sack and used saddle as a pillow. At 3 a.m. a little mist in my face awoke me. I jumped out, grabbed my little hatchet (how I longed for a pick!) and by 4:30 had a trail made up the side of the bank that Queen could climb. I carried most of our freight to the top. Then—say, you should have seen Queen climb!

It was daylight. The rain had not come. There were the rocks which we thought we must have passed, still a little to the south of east. And there to our right lay Mancos Creek, the bridge, and the Post. We had not crossed Mancos Creek—but a tributary. * * * * Instead of 22 miles, we had traveled 34. We arrived here 6 o'clock a.m. and are resting here today.

(Frank).

We were resting on the bank of Mancos creek (which, by the way, was very muddy) down below a little bench some fifteen or twenty feet higher, upon which was located the Trading Post, on the other side. We had plenty of good alfalfa and oats for Queen. I had a fire and a big stew, and was sitting on an old box. Before I started to eat I slapped my teeth into my mouth, when I heard a scream that was half laugh. I looked up. Upon the table land across the creek stood a big fat Indian and his squaw observing us. I have no doubt that in these days they knew about false teeth, but they seemed to see something funny about my slapping 'em into my mouth, or something. Pretty soon the buck came down across the bridge to where I was eating. Without a word he sat down on another box or something five or six feet in front of me, looked at me a while, peeked at me, stroked his own (imaginary) whiskers, indicating my whiskers, of course. He asked, I hardly know whether impudently or comically, "Jesus?"—giving his whiskers another stroke, indicating mine. I barked, "No!" He looked at me again for a few minutes, and giving his imaginary whiskers another stroke, indicating mine—he had humped himself along until he was squatting almost under me—he said "Domingo?" I guess I felt cranky.

I was just about to give him a good swift kick under his fat old chops when—suddenly it occurred to me perhaps that wouldn't be just the thing to do. There were not more than three white people within many miles of us. So I decided, after all, a little tact might be the better part of valor. And then too, suddenly I began to see the humor of it. So with a little laugh I said, "Oh, go to hell!" "All right," he said. He laughed too, got up and went away.

From Signature Book: "Mancos Creek, Colo. Frank M. Heath arrived here about 6 a.m. riding Gypsy Queen. Horse has wart on right ear.

(Signed) D. W. Tice Jr.

Towaoc Cole Ute Res."

From Notes. April 9, '27: Cool, windy. Needed all bedding last night. Leaving Mancos Creek 7:40 a.m. Noon, Nosebag on N. bank San Juan about 7 mi. N. of Shiprock. Very windy. Fire inside hollow cottonwood stub 6 ft. across at roots. Bark 5 in. thick. River muddy. All creeks since Bluff muddy. Have passed two large prosperous looking bands sheep and goats. Lambing. One Navajo herder speaks excellent English. Two camps on river. One of same bands here now. Met Mr. Hans Aspass, full Navajo, P. O. Shiprock, graduate school at Carlyle, Pa.—says have angora goats, sheer long mohair, 40 cts., wool, 30 (?)—Goat brings most—says using Rambolet bucks. * * * * Very large, level river bottom bench. High, perpendicular slate-colored bank on N. of river flats, resembling huge ancient ruins of brick masonry. 3 p.m., Entering irrigated district. Pretty fair alfalfa, some corn stubble, good fences. Round hogans giving way to square huts. * * * * One place ½ mi. to north has good stack alfalfa, large bldgs. In about a mile soil is poorer. Alfalfa making a desperate struggle for existence. 4 p.m., Ar'd Shiprock. * * * * Ar'd large Indian school—other Gov't bldgs. * * * * Wrote Joe to try to get loan on bonus certificate. If other means fail (get mortgage) 2-3 years on place.

From Signature Book: "Shiprock, New Mex., April 9, 1927. Frank M. Heath arrived here at 4 p.m. riding mare Gypsy Queen. Mare in good shape.

(Signed) William Evans,
U. P. Lipscomb, Indian Trader
Agnes C. Evans, Postmaster."

From Notes. Sunday, April 10, '27: Cold S.E. wind. Slept
well in hogan with Navajo who lives 40 mi. toward Gallup and
is hauling hay for cattle, sheep, goats, from 10 mi. E. of here, 5
days trip. Queen in lee of hay shed, did not lie down—is little
sore—have her in creek 1 hr. Met Dr. O. P. Goodwin—told him
of "bones." Also Mr. B. Evans, Dr. Lipscomb, Towaoc, N. M.,
c/o Ute Mt. Ind School, naturalists. (Evans wants story C.O.D.)

I believe this doctor was the Government Indian doctor. I called
on him at his office, showed him these cuts mentioned above, of the
jaw bone, as shown in the notebook, and told him about the cannon
bones, and he appears to think that without doubt they were part
of the remains of a prehistoric person.

From Notes. April 10, '27 continued: 1:30, Leaving Shiprock. Hard east wind. 5 p.m., Came to spring and Rd. camp 10
mi. S. of Shiprock. Blowing a gale. No shelter. Filled canteen
and struck for lee of large rocks 3½ mi. ahead, ¾ mi. to left of
rd. 6 p.m., Came to deep wash, bridged. Found place where I
got Queen down (out of wind). May rain but can get out in
time. Sleeping with boots on. Not unrolling. * * * * Dusk.
Looks, feels like rain. Moving onto ledge. Colder but safer.
Would be difficult getting out up slippery bank in dark. Sleeping under bridge. Queen in "pocket" against upper bank. Little
alfalfa, cut little saccaton.

April 11, '27: Cloudy, cold S. wind. Up 5, leaving camp
7. * * * *

April 12, '27: Slept snug in old hogan—fireplace—wood. Queen
full of hell. Leaving Nova 8:45. Noon, Nosebag, hot coffee in
wash 8 mi. S. of Nova (later wind changed west, sweeping up
wash.) A squaw with little girl behind her on pony came down,
tried to trade me fine silver bracelets mounting several green
stones and her horse for Queen. (Later offered several pieces
jewelry to boot.) Had little lunch with me. Rode double straight
up 45% grade.

Just after I had this hot noon lunch ready, I heard someone laugh,
looked up, and just at the end of the bridge (all these arroyos were
bridged on this road) saw a squaw on a good-looking, though rather
thin sorrel horse. Riding behind her was a ten-year-old nice-looking
little Indian girl. I was presuming that they would like a cup of hot

coffee on such a cold day. I dished them out a cup of coffee each. I soon learned what the old girl was after. She wanted to trade me out of Queen. She made her object known by signs. She pointed to first one very fine bracelet with several turquoises. From there she pointed to her horse and then to Queen, then from Queen to herself and from her horse to me. I took this to mean that she wanted to swap horses. I shook my head, "No." She started all over again, pointed to the same bracelet, another bracelet on the other arm, her horse and Queen, and went through the same rigmarole. Again I shook my head. Starting the third time, she pointed out these two bracelets or wristlets mentioned, and a very elaborate neckpiece of turquoise and it seems to me a few garnets. (By the way, the Navajo had a turquoise mine up in this country somewhere and garnets were frequently picked up off the ground.) Then through the same motions indicating that she had raised her ante from the horse and one ordinary bracelet to her horse and both wristless and that wonderful neckpiece. I shook my head very positively, although to be perfectly frank her horse was really worth more money than Queen, even if thin.

The notes give a brief account of this, stating that they departed up this bank, which seemed to me 45 degrees, the horse carrying the big squaw and the little squaw. Nothing had happened—she didn't even stroke my beautiful whiskers! I never in my life saw a horse climb so well under a load. Many times I have seen an Indian deliberately straddle a horse, and make it carry him up a steep bank, where I certainly would have dismounted.

From Notes. April 12, '27 continued: It is spitting little snow. 3:40, Ar'd Roulette (?) a trading post. Also big rd. camp for an outfit working on the new Govt. 100% aid road—about 100 mi. (?).

Traveled: 17 mi. Level to hilly. Dirt 12 mi. R. I. 5 mi. Some saccaton, some gramma grass. Shad-scale, sagebrush, R. thistles. "Broken" mesa, hills E., Mts. W. snow covered. Very few cattle, too many wild horses, plenty sheep, goats. Herders all on foot today—blankets mostly. Boys, one squaw. Hogans mostly giving way to cabins, some of stone. 2-3 log, 1 painted green. 1 very small field—corn stubble. Mostly Navajo labor on Hy. Pretty good workers. (At least one gang of Mexicans.) Cold wind continues. Spitting snow. Queen, open corral, bldg. on E. Wind whips about.

April 13, '27: 2, 3 inches snow fell in night. Queen little wet and cold—not bad. Slept in hay room. Breakfast under dobie bank of draw. Noon, Nosebag, hot lunch, lee of a rock. 8 mi. S. of Roulette Trading Post. 6 p.m. Ar'd store of James N. Halona, full Navajo. * * * * 1 mi. S.E. of Tahatchi Ind. School, P. O. Local.

Traveled: 20 mi. Snow and mud A.M. Hilly, dirt, 18 mi. R. I., 4. * * * *

April 14, '27: Cold, clear. Cold wind from S.W. in night. Queen fair in partly enclosed shed. I slept in house (not hogan— bldg. new addition)—good fire, cover. Halona has 5 acres in good cult. Good fence. These folks speak good English, teach it to children (2) and feed the horses. Dress modern. Leaving the Halonas 8. No chg. for sleeping, cooking in house. Noon, Nosebag, hot lunch in lee of sand hill 9 mi. S. of Halonas. 5:30 Ar'd Gallup. Putting up at corral of Herman White (local). Box stall, alfalfa, oats, $1.00.

Traveled: 24 mi. Hilly, gravel, 10 mi. (dirt side). Paved 3 mi. (dirt side 1 mi.). Dirt 11 mi. Saccaton grass, gramma grass, sagebrush, shadscale, juniper—in mts.—1st 12 mi. "broken mesa," —Bal. mts. and high plateau—down again to Gallup. Sheep, goats, horse. Power house, aerated water works.

Special Note: Shiprock to Gallup, 98 miles.

Total to Gallup, N. M., 8,712 miles [as corrected].

Note: Traveled 470 mi. (Flagstaff to Gallup) without seeing a R. R. or a bathtub—(or a barber)—except at Tuba City, saw a tub.

From Shiprock to Gallup we had no difficulty in finding our way. We simply followed the main road. In several places they were working on this road, as mentioned in the notes. The footing, except in a few places, was not what you would call bad. There were as yet some fairly steep places, in spots. (It seemed to me that one object of this new road was to eliminate some of these steep grades.) It was on some of these down grades that I believe I solved a problem which had been bothering me for quite a while, in regard to Queen and her left knee.

It was plain to me and it is plain to the reader, and ultimately it was proved definitely, that there was nothing wrong with Queen's knee joint. Sometimes she would go along for days without a limp, although as I have stated, previously the left leg or foot was her weak point. But in going down some of these grades just mentioned, she would almost go on three legs. That is she wanted to half drag this leg and catch herself on her right foot. I figured out that this must be purely habit, accentuated by stubbornness, for Queen certainly had a very strong streak of stubbornness in her nature. As an expression of this she would sometimes stick her tongue out of her mouth partly, on the left side where I would be most likely to see it, I believe simply because she found I didn't want her to do it. I partly broke her of this by saying, "Put your tongue in your mouth!" and slapping it a little with the end of the reins. She knew what I meant. Well, she had found out somehow that her limping extremely and unnecessarily in the left leg bothered me—explain that if you can. You might use the word psychology. Partly this, and we might say I guess partly a habit, for she had been lame way back. Thus I reasoned.

I could see no reason in this lap for her limping. The hoof I kept soft by soaking and as we had done it for a thousand miles or so, by means of lard, now, especially when the hoof was soft, it wasn't a case of being hoofbound. So I cut a little switch. I would be walking along beside her with her lead rope in hand, so she wouldn't get away. When she would start this business of buckling the left knee and catching herself on the right foot (and I had noticed this half stubborn, half insolent expression in her eye) I gave her left front leg a little crack with that switch, commanding her at the same time, "Come back with that knee!" She soon learned what I meant and what it meant when she needlessly resorted to this trick. I broke her of it in a short time. After that, if she would start this, I had but to say, "Come back with that knee," severely, and maybe wave the little stick at her, or the reins, or the rope, or whatever I had in hand. In that case she could walk as well as any horse.

From Notes. April 15, '27: Blustery, snow in night. Laying in. Set rt. front. Laundry etc. Batching in camp house with Mike McCann—old-timer.

April 16, '27: Partly cloudy, N.W. wind. Leaving Gallup 8:45. *Note:* Met several men from Montezuma Valley. They all tell the same story of hard times. Crops grow O. K. with irrigation, but no market. Carload cattle to Kansas City did not pay freight. On 14th fell in with old man, young man with pretty good horses, trailing farm wagon and light one. Good baled alfalfa worth $5.00 per ton in valley, $24.00 in Gallup.

Pigs, chickens, farm implements, going to Ramah where young man has farm. Noon (Apr. 16), Nosebag, hot lunch 9 mi. S. of Gallup in lee of rocks and "thorny greasewood." 4:15, Ar'd Carson's Store, Fred A. Carson, Prop., P. O., Gallup, N. M., Zuni Rt. (route) Necklaces, bracelets, made by Navajo Indians.

Traveled: 18 mi. Hilly, R. I., 6 mi. Dirt, 12. Broken mesa, juniper, pinyon, sage, greasewood, little grass (few yellow places). Few cattle, horses, flock goats, few sheep feeding on sage. Many Indians hauling pinyon posts to Gallup with little rats of tough horses. Haul 25 to 40. Get 25 cts. (each). Alternate secs. Santa Fe R. R. Bal. Navajo allotments. Colors yellow, gray, brown almost to red. Passed 1st store of Newman, originator of Gallup Mercantile Co., 60 years old. Pass two Navajo square log houses —2 summer hogans. (Continued short curves, Gallup to Carsons.)

Note: Altitude at Carson's Trading Post, about 7,900 feet. 18 mi. E. of S. of Gallup, 3 mi. N. of Hogsback of Rockies, Colo. to Old Mexico. Plenty Navajo fences. Passed field in cult. (Mexican homestead.) Corn, oats, wheat, barley, spuds, yield fair. [Illegible word.] Also abandoned field. Carson cultivates 60 acres crops as above. Hire Navajos, $1.50, dinner. Gets a large pinyon crop every 7 years, gathered by Indians. They get 15 cts. from traders—New York Market.

April 17, '27: Leaving Carson's 9. No chg. for camp house, nicknacks. Accompanied by Fred Jr. Noon, Dining with Napoleon, (head man) in Zuni village of Nutria. These people dress well, seem clean, are industrious. Good horses well fed. Irrigate, raise corn, wheat, oats—thresh on stone floor with horses. Good gardens, poultry, sheep, goats. Seem hospitable. Mostly good-looking. Make much jewelry, pottery. Beautiful rocky hills to E., brown, gray, pink. Met Bill Poncho, P. O. Zuni, N. M. Speaks and writes English. Zunis live in village, cooperate in farming. No objections to photos. Dutch ovens, salt rising bread. Flat top houses. Stone or adobe bricks. Logs, stones, straw, dirt roofs. Straw covered stables. Polygamy. 7 p.m. Ar'd ranch, place of R. H. Bloomfield.

Traveled: 24 mi. Hilly, dirt, 18 mi. R. I., 6 mi. Description as yesterday, to 3 mi. N. of ranch. White men's ranches in Ramah Valley. Irrigate from storage reservoirs. Gov. farming 2,000 acres. Several "regular" farms—straw stacks. Alfalfa $20.00.

In a Navajo Hogan on or near the
Continental Divide, 23 mi. S.E.
of Ramah, N. M.,
April 19, '27.
(If you don't find Ramah on your
map, we are 65 mi. S.S.E. of
Gallup, N. M.)

Dear Cousin Esther and Family:

I wrote you last about 10 days ago. That was some distance
back, but I'm going to skip over all that, as I either have it in
my notes or else have written it home.

I'm going to confess that one reason I am availing myself of
your proposition to record parts of my small adventures by writing them to you, is because, should I write these little difficulties,
or whatever you choose to call them, to my old Mother and
Dad, they would have the jimjams same as when I told them
I was going to cross the desert (which I did). These little matters have a slight tendency to put a "kick" into the trip for me—
so I assume they'll not worry you—especially as I decided by
your cheek bones (excuse my noticing it) that there is in you
the same love of travel and adventure that there is in me. I
believe we inherit it from our beloved grandmother. * * * *

Maybe I'd better tell you briefly what a hogan is. It's the kind
of dwelling in which most of the Navajo live. It is round,
hexagon or octagon, and is usually built of logs running around
and joined at the many corners to 5 or 6 feet (high), then
other logs just across the corners, other logs across from one of
the benches so formed to the other, and so on until only an
opening of about 3 feet remains in the center of the "roof."
These timbers are covered with earth, leaving a hole for light,
smoke and air. Sometimes they set the poles up and down and
cover the whole with earth—except an opening, a kind of
"dormer window" in the E. side. The one of which I am the
sole occupant—an uninvited guest—is rather elaborate, being of
hewn logs. I mean the walls. I am to build a fire of juniper,
which is abundant here, in the center, roll up in my blankets in
one corner, and Queen in another.

I have raked together the "remains" of a little corn fodder
(an unexpected luxury for Queen). I was told there was grass
but there is none growing yet—(altitude) too high. Oats we
have to last tomorrow, and grub. Tomorrow we follow a dim

auto track to a ranch 24 miles E. of here. By cutting across here we hope to save about 75 miles and have more experience. * * * *

I am up against another of those problems that beset all who leave "the ways of civilized man,"—I mean the main highways. Yesterday morning I left Ramah in a snow storm, headed for the White House Trading Post, 15 miles. I had quite a complete sketch of the road and side roads, fences, etc. As usual one or two side tracks were not recorded, but we made good guesses and arrived O. K. We laid over at the (White House Trading) Post until noon today, resting Queen after her hard day in the terribly sticky dobie mud during and after the little fall of snow. Today at 12:30 we started to this place—at least I hope this is it—8 miles, in order to cut down the otherwise 32 miles tomorrow to the nearest feed or grub.

The Trader drew me a map. In addition to the map he told me to follow an auto truck track which he recently made in coming across country from Hot Springs. Auto truck tracks across here are by no means common. But the trader is an old-timer here and knows the country.

"Follow the truck track," he told me, "and you can't miss it. Watch for the marks of the chains. We used chains all the way."

I got along fine and dandy. Only—there seemed to be chains only on one side. We came to a certain pond of water that he had described. A short distance beyond this pond, close to the "road" I was to find the hogan which I hope is the one I'm in. But—here the road forked. No fork is indicated on the "map" at this point. And—in each "road" is the track of an auto truck with chains. The track taking the left fork is fairly fresh but the chains are on only one side. The one taking the right fork had both chains, and the track is not so fresh. The latter points in the right direction. But roads running in a "general" direction here often twist in *all* directions so there is no certain reliance to be placed on that. Then too, right slap dab across the one running in the right direction is a fence with the gate closed— but not padlocked. *This* fence is not in the "map," though all fences were supposed to be. The hogan was not in sight on either "road." I came near taking the road across which there was no fence (and goodness knows where it leads to). I have, assuming that I am right, 24 miles tomorrow—through the wilderness, without a habitation. But the word "chains" kept dancing a jig in my cranium. I felt sure that had the Trader used only one chain he would have mentioned the fact, whereas he might have forgotten about this last fence. (While I think of it, the fresher track with one chain seemed to have obliterated the older track with two chains up to where the two tracks parted company. This is not strange here where one machine often holds to the ruts of another for miles on account of the dobie mud.)

And there I was. "It's an easy matter to try both roads," I said to Queen, "only when a fellow gets started—maybe on the wrong one, he keeps thinking he sees a clue, and goes a long way. That don't get us back to Washington."

Peering into the woods through the fence I spied an old "sweat cave," a miniature hogan in which the Navajo makes it hot for the devil that is in him regardless of the fact that it makes him (the Navajo) sweat. "This is a deuce of a hogan," I thought, "if this is the one referred to, but even so, where is the corral mentioned." Still, not far from one of these sweat caves, as they are called, but yet far enough so that the devil has plenty of room in which to cool his heels between them, is usually a hogan. With this as a clue I proceeded to follow the dimmer but double-chained tracks deeper into the juniper and pinyon woods. And there, two or maybe four times as far from the pond as the crude sketch would indicate, I found this hogan and corral answering the description.

To make uncertainty a little more certain I left Queen at the gate and followed the fresher track a little way, but saw no hogan. And so, if I have made no mistake in my deductions and nothing leads us astray tomorrow, we'll probably arrive at the ranch 24 miles distant through the wilderness before dark tomorrow.

And now I must close, and warm a bit over the fire in the middle of the hogan, eat it, and hit the hay—rather the ground.

Trechada, N. M., April 21, '27.

Yesterday morning I left the hogan 6:40. Took chances on finding water to save going back a mile to the pool I mentioned yesterday. We had not gone far when we came to a large puddle of rain water. That was what we had guessed at. It was a slim guess, though this was not the only one we passed. Yes, I know it was a wicked risk. But—as it turned out—to backtrack would also have been a shame. We had not traveled a mile when the "one chain track" we told you of converged with our "two chain track." Had we followed the former, and kept on, this is what would have happened. (Sketch will be found in the original letter.) You see we would have passed the hogan. (A similar divergence and convergence of roads caused us many weary rough miles in a bitter cold wind once in the wilderness north of Flagstaff, Ariz., in looking for a water hole.)

Well, yesterday I thanked luck—or hoss sense—and on we went. As before, the "one chain track" wiped out the other except once or twice we caught the double. Finally both chain tracks were obliterated by the "running together" of the dobie mud following a heavier fall of snow. But while the more delicate marks of the chains were gone, I still could follow the deeper imprint of the large tires.

We made a wide swing to S. E., then S. a little way, then S. W., passing W. of the Serias Majeres, two rather beautiful tall mountains. The name in Spanish means Beautiful Women. Then we swung S.E. again. Why these large curves I didn't know—some obstruction to autos I suppose. Possibly had I been familiar with the country I might have saved much travel. Besides the wide curves there were continual small curves.

At 1 p.m. we took refuge from the cold N.W. wind on the sunny side of a large rock. As I was a little uncertain of finding the ranch we were making for, with the chain tracks gone and roads running and branching off in all directions, I cut Queen's noon ration in half and ate rather sparingly myself. The only grass here at this time is a little of last year's gramma grass, and it is very short.

About 4 p.m. we spied off to our right a ranch. I took it for that of "The Nice Old Man" the Trader had told us of. We came to a fork in the road, or rather a cross, like this. (The double mark shows, on our sketches, the road we traveled.) Here the auto tracks turned right, or S.W., into the dim track running in that direction, and through a gate to the ranch in sight. I turned into them and went a short way. Wishing to be quite sure, for the track we left pointed in our general direction, I went back and looked again. There was at that time not a sign of an auto track. It turned out later to be the one we should have taken. But the melting snow had wiped out the track of the single light truck.

We arrived at the wrong ranch to find no one at home. Evidently no one had been there for a day or two at least. The unfinished log house was open. (There are many log houses here, and barns and corrals.) There was a good sized stack of good corn fodder—raised on this ranch. This verified our expectations, as the Trader had told me that our feed would be corn fodder and corn. There was a feed room, padlocked. I watered Queen from the cistern, turned her in the corral in lee of the stack, and fed her—cutting the ½ feed of grain in two.

After making myself a nest close to the stack and spreading my blankets, I went to the house, built a fire, and proceeded to investigate. There were flour, baking powder and sugar, beans (but it would take too long to cook beans) and corn meal. That was all. And that was enough had I only had something with which to shorten some biscuits. Oh yes, there was blackstrap molasses. I took a chance on using the latter in place of shortening. I know from past experience that had I had about 4 eggs this concoction would have resulted in a kind of ginger bread. But it was the sorriest, mess, nearly, that I ever tackled. I ate a little with coffee and jam and raw onion, and my intestinal adhesions are growling about it now, 24 hours later. I gave Queen the rest of it. She has good horse sense. She refused it, hungry as she was, though she is very fond of good bread and molasses.

This morning we left the corral at 8 a.m. We felt a little dubious. We had absolutely nothing to guide us but general direction. Of course I had expected to get directions of the "Nice Old Man." By the way, the ranch at which we stayed belongs—we learned later—to his son.

I saw a track running east. We took it. It ended in a field where the corn grew (had grown). Back we came. We circumnavigated the buildings in search of auto tracks, but found none. The track we had taken into the ranch continued S. We took that, hoping it went only around the hill to the south. We followed it quite a way. It kept S.W. I didn't like this, as our general course is E. of S. I turned Queen and came back to the house. I had determined to take from the house the corn meal and beans, leaving a good round price in the bean can. I forgot to mention the fact that in any honest-to-goodness "cow country" it is the custom for any traveler to stop at a ranch if no one is there, feed and eat in welcome—but take nothing away. Seldom are the buildings locked. And seldom, if ever, is this generous custom among generous people abused. That is why I was going to leave the price for what I was going to carry off. And the reason I was going to take it was because I knew I was taking a chance of going a long way before striking a habitation. Queen could live on grass and beans. She loves beans. Had I taken the S.E. trail, as I intended, I learned later I would have struck old Mr. Whitley's—if we didn't miss it. Had we missed it we'd have gone a long way indeed without a habitation—60 miles or more.

But—I stepped out to get a small bag out of my pack. I looked over toward the gate where we entered last night, and there stood a horse and rider. It seemed a long time since I had seen a human being, although in reality it had scarcely been 24 hours. I met a Navajo yesterday morning. He was the only person I'd seen since we left the Trader. This Indian, by the way, happened to be the one in whose hogan I had camped. Bartecilo is his name. He speaks a little Spanish and owns many sheep.

When I spied the lone rider, the situation changed in the twinkling of an eye. I hurriedly sat the grub back in place, mounted Queen and put her into high. The rider had passed on at a trot. We gained on him rapidly. Seeing that we wanted to see him, he stopped and waited. Hugh Moore is the man's name. He is middle-aged, was raised in these parts, rides a fine horse, and was very obliging. He studied some as to the most practicable way for a stranger to find his way to Trechada, the store where I now am, having first discussed the feasibility of taking this instead of the slightly nearer but much more difficult trail to the east.

Finally, on account of the many and confusing "tracks" involved in cutting across, we decided that the "longest way round" would be the shortest. So under his direction I drew the accompanying sketch. Each square represents a section or mile square. W. M. stands for windmill. The ink marks are later corrections. (This sketch may be found in the original letter.)

In cutting around the corner of the last fence I would have gotten tangled again in the dense juniper and pinyon woods had it not been for the sun and my old Ingersoll.

1 p.m. we arrived at the Chock Brannin Ranch. We were now in the edge of quite a settlement. Chock, as everybody calls him,

(Mr. is not a common title here) was away riding after stock, but Mrs. Brannin made us feel welcome in true Western fashion. She was very sorry they were entirely out of grain (so were we) but we were welcome to all the hay Queen could eat, though hay is scarce here. This hay was a new addition to the long list of different forage Queen had eaten on the trip. It is a weed. They call it Yellow Annual, a little like wild sunflower, and is quite nutritious. Mrs. Brannin also presented me with something to supplement my own slim lunch. I stuck my coffee bucket onto an out-of-door fire she was using for washing, and we chatted while I ate. In these parts no man needs a formal introduction to the folks of the "old-timer." * * * *

At 3 p.m. we left the Brannin Ranch. Poor Queen, she was much disappointed at not having had her oats. She is almost human in intelligence, but it is a child's intelligence, so of course I couldn't make her understand. But I promised her "oats pretty soon" and she knows what that means. I never promise her "oats pretty soon" unless I'm sure about it.

At 4:15 we arrived here. Queen has her oats and is happy. We have plain sailing from here on, for quite a way at least.

(Frank)

From Notes. April 21, '27: * * * * 4:15 p.m., Ar'd Trechada Store and P. O., M. E. Miller, Prop. Plenty oats and hay, here. * * * * Queen fine. I slept well under shed. Leaving Miller's 9:45, having taken time to write 1½ hrs. Chg. for feed very reasonable. R. R. 80 mi., Magdalene. Noon, Have come 1 mi. N. from rd. to see ancient spring. Feeding, cold lunch. Leaving spring 2 p.m. * * * * (Fed millet hay last night—seems upset stomach.) 5 p.m., Ar'd ranch of Mr. E. V. Taylor, 2 mi. N. W. of Tres Lagunas, local. Discard galoshes.

Traveled: 13 mi. (2 to see spring 1 off rd.) Rolling, dirt. Description as yesterday. A log schoolhouse. 75 mi. to a Dr. Taylor farms little—mostly cattle. Here 10 years—hauls water. Met Mr. R. L. Keller, Trader (General, not Indian Trader.) Homesteader. * * * * Note: ⅛ mi. E. of the Taylor home is the summit of the * * * * divide at this point. Want book.

April 23, '27: Leaving the Taylors, 8:00. Meals, corn, fodder, no chg. (Formulas.) Noon, Feeding—invited to dinner at Tres Lagunas, Mark Webster, Prop. (Webster trades some with Navajo, principally buys pinyon nuts in fall. Is starting with cattle. Hopes to obtain water by digging—is trying.) Lakes dry—

hauls water—about gone—bucket, Queen. 3:30 p.m., Ar'd ranch of E. P. Ridgman, Mt. View Ranch (sheep), P. O., Datil, N. M.

Traveled: 18 mi. (1 by error). Rolling—dirt. Description same. * * * * Note: The * * * * divide at this point is ½ mi. S. of the Ridgmans' home. The "Sawtooth Mt." is about 1 mi. E. [As far as the immediate topography of the country was concerned you would not realize we were on a summit. Here were these little places, generally more of an attempt than a success at farming, some fences, and all that. A ridge there is called a dike. The theory was that the region had been under water originally, in a prehistoric age.] This is a beautiful home, consisting of the house, detached kitchen, bunk house, shop, stables, granary, poultry house, all built of logs, and a lumber sheep shed. They farm about 80 acres. Gen. crops, including corn. Young orchard. Several pack animals, cows, etc. 3 mos. growing season. Some dry seasons. Trees all trimmed up—everything orderly. 2 boys, 2 girls. Mrs. semi-invalid. Amiel Dauen, farm hand.

I had met this young fellow, Ridgman, before arriving at Tres Lagunas, driving his fine automobile. He was coming from the ranch, and I was going toward it. He invited me to stay at their place over night. He was to put up a stick where the road branched off. But Queen *would* sheer off to the left through a patch of timber. I was walking. (I missed young Ridgman's sign.) I couldn't get hold of her, and she wouldn't listen. I was supposed to go one way, and she *would* go off another way. About a mile or two from nowhere we came to a dugout looking like an old-fashioned root cellar, half in, half out of the ground. Queen led me right to this. This took us at least a mile off the trail we should have followed. What could have possessed her? I have often wondered, and it is suggested to me by a friend who has been around, "Why, maybe she smelled something there,"—or something like that. And I said, "Well, I wasn't going to mention it." But I had been told a few miles back that somewhere in there dwelt the principal bootlegger for the whole country about—and if a bootlegger, why not a moonshiner? Come to think of it, Queen was a little bit hungry, and a horse just loves mash. Also, as previously explained, a horse, compared with us, has an abnormal sense of smell. However, I wasn't looking for moonshiners or bootleggers—that wasn't my business, and I didn't want to know anything about them. I got hold of Queen and left another way without examining this place. Knowing that we had veered off considerably to the left, I struck off again to the right and arrived finally at this sheep ranch.

From Notes. April 24, '27: Fair. Leaving the Ridgmans, 8 a.m. Meals, feed, hospitality, no chg. (Formulas). Noon, nosebag, cold lunch under yellow pine, 12 mi. W. Datil. Two men, 1 woman in 2 cars halted us for photos. Dog Gretchen killed by passing car—lady hysterical. Mrs. Florence B. Rucker, Kansas City, Mr. J. H. McPherson, ex-sgt. Engrs., W. W., Mr. O. J. Leihy, ex-sgt. maj. Canadian army, 1 a.m. 2 p.m., at * * * * divide. Elevation 8,300 ft. Forest Reserve. * * * * 6 p.m., Ar'd Datil, N. M. Putting up at Morley's place.

Traveled: 23 mi. Hilly, dirt, 8. Gravel, 15. (Good side 3 mi.)
Note: Datil, N. M., 8,230 mi. [as corrected.]

Mr. Morley was said to have thousands of acres of land, thousands of head of cattle, some sheep. He had and was maintaining a band of the regular Navajo sheep. His place, where we stayed, was also a hotel. He had Navajo blankets and the like of that, which he sold to tourists occasionally. I don't know how many cowboys he had. About half a dozen were staying right here at this hotel, which was also headquarters for the cattle business. One was a Mexican. In the evenings they all sat around and talked on almost equal terms, that is, Morley and the cowboys and the cook. At this headquarters he had quite a large pasture used for calving, as they called it. He had quite a lot of wild hay. They were feeding apparently tons of oil cake to the cows, and particularly to the bulls, of which I believe he had about twenty, white-face.

From Signature Book: "Datil, N. Mex., Apr. 25, 1927 (Postmark) Frank M. Heath arrived here at 6 p.m. April 24, 1927 riding bay mare, Gypsy Queen. Man and horse both in good shape. Stayed all night. In the A.M. Apr. 25th I weighed his saddle, blankets and pack and all told he had 101 pounds dead weight. Heath left Datil for Hot Springs, N. M., at 9 a.m., Apr. 25, 1927.

(Signed) Wm. R. Morley,
Postmaster and Rancher."

Chapter VI

SOUTHERN NEW MEXICO AND TEXAS

From Notes. April 25, '27: Leaving Mr. Morley 10:30 a.m. Horse, feed, meals, groceries, no chg. (This was a case of genuine hospitality.) * * * * Mrs. Roberts taking photos. Noon (1:30 p.m.) Nosebag, cold lunch * * * * 6 p.m. Ar'd at what I take to be Three Bar N Ranch after passing (and stopping at—going ½ mi. out of way) W. M. (windmill) shown on Mr. Morley's sketch.

Traveled: 17 mi. (1 to ranch and water, 1 to W. M.) Mostly level. Dirt. Timber to W. Crossing plain after cutting through woods. Pretty fair grass—saccaton in bottom, gramma higher up. Plenty white-face cattle, few horses. A lot of burros in large pasture around 3 p.m. No one at Ranch—signs of recent occupancy. Door to house locked. No feed outside. See alfalfa through window. Little stubby saccaton. Some green in abandoned tank. Dividing the last ½ of oats and corn. Sleeping under shed. Discard wool sox.

Must have feed and oats for today. Removing some glass—evidently the usual way—removing "prop"—opening sash. Ate rutabaga, spuds last night—save grub. Entering, taking little corn meal and beans for Queen. Rice, coffee, for self. Leaving Ranch 7:15, making a guess at direction. Heading W. of south, little W. of gap—on map—following old double track not traveled recently except by stock. Queen refused water in tank of W. M. —also in pond.

To people brought up in some parts of the United States this act of mine in going into the house might seem like robbery, but in this country it was not so considered. I was just getting out of a large area, mostly stock, where what is known as the "sundown custom" still prevailed more or less. The "sundown custom" means that seldom is ever is a man turned down or sent away from a ranch or any other habitation after, broadly speaking, anywhere near sun-

342

down. Even if the man is broke, he is not sent away, unless he shows signs of being a professional bum—maybe not then. If no one is at home, it is the unwritten law that a man may enter, so he breaks no locks, helps himself to feed for a horse, if available (without breaking a lock), enters the house, if not locked (chances are four to one it isn't), cooks, and eats. If he is a gentleman he is supposed to wash up the dishes and sweep up, and absolutely carry nothing away with him unless it would be in an emergency such as I have just mentioned. If a man went to ransacking or lugging something away merely for its value, I wouldn't advise him to tarry around there very long.

From Notes. April 26, '27 continued: 8:40, Letting Queen feed on last year's gramma grass outside pasture on W. Consulting map (large map)—see Hot Springs back to E. as per Morley sketch. Making S.E. for gap when pass S.W. Cor. fence as going through. Double track kept S.W. outside fence. 9, came to S.W. corner fence. Spy W. M. 2 or 3 mi. E. Turning, 10 a.m., at W. M. pumping good water. Camping. Queen refuses mixture oatmeal [error, cornmeal], beans. Drinks moderately. Nosebag, 11 a.m. at W. M. tank and sheep corral, 1½ mi. No feed, Nobody there. Found dim, unused double track running Montocila Sheep Co. 12, Leaving W. M. Taking track S. 12:30, Crossed E. W. track, slightly used. W. M. to E. of S. Track holding S. 12:45, Another W. M. little E. of track which, by the way, has not been traveled in long time except by stock. 1:15, Entering pass. Swung S.E. for short way. 1:40 p.m., Crossing well traveled rd., S.E. E. to N. W. W. (wrong quarter for Fairview Hy.—no sign). Keeping old track until see whether it bears E. when pass a certain ledge. Queen nibbling old gramma grass. 1:30, A track converges from N. W. carrying single auto track. 1:45, Fairly well traveled rd, converges from N.N.E. We are still bearing little W. 2 p.m., We have converged with a "main" rd., probably Fairview. Where it passed through a fence a light double trail turns S. E. We take the trail. We had decided to cut through if rd. continued S. W. This is getting interesting. We enter a small canyon inclining upward. Pinyon, juniper, pine, a kind of scrub ash. We reach the summit and go down a steep long grade 1½ mi. Come to old lumber camp. 4:30 p.m., Come to a well in draw and a dry "tank" (a canyon damned across). 5:30, Ar'd ranch Will McCracken, 40 (?) mi.

E. of S. of Datil and 4 mi. S.W. of Tucker Ranch, for which I was making. It is over a black range of mts.

Traveled: 25 mi. (5 by error). Hilly, dirt, 2 mi. R. I. 5 mi. Sandstone, gramma grass, sage, cattle, horses. No hay. Queen still dainty.

April 27, '27: Slept well in wagon under shed. Queen in corral lot—restless, dainty. Eats little better.

In Will McCracken's pasture was a lot of loco weed. He was concerned about leaving a horse in there too long, for fear it would acquire what he expressed as "the loco weed habit," just as a person acquires the drug habit. For that reason Queen was kept in the corral lot.

From Notes. April 27, '27 continued: Taking breakfast with the McCrackens. Leaving the McCrackens 8:40—no chg. 10, Watering at W. M. Grazing ½ hr. on old gramma grass starting green. Washing cupboard at trough.

By cupboard I mean that before starting on the trip I had got hold of some kind of a Red Cross kit, within which I had put two cross partitions, making three main compartments besides a little pocket in which I carried a little round pocket mirror two or three inches across, a comb, and so on. Another minor pocket I had for matches. This was fastened to the saddle by two hooks, and was waterproof.

From Notes. April 27, '27 continued: Noon, Just watered again at W. M. near Henderson Ranch—drinks heartily. Feeding alfalfa, procured at ranch, also mixing beans with oats, red beans. By mixing alfalfa leaves, getting her to eat some. Alf., qt. bran, qt. milk, 50 cts. Queen stands it well in spite of feed troubles. This is 1st hay in 60 hours, 1st feed oats, with "mixture" in 60 hrs. 4 p.m., Ar'd Gables Store. No oats. Buying 5 lbs. shelled corn (have 10 lbs. alfalfa)—grub. 5:30, Ar'd at old Fort at head of Box Canyon on Monticello Creek.

Traveled: 15 mi. (1 mi. by misdirection). Hilly, R. I., 9 mi. Dirt, 6 mi. Timber as yesterday, 2 mi. Bal. gramma grass, little sage.

April 28, '27: Fair. Leaving old Fort. 6:40 a.m., Enter canyon. 11:30, Ar'd ranch of Celso Frugillo, 5½ N. of Monticello— cattle ranch—also raises English walnuts, chestnuts, in commercial quantities. Apples, peaches, grapes, some corn, alfalfa, wheat. This place 75 (?) years old, belonged to Mr. Frugillo's father. 2 p.m., Missed canteen. Mr. Sanchos lent me white pony to go back after it. Men weeding wheat. 4 p.m., At old water power custom mill—bought 10 lb. mill run, 20 cts. 4:30 p.m., Ar'd Monticello, a typical Mexican barrio of adobe—only stone bldg. is chapel. 1/3 dilapidated, ½ deserted. 1 store open. A comfortable looking adobe hotel. Corrals facing the narrow crooked st. Trees. Tourists should visit this quaint place. 6:15, Ar'd ranch of Mr. Geo. Berner, P. O. Hot Springs, a fine, well-kept place.

Traveled: 21 mi. Rocky, R. I., 16, dirt 3 mi. Loose sand, 2 mi. Irrigated farms all along canyon after getting out of "Box." Owned at least mostly by Mexicans and Spaniards. Cactus, sage, wheat, corn, orchards, grapes, alfalfa, gardens, cows, cattle, poultry. Some range in hills. 15 A. per head. Discarding canvas gloves. Desert flowers in bloom. Alf. 10 in. high.

Much of our trail from about where we struck Nevada was over earth more or less charged with chemicals that were ruinous to a horse's feet. Especially was this so where, approaching Pyramid Lake, we ran into surface mines of chemical fertilizers and all that, and on as far as central Texas. More particularly was the region from Hawthorne, Nevada, to Hot Springs, New Mexico, a distance of over fifteen hundred miles, hard on a horse's feet.

There were salt marshes where you could pick up alkali or salt lying in crusts on the ground, or in the mud when rainy. We sometimes worked an hour with water and brush in removing the mud from around the top of Queen's hoofs lest the chemicals and dirt together cause quitter. At the least sign of a break at the coronary band we rubbed in zinc ointment after the part was thoroughly cleaned and dried. This peculiar mud at the same time seemed to extract moisture from the foot rather than impart it. We combated all this largely with lard in cold weather or tallow when it was hot.

So charged with different chemicals was the ground for a few hundred miles that some of the nails corroded or rusted and broke in two between the shoe and the hoof. I shiver even now when thinking of the danger of tetanus that we were running about this time, and how fortunate we were that I had always insisted upon having the shoe so fitted that the nails would come a reasonable distance outside the white line. It is my belief that had we under these conditions gotten the nails near the sensitive parts, inside the white line, that is, the junction of the sole with the wall of the foot, the chances are two to one that tetanus would have been produced by these rusty nails.

At one place we got a boy to hold a heavy hammer against the toe of Queen's shoe to take the jar off while we extracted the stubs of these nails that were broken off. That tightly were they corroded or rusted into the shoe that it took considerable work with a special narrow key slot chisel to remove them. When finally removed, we nipped the point off the nail that was to replace the broken one and used it as a punch, carefully following the broken upper part of the old nail out and then clinching the new nail. There was not hoof enough to warrant a regular resetting of the shoes. Meanwhile we preserved the hoof and the frog with lard, tallow and pine tar.

In one section in particular we heard range riders complain of "tearing the frogs out of their horses' feet." This was west of Elephant Butte, New Mexico, and not only the horse under saddle, but more particularly the horses that were being rounded up were affected. The ground in there is stony, but no more so than in many parts of the States where horses do not "tear their frogs out."

For some distance before we ran into this, we had noted a peculiar soreness, apparently "at the roots" of Queen's frogs—in other words, in the sensitive frog, or about the plantar cushion. We knew the flinching upon pressure of any of the frogs was not caused by navicular disease. If we are not mistaken, we saved Queen's frogs with turpentine poured in around the edges and into the cleft (after cleansing) and followed by hot pine tar. It is our belief that in these horses that "tore their frogs out" an inflammation caused by the poisonous mud and followed by suppuration (or a gathering of pus) had put the frog in pretty good shape to be "torn out." If wrong, we wish to be corrected—by a veterinarian.

From Notes. April 29, '27: Fair. Slept well on straw stack bottom. Queen had 1st straw bed since Kent, Ore. Plenty alfalfa, good water. Mill run—feels O. K. This morning feeding some plus 1½ lbs. shell corn. Taking some for noon. Leaving Berner 8 a.m. Alfalfa, 3 lbs. corn, 50 cts. * * * * Want lard. Noon, Nosebag by Hy. 12 mi. N.W. Hot Springs in shade of large greasewood. It's hot. Saw a young lark. A large B. Eagle. 2 p.m., In sight of Elephant Butte Lake. 5 p.m., Ar'd Hot Springs. Putting up at 1st corral (2nd service station) and store.

Traveled: 24½ mi. Level to very hilly. R. I. (mostly stony)

10½ mi. Gravel, 14 mi. (dirt side 6 mi.) Up side of canyon to mesa, 1 mi. Level mesa 12 mi. Bal., Brakes of Rio Grande. Greasewood, little gramma grass on mesa. Few cattle. Hot Springs is a quaint place. No sidewalks. Many "mineral baths" places. Rooms. A tourist town. Discarded O. D. shirt and both pair breeches. Took mineral bath (1st bought pair new breeches).

April 30, '27: Fair. Slept little cool in corral after getting rid of surplus clothing and a large number of animals acquired somewhere between Flagstaff and here. (For quite a while they've kept me warm entertaining them.) Discarding my whiskers. Leaving Hot Springs 9:30 a.m.

Special Note: Datil to Hot Springs, 193 mi.

Total to Hot Springs (as of April 29)—8,333 [as corrected].
* * * *

Noon, Passing through Las Palomas, another half tumbled down adobe Mexican barrio. 2 p.m., Feeding, hot lunch by a ditch, shade of large poplar tree, Rio Grande bottom, 11 mi. S. of Hot Springs. 2 p.m., Passing Caballo, filling sta., store. 6 p.m., Ar'd ranch of Jack Salsbury, P. O. Caballo. Roy Johnson lives on place. Robt. Johnson, 17, lover of horses. Irving Jewell, Garfield, rides. Johnsons had me in to supper.

Traveled: 20 mi. Level to hilly, gravel or loose sand. Followed Rio Grande bottom. Fair ranches, irrigated alfalfa, corn. Cattle.

Sunday, May 1, '27: Fair. Queen good shape, slept outside. Leaving Johnsons 8:30 a.m. No chg. Formulas. Noon, Nosebag, cold lunch by a ditch under large cottonwood. 2:15, Ar'd Garfield. 2:30, Ar'd place of Mr., Mrs. E. R. Thomas, 1 mi. S. Gar.

Traveled: 13 mi. Hilly to level. Gravel 12 mi. Dirt 1 mi. Following environs of Rio Grande. Good little farms, mostly Mex. Adobe house, some very simple. All kinds truck, alfalfa, wheat, few cows. Garfield is ½ modern, ½ Mex.

Special Note: Hot Sprs. to Garfield, N. M., 33 mi.

Garfield, N. M. (Thomas Place)—8,366 miles. * * * *

From Signature Book: "Garfield, N. M., May 4, 1927. Frank M. Heath arrived at our place 1 mile S.W. of Garfield Sunday P.M., May 1 with his bay mare Gypsy Queen. They are visiting us a few days. Intend to leave for Carlsbad, N. M. morn of May 5th.

(Signed) Mr. & Mrs. E. R. Thomas,
By Mrs. E. R. Thomas."

It will be inferred that for a day or two we had been traversing the northern part of the irrigation project under Elephant Butte Dam. A great deal of this distance we had excellent footing, particularly because they were just finishing a new road grade.

We left Thomases at 7:45 a.m. on May 5th. We had enjoyed the visit.

From Notes. May 6, '27: * * * * 5 p.m. Ar'd Las Cruces. Putting up at old feed yard. Now parking camp of Frank L. Oliver—after looking 1 hr. for camp or yard. * * * *

We had followed the Rio Grande from Garfield most of the way to Las Cruces. Some parts of this valley below Garfield had been reclaimed and were handled about the same as that above Garfield. Other parts were not reclaimed yet. We had no difficulty about feed, grub or footing.

From Notes. May 7, '27: * * * * Having Queen shod A.M. at Candlers—only $2.00 for a $3.00 job. * * * * Leaving Las Cruces 1 p.m. 6:30 p.m., Ar'd Organ. Strong cool wind on back all the way. Putting up in shed of S. O. Chapple—old-timer. An hour for coffee and talk. (There was a little store at Organ.)

Traveled: 15 mi. Rolling, gravel. Mesquite, greasewood, other shrubs, little grass. Large cactus. Last ½ no habitation. An old mine or two—dead town across mesa 12 mi. Looks like rain. Cold. No water for Queen.

May 8, '27: Leaving Chapple 8:30. * * * * 11:30, Nosebag, hot coffee, lee of brush under hill about 8 mi. N.E. of Organ. We are just to cross 6 or 8 mi. of the N. end of the "White Sands," a desert.

These were not the now notorious White Sands—sand dunes—south and southwest of Alamagordo. The sands referred to in the notes had better have been referred to as "loose sands." They were the north end of the stretch of sand to avoid which we changed our route at Las Cruces. This "rim" was not really bad. We did not cross these loose sands except the northwest corner, of which eight to twelve miles were not really bad.

From Notes. May 8, '27 continued: In order to miss the 40 miles stretch of loose sand without water we are detouring via Alamagordo some 30 mi. N. and return. It is easier. A.M., very strong cold wind still blowing. 2 p.m., Road bearing more to W.

than I like. Hailed 3rd auto before one stopped. * * * * 3, Watering at old ranch, W. M., ½ mi. E. of rd. No one living there, no feed. 5:30, At a ranch 1 mi. W. of Hy. No feed, 6:15, At sheriff's ranch, 2½ mi. to north of 2nd ranch. Here was one old one-eyed Mexican—speaks very little English. No feed. No grass. Offered corral. Said alfalfa R. (ranch) 3 mi., described rd. Dusk, Struck dim rd. Took it for one to ranch followed for a while—saw no ranch—getting too far. Believing chance for feed slim, made back to Hy. 8, Grazing 10 minutes. 8:25, Grazing 10 minutes. No windbreak for Queen. Severe cold wind. 8:30, Dry camp in "shade" of mesquite. Queen grazing until 10. Tied to mesquite. Fed ½ of ½ loaf.

Traveled: 28 mi. Gravel 12, Bal. dirt. Level mesa. Cattle. See above.

May 9, '27: Fair, not so windy. Up at 4 a.m. Turned Queen on grass. Fire, coffee, last of grub. Short on water. 5, Wild cattle threatening. 5:10, I made a break for Queen. O.K. 5:15, Feeding Queen remainder of bread. 5:30, Leaving camp. 6:45, Spied ranch to S. E. Something looked like 2 gate posts. (Ranch old Mex. told me of, visible far to west.) Demurred (or procrastinated) 15 min. while Queen grazed. (The "gate posts" proved to be windmill towers. Strange they looked so small at 2 miles.) * * * * 7:30, Arrive ranch of Walter M. Baird, P. O. Tularosa. Found Estevan Escarza in charge. * * * * (Details of stay at ranch given in letter.)

20 or 30 miles southwest of Alamagordo, N. M.,
On the Desert, at Ranch of Mr. Baird,
May 9, '27—10 a.m.

Dear Sister and Family:

* * * * Though Queen seems to be much attached to me—especially for eats—like most of us she seems to crave the society of her own kind. I have often wondered just what would happen to her if she ever made a break, as she often shows an inclination to do, and got with a band of wild horses. Especially might this be disastrous should she get with such a bunch with saddle and pack on, for as I do not cinch her very tight she would become badly entangled. So I've managed to keep her pretty well in hand until now. But now—well, I'll begin yesterday.

Yesterday, as more fully described in my notes, we had a fairly hard day, went 6 miles out of our way to try to be sure to obtain feed and didn't get it. We laid out last night without grain for Queen, and this morning by accident came back to the very ranch we should have hit last night, to receive a royal welcome from Estevan Escarza, bronco buster. He is a Mexican American, lives in El Paso, travels from ranch to ranch and opens the ball when it comes to breaking horses. He is a modest man and a good fellow.

Here "Steve" set us up hot coffee and eats and a liberal feed of oats and welcomed us in his broken English—and my meager understanding of Spanish—to stay as long as we pleased.

I pulled off the saddle and pack, gave Queen the oats and a good leg rub, and took off the nosebag to let her pick the good grass that grows too close to the ranch house to suit the wild ones.

Scarcely had I finished my notes, when looking out the window I noticed that a wild horse or two and some little range mules had slipped in off the range and were in the main corral where is situated the watering trough. Queen was with them. I tried in vain to reach the gate before they came out but they beat me to it. I tried to talk to Queen but she paid me about as much attention as a street Arab does a disreputable parent. She had stirred up about all the devil there is in these wild broncs and mules and away they scampered, Queen the biggest romp in the bunch—and I had believed she was tired! Steve says they range only two or three miles away and that when his saddle horses come up to drink he will bring in the bunch. Today the boss is away and Steve is taking a day off from riding, hence no saddle horse on hand.

Meanwhile 4 things let us hope. 1st, That the instinct of many to remain on the native range will outweigh the wander-lust Queen has acquired from much travel. Imagine her piloting the unseemly bunch back over our long, long trail! 2nd, Let me be glad she has not the saddle and pack on. 3rd. Let this be a lesson to me. And 4th, * * * * I have dreamed of "perpetuating" Queen after this trip shall have been accomplished and thus her reputation established. As to the male parent, or sire, I've been giving that matter much thought. * * * * There is on the range everything from just a *fairly* good range horse to the orneriest looking burro of the masculine gender that Nature ever put a breath into. And there you are. * * * * Still, after all, the Goddess Chance does sometimes head man off—he and his measly little science—and produces a wonder. * * * * After all, should "anything happen" from this escapade of Queen's, it will probably be tougher than a cheap beefsteak. * * * *

12:30 p.m. Steve's saddle horses have come in for water. He has the one he wants. Doubtless after partaking of the pork and beans, which smell mighty good, he'll bring Queen in and we'll go on our way rejoicing that matters are no worse, while the Good Old World wags on regardless of what happens to a little atom like yours truly, and Mother Nature does her work in spite of us.

I must close and apologize. Hoping that all are well or continuing to improve,

As ever your brother,

(Signed) Frank.

May 10.

Steve didn't bring in the bunch yesterday p.m. Instead, it was suggested by the other Buster, who returned about noon with the boss, that possibly I might catch her on the prairie with some oats, if I could locate the bunch, and save a lot of racing the bunch with a saddle horse. No, it wasn't a joke. They offered me a saddle horse if I preferred. It was a reasonable proposition. The worst trouble was, I walked from 3 p.m. till 8:30 p.m. as fast as I could—about 13 miles, and didn't find the bunch. I'm tired.

This morning at 7 Queen came in with the bunch—closely pursued by a not very respectable Jack. I fear she has disgraced the whole family.

Alamagordo, N. M., May 11.

I arrived here last night at 8 o'ck. Laying in this A.M. Cleaning up. Giving Queen a good bath, etc. Came this roundabout way after having planned to strike E. from Las Cruces, to avoid almost impossible conditions as to footing, feed and water. Traveling this P.M. Love,

(Signed) Frank.

From Notes. May 10, '27: * * * * 3 p.m., At White Water Springs, an artesian well 8 in. in diameter, warm and strong with alkali. Formed quite a pond or lake. 2—3 hundred horses in sight, some drinking—good horses. Many skeletons and carcasses. Few cattle. A large old boiler.

I did not dare let Queen drink. Some of this stock about here, it must be, were somewhat inured to this water. At the same time many had died, and Baird had particularly directed me to "go damn light" on the water at White Water Springs.

> *From Notes.* May 10, '27 continued: Sighted Alamagordo. Striking direct for it over large level mesa, through 6—8 fences, past many abandoned places. None inhabited until about 2 mi. of Alamagordo. Good bunch (?) grass, some saccaton, little gramma, little mesquite. * * * * 7:15, Hit into main road. (Many cactus in bloom—great red blotches.) Other flowers, 9 p.m., Ar'd feed yard of Alamagordo. (Alamagordo a pleasant, sleepy, shady old town.) * * * *
> *Traveled:* 27 mi. Dirt. Mostly prairie. See above. * * * *

Leaving Alamagordo, looking back from an elevation about four miles up in the mountains, I saw a clear, beautiful river, running north and south in the valley north of Alamagordo between St. Andrea to west and Sacramento Mts. to east. But on inquiry I found that the river positively does not exist, nor is there any water whatever where this seemed to be. It was purely and simply a mirage, the most real I have ever seen. It is claimed by some to be an atmospheric reflection of a long series or chain of wet weather lakes over the mountains to the west. I did not take this from one person, but several, so it must be a fact.

After passing through wonderful mountain scenery in the afternoon, we camped that night, May 11th, at the head of Box Canyon. Leaving camp early the next morning, we arrived at High Rolls at 8 a.m., and at 8:30 were at the farm of Mr. S. J. McCracken, father of Will McCracken in Mountain Park, to whom we had an introduction. We left the McCrackens the next morning at 8 o'clock, and at five that afternoon arrived at Cloudcroft.

10 miles E. of Cloudcroft, N. M.,
May 14, '27.

Dear Folks:

We are thus far in pretty good shape. And I believe that we are past all of our worst difficulties. * * * * We came upon a phenomenon in the way of grass. It is called "sleepy grass," grows in large, tall bunches, has a stem about 3 or 4 feet high, with a tassel something like wild rice. It grows abundantly here in the valley on the E. slope, and I am told elsewhere for quite a distance about. If a horse or cow eats much of this, he lies down and goes to sleep and sleeps 3 or 4 days. It is nearly impossible to get him awake at all, even to eat or drink. In fact, he is thoroughly drugged. For a long time after he comes out of this sleep he is dopy. He gets poor, his eyelids are puffy. One strange feature is that a horse, once the victim of this sleepy grass, never eats it again. It may grow in abundance all around him, but he'll never touch it. Unlike "dope" with a person, or loco weed with a horse, it does not become a habit. Whether the one feed of it creates a loathing of it, or the terrible effect is remembered by the animal to the effect that he says "never again," science has as yet been unable to discover. Could we comprehend a horse's mind—definitely read his thoughts, for he does think—what a lesson we might gain. However, it is my theory—and it is only conjecture—that the former is the reason why he becomes a total abstainer from "sleepy grass." For is it to be expected that a horse should derive a moral lesson from an unpleasant experience while his master repeats his mistakes? Whether this sleepy grass contains a powerful anesthetic or a powerful sedative, does not seem to be quite clear.

Gypsy Queen is fat and sleek. She is very happy this morning after feasting on Farmer Hamlett's excellent oat hay and corn and sprawling on a bed of straw—the second since leaving Alturas, Calif. on New Year's night. I too am standing it pretty well. From now on we expect to travel through civilized parts. The heat may check us a little at times, but then we are gradually discarding our winter outfit, so we have less load.

Next address, Big Springs, Tex. Love,

(Signed) Frank

Mr. Hamlett, with whom I stayed east of Cloudcroft, told me about this sleepy grass and gave me its local history, and definite instructions as to how to distinguish it from other grass that grew in bunches, that to the casual observer would look the same.

From Notes. May 17, '27: Clear, warm, Up 4:45. Still tired but decide to travel. Slept fairly well in hay shed after putting them to a lot of trouble. Queen rested well on bed of trash tied

to shed. Leaving Hope (a forlorn Hope I call it) 5:45 a.m.—
6:45, Making a cut-off through a lane and across fences—saved
1 mi., better footing. * * * * 11:30, At a windmill—pumping
bad tasting water. 2 p.m., Ar'd Artesia, a thrifty appearing town.
Plenty of "oil land offices"—oil district to E. 3 p.m., Leaving
Artesia with 3 feeds, 2 meals. 4:15, Ar'd farm pumping plant of
Mr. Jas. Zeleny, 3 mi. S. of Artesia. A prosperous man of
Bohemian birth, and a good fellow.

Traveled: 24 mi. * * * * mostly level. Gravel 23 mi.—but
prairie side 19 mi. Dirt 1 mi. Level plain soon after leaving
Hope, to Artesia, 22 mi. Gramma grass. A ditch but no water.
Cattle. No habitation 20 mi. S. of Artesia. Little stock. Cotton.
Local irrigation from "artesian" wells that are 950 feet deep and
[water] comes within 24 feet of surface. Good camp, plenty of
grass, different varieties, including alf. in rd. Queen in ditch to
½ way to knees, grass to her eyes, same time. She seems happy.
Also have suitable dirt for packing her feet. * * * * Mr.
Zeleny has 65 acres all under irrigation from well 950 feet deep.
Raises water 26 feet with a 25 horse power fuel oil engine
centrifugal pump—throws nearly a full 8 inch stream. Costs $2.50
per day, including wear and tear, but no wage. Winter time, 4
mos., well overflows. There are a few orchards around Hope,
some here. 3 mi. N.E. Artesia Hy.

May 18, '27: Fair. Leaving camp 7:30. Stopping at Zeleny
farm for 4 lbs. corn, ½ doz. eggs. Rather embarrassing to find
am out of cash. Will return stamps. Mrs. Zeleny fine about it.
10 a.m., In Dayton for groceries to cash check $36.00. 11 to 1, In
shade of large poplars—surround a tank fed by artesian well
about 11 mi. S. of Artesia. 3:30, Ar'd [name omitted], 15 mi. N.
of Carlsbad. Camping. Plenty of grass. Sleeping in open acct.
snakes.

Traveled: 19 mi. * * * *

May 19, '27: Fair. Up 4 a.m. Queen did not lie down. Noises.
Leaving camp on creek 6:30. * * * * 3:15, Ar'd Carlsbad.
Spent 15 min. looking for camp. Putting up at feed yard of
[name not recorded.] * * * * No mail from Joe. (Bees all way
up valley.)

Traveled: 15 mi. Rolling, dirt, 5 mi. Gravel 10 (dirt side 5
mi.) Abandoned Ir. system few mi. Mostly arid plain. Gramma
grass. Cattle. Few horses. Some farming, dairying, 1 mi. W.
Carlsbad.

Special Note. * * * * Total to Carlsbad, N. M., 8,654 miles [as corrected].

May 20, '27: Fair. No mail from Joe. Laying in. Dinner, supper, with the Luther Thomases. (Luther Thomas was son of Mr. and Mrs. E. R. Thomas.) Had made 1 horse boot.

From Notes. May 21, '27: Laying over. No mail. Another boot, making a pair.

About these horse boots: The reader will understand that we still had to combat the road fever, as I call it, that is, fever in the foot usually extending up the leg, from too much travel on hard or rough road, especially under a load. If not combated, and if the irritation persists, this leads to acute inflammation of the sensitive parts of the foot, particularly the sensitive laminae. If this is not soon relieved it may result in road founder or laminitis, caused by the constant pounding on the road. It is well known that the best antidote to offset this is, if reasonably possible, to stand the horse in a creek (but watch that he does not stay there too long after the fever has subsided). Another way, as I have described away back, where water and a hose are convenient, is to shower. This is a very good way. (However, in this case of hosing, or of standing a horse in a creek, the horse must not be suddenly cooled off and then left standing.) Hose the horse with cold water, and then start him on. Ride him through a cool creek or a cold creek even, but keep him moving. Regarding the boots, you are not supposed to put in ice water, of course. Still another way that I have described, the reader will perhaps remember, is to wrap the leg loosely with burlap, being careful not to cord the leg. Remember I sometimes used what might be called a suspender, described at Miles City. But in this desert-like country water was usually very scarce. There was none to throw away. This was the case, as I remember it, at Carlsbad, and I knew that it would be the case for quite some time, at least until we should have traveled half way across Texas. Another point—perhaps the reader is aware that after sundown or in the early hours of the night, if there is any coolness at all, it is near the earth. If the earth is baked hot, then the horse wearing the boots I am about to describe should be stood if possible where there is shade or where in some way the ground is as cool as can be found.

Now for the boot. A leather boot would not answer the purpose that I was aiming at for the reason that leather is to quite an extent a non-conductor of both heat and cold. Cotton canvas is more nearly a conductor of cold, while on the other hand it will not retain excessive heat. So in making these boots I cut a sole for each, out of a heavy auto truck inner tube. Then I made, you might say, a canvas tube roughly six inches in diameter (for a horse that carries a number 1 shoe). This tube I had sewed strongly to the sole. When completed, the boot somewhat resembled a golf club bag. This, of course, was cotton canvas of about 14 or 16 ounce duck. This I held from sagging down by taking a piece of galvanized clothesline wire (solid), and making of it a tall inverted U. (That is, had two prongs about 2½ inches apart.) The two ends I turned at right angles and curved them to conform to the rounding periphery of the sole. These I had sewn strongly to the canvas just above the sole. It will be understood that this double support, one in each boot (not necessarily two) ran from the sole of the boot to within an inch or two of the top, so that it held the boot up to the horse's knee. About four or five inches above the union of the sole and the canvas wall, I attached a strong cord (in this case torn out of the same canvas), and the boot was complete.

You pick up the horse's foot, simply slip the boot over the foot, set the foot down, tie this string last mentioned around the pastern, and there you are. We filled the boot with cold water to just below the knee joint. The heat of the foot and leg worked out through the canvas. The coolness of the atmosphere near the ground exchanged in the water inside the boot with the heat of the foot. That is about all there is to it. I tried to leave this on from the time it got cool in the evening until about bedtime, feeling once in a while whether the foot was sufficiently cool to remove the boot. This not only reduced the fever but also moistened the hoof, and the frog, which, if dry, absorbs water like a sponge to some extent.

In crossing the Texas plain, we had a fairly hard fight to keep the road fever down. There we used to put in the bottom of these boots a pint or a quart maybe of what I believe away back in New York we described as "barnyard poultice." I found this very effective. Afterward, of course, the boot should be thoroughly rinsed.

Such a boot makes a convenient receptacle for bandages, medical cotton, or anything in that line, or any light article to be carried along. They can be put inside one boot, which can then be put inside the other, so as to telescope them in such a way that the soles are at each end. This is very convenient to lash onto the cantle or back of the saddle. I am presuming that the College will exhibit one of these boots—what is left of it—for anyone who should wish to see it. We wish more people out for riding strenuously would use these. Once a horse has had them on, he will cooperate with you in getting into them.

From Notes. May 21, '27 continued: * * * * Sending outfit to Big Spring, Texas. Surplus to Norred. Carlsbad Ir. project partial failure. Carlsbad is "nuts" about caverns. * * * *
From Notes. Sunday, May 22, '27: Fair. Leaving feed yard 7:00. A good place to put up. 11 a.m., Nosebag, cold lunch, 1 mi. N. Loving. Queen in ditch. 3 p.m., In Malaga—autobus failed to deliver oats. Bought 6½ lbs. corn—bran—had 1 lb. oats. 6:45, Ar'd ranch of Mr. C. J. Queen, P. O. Malaga, Red Bluff Canyon.
Traveled: 30 mi. Rolling. * * * *
Monday, May 23, '27: Fair. Leaving camp 6 a.m. ½ doz. eggs. (Formula No. 5.) Salty water, no chg. 9, Autobus leaving us feed, oats, can milk. Order surplus to Pecos. 9:15, Watering filling canteen at a good creek. Queen in 10 min. 9:30, Met Commander West, Post No. 7, Carlsbad (overseas Capt.). 10:50, Crossing line into Texas. 11, Nosebag, cold lunch by rd. side. No water for Queen. 40 min. only. * * * * 3:45, Ar'd Orla, Tex. Rolling. (Most W. M.'s gone or out of repair.) 2:45, A little very salty water in pools—live minnows. Queen 3 swallows.
Traveled: 22 mi. * * * * Dirt, plains, some grass—thorn bush, other des. veg. Very hot. Greasewood. Some cattle. Oats at Orla O.K. Buying water shipped from Carlsbad.

From Signature Book: "Orla, Tex., 5/23/27. Frank M. Heath and Gypsy Queen arrived here this P.M. and staying over night. In good shape.

(Signed) R. M. Atwater, P. M.
(P. O. Stamp, Orla, Tex., May 23, 1927)"

From Notes. Tuesday, May 24, '27: Fair, cooler. Leaving Orla 7 a.m. Water, 10 cts. 11:15, Ar'd at W. M., steel tank, good water. Feeding, cold lunch. Found oats, milk intended to be left at "Tin Mill" 3 mi. S. 3:15, Watering at a W. M. ½ mi. S. of Hy. Salty, hot. Find oats over at right mill. (Misinformation—traveled faster.) 4:45, Ar'd at an oil drill. * * * * 20 mi. N. W. of Pecos. (1,300 ft. expect 4,500.) S. A. Burks running 12 in. drill. Let us have water. Camping. Dry gramma grass.

Traveled: 25 mi. (1 side to W. M.) Rolling, dirt, as yesterday. Cattle. Most W. M. running. Several oil derricks around here.

Wednesday, May 25, '27: Fair. Leaving oil well 7 a.m. All good fellows. No chg. for water. 10, Watering in ir. ditch. 11, Nosebag, lunch at a ditch—bathing Queen. Judge D. G. Grantham of Carlsbad contributed to lunch and 15 cts. (2nd offered in cash—1st accepted, since Searchlight, Nev.)—(i.e. the one at Searchlight) was 1st since Butte, Mont. 3 p.m. Ar'd Pecos. Putting up, old corral of R. S. Johnson. * * * *

Traveled: 19 mi. * * * *

Thursday, May 26, '27: Fair. Leaving old corral, 7 a.m. Queen well fed, oats, alfalfa. 9:30, On bank of ditch by Hy. at Barstow, 7 mi. E. of Pecos. Bathing Queen, bathing self, washing up. This land is bad with alkali. Beautiful tall cedars. Leaving 12 noon. 5:15, Ar'd at a ranch. W. M.'s—several ranches. * * * * 7:15, p.m., Ar'd Pyote, a new oil town. Oil 20 mi. or so. N.E. About 2—3 wells in operation. Many tents here. Laying a pipe-line Pyote. Men of whom I inquired for feed all talk at once. Trucking a big feature. Water free, feed reasonable. Hunted 45 min. for hay. Found it at Neil Moreland. Very reasonable. * * * *

Traveled: 25 mi. (1 side to Pyote—and all over for hay.) Hot. Mostly level Texas plain. * * * * Also some horses. Mostly poor soil. Rock comes to top some places, kind of limestone rock. Pass red sandstone quarry.

Friday, May 27, '27: Fair, hot S. W. wind. Leaving Pyote 10 a.m. * * * * 1 p.m., In Monahan. Difficult finding shade. * * * *There seems to be a boom here too. * * * *

Dear Folks: Monahan, Texas, May 27, '27.

Two letters from you reached me at Carlsbad. We are now making for Big Springs via Pecos (which place we passed) on account of water and better opportunities to get feed. The shorter route would have been very hard on us both. We are following the Bankhead Hy. The country through which we are passing now is very barren—just Texas plains. But, following the highway and just now the R. R. gives us a chance to buy eats and oats and get water. Today the Hy. has run through the sand drifts, mesquite, other desert vegetation and little else. Ahead of us I see sand, sand, sand. But the footing beside the paved Hy. is good to fair, mostly.

We cut the day's travel to what Queen can stand. Several times recently I sent oats and corn ahead by the bus drivers. Sometimes I have them left at a windmill and well, where there is no town or house. (The windmills pump water into tanks for stock.) I put on the tag the following: "Frank M. Heath, Windmill (so many miles in such a direction from such a place). This bag contains oats for Gypsy Queen, the Horse that is Touring the U. S. She Needs Them." I offered to bet a man $10.00—the last I had—that he couldn't find a man in the State of Texas mean enough to swipe them with that tag on them. Nothing especial to write. Hope you stand the heat. Next address will be Eastland, Tex. Love.

(Signed) Frank.

From Notes. Saturday, May 28, '27: Leaving Monahan's. * * * * 3:30 p.m., Ar'd at Jones Well, 22 mi. E. Rolling plain, sand hills. Desert veg. Some grass, sev. kinds. Few cattle under fence. Mesquite.

Traveled: 22 mi. Pavement (gravel side 18 mi., dirt side 2 mi.). This is a good well of good water. W. M., very little grass. I don't feel good. Weak every p.m. Eating R. oats, milk and bread for a change. Warm W. wind all day.

Sunday, May 29, '27: Hot. Leaving Jones Well 6:45. 9 a.m., Queen on good grass by rd. side 15 min. 11:30, Ar'd Odessa. Tried 1 hr. to find a store that was open where they had feed. Wherever I ask about shade they say: "Shade?" Town seems to be booming in tourist business, or oil boom business. Many new cheap bldgs., mostly tin—many tents. Much large oil well equipment moving mostly on large trucks. 12:30, Pulling out for a farm 3 mi. E. after eating a pie, watering Queen. Everybody talks about "maize" or Kaffir corn.

About this maize: If some of us old-timers get back to what we learned in our school history, we will remember that maize, properly speaking, means—or meant—Indian corn. It is my opinion, though I am not quarreling with Noah Webster about it, that so far as Indian corn is concerned, the word maize is long out of use. This maize that we speak of here, which from now on for a long stretch is the principal feed, has no ear, no cob, like Indian corn. The grain is in the head of the stalk, more resembling a large, bushy tassel. In fact, it much resembles Kaffir corn. This is raised extensively from here on to considerably beyond Big Spring, and overlapping the cotton area. It is sown in large fields, I believe with grain drills. It seems to me that I remember the rows were from a few inches to a foot and a half apart. It is sometimes cut when ripe enough for feed with a header as low down as convenient, sometimes with a binder, and usually put in sheds. For a long distance it was about the only feed available. The native stock was fed this mostly altogether, there being enough stalk to provide roughage. They worked the horses hard on it. It was pretty rich for Queen at first, as she was not used to it, and when I fed her too much it used to cause her to belch. There are several varieties of this maize, all pretty much alike.

> *From Notes.* May 29, '27 continued: 1:15, Procured 1 feed oats at last service sta. out E. of town. It's hot. The only field I've passed since Pecos is one W. of Odessa, showing corn stubble—not now in crop. 3:05, Ar'd ranch of——— Newman, 3 mi. S. Odessa. Not at home. Borrowing tools (from family) to tighten shoes, replace 1 nail. Leaving 4 o'clock.
> *Traveled:* 21 mi., mostly gently rolling. Bankhead Hy. * * * *

On May 30th we left Odessa, and proceeded through the oil country, finding everything very dry. The main crop continued to be maize, though there was some cotton. At this time, perhaps owing to the water, I was feeling very sick, had no appetite, and was not able to walk very much. On the 1st of June we arrived at Big Spring.

> *From Notes.* June 1, '27: Fair, S. W. warm wind. Feeling just a little better. No supper last night. Had a long tramp and chase in pasture for Queen. * * * * 12:45, Ar'd Big Spring, putting up at feed yard.
> *Traveled:* 11 mi. * * * *
> *Special Note:* Carlsbad, N. M., to Big Spring, Tex., 232 mi. Total to Big Spring, Tex., 8,886 miles [as corrected].
> June 2, '27: Fair. Laying in a.m. Writing Thomas, also Norred. Cashed last traveler's check. Leaving Big Spring 12:20. 4:30, Ar'd Coahoma. Renailing left shoe at shop of old Mr. Hull. No chg. * * * *
> June 3, '27: Fair. Leaving Coahoma, 6:45. * * * * 6 p.m., Ar'd ranch of J. M. Henderson, 3rd try. * * * *
> *Traveled:* 27 mi. St. Hy. No. 1, Pave, 8 mi. (gravel side), dirt 14 mi. Gravel, 5 mi. Slightly rolling, less mesquite, more

wild sunflowers, R. thistles, some bear grass, gramma grass, Johnson grass, few Spanish dagger. Some broken land. Some local rain about Westbrook recently. Some dobie. Bal. mostly in cult. Some idle. All crops need rain. 1 man planting cotton. More cows. Good mules. Road full of oil equipment. Many oil tanks N.E. of Coahoma. 90 derricks in sight N. of Westbrook.

June 4, '27: Leaving Henderson, 8. Bundle maize, 2 feeds maize heads, only 25 cts. * * * *10:45 Queen feasting on Johnson grass which grows rank in rd. way—also in most fields. Soil here little less dobie. Some cotton and Kaffir corn pretty fair, but farmers say it will not "make" without rain. No rain here for two months. Most all here under plow. Still little mesquite and wild sunflower. Noon, Nosebag with maize, cold lunch, glass buttermilk at ranch of Tom Comer, 6 mi. E. of Colorado. This is typical rolling prairie on divide between Colorado River (Crossed at Colorado) and Clearfork River. 5:30 p.m., Ar'd place of Mr. Stewart. * * * * 5 mi. of Lorraine. * * * *

Sunday, June 5, '27: Fair, S. west wind. Leaving Stewarts 7 a.m. Slept in empty house. Maize, sorghum hay, buttermilk, no chg. Formula No. 5. * * * * 4:30, Ar'd farm of O. C. McDonell, 7 mi. E. of Sweetwater. * * * *

Traveled: 21 mi. * * * * Conditions to Sweetwater as yesterday. E. of Sweetwater more pasture and mesquite. Cotton. Many cows. Need rain badly. Looks, feels like rain now. Soil good. Faced dust storm, high wind, most of P.M. 5 p.m. shower.

Note: Maize produces, here, ½ to 3 tons of heads per acre, 1 ton average. Not very hard on land. Stalks and all, it averages 2½ tons or from 1 to 6 tons.

Note: Prickly pear, cactus, grows very large here. Clusters 6 ft. diameter, 4 ft. high. Tongues often 4 x 8 x 2 in. Leaves 6 in. thick at butt. Stockmen feed them to cattle when grass is short, by burning thorns with gas or coal oil burner, or by cutting and holding in fire.

Note: Cotton averages ½ bale per acre, or 800 lbs. Must be hand hoed.

From Signature Book: "Sweetwater, Tex., June 5, 1927. Frank M. Heath is feeding his bay mare, Gypsy Queen, here at Wade Bros. Packing Plant, noon today.

(Signed) T. C. Canthen, Butcher."

From Notes. June 7, '27: Cool. * * * * 3:30 to 4 p.m., In Abilene. No mail. * * * * 6:45 p.m., Ar'd farm of Mr. John Warren, 7 mi. E. Abilene, 3rd try. Via St. Hy. No. 2. Rolling. * * * *

June 8, '27: Fair. Leaving Mr. Warren 8 a.m. No chg. for corn, hay, meals. Slept in porch on cot. But made him take 75 cts. (Formulas.) Mr. Warren recently met with an accident which wholly incapacitates him for work, he has large family, is a tenant and very poor. Yet they treated me hospitably to "the best they had." The Warrens were born and raised in Tex. * * * * 3 mi. S.E. Clyde we almost suddenly came into oak instead of mesquite. Vineyards, orchards, rank growth of corn, fields of oats in shock, showing good yield. Soil varies from dark loam to red dobie, and sand in places. * * * * Signs of recent rain W. of Clyde. Raising little sweet clover. 3 p.m., Back in mesquite. 13 mi. E. of Clyde, place of Mr. H. A. Vines, P. O. Baird. * * * *

June 9, '27: Pleasant. Leaving the Vines. * * * * Water is scarce along here. * * * * Feeding bearded wheat. I am very tired—so is Queen, 5 p.m., Ar'd at Old Gin, Cisco, via No. Rolling. Hot.

Traveled: 22 mi. * * * *

June 10, '27: Fair. Leaving Cisco 6:40 a.m. Slept well under shed of gin. 10:30, Ar'd Romney, Tex., an inland town of P. O., 2 stores, garage, filling sta., 11 mi. little E. of S. of Cisco.

Note: I find I made a damned blunder. On inquiry was told to take "Main Rd. to Eastland." I failed to turn to left just S.E. of Cisco (no one to tell me) and I am thus now 21 mi. S.W. of Eastland, my *mail* point. Saved a little for Queen but must spend $1.00 probably, of my last $5.00, in getting from Carbon— 10 mi. E. of here—to Eastland and return. * * * * 3:30, Ar'd Carbon, Tex. via county road. Queen in corral of Carbon Trading Co. * * * *

Traveled: 21 mi. (1 by error in not hitting Eastland)—see above. Pave 11 mi. (gravel side 4 mi., dirt side 6 mi.) Dirt, R. I. 3 mi. Dirt 7 mi.

Note: From Romney traveled at least 2 mi. S., back N. Went in every direction except W. Passed through oil fields. 10 derricks in group on S., 13 to N.—few others. Post oak continues. Some good fields corn in tassel. Cotton fair. Lots of melons, cantaloupes, etc.

From Signature Book: "Carbon, Tex., 6/10/27. Frank M. Heath is staying in my lot tonight, feeding a bay mare whose name is Gypsy Queen. Will rest until 11th, when he expects to leave.

(Signed) Manager Carbon Trading Co.,
W. W. Speer."

From Notes. June 11, '27: Fair. (Laid in.) Side trip to Eastland. Caught ride both ways. Back 10 a.m. No word from Joe, though letter addressed to Eastland and forwarded from Carlsbad, Big Spring and Abilene. Got check for $10.00 from E. R. Thomas—cashed by Mr. S. P. Rumph, 1st State Bank of Carbon. Writing S. S. (Silver Spring) for 20 dollars and bonus certificate, address Corsicana. Writing Joe for a showdown regarding address. P.M., Having Queen shod new behind, reset front leg, J. C. Martin, $1.50.

Special Note: Abilene to Carbon, Tex., 73 mi.

Total to Carbon, Tex., 9,072 miles [as corrected].

We left Carbon at 6:40 a.m. on June 12th, and arrived at noon the next day in Dublin, Texas. Dublin is said to have been so named because of its having been in early days a kind of meeting place for Indians from both north and south, who were said to "double in" at this point—a natural camping place of alternate open land and timber, also a creek. It seems to be a peculiar fact, however, that the locality is largely populated by people of Irish descent!

The next afternoon at 5:30 we arrived at Iredell. I slept here on a cement floor—plus a few rocks and a little loose cotton, and breakfasted the next morning under a bridge. I had found for some distance around here eggs ranging around 12 cents a dozen. Here I bought 5 for five cents, and milk only ten cents. It seemed as though we had at last got back where they raised something besides hell. We left Iredell at 7 o'clock, and Queen seemed well rested. At half past two that afternoon we were at Meridian, Texas, which was a town before the Civil War. We traveled on five miles beyond Meridian and stayed at the farm of Mr. F. M. Jameson. The Johnson grass in this region seemed to be taking the grain fields. There was a great variety of trees, including mesquite, willow, juniper, cottonwood and post oak, and also much wild sunflower. Queen spent the night in the pasture of ex-Governor Ferguson. I slept in the Jameson's granary on loose Johnson hay.

On the night of the 17th we slept in the open, and on the 18th at the home of W. H. Thorn on the Alexander farm. At noon on June 19th we arrived at Corsicana, Texas, our next mail point, and laid over on account of mail. It rained hard about 4 p.m., in Corsicana.

Corsicana, Tex.,
June 19, '27.

Dear Folks:

I arrived here today at noon. It's pretty hot. Queen is O. K. but she gets pretty warm the last few days. I let her take it as easy as she will, but the racehorse blood in her makes her want to go. I am going to start in now traveling early in the morning and late afternoons.

One thing we are thankful for and that is that we are out of the arid regions. A few hundred miles more of drouth, and sand, and all kinds of chemicals in the soil, alkali, lime, salt, gyp. (gypsum), and something that I can't name in the red dobie, and I fear Queen would have had no feet left. I resorted to every means I knew of but her hoofs were getting very brittle. In fact I had a hard time making the last (and 19th) set hold on until she grew barely enough hoof to nail the 20th set onto.

Her frogs at one time were as hard as horn and chipping off much like horn as a result of drouth, sand and chemicals. For roughly 2,000 miles there was no mud fit for packing the feet. One time I paid 50 cts. for a little flaxseed meal, but soon I got into the farming country where I could get "barnyard" pack or cow dung. That helped a little. And now we are over the danger of drouth and chemicals in the soil and the feet are coming along fine.

I forgot to mention, I helped them a little first with lard or tallow, but one can overdo the grease, especially when it's hot. I believe at one time I saved the frogs of the feet from certain destruction with tar, but the use of it has a limit too. I believe there is nothing else under the sun as good as Mother Nature's own remedy, water and mud—that is, the right kind.

I am in the cotton belt. Cotton is the major crop. Back west a hundred miles or so they needed rain badly. Around here just now it's too wet.

I'll finish this tomorrow after I get the mail. Next address after you get this will be Mansfield, La.

20th. Yours of 13th rec'd. Next address: Shreveport, La. Love,

(Signed) Frank.

Leaving Corsicana on the afternoon of the 20th, passing through a number of small towns, Powell, Malakoff, Athens, Chandler, Tyler, Browning and Longview, we arrived in Hallsville on June 26th. The country through here was level, and everything was very wet. There was too much rain, and we suffered from heat. We noticed that some peanuts were being raised through here, and that the colored people seemed prosperous. In Longview I slept in the Courthouse, which is on the site used for that purpose since before the Civil War. This is on the old Greybull Plantation of 8,000 acres.

Note: The man at whose place we stayed, night of June 24-27, was John R. High, P. O. Winona, Tex. The son Charles E. High, 16, is blind—but not born blind. Charles got a wonderful thrill out of interviewing me all about the trip, in feeling Queen all over, her fleet limbs, her silky coat, shape of her head, texture of her mane. He asked me if I were going to write a book. I told him I meant to try it.

From Notes. June 25, '27: Fair, leaving the Highs 6:30. Maize, eggs, tom, cot, no chg. (Formula No. 5). Blind boy, Chas. took notes for story for "blind" paper N. Y.

Sunday, June 26, '27: Fair, warm. Leaving camp in Longview, 5 a.m. 9:30 a.m., Ar'd Hallsville via Hy. Hilly, pave (gravel side) 10 mi.

Traveled: 11 mi. (called variously 10 to 12—took "time" of 11 mi.). See above. Conditions as yesterday P. M., except no swamp. Camping under pines N. Hallsville. Bathing Queen, cleaning up.

Note: For several days I have noticed quite a lot of cows of a very light, sometimes a light buckskin, yellow Jersey. I have never seen this peculiar color cow * * * * elsewhere. They and the other cows, most Jersey, look good.

Hallsville, Tex.,
Sun., June 26, '27.

Dear Folks:

I received a letter from you at Athens. Glad all well and the garden coming on. Two or three weeks ago I had green corn and saw some green peas. In this section everything seems later unless it is tomatoes. Besides cotton and corn they raise quite a lot of tomatoes here. I see them packing them green into nice little baskets or boxes. They'll be ripe when some city person gets them, of course.

We are having no trouble about—or with—moisture now—that's past. And with it most danger of road founder. Now it's the heat. Queen sweats profusely. I am very careful about her back—not to scald it. We aim to hit the road about 5 a.m. and travel until 9—or 11 o'clock, lay in until about 2:30 p.m., then travel very leisurely until 7:30 or 8 o'clock. In the P.M. we make several halts in the shade. Generally about the middle of each half day I take off the pack and saddle in order to allow Queen's back to cool and dry. So far her back is steadily improving from the scald I gave it in the desert.

(It will be remembered that in approaching Mina, Nevada, heavily loaded and making long jumps, Queen had a slightly sore back. I took the soreness out of the back temporarily with strong salt water.) (By the way, if you ever use salt water for this purpose, be very sure that you remove all signs of salt from the skin before applying either a collar or a saddle.) We went along very nicely then until we were crossing a long stretch after Carrara in two days, the days being very hot, while the nights were cold. The second of these days I noticed upon unsaddling Queen, who was pretty well heated up, that her back was slightly scalded in one not very large spot. This scald, however, did not go below the epidermis except in a very small spot, perhaps the size of a half dollar. I at once relieved the pressure on and around this spot. The reader perhaps will remember that beginning with the next day Queen had approximately a week's rest at Indian Springs and Las Vegas, which gave the back a pretty good chance to recover. Then too, I got at Las Vegas the material for one of the best remedies for a local surface gall that I have ever used or known of. I had gotten this prescription from an army veterinarian while I was in charge of horses and mules in France. I carried a small bottle of this continually from this time on. This back was, in fact, beginning to make us trouble again when we got to Shreveport, not on account of neglect, but on account of the everlasting heat under an overloaded saddle. And here comes a little point about saddle blankets and pads. I quote from my article, "What One Horse Did" in the Cavalry Journal, July, 1930: "When it came to long hot stages under pack, I had trouble with Queen's back. I tried everything. Finally, at Shreveport, Louisiana, I got a Felt-Less pad. It is all simple when you think of it. This pad is made of *cool* instead of *hot* material. In the hottest parts I cured the back. I might add here, I have no brief for advertising this pad."

Since 9:30 today I am camped among the tall pines. It's a restful spot. Plenty of grass, water and shade. I've been washing saddle blankets and about all my own duds, besides a bath in the creek, and I thoroughly washed Queen.

I am considering getting up at 2:30 a.m. tomorrow and starting out at 4. I am not sure whether this will pay, as sometimes Queen does not get up until 4:30 or 5 o'clock, if not aroused, and after all she must have her rest—and sleep. I've heard a lot of talk about when a horse sleeps. Some fellow seems to have given us to understand that a horse sleeps from 12 midnight to 4 a.m. That may have been his observation of his horse. As for Queen, I've found her sleeping soundly at 10 p.m. when she had a good bed, and she would lie stretched out until about 5:30 a.m. Then again, when she has not a good bed she often does not lie down at all and sleeps little if any. I've known this to continue three nights when we were in the wilds. But that was rather long for a horse to remain on feet. The more we have of such a life the longer rests we require when we get a chance. I mean that she needs more rest in proportion.

Well, about day after tomorrow I should hit La.—the 40th state. I'll hear from you of course at Shreveport. Our next regular address will be Vicksburg, Miss. By the way, we are going about 100 miles farther north than we intended, on account of the second rise in the Mississippi. By the time we reach Vicksburg we hope transportation will have been restored on the main Hy. If not there should be some ferry or something. I don't aim to go farther N. than Vicksburg.

Well, I must close, get a bite to eat, take care of Her Royal Highness and hit the pine needles. Love,

(Signed) Frank.

From Notes. June 27, '27: Fair, cooler. Leaving camp 4:30 a.m. Trains passing through kept Queen awake. She did not lie down though she had a good soft bed. I had everything fixed and my mouth all set for a good hot breakfast, but matches, damp, would not light. Ate little milk and bread. * * * * 6 p.m. Ar'd Scottsville. Camping under cedars, leaves for bed.

Traveled: 22 mi. * * * *

June 28, '27: Fair. Leaving camp under cedars and oaks, 5:30

a.m., after good night rest on bed of oak leaves. Queen lay down, rested well. She got up at 4:30. 7:45 to 8:15 a.m., Unsaddle in shade giant oaks to cool Queen. Note: I see more Johnson grass yesterday and today than of late. Injures cotton, corn. Mostly colored working in fields, living mostly in shacks or old houses. 9. Met refugee with covered wagon, mule team, wife, from La. Wants work. 11 a.m., Ar'd Waskom, via Hy. 15—2. Hilly to level.

Traveled: (A.M.) 12 mi. * * * *

From Signature Book: "Frank M. Heath stopped at my store at Waskom, Tex., June 28, '27. Riding bay mare called Gypsy Queen. Left for Shreveport in afternoon.

(Signed) A. J. Mitchell,
Waskom, Tex."

From Notes. June 28, '27 continued: P.M., Leaving Waskom 2:15. * * * * 6:20 p.m. Ar'd at vacant place 8 (?) mi. E. Waskom, in La.

Traveled: P.M., 8 mi. Pave, dirt side, 5 mi. Oak and pine timber. Patches cotton, corn. Some cows, etc.

Chapter VII

THE MISSISSIPPI FLOOD AREA

From Notes. June 29, '27: Fair. Leaving camp under shed, 5 a.m. 8 a.m., Ar'd Shreveport, La. Camping at city farm of Wm. Brewer in W. suburbs, P. O. Shreveport, c/o J. E. Brewer, Shreveport Traction Co.

Traveled: 10 mi., counting to city of Shreveport. * * * * Called Chamber of Commerce to select road. Called on Journal. Called on Vet. Bureau man. Nothing doing on Bonus without certificate.* * * *

THE SHREVEPORT GAZETTE
Shreveport, Louisiana
Wednesday, June 29, 1927

HORSEMAN ON TOUR OF 48 STATES HERE ON LAST LAP OF TRIP

Having covered 40 of the 48 states of the Union on his self-imposed two-year horseback tour of the United States beginning April 1, 1925, Frank M. Heath, of Silver Spring, Md., reached Shreveport Wednesday morning. So far his mileage is 9,389 and both he and the horse, Gypsy Queen, a 12 year old dark bay mare, are in good condition. He has yet to traverse Mississippi, Alabama, Georgia, Florida, the Carolinas, Virginia and West Virginia.

Traveling light and with sufficient income to meet ordinary expenses, Heath, a member of Cissel Saxon Post 41 of the American Legion, employs his veterinary skill to tide him over when the weather is too wet or cold to camp under the nearest tree or at the closest spring.

From Signature Book: "W. H. Smith, 304½ Texas St., Shreveport, La., July 1, 1927.
(Signed) Fox News Cameraman."
From Signature Book: "Shreveport, La., July 1, 1927. Frank M. Heath arrived at my place in W. suburbs on June 29, '27,

with his bay mare Gypsy Queen, and is keeping her in my pasture a few days while attending some business.

(Signed) W. M. Brewer."

From Notes. July 2, '27: Cloudy. Rained hard last evening. Old barn in which camped leaks like a sieve except one little corner. No word from Joe. * * * * Taking 7:50 p.m. train for Washington, leaving Queen c/o Mr. Brewer. * * * *

St. Louis, Mo., July 3, 1927

Dear Folks:

Yours of June 25 rec'd at Shreveport. Am on way to S. S. (Silver Spring) to straighten out my finances which have gotten into a bad tangle. Will return and finish trip. Do *not* worry and do *not* send me any money. I'll come out O.K. Address, Silver Spring. Love,

(Signed) Frank.

Rockville, Md. (near Washington, D. C.)
July 6, 1927.

Mrs. Frank Hughes—Family
Bowie, Ariz.
Dear Mrs. Hughes:

I just happened to be in Washington when your letter of June 30 arrived. I have not finished the trip yet, but came here to attend to some urgent business and am going back in a day or so to resume our journey where I left Queen in good hands, at Shreveport, La. I expect to finish in Oct. * * * *

When I left Shreveport on July 2nd the water was still ten or twelve feet deep for several miles west of the approaches to bridges. So I took advantage of the time I'm waiting for the water to recede to so arrange matters here at home that I will not have to kill the Queen off or worry myself to death to get back to attend to matters here at "home." (Home?—I have no home except my saddle for a pillow and the blue sky for a roof. I feel free that way, and as though I have more room in which to grow. Headquarters I'm afraid would be a more fitting term for the place most people would call home.)

I first changed my general course to one which should have taken me across just north of Waco, Tex. to Natchez, Miss., believing that I could cross there by the time I arrived. Then, on news of the second rise, I swung north, believing transportation would be restored more quickly on main Hy. via Vicksburg. If by the time I reach the Mississippi, which should be about two weeks, road is still blocked, I shall probably have to ship Gypsy Queen over in a box car. This last I dislike to do, as my intention is to "hit every state, traveling the entire distance under saddle, and except ferries (which distance I deduct) on her own feet." Now of course putting her over the Mississippi flood on a box car in absence of either bridge or ferry would be legitimate. But people these days demand uncomplicated results, not explanations. We are an impatient world and want everything "in a nutshell." Nor do I want to have to spend my time and energy in explaining to some dumbell who might say: "I saw Gypsy Queen in a box car." I shall probably have to put time of completing the trip forward as much time as I am losing on this last count. For in laying out our schedule I purposely crowded it to a horse's limit—and a new limit. And barring these delays it has been and will be until the last, one constant "race" to keep up with that schedule. Fortunately there is no money up. And putting the finish forward to cover these delays will be understood. Psychologically it will be "different."

Still, as we are out to "Prove by Actual Test the Capability of a Good Horse" we will not "beat about the bush" but admit frankly that it actually took exactly so long, and challenge the wide world to beat it. * * * *

(Signed) Frank M. Heath.

P.S. By the way, I'm writing my story as I go along. Diary, letters to different parties, clippings, photos, etc. Come to think of it, that part giving reasons why we delay for flood is probably more adequately described in this than any other letter I've written. I'm collecting these letters at the address I gave you. Will mail self-addressed envelope.

July 8. Starting back tomorrow. Next address will be Gen. Del., Vicksburg, Miss. (Hold 30 days.)

Shreveport, La., July 14, '27.

(Dear Folks:)

Arrived here O. K. last night from side trip to Washington, D. C. Found Queen O. K. Starting on tomorrow morning early. Hope water which still covers highway some distance west of Vicksburg will have receded by the time we arrive there.

We expect to be in Tallulah, La. about July 23rd—write me

there. Tallulah is the last town we will hit W. of the River.
With love,

(Signed) Frank.

As we were leaving the Brewers, I went out about midnight into
the wooded pasture. There in a fence corner stood Queen, wide-eyed
and alert in the moonlight. Skinny and Nellie, Mr. Brewer's two
horses were with Queen in the pasture, and were both sleeping
soundly with their muzzles resting on the soft turf. Midnight is
when a horse usually sleeps soundly—if undisturbed. They did not
wake up. Queen stepped lightly over to first one, then the other,
touching each with her muzzle. It was her "goodbye" to her two
companions of a fortnight. Without a sound or a word from either
of us Queen followed me down the path toward the old barn. She
knew that we were hitting the trail.

I hear someone say, "Phuey, how the devil could a horse know
she was leaving old Skinny and Nellie for good? How could a horse
know what was in Heath's mind—without a word?" It is such doubts
as that which sometimes make me almost glad that I have acquired
the larger part of whatever education I have through experience,
first hand observation and—living close to nature. Sometimes I
sorely regret not having mastered more of the technicalities of the
sciences—especially when I find it hard to express myself.

But just the same I am glad that I am not stuffed so full of
dogmas, of so-called "unquestionable facts" that I cannot believe
my own eyes. I am glad that, because I walk on two legs and read
and write—some, and can "calculate" or reason: I am glad that in
spite of all that, I can understand and appreciate the fact that some—
perhaps most—animals have in their mental make-up, very deep
within them, instincts that guide them very correctly, generally.

Queen knew that she had had a good rest and a good time with
these two old cronies. She knew she would never see them again. In
her own way, quietly, unobtrusively, she bade them an affectionate
"goodbye."

Soon, in the cool of the small hours, we were on our way—home.

Gilsland, La., July 17, '27.
Dear Folks:

I've taken to getting up in the "wee sma' hours" and hitting
the pike anywhere from 2:30 a.m. to 4:30 a.m. That way we
cover about half our day's journey before the sun's out of bed.
The son can beat the sun up for a while, but he can not keep it
up for long—as the sun reckons time.

Contrary to my preconceived notion the nights here even in July are fairly cool—and damp. So the Earth—this wee part of her—being cooled over night, the morning breezes are quite pleasant. But Queen? Foolishness aside, I am "experimenting" on her. Some time ago we said something about a horse and his sleep. It is generally believed—and I concede—that a horse sleeps best, generally, early in the morning. Queen these three days since leaving Shreveport seems to enjoy and is refreshed by the four hours rest at midday. But she does not sleep. She is drowsy now but not sleeping. There are too many flies and too many noises. Not the noises of the song of the night but "waking noises." One thing is certain, a horse *must sleep*. The next question is: Can a horse's hours of sleep, four or five, be changed successfully from about 11 p.m., or midnight to 4 a.m. or 5 a.m.? Milk rt. horses do, but they have a regular hour. In most things there is a limit as to how far we can with impunity overstep the laws of Nature. This is going to be a test of how far we can overstep this law of "the horse and his sleep," without abuse or injury to the horse.

I am not telling you much about the country—I haven't the time. My notes take care of that and you'll get it all later. Suffice it to say we are in the woods—largely pine. Passed a *large* sawmill today, a few smaller ones past two days. Out of the woods are carved small farms. Many of these are full of stumps. The principal crop is cotton and the colored fellow does most of the work. Some corn is grown and a few sweet potatoes and garden truck and melons.

Getting back to the horse's viewpoint. Queen does not drink as much water as where a dry heat prevails. In that at least we have an advantage. Oats are not grown here at all. But I am usually able to get them at some store—with some difficulty. They don't like to "break a sack." Usually in a town there is a grocer or feed man who will reluctantly open a sack to be obliging.

I must hit the road now. Address Vicksburg, Miss. Love,

(Signed) Frank.

Ruston, La., Monday, July 18, 6 p.m.

I got wet, outfit and all. Outfit was out in the woods. I was over town on my everlasting quest for oats which I procure through here with great difficulty. It came up a sudden and hard rain. Now we are in an old shed with a good fire, drying out.

About four weeks ago, at Corsicana, I swung northwest to cross Miss. at Vicksburg. As nearly as I could learn, on consulting Chambers of Commerce, crossing seemed certain to be restored at Vicksburg earlier than at Natchez. Then too there was the Red River, crossed at Shreveport. I couldn't find out about it and other streams. I crossed the Red at Shreveport. In leaving Shreveport I heard that light traffic was crossing at Natchez. But I could not learn much of roads across swampy country between Shreveport and Natchez direct. This way I was sure of the highway to Monroe, La. at least. Just today I learn on what seems dependable information that they are crossing at Natchez and it seems they may not be crossing at Vicksburg for perhaps a month. Anyhow I go on to Monroe, 36 miles from here. If then it develops that the ferry at Vicksburg is not yet running I'll have to swing back south to Natchez, having come about 75 miles too far north. If the ferry (which lands on ground considerably higher than the broad bottom west of the ferry) is running, I believe I can find a way to the ferry. But I'll not run any undue risks. Mail will be waiting us at Tallulah some 30 mi. west of Vicksburg. I can have that forwarded to us of course, but now that I have come north I'd like to strike across the higher country rather than the lower via Natchez. At least I believe there is more swampy country—and a few billions more mosquitoes on the latter route. And so you see it's a constant case of manoeuvre.

July 19, '27—5 p.m.

I certainly intended to mail this early this morning as I passed through a little sawmill town called Calhoun. Last night I was out of envelopes and I was so wet I did not get them while in town. I missed Calhoun. This morning I thought it was on the Dixie Highway, which I'm traveling, but it is some half mile off to S. and over a hill. Finally, knowing by the time we had traveled we must be near or past it, I inquired and found we had left it two miles behind. Leaving Queen resting in the shade of a chinaberry tree—and by the way, the "china" makes the coolest shade I ever saw—I caught a ride back to Calhoun. There I met the same difficulty that I most always meet in these small town. The oats are in three-bushel sacks, and the merchant hates

to break a sack. He would not either as far as the money goes.
But I've yet to find the small town where someone will not
break a rule for the sake of a horse, and that same thing happened in little sleepy old Calhoun. Just at noon we arrived at a
tourist camp in the woods. Not the high road tourist camp, but
just a plain unpainted building among the pines and oaks. This
is free. The homefolksy people, a filling station of course, and a
small grocery. This is the kind of place I love, you know. And
Queen is resting well—I guess she is either sleeping or drowsing,
standing in the shade, having filled up on grass. I wish she would
lie down—something she has not done that I know of since the
night of the 13th. We left Ruston at 2:15 this morning and
made our average—21 mi. I still believe that is much better than
traveling in the broiling sun. Only I hope Queen will soon learn
to adjust her sleep and her lying down to the P.M. or the first
half of the night.

We are 12 mi. W. Monroe and should reach there tomorrow
early. I'll probably mail this before I figure out definitely which
route we take from there. Will let you know later. I've been
busy all P.M. washing out every rag I wear. So I'm tired.
Must hit the hay soon as expect to roll out about 1 a.m.
tomorrow. Love,

(Signed) Frank.

P.S. July 20th. Overslept and so Queen got a night's rest. Here
at Monroe I find we must cross river at Natchez—the reason is
that the break in the levee above Vicksburg being still open
keeps the lowland W. of Vicksburg inundated. Address me at
Natchez, Miss. Love,

(Signed) Frank.

From Signature Book: "West Monroe, La., July 20, 1927.
This is to certify that Frank M. Heath is stopping in this city
today with his bay mare Gypsie Queen on tour of U. S.

(Signed) A. King, Marshal and
Chief of Police."

From Notes. July 21, '27: Fair, hot. Left camp at old gin
(Monroe) 12:20 a.m. 7 a.m., Nosebag by rd. side. 11:30 a.m.,
Ar'd Rayville. Camping back of garage of W. E. McCoy, under
large trees.

Traveled: 24 mi. * * * * 1st 10 mi. in "dark" suburbs. Then crossed part of recently flooded district, a few fields not planted. Saw water marks 4 to 7 or 8 feet on bldgs. which are mostly "nigger shacks." Then quite a stretch of wood, mostly oak— inundated lowland. Later some farms planted to cotton, corn, cow peas, etc. Refugees back. W. D. Bird gave Queen 3 feeds oats. * * * *

July 22, '27: Clear, hot. Left Rayville 1 a.m. 5:30, Feeding and hot coffee by rd. side. 7 a.m., Crossing Big Creek. Concrete bridge collapsed—one set pillars undermined. Grade was under water 1 mo. Pools beside grade full of minnows. Some places school large fish were trapped by falling water—they now smell rich. * * * *

Traveled: 23 mi. * * * *

From *Signature Book:* "Winnsboro, La., July 22, 1927. Frank M. Heath arrived here 11 a.m. today with bay mare Gypsy Queen and camped under pines near my store. I have just weighed his outfit and find he is carrying 63 lbs. dead weight, including 1 camp meal, canteen and no water, no feed.

(Signed) J. C. Cobb."

Harrisonburg, La.,
Sun., July 25, '27.

Dear Folks:

I got in here yesterday noon, crossing Ouachita (pronounced Washita) River from the east on the ferry. "Way back yonder" I had been told repeatedly that I'd probably have to pay heavily for crossing ferries through here as they "had the cinch on me." I had heard that until I had assumed almost a belligerent frame of mind, but had decided to pay whatever they soaked me as though a few dollars were a mere nothing to me, and then ask the ferryman where he expected to go when he died. So you may imagine my surprise when they charged but 15 cts.—I believe that is the lightest ferriage I've paid on the trip.

As you know I turned south a few days ago at Rayville. I came through Winnsboro, Gilbert, Wisner and Cissely Island. All the above places border on the recently flooded district but were not hard hit by the flood except as some of the farmers tributary to those towns were entirely or partly "washed out."

It is only after leaving Cissely Island that the terrible effect of the flood makes itself manifest in views of the aftermath. First I began to notice the damaged condition of the crops.

Some of these were not inundated long enough to obliterate the first planting, but the ground is more or less water-logged and the corn especially looks as though it has "yellow fever."

The range is nearly ruined. The grass survived in its last gasp for air, and is recovering its breath very slowly. It has about all it can do to live. So you can imagine the condition of the stock that depends upon it for subsistence. 1st there is the hog. True to Southern traditions he is to begin with somewhat of the razor-back type. Today he is a parody on a real hog. The cattle largely of very common stock are today a burlesque on the long-horn. The horses are a joke—if misery is ever a joke. And the mules are a comic opera. The people along the "borderland" as I call it, or those who suffered but little, are placid in the knowledge that this only happens in its intensity about once in 30 years and in part about once in six. And that the soil is rich. Those a little lower down, those who were "covered" have replanted some of their ground. But the worms have taken the second crop of corn, leaving the farmer only the toll, like a modern miller. Some have planted the third crop, which is in a precarious condition. His cotton is a little better, but bad. This "borderlander" has fallen into a state of patient, hopeful waiting upon fate, while he is profuse in his praise of the Red Cross which stakes him. They stake him to feed for his team, for one thing. Today—the camps having been discontinued—these oats go out through some business house. I could not get the business man to whom they are intrusted to go into a sack to save Queen's life, or for love or money. They are relentlessly true to their trust.

A little farther down on the flatland the scene is one of desolation. Houses are washed off their foundation—usually piers or piles, and are anywhere from a few hundred feet away in any imaginable angle, out of plumb in all degrees, just as the flood left them. Families are living in some of these. Other houses, they tell me, are fifty miles down stream. Some of those we see come from nobody knows where, like a stray cat. Ownership seems to have been lost sight of. They stand, sit, or lean there in the mud or perhaps partly under water, in a state of utter indifference. Then of course there are sides of houses, roofs of houses, parts of stables, feed boxes, gates, fences and vehicles, all tangled up together. (Some bldgs. on little rises of land are still in place, but mostly more or less wrecked.)

Transportation has been re-established here only three or four days. The last few miles we came over a grade little above water and newly graveled. From here on to Natchez it is the same. Yesterday I hunted in vain here for oats for Queen from noon—when we arrived—until night. I found oats (except Red Cross oats, which are unavailable to us) in only one place, and that after calling at several places several times. These oats—part of a sack—belong to a farmer merchant—for his own use. He would not let me have an oat yesterday on a bet, but promised me a couple of feeds this morning. The man believes in the Sunday closing law. He started the Sunday closing game himself and now does not propose to "give anybody a chance to come back at him." I might say, even though a horse might starve. Let us hope the Lord will take care of him. I am now, at 8 a.m., sitting on his store steps, waiting for him to open up, so I can feed Queen before hitting the loose gravel. I wish the Lord would help him get a move on him. We *should* have been 12 miles on our way. It's getting *terribly* hot. Still we can't start Queen out on an empty stomach to go into a land of desolation where oats may or may not be available for 36 miles. I could get "chop"—ground corn—but that would bring on digestive troubles. And the main thing, especially just now, is to keep Queen in the healthiest condition possible and at a high point of resistance. To allow myself to become excited and overdo her might prove fatal. "What is the particular danger just now?" you ask. Well, it's charbon (a French word, pronounced char-bone). [In United States it is Anthrax, but as down here it is invariably referred to as Charbon and the fly that has to do with distributing the disease is referred to as Charbon fly, I naturally in my letter used the local term charbon.]

It comes from a germ that may be transmitted to the animal from a fly bite (the charbon fly) or from eating grass upon which the fly has deposited the germ. It lives in sod twenty years, especially on tall dank grass. (Or it may be taken from drinking stagnant water.) The disease first shows up on the belly or breast, swells until it chokes the animal, and is usually fatal. The natives here inoculate against it. Queen has not had this inoculation—in fact I never heard of charbon until day before yesterday. The nearest point at which I can get this done is Natchez.

[After I learned all this, I kept Queen off the infected grass, gave her only well water, fought the flies, kept her toned up with nux vomica, kept her vitality up—and thanked Heaven when we were out of it.]

Why did I come into Harrisonburg *from* the east when I am *going* east? It is the only way open. The road running east from Cissely Island via Clayton is still largely under water. Bridges are gone and there are dangerous channels. This obstruction is caused by the overflow of the Fensas River, a tributary of Ouachita. (One thing they have in abundance here is rivers.) So you see we made from Cissely Island southwest, crossing the Ouachita at Harrisonburg. From Harrisonburg, we must go South to Jonesville, crossing Little River over a bridge, having passed the junction of the Fensas (Fensaw) with the Ouachita. From Jonesville we'll cross the Black, an extension of the Ouachita, on a ferry, on east to Faraday, having traveled nearly every direction except straight up and three or four times the distance gained between Cissely Island and Faraday. From Faraday we are to go southeast to Vidalia, where, if Providence has no objection, we will cross "The Father of Waters" over into Natchez on a ferry.

8:30. Met Mr. T. W. Sargent, who readily gave Queen 2 feeds oats. (But he's badly in need of them; I made him take some pay.) Will close now and swelter along to Jonesville, 12 miles. (Store not open yet.) With love,

(Signed) Frank.

Jonesville, La., July 27, '27.

Dear Folks:

In my last, July 25 and 26, we were about to start from Harrisonburg to this place, crossing the Burkley Bayou over a good bridge, only the wooden framework of which seems to have been slightly damaged by the rush of water over it. The entire distance of 12 miles between Harrisonburg and Jonesville was under water during the flood, which left desolation in her wake. A great deal of the distance is large timber, the land apparently being considered too low for safe cultivation.

We saw a few of the runaway houses peeking out from among these trees as though ashamed to be seen so far away from home, most of them still partly submerged.

In some clearings bordering the Hy. nothing remains but the fences, and still some water. The fences seem to have main-

tained their hold on Mother Earth while the water seems to
have been deep enough to carry all floating matter clear of them.
In a few of the higher spots the buildings are only more or less
wrecked but remained at home or near at hand. On these farms
the farmer is working away in his dubious fields with his half
starved horses or mules. (By which I mean they were half
starved—the Red Cross is feeding them now.) He may get
some cotton—his corn the worms have taken.

All along the Hy., which is now passable, are temporary
bridges, gangs of men working and whole families catching a
few tiny fish. Some of the adults—both sexes—as well as the
kids and geese, are barefooted.

About 1 p.m. we crossed Little River into Jonesville over a
"musical bridge" that was built for wagons, not auto trucks. The
only fault Queen found with the noises it gave up under her
nimble tread was that the noises do not harmonize. Still she
soon seemed to realize that the dismal sounds were in keeping
with the dismal scenes left by the flood. She walked the planks,
which are laid lengthwise with bridge to reinforce the old bridge
floor, like a good soldier. In some places, to have stepped off
them would very likely have meant a broken leg.

[In some localities the old floor of the wooden bridges was
badly rotted, sometimes full of holes. Queen had learned to look
out for the holes, especially if told. But of course the question
of whether the planking would bear her weight was beyond her
power of deduction. So we taught Queen to "walk the plank"
that has in most cases been laid lengthwise for the auto traffic.
In those thousands of miles she never once stepped through a
bridge.]

Arriving in Jonesville we tied up under the nearest tree and
proceeded to replenish the inner man—and horse. The high-
water mark in the buildings is anywhere from half way up to
near the ceiling. All merchants built scaffolds in their stores
during the flood and placed their goods thereon. Most families
moved out of here to higher ground in locally owned boats
before the arrival of the Red Cross. They are used to it. Some
remained—some on the scaffolds, some at the hotel, which is on
a slight elevation, others in the second story of the large brick
school bldg. (Some sixty people and a lot of cattle, horses and
pigs were camped on an old Indian mound of less than an acre.
I cannot learn whether these Indian mounds are the work of

the Mound Builders or of later Indians. Some have been partly leveled for building purposes. In them they find human bones, arrow heads, and pottery. They probably were built for refuge in time of flood. It's too bad to level them.) All this is now a matter of recent history, though water still stands in some street gutters for the convenience of frogs and mosquitoes.

About 2:30 yesterday (that is, the day we arrived here, though it seems a week) after answering the same questions over and over—as usual—until I was black in the face, we started to proceed. We got as far as the ferry over Black River (an extension of the Ouachita. It seems the river could bear its Indian name no farther) when—"biff"—"I can carry you across, but I can't take your horse" quoth the ferry-man.

"How is that?" I asked.

"Quarantine," said he.

"Quarantine? I thought that was at Vidalia before crossing into Mississippi?"

"Yep. Here too. Ticks—outlaw parrish."

"All right, if I'm quarantined, we are ready to be inspected. We have no ticks. Where is your inspector?"

"Over at Monterey. Man named Robb. You can phone him long distance."

"Well what the hell is the inspector for this 'part' doing at Monterey?"

"Don't know. You may be able to get over today. Sometimes it takes longer."

I went to the long distance telephone office and got in touch with Dr. Robb. The minimum charge was 30 cts. for 3 minutes.

"Where are you?" asked Robb.

"Touring the states," I told him. "This horse is in the 40th state and has traveled over 9,500 miles."

"Can't do anything for you," answered Robb, "I'm just a local man. I pass the refugee stock."

"Well, can't you tell whether my horse has ticks as well as a horse belonging to a refugee?" I asked, in I'm afraid somewhat of a huff.

"No use of any argument," came the reply, "you come under the Federal. You'll have to see Dr. Flower at Baton Rouge."

Taken by surprise, I'm afraid I gave voice to words that are not supposed to be used over the phone because ladies may be listening in. In fact I suppose I used words that if persisted in might lead to cussin'!

"_____ _____ _____ I can't take my horse to Baton Rough! I never heard of such Blank foolishness. There must be someone to inspect a man at a port of inspection."

"You might call up Mr. Bruce of Lee Bayou." (The natives pronounce it "by-o.")

"Forty cents," says the operator.

"The Dickens," said I. "Was I talking 4 minutes?"

"You had the line for four minutes," she replied. I paid the damage.

Then I tried to get Bruce at Lee Bayou, only to find that the wire was down. The operator said she had no idea whether it would be repaired in an hour or a week. It was under water. If it (the wire) came up, they maybe could use it.

Meanwhile I had learned that Lee Bayou was not far from Cissely Island. Why, I thought, had I not been informed back there, the inspector residing near there, of this inspection.

(Knowing that we were in the tick area, which includes a large part of Texas, just before crossing the line into Louisiana, I deliberately went to see some Federal inspector as to the best method to pursue in getting from one state to the other, as I did not wish in any way to evade any law. His opinion was that as long as I was traveling in the road, I need not worry, that they did not bother work or saddle horses that were traveling the road. We kept the road religiously. Imagine my surprise then, when I found we were quarantined at the Black River!)

I rushed over to the Postoffice five minutes before the mail to Lee Bayou closed. But the Postmaster told me that I could get a letter into the mail for half an hour yet. (I learned subsequently that the depot is nearly half a mile distant.) I got a stamped envelope and rushed back to the ferry, where I had left Queen tied in the hot sun, to get writing material from my haversack, and Bruce's first name from the garage man near by who knew him. Just as I had written and addressed an "earnest appeal" to Bruce to come as soon as possible (I'd learned that at best it would take several days for the letter to reach Bruce and Bruce reach the ferry) I got what seemed reliable information that "Bruce could not do a darned thing for me without first communicating with Dr. Flower and getting from him by mail or in person a signed permit for me to cross." But I was told that Mr. Guss, owner of the ferry, could and probably would phone Dr. Flower for me, and being well known by Dr. Flower, probably facilitate matters for me. The idea seemed to be that were we (Queen and I) properly vouched for, Dr. Flower might at once send Bruce the necessary signed permit with a friendly suggestion that he (Bruce) interrupt his somewhat leisurely habits and "shake a leg" over here some thirty miles to inspect my horse.

By this time I reasoned that the train by which I had intended to send the letter to Bruce—not knowing anything of my troubles—would have pulled out, so I decided to see Mr. Guss. Mr. Guss lives in a big white house across Little River, over which we had come. I took Queen back to the big tree near the town end of the bridge and tied her in the shade. Then I recrossed the musical bridge, walked a few planks over some wet ground and mud, and finally arrived at Mr. Guss' place. Mr. Guss was not at home. But Mrs. Guss, after hearing my tale of "woe" believed that Mr. Guss "might be able to help me out." I was to return about sundown, which I did.

Coming back across the bridge of discords I soon had us domiciled for the night, myself in a small, partly-covered fishing boat on the river bank, where prevailed the softer, but more exhilarating music of the mosquito, and Queen out on the common where she utterly ignored the scrawny horses and mules that were grubbing a precarious existence from the strangling vegetation.

I returned to see Mr. Guss as per appointment. He returned home about 7:30. I found him a very pleasant man. But he could not help me.

The only thing remaining for me to do was to get in touch with Dr. Flower at Baton Rouge. I got back to the telephone office about 8:30 p.m. The wire to Baton Rouge was also out of commission. It might or might not be in order by morning. The Western Union has no night service here.

So the next morning (yesterday) I wired Dr. Flower:

"Going to Natchez. Please instruct Bruce inspect my horse Queen."

(Signed) Frank M. Heath,
Horseback Tripper. (65 cts.)

I heard this painstakingly phoned to the W. U. and then went about getting settled for a few days wait. I understood that if Dr. Flower got the wire promptly and was obliging enough to write Bruce at once, and there is no hitch in the mail service, and Bruce should be on hand to get his mail and should happen to come right on over here he *might* arrive here sometime this P.M., at best over two days after I learned we must be inspected. And if you ask me "how come" as the modern vernacular goes, all I can say is "God knows."

I am told by apparently reliable people that whole families, whole bunches of logging teams, have been held up here for a week. One outfit, I'm told, had to leave a team as security for debts incurred while waiting.

The worst of it in our case is that this wait will be a damage to Queen rather than a benefit. She does not need rest—has had too much. She'd be much better off on the road than fighting flies. I've taken her off the grass upon learning that the short grass is more liable to produce charbon than is the tall grass, as it's in the sod. Upon getting a place to keep her in a corral where she can run under a shed I learn of still another terrible disease that prevails here called "foot-evil." This comes from a germ—or worm—that lives in the refuse from the overflow and attacks the feet, by entering at the coronary band. Infection follows. The hoof comes off. Often the horse dies. I avoided this by avoiding places where the sun was excluded, keeping the feet clean and daubing the top of the hoofs with zinc ointment. I have taken every possible precaution against this, and will I trust escape both it and charbon. But I certainly will feel a great relief when we get across the old Miss. on into the hills.

I expect there is mail waiting me at Natchez, at which place we should have arrived yesterday. I've written them to hold it —forever.

You better write me there, as I certainly should be out of here before a letter could return.

And now folks, if you are inclined to censure me for using a few words that were not taught me in Sunday School, please remember that Job never was held up for inspection at a port where there was no inspector. With love,

(Signed) Frank.

Jonesville, La., Fri., July 29, '27.

Dear Folks:

You see I'm still here. In fact, I'm getting used to being here in spite of my impatience. Jonesville is a typical old Southern town. Had I the ability to describe it I would make it a spot dear to any lover of easy romance. Cows and horses roam the streets at will. The favorite "resting place" for the cow here and for miles back is the side of the road on top of the grade—out of the mud. The sidewalk, or parking under the giant pecan trees is where the cattle and horses love to stand and dream of better days and fight flies. The people speak in soft tones, slightly bordering on a drawl. But the unspeakable jargon attributed to them by some writers is not heard.

I waited about thirty minutes this morning for a stack of hot cakes, after giving the order. No one ever seems to be in a hurry.

That brings me back to my delay here. While I've been waiting over three days, at least two "local" inspectors have been here, passed "local" stock, and gone. They could do nothing for us. The local stock was passing out of a tick-infested parish. There seems after all to be nearly as much difference as there is between "Tweedledum" and "Tweedledee." So it seems a *Federal* inspector must pass upon "Tweedledum," notwithstanding we must pass an interstate inspection at Vidalia, less than 30 miles. Yesterday made two days of waiting on Bruce after he should have been here if Dr. Flower wrote him from Baton Rouge on receipt of my wire (and the "returns" show that he got it about 10 a.m. Tuesday). That is assuming Bruce gets his mail each morning, as you will agree an official who has no telephone communication should. Yesterday also I learned that a son of the Swayzes, at whose barn we are camping, is a local inspector under Bruce. He had been here and gone before I knew about it, but I learned he will be in Jonesville again tomorrow—Saturday. Thereupon last night at 8 o'clock I got Dr. Flower at Baton Rouge over long distance and to the tune of 85 (cents) and I believe the operator let me off easy at that. At first I could not hear. When I did hear it seemed Dr. Flower was trying to tell me of an inspector I'd have to pass at Vidalia before crossing the Miss.

"The Mississippi!" I exclaimed. "I can't cross that until I reach it. I'm trying to get across *this* river. You got my wire?"

"Yes, and I wrote Bruce to inspect you. He'll go over when he gets around to it," or something like that.

"But he has not showed up yet, and I feel I've been detained too long already. Henry Swayze, who I understand works under Bruce, will be in Jonesville Saturday. I am asking you if you will write him to this place, authorizing him to inspect my horse and pass her if he finds her all right."

"I'll write him as soon as I get back here," came the reply. "I'm leaving here four o'clock tomorrow morning and will return Saturday."

"But Dr. Flower," I remonstrated, "Swayze will be here, and leave, Saturday. If you write him Sat. I'm afraid he won't get your letter. Couldn't you please write him *before* you leave tonight?"

"No."

At that point, a lady's voice came over the wire and I seemed unable to get anything more from Dr. Flower. I thought at the time it was one of those cases where two conversations became tangled. I remembered the 85 cts. for three minutes, remembered the financial difficulties which seemed to pursue me like a shadow, and hung up in despair. No sooner had I left the booth than I was motioned back by the operator. I took down the receiver, and there came from Dr. Flower: "Tell Swayze to inspect your horse and pass her if she is all right. Tell him I said so."

"Thank you, Dr. Flower. Thank you very much."

Now about that lady's voice: I've decided since I've had time to think it over that the voice was that of a secretary who overheard the conversation—perhaps had knowledge of my telegram of Tuesday morning—grasped the situation I was in, and so interceded. Or perhaps the operator in his office. I am sure the voice was addressing Dr. Flower and in slightly remonstrative tones, though in that sweetly refined voice characteristic of the gentle Southern woman. Romancing, you say? Raving over a woman's voice over the long distance? Not at all. I'm too young for that—yet. I'm only 58. Please remember that that is one of the many instances where some little thing has popped up or come in just at the last minute and—saved the situation. This time it *seems* likely to have been a woman's voice backed by a woman's quick intuition—or proven deduction, and a womanly sense of justice. So, as such, I shall continue to believe—unless

I learn differently—that "the mysterious lady's voice" had to do with this one of the continuous string of our ever changing small adventures.

So here we are, nearly four days by the watch after we first learned that we couldn't cross without Federal inspection, simply because we came across instead of from a "tick parish." We must stand a *regular* inspection upon leaving the next parish into another state. Can you beat it?

I have a cordial invitation to a picnic of the people of Jonesville and surrounding country. A kind of jollification in the knowledge of "how much worse it might have been." Isn't that the right spirit? The people appreciate what is left. The crops are entirely or largely ruined over a great sweep of country tributary to Jonesville. But no lives were lost. Most buildings were more or less damaged—but they *could* be worse. There still remain the fish—most kinds in abundance. Bull frogs, the largest I ever saw, in great abundance, find a ready market. Raccoons are plentiful in the woods. Wild honey, too, although I understand the large timber owners object to having the "bee trees" cut down. There are cattle, who are beginning to pick up a bit on the slowly reviving grass—though I hear that charbon is raging not many miles away. There is the "razor-back" hog. To the casual observer it might seem questionable as to whether he is more valuable for ornament or for actual use. Still I believe they make bacon and don't cost much. The horses and mules are a questionable asset. * * * * And there is the inevitable Good Cheer.

Queen is "raring to go." I'm taking every precaution against both charbon and foot-evil. I guess this is all for now. Love,

(Signed) Frank.

4 p.m. Bruce came at last. And the worst of it is, he found fever ticks on Queen's belly—lots of them. They are new to me. Never saw one before. Little gray devils. Bruce found them at once. The only kick I've coming is that it took so long to get him. He said he got Flower's letter yesterday or day before, he had forgotten which.

Now the only thing I can do is to go back west about 60 miles to a Central Federal Dipping Sta. at Alexandria, and have Queen dipped. If they, on my arrival there, find any ticks on her, they dip her, hold us 7 days, dip her again and let us go. In order to get into Mississippi I will in either case have to *ship* her from Alexandria to Natchez. * * * * Love,

(Signed) Frank.

* * * * I am now on my way back S.W. to Alexandria, La., a distance of about 75 miles. If at Alexandria they find one tick on her, they will dip her, hold us 7 days at my expense, and dip her again. Then they will probably let me *ship* her but will not let me travel her back across La. and the Miss. River to Natchez. I hear that "maybe" I can take her S.E. to St. Francisville through "tick free" territory and finally pass into Miss. overland. This I doubt.

Well, there is this to offset to some extent the fact that for the 30 miles between Jonesville and Natchez, I will have backtracked about 75 miles, and that after having tried every other lawful means. And that's that.

I had not proceeded more than five miles yesterday (having started at 1:30 a.m. to avoid the heat) when Queen began to slacken her pace and otherwise show signs of soreness and a little pain. She continued getting worse. The symptons showed complications. The tendency to knuckle in her hind legs and fetlock joint would indicate azoturia—a disease that usually attacks a horse that has been standing still on too much feed, upon starting him out. About the only chance—1 to 100—in azoturia, is to stop the horse at the first signs of the trouble— and some other treatment. But first, the care Queen has had the last few days should not produce azoturia. Secondly, I could not possibly care for her in the middle of a mosquito, charbon infested swamp on a narrow highway. I proceeded at a slow pace —myself walking all the way—while I shuddered at the possible consequences. Then there was the disease, foot-evil. * * * * I doubted its being that.

But the plainest symptoms were of a kind of founder or congestion of the laminae, or connection between the bone and the hoof. And—the cause? Five miles of gravel—bad as gravel is— should not in itself produce inflammation of the sensitive laminae. Tracing the cause a little farther—in order to try to determine the trouble—I remembered that all the time I kept her in the small corral on the lately overflowed ground floor of the Swayze's stable, on some indigestible hay and ½ ration of oats, I had feared ultimate trouble. I had fed the poor hay—

which was the best obtainable, sparingly, and exercised her regularly twice a day. Bran I could not get. The grass is charbon-infested. Animals were already dying all about us. I believe I had done the best that could be done. Nevertheless, Queen was showing by now, distinct signs of obstruction colic. And where there is obstruction there is usually congestion more or less all over the animal as well as gas pressure. In fact, who knows to what degree gas pressure causes congestion, even in the feet?

Meanwhile Queen was stepping shorter and shorter, beginning to breathe with more or less difficulty, looking at me as much as to say, "Frank, I'm sick," and plodding along like the plucky girl she is. Whenever I stopped her for a moment to let her recover her breath she started on with difficulty. I don't believe in "doping" a horse, except as a last resort. But now I took from my haversack the emergency dose which I am seldom without. I had carried this dose from Needles, Calif., I believe, having given the last previous one about the time I entered the state of Nevada way last winter. It consists of Tinct. belladonna ½ oz. and Tinct. aconite ½ oz., which is about ½ a full dose. (Don't give fluid extract of the same drugs as the same amount of the fluid extract might *kill* about three horses.) I carry this in two little vials in a safe little pocket, in the haversack.

I gave Queen one-half of this small dose with a syringe which I always carry, and in 15 minutes gave her the other half. * * * * I also resorted to another means which sometimes induces action of both bladder and intestines.

We kept moving. Soon the gas made itself heard. A slight relief had been obtained—temporarily. But I knew the cause had not been removed.

A little after 7 a.m. we got into Harrisonburg, having given Queen half a bucket of water at a garage a mile back. At an old brick store building near the river I tied, removing the pack. I got a beer bottle at a nearby house and went in quest of it full of raw linseed oil. I found about two ounces by scouring the whole town. I don't like castor oil for a horse so I got 3 oz. of Epsom salts (the Glauber salts were not obtainable). I made a drench of the salts and proceeded to drench Queen. I was getting along pretty well when—craunch—she had ground the neck of the bottle between those excellent teeth of hers. I was much alarmed for fear she might swallow some of the crushed glass. That I believe would have terminated our trip indeed.

Quickly seizing her tongue and pulling it out the right side of her mouth with my left hand, I raked the pieces of glass off the roots of her tongue with the right. I must have gotten them all. At least she is still alive 24 hours later.

After trying every store in town I got 20 lbs. of wheat bran off the same Mr. Sargent of whom I had gotten some oats a few days before. It was Red Cross bran. He didn't care to sell it, but felt it would be all right under the circumstances to "swap" it for other cowfeed. Accordingly I bought for him its value in cottonseed meal.

I made our 16-quart canvas bucket nearly full of bran slop, putting into it about two drams of nux vomica and just enough ginger and salt to make it appetizing. This I induced Queen to eat. She seemed a little better at once. Still I was in a quandary. Hay is unobtainable here for love or money. Stock is dying around here every day of charbon. The grass is infested with that dread disease. By chance I met Dr. P. W. Callahan, who owns the drug store. Mrs. Callahan, with whom I'd been doing some trading yesterday and also upon my previous passage through here (they also keep groceries) had told the doctor about our trip. The doctor is interested in horses and also in stunts. And so it happened that the Doctor came to the rescue. To try to move Queen on to the next town, Manifest, 12 miles, was much of a hazard. To let her starve until fit to travel was out of the question. To feed her altogether on bran for several days was not the thing, and you know about the grass.

The Doctor showed me his fine clean grass plot back of the store—nearly half an acre, well fenced and kept mowed.

"This is clean of charbon," said the Doctor. "I've never allowed anybody to put any stock in here, beg as they would. It is not infested. The outside range is. Charbon is an infectious disease. Turn your horse in here and welcome. And keep her here until she is able to travel. I like the stunt you have undertaken. In my opinion your horse has had a close call. It's hot and this is not the healthiest of places for a horse. It's too bad you were caught in this quarantine. In my opinion your horse would be better off with several days rest in this clean lot. You are welcome," he repeated with genuine hospitality. He also replenished my drugs—free.

So here we are today. Queen is much better. The bran slop, with the little oil we could get, the nux, salt and the ginger, followed by the bran mashes with nux and salt, are producing the desired results. The stoppage in stomach and intestines has fortunately been overcome. The soreness resulting from the congestion is not entirely gone, but I trust the congestion was not of sufficient duration to produce chronic laminitis or founder. I spread her shoes early yesterday to relieve the pressure and am keeping her feet fairly cool with water.

Whether Queen should travel tomorrow is doubtful. I've asked Dr. Callahan to "check" on my anxiety "to be moving." I am certainly anxious to be getting on out of these unhealthy flatlands on account of flood.

* * * * After feeding her the bran slop I had had her down to the ferry to "wash her up," so the flies wouldn't bother her so bad. I had also wrapped her lower legs lightly and loosely with burlap which I kept moist for the purpose of cooling her legs and imparting moisture to her feet—as the water drains off. As I was leading her up the street to the Doctor's lot, some fellow who had not yet been heard from, asked: "What's the matter with yo' hoss'es laigs?"

"Not a damned thing!" I replied.

"He just put them on to keep the flies off her laigs," said the questioner to his nearest neighbor on the store steps.

That night I camped and am still camped, in the dirty old brick store bldg. near the ferry. During the flood the floor was covered several feet in water. The water receded through the battered floor which made a convenient trap for all kinds of rubbish. I kicked a spot in the middle clear of the worst refuse, laid down a lot of paper, and stretched my "bar" which I found it necessary to procure as protection against the Louisiana humming birds (erroneously called mosquitoes). The "bar" (mosquito net) also is protection against a thousant bats or vampires that are lodged in one end of the bldg. and keep up a constant chatter, while an old man who talks to himself occupies the other end. These little instances only lend variety to my small experiences.

After all is said, Harrisonburg is another of those dear old Southern burgs. Horses, cattle, hogs, dogs, geese and goats are equally at home in the streets. If people are a little easy going it only counter-balances the senseless rush of some other places.

I hear a lot of farmers say that the worms are taking their late crops—planted after the flood. The principal redeeming feature

of the surrounding country is that the soil *is rich* and produces
bumper crops of cotton and corn when the flood does not drown
them or the worms eat them. Anyhow, while the World wags
on, Harrisonburg seems to wag along with it.

I guess this is all for today. With love,

(Signed) Frank.

6 mi. N.E. of Gena, La.,
Mon., Aug. 1, '27.

Talk of one disaster following another I got up at 1 a.m. this
morning and made Manifest, 10 mi., by 6:30. When I unpacked
I found I had either left behind or lost on the road—probably
the former—my horse kit—that is, grooming tools, medicine,
etc., which we carried all the way in an old nosebag hooked on
pommel of saddle. Its value was only about $2.00, but I need the
stuff. Sore back dope, zinc ointment, nux vomica, turpentine,
ginger, grooming tools.

I caught a ride back to Harrisonburg with a local Doctor, and
went to the old warehouse, but the kit was not there. I asked
about all the boys in town. None of them knew anything of it.
I asked the old man who talks to himself. He brought me out a
torn old gunny sack which I'd left. I got a ride most of the way
back to Manifest. I had left my pack hanging on the box of
an old sled, well covered in case of rain. It was gone. A man
soon told me he had put it into a nearby shed. A bunch of hogs
had been helping themselves to the contents. Not a great deal
of damage was done.

Still I am lucky. Suppose Queen had had something worse
than ticks to turn back for? Suppose she had died with that
obstruction? Suppose she had swallowed the glass? Suppose I
had lost my haversack with Traveler's Checks, book of signatures,
notebook and all?

August 3, '27, 11 a.m.
8 mi. N.E. Alexandria

Yesterday morning I had rigged up an old tin lard bucket to
use temporarily until I got something more suitable for my
horse kit. Luckily I had not yet replaced many of the articles,
for somehow it too was lost off the hook on the saddle. This is
the third disaster, large and small, since we were turned back.
If I believe in the old superstition I'd say this ended the
accidents for a while.

Just now we are camped during the heat of the day under some pine trees beside a creek. Many of the creeks we've passed the last day or two were really nice and clear. We were coming through some hills. But now we seem to be getting back into swampy country.

Last night and again now I took a chance on letting Queen eat grass. No cases of charbon seem to have been heard of within twenty or thirty miles. Hay that is fit to feed a horse is very hard to procure. Oats I can generally get at about three cts. While waiting here we've been taking a general wash-up. With only the clothes I wear this is some little problem, beside the highway. And I don't care much about playing Adam in the Garden of Eden back in the woods for fear of poison vegetation and possibly poison snakes and insects, and mosquitoes. I've been promenading about with my old raincoat as a dressing robe, but it's awful hot for that. Just now I am sitting on a log, back to the road, in my light underwear and the old raincoat draped gracefully over part of me like Adam's fig leaf. Some of the passing tourists glance at me as though they thought me a "Nature faker." Still, as I've some clothes on they haven't anything on me—in fact I haven't much on myself.

Aug. 4, '27, Alexandria.

Got here to the Central Dipping Station at R.R. terminus, 3 mi. S.E. of the city, last night about 6 o'clock, after having gone 2 miles out of my way by suggestion of a policeman. Everybody had just gone home. All I could do was tie Queen to a fence and feed her some hay. I hit the loose gravel under a shed and so put in rather a "rocky" night of it.

I got up early and resumed my regular occupation (of late) of looking Queen over for ticks. I found some too, that must have gotten on her during the night. As this is where the cattle are brough to be dipped for ticks it is not strange that the outside and outer pens are "dirty."

About 8 a.m. Mr. Cotton, Federal Inspector, looked Queen over. Once I feared I'd be held 7 days when he seemed to have "found something." But he said it wasn't a fever tick. So they dipped Queen and gave me a tick-free certificate. I also have a health certificate from Dr. H. S. Burton.

And now we are ready to give Queen a ride to Natchez, 100

miles, after we have been within thirty miles of there. We
backtraced a weary 82 miles. I considered changing our course
back to the original, that is, via Baton Rouge. But that would
take us through one tick infested district after another and
there would not be much chance of traveling her through. I'd
be held up at Baton Rouge, again at the Alabama line, probably
at Fla. line, and finally going from Fla. into Ga. At all or any of
them we'd be held from 1 to 7 days. Added to this the fact that
these ticks sometimes *kill* a horse, and the danger of both charbon and foot-evil—which really is not "Foot and Mouth
Disease,"—both of which are prevalent and some places raging
(especially the charbon) in most of the low-lying country
through which we would pass, and I don't believe there would
be any chance of getting Queen through. As it is, going the
other route, we can by detouring still further north about 100
miles, go clear around the tick infested areas and come back
south, and as luck will have it, just touch one little part of
northern Florida that is "tick free" and then north.

On account of all this delay and all these detours our original
schedule is "shot all to pieces." We mean to get back *sometime*,
and will do well at that.

Besides lost time *this* side trip is only costing $32.35, most of
which is freight. And the boys here "saved" me all unnecessary
cost at that.

The fight against the Texas fever tick has been long and
arduous on the part of states and Fed. and the area has been
narrowed down greatly. I am told by Dr. Burton that if every
last animal in all infested areas were properly dipped every 30
days for one year the Texas fever tick would be eradicated. Every
tick "picked up" would thus be killed and any chancing to
remain in the ground would starve to death. So much for ticks.

We expect to get our mail in Natchez tomorrow so I'll not
mail this until then. Love.

(Signed) Frank.

From Signature Book: "Alexandria, La., Aug. 4, 1927. Frank
M. Heath arrived here at the Central Dipping Sta. at the stockyards last night with bay mare known as Gypsy Queen. We
dipped her at 9:15 a.m. today after inspection by J. W. Cotton,
Federal Inspector. Mr. Heath is shipping his horse via M. P. to

Natchez tonight as the only possible way of getting her out of the Tick Infested Area.

(Signed) L. P. Jordan, Mgr. R.R.,
Alexandria, La.
4 p.m., Aug. 4, 1927."

How do they go about dipping? The animals go down out of the pen or corral into which suspected animals are taken, then through a chute which must be ten or fifteen feet deep in the deepest place, that is in the middle, then up at about the same grade, and into the pen that is intended to receive the animals after dipping. The chute is, I would say, about three feet wide—anyway wide enough for any animal to go through, the slope being about 20 or 30 degrees, supplied, of course, with cleats to keep the animal from slipping. The partitions between the two pens, and in fact all round each pen, consist of corrugated galvanized iron, set on end well imbedded in the earth, so as to make it impossible for ticks to escape from the dirty pen or get into the clean pen.

In preparing to dip Queen, I noticed that the men sized up her height with her head as high as she could hold it, and added to the dipping fluid in the chute or vat enough to insure that Queen would have to be entirely immersed in it, including her ears. We started Queen down, myself after her with a rope in my hand. I preferred to do this chasing myself, to keep her moving. She went part way up, stopped nearly exhausted. I punched her along. I was keeping out of the liquid myself by having one foot on each of the girders that supported the tank on each side. I was glad when she was out of it, and I guess she was too.

Soon after this dipping, Queen's epidermis began to peel off somewhat. If I curried her ever so lightly, there was a little sloughing off of the skin, one might say a fine black dandruff, if that expresses it. I had to be very careful how I handled her skin. She was very nervous. I can't say that it affected the hair adversely.

Of all the friendly people, whether officials or merchants, railroad men or others, that I have ever met, in a pretty good sized city, I never met any better than in Alexandria. The boys at the plant saved me, legitimately, quite an expense that I would ordinarily have had in sanding the car.

Nobody treated me with charity, but I bet the oats I bought weighed much more than they were supposed to weigh, and so on.

Collinston, La., Aug. 5, '27.

Dear Folks:

Left Alexandria last night. 5 a.m. found me here, where we lay until 10 a.m. We are about 92 mi. N.W. of Natchez, so we must not have progressed far during the night. Queen is O.K. though restless. It's rather too hot in the car. But fortunately it's partly cloudy. I packed water quite a distance for her, and must carry more. This is low-lying country. Some darkies are cultivating corn by the track. It is only about knee high. Planted late on account of flood. They say it may "make" by some time in Nov. —if it don't freeze. We have passed corn the last few days that was about ripe, on the higher land.

There is a little red "jigger" or something like it, all through this country that gets onto a fellow, takes a firm hold and hangs on like a mortgage. They are quite interesting.

Later, P.M. We have turned S.E. and are paralleling the H'y. over which we came about 10 days ago.

6 p.m. We are at Cissely Island. Here we keep across the river to Clayton. You recollect here is where we detoured via Harrisonburg and Jonesville in trying to get to Vidalia across from Natchez. We—on the R. R.—are paralleling the Hy. over which we could not pass. It is still impossible. They are restoring the gravel from both ends and putting in a temporary bridge or two. The water has mostly receded. But still, in the gaps where the bridges were, are great muddy, slimy chasms. * * * * The grade is cut into ridges by the flood in every conceivable fashion, as though the devil had wreaked an unholy vengeance upon it. At the time we detoured around this grade I had to curb my impatience. I had had—just for a minute—a notion to try to wade the water on the grade and swim the gaps where once were bridges. But I gave it up as a foolhardy risk. Now as I view the gruesome effect of flood on grade I shudder at the very idea of having considered it.

7 p.m. We are in Vidalia. The watermarks high up on the Bldgs. have mostly been removed. The town has resumed activities. The big sawmill is running. The side tracks are full of carloads of great hardwood, products of the surrounding country. All day we have been passing carloads and trainloads of logs. Also we passed a number of sawmills. Lumbering is indeed one of the chief industries of these parts.

Here at Vidalia I parted company with one of the finest men

I have ever met. He is Mr. L. R. Conner, conductor on local freight, Collinston to Vidalia. He is a great lover of horses and anything beautiful or noble. * * * *

(Toward the last of our ride together Conductor Conner began asking me some questions about my financial affairs, if this dipping wasn't making a hole in my schemes, and so on. I told him that it sure was setting me back, counting cash, including expenses during delay, etc., probably fifty dollars.

"Can you make it on through?" he asked me.

"Lord, I hope so. I'll have to do something. I can't give it up now."

"I like that. And for the reputation of the horse I want to see you win. Now for instance—" and there he hesitated.

I came right to the point. I said, "If you mean that if you were certain I was all right, you would advance me some money, I am going to give you some references."

"That is what I wanted to say," he said, "but I didn't want to offend anybody. Mind, I seldom have much loose change, but—well, suppose you give me two or three references from your home town, and later send me your forwarding address, and so on."

I have no record of the references I gave. I am sure one was Brooke Lee, at that time Speaker of the Maryland House of Representatives, another was Joseph C. Cissel, and I believe also the Silver Spring National Bank.)

9 p.m. They are moving us over to Faraday to the R. R. ferry.

Aug. 6, '27. Cloudy, warm. 5 a.m. finds us on R. R. track at Faraday. We slept in the car—under our "bar."

7:30. We are crossing the Miss. R.

8:15. We are across on the Miss. side. Queen is all saddled and packed and "rearing to go" whenever we get to stock yards at Natchez.

Noon (Aug. 6). Got over ferry and out on the ground again about 9 a.m. Find people at C. of C., newspaper and all very courteous. This is a nice city.

Got all kinds of mail. Five letters from you. Have read only the last as yet—will peruse the others after getting started, while Queen rests in the shade. I doubt if La. is any hotter than you reported there. We are through the *pests* now, I believe. We hit Jackson from here—going that far N. to avoid tick area. (We hit Tenn. in 1925.) Must hit N. W. Florida. Address us next at

Meridian, La. [Error—I meant Meridian, Miss.] Must close now.
Love,

(Signed) Frank.

From Signature Book: "Natchez, Miss., 8/6/27. Frank M.
Heath with bay mare Gypsy Queen passed through Natchez today en route to Alabama and Florida. Both in good shape.

(Signed) W. G. Powell, Manager,
Natchez Association of Commerce."

20 Mi. N. E. Natchez, Miss.,
Sunday, Aug. 7, '27.

Mr. & Mrs. E. R. Thomas,
Garfield, N. M.

Dear Friends:

* * * * Yesterday after getting into Natchez about 9 (?)
a.m. I went to the C. of C. to get a map rigged out to guide us
around all "tick areas." This route takes us way north again to
Jackson and Meridian, Miss., E. to Montgomery, then south to
Florida. I was interviewed by the Natchez Democrat. Next I
called at the Postoffice, got my letters, sent off two, wrote five
postal cards, took out my parcels post package, which I'd forwarded from Vicksburg, got what I needed out of it and remailed it to Meridian.

This done, I got a bite to eat, bought a few eatables to replenish my grub kit, found some oats for Queen, and started
back to the stock pen where I'd left her tied in the shade of an
oil tank. It was 3 p.m. when I found her among the somewhat
intricate tangle of ferry landings and R. R. yards. Queen is not
feeling well since her dipping at a Federal Dipping Sta. at
Alexandria. She refused her oats. But we started at 4 p.m. Queen
suffered much from the heat, though I walked most of the way
and held her back. She panted badly and did not sweat—a bad
symptom. We only made to a creek E. of the little town of
Washington, about 9 miles. The first mile or two after leaving
the heart of the city was through a colored district. I never before saw such a conglomeration of small shops presided over by
African-American negroes. I've seen many Mexican quarters and
Filipino quarters in which the populace were catered to by their
own race. Heretofore I've most always noticed the American

negro patronizing a middleman of a lighter complexion. Out about 2½ miles east we took a dirt road that is admittedly ½ mile longer in order to avoid 4 miles of gravel. This road is rather a narrow lane shaded most of the way by tall trees. The small farms that are carved out of the woods along the way are cultivated mostly by the negroes. I passed the residences of but two white families that I know of in about 4 miles.

An understanding seems to exist between white and colored. They do not "mix." The black may work for the white, rent land of him, trade with him—but not get familiar.

Queen seemed suffering for water on this 4 mile stretch. I was pretty thirsty myself. I hailed a negro who was passing in his inevitable one-hoss wagon. "Next house to the left, suh. White folks live there. You'll be perfectly safe stoppin' there."

When I came near, the old negro hailed me with "White folks not home." (He'd tried to hail them for me.) "Stop at this next place to the right. She'll give you a drink." A neat looking young colored woman met me half way to the gate with a glass of cold water. We found water for Queen at a pool. Some time after I arrived at the creek near Washington, Queen again refused her oats. Again this morning at 3 o'clock she refused her oats. 4 a.m. we hit the pike. Queen seemed in good heart in spite of her fast. We made 11 miles to Coles Creek, arriving about 8 a.m. About 6 miles back we again left the graveled highway—No. 61—and are saving about 7 miles in distance, all of which would have been gravel, in reaching our next town, Fayette. About 6 a.m. I hailed the broad side of a whitewashed house. An old gray negress appeared—barefooted—which is nothing uncommon in either sex of any age. I had been directed to take a "right fork." I thought I was a little previous, counting the time we had traveled and the probable distance to the fork. But miles, like time, in the country, are loosely considered. So I inquired.

"I's been yah evah since I's bo'n'd" quoth the old negress, "I's nevah been three mile up dat road. But ah reckon de sto' you speak of am about 2 mile up de road. De man dah can tell you about de dirt road."

"The "sto" is run by a colored man, also a filling sta. He was both courteous and concise. By his direction I passed certain land marks and turned abruptly into a deep narrow cut. The road from there runs for the most part between trees large and small of many varieties. The branches interlocked overhead much of the distance. Wild grape, Virginia creeper, trumpet vine and other vines festoon the leafy ceiling. The sumac turns up a red nose at one. The faint odor of sassafras is in the air. Pine, oak, (many varieties) cedars and maple, ash, walnut, hickory, willow, locust, sycamore, cottonwood, sweet gum, elm, wood of paradise and some other trees all get along harmoniously together in wild profusion. I'll not attempt to name the profusion of undergrowth. Wherever there is a little opening, Johnson grass and Bermuda seem to be vying with each other. The steep banks of the deep cuts through the hills are reinforced in many instances by the shrubs and roots of trees. In the little valleys nestling among the hills are little farms or patches. Upon some of these the crops of cotton seem rather indifferent as to whether we shall wear clothes or not. Style seems to be contagious. In other patches the outlook is a little better. Negroes seem to be working most of the land (some of them own it) in a more or less indifferent manner. Some corn too is very poor, though I saw one or two small pieces of excellent corn nearly ripe. Sweet potatoes do very well, and are largely grown, as is other "truck."

This is a lovely spot in which we are camped, a beautiful opening on the north bank of Coles Creek. Water, grass, shade and wood are in abundance. A kind of gray moss that I can't name hangs in great strings from some of the largest trees. The place is part of the farm of Jim Perryman, colored.

* * * * I thought we were about out of the dangerous places, but Jim Perryman just told me of a horse having dropped dead yesterday, over on the main road about a mile from here, presumably from charbon. * * * * We find we are still in the post-flood area, which means this whole country about here is more or less infested with the dread disease. There only remains this township in which we are that is not quarantined. Ticks on our right, charbon on our left along the Miss. river. And it is strongly rumored that the authorities will declare a quarantine early tomorrow. I've been told that by half a dozen people. But whether the lid will be clamped down at 12 midnight or later is not certain. If they catch us within the line it means we stay here indefinitely. They had a similar quarantine not many years ago. An animal is not allowed to move off the farm on which it belongs and the law is rigidly enforced. Just what that would

mean to us in case we should be caught in this trap—well, we don't intend to be so caught if we can help it.

Aug. 8, '27, at Loman, Miss.

This is about 20 miles from where I wrote you yesterday. We pulled our freight last night at 10:30 p.m. We had gotten detailed directions from Jim Perryman as to getting on through the "back country" to Fayette. First we were to follow the dim track to the first "right fork" at which place there is a church on the right and a schoolhouse on the left. Here by crossing the Hy. and taking a lane to our right we would again avoid the hard footing. Then more intricate directions, all of which I scrawled largely on an old envelope.

Well, we started. * * * *

I inquired whether we were on the right track, and found that we were. * * * *

I came to a bunch of rural mail boxes Perryman had told me of. I struck a match and glanced at the "chart." We were right. Another "fork" or two and another look or two at the chart, and we were on the Hy. leading to Fayette, the county seat. Soon we reached the suburbs. Most all night the country had reminded me of some weird story of the jungles. The sudden contrast of the beautiful plaza seemed almost unbelievable.

I had intended to slip quietly through the county seat but— just another of those little surprises that make life interesting.

Our map of Miss. shows the Hy. running *straight* on through Fayette, but actually the Hy. made an abrupt right turn southward. Now we could not well afford to bear south across our general course for the simple reason that to do so would take us across the well patrolled line back into the tick infested area from which we had with such difficulty escaped. It was 3 a.m. Not a soul was in sight. Finally I saw a light in the back room of a bake shop and entered. I ran slap dab into the city marshal. He put me on the right track, which was the one that jogged— in spite of the map—for half a mile, then on again on the course shown on the map. The marshal seemed a right fine fellow. As he made no sign of detaining us I knew the quarantine was not yet declared.

"Not yet," he replied to my guarded inquiry. " 'Fraid they'll have to. You'll be well out of this township by daylight. Luck to you." And as we were now out of the post-flood area we hope we are now done with charbon.

At 6 a.m. we stopped and fed and made a cup of hot coffee at another point in Coles Creek, which we crossed on a bridge. Queen's appetite was a little better. At 9 a.m. we pulled into the shade of some giant oaks at Cohen Bros., at Loman, Miss. This is a one-firm town but they are reasonable and very obliging.

We had traveled 20 miles (possibly 22). The resources as I jot them in memorandum book are, "patches" to near Fayette, then larger farms. Cotton, corn, truck, dairying, crops fair, some lumbering, all kinds timber including a little good pine.

Later: Queen and I are both dead for sleep. I just approached her where she was chumming up to an old horse under a tree. She seemed in a troubled doze. As I stood looking at her in sympathy, she half awoke and made for me like an infuriated tiger, as though I had submitted to her subconscious mind some terrible dream. Poor Queen—I kept the old buggy between us until the spell was broken, then led her off and tied her to a swinging limb in more restful environments. She *must have* a little more sleep. And I too must hit the sod, where the little red ants will awaken me soon enough, sleepy as I am.

Very truly yours,
(Signed) Frank M. Heath.

From Notes. August 12, '27: * * * * 7 a.m., Ar'd place of Jessie Hurst, W. side Jackson.

Traveled: 10 mi. * * * *

Special Note: * * * *

Total to Jackson, 9,828 miles [As corrected]

Later: over to city. Saw Police, arranged to go through unmolested. Saw Jackson News. Also got tick map.

It was at the Chamber of Commerce in Jackson that I got a map showing the tick quarantine area, the line between the free area and the infested, or red area, as it was called. In fact, the so-called "red area" is marked red on the map. This map shows also the former quarantine area at the time the work began in 1906, twenty years before, by a red line.

3 Mi. W. Merton,
36 Mi. W. Meridian, Miss.,
Aug. 15, '27—4:45 p.m.

My dear Mr., Mrs. Thomas—Family:

I've not heard from you since I last wrote. In fact, I've not reached my "next address"—so how could I?

But here goes for a few lines anyhow. So many little (?) things have happened to Queen lately, any of which might have ended disastrously, that I feel like voicing my wonder at our narrow escape. All at once the "luck" changed from petty annoyance at small losses financially to real trouble.

On Aug. 9th we had traveled 29 miles. We had escaped being caught by the charbon quarantine by a margin of a few miles. A comparatively narrow strip let us out between that and the "tick area." It being cool that day we had traveled until nearly night, notwithstanding we started 11:30 the night before. The farther we put the flooded area behind us the better. * * * * *

Queen seemed to be holding up pretty well in spite of her loss of appetite after her dipping. But we were both half dead for sleep. It had been raining all day and looked like more rain. With the permission of the owner, Mr. D. R. Young, we were camping at an old house in a large pasture on a large farm. I had grassed and fed Queen well and tied her to the one end of the old house where she had a nice sod for a bed. I'd stretched the "bar" and hoped for one long solid sleep until about midnight. It was hot and I was dressed very scantily indeed. I had hardly closed my eyes when a commotion outside announced the arrival of a few horses and mules that were in the large pasture. I had hoped they would stay away. Queen, like myself, was not in a humor to entertain company, while the other horses and even mules seemed intent upon hearing all about us. There was no getting rid of this gossiping bunch except to move Queen. In the road there was a wide grassy place and many small trees. I was just about to dress and tie Her Royal Highness to one of these trees, when appeared the farm teamster, an obliging darky. To save my dressing he volunteered to take Queen out and tie her for me on his way home. I knew better, but weakly I consented, impressing upon him the vital necessity of tying Queen short so that she could not become entangled. Scarcely had I closed my sleepy eyes when I heard someone (I believe it was a man camping just over the fence) say, "That old man's horse is tangled up." Sticking my head out of the door I asked him to please untie her quickly. I met the colored fellow who keeps a small store near by leading her. In the semi-darkness I felt a moisture under her left hind fetlock—a rope burn. That was six days ago, and with persistent care and zinc ointment the sore-

404 FORTY MILLION HOOFBEATS

ness is getting out of it. We have traveled right along. I'll never trust anyone else to tie her.

On Aug. 11th, the next day but one after getting the rope burn, we were camping at a shack where had once been a saw-mill, 10 miles W. of Jackson. We had started that morning at 1:30 and covered 26 miles, largely in the hot sun, arriving at 12:30 p.m. Mr. P. Y. Hammett, owner of the shack, had corn right up to the road on one side, and a Mr. O. M. Gelp, who proved very neighborly, on the other. A little grass grew between some logs in the roadway. I tied Queen to the rim of a very heavy old logging truck wheel. In her normal state she probably could not, certainly would not, have moved it a foot. I heard a noise and looked up just in time to see Queen flying down the road, the wheel bumping her heels at every jump. I came up with her in about a quarter of a mile. The rim had bounced off the grade into the mud of the broad ditch. Queen was badly unnerved and her hind legs and ankles badly bruised and skinned, especially the left, on which side she had "drug" the wheel by the neck rope. But what gave me the most concern was a rent at the top of the opposite hoof on the inside, about two inches in length. This was a nasty wound in a dangerous place. I got Queen quieted down, washed the mud off her, trimmed the loose pieces of skin with my pocket knife, and daubed the wounds well with zinc oxide powder—which I am seldom without—mixed with lard.

Poor Queen! I just then began to realize fully how terribly she had been upset since her dipping. I wonder if in addition to the effect of the dip on her delicate skin she did not absorb too much of the poison. Certain it is that she seemed to possess a false energy. I petted and consoled her as best I could. She seemed in considerable pain, did not care for grass, but begged for oats. Then she was determined to strike out on our backward track. Time and again I headed her off and tried to get her to pick a little grass. But she seemed to say plainly: "Frank, I'm going home. There have so many things happened to me in the past two weeks that I'm plumb discouraged." She has never acted so before—or since.

"Poor old girl," I said to her, "I don't blame you. I want to go home myself. Everybody always wants to go home when they're out o' luck. But the way we came is a long, long trail. This is the best way home, the shortest now," pointing in the direction we were traveling. (And I want to tell you that always when we hit the trail she takes the trail in the right direction.) Finally I seemed to make her understand and she seemed reconciled to her task. I've promised her, you know, her ease the rest of her life after she finishes, in spite of all handicaps, this trip. Several times recently people have tried to buy her "after the trip is ended." She is not for sale—or ever will be.

Once more I note that a great many people, some of whom really understand a horse pretty well, would pooh pooh the idea that I made Queen understand that backtracking would be the wrong and the long way home, whereas straight ahead would be much shorter. As the horse's mental make-up is generally understood even by those who do understand it well, my statement that she understood what I was trying to tell her might seem like bunk. It would have seemed like bunk to me before I had this continued experience of studying a horse's psychology, for we can call it nothing else. Candidly and sanely I believe that while she could not understand all this language, she got my *thought* psychically.

Early the morning after this last accident we hit the trail; slowly we crawled along into Jackson (10 miles) and arrived there 7 a.m. I thought best to get her to where I could take care of her. But a good place seems hard to find. She was not as sore as I had feared she would be, so we left Jackson the same night at 7 o'clock, intending to make it to some sylvan spot some one had told us about, just across Pearl River. Bivouacked several hours in the night. Paused again for breakfast. But did not reach a suitable camping place until noon. We had traveled 25 miles to a creek in the W. suburbs of Palahachie. Here indeed was a place in which to rest, one of those lovely spots we read about. A creek, deep shade, and open spaces with beautiful grass. The town too seemed "friendly" and not overly inquisitive. And to my joy Queen seemed no worse for the travel. In fact I believe a little travel is good for her (but I don't like these long days). I give her time, feed her moderately, "tone her up" with a little nux vomica, and keep the wounds well anointed. She is drawing on her wonderful stamina.

From Notes. August 17, '27: Clear, hot. * * * * 10 a.m., Ar'd Meridian. Camping near Morgan Hardwood Co., ½ mi. S. of depot.

Traveled: 24 mi. (1 to camp and return) No. 80. Hilly, few mi. under construction. Pave 5 mi. gravel (side 2 mi.), R. I. dirt 4 mi., dirt 15 mi. First few mi. good places, large fine houses. Cotton, corn. Then a stretch of wooded hills, little cultivation.

Special note. * * * *

Total to Meridian (counting extra mile camp and return) 9,929 [as corrected].

Later went to city C. of C. (Chamber of Commerce). Saw State and Federal Inspectors. (Name on map.) * * * *

From Signature Book: "Aug. 18th, 1927. Frank M. Heath passed through Toomsuba, Miss., 13 miles east of Meridian, Miss. on So. Ry. I saw the bay mare Gypsy Queen and she was in fine shape as well as rider. I enjoyed a chat with Frank.

(Signed) G. A. J. Price,
Toomsuba, Miss."

Cuba, Ala., Aug. 18, '27.

Dear Folks:

Yours of 11th reached me yesterday at Meridian, Miss. My next address—about Aug. 29, will be Tracy, Ala. * * * *

Well, I had quite a scare yesterday. We got into Meridian, Miss. about noon. I soon found a good shady place in the S. suburbs. After dining upon a log and feeding Queen, I piled saddle and all things that would be damaged by rain on the log and covered them with the old rain coat. Mr. Smith, at whose corral I got water, advised me to put the things in his shed. But as I've never had anything stolen but once (a fountain pen—oh yes, and a Bob Ingersoll at the Carnival in 1925) I had formed the habit of believing our outfit bore "a charm against thieves."

I went over to the city and spent more time than I expected in finding both state and federal inspectors. If there were any rigamarole to go through in passing into Ala. I wanted to know it. I also went meanwhile to the Chamber of Commerce to get an Ala. map and mark out the tick infested area on it, so I could lay out our route around it. The "Federal Tick Map" gives only the counties, which leaves a stranger all at sea as to the cities and roads until the two maps are coordinated. I found out finally that all I have to do here is to keep out of tick area—or rather quarantine area. Passing from Ala. may be different. While we are on the subject, "tick free area" does not always mean that there are no ticks in that area. It means—along the border—that those counties that are not quarantined are *dipping*. I passed through two and yesterday morning I picked 8 or 10 good healthy ticks off Queen. I am a little surprised that I did not require an inspection before coming into Ala. *Had* they inspected us and found a tick it would have been one that I could not find—beforehand.

In these counties that dip I understand that dipping every so often is compulsory. Lines are ridden by county employes, they tell me, and all cattle that are not brought in by the owners are rounded up, dipped and sold to the highest bidder. I am told this has been going on for many years, and still there are ticks. Comment withheld.

Well, getting back, I got back to camp. I found everything thrown helter skelter, and it had been raining—except the saddle and bed roll. They were gone. Mr. Smith, team owner, and a Mr. Harp came to try to solve the problem. I was nearly sweating blood. It would take my last dollar to replace the stolen articles—and then some. * * * * "I told you they were not safe out here," said Mr. Smith. "These niggers will steal anything that is loose, sell it if they can."

"It's probably hidden somewhere about in the brush, waiting for darkness," quoth Mr. Harp.

"It was here not over half an hour ago," said Mr. Smith.

I started hopelessly looking about in the weeds. I wanted time to think—to find some clue. I knew it would be useless to speak to the Police without a clue.

"See this track?" I heard Mr. Harp say to Mr. Smith. Pretty soon Smith called to me, "Here's your saddle!" They had followed the faint trail through the wet weeds, grass and brush.

I tried to express my appreciation of the recovery. After a hurried consultation it was decided to leave the bait, but watch it, while Smith went to the Police, although we knew that the thief might be taking in our movements all the time from cover.

Anyhow it proved to be just outside the jurisdiction of the City Police. A justice of the peace in the district suggested that "I better get my saddle and bed roll while the getting was good." I did so—and slept under a garage shed out of the rain. I left there 1 a.m.

Coatapa, Ala., Aug. 19, '27.

Nothing more has happened. Making good time now. Queen fine. Love, (Signed) Frank.

Chapter VIII

DIXIELAND

8 Mi. W. Demopolis, (Ala.)
Aug. 20, '27.

Dear Folks:

* * * *

Nearly all day yesterday and today I passed "patches" cleared
out of the woods and planted to above mentioned crops. Except
some fields are vacant. Many log shacks there are and board
shacks and old houses. In most of these lives a family of darkies.
If the colored race is depreciating it don't look like it here. And
they seem quite satisfied and happy in their own peculiar way.
The white people too seem well pleased at the way things are
going. Leave them alone, say I. A few own their own places. If
they as a whole are "well controlled" they don't seem to know
it.

A fairly bright looking colored boy of about 14 (I should
judge—though he does not seem to know his age) just stopped
to tender us the use of their well, "if I needs any watah." The
conversation turned upon our trip. He pronounced Queen to be
a "sho' nuff fine hoss." When I told him she had traveled
nearly 10,000 miles he could hardly realize so great a distance.
He began to remonstrate: "Nine thousand, ten hund'ed an—
how fah did you say, boss?"

"Say, boy," I asked, "How many hundred does it take to make
a thousand?"

"I don't know, suh." Yet as he wears glasses I had thought
him a student.

"Don't you go to school?"

"Yes suh."—And there you are.

"What do you do?"

"We fa'ms—dis nex' place yah."

"Own it?"

"No suh."

"Oh, you rent it then?"

"No suh, we works it on de halves." And this is a true conversation.

I forgot to mention, the houses or shacks for the most part have no windows. They have board shutters on hinges. Some have gauzy looking curtains showing artistic-like when the shutters are open. I do not mean to say this is a hardship or necessarily a sign of extreme poverty. Why after all shut out the balmy honeysuckle-perfumed breezes? This is Dixie. Some, but not necessarily all, go bare-footed. Hookworm is not so evident. The darkies seem rather neat, and look to be well fed and content. Why worry? Love,

(Signed) Frank.

[Conclusion of letter to the Thomases, beginning August 15th.]

Prairieville, Ala.,
9 Mi. E. Demopolis,
Aug. 21, '27 (P.M.)

No more accidents—to Queen. Going right along. Queen's legs nearly well. Back on her appetite. Write me at Troy, Ala. Best wishes,

(Signed) F. M. H.

From Signature Book: "Selma, Ala., Aug. 23, 1927. Frank M. Heath arrived here at 1 p.m. today riding his bay mare Gypsy Queen and is staying until tomorrow.

(Signed) J. I. Sadler,
Proprietor K Shoe Shop,
526 Jess Davis Ave."

From Notes. August 27, '27: Clear, fairly cool. * * * * 4:15, Ar'd Ramer via New State Rd. to Snowden, 11 mi., cross country road to Ramer, 15.

Traveled: 25 mi. (maybe 26)—Hilly to level. * * * * Blacksmith at Ramer wanted to tell me how I wanted Queen shod. Am passing on. * * * *

Sunday, August 28, '27: Fairly cool. Leaving camp 5:40. 10:45, Stopped in pasture 2 mi. E. shady grove, 2 lbs. oats, 3 ears new corn, boiled rice, bread, coffee, onion, wild crabapple. The latter

the sourest damned thing I ever tasted. Cash getting low—eking
out on most anything. 2:30, Ar'd Shellhorn, Ala., 9 mi. N.W.
Troy, store of Mr. J. R. Cochran, local, via country roads. Hilly.
    Traveled: 17 miles. * * * *Alternating dotted prairie, pine,
oak, mostly poor soil. Cotton, corn, sweet potatoes, peanuts,
cows. Lumbering. Camping near mill pond—grist mill of Mr.
J. R. Cochran. Cleaning up Queen—1 hr. in pond.

From Signature Book: "Shellhorn, Ala., Aug. 28, 1927. Frank
M. Heath and his bay mare Gypsy Queen staying over night.
                                              (Signed) J. R. Cochran."

THE MONTGOMERY ADVERTISER
(*Montgomery, Alabama*)
Sunday, August 28, 1927

HORSE AND MASTER VISITS 42 STATES ON
COUNTRY TOUR

An unusual, or rather two unusual travelers, spent Friday at Montgomery. They were Frank M. Heath, of Silver Springs, Md., and his
saddle horse, Gypsy Queen, who are making a horseback tour, touching the 48 states of the union and claim to have accomplished travel
in 42 of the 48 states. * * * *

    From Notes. August 29-'27:—Fairly cool. * * * 9 a.m. to
10 a.m., in Troy.—Hard time getting feed.—5th store found
"sweet feed" retail.—Others would not break sack.—Interviewed
by "Standard. * * * * 5 p.m., Ar'd Brundige, via country roads
and 2 mi. H'y.—Hilly.
    Traveled: 23 mi., Pave 2 mi.—Dirt, R. I. 10 mi.—Dirt 11 mi.—
Dotted prairie.—Red, sandy soil, sandstone subsoil.—Cotton,
peanuts, corn, sweet potatoes.—All poor to fair.—Cows.—
Brundige is a live place, live people. * * * *
    Aug. 30-'27:—Fairly cool.—Having Queen shod all around
new.—Leaving Brundige 10 a.m. * * * *

    From Notes. September 1-'27:—* * * * 8 a.m., in Midland.
—Bought 4 lbs. oats, 15 cts.—9 a.m., Met Mrs. Wm. M. Mc-
Pherson of Pinckard, Ala., local, 2 mi. E. Midland City, straw-
berry farmer, hubby, farmer.—Wants story or stories.—Invited

me back to dinner—rd. side, 5 mi. N.W. Dothan.—Later Ar'd Dothan via No. 7.—Rolling.

Traveled: 18 mi.—Dirt or rock.—Better country, mostly grayish soil.—Timber.—Cotton, peanuts, corn, cowpeas, hogs.—Few prosperous looking fruit trees.—Little Johnson grass, Bermuda crop.

Special Notes: * * * * TOTAL TO DOTHAN, ALA., 10,219 miles [as corrected].

Note: All across La., Miss., Ala., have been a few scattering fig and peach trees, sorghum cane, or farther S.E. little patch sugar cane for local use.—A few cows of course, chickens and pigs.—Colored churches, school houses, mostly ramshackle.—Cotton pickers here get $1.00 per bat.

September 2-'27:—Hot.—Slept bum in open near service sta., N. suburbs Dothan.—Ants.—Some rummy raving about "That man traveling for health—he'd show him, etc.—I paid little attention except that the fool kept me awake.—Queen rested well.

Leaving (Dothan) 5:30.—Met Mr. Powell on Hy., invited stay at his place returning from Fla.—9:30, Camping at Big Creek, 12 mi. S. Dothan.—Washing all clothing.—Leaving 1 p.m.—"Some boys."—4 p.m., Crossing into Fla.—5:30 p.m., Ar'd Campbellton, Fla., (Signature from Mayor White.)—via No. 7. —Rolling.

Traveled: 22 mi.—Dirt or sand, 17, pave 5 mi. (gravel side 4 mi.)—Fairly good land, cotton.—(Weevil taking lots of it.)— Corn, peanuts—harvesting them.—Corn, cotton nearly picked.— Sweet potatoes.—Some turpentine.—Little lumbering.—Camping N. of Campbellton in open.—No feed attainable except corn and middlings.

Special Note: * * * * TOTAL TO CAMPBELLTON, FLA., 10,241 miles [as corrected].

From Signature Book:—"Campbellton, Fla., Sept. 2, 1927.

Frank M. Heath arrived here at 5:30 p.m. today riding his bay mare Gypsy Queen and is staying in this town tonight.

(Signed) J. W. White,
Campbellton, Fla., Mayor."

From Notes. September 3-'27:—"Hot.—Leaving camp 3:30.— Again at Big Creek on way back to Dothan.—Out 10:15.—

Washed Queen thoroughly.—p. m., Ar'd farm of Mr. C. Powell,
2 mi. S.W. Dothan, via No. 7 except last mile.

Traveled: 21 mi. * * * *

Sunday, September 4-'27:—Hot.—Laying over today.—Queen
in pasture.—Powells had me in to supper. Note: Dothan is nice
live place—15,000.—Everybody sociable.—Traded at Weathers.
They are liberal.—Met Mr. J. M. Byrd, Box 485, representing
Purina Mills.—Writing Mr. L. R. Conner, Collinston, La.
* * * *"

From Signature Book:—"Dothan, Ala., Sept. 4, 1927.
I met Mr. Frank M. Heath on Fri., Sept. 2, as he was riding his
bay mare, Gypsy Queen, from Dothan south to Campbellton, Fla.,
and had a talk with him. Yesterday, September 3, he came (by invitation) to my farm here—2 mi. S.W. of Dothan—to lay over today Sunday, and rest his horse. He is returning from Fla. via Dothan
on his way into Ga.

(Signed) C. V. Powell,
By A. L. Childers, Neighbors."

Dothan, Ala., Sun., Sept. 4-'27.

Dear Folks:

Your letter addressed to Troy overtook me here yesterday. It
finds us headed straight for Washington. Friday we went 22 mi.
S. from here to Campbellton, Fla., thus hitting the 43rd state.
We just nicely had room to enter Fla., "and turn right around
and walk right out again" as the old song has it, without brush-
ing elbows with ticks. We are done, now, with ticks. Ticks! The
nasty little devils! What a lot, in many ways, they have cost us.

We backtracked to Dothan to keep as far away from ticks as
possible. Some time ago I "withheld comment" on ticks, quarantine, etc. I wanted to learn first what I was talking about. Now I
want to say that since we got miles away from the quarantine
line we have not encountered a single tick, though traveling in
territory that was once alive with them. The tick infested area
is only about half its original size. Let us hope the people will
continue to cooperate diligently with states assisted by the Federal until this scourge shall have been choked out.

From Dothan, long before the sun shows red above the horizon tomorrow morning we will be well on our way toward
Waverly Hall, Ga., (Get that—our next address). Atlanta we
hope to make late in this month.

In leaving Ala. I will say that in no state through which we have passed have I been more agreeably surprised. In lieu of the Alabaman who is the joke of the old time traveler, I find an industrious, open-minded—even liberal-minded people. Not once have I met with indignities from suspicious persons. In fact the attitude is almost entirely very friendly.

Friday, in going to Fla. I fell in with Mr. Chas. V. Powell, a man of 57 who was born near here and who has lived here most of his life. He invited me in returning to stop at his farm over Sunday—today—and as much longer as I would. So Queen today is having a good rest in grass to her eyes and fine deep shade whenever she cares to avail herself of it. Me, I am sitting in the shade of one of those grand old oaks so characteristic of the sunny South. This is the first day we have had off in over a month. It's hot and we enjoy the rest.

Mr. Powell is a character. So is his good wife. Each day I meet some adventure. If it is not of some other nature it is "human nature." Friday as I was hiking along beside Queen on a pretty fast walk, I heard for some distance the steady tread of a single animal which I knew instinctively to be the inevitable mule. Soon the mule passed us, walking "a blue streak." Seated each in a splint bottom chair—the common wagon seat in these parts, were Mr. and Mrs. Powell. Mr. Powell, rather interested in our unique way of travel, turned the mule over to the tender mercies of Mrs. Powell—or Mrs. Powell over to the tender mercies of the mule—slipped off the wagon and joined me for nearly a mile, ending in the invitation to their place.

The soil here—unlike some over which we have traveled in Ala., is pretty good, a gray sandy loam. Cotton, corn, peanuts, sweet potatoes, cowpeas, some kinds of beans, melons, yield a good return for the labor spent upon them. Hogs, cattle, horses, mules and poultry do very well.

When Mr. Powell was a boy roads were few and far between, —in fact there were none. The common means of transportation was the little old cart of wooden axle and wheels, home made drawn often-times by a "poor little yoke o' yearlings." It took as high as four days to make a trip to Columbia (20 mi.) the nearest trading point, or Eufala (?) a little farther away. Feeding on the dark, unnutritious wire grass of those early days, toiling through the unmarked trails, was not conducive to speed.

Today it is different. I haven't seen a team of oxen in Ala.

(There may be some—I don't know.) In Miss. I saw some in the lumber woods, but they are getting rid of them, and one—and only one—team of oxen in use on a farm. Mule teams in chain traces, driven with rope lines, seem to be the rule, horses sometimes, of course, or occasionally a horse and a mule.

Yesterday, Sat., P.M., being a self-appointed half-holiday, the roads—and they have roads here now—were full of these rigs going to or from town. White and colored about equally divided, and the rigs all pretty well loaded, for nearly everybody goes to town on Saturday afternoon. Sitting on sometimes a spring seat, but more often a board laid across the wagon box, or a cane bottom chair, all ages and both colors are having a good time. Often the colored folk are "catching a ride" with the white folks. And there seems to be no animosity, while there is a distinction.

In the city of Dothan, as in most Southern cities I have seen, is a large wagon yard. This, yesterday P.M. was literally full of horse and mule drawn rigs, including the old time buggy, which I had forgotten. Many is the rig that passed us with "head—(driver's head)—erect and feet stepping high." I was catching a ride with a man named Taylor Powell, a nephew of Mr. Chas. Powell, seated on the edge of the wagon box which seemed always at the point of buckling over and letting me down, while the one mule plodded happily along with this driver, the two boys, a neighbor and his fat wife whom they had "picked up" and yours truly. Being 2 miles out of the city I was on my way to lay in a week-end supply of Omolene, the best prepared horse-feed I've ever tried. We no doubt would have been welcome to a few feeds of Farmer Powell's corn—but I steer clear of corn for Queen when I can.

The young Mr. Powell, on learning that I had a horse, promptly tackles me for a swap. Swapping hosses is one of, if not the, favorite pastimes. All over the feed yard were little bunches of men bantering each other on a "hoss trade." Grinning darkies looking on—or perhaps participating. * * *

The grotesque language one hears related by people who never have been here—at least in recent years—one does not hear, specially among the younger generation. That different expressions as well as different customs and traditions prevail in different sections of our good old U. S. A. is true. That the people of Dixieland, probably unconsciously, through environment acquire a slight "dialect" from hearing the picturesque darky or perhaps from indulging in the amusing habit of mimicking them, is quite true. But the impossible jargon one never hears.

One thing sure, I'm getting a great kick out of Dixieland.
* * * *

Yes, you will both feel better as the weather cools.

Queen and I are both as well as usual. I'm afraid I'll have to again interrupt our trip to go for an exam. by Vets. Bureau. With love,

(Signed) Frank.

From Notes. September 5, '27: "Hot. Slept fairly in wagon shed. (No chg. formula.) Leaving 4:30. * * * * 3:30 [p. m.] Ar'd Columbia via No. 20. * * * *

Traveled: 24 mi.

September 6, '27: Leaving Columbia 4:15 a.m. 4:35 a.m., Crossing bridge over Chatahachee. Passing us free—toll 25 cts. 9:30, Ar'd Blakesley, Ga. * * * *

Traveled: (a.m.) 15 mi. * * * *

September 7, '27: Fairly cool. Slept in porch old house—good. Queen loose, mostly. * * * * 4:30, Ar'd Cuthbert. * * * *

Traveled: 21 mi. * * * *

September 8, '27: Rather hot. Little red ants chewed on me most of night in open in Pine Park. They seemed to take a rest 3 a.m. to 4 a.m. Queen tied to tree. Leaving camp 5 a.m. * * * * 4:20 p.m., Ar'd old house ¾ mi. (or more) N. Lumpkin. Camping. Water ¼ mi. Good grass.

Traveled: 21 mi. * * * *

September 9, '27: * * * * 12 noon, Ar'd Cusseta, Ga. * * * *

From Signature Book: "Cusseta, Ga. 9/9/27

I certify that Frank M. Heath together with Gypsy Queen is here camping on Court House Square. Both seem to be in first class condition and Frank is an interesting talker.

(Signed) F. M. Gordy, Mayor."

From Notes. Sunday, Sept. 11, '27: "Leaving camp under bridge, 1 a.m. 6 to 7 a.m., Nosebag, lunch, 12 mi. N. Columbus. 12 noon, Ar'd Waverly Hall via a tangle of roads getting by Columbus and New State Hy. to Atland. Hilly to level.

Traveled: 23 mi. Dirt. Pine, oak, other. Johnson grass, other grass. Cleared patches. Cotton, corn, etc. Many abandoned places. Red land, sassafras. Waverly friendly place. Old Wilson Rolay, colored, very obliging. A. C. Alexander gave out hay."

P.M., Whitehead opened office. Rec'd $20.00 from Conner, Collinston, La.—other letters. None from Joe or S. S. B. Boys fine.

From Notes. Sept. 12, '27: "Hot, slight shower in night. Queen lay down. Leaving Waverly Hall 3:30 a.m. 7:30, in crossing by bridge site on new Hy. to save detour, Queen slipped into narrow trench with left hind, front feet in a ditch. Greatly assisted by Amos Cartwright, a colored trusty in stripes, 3 mo. to do. This man was working alone. Send card to Hamilton, Ga., c/o W. P. Langford, Warden. Took nearly 1 hr. to wash red mud off Queen."

"You caint cross yere wid dat hoss. You has to go back roun' de detour," warned the colored trusty. The trusty, one of the hundreds of colored convicts working on the state highways in the South, was bailing the water out of a trench where the forms were in, ready for the new concrete abutments. On the opposite side of the small creek from us was a ditch into which the water of the creek had been "switched" (by means of the usual coffer-dam). This left a ridge (the coffer-dam) some two feet from the opening between the form and the bank of earth. This ridge, part of the coffer-dam, owing to a double turn in the dam, was, *at this place,* at right angles with the trench, just right for a trap for the hind foot if it slipped, and we should have noticed that. But at a casual glance it didn't look nearly so bad as many places we had crossed in saving a wide detour. It was necessary to follow that part of the dam running at right angles to the form, on account of other obstacles. I should have known that this little "grade" was slippery. Queen didn't like the layout, but I unintentionally lied to her—I told her it was "all right." Queen had a habit of treading a moment before leaping—a kind of fidgets. In treading this time, her hind foot slipped and wedged quite firmly between the bank of earth and the wooden form. Most horses very likely would have wrenched their leg out of joint—especially a high strung horse. But Queen lay right quiet in a very uncomfortable position, with one hind foot on the path, the other in the trap, and both front feet over in the ditch ahead of her. Her belly was resting on that part of the coffer-dam just beyond that which ran parallel with the trench and forming the second turn (the two turns forming a kind of abbreviated S).

"I tol' you you couldn't git dat hoss 'cross yere!"

"I'll admit I'm a damned fool and ought to be wearing your striped suit, but for Heaven's sake get a shovel quick."

He did so, and working dextrously, soon removed earth enough to release the foot. I packed clay under the foot.

"We's gwine have a hard time a lif'in' her out o' dat. I'll take hol' o' her tail an—"

But with one tremendous double leap, if that expresses it, Queen, from her very unnatural and unheard of position, had cleared that ridge across which she was lying, the ditch of about two feet in width in which her front feet had been, and the slippery bank of loose earth on the opposite side.

"Well suh, I'se been brung up wid hosses and I be darned if I'd a believed it, an' she done it herse'f widout no 'splainin'!"

"Do they give you tobacco in the—where you are?"

"Dey gives us all de chewin' we wants, or all de smokin' we wants. Dey don' give us bofe."

"Which do you do, chew or smoke?"

"I chews an' smokes bofe—when I kin git it. Dey gives me all de chewin' I wants."

Needless to say that darky got the price of some smokes.

Down in this same section of Dixie is in many respects the most vicious horsefly in the United States. They resemble to some extent a kind of yellow wasp. In fact, we are not quite certain whether they bite or sting, or both. I am not a fly-ologist. But they certainly did deal Queen a lot of misery, especially near sundown. They were almost impossible to dislodge, in that they would cling to the inside of the hind legs or thighs, or under the belly. They were alert and very hard to catch. Wherever they bit, or stung, they left a great welt. Queen would actually pound her belly with her hind feet, but seldom could dislodge the fly. He dodged. Finally we noticed that if left to her own devices she would soon be rid of the two or more flies. We discovered that she would start out on a trot, flies following (or riding). She would come to a nice big dust pool, stop and throw dust onto her belly as does a bull. This evidently either strangled the flies or blinded them so that she killed them with her hind feet. Anyway we sometimes found dead flies in the dust afterward.

Queen became very observing. She seemed to acquire a love of travel. She noticed any peculiar scene. She was always anxious to start on the day of new adventure. Once in the Bitterroots she evinced a strong desire to look over the embankment into a deep dark canyon, but was afraid of the edge of the grade. She watched me test the grade with my foot, then, approaching closely, gazed all up and down.

"That's a hell of a place down there," she finally concluded. "Let's go!"

From Notes. September 14, '27: "Warm. * * * * 1 p.m. Ar'd Palmetto, Ga., via No. 41—rolling to hilly. [At Palmetto and all through here, were dwarf palmettos.]

Traveled: 27 mi. * * * * Alternating, rather scrubby pine, oak, sassafras, persimmons, other trees. Broom grass, or broom straw heretofore mentioned, or a "kind of blue joint." A little Johnson, Bermuda, etc. Cotton (poor) corn, peaches, etc. Hogs. (For quite a stretch before daylight, numerous hogs made themselves manifest by their perfume.) Red land. Colored and white farmers. Laying in under oaks, N. suburb. Good water all along here.

September 15, '27: Leaving camp at Palmetto 1 a.m. 8 a.m., Spreading front shoes at shop of Mr. Orr, S. College Park, Ga., 9 a.m., Ar'd College Park."

From Signature Book: "College Park, Ga., Sept. 15 (1927) (8 miles so. of Atlanta, Ga.) Frank M. Heath arrived here about 9 o'clock riding Gypsy Queen.

> (Signed) Smith Bros.,
> Purina Dealers."

From Notes. September 15, '27: continued: "* * * * P.M., Went to Atlanta—no mail. In the evening, a bunch came out to our camp 1 mi. S. of College Park. Bonfire, talk.

September 16, '27: Hot. Laying in. Washing up. Repairing. Treating Queen's legs with burlap bandages and cold water. 2:30 p.m., Going to College Park.

September 17, '27: Hot. Leaving camp 2 a.m. 6 to 7, feeding hot lunch in S. environs Atlanta. 9:30, in S.E. suburbs Atlanta. 11 a.m. Ar'd warehouse Smith Bros., Purina dealers, Oakhurst (E. Atlanta) via Hopeville.

Traveled: 18 mi. (4 by misdirection) 1 detour to avoid R.R. traffic. Pave. 14 mi., city traffic and pave., 2 mi. (equal 30 mi.)

Camping in grove near Smith Bros. Going to Atlanta after mail. Smith Bros. gave all the Omolene we wanted."

For quite a stretch through here the principal grain concentrate or feed for horses and mules was Omolene. I ran across some places, or what you might call plantations, where considerable stock was used, horses and mules, where they simply kept great troughs full of it. Every animal helped itself to Omolene, and sometimes alfalfa, sometimes other hay. They seemed to thrive on it, as well as horses and mules can thrive in this enervating climate. I believe this continued clear across Alabama and Georgia, and of course was not confined to those localities.

Of all the feeds we fed, aside from good, heavy, clean oats, Omolene seemed to me to be the best for Queen. There are other kinds of so-called molasses feeds, of course, good, bad and indifferent. By the way, I have no brief for advertising Omolene. The merchant usually sold this in no less than sack lots—I forget how large—a hundred pounds or more. Of course we couldn't handle a hundred pound sack. I do not remember passing through one town where some merchant would not break a sack for Queen, though he was aware of the fact that his customers did not like to buy a sack that had been tampered with.

From Notes. September 20, '27: "* * * * 4 p.m., Ar'd Oakana River, 6 mi. N.E. Gainville, via R. 13 and detour. Hilly.

Traveled: 25 mi. * * * * Queen in river (creek) 1 hr. for inflammation in feet. Bermuda grass. * * * *

September 21, '27: Heavy dew, wet, little cold at night. Leaving camp 2:30 a.m. 11:30, Bought oats, eats. Met Miss Helen Bellhouse, high school girl of Alto, local. Interested (wants story). Later called at camp with Mark Sheridan, high school kid. Both interesting. 11:30, a.m. Camping in a beautiful shady spot on a fine creek, Wheeler's Branch 3 mi. S.W. Cornelia. Hilly.

Traveled: 18 mi. * * * * Description as yesterday. * * * Peach orchards, apple orchards, little cotton, corn, beans, peas, onions. Better homes. Bermuda, broom, other grasses. Soil reddish clay. Great variety trees, oak, pine, lead. Much goldenrod past few days.

September 22, '27: Cool. Leaving camp 3 a.m. * * * * 12:30 p.m., Ar'd Toccoa.

Traveled: 23 mi. * * * * Hills, timber as yesterday. Peach, apple orchards. * * * * as yesterday. Cotton just started picking, fair to light. Corn fair to very poor. Some Sudan grass. Cowpea hay, cowpeas, etc. Soil, red sandy and gray sand deep washes. Furniture factories at Toccoa. Queen very tired. Feel bum myself—Abdomen bothering me more. * * * * Some terraced fields. Camping in small timber—no protection. Bed of leaves, self and horse."

From Signature Book: "Frank M. Heath is in Toccoa, Ga. with Gypsie Queen today, September 22, 1927. Glad to have him.

(Signed) R. C. Jones,
Toccoa Grocery Co."

This reminds me: On this occasion, the morning of September 22nd, as on some others, I was leaving in the dark. I led Queen up pretty close to the small creek, scratched a match, which was the only light we had—this gave her a chance to view the distance. As the match flared I said "jump!"—Over she went, landing safely on the other side. After that she would wait for me to strike a match.

From Notes. September 23, '27: "Cool. Slept well. Queen rested but did not lie down. Leaving camp, 3:45 a.m. Sunrise finds us just over in S. C. 8 a.m., Feeding, cowpeas, sorghum hay—own oats and 3 very large plump ears of corn "borrowed" from a farmer—name unknown—early this morning. * * * * 1 to 1:45, in Westminster. Oats, groceries. * * * *

Traveled: 20 mi. * * * * Few farms, some patches cleared from timber, various kinds. Bottom of river—corn etc. is wonderful. Cotton on upland fair. Lot of cowpeas, sorghum hay, put up in tall, round stacks around a pole. Few good hogs. Little valleys very fertile. * * * * Much tulip poplar and goldenrod (bee range)—no bees. Camping in dense small timber. Bed of leaves. Plenty muscatine. Queen in pool made by damming branch, 1½ hrs. Plenty of grass.

September 24, '27: Leaving camp 2:30 a.m. * * * * 2:30 (p.m.) Ar'd at a wood 2 mi. N. E. Norris. Buying oats, groceries. Via 17-2. Rolling. Camping. Water at a well. Bum grass.

Traveled: 23 mi. * * * *

Sunday, September 25, '27: Fair, cool. Leaving camp 2:30. * * * * 2:30 Ar'd at a branch ½ W. Saluda R., 5 mi. W.

Greenville, via No. 2 to Liberty, then a tangle of country roads to present camp, on old Easley Rd. Rolling.

Traveled: 24 mi. * * * *

September 26, '27: Cool, cloudy. Leaving camp 5 a.m. 6:15 Ar'd Greenville via old Easley Rd. Camping at Malard's Feed Yard. * * * *

Special Note: College Park-Atlanta to Greenville, 200 mi.

TOTAL TO GREENVILLE, S. C. 10,691 miles [as corrected].

Mail from home. Letter with my. [money] from Mr. Conner. Writing Mr. Conner, Joe, Hall of Purina, others, home. * * * *"

From Signature Book: "Greenville, S. C., Sept. 26, 1927.

Frank M. Heath arrived here, at our feed yard (Malard's Tie Yard) at 8:15 a.m. today riding the bay mare Gypsy Queen. This mare has a small "teat" somewhat resembling a wart, on her right ear, a scar on left ear, a plain scar on each "buttock," a scar on back of left front pastern, and a scar on back of each hind pastern (the right one scarcely healed.) She has white saddle mark on left just back of withers and two on right. Two white dots on right rump.

(Signed) Josiah Johnson,
Prop., Malard's Tie Yard."

Greenville, S. C., Sept. 26, '27.

Mr. Joseph C. Cissel,
Rockville, Md.

Dear Comrade Cissel:

I have written you several times since I was there in July and have had no reply.

Now I am going to try to make my situation quite clear, so as to see if you won't get it.

I am nearly out of money.

I have nothing in the bank.

A friend loaned me $20.00 for a short time, and probably will let me have $20.00 in October and again in November. That and the $12.80 per from Vets Bureau is all I have in sight (and I've drawn that for Sept.) unless I can get you to get some kind of action on the loan for which as you are aware I have already signed.

As I travel north and have to put my horse up on account of

colder weather and mountainous country in approaching W. Va. this $1.00 per day will scarcely more than pay the horse's way, for feed is high and she must eat. At present I am barely making out on it by laying out and camping.

Even if I *could* subsist without some money through you, I am destitute of clothing. I actually have on the last shirt and the last pair of breeches (and they are out at both knees) I have to my name (having lost all extra clothing in the mail) and an old straw hat is the only cover I have for my homely head. The only pair of shoes I have are going to pieces. My only pair of socks wouldn't hold potatoes. My one B.V.D. union suit I wash occasionally with my other rags and dry them on the bushes while I adorn my shapeless personality with my old rain coat, and you could throw a live chicken through it most anywhere. I have still five or six weeks to travel. Won't I look sweet with just the little bit—if any—of my present apparel that will yet remain—riding cheerfully down Pennsylvania Ave.? Joking aside, I had hoped by not being stingy with my resources, and you know I have them—to return to Washington and "the Old Home Town" dressed decently as becomes the man that escorts Gypsy Queen on her World Record Breaking Trip. I'm going to finish if I have to ride up to the Mile Stone past the White House and up the Main Street of Silver Spring dressed in a bathing suit and barefooted.

Now Comrade Cissel, I hope you'll take this seriously and send me $50.00. With the signed mortgage in your hands you should, it seems to me, be able to manage it *somehow*. Anyhow you know I am good for it, and I don't care what it costs—any kind of bonus—in reason—would be much cheaper for me than exposure to the weather or exposure to ridicule.

I should not wonder if they would film us too. What the heck would the people of 35,000 theatres make of it? Me in a battered straw hat and little else, late in Nov. returning home riding the famous horse.

I expect to be in Winston-Salem, N. C., on Oct. 4th. Please address me there, Gen. Del. If you can send me some money please send it P. O. order.

Hoping to hear from you *without fail*, I am

Very truly yours,

(Signed) Frank M. Heath.

P.S. If you *can't* send money, I'll phone you just before entering the Capital. (If I can get to a free phone.) And you might have a committee from our Post meet me at the Mile Stone with a blanket and a safety pin! H.

From Notes. September 27, '27: "Hot after threatened rain. Slept well in shed with Queen. Queen laid down—rested. Leaving Greenville, 6:30 a.m. * * * * 5:30 (p.m.), Camping at a creek 4 mi. N. E. Greer.

Traveled: 19 mi. * * * * Greer, peach orchards."

September 28, '27: "Some small animal kept me awake some. Woke me 3:30 a.m. trying to steal. Leaving camp 5 a.m. * * * * 1:45 to 2 p.m. in Spartanburg. 3 p.m., Camping at a wooded creek 2 mi. E. Spartanburg. * * * *

Traveled: 19 mi. (½ by trying to avoid pave in Spartanburg and to camp and returning). * * * * Few fruit trees. Better homes. More old fashioned fireplaces, especially in old buildings.

September 29, '27: Warm. Leaving camp 5:30. * * * * 4:45 p.m., camping at a lovely creek (or branch) 2 mi. E. Giffeny. * * * *

Traveled: 21 mi. * * * *

September 30, '27: Leaving camp 6:15 (Delayed by lost bridle). 5:30 (p.m.) Camping at a branch 5 mi. N. E. Shelley. * * * *

Traveled: 23 mi. * * * *

October 1, '27: Leaving camp 6:30. 4:30 to 5:15 (p.m.) in Lincoln [Lincolnton]. Oats, groceries. Saw Lincoln [Lincolnton] News. * * * *"

From Signature Book: "Frank M. Heath is in Lincolnton today with a bay mare called Gypsy Queen. This is the 1st day of Oct., 1927.

(Signed) J. W. Farier (?), C. P."

From Notes. October 3, '27: "Drizzling rain. Leaving camp 6:30. * * * * 1:30 p.m., camping in old garage of Claud Setzer. * * * *

Traveled: 15 mi. * * * * 2 p.m., Rain ceased. Staying in, drying out. No oats. 4 ears new corn, night, morning. Grass, hay. Apples (trees in bad shape). Peaches, strawberries. Bermuda grass nearly out. Little Johnson, other grasses. Crab grass.

October 4, '27: Partly cloudy. Leaving Setzer 6:15. * * * *
3:15 to 4 p.m., In Statesville. * * * *
Traveled: 19 mi. * * * *
October 5, '27: Fair. Leaving camp 6:30. Queen, self, rested
well. * * * * 4:45 p.m., Ar'd at farm of John Clement, Maxville, N. C., R. 5, 4 mi. W. of Maxville. Prosperous colored
farmer, owns 200 acres. Raises cotton, corn, wheat, truck.
* * * *
Traveled: 21 mi. * * * * Dirt all the way. Large and small
farms cleared out of small mixed timber. No more terraces.
Cotton, corn, tobacco, sweet potatoes. Clover, some Johnson,
little Bermuda, other wild grasses. Mr. Clement was a slave, less
than 3 miles from here. Is 78. Wheat, oats, barley, rye, old
orchards.
October 6, '27: Fair. Slept well on corn fodder in shed. Queen
well rested after bed of straw. Corn "blades," bran, corn.

These corn blades we had had for feed off and on (but not often),
since the Missouri Ozarks. (Harry La Mere fed them.) They consist
simply of the leaves that have been stripped from the corn about
the time it was filling. It might include also a few suckers off the
corn stalks. This stripping was done with the double purpose, first,
of throwing the strength into the ear, and secondly, to conserve the
feed. Corn Blades make pretty good roughage, at least occasionally.

From Notes. October 6, '27 continued: "Leaving Clements
7 a.m. * * * *4 p.m., Buying "mill run" at a store (stores all
along here). 4:45, Buying 4 lbs. at Muddy Creek, Sides Roller
Mills. A. F. Sides. Winston Salem, R. 1, Prop. 6 p.m., Camping
near home of Mr. A. F. Sides (after finding 2 people away at
Fair.)
Traveled: 23 mi. * * * *
October 7, '27: Fair. Leaving camp in woods 8 a.m. Mr. Sides
gave hay—no chg. 10:45 a.m., Ar'd Winston Salem.
Traveled: 7 mi. Pave 7 (dirt side 5 mi.), Environs of Winston
Salem, *large city.* * * * * Getting Queen shod all round by
C. A. Bryant, 419 Cleveland Ave.—Good job, $3.00. Mail from
Joe, $50.00, Conner, $10.00 * * * * Laying over tonight. This
is a manufacturing city. 'Honey combs.' "

From Signature Book: "Oct. 7th, 1927. Winston Salem, N. C.
Frank M. Heath arrived here at our place at 1100 North

Cluny St., Winston Salem, N. C., riding a nice bay mare known as Gypsy Queen, at 10:45 o'clock a.m. today.

(Signed) W. E. Bowen & Bro.
W. E. Bowen."
(Postmark, Winston Salem, N. C., Oct. 7, 1927,
John T. Benbow, P. M.)

Collinston, Sept. 30, 1927

Mr. Frank M. Heath,
Winston Salem, N. C.
Dear Mr. Heath:

Your letter of the 26th, written from Greenville, S. C., was waiting for me when I got in today. Glad to know that all is going well with you and your horse.

No news of importance to write. We are at this time having a little cooler weather. Will endeavor to give you another lift the next time I write you. Trusting that all goes well with you and with kind personal regards I am,

Yours very truly,
(Signed) L. R. Conner

In writing me, suggest that you let me know how you are fixed for money and what amount you need and to what point it should be sent. About how are your expenses running per day?

On second though I am enclosing a ten dollar ($10.00) bill for fear that you may be broke when you get this letter and again I might be out of money when I hear from you again.

(Signed) L. R. C.

SERVICE CO. 1st INF.
MARYLAND NATIONAL GUARD
Silver Spring, Md.

October. 3rd, 1927

Mr. Frank M. Heath
General Delivery
Winston-Salem, N. C.
Dear Comrade Heath:

For some unknown reason your letter written on Sept. 26th was just received this morning. I am trying to make up for the lost time by getting this out from the Armory at once, and trust that it will reach you at Winston-Salem. I am enclosing Postal Money Order for Fifty Dollars, representing two months' rent for the place, which I was able to rent for that period, for a family which moved at the expiration of their second month, much to my chagrin, since I confidently expected that they would be good tenants. However I suppose that half a loaf is better than no bread, and it is fortunate that I have this sum at hand.

You may feel at liberty to call upon me for any personal assistance that my means will permit in order to render the conclusion of your trip the success which it has manifested throughout. Trusting that this will reach you in time to be of some assistance,

Fraternally yours,
(Signed) Joseph C. Cissel

From Notes. October 8, '27: "Put up last night boarding stable of John Hester, horseman, under Brown Tobacco warehouse. Leaving Winston Salem 6:15, barn 50 cts. * * * * 5:45 p.m., Ar'd in drizzling rain at farm of James Massey, P. O. Walnut Cove, R. 2 (Colored). 7th try—(some couldn't, some wouldn't). (Send a card.)

Traveled: 15 mi. * * * *

Sunday, October 9, '27: Drizzling rain. Queen comfortable in shed on straw bed, hay. Self fine on lounge in cabin. Fire place. Supper at W. M. Warren, colored. Father in law of Massey. No chg. Gave kids a "treat." * * * * Mr. Massey owns own home, is full voter. 3 adopted boys. Mrs. Massey also voter—does not vote. Leaving Mr. Massey 8:30. No chg. (asked to breakfast but cooked own by fireplace.) Formula—advice on chronic sore shoulder. * * * * 5:30 p.m., Ar'd Madison, N. C., via various country roads. * * * *

Traveled: 18 mi. * * * * Country resembles yesterday—more "chocolate" soil.

October 10, '27: Leaving 7 a.m. * * * * 6 p.m. Ar'd filling station and home of Hardy Scales, colored, 12 mi. S. W. Martinsville, Va., P.O. Spencer, Va., R. 1, Box 60. 5th try, 4 white, one colored. * * * *

Traveled: 21 mi. Fairly good homes mostly. Few colored farmers—own farms."

From Signature Book: "Oct. 10, 1927. Stoneville, N. C.

Frank M. Heath arrived here at 11 o'clock today riding a nice bay mare known as Gypsy Queen.

(Signed) W. E. Smith."

From Notes. October 11, '27: Leaving Scales 8:30 a.m.
Supper, breakfast, feed, bed, no chg. (Gave kids change.)
* * * *"

From Signature Book: "Spencers P. O. (7 mi. S.E. of)—12
mi. S.W. of Martinsville, Va., Oct. 11, 1927.
Frank M. Heath arrived at our store and filling sta. here at
6 p.m. yesterday riding bay mare Gypsy Queen and stayed over
night.

(Signed) D. H. Scales."

From Notes. October 12, '27: "* * * * Noon, Feeding corn
and 'blades' at farm of Fred Owens, 10 miles N. Fieldale, P. O.
Henry, Va., R. 3. Mr. Owens was a slave, owned by, 1st, Rubin
Witcher, Pennsylvania County, Va., sold at age of 10 on the
block to Wm. Owens. * * * * This was about 1863. He is
about 74. Mrs. Owens also was a slave, owned by Mrs. A. L.
Burrell. She was a very kind mistress—Gills Creek near Rocky
Mt. Also met Mr. R. D. Williams (same address). Can get
photo of Owens and home through Mr. Williams. 2 p.m. Rain-
ing, driving fine rain. Laying in, Feeding corn "blades," corn.
Sleeping in corn crib. Writing letters—Dr. Cox of Purina Mills.
Traveled: 10 mi. * * * *
October 13, '27: Clear, cool. Leaving Mr. Owens, 7 a.m.
"Blades," corn, straw, some grub—gave the old man 90 cts. (No
chg.) Formula. * * * * 3:30 p.m., In Rocky Mt.—no oats.
4:30, Camping in stable of Mr. Moss Weaver, ½ mi. N. Rocky
Mt. * * * *
Traveled: 19 mi. * * * * Logged-over mixed timber. Cleared
patches. Tobacco, corn, wheat, sweet potatoes, clover and alfalfa.
Broom straw. Some fairly good homes. Old orchards. Furniture
factory, R. Mt. Bought 3 qts. (5 lbs.?) shelled corn, 10 cts., of
neighbor boy. Plenty grass for bed. Later about a dozen boys and
men called—round camp fire. One invited me to his home for
the night but being comfortably fixed, declined with thanks.
October 14, '27: Leaving Weavers, 6:30 a.m. * * * * Note:
Cars passed between 6:20 a.m. and 4:35 (2½ hrs out) 327.
Circus in Roanoke. 6 p.m. Ar'd Roanoke, wagon yard of J. R.
Garrett, via No. 33. Mountainous—Blue Ridge Range.
Traveled: 25½ mi. Pave. 24 mi. (gravel side 14 mi.) Gravel

1 mi. Mountains—fertile little valleys—some clearings high up sides of mts. Corn, wheat, sweet potatoes. Some pretty good homes. * * * *"

From *Signature Book:* "Roanoke, Va., Oct. 15, 1927.
Frank M. Heath came into our wagon yard last night about 6 p.m. riding the bay mare known as Gypsy Queen and stayed until 1 p.m. today. Horse apparently in good shape.
(Signed) J. R. Garrett, Prop."
(Postmark, S. Harris Hoge, Acting P. M., Oct. 15, 1927.)

THE WORLD-NEWS

Roanoke, Va., Saturday Afternoon, October 15, 1927
RIDER AND HORSE, GYPSY QUEEN, TRAVEL HALF WAY AROUND WORLD * * * *

From *Notes.* October 15, '27: "Fair. Laying in A.M. Drew coat, sweater, from P. O. Bought shirt, sox, U suit. * * * * [Somewhere previous to this I had bought a good so-called five gallon hat, to replace the old straw sombrero. I wore this good hat to the end of the trip, a good deal since, and still have it.] 1 letter from "Tim" at I. Spring [Indian Spring, Nev.] Leaving Garrett's Wagon Yard, 1 p.m. Only 15 cts.for stall slept warm in hay. 6 p.m., Ar'd farm of W. B. Wills (Old Billy Wills), 2 mi. S. Troutsville, Va., R. 1. * * * * 4th try.

Traveled: 10 mi. * * * * Mr. Wills is 82. Been here 53 years. Drove 4 horse stage, Bontox to White Sulphur Springs, W. Va., 1870-74, Lexington to Bontox (to Natural Bridge), '75 to '80 7 miles average speed. Fifteen miles was a day's work for a horse. 6 days a week. Apples good—spray 3 times year.

Sunday, October 16, '27: Leaving the Wills 9 a.m. No chg. Supper, breakfast, 1 big feed corn, hay—slept in hay (cold). Advice on lame horse, (formula.) * * * * (Sunday, October 16, fair, cold.) * * * * 4:30, Ar'd farm of Mr. B. S. Williams, W. suburbs Buchanan, Va. Via R. 33 (Lee Hy.) Hilly. Spread shoes, shop of J. H. McCleland, Buchanan, Va., G. H. Watts helped. Send card.

Traveled: 17 mi. * * * * Note: Yesterday I saw 1st colt since La. 2 more today—good ones.

October 17, '27: Cloudy, may rain. Leaving Williams 7 a.m.
Hay, corn, slept warm in hay, only 50 cts. Lady gave some lunch.
8 a.m., Drizzling rain. * * * * 4:30, Ar'd in rain at farm of
Mr. G. W. Hostetter, 7 mi. S. Lexington, Va., P. O. Glasgow,
R. 1, Box 53, via R. 33. Hilly.

Traveled: 20 mi. Pave. 20 mi. (dirt side 5 mi., gravel side, 12
mi.) Shenandoah Valley. * * * * Most all good farm homes.
* * * * Practically all white farm owner. *Note:* Came in here
soaked to my knees. Have shoes and socks drying by kitchen
fire while the good lady cooks supper."

Near Lexington, Va., 17-'27.

[Dear Folks:]

We'll get into Lexington tomorrow A.M. Traveled in rain
today up to 4 p.m., and now I am sitting by a kitchen stove in
the kitchen of the farm home of one of these Shenandoah
Valley farmers, with my shoes off. I'm going to sleep in the
house tonight too—after eating in the house. This is some
change from the way we've been living. Queen is in a comfortable place with plenty to eat.

I'll pay of course. But I'll bet you two to one that these people
won't overcharge me.

Well, the end of our trail is drawing near. And I guess we'll
be glad to get back. I'll finish after I get mail tomorrow.

Harrisonburg, Va., Oct. 18-'27.

No mail from you either here or back at Roanoke. Address
me next at New Market, Va., Gen. Del.

It is drizzling rain these days, but we are pluggin' along—short
days. Hope to "arrive" early in Nov. Both well. Love,

(Signed) Frank.

From Notes. October 18, '27: "Rainy. Leaving Hostetters 8:30
a.m. 2 meals, bed, horse, $1.50. 11:30, Putting up at barn of
Tom Sheridan, Sheridan Trans. [Transfer] Co., [Lexington, Va.]

Traveled: 7 mi. * * * * (Description as yesterday.) Laying
in, P.M. [Lexington]. $6.25 for raincoat and rubbers. Visited
Stonewall Jackson Memorial Hospital, Lee Tomb. Packing
Queen with linseed meal. Making * * * * brace [leg wash]"

THE GAZETTE

Lexington, Virginia, Tuesday Afternoon,
October 25, 1927

TRANSCONTINENTAL TRAVELER PASSES
THROUGH LEXINGTON ON LAST LAP
OF LONG JOURNEY

———————

Frank M. Heath, of Silver Springs, Md., who left the Milestone in the city of Washington, D. C., April 1, 1925, spent Wednesday night in Lexington having almost attained his objective and expecting to realize his ambition of visiting every state in the Union riding and walking beside his little bay mare under saddle. Mr. Heath is fifty-nine years of age and weighs one hundred and twenty-five pounds. The mare weighs one thousand pounds now, having gained fifty pounds on the trip, after carrying her master part of the time and seventy-five pounds of equipment including the saddle all the time through forty-seven states. Both are full of pep and bright of eye. The mare is a Kentucky Morgan, twelve years old. * * * *

Mr. Heath is a very entertaining talker and is something of a philosopher. He left this parting observation to be handed on to the readers of the Gazette: "If any man who is a man himself will start out and make a trip of this sort, traveling leisurely and rubbing elbows with all classes of people, as I have done, his stock in his fellow Americans will jump up at least fifty per cent in two years."

From Notes. October 19, '27: "Cloudy. Leaving Mr. Sheridan, 7:45 a.m. Horse, feed, bed in office, no chg. (Advice, formulas). * * * * 4:45, Ar'd farm of W. W. Umberger, 3 (mi.) S. Greenville, R. 2, via 33. Hilly.

Traveled: 21 mi. * * * * Mixed timber in mts. on either [side] Shenandoah Valley. Few "woods" lots, bal. Cleared farms. Larger field fairly level. Soil grayish clay—lime subsoil. Wheat corn, hogs, cattle, dairying (largely Jersey). Hay, timothy, clover, alfalfa, oats. Spuds, excellent gardens. Commercial apple orchards. Poultry. Good horses, largely percheron. Some colts. Sheep. Blue grass. Good homes, well kept up. * * * *

October 20, '27: Clearing. Leaving Umberger, 8:15. Horse, 2 meals, bed, $1.00 (Formulas, advice). * * * * 3:30 to 4 p.m. in Staunton—oats, eats. 5:30 to 6 p.m., Considering camp at vacant place 3 mi. N.E. Staunton. Gave it up. 7 p.m., Putting

Queen in box stall, hitting hay, after cold lunch at Verona Inn, Mr. J. S. Sutton, owner. * * * * Oats, hay. 3rd try after vacant place.

Traveled: 20 mi. * * * *

October 21, '27: Clear, cool. Leaving the Suttons, 7 a.m. * * * * 5:30 p.m., Ar'd Harrisonburg, Va., stable of A. S. Whitsel, 62 Federal St., via No. 33—Hilly.

Traveled: 20 mi. * * * *

October 22, '27: Slept in office of barn. Queen rested well in her stall. Writing Conner, folks, sending stamps to Meridian, La., to forward package. Leaving Whitsel, 11:45, $1.25. * * * *"

From Signature Book: "Harrisonburg, Va., Oct. 22-1927.

Frank M. Heath put up here last night with his bay mare Gipsy Queen, leaving today for Mathias, W. Va.

(Signed) Aldine S. Whitsel,

Prop., Whitsel's Stable."

From Notes. October 22, '27 continued:—"6:30 (p.m.) Stopping at farm of Mr. Baylor C. Dove, 3 mi. W. Broadway, R. 3, via local rds.

Traveled: 17 mi. * * * * Beautiful sparsely wooded hills (once timber). Grayish clay soil, blue limestone subsoil. Grassland. Blue grass. Herds of fat cattle, largely Durham. Dairying. Some poultry. W. leghorns. Corn. Hogs. Good horses. Fine homes. Land very stony. Well watered. *Note:* All land N. Winston Salem more or less stony.

October 23, '27: Fair. Slept in fine bed. Queen good bed, well fed, corn, oats, fodder. 2 fine meals, hospitable. Leaving the Doves, 9:00. No charge. Gave kids $1.00 for Christmas. Formula. Want book. Send card to Doves, also one to Mrs. Lillian Dove. 1 p.m., Ar'd farm of J. R. Breneman, member Va. Leg. [Legislature], 12 mi. N.W. Broadway, Va. Feeding "mix feed." Fine lunch. Miss Breneman takes pictures. Leaving 3:15—no chg. 6 p.m., putting up at farm of Mr. Moses B. Halterman, 8 mi. S.E. Mathias, W. Va., *in* W. Va., P.O. Bergton, Va., R. 1, B. 55.—15 mi. N.W. Broadway, via local rds. Hilly. Into Brock's Gap.

Traveled: 13 mi. * * * * Brock's Gap, Appalachian Range, not yet at summit. * * * *"

From Signature Book: "At my farm in W. Va., 7½ miles S.E. of Mathias, W. Va., Oct. 22 [should be 23], 1927.

Frank M. Heath arrived here at 6 p.m. today riding his bay mare Gipsy Queen and is staying here with his horse tonight.
(Signed) M. B. Halterman."

From Notes. October 24, '27: "Fair * * * * Leaving Halterman 8:10—only 50 cts. (Formula). 12 noon to 2 p.m., on bank of beautiful N. fork Shenandoah R., 9 mi. N.W. Broadway, feeding 5 good ears new yellow corn contributed by Mr. Dove. Hot coffee, roasted apples. * * * * 5 p.m., Ar'd Couch's Store, 4 mi. N.W. Broadway (1 mi. N.W. Baylor C. Dove's) having retraced yesterday's rt. so far.

Traveled: 12 mi. * * * * Invited to spend the night with Mr. E. A. Couch and family. Queen loose in old stable—clover hay, new corn.

Note: Weighed saddle and pack—no water, no feed, no grub —total pounds, 64. Mr. E. A. Couch represents the fourth generation of Couches who have dwelt in the house in which he now lives. Family ran store all this time.

October 25, '27: Fair. Couches entertained us royally. Leaving 8:30. Hospitality. 9:15, Ar'd back at Baylor C. Doves.

Traveled: 1 mi. * * * * Laying over today. Cleaning up self and Queen. Writing letters. Wearing Mr. Dove's overalls—4 sizes too large."

Broadway, Va., Oct. 25, '27.

Dear Folks:

Was going to write long letter today as am laying over, resting. But my arm has one of those numb spells. We spent night before last in W. Va., our last state, and are now headed straight for the Mile Stone. Hope to arrive Sun., Nov. 6th.

The people all about here nearly ovrewhelm us with hospitality. Weather fine at present.

Write next to Warrenton, Va., Gen. Del.

Oct. 26th—at New Market.

No mail yet—Don't understand it. Weather fine. Address us above. Love,

(Signed) Frank.

From Notes. October 26, '27: "Slept in bed. Queen good bed. 2 feeds corn, 1 oats, 3 meals, no chg. Made lady take $1.00,

poultry dope. Had to force $1.00 on them "for Xmas." Mr.
Dove works hard in rock quarry for rd. dept. for 10 hr. day,
$2.50, $1.00 for horse. Farms little home place, 10 acres. 4
children, wife, mother. Send book free. * * * * 4:30 p.m.,
Country summer home of Mr. W. P. Runion and family (Valley
View), 2 mi. N.E. New Market, via local rds. to New Market
* * * * Lee Hy. E. Hilly.

Traveled: 14 mi. * * * * Out to a wiener roast with the
Runions—fine time. Description same, and many fine black
percheron horses."

From Signature Book: "Frank M. Heath through here on
"Gypsy Queen bay mare," New Market, Va., Oct. 26, 1927.
(Signed) Mary B. Wicker, P.M."

From Notes. October 27, '27: "Leaving Runions, 8:30 after
taking photo. Corn, no hay, grass, stall, no bedding, bed, breakfast, $1.75. 11:30, At farm of W. M. Long, 6 mi. S.W. Luray,
P.O. Luray, R. 5. *Note:* Mr. Long has a good 5 year old "Den-
mark grade" Ky. saddle horse. Would consider $200.00 (gave 5
ears corn). Noon to 1:45 p.m., In a little cove with creek. Blue
grass. 5 mi. S.W. Luray. Traveled at least 1 mi. extra, A.M., in
following one of those damned "cut-offs" and the way was
mostly very steep—every way—and stony. Weather fine. 3:30 to
4:40, in Luray. Oats, eats. 6 p.m., Camping in vacated stable
2 mi. N.E. Luray 2nd try. Via No. 21—mountainous (Crossed
Massanutten Mt.), too hilly.

Traveled: 15 mi. * * * *

October 28, '27: Fair. Leaving camp at old stable 6 a.m., after
restless night. * * * * 3:30 p.m., Ar'd Sperryville, Va. Very
inquisitive bunch. Had to "close up." Spreading Queen's shoes
all around, at Mr. Jenkins' Blacksmith Shop. No chg. (Lecture
on feet) 6 p.m., Putting Queen in cow stable of Mr. ———
who runs store. 8 ears corn, 6 lbs. bran, little corn fodder, $1.00.
Slept in stall. *Note:* Down ——— Creek, after getting ½ way
down E. slope Blue Ridge Mts.—one sees many little mt. homes
literally "hewn out" of the logged-over land, and generally out
of the boulders. Poor shelters largely. Twice I met a boy carrying
meal in a bag on his back. A few tall woods or timber. Jerk
lines. Nearly every place has a few old apple trees, usually a pig,
few hens—sometimes a cow or two—little patches corn—gardens
—sweet potatoes. The Atkins boy told me both he and his father

were born in the old house nearly 100 years old where they live. The house was never painted—partly log—two fireplaces.

Traveled: (Oct. 28) 15 mi. via No. 27—mountainous. Pave. 7 mi. Dirt, R. I., stony, 8 mi. * * * *

October 29, '27: Fair, warm. Good breakfast at Dewdrop Inn, 50 cts. Leaving Sperryville 7:30 a.m. 9:30 to 9:40, Queen, feet in creek * * * * 4 p.m., Met Aubry Brown and Pink Low of Culpepper in auto. They had Granville Kelly of Culpepper stop me as I went in and put up horse in his barn. 6:15 p.m., Ar'd Culpepper. At Thomas Garage, Granville Kelly accosted us and had me up to his parents' place, D. W. Kelly.

Traveled: 21 mi. * * * *

Sunday, October 30, '27: Fair. Slept well in barn. Queen fared fine. Hay, ground mixed feed. Queen very tired, feet hot. Kellys had us up to breakfast. Leaving 9:30, no chg. for meal.—Queen 50 cts. Send card—also to Aubry Brown. 1:30 p.m., Ar'd Remington, Va., via 32. 1:45, At home of Ed. B. Mills, former owner of Gypsy Queen, with son Clarence, deceased. (This son Clarence was the grown son accompanying Mills at the time I traded for Queen. Meanwhile he was deceased.) ½ mi. W. Remington, on R. I. road. 2:15, Back in Remington at home of Mr. A. E. Hall.

Traveled: 13 mi. * * * *

October 31, '27: Mills had me stay after getting his signature —also to breakfast. [Left Queen in stable. Stayed at Mill's.]

From Signature Book: "Remington, Va., Oct. 31st, 1927.

About Feb. 15, 1925, I let Frank M. Heath of Silver Spring, Md., have, in exchange for a black mare, one bay mare about ten years old at that time.

At that time Mr. Heath declared his intention of "Hitting every State in the Union" with horse. We traded on the road about 13 miles west of Warrenton, Va. Heath at that time renamed the mare Gypsy Queen.

Today at 1:45 p.m. Heath rode into my yard here on the same mare. Several members of my family recognized the mare at once, though they had never met Mr. Heath. The mare had been owned in our immediate neighborhood for several years. We had owned her for some time, and am positive this is the same mare.

(Signed) E. B. Mills."

From Notes. October 31, '27 continued: "Leaving Hall's stable 9:30 a.m., $1.00 * * * * 3:30 p.m., Ar'd Warrenton, Va., via R. 32. Rolling.

Traveled: 15 mi. (including 2 trips to fairground and return). Pave., 14 mi. (dirt s. 12 mi.), Dirt 1 mi. * * * * Met Dr. Shirley Carter of Warrenton, who with Mr. C. Ullman, saw us into the fairgrounds, where we spent the night quite comfortably, each in a box stall. Bought oats and a bundle of corn fodder from old man at grounds."

Collinston, La., Oct. 26th, 1927.

Mr. Frank M. Heath,
Warrenton, Virginia.
Dear Mr. Heath:

Your letter of the 22nd, written from Harrisonburg, Va., was here for me when I came in last night. Am enclosing you herewith the $25.00 you asked for, which I trust will reach you all right. * * * *

Very truly your friend,

(Signed) L. R. Conner

You know without my saying that we are wishing you Good Luck and a safe journey. L. R. C.

From Notes. November 1, '27: "Fair. Leaving fairgrounds 6:30, Warrenton 7 a.m. * * * * 6 p.m., Ar'd farm of Mr. Frank Wells, 15 mi. W. Fairfax, P.O. Gainesville, Va., R. 1, via Lee Hy. * * * *

Traveled: 17 mi. * * * *"

Gainesville, Va., 33 mi. W. Washington,
November 1, 1927

Dear Folks:

Three letters reached us yesterday at Warrenton, Va. Jogging along very slowly account rough roads. Look for a wire when we reach the Mile Stone.

Both are O.K. Excuse haste, Love,

(Signed) Frank.

From Notes. November 2, '27: "Foggy, may rain. * * * * Leaving 7 a.m. * * * * 4:30 (p.m.) Buying oats in Fairfax. Out 2:30. Rec'd 3 parcels. Doubling them into 1, sending to Washington.

Traveled: 15 mi. Putting up, dairy farm of Mr. J. W. Sims, Oak Farm, P.O. Fairfax, 1st try. * * * *

November 3, '27: Foggy. Leaving Mr. Sims, 7 a.m. Hay, milk, no charge. Send card 11 a.m. Ar'd Arlington, via No. 21. Rolling.

Traveled: 11 mi. * * * * Leaving Queen in old stable back of grocery. Bail straw, $1.00, 10 lbs. bran, 30 cts. Taken very sick. Throwing up. Took car to V. B. [Veterans' Bureau]. [They asked me if I wanted to go to the hospital. I told them "not at present anyway."] Some relief. Spent night with the Norreds, 1633 A St. N.E. It is cold and drizzling rain."

While this trip was largely for health, and improved my health ultimately, it had developed at this time, that is, shortly previous to finishing, into "too much of a good thing" as they say. It had been strenuous of late for several reasons. First: As we hit the rougher, harder roads in approaching Washington, it was again giving me my hands full to keep Queen going, on account of that foot and leg. Second: It will be noticed that a good many people along this stretch were hospitable and often had me in to meals. A favorite local breakfast through here consists largely of nice white hot biscuits and bacon. Now I like biscuits and bacon, and it is a fine breakfast for a man with a good stomach and good digestion. But it sure upset me, with my bum stomach and digestive trouble. It must have been the worry over Queen going lame again, slightly, so near the finish, this unfavorable diet, and probably the reaction, or let-down as it is sometimes called, as I neared the goal. I sure was sick.

From Notes. November 4, '27: "Cloudy, colder. Decided to bring Queen in while both able. Feeling some better. Spent several hours on phone. Leaving Arlington 10:30 a.m. Ar'd at Mile Stone, D. C.

Traveled: 4 mi. Pave. * * * *

TOTAL TO MILESTONE, D. C., 11,389 miles. Major Scott identified Queen. * * * * Photographers, later reporters. * * * *"

The Major looked Queen over thoroughly and identified her positively. The fact that the left foot and leg were on the bum didn't escape his notice, you bet. He also remarked that the old girl certainly realized she had done something. She stood there looking mighty wise and satisfied.

Small articles with pictures appeared in most of the newspapers in and around Washington. Announcements of the finish were evidently published pretty much all over the country, for I got letters from the four corners of the U. S.

And so finished the trip.

Chapter IX

CONCLUSION AND SUMMARY

From Notes. November 4, '27 continued: Later reported V. B. Exam postponed to any time up to Nov. 15. Stayed the night with Norreds, 1633 A St. N.E.

November 5, '27: Cloudy, cold. Leaving Riding Academy, 1202 (?) Ohio Ave., 9 a.m. * * * * 12:30, In Silver Spring. 4 p.m., Home on Sligo Creek."

In a day or two Captain Cissel came down to our place with a small delegation from our Post and our town. In the conversation Joe asked me, "Sergeant Heath, what is the biggest thing you learned on your trip?" "The biggest thing I learned," I replied, "is that I know nothing."

We started at once trying to get matters straightened out.

The reader will realize that this is far from a complete story of this trip. As I previously stated, had we attempted to give anywhere near a complete story, it would have run into about four million words, which would of course be impossible as far as the book is concerned, and also it would have entirely worn out the reader. Even an abbreviated story would have run into two million words. The best we seem to have been able to do is some few thousand words, which in a sense is little more than a synopsis. In other words, the trail might be likened to a string upon which the outstanding facts are strung, together with enough of the local color to make the picture more complete. Also we have given something of the comparatively recent history of some parts with which the writer has been personally conversant over quite a period of time. This, I hope, could be likened to a background upon which a picture is portrayed in words. Many instances that might be considered a part of the story were not even written down in the notebooks. Some of these omitted instances, however, came so near to vitally affecting the outcome, that I am giving a few as examples.

Somewhere in the semi-arid Oregon country, about the only

resource of which was cattle, along in December, 1926, during the noon halt, we were on the bank of a small creek which was frozen over. There was a bridge across the creek. By some means, probably a rock, I had broken the ice. I had fire and was making a cup of coffee and giving Queen the nosebag. On the south of us was a good wire fence. There was a gate there which was open. Hearing a devil of a commotion I looked up. Here came a mad wild cow. Two men and a boy, well mounted, were chasing her. They were trying to get her in through this gate. She had broken out. Like a dumb bell I tried to obligingly head her in (though I knew that a man on foot has no business where there are wild cattle about, mad or otherwise). Thoughtlessly I stepped in to undertake to head her off. She was of the shorthorn Durham type. The short horns in this case at least, pointed right straight ahead, reminding me of a two-tined fork. Instead of stopping, she lowered her head slightly and made right at me with an ominous bellow. If ever I saw a devilish expression in an animal's eyes it was the eyes of that mad cow. I side-stepped her and she went by, turned and was making back at me furiously. How many times I could have side-stepped her without being outwinded or perhaps losing my footing, I don't know. But here came the kid roaring up on his very good bronco, swinging his lariat. He stopped the cow. It is well known that a wild cow respects a man on horseback. I believe it is fairly certain that had not this kid showed up in the nick of time, I would certainly have become an ornament on that cow's horns. We would never have finished our trip.

Somewhere in Dixieland, it may have been somewhere in western Alabama, we were making the noon stop under some tall pines by a little country garage. There was a well there. A couple of fellows were out talking with me. Queen was standing munching oats from the nosebag. One of these fellows said, "Look at that snake making right for that horse!" It was in the dog days. The snake was a copperhead, slithering right directly toward Queen. Queen had not noticed the snake. Whether she would have, in time, I don't know. I grabbed a club and dispatched the snake with one blow. It was within ten feet of Queen when I got it. The boys told me that one bite from this snake would have ended that horse—quick!

By the way, another time, in the post-flood area, we were traveling along a grade that had been flooded, and now was a little above water. Of all the croakings and bleatings you ever heard, the loudest was along there. Some of these sounds were from the mammoth frogs, others were said to be from the bullsnakes. Queen was sleepy.

There was something lying across the road, which could be taken for a crooked limb or something, at a glance. It was as large as your arm. It was a bullsnake, the largest I ever saw. Queen nonchalantly stepped over it. This was no hazard, as they are said to be non-poisonous. I don't know why I am telling it, unless it is that it was a kind of peculiar incident.

Once while bathing in one of those mud bottom creeks, I had laid down my old black slicker upon which to stand, to avoid the mud. Just as I was wiping up, ready to put on a few clothes, an adder about eight inches long wriggled out from beneath the old black coat. This adder was deadly poisonous. This did not have anything to do with Queen—except that she might have lacked a pilot.

Another time I had Queen tied to a low bridge that crossed a creek. It was somewhere in Dixieland. Queen was in the water to her knees, an opportunity I seldom passed up. Having lost the nose-bag, I had converted the canvas bucket into double use. As a nose-bag I had simply tied a strong leather thong, each end onto each side of the pail, so that the leather strip went over back of her ears, while the top end of the pail made a kind of nose band. This made a very convenient nosebag. I could use it otherwise, of course, for a bucket and, partly collapsed, as a receptacle for various articles while traveling. Queen was munching her oats. I was also lunching, on the bank, when suddenly there was a terrible commotion. Before you could say Jack Robinson, Queen had pulled back, broken the small rope with which she was tied, and bolted right up to me. Fortunately the bank was low. She had stuck her nose, with bucket attached, down into the water. The bucket had filled with water. She had no way of getting it off. She was drowning. Needless to say, I quickly slipped the bucket off her head.

Another comparatively small incident that will insist on bobbing up in my memory is as follows. In approaching either Harrison or Jonesville, Louisiana, it doesn't matter which, looking across the stretch of desolation on the opposite side of this still partly flooded area, standing or meandering about were some half dozen or so white egrets. These, at that particular time, constituted the only life in sight.

It is obvious to the reader that much of the time we were very short of cash. We will say that even when living in the open our cash outlay could not very well be less than a dollar a day. If I didn't make, or get hold of a dollar in some legitimate way, my balance of, we will say $5.00, was cut into to the extent of a dollar. One afternoon up in the Northwestern Montana country somewhere, we were moseying along worrying slightly about that day's balance, when suddenly my eye lighted upon—what do you think? A bright silver dollar lying tipped up against a little shrub about a foot from the edge of the road. This is true. I didn't hunt for the owner of the dollar!

Then there was the time—but I must ring off. I can't keep on forever bringing up these unrecorded instances.

THE MARYLAND NEWS

Friday, November 11, 1927
SILVER SPRING

SILVER SPRING MAN RETURNS AFTER RIDING THROUGH 48 STATES

W. D. [Misprint, F. M.] Heath Rides 11,389 Miles on Same Horse and Establishes Record for Touring

Although this is the era of trans-oceanic flights and other great achievements in the development of mechanical means of transportation, it remained for a Montgomery county resident, Frank M. Heath, of Silver Spring, to be the first man in history to make a tour of the United States, visiting every state, on horseback, with the same horse.

Mr. Heath, 57 and a veteran of the World War, returned to the zero milestone south of the White House November 4, 1927, on his horse, Gypsy Queen, the same point he left April 1, 1925, exactly two years, seven months and four days after he began his tour of the nation.

In making his swing around America, Mr. Heath visited every one of the 48 states and traveled a distance of 11,389 miles. His achievement not only gives him the distinction of being the first human being ever to ride a horse around the United States, but also gives him the long distance record on horseback.

The arrival of the Silver Spring man and Gypsy Queen was witnessed by Major General Cheatham, Quartermaster General of the U. S. Army, and Major Scott, Chief of the Remount Division of the Army, who made a thorough examination of the animal before she started on the tour over two years ago, and positively identified her as the same horse.

Both Mr. Heath and the horse were in excellent condition when they returned to Silver Spring. Their accomplishment is regarded as even more remarkable when it is learned that the horse made the entire trip under saddle except in crossing ferries and for a distance of 30 miles between Jonesville, La., and Natchez, Miss., when State and Federal quarantine laws required the horse to be shipped because of the precautions against Texas fever ticks. To offset this 30 miles, Mr. Heath and the horse backtracked 82 miles.

In starting his trip, which was to lead him into every state in the Union, Mr. Heath's avowed objective was to complete the tour by July 1, 1927. His reason for not making it in this length of time was because he was detained unavoidably by reason of a broken knee, heavy flood waters throughout the south, and detours around quarantined area. His actual traveling distance, however, was made in the number of days which he had given as his objective before beginning the tour. In other words, the horse stood the test and made good, completing the actual trip exactly on schedule. Mr. Heath was forced to delay the trip for two months and twenty-one days back in 1926 when he broke his knee, being kicked by another horse in Yellowstone Park.

At Shreveport, La., he lost 15 days waiting for the flood to recede; at Jonesville, La., he was delayed another eight days waiting for inspection. A detour of 150 miles because of the flood set him back another eight days; a Federal dipping plant caused another two-day delay, and a detour of 250 miles around a tick infested area caused another 14-day delay. This was a total of four months and four days delay and he arrived at the milestone exactly four months and four days behind his schedule.

The rider said that these delays did not afford his mount anything that could be counted as a beneficial rest, for the reason that conditions in each case were not favorable. All "rest periods" running from one to ten days, together with four months and twenty-two days in winter quarters at Princeton, Ill., in 1925-26, which he counts as part of his regular schedule.

Mr. Heath made the tour of America on horseback for the following reasons: To improve his health, which was greatly impaired by his experience in the World War. To prove by actual test the capacity of a good horse. To give the rider education and experience by travel.

According to Mr. Heath the trip was full of thrills, dangers and hardships which tested the horse and rider on many occasions. Gypsy

Queen, a beautiful dark bay, crossed 12 mountain ranges, including the Rockies twice and the Blue Ridge three times [Slight error: Blue Mountains once in West; Blue Ridge twice] reaching an altitude of 8,900 feet. At one time the horse and rider traveled 65 miles between watering places and on the same occasion 72 miles without seeing a sign of habitation. This was in the Amargosa desert. The horse was compelled to eat about every kind of grass and grain grown in the United States during the journey, and drink all kinds of water, stay under all kinds of shelter, if any, and be exposed to many dangers and diseases. The fact that she came through in excellent condition and weighed 1,025 pounds when she returned home as against 950 pounds when she left here two years ago, speaks well of her stamina and endurance as well as the excellent care and attention given her by her rider.

Before leaving on his 11,000 mile ride, Major Scott carefully inspected the horse and identified her by means of marks, scars and other characteristics and made a similar inspection upon her return. Several other well known horsemen also identified her as the same horse.

Gypsy Queen now is to be rewarded for her great work, Mr. Heath says, by having an easy time from now on for the rest of her life. Mr. Heath is a member of the Cissel-Saxon Post No. 41 of the American Legion of Silver Spring. He paid his own expenses on the trip and frequently made extra money by treating animals for farmers along the roads where he traveled.

In hitting every state in the Union Mr. Heath started by first going through all the North Atlantic states, passing west [misprint: north] across New York City and Boston. Thence to New England, returning west across New York and over the Adirondacks.

From there he crossed the lake states, going through Omaha and Nebraska. He then made a loop through Kansas, Oklahoma, Missouri and Arkansas, Tennessee, Kentucky and Illinois. From here he made Wisconsin, Iowa, South Dakota [North Dakota], Yellowstone Park, [Wyoming] and Montana; from Montana he toured Idaho, Washington [Oregon], Northwestern California [Nevada]. Arizona was next on his route, and after passing through numerous Indian reservations and experiencing a number of thrills, passed safely through Utah, Colorado, New Mexico and reached Texas. [Louisiana], Mississippi, Alabama and Florida were then visited in the order named, but not without the Silver Spring rider being delayed many days by high flood waters. He then began his homeward march, including

Georgia, North and South Carolina, West Virginia, Virginia and the District.

Upon his return, Mr. Heath, who is by this time certainly a widely traveled man, declared that he saw no town or community that appeals to him [as] much as a place for homes as Silver Spring, Md.

Collinston, La., Nov. 13th, 1927.

Mr. Frank M. Heath,
Silver Spring, Md.
Dear Friend:

Received your letter saying that you had reached the end of your journey all right and we rejoiced with you to know that all had ended well with you and Queen. I have not written you sooner feeling that I could not be of any more assistance to you since you were at home and among friends. We are however always glad to hear from you and if you ever come south be sure and tie up for rest at our house. * * * *

No news worth writing you at this time. Hope you are enjoying good health and that all is going well with you.

Very truly your friend,
(Signed) L. R. Conner.

From Signature Book: "Wash., D. C., Nov. 16, '27.

On April 1st, 1925 I saw Mr. Heath start on a ride to every state in the U. S. and was requested to identify his horse at the start of the ride and upon its return.

At noon on Nov. 4, 1927, I met Mr. Heath at the Zero Milestone, Wash., D. C. and positively identified the horse as the same one that started April 1, 1925.

My identification was based on the general size and shape and color of the mare and the following indicated peculiarities. (a) a small peculiar teat on the right ear caused by a cut. (b) two small scars, 1 on each side of the croup. (c) two small white dots on right croup."

(Signed) C. L. Scott, Maj.

From Signature Book: "Silver Spring, Md., Nov. 20th, 1927.

This is to certify that on Sunday, March 22nd, 1925, I examined to the orders of Mr. Frank M. Heath of Silver Spring, Md., one bay mare. As he was about to start on a tour of all the states he requested that I make a further examination, when I found her in good health and also noted markings.

I have just re-examined the animal on his return and find her the same one, still in good health.

(Signed) Charles J. Frey,
Veterinarian."

The figure (11,389 miles) which I gave reporters at the Milestone on finishing was wrong by 33 miles. As stated in the beginning of this narrative, I later discovered a slight error.

Setting down the single items of each day's travel was a simple matter. Figuring up the laps was different, especially when one was in a hurry. (After all, we probably traveled much more than thirty-three miles which is not recorded. I always set down each day the miles that I was sure we had traveled, if in doubt as to whether there were that many or more.) When in reviewing later, I discovered errors, I had the whole seven notebooks gone over by an expert mathematician, computing only the daily items. The distance so recorded was found to be 11,356 miles, a difference of 33 miles in 578 days under saddle.

I am submitting this explanation, trying to be frank. There is no intention of misrepresenting or exaggerating anything. In all subsequent articles or interviews I always gave the distance as 11,356 miles. Meanwhile in having a zinc etching made for card showing us at Milestone on return, we somehow got the miles mentioned as 11,532. This was while I was still trying to get my affairs straightened out. These were worrisome days. I have corrected the distance on all cards I have handed out since.

SUMMARY

Correct actual miles as computed by expert........ 11,356 miles
"Theoretical" miles (for explanation of this term see Book I. I went over each day's travel as computed from taking note of handicaps of road owing to various kinds of unnatural footing) .... 4,804 miles
(roughly)

Number of days for entire trip, (Sundays and lay-over included) .... 948 days

Average per day, actual miles for each day of the entire trip .... 11.98 miles
(Approximately)

Number of days that we actually traveled one mile or more .... 578 days

(I thought I had checked this correctly when I was checking for several other points. In my article "What One Horse Did," Cavalry Journal, July, 1930, I gave the number of days as 580. Just now, in compiling this record, each days notes were examined closely by my secretary in a thorough and painstaking manner, and double checked by myself, and the number 578, given above, was found to be correct.)

Number of miles per day actually on the road under saddle .... 19.64 miles

I estimate that Queen was under saddle an average of seven hours for each day on the road, making an average of 2.80 plus miles per hour. This would include many short stops such as being interviewed, or stopping to let her cool off in the shade, or stand in the creek a few minutes or half an hour, or letting her nibble grass a while. It is reasonable to presume that while in motion she had, on an average, better than a three mile gait. On rough and inflexible roads she did not travel three miles an hour.

Expenses above earnings for the entire trip, including one side trip from Las Vegas, Nevada to Pasadena, California, and one to Portland, Oregon, by rail, were about $1020.00, or about $1.08 per day, above earnings in treating and advising on horses, etc., or about 9 cents per mile. This does not include the original cost of horse and outfit. The expenses borne by the Veteran's Bureau while I was in the hospital would about offset the expense of my side trips to Portland and Pasadena.

Counting out unforeseen time lost by accident to knee, time held up by flood and quarantine, and extra travel on account of same, we made the trip in one day less than the original schedule, which had been two years and three months.

It is my candid opinion that I could take a horse, as nearly as possible the counterpart of Gypsy Queen, select my own route, that is, my own conditions of footing, climate, etc., ride with stripped saddle, having pre-arranged to be rid of the handicaps of no certain feed, water and shelter, with a certainty of having the horse shod as I ordered—under such conditions it is my candid opinion I could easily ride this new horse twice the distance in actual miles that I rode Gypsy Queen in actual miles, in the same number of days we were on the trip. In fact, I offered, to a very outstanding horseman, to wager any reasonable amount that I could do this, taking my own risk on the health of the horse—that is, if the horse broke a leg or died that would be my hard luck. My reply to this proposition to Major Benton was that "he believed I would be safe in making that bet if anyone that knew anything about horses was fool enough to take me up."

I claim for Gypsy Queen the world's record for endurance, durability and adaptability. If any horse anywhere ever made this number of miles within the same time, under conditions and handicaps approximating those endured by Gypsy Queen, I want to see the proof. I am, in this book, offering indisputable proof that Gypsy Queen accomplished what I claim, and under the handicaps as set forth.

(Signed) Frank M. Heath,
Silver Spring, Md.
March 1, 1940.

Chapter X

THE AFTERMATH

WHEN I got back from the trip, the man who held the first mortgage on my place was crowding me pretty hard. He had given the extension with the understanding that I was to pay the mortgage as soon as I got back. Somehow the mortgage I had signed through Captain Cissel, by which means the thing would all have been settled, went haywire, perhaps through some technicality. The man holding the mortgage was threatening to foreclose. That would have wiped me out. So we had to go after a new mortgage, which at this particular time seemed a little hard to get. Finally, just in the nick of time, and by the intercession of a mutual friend, Joe got the loan of fifteen hundred dollars.

With the balance, after paying the first mortgage of a thousand dollars, I straightened out the obligations that I had incurred on the trip, including that to Conner, and had a little left to go on. These small obligations had been worrying me.

The house or bungalow, which was vacant, I finally rented, and it was off and on during the three or four years I still had the place.

During the few days that I was in Silver Spring in July, Brooke Lee had interested Senator Millard Tydings in trying to get me some kind of a reasonable raise in my veteran's compensation. Tydings was instrumental in getting me a raise up to about twenty-nine dollars. This helped a little. The half acre of garden on the place helped a little. So by one means and another I worried along.

About 1930 the Park people began angling for part of the three and a half acre place I had. Finally the Park got approximately two acres. This left me a few thousand dollars balance after cleaning everything up, most of which I spent on what remained of the place.

Meanwhile I got a couple more raises in compensation as the laws were amended and as various examinations clarified my case. So I managed to get along.

Getting back to about the time I finished the trip, I spent every bit of my odd time and surplus energy in perusing notebooks, writing articles, a number of which were called for. Where I fell down principally was that most magazines asked for a story of about four thousand words. It took me nearly two years to get this story down to less than twenty thousand words. Finally I did get two articles down to about four thousand words. These were accepted, as mentioned, one in the *Rider and Driver*, April, 1929, and one in the *Cavalry Journal*, July, 1930. Once, in 1932, after this Park land deal, having a few thousand dollars, I did make one attempt and spent considerable money and a lot of energy in an attempt at a book manuscript, and got nowhere. In spite of all I could do, it was running into four times too many words. Besides, it was getting on both my nerves and my finances. Seeing that I could not make ends meet, I laid the matter aside indefinitely. Finally, by making some sacrifices in regard to the estate I had left, I saw my way clear to at least leave a comprehensible manuscript, whether acceptable to a publisher or not. This is what I am doing.

Finally, by chance almost, I did find a person who was experienced and capable of this work. The task is very exacting—so much data to examine and copy, and everything to keep in order.

During the last few hundred miles of the trip, the road being again hard, rough and difficult for a horse, Queen's left front foot went bad again, as stated. The knee again began to buckle. After we arrived home and I was busy as the devil preventing a financial collapse, Queen did not get nearly enough exercise. True, she had nearly three acres to ramble about in. But she believed she had done enough rambling for a while. When cold, stormy weather set in, and she was in the stable most of the time, that was still worse. More and more Queen got to leaning on her right front foot, first no doubt from some soreness in the left, recurring toward the end of the trip. But certainly, after I had gotten her over the soreness, by standing her to the ankles in Sligo Creek quite a lot, she did it as a matter of habit. This throwing the weight on the right foot with the left knee buckled was doing Queen a great deal of injury. The muscles of the left fore-leg again began to shrink as they did in winter quarters in Princeton, Illinois. This leaning also threw her whole frame out of alignment, and this position caused her to 'rest' her left hind in a position that caused the foot to stand out too much.

What was to be done? I could not ride Queen any to speak of without keeping her shod. I did not feel like shoeing her myself, and it was hard to get any shoer to do the difficult shoeing exactly as I wanted it done. Besides, I wanted to give her a long barefoot spell. I was puzzled as to how to handle this situation. Queen was still too good a horse, too full of vitality, to be allowed to go to the devil.

Here is what I did; I got her shod all around as best I could. Then, in order to make her stand her weight on her left front foot part of the time, to give her sort of balance, I took a block of hardwood about an inch wider than the shoe, a little longer than the shoe, and about four inches high. I next made a kind of rocker of this by nailing a cleat about an inch thick crosswise in the center of the ground surface, and tapered off the ends of the block. I then set the foot on the block and marked a line on the outside of the shoe. I next drove a row of nails just outside this line, with the heads inclined inward. Into this space I shoved Queen's foot, that is, the shoe, from the back. Then by a series of straps, one going around the pastern and buckling, another passing simply in front of the pastern and buckling, and still another over the top of the hoof, it will be seen that I had this fastened to the foot. This would cause Queen to throw her weight in walking onto the left foot eventually. It would allow Queen to walk or rather limp off her right foot onto the left, bearing her weight principally on the left foot most of the time. While she could step and roll off from the rocker she could not stand still on it. This I made her wear several hours a day, and usually, when standing in the barn, twice a day for several hours. In addition to this, I so rigged up the manger and feed box that whether this apparatus was on her foot or not, she had to lean away over and reach around to the left to reach either the feed box or the manger. By these means she began to come back into something like proper alignment. Later I had more time and took to riding her more. In the summer of 1928, or less than a year from the time we finished the trip, her leg was practically straight. If, during enforced idleness, I saw in her an inclination to get back into the old habit of leaning on the right foot, I either saw that she had more exercise under saddle, or barring that, I used this apparatus.

Now for Gypsy Princess. Queen had evidently been a mother before I acquired her. I have no record of any offspring. You might presume that some way or another she had been deprived of this colt. Never would we pass in sight of a trim bay or near bay little colt, but that Queen seemed bound to adopt it. This probably was one reason why I thought it was no more than right that she should be allowed to have a colt of her own. And of course naturally I was anxious to perpetuate her. Beginning with 1928, several trips were made in trying to mate her with the proper kind of stallion, from my point of view. A Morgan was not available in our region. Once I took her on a whole two-day jaunt, going and coming, to a farm where was a thoroughbred belonging to the Remount. This trip was futile. I finally, after much scouting around, bred Queen in 1929 to a standard bred, Old Kinster, belonging to a Mr. George E. Nicholson of Olney, Maryland.

This attempt proved successful. Queen was fourteen and the stallion was twenty-two at the time of breeding. By the way, I had investigated some of the get of Old Kinster, and they were quite wonderful horses, especially as to vitality. Kinster, of course, was a trotter, and I was deliberately aiming to breed a good road saddle trotting horse. This Gypsy Princess proved to be. She was broken to ride when she was three years old, and now belongs to Mr. Whitney Aitcheson, near Laurel, Maryland, who owns a string of saddle horses. She is still a very strong, able horse at nearly ten. She will take a smooth trot, what I explained early in the book as a dog trot. She is easily urged into a slight posting trot, by which I mean a rider just naturally takes a short post. She can be advanced into a very good canter. She can run quite a clip, but probably not fast enough to win money on the track. She easily jumps three and a half or four feet, sufficient to make her a good hunter. When a bunch of horses goes out from this stable under saddle, she invariably leads the bunch if allowed to do so. No matter whether she goes out every day in the week, or sometimes two or three times during the day, she has never been known to show any signs of fatigue. She is tougher than a boiled owl. One thing more: With this smooth little trot mentioned, she will put the other horses of the bunch into a keen lope, as would Queen when I got her.

Gypsy Princess is ten years old this spring, 1940, and is still going strong. She is a beautiful mahogany bay. You never saw better knees on a horse.

THE MARYLAND NEWS
Friday, May 8, 1936
TWENTY-FIRST BIRTHDAY OF HORSE THAT
TRAVELED THROUGH U. S. CELEBRATED
GYPSY QUEEN FETED FRIDAY AFTER-
NOON AT THE HOME OF HER MASTER,
FRANK M. HEATH FAMOUS FOR 11,356
MILE JOURNEY

Almost nine years ago, November 4, 1927, to be exact, Sergeant Frank M. Heath, World War veteran of Silver Spring, rode his bay mare, Gypsy Queen, to the zero milestone in Washington to complete the longest trail ever traveled by one horse under saddle.

Since that time the handsome mare has been in virtual retirement, but she blossomed forth as a gracious hostess two weeks ago to celebrate her twenty-first birthday at the home of her master in Silver Spring.

Guests of honor at the party were a host of local children with whom Gypsy Queen is a prime favorite. Entering into the spirit of the occasion Gypsy Queen contentedly munched oats while her youthful admirers consumed hot dogs.

Sergeant Heath purchased his famous horse, of the well-known Kentucky Morgan strain, in Virginia for $110. She has been his faithful steed and pet ever since.

The historic trip around the country which was to consume 11,356 miles and include a visit to each of the 48 states, started April 1, 1925, from the zero milestone in Washington, where the tour also ended.

Sergeant Heath conceived the idea of the tour, partly to improve his health, which was greatly impaired by his World War experience, and to prove by actual test the capacity of a good horse. At the same time he gained wide education and experience on the tour.

Both Sergeant Heath and the horse were in excellent condition when they completed the trip. They were greeted in Washington by Major General Cheatham, then Quartermaster General of the United States Army.

The horse was checked by Major Scott, chief of the Remount Division of the Army, who had examined the animal at the start of the trip. He positively identified her as the same horse, thus eliminating any possible doubt of her endurance throughout the arduous journey.

A chart of the route followed by horse and rider is shown in a map that appears in this issue of the Maryland News. During the journey Gypsy Queen was reshod 22 times and carried an average of about 70 pounds deadweight, the rider walking and riding alternately.

Sergeant Heath describes his historic trip as being full of thrills, dangers and hardships which tested both him and the horse on many occasions.

They were required to cross 12 [15] mountain ranges, or spurs of same including the Rockies twice and the Blue Ridge twice. At one time they traveled 65 miles between watering places and on the same occasion 72 miles without seeing a sign of habitation.

As time progressed Gypsy Queen was getting along in years, but did not feel her age. My own health was not good. There was no longer much of an opportunity for me to keep her on what was left of my place. The roads were becoming such that there was not much of any chance to ride her as a horse should be ridden. One trouble was that about the only place I could ride was alongside the various paved roads, the shoulders of which were mostly treated with fine crushed rock. This meant that I either had to keep her shod, or else the fine particles of crushed rock would become lodged at the union between the sole and the wall of the foot, the white line. It is well known that the white line is soft. A large sharp grain of sand for instance, or small sharp gravel, becoming imbedded there, makes a horse lame, [after having worked through the union of the soles and the wall of the foot, the white line] sometimes very lame. If it gets beyond a certain point, a horse is what is known as "graveled." (Sometimes the expression is "sanded.") In other words, the particle of sand or gravel has gotten up into the sensitive laminae. I have known of such cases, where the horse would be extremely lame for quite a long time until such gravel or grain of sand eventually came out at the coronary band. I have myself, but not with Gypsy Queen, successfully poulticed a horse in a case of this kind to facilitate the exit of the grain of sand or gravel. While this is an extreme example, the reader may well judge that this treatment to which Queen was subjected when taken on the road did not add to her comfort in traveling. The risk did not add to the peace of mind of the owner. I tried, and so far succeeded in keeping these small particles of gravel and so on from penetrating to such a depth that they would keep on going. I kept them picked out as best I could. But even this was causing soreness all around. It was gradually causing a parting at the white line, which in turn was causing what is known as "rim-thrush." That is, this cavity would gather filth, which causes thrush.

As to shoeing, I had had one job of shoeing done up country, as they call it. Contrary to my orders they had thrown Gypsy Queen's left hind foot badly off balance, to the extent that she had serious stifle trouble—what is known as a slight stifle slip, from walking a few hundred feet, before I made the shoer pull the shoe and put it on as nearly right as conditions would allow. I made up my mind right then that I never would allow anyone other than myself ever to shoe that mare again, and I never did allow anybody again to shoe her, both on account of the hind foot and the front foot. I know how to shoe a horse, but owing to my physical condition, the job of shoeing a horse was very painful and also injurious to me. I knew I couldn't keep it up.

It took over a year to get Queen's stifle region back to normal, if indeed it ever was quite strong. Soon after this accident from the shoeing being done wrong, I was letting a boy that used to help me about the place ride Queen sometimes. I noticed Queen coming up the bridle path toward the stable all pepped up, walking snappy, as they call it, and the stifle snapping somewhat at every step. That is the time that I further resolved to let no one ride her but myself. By restraining her, making her take it easy and trying to keep the shape of the foot right, she got about over this in a year. A part of this treatment was in keeping the outside of this hind foot a little low, right the reverse of the way I was paring and shoeing the left front foot.

Owing to various reasons, possibly the fact that the circulation in the extremities of a horse is not quite so good as the horse ages, the action of the limbs is not quite so nimble. He may wear the toe, if bare, unduly by not properly raising it in stepping. Thus the toe wears off too much in relation to the heel. This, if left alone, may accentuate what is commonly known as buck knee. Queen's left knee had again begun to go over, and she again had gotten the habit of leaning on the right front. Perhaps this was largely through lack of proper exercise.

Something that I have not mentioned before, Gypsy Queen was beginning to be threatened during the last year or two of her life with mange. Once the mange gets a hold on a horse along in years, especially a horse that throws out long hair in winter, it is hard to keep down. I had kept it down, but I was afraid of it.

I, to be perfectly frank, had begun to worry about what would happen to that horse in case I should "kick in" as it is sometimes expressed. I had a feeling that she would not be properly handled, that she would not be properly understood. No telling what hands she would get into. Some fool might try to make her jump, and she was a wonderful broad jumper. I couldn't bear the idea of what might happen to her in such a case. I couldn't bear the idea of her being fed to the dogs or just simply hauled out and dumped some place after she herself passed. I investigated different possibilities of having a statue made of her, but the best sculptor I could contact locally seemed bound to emphasize this point or that point, until I become disgusted in that line.

I either wanted a statue of Gypsy Queen or none. I didn't want just a horse. I considered mounting her, but that did not seem feasible, either. After investigating the matter I found that a real horse mounted would eventually go haywire if it was not properly preserved. I don't know why this idea came to me so belatedly, but I suddenly conceived the idea of having her skeletonized, so as to show the framework of this particular horse that did this stunt— her strong jaw, her wonderful teeth, the wonderful bone, her actual build and proportion; that she is on balance as far as the framework is concerned, and also properly on axis; the corrective shoeing, that is, a departure from the way a perfectly sound horse should be shod, the extension on the left front foot, and the left side of the left hind slightly lowered to take care of the affected stifle.

The next question, as I thought it over, was, where did this skeleton belong? All at once it occurred to me that perhaps the University of Maryland might like to have this skeleton in its Department of Animal Husbandry. Not that I presumed the mere skeleton of a horse would be very much of a contribution, but that perhaps they would appreciate the skeleton of this particular horse. I called up my old professor in horticulture, Professor Vierheller, and was soon in touch with the proper authorities, the professors in Animal Husbandry, and they took to the idea readily. After several interviews, arrangements were finally made. The Horse Breeders' Association of Maryland contributed most of the funds for the mounting, which was done by W. Bryant Tyrrell, Osteologist.

Now comes the most painful part of it. When the arrangements were all completed, they sent a truck over for Gypsy Queen, on October 29, 1936. She seemed to know what was going to happen. Several times, in taking her and the colt up country and back, and so on, when I was an out-patient in the hospital, trying to find a place for them, Queen had been in and out of trucks, so she had no fear of a truck—but it took all three of us, all we could do, to get Queen into this truck at this particular time, although it was backed up to a high bank where all she had to do was to walk in. The expression of her eye intimated to me that she had an inkling of what was going to happen.

After arriving at the college grounds, unloading her at some stable near what was at that time the Animal Husbandry Building, I had again all I could do to get her into that stable. I finally got her in and gave her a nice feed of oats that I had along, which pacified her somewhat. Then somehow I couldn't stand it any longer. I got out.

I had not gone twenty feet from the building until she called me. I said "All right, Queen." She quieted down.

I got word somehow that the veterinarians, who were having a convention there, at that time, were taking measurements of her, and so on and so forth. I considered this was all in proper order and stayed away. I knew they would not subject her to any abuse.

When the time came, they led her out into a grass plot nearby. I mounted her, and she willingly, almost eagerly, went through her paces, seeming to be very desirous of posing as I wanted her to pose. Bryant, who also is a photographer, got some pictures of her.

The appointed time arrived when they were to administer some anaesthetic which they told me would be painless, and I slipped through the gate.

It developed, and the skeleton is there to prove it, that there was nothing wrong with the knee joint, or with the ankle joint, or with the shoulder joint. It is a fact that there were signs in preparing the skeleton that the circulation in the left front foot was not perfect. This was as I had presumed. The blood coagulated in that foot to a greater extent than in any other foot. There was a slight, but only a slight, indication that there may have been a very slight chronic inflammation about the navicular. There was some sign that there had been some unnatural irritation in the left side of the foot, but the bone had never reached the stage of ossification. There was a slight thickening of the upper part of the left front hoof. Neither was she hoofbound at the time of her demise, or in her later years. The top of the hoof had always been flexible. So much for the front.

Getting back to the left hind, the skeleton does bear indications that something had happened to that leg. Come to think of it, there was, when I obtained Gypsy Queen, almost an imperceptible —what is called a "dead jack" or arrested spavin. This never had bothered her until this particular shoeing previously mentioned. That, as well as naturally affecting the stifle region, had also seemingly aggravated this old spavin. I had killed that with a double blister of biniodide, or red iodide.

THE TIMES-HERALD

Washington, D. C., October 30, 1936

"MERCY DEATH" ENDS GYPSY QUEEN

Champion Horse Gone at 21

PRIZE HORSE MARTYR

A martyr to the cause of Science, Gypsy Queen, for whom the title of World's Champion Long-Distance Horse was claimed, yesterday was put to a "mercy death" at the University of Maryland. * * * *

Eleven years ago Gypsy Queen and her master, Frank M. Heath, of Silver Spring, Md., set out from the Zero Milestone in the Ellipse to claim the long distance championship. They traveled 11,356 miles through every State in the Union, and Gypsy Queen cinched for herself a niche in the Hall of Fame of the horse world.

The horse was 21 years old last April 1. Due to her triumphant tours, Gypsy Queen was bothered with a knee ailment and in recent years a skin disease broke out to torture her. Heath, broken-hearted over being forced to part with the once stately mare, deemed it best that she be put out of her misery.

*   *   *

Speaking of Gypsy Queen's being put out for the benefit of science —there were many press notices mentioning this. In addition to what I have already told about not wanting to let her get down or trusting her to anyone else when I was gone, "the benefit of science" from my point of view concerns what developed at what you might call the post mortem, that is, the preparing of the skeleton and what the skeleton shows, including the fact already mentioned that there was nothing wrong with the knee joint, and particularly showing the condition of the feet, how I kept her going by practicing what I call corrective shoeing, which corrective shoeing shows as she stands mounted at the University. She was really happy during the nine years after our return from this trip, in spite of little temporary accidents, very full of pep and energy until about a month before her death, when finally this rim thrush of which I have spoken began to get her. Had it not been for this, and my physical inability to shoe her, I believe she would have lasted another ten years.

The movies taken of her in February, 1935, which are now in the possession of the University of Maryland, show her at that time very full of pep, able, with scarcely a limp, alert and in good condition.

THE MARYLAND NEWS
Montgomery County, Friday, July 8, 1938
TABLET IN HONOR OF GYPSY QUEEN

A bronze tablet erected to the memory of Gypsy Queen, the world-famous horse owned by Sergt. Frank M. Heath of Silver Spring, will be unveiled at the Rosa Bonheur Memorial Park tomorrow afternoon at four o'clock.

Governor Harry W. Nice will head the list of state dignitaries who will take part in the program which also will feature the formal opening of the modern burial park for pet animals at Washington, Baltimore Boulevard and Dorsey Lane.

Gypsy Queen gained world wide fame for herself and her master when they completed the longest trail ever traveled by a single horse under saddle. The trip covered 11,356 miles and touched every state in the Union.

Sergeant Heath, a World War veteran, started with his noted horse on his memorable trip from zero milestone in Washington on April 1, 1925, and ended at the same point on November 4, 1927. Gypsy Queen died for the benefit of science October 29, 1936, at the University of Maryland.

Tomorrow's program will include selections by the Maryland Training School band and will open with the introduction by Edward Gross. Governor Nice will unveil the Gypsy Queen tablet and Sergt. Heath will be introduced. A talk will also be given by Charles E. Moylan.

PROGRAM OF EXERCISES
Processional March—Aida, by Verdi
Maryland Training School Band

Introduction ....Edward Gross
Unveiling of the Gypsy Queen Tablet
By His Excellency Harry W. Nice*
Governor of Maryland

Presenting Sergeant Frank M. Heath
Presenting Mrs. Roslyn Terhune of Station W.B.A.L.
(Courtesy of Baltimore News-Post and Baltimore Sunday American)
*Governor Nice could not be present.

Selection—Melody in F .... by A. Rubenstein
                     Maryland Training School Band
Presentation of Distinguished Guests
Presenting Mrs. Ruth M. E. Dean (Malinche Macevoy)
Solo Selection—"Gypsy Queen," (Melody, Old Faithful)
              by Edward Walker, Tenor, Accompanied
                  by Jack Decker at the Piano
Oration .... by Honorable Charles E. Moylan
Finale—National Anthem "The Star Spangled Banner"
                  by the Band and the Audience

COPY OF INSCRIPTION ON TABLET
ROSA BONHEUR MEMORIAL, Inc.

*   *   *

ERECTED AND DEDICATED
IN MEMORY OF GYPSY QUEEN

Sergeant Frank M. Heath, U. S. Army World War
Veteran, and Queen Traveled 11,356 Miles on the
Longest Trail Ever Traveled by One Horse under
Saddle covering each of the 48 States of the Union.
They started at the Zero Milestone in Washington
D. C., on April 1st, 1925, and ended at the Same Point
On November 4th, 1927,
Queen Died for the Benefit of Science
On October 29th, 1936

A FAITHFUL AND LOYAL COMPANION

*   *   *   *

ROSA BONHEUR MEMORIAL, INC.

Washington Blvd. at Dorsey Lane

July 26, 1938.

Mr. Frank M. Heath
Silver Spring,
Maryland

My Dear Mr. Heath:

Enclosed you will find the Deed to the Burial plot of your
faithful companion, Gypsy Queen. Our Engineer has just
recently completed the final and accurate survey of the Park.

This was quite a task and is the reason for the delay in sending you the Deed.

The entire developed property is under perpetual care, which will insure that the lawns will be kept trim and looking beautiful at all times.

The future development of the Park will be completed as rapidly as conditions will permit.

Assuring you of our keen appreciation of your encouragement in behalf of our efforts, we are

Sincerely yours,

ROSA BONHEUR MEMORIAL, Inc.,

(Signed) Edward Gross,
President.

After exchange of many letters for several years with the University, the following letter was received, accepting custodianship of the skeleton and data pertaining to the trip.

UNIVERSITY OF MARYLAND
College Park

College of Agriculture
Department of Animal and
  Dairy Husbandry

June 30, 1939.

Sergeant Frank Heath
8310 Sligo Drive West
Silver Springs, Md.
Dear Sergeant Heath:

Professor Fred H. Leinbach has written me under date of June 26 that you desire us to be custodian for the records that you obtained on your tour through the United States with the saddle mare, Gypsy Queen.

Inasmuch as you have given the skeleton, mounted through funds of the Maryland Horse Breeder's Association, to the University of Maryland for educational purposes, we shall be glad to keep the related records in our files where they may be available to those interested in them. However, the rules of the University do not permit the acceptance of any special or financial responsibility in the matter.

Thanking you for your interest in this matter, and assuring you of our desire to cooperate with you, I am

Yours faithfully,

KCI:RMB

cc: H. T. Casbarian   (Signed) Kenneth C. Ikeler,
    H. S. Finney   Head Animal & Dairy
    F. H. Leinbach   Industry Section

THE MARYLAND NEWS
October 27, 1939, Friday

* * *

SKELETON OF GYPSY QUEEN IS GIVEN
MARYLAND UNIVERSITY

The Block and Bridle Club of the University of Maryland was the scene of an interesting meeting last Thursday when Sergt. Frank M. Heath of Silver Spring formally presented to the University the mounted skeleton of his famous horse, Gypsy Queen, who held the world's record for long distance travel.

Sergt. Heath was introduced by Prof. A. F. Vierheller and the skeleton was officially accepted by Kenneth C. Ikeler, head of the Animal and Dairy Industries Section.

Other speakers included Maj. Goss Stryker, secretary of the Maryland Horse Breeders' Association, and Prof. F. H. Leinbach. Refreshments and a social hour followed the program.

Sergt. Heath also presented all the data pertaining to the momentous trip he took with Gypsy Queen which included visits to every one of the 48 states in the Union. The material included seven note books, a signature book, three scrap books, a large number of newspaper clippings, about 100 letters written during the course of the trip, the manuscript account of the trip later to be published, and a map showing the route.

Prof. Vierheller in introducing Sergt. Heath, with whom he became acquainted after the World War, recalled how the owner of Gypsy Queen used to ride horseback on University Lane, then a muddy country road.

Sergt. Heath opened his remarks with a request that the film of Gypsy Queen, taken in 1935, be shown. The film showed still pictures of Sergt. Heath and his horse at the beginning and end of the long trail, and other views, a moving picture of Sergt. Heath on his horse showing off her various gaits eight years after their return from the trip, and a moving picture showing the dedication of a memorial tablet to Gypsy Queen at the Rosa Bonheur Memorial Cemetery in July, 1938. * * *

Professor Ikeler expressed appreciation for Sergt. Heath's gift and said the skeleton and data are already being used by the University in actual class instruction.

Major Stryker, who spent many years with cavalry units in the Dakotas and some of the western territory covered by Sergt. Heath on his trip, expressed amazement that one man alone could accomplish what Sergt. Heath had accomplished.

Complimenting both rider and horse on their gallant conduct, he said: "Only a gallant man could have accomplished such a feat and he could have done it only mounted on a gallant horse."

Just as I believed we had finished, a friend of Queen—and myself brought me the following clipping.

WASHINGTON EVENING STAR

Washington, D. C., February 7, 1940
Haskin's Answers to Readers' Questions,
By Frederic J. Haskin

A reader can get the answer to any question of fact by writing The Evening Star Information Bureau, Frederic J. Haskin, director, Washington, D. C. Please inclose stamp for reply.

Q. What became of the famous horse Gypsy Queen? L. W.
A. Gypsy Queen died on October 29, 1936. The horse has been honored by a bronze memorial tablet in the Rosa Bonheur Memorial Pet Animal Cemetery in Maryland. Gypsy Queen's fame was established by carrying Sergt. Frank M. Heath, United States Army and World War Veteran, 11,356 miles on the longest trail ever traveled by one horse under saddle, covering each of the 48 States of the Union. They started at the Zero Milestone in Washington, D. C. on April 1, 1925 and ended at the same point on November 4, 1927.

This, from such a reliable Bureau, is rather gratifying as, with all these other recognitions of Gypsy Queen and her performance at this late date it indicates an interest in the history of the feat.

Some of the other titles in the Equestrian Travel Classic series
published by The Long Riders' Guild Press.
We are constantly adding to our collection, so for an
up-to-date list please visit our website:
www.thelongridersguild.com

Title	Author
Tschiffely's Ride	Aime Tschiffley
The Tale of Two Horses	Aime Tschiffley
Bridle Paths	Aime Tschiffely
This Way Southward	Aime Tschiffely
Bohemia Junction	Aime Tschiffely
Through Persia on a Sidesaddle	Ella C. Sykes
Through Russia on a Mustang	Thomas Stevens
Riding Across Patagonia	Lady Florence Dixie
A Ride to Khiva	Frederick Burnaby
Ocean to Ocean on Horseback	Williard Glazier
Rural Rides – Volume One	William Cobbett
Rural Rides – Volume Two	William Cobbett
Adventures in Mexico	George F. Ruxton
Travels with A Donkey in the Cevennes	Robert Louis Stevenson
Winter Sketches from the Saddle	John Codman
Following the Frontier	Roger Pocock
On Horseback in Virginia	Charles Dudley Warner
California Coast Trails	J. Smeaton Chase
My Kingdom for a Horse	Margaret Leigh
The Journeys of Celia Fiennes	Celia Fiennes
On Horseback through Asia Minor	Fred Burnaby
The Abode of Snow	Andrew Wilson
A Lady's Life in the Rocky Mountains	Isabella Bird
Travels in Afghanistan	Ernest F. Fox
Through Mexico on Horseback	Joseph Carl Goodwin
Caucasian Journey	Negley Farson
Turkestan Solo	Ella K. Maillart
Through the Highlands of Shropshire	Magdalene M. Weale
Wartime Ride	J. W. Day
Across the Roof of the World	Wilfred Skrede
The Courage to Ride	Ana Beker
Saddles East	John W. Beard
Last of the Saddle Tramps	Messanie Wilkins
Ride a White Horse	William Holt
Manual of Pack Transportation	H. W. Daly
Horses, Saddles and Bridles	W. H. Carter
Notes on Elementary Equitation	Carleton S. Cooke
Cavalry Drill Regulations	United States Army
Horse Packing	Charles Johnson Post
Mongolian Adventure	Henning Haslund
The Art of Travel	Francis Galton
Shanghai à Moscou	Madame de Bourboulon
Saddlebags for Suitcases	Mary Bosanquet
The Road to the Grey Pamir	Ana Louise Strong
Boots and Saddles in Africa	Thomas Lambie
To the Foot of the Rainbow	Clyde Kluckhohn
Through Five Republics on Horseback	George Ray
Journey from the Arctic	Donald Brown
Saddle and Canoe	Theodore Winthrop
The Prairie Traveler	Randolph Marcy
Reiter, Pferd und Fahrer – Volume One	Dr. C. Geuer
Reiter, Pferd und Fahrer – Volume Two	Dr. C. Geuer

The Long Riders' Guild
The world's leading source of information regarding equestrian exploration!
www.thelongridersguild.com